Religion in Childhood and Adolescence

Religion in Childhood and Adolescence

A Comprehensive Review of the Research

KENNETH E. HYDE

Religious Education Press
Birmingham, Alabama

Library of Congress Cataloging-in-Publication Data
Hyde, Kenneth E. (Kenneth Edwin)
    Religion in childhood and adolescence: a comprehensive review of the research/Kenneth E. Hyde.
    Includes bibliographical references and indexes.
    ISBN 0-89135-076-4
    1. Children—Religious life. 2. Teenagers—Religious life.
I. Title.
BL625.5.H93   1990   90-42006
291'.083—dc20   CIP

Religious Education Press, Inc.
5316 Meadow Brook Road
Birmingham, Alabama 35243
10 9 8 7 6 5 4 3 2

Religious Education Press publishes books exclusively in religious education and in areas closely related to religious education. It is committed to enhancing and professionalizing religious education through the publication of serious, significant, and scholarly works.

PUBLISHER TO THE PROFESSION

IN MEMORY OF BEATRICE HYDE
WHO LOVED AND UNDERSTOOD CHILDREN
AND SPENT HER LIFE WORKING AND PLAYING WITH THEM

Acknowledgments

The production of this book in my retirement has involved the help of many people and institutions. It would not have been possible but for the encouragement and assistance of John M. Hull and Michael Grimmitt at the Centre for Religious Education Development Research (CREDAR) at the University of Birmingham, England, and the facilities the university provided. The Edward Cadbury Trust generously made a grant to defray the costs involved. The extent of the references bears testimony to the help freely given first by the staff of the School of Education Library of the University of Birmingham and more recently by the staff of the Brynmor Jones Library of the University of Hull. Many helpful suggestions came from William Curr, Ralph W. Hood Jr., H. Newton Malony, David Palliser, Donald Ratcliff, and from James Michael Lee, editor and publisher of the Religious Education Press. The SCM Press gave permission to quote from Harold Loukes *Teenage Religion*. Glynn Doran, Ronald Goldman, Graham Miles, and Harold Taylor have allowed the use of material from their theses. To all of these I gladly express my sincere thanks.

Contents

Preface

For a long time the psychology of religion was dominated by animated discussions about depth psychology. Freud was alleged to have undermined religious belief while Jung was supposed to have sustained it. When Freudian psychology was reinterpreted to provide a psychological basis for belief, educational psychology was hardly mentioned, if at all. Yet while studies about Freud became the longest entry in the bibliography of psychological writings, those by Piaget came next. Behaviorism became fashionable, again with its dismissal of religion. In time, the empirical approach which had become prevalent in the general field of psychological studies was applied to the psychology of religion, with journals about the scientific study of religion and religious research. It is this type of research which forms the basis of this review. No attempt has been made to adopt a particular stance toward depth psychology or its bearing on religion; that has been done many times, most recently by Caputi (1984). It will be seen that relatively few empirical studies of childhood or adolescence relate directly to the theories of analytic psychology.

Over the years, the psychological study of the religious development of children and adolescents has attracted a great deal of attention from parents and teachers, church workers and clergy, educationists, psychologists, sociologists, and theologians. Many studies have been made that bear upon it, some of them well-known and others largely overlooked in academic journals or dissertations. In the pages that follow an attempt has been made to review this extensive and disparate field and to impose some sort of order on it. Deliberately, rather more attention has been given to lesser-known works which appear to be important and are not easily available to the general reader. The feature that is common to almost all of them is that they are based on the results of empirical tests with children and adolescents. Bringing together results from a range of studies about the same topic

9

enables the validity of the conclusions to be better assessed. A landmark in this area was the publication of *Research in Religious Development* (Strommen, 1971) with the critical discussions of its distinguished contributors, but even this gave no simple survey of what had been undertaken, as did the brief survey of Wright (1972). For this reason, some reference to major work before this date has been included in the present review, while the main endeavor has been to make at least a brief reference to as many as possible of the studies that have followed it. Their number is such that all too often it has not been possible to deal adequately with them but only to mention their main thrust. An attempt has been made to indicate the field covered by each study, rather than only citing details appropriate to a topic being considered. The considerable continuing interest in many areas of the subject is indicated by the extent of the bibliography, which it is hoped will provide a tool for future research studies, building on Pitts (1977) and Ratcliff (1985b).

At the outset, some difficulties must be noted."Religion" has proved to be an amorphous term; definitions vary greatly, not only among theologians and philosophers, but also among psychologists and sociologists. The problems are discussed in Appendix A. The snags of using numerical scores in tests of religiousness are considered in Appendix B. These are not always recognized, so that misleading interpretations of test results can be found. The psychological approach to defining religion has been more objective, and tests of adolescents and adults over a long period have shown that different aspects of religion function with a degree of independence. An early and influential investigation by Glock and Stark (1965) showed five different dimensions of religiousness: the ideological, intellectual, ritualistic, experiential, and consequential. And in England, teachers are familiar with Smart's (1969) philosophically based six dimensions of the ritual, mythological, doctrinal, ethical, social, and experiential. Some account of this important research about dimensions of religion is given in Appendix C. Failure to recognize the dimensionality of religion gives rise to confusion and the misinterpretation of results. All aspects of religious development need to be considered; neither the intellectual nor the experiential should be stressed at the expense of the other.

In addition to recognizing what aspect of religiousness is being considered in any particular situation, the religious orientation of those who make up the group being investigated is also important. Two different orientations have emerged in many studies since they were first identified by Allport (1950), who distinguished between the extrinsic religiousness of individuals who used religion for some sort of personal benefit and the intrinsic religiousness of those who were concerned for religion for its own sake. An account of this, and of other orientations, is given in Appendix D. Every religious person exhibits both orientations to some extent, but the differences between the predominantly intrinsic and the predominantly extrinsic are marked. In most research, no account is taken of this difference, and some conflicting results may be due to them.

Argyle (1974) contended that it did not follow that because a belief had psychological roots it was therefore false and went on to discuss belief in such terms as the reduction of needs, anxieties, and internal conflicts. It was influenced by parental figures, it assisted ego identity, and provided cognitive clarity to understand life. It was possibly influenced by biological factors. This present survey shows that religiousness—or the lack of it—has its psychological origins in infancy and childhood, when newly born children begin to react to the environment created by their family. From the beginning of life, if their feelings of hunger and discomfort receive attention they develop a sense of security about life. With the growth of thought and speech they not only learn the language of their families but also adopt their ideas and attitudes and in the early years remain ignorant of alternative sources of information. At home they first hear of God, reverently or irreverently, and begin to perceive the significance of religion to their parents. Before long their environment is enlarged through the wider society to which the family belongs, which might include a church, mosque, synagogue, or temple. They become exposed to prevalent social trends and to the media. When these are at odds with parental beliefs and attitudes, then children are shielded from them as far as is possible and are taught to resist them; these families hold religious belief strongly, and their stance is vigorously supported by the religious groups to which they belong.

The style of family life, the manner by which children are nurtured, encouraged, guided, corrected, and punished all have their influence on children's consequent religiousness. It is from their parents that children inherit any genetic personality dispositions. Taken as a whole, studies of personality and religion demonstrate that religiousness is not due to particular personality traits, but its expression is strongly influenced by some of them. Dogmatic people are not necessarily religious, but when they are, their religiousness is dogmatically expressed. In every faith fervent believers, whatever their theological position, hold to their belief with similar absolute certainty. The binding authority of all of their scriptures and of each of their religious traditions is not demonstrable objectively but has been accepted as self-evident in the process of their religious development. In this sense religion is also a product of social learning, transmitted from generation to generation by religious groups through the families of their adherents. Brown (1966b) argued that although emotional dependence might account for the acceptance of some religious explanations of life, belief was predominately a somewhat isolated cognitive activity. It was acquired and sustained by social influences within a supportive context, and the affective aspects which influenced the manner in which belief was expressed were not specific to religion.

Social influences on religiousness increase as children grow to adolescence and adult life. Just as relationships with parents were of prime importance in earlier years, relationships with adults regarded as important assume a greatly increased importance in adolescence. This is especially true in the church, where a good relationship with a trusted adult greatly strengthens a commitment to religious belief and practice but where the perception of adults as hypocritical can be most damaging. Most children regard worship as uninteresting and boring, nevertheless, it is the children who have been regularly involved in it who are more likely to retain the habit of church attendance when free to abandon it. Here again, parental example is of prime importance, and the early corporate experiences of the symbolism of worship and the mythology of the liturgy and the scriptures also have a positive effect. To those who lack this and have little or no personal experience of the power of symbolism in the arts the language of religion is particularly arid and void of significance.

The religious influence of schools on their pupils varies greatly. It proves to be not a contrast between church schools and state schools, or primary schools and secondary schools, but a product of school climate. The attitude to religion of groups of children in different schools ranges over a wide spectrum. Some schools which set out to enhance the religiousness of their pupils succeed to varying degrees, but others fail to do so. How long such religious influence holds when school days are over is uncertain, and evidence about it confused, although some church-related colleges, but not all, appear to have a continuing influence. Good religious teaching can hold back the normal decline in religiousness observed as adolescence advances, but poorer teaching has no such effect. The religiousness of Catholic pupils, whether or not in Catholic schools, is greater than that of non-Catholics. This has little to do with the schools and most to do with their homes; in surveys of religiousness, Catholics, except for ardent evangelicals, score more highly than any other group.

The verbal expression of religious belief develops in the same way as other cognitive skills. In early childhood spontaneous religion is dominated by ideas of magic; preschool children can be very sensitive to atmosphere, but their religious statements demonstrate that theirs is a different world from that of adults. What is concrete in religion is better understood from the age of eight, so that parables can then be understood at an elementary level. Not until well into adolescence—if ever—can theological statements be adequately comprehended. This is the pattern of normal mental development. "Understanding" in this context is often used ambiguously. It may imply no more than a grasp of what the words mean—in the sense that even theology is not a religious activity in itself—and can be undertaken by unbelievers. But religious understanding is often taken to imply some measure of personal acceptance of religious ideas and commitment to them. The confusion this causes is discussed in Appendix E.

Faith has the potential to develop throughout adult life, no matter how such development is described. Descriptions of the development of belief have given but scant attention to its modification or abandonment, not under secular pressures in adolescence, but in later life and with fuller experience. "The dark night of the soul" which many mystics described is still a contemporary experience for some believers; there is no lack of newspaper columns, articles in the rationalist press, or of books written by those whose faith did not develop in conventional forms, and their integrity should not be questioned. A better knowledge of the factors associated with a loss of belief in mature life would be of value in appraising their influence on the formation of belief in adolescence. The expression of belief by adolescents depends on their personal development; when moral insight remains at the level of law and order, accepting externally imposed regulations as a matter of course, then religious belief is also similarly restricted to a legalistic form.

Here, we set out to chart the development of religiousness and account for it in psychological terms. The image of God held by a believer can be seen to have grown from parental images acquired early in life from both the father and the mother. Ideas of God will have been enriched by religious education and worship and better understood with growing mental powers. Life's actualities and happenings will be explained in terms of the beliefs that have been acquired and attributed ultimately to the activity of providence or of God. Patterns of religious practice will have become established, and the judgments and choices that have to be made on many issues will be informed by religious insight and feeling. But here psychology comes to an end. It can describe and account for belief, but it cannot say whether ultimately God is only a projection of our minds, however valuable the image may be to some, however inhibiting to others, or whether our images of God correspond to an eternal transcendental reality, external to our world yet immanent within it, as believers have always claimed.

Chapter 1

Religious Thinking—Before and After Goldman

The study of religion in childhood and adolescence has been dom-
inated for thirty years by investigations of the process by which reli-
gious thinking develops. This is largely owing to a broader educa-
tional interest in cognitive development which has been stimulated
by the considerable number of studies of children's thinking made by
Jean Piaget and his colleagues in Geneva. The relevance of his the-
ory to religious thinking was first brought to attention in the United
States by David Elkind and in England by Ronald Goldman. It is the
work of these two pioneers, and the studies of those who followed
them, that must first be considered.

No other psychologist has produced such a body of books and articles over so
long a period as Piaget—they are only exceeded in volume by writings about
Freud which come from many authors. His single purpose was to trace the way
children's thought forms and logic developed from the maturation which is genet-
ically built into the human race. His earlier writings, which were influential for
the studies of religious thinking, were almost entirely restricted to studies of number and conservation. He wrote one book about moral judgment (Piaget, 1932)
but nothing at all about children's religious ideas, despite his own religious interest
(e.g., Piaget, 1930). Some of the relevant aspects of his theory, and recent criticisms of it, are discussed at greater length in Appendix G. It is sufficient for the
present to take note that he regarded intellectual growth as developing in a series
of progressive stages of an invariant order, each building on the previous stage.
Central to his theory is that a stage is marked by an equilibrium. The world as it
is encountered is assimilated to fit the structures of children's minds; new expe-

15

riences are absorbed and integrated into the existing schemata of mental structures. At the same time the structures have to be modified to accommodate in a better way new information; the schemata are modified by new experiences or new schemata built. When this equilibrium is overthrown there is progress to the next stage. The goal is formal operational thinking. The objects of thought are symbolic, and the extent of the development depends on children's capacity to deal mentally with reality. The process starts in an unorganized situation when all activities are directed by egocentric emotions. An important level is reached when they are able to deal consistently with objects of thought, and another when they can deal with mental images in the absence of the objects to which they refer.

In the earliest sensory-motor stage, up to the age of two, children are largely concerned with themselves, and other things do not matter unless they affect them in some way. Children from two to four are in a stage of preconceptual thought, not yet clearly distinguishing between an object and its class or able to think logically. From about four to seven children are characterized by intuitive thinking, which is dominated by what they see and how they interpret it. They are able to grasp only one relationship at a time and are confused by irrelevant details and ideas of magic. They have not yet understood the unchanging quantity of objects, which Piaget called conservation. From about seven to twelve comes the stage of concrete operational thinking, an important concept to Piaget. Babies do not think out problems; if they want to hold an inaccessible object they will reach out toward it. Later, children begin to think how to do such things, and the action is internalized and becomes an operation. The logical process by which a conclusion to a problem is reached can be thought backwards to the start, and this concept of reversibility is again of importance to understanding mental processes. The quantity of water poured from a tumbler into a tall, narrow vase seems to a five-year-old child to have become greater. An eight-year-old knows this is not so, because he can envisage pouring it back again to show that it is the same. Logical ability and reasoning become prominent in dealing with concrete ideas, although abstract thought is not yet possible. Children become aware of the sequences of their thinking and see that other actions would give the same result. Thought becomes consistent, and concept building is extended, but only about concepts that can be derived from first-hand reality. At eight a child knows that iron sinks in water because it is heavier than wood, which floats. Not until adolescence is the concept of density established to allow an adequate account of the difference.

With the approach of adolescence abstract thought becomes firmly established. This is the characteristic of mature adult thinking, and it enables the full logical activity of formal operational thinking. Reasoning from a hypothesis becomes possible, and the mental manipulation of a number of variables in turn. Generalizations can be made, and an expanded time scale allows thinking about the future as well as having a better grasp of history and the past. Symbolic thinking allows ideas not directly related to the real world to be considered. A capacity for hypothetical reasoning develops, enabling generalizations to be made as well as critical appraisals. Less able adolescents do not reach this stage of thinking and cannot adequately deal with the abstract arguments and concepts that make up much of the learning process of their peers. Adolescents seldom achieve full maturity before adult life.

This process of mental development affects every area of thought, including that of religion. Because religion has more than a single dimension it follows that its development is not limited to its cognitive aspects but equally it cannot exclude them. Batson (1971) argued that religious development was a process of creative growth through imaginal thought by which individuals could deal with an increasing range of needs with greater responsibility, rather than a process of cognitive development or socialization. Dunning (1973) gave support to this theologically and described five themes of creativity which were: openness to experience, integration with the environment, a search for meaning, self-actualization by realizing one's potential, and self-transcendence, especially in receptivity to mystery and the future. But creative growth cannot be unrelated to cognitive development, especially if it is to be interpreted in these theological terms. These issues will be taken up later, but at the outset the manner and content of cognitive development must be clarified.

It had long been recognized that young children had a very limited understanding of religion and that only in adolescence the ability developed to deal with abstract theological concepts. Beiswanger (1930) had used experienced judges to evaluate Old Testament materials frequently used with children, and, apart from criticisms about its ethical and religious content, they regarded none of it as suitable for children below the age of nine. The first attempt to relate religious understanding to the insights of Piaget was made by Ainsworth (1961) in a study of children's understanding of parables. In a series of interviews she first told children a parable and then asked them to choose which of two more stories was like it; in the two stories, one used the background material of the parable but without its meaning, while the other replicated its meaning in a different situation. Only from about the age of nine could children identify the story concerned with meaning.

However, Ezer (1962) was critical of Piaget's studies of children's explanations of causal events on the grounds that his sole criterion was that of age, whereas experience with the phenomena involved might have had an effect. To ascertain the effect of religion on boys aged six to eight he used four tests describing situations which posed problems to which they had to suggest solutions. Thus, what should a non-swimmer do when drifting at sea in a leaking boat beyond help brought three types of responses: animistic—"The ocean would send a big wave to push me to shore"; anthropomorphic—"I would pray to God to help me"; or scientific—"I would stop up the hole with my finger and throw the water out with my other hand." Children from devout homes and children who had received a greater amount of formal religious education offered more animistic or religious explanations, and this greater recourse to animistic thought forms indicated that this group was regressing to earlier modes of thinking. Denominational differences were less than the effects of religious background and religious education. Causal thinking at this age was affected by religious training, and the development was not due to maturation alone. Scientific explanations were also offered, contrary to Piaget's suggestions. Shaw (1970) carried Ezer's findings further with students described as fundamentalist, devout, or of the indiscriminately proreligious orientation. They made significantly less use of psychological approaches to human behavior. Their theological conception of it was incompatible with a psychological one, since this religious view considered the causes, cures, and nature of much human behavior in terms of will, sin, prayer, and virtue.He found support from Brown's (1966b) conclusion that religious beliefs were categories used to explain, interpret, and cope with the natural world, and differences in religious orientation showed that people who lived their religion tended to be theologically oriented, not illness oriented or psychological in their thinking about the behavior of others and in responding to their needs.

David Elkind had played a prominent role in bringing the work of Piaget before an American audience, replicating a number of the Genevan studies, and his were the first published studies about cognitive development in religious understanding (Elkind, 1961, 1962, and 1963). They were about children's understanding of their religious identity and were followed by summaries (Elkind, 1964a, b) and a description setting them alongside other original developmental studies (Elkind, 1978). His concern was to investigate the nature of their spontaneous religious ideas. The first study was with Jewish children, but the method and the questions were repeated with little change with Catholic and Protestant children, aged five to fourteen, from homes in which religion was practiced. The Jewish children aged five to eleven were interviewed and asked: Is your family Jewish? Are you Jewish? Are all boys and girls Jewish? Why? Can a cat or dog be Jewish? Why? How do you become a Jew? Why or what makes you Jewish? What is a Jew? How can you tell a person is Jewish? Can you be Jewish and American at the same time? The responses met Piaget's criteria; there was uniformity in ideas at a given age and these often extended over several years; the appearance of ideas from an earlier-year level were part of, or added to, the more advanced ideas of a higher level. There was an increased correctness or conformity with adult conceptions with increasing age. Religious concepts were thus regarded as being no different from those of mathematics or science that Piaget had studied, and it was the manner in which children progressively reconstructed institutional religion, with its beliefs, practices, and dogmas, that was under scrutiny and not the feelings, attitudes, and concepts of personal religion which children may experience, even toward living people or nature or even animals.

Very similar response patterns were obtained from Catholic and Protestant children. From five to seven the children's responses were global and undifferentiated. A Jew was "a person," as was a Catholic. Jews and Catholics differed because "some have black hair and some have blonde," or "he comes from a different country. "Another child did not know how Catholics differed from Protestants; Protestant was a term not yet understood by young Protestant children. A cat could not be a Catholic because cats walked on four legs. Not all boys and girls could be Jewish "because some were colored, they spoke another language," nor could all be Catholics since "some are Irish, some are Russian." A boy was a Protestant "because he fights." These children lacked the ability to distinguish between religious and nonreligious class designations. Denominational terms had a kind of physical existence, and because you could not be two things at the same time multiple group membership appeared to be impossible, so that they gave such replies as, "Are you an American?" "No"; "Are you a Jew?" "Yes." Elkind commented that Piaget had found the same type of reply when he had asked children whether they were Swiss or Genevan. At this first stage there was an absolute conception of denominational allegiance, as ordained by God; you could not change to something else because "God made you a Catholic." The origin of religious identity was described in the first place in terms of Piaget's concepts of artificialism and moral causality; "God makes you Jewish," "Your mother turns you Jewish"; it is of necessity, just as one of Piaget's children said, "the clouds must move." To young children, religious identity was no more than a name for race or nationality. Some children did not know how to recognize one of their number. Many looked to such things as pious actions: going to synagogue or church, or crossing oneself; or to ethical actions: doing right things or not saying bad words.

At the second stage, from about seven to nine, religious identity was seen to be by generation and by participation; "You are born Jewish." It came to mean a form of behavior or a characteristic manner of action, including the wearing of particular symbols. Frequently, use was made of the concrete behavioral pious actions and ethical categories. People behaved in certain ways: They went to synagogue or attended Mass or a Protestant church. Religious terms were now understood in the light of actions. A cat or dog belonging to a Protestant family was also a Protestant. Some thought cats or dogs could share the denominational adherence of their families; others were equally clear that animals were not human and so could not attend a place of worship or say prayers. Even so, one child commented, "They can't go to the synagogue . . . but I guess if it belonged to a Jewish family it could be Jewish." Asked if a lion or tiger could be Jewish, the reply was, "No, because they are wild. Nobody owns them." This is correct, but concrete. Being Jewish depended on the ability to carry out certain actions. Jewishness was correctly perceived as being a family quality, but the conception of a family was undeveloped. It was all the people living together, and it had a primitive idea of participation in it. Similarly, Catholicism or Protestantism was understood in terms of a group of people with characteristic ways of behaving which animals could not perform. Proportionally more Jewish children said they were Jewish because their families were than Protestant or Catholic children. This bears out Ash's (1969) suggestion that Jewishness was not only religiously but culturally distinctive. When asked about religious affiliation and nationality at this middle stage the children displayed much more insight, recognizing that you were "born a Jew but live in America," or "I was born in America but I was baptized." You could not be a Catholic and a Protestant at the same time because "you could not go to two different churches." But they also recognized that change was possible since you could stop going to church or go to a different one.

At the third stage, from about ten to fourteen, just before adolescence, the children spoke of initiation, practice, and ritual: "You are bar mitzvahed." Religious identity now could be established by asking individuals directly about it: "You can't tell unless you ask them." Only now did religious identity come to be thought of as something emanating from within rather than from without the individual. Development of recognition of membership was not sufficiently precise to show a clear stage development, although results pointed in such a direction. The children displayed abstract and differentiated concepts; classes were now explained as compatible by means of their general properties rather than by personal experience: "You study your religion," "you study the catechism and receive communion," a Jew is "a person who believes in one God and doesn't believe in the New Testament," and a Protestant "believes things" and "is a faithful believer in God." Religious groups were distinguished by differences in the content of their belief and denominational differences were seen, not by means of the religious subject, but by means of the religious object. A denomination was now perceived as one sub-category within the category of all religions. Animals could not have a religious affiliation because "they are dumb, have no brains, and can not understand things like that." The use of terms such as brain and mind showed that belief was understood as a mental quality and the children were not parroting an adult verbalization. Once children had discovered that people of all denominations had in common a belief in God they were able to form the general category of religion, so that : "Being Jewish is a religion and being American is a nationality. They are two different things."

Elkind's final word was that while adults believe children and adolescents are most like them in their thoughts and least like them in their feelings, it is the reverse which is true. Before eleven or twelve most children were not able to understand religious concepts as they were understood by adults, but instead they gave meanings to them which reflected their own views of the world.

When Elkind examined the homogeneity of the children's replies he found a pronounced consistency. About a third of all children tested answered all questions at one stage and another third answered all but one question in one stage. Only a very small group, less than 3 percent gave answers at all three stages. The greatest variability occurred at age ten, with children in the transitional period between the second and the third stage, aware of the inadequacy of their former ideas but as yet unable to replace them. These stages, Elkind said, should not be regarded as absolutes, but they contain subtle gradations. Some of the variability should be seen to be due to the unequal difficulty of the questions, for, as he remarked, the nature of the materials and the questions asked can affect the level of children's performance quite independently of their level of intellectual development. Dittes (1965) commended Elkind's method for meeting the two fundamental research requirements of objectivity and fidelity to religious experience itself and regarded it as capable of being adapted to many other questions in the study of religion.

By conflating Elkind's tabulation of Jewish, Catholic, and Protestant responses, it is possible to obtain an overall conspectus of the development:

PERCENTAGE OF ALL RESPONSES ABOUT DENOMINATIONAL AWARENESS								
Stage				Age				
	6	7	8	9	10	11	12	13	14
I	62	22	11	3	3	0	0	0	0
II	30	76	78	75	62	50	39	24	8
III	0	4	10	20	36	50	61	76	92

It is of interest to notice the rapid transition from stage I to stage II after the age of six and to compare this with the quite gradual transition to stage III, which is in fact linear, something not expected from a popular understanding of stage theory.

Elkind's interest in religious development was continued in a subsequent study of children's conception of prayer carried out with two other colleagues (Long, Elkind, and Spilka, 1967; Elkind, Spilka, and Long, 1968). Boys and girls from five to twelve were interviewed about two pictures of families engaged in prayer and were asked to describe what was going on, by a series of questions and incomplete sentences. These were: Do you pray? Does your family pray? Do all boys and girls in the world pray? Do cats and dogs pray? What is a prayer? Can you pray for more than one thing? What must you do if your prayer is answered? What must you do if it is not? I usually pray for . . . Sometimes I pray for . . . When I pray I feel . . . When I see someone praying, I . . . Where do prayers come from? Where do prayers go? Global and undifferentiated answers were scored 0, 1 if they were concrete differentiated, and 2 if they were a differentiated abstract category. Analysis showed a number of distinctive age clusterings. At five, responses were at a global, undifferentiated stage, followed at six or seven by a transitional stage, leading to concrete differentiated levels at age eight. This was followed by another transitional stage from nine to eleven before the abstract differentiated stage started at about twelve. Some questions were "easier" in the sense that they tended to have more advanced replies than the others. Overall, the developmental process for the whole group was shown to be a gradual one.

From five to seven, prayer was understood only vaguely as a verbal activity about God, rabbits, dogs, fairies, deer, Santa Claus, Jesus, Mary, and Mary's little baby. Cats and dogs were said to pray, if prayer was thought to do with speech;

when it was seen to relate to people, then animals did not pray. All the boys and girls in the world prayed. "Can you pray for more than one thing at once?" The children guessed at random and gave no rational explanation for their judgment. They were primarily concerned with the gratification of personal desire. They associated prayer with certain fixed times—going to bed, before eating, or going to church; but their attitude was neutral. Unanswered prayer distressed them more than the older children and was sometimes associated with immature frustration responses—"be mad at God," "cry," or "scream"; but some would "thank him anyway" or "keep praying for it." They had many fantasies about prayer; they thought it came from God, or from heaven, or even from fairyland. Prayers were said to fly, float, or jump up to heaven.

Between seven and nine prayer was regarded concretely, in terms of requests for particular appropriate activities and things, but the children never rose above the actual behaviors they associated with prayer. "We should have water, food, rain, and snow. It's something you ask God for." Cats and dogs were excluded because they could not talk, suggesting that the form of prayer was mistaken for its substance. Not all children in the world prayed because some forgot, or were too sleepy, or didn't want anything, or didn't like to pray. When asked if they could pray for more than one thing, their replies indicated that they thought God had a limited capacity to do things and not everyone could be served completely at once. Now they showed a shift to thanking God for things already received and an increasing concern with humanitarian and altruistic requests—for peace, the poor, and the sick. There was also a tendency no longer to recite standard prayers, so that prayer became more personal and individualized and less egoistic and self-centered. They often said that prayers came from people living in former times, made by Moses, Abraham Lincoln, or the Pilgrims, passed on by books such as the Bible.

About the age of ten, and increasingly thereafter, prayer came to be understood in terms of thought, as a private conversation with God, involving matters not discussed with other people. The distinction was now found, seldom seen before, between what was said and what was thought. It was recognized that prayer involved belief; not all children prayed, some did not believe in God, or did not know about the Christian religion. So, starting from a stage when prayer was simply a word associated with other religious words such as God, that had as yet little meaning to children, it came to be conceived as a mental activity associated with a system of religious beliefs not shared by all others. Now they viewed prayer more abstractly, objectively, and in a more differentiated fashion than younger children. Similar trends were observed in the contents, affects, and fantasies associated with prayer. Prayers were regarded as originating within oneself and heard directly by God as a form of direct communication. Prayer could arise spontaneously in response to particular feelings, as when they were worried, upset, lonely, or troubled. Empathy also affected the older children—they thought that others prayed for the same things and for the same reasons. At each stage of development children constructed a new concept of prayer that was neither entirely learned nor entirely spontaneous. The process was continuous, and the successive conceptions progressively approximated to those held by adults. At every stage the concept represented the product of the children's thought and their experience. Elkind clearly did not regard this continuous development as inconsistent with Piagetian stage theory, which less-informed commentators have considered as requiring abrupt transitions between stages.

The study was replicated by McGrath (1974) with Catholic children, which confirmed the results. He regarded the somewhat more rapid progress through the stages he observed in his sample as the result of their increased experiential learning. Worten and Dollinger (1986) also replicated the study and confirmed the age trends but did not find support for the other theory they tested that more abstract thought would be associated with reason-centered rather than power-centered discipline or with the mothers' intrinsically oriented religious motivation. The study of prayer generated much interest, and subsequent research on the topic will be described in chapter 5.

These studies of religious identity and prayer directed attention to Piagetian theory; an approach to religious education which took account of stage theory was receiving growing attention among those concerned with religious education in the United States. Isert (1969) argued that the general conclusions about religious education made by a number of well-known authors could best be understood in the light of Elkind's interpretation of Piaget. Williams (1971) described Piaget's account of artificialism in children's development of their understanding of the world of nature and suggested that at the age of six they might be ready to begin to understand concepts about God.

In New Zealand, Lawrence (1965) was concerned with concrete operational thinking; the level of children's understanding was influenced by what had been learned but not understood, so that while church members' children might have a more sophisticated understanding of religion than others, they would later need to achieve a deeper and richer understanding of concepts already familiar in symbol, allegory, metaphor, abstraction, and theological subtlety. Parents supplied information regarding their children's religious questions; they were mostly about the nature of God, suffering and death, the church and the world, and the supernatural. They showed that children's interests were not metaphysical but matter-of-fact and materialistic in a concrete style. At this stage of development they were not yet prepared for theological answers to their questions; since rote learning would not be understood, the problem for religious education was in the doctrinal content of religious teaching and not merely in providing better teaching materials.

It was the work of Goldman that brought to the forefront questions regarding children's ability to understand religious ideas. His research came in a thesis (Goldman, 1962) followed by two books (Goldman, 1964, 1965a) and a range of articles (Goldman, 1963a, b, 1965b, 1965c, 1966). In a series of carefully structured interviews, children aged five to fifteen were asked questions about three line-drawings and three Bible stories. The drawings were of a child kneeling at a bed, obviously praying; a child standing at a Gothic doorway with two adults, as if entering church with them; and a child looking at a mutilated book which was labeled "Holy Bible"; there were four versions of each drawing, for younger and older boys and girls. The three Bible stories were paraphrases of Moses at the burning bush, the Israelites crossing the Red Sea, and the Temptation of Jesus, stories which at the time were still suggested for children of these ages in some English agreed syllabuses of religious education.

Responses to five of the questions were classified according to the development they indicated when judged by Piaget's stage theory. Three were from the burning bush story: "Why was Moses afraid to look at God?" "Why do you think the ground on which Moses stood was holy?" and "How would you explain the bush burning, but not being burnt?" and a question from each of the other two stories: "How would you explain the dividing of the waters of the Red Sea?" and "Why wouldn't Jesus turn the stones into bread?" The classified responses were then subjected to a scalogram analysis, following Peel (1959), who had successfully used this technique to establish the presence of stages in children's responses about history, geography, and moral judgments. In addition to this, all the responses were theologically classified, with criteria "based upon the current theological approach of biblical theology, interpreted from a central-to-liberal position" (Goldman, 1964). It was recognized that those who differed theologically would find that the research had little to offer but no other criteria were available. In view of subsequent controversy this proved to be of some importance.

The result indicated that children's religious ideas followed a stage development. The responses of the youngest children from five to seven were consistent with other Piagetian studies, showing the characteristics of intuitive thinking, absorbed by details often irrelevant or misunderstood: God had a funny face; the ground was holy because grass grew on it, or because it was hot; the Red Sea divided by magic, and magic also would enable Jesus to turn stones into bread. The Bible was regarded as significant because of its physical nature or its particular use; it was a big book, with small print, big and black and holy. About seven to eight concrete operational thought developed; from thirteen to fourteen formal operational thought was found. It seemed that for many people religious development had stopped at the level of the second stage of "sub-religious thought," appropriate for a mental age of ten, and the crude religious ideas of this stage were subsequently rejected. By ten most children had developed a two-world mentality; one was a theological world where God existed and was especially active in biblical times, in which anything could happen, and in which God intervened to help the "goodies" against the "baddies," and the other the world of emerging scientific thought where God did not exist and in which the mysterious and the supernatural were irrelevant. This divorce between the two worlds seemed to be a major cause of widespread misconceptions about the Bible.

It is of interest to compare the ages of Goldman's stages with those indicated above in the study of prayer (Long, Elkind, and Spilka, 1967) or with denominational understanding (Elkind, 1964a,b); the children with church affiliation showed a similar developmental process, but the stage transitions were at earlier stages. Age boundaries have shown variations in a number of other studies.

Goldman had shown that mental ability and age were the major factors associated with the development of religious thinking, rather than other religious variables. Confirmation of this came from the study of Kingan (1969) who looked at the factors which might influence the religious understanding of a class of able eight-year-old children from varied backgrounds in a Church of England primary school.[1] She devised a test based on four biblical passages—Joseph and his brothers, David and Goliath, Jairus' daughter, and the parable of the lost sheep, with five questions about the factual content and three about the significance of each passage, and related scores to a number of variables. Intelligence and reading comprehension scores showed a significant association with religious understanding scores; religious background and age showed a weaker association lacking statistical significance, and reading accuracy was without effect. Emotional adjustment did not have any general influence, but sometimes it inhibited children's ability to express themselves adequately. The small age differences in the group were also without effect. Girls scored higher than boys on the test, and more of them attended church or Sunday school. It appeared that while a good religious background did not necessarily facilitate religious understanding, the lack of such support hindered its development.

Before further consideration is given to the significance of this work, an account must be given of other similar research undertaken subsequently. It has not been possible to obtain information regarding the work of Martinsson (1968) about abstract thinking and understanding of parables and religious symbols, and of Pettersson (1970) on readiness and abstract learning in Sweden. Studies on the parables and related material have been grouped in a later chapter, but some other contributions need first to be mentioned.

MacCuish (1970) replicated Goldman's test in its entirety, adding an extra question to the first story, and following criticism by Howkins (1966), using different line drawings for the pictures. Minor amendments were also made to the wording of the first two stories. Children aged eleven were interviewed; they had previously been taught the material tested by their class teachers. Responses were scored on the five questions Goldman had subjected to a Piagetian analysis. No significant difference was found between boys' and girls' scores; chronological age differences, within the year group, did not affect the scores but mental age had a significant effect, showing that religious thinking had a progression as in any other field of thinking and was positively related to intelligence. The results did not give sufficient evidence either to confirm or deny Goldman's theory, although they fitted it within their limits. The interviews showed a wide range of

---

1. See Glossary for nomenclature of English schools.

ability in religious thinking; some had very limited ideas, but others were beginning to think propositionally. Most accepted the miraculous, but with considerable variations in understanding it: Some regarded it as an isolated event in the past, others questioned certain literal elements, and yet others advanced a simple theory of miracle by which they tried to account for all the facts as they knew them. Some of the children had reached a formal operational level of thinking; this was before the age suggested by Goldman, and this was probably due to favorable environmental influences through home and church.

Because Goldman's material had been criticized for its reliance on miracles, Whitehouse (1970, 1972) chose the nonmiraculous story of Zacchaeus to test children aged eight and eleven in a Catholic school and a local authority school. The interview was based on three key concepts in the story: 1) sinners welcome Jesus, 2) Jesus welcomes sinners since his mission is to the lost, and 3) a prerequisite for salvation is repentance, seen as a change of life and restitution. The younger children responded as expected from previous findings: Zacchaeus was not thought to be a good person because he wore a red cloak, or hid up trees. Confusion was found even in the older children tested. The responses showed that there was little difference between the eight-year-old children from either school, but three girls aged eleven of high ability in the Catholic school had reached a stage of formal operations. Even this nonmiraculous, personal-encounter style Bible story gave rise to many confusions and difficulties with primary school children, and because of their limitations of thought this particular story did not help to develop religious insights.

Further replications of Goldman's work continued. Morley (1975) used the test with educationally subnormal children in a special school, finding the same stage sequence but at a much later chronological age; none of the children in the last years of school had reached the level of formal operations, although some gave answers at such a level to one question at least. The mental ages for the stage transitions were below those of Goldman's sample, showing that experience of life partially compensated for lower mental ability.

In the United States, Cater (1976) also used the test. His research was set against the background of theological criticisms of Goldman, and he took precautions to overcome this. A theological statement was devised for a reference to rate children's responses; religious orthodoxy was regarded as the degree of accuracy with which a particular set of religious concepts and propositions were used. The rigorous training of his assessors produced a high test-retest reliability for them. Two groups of children, aged six to eleven, and adolescent volunteers aged fourteen to eighteen were tested; in addition, after a month they were also given a personality test and tests of verbal ability and background variables. Goldman recorded a high level of agreement between assessors' scores on Piagetian and theological ratings of responses, and Cater found a similar, though weaker, agreement between scores on conceptual religious thinking and scores on religious orthodoxy as judged from the responses. These scores were associated with verbal ability and also with daily prayer. Nothing in the results questioned the findings of Goldman. Very little association was found between any of the personality traits tested and conceptual religious thinking, apart from religious orthodoxy being associated with a tendency to be outgoing in children, and with a tendency to be relaxed in adolescents. Religious concepts in children seemed to be the product of memory and verbalisms and of what they had been taught. General verbal ability and vocabulary skills were essential for the acquisition of conceptual religious thinking and religious orthodoxy both in children and adolescents; for both groups, the frequency of daily prayer was an important influence. Chronological age was significantly related to religious thinking and to religious orthodoxy, as was the number of years spent in religious education. Religious thinking was also associated with the ability to talk about it, measured by the response length to five of the test questions, and religious orthodoxy had some relationship to the grades secured in religion classes. Goldman's test was also shown to be of a high level of reliability.

A notable study was made by Miles (1971) of logical thinking and moral judgments in candidates for the Bible knowledge examination of the General Certificate of Education. He set out to measure the effects of conventional teaching on two groups aged sixteen and a final year advanced level group aged eighteen. An experienced teacher taught the normal ordinary level and advanced level groups, and an inexperienced probationary teacher taught an ordinary level group retaking the examination. All candidates were tested at the beginning and at the end of the school year, as were similar groups in matched samples. Attitude to religion, religious concepts, the image of God, declared religious behavior, and logical thinking were tested, using the tests of Hyde (1965) and Goldman (1964); two biblical passages from Hosea and the parable of the Prodigal Son were added to Goldman's material. From the six passages, two from both the Old and the New Testaments were available for testing so as to include material that would be subsequently taught. The question in each story that raised a moral problem was used to provide a test of growth of moral understanding. There was no significant difference between results from Goldman's material and from the nonmiraculous passages added. Among the advanced level students, with whom logical thinking was firmly established, there was a significant relationship between clearly understood concepts and the ability to think logically.

With the normal ordinary level group maturation accounted for more of the increase of logical thinking than the effect of the course. By the end of the course, I.Q. scores had ceased to be significant; the leveling-up effect of the course was due to the less able working harder or showing later intellectual growth. Attitude scores were not significant. Knowledge proved to be a significant factor; the taught group gained higher logic scores than the control group partly as a result of their knowledge of the subject. Religious behavior scores were not significant; lower scores were compensated by teaching during the course. The "retake" group, taught by the inexperienced teacher, gave very different results; the course had no effect on logic scores, and while attitude, knowledge, concept, and behavior scores were all significant factors at the start of the course, all traces of their effect were obliterated by its end. The religious education of these students would have been better served if they had not taken the course, and in the event, all of them failed the examination. Thus it was possible to delay the decline in attitudes to religion by an examination course, although a poorly taught course could accelerate a deterioration of attitudes. Maturation effected a significant improvement in logical thinking scores, and teaching was not significant apart from its interaction with maturation; however, a course could depress the increase in logical scores that might be expected from maturation.

The advanced level group of only ten students, eight of whom had high religious behavior scores, showed significant differences from the control group both at the start and at the end of the course. A small but significant gain in logic scores of taught stories in comparison with the untaught stories was noted. Not only were I.Q. scores significant at the start of the course, but they were more significant at its end. They influenced the achievement of formal operational thinking, which only was secured by this group. Those with more favorable attitudes made the greatest increase in logic scores; attitude scores were a factor of considerable importance, as was also religious behavior. Variance analysis showed by the interactions that the course had an effect on the development of logical thinking, but it was less than the effects of mental ability, favorable attitudes, more developed concepts, higher religious behavior scores, and maturation. Goldman had stated that formal operational thinking did not appear to develop before the mental age of 13.5 for most pupils and later still with some stories, assessing the stage on the best single judgment offered. Miles, following Piaget, used global scores for this assessment and found that at the end of the course the "retake" group and the ordinary level control groups were at the concrete operational stage, while the normal ordinary level group had reached the intermediate-to-formal level. The students did not attain formal operational thinking in religious studies until age seventeen or more. The course made a significant difference to moral judgment scores in the normal ordinary level group but had no similar effect on advanced level students. Almost all students in all groups were between the stages of concrete and formal operations, but the majority of the advanced level group had achieved the formal operational stage by the end of the course. This age for the attainment of full operational thinking is not perhaps as late as might be thought, similar findings are known in other fields. For example, Sutherland (1986) found the mean age for achieving full operational thought in physical and biological science was seventeen. It may also account for the lack of success recorded by Arbour (1977) when teaching theological ideas to high-school girls; the course gave better understanding of content but not in relating knowledge to life experience. Earlier, Davies (1965) had shown that concrete and circumstantial thinking was characteristic of a group of average ability boys and girls aged fourteen, and linguistic poverty was an important factor in their failure to attain formal and abstract levels of thought.

Bagshaw (1966) followed the approach of Peel (1971) and his methodology in his studies of adolescent judgment. Peel had modified Piaget's theory and suggested that there were three appropriate levels of adolescent thinking. These were used to assess the written responses of a group of forty-eight adolescents to three biblical passages. The sample consisted of three boys and three girls in each of a more able and less able group aged twelve to fifteen. Three questions were asked about each passage, for example: "Why didn't Paul command Philemon to take Onesimus back?" about the epistle to Philemon, and "Why did Naboth refuse to sell his vineyard?" about the story of it. Responses were classified as prelogical, partial and circumstantial, transformation, logical possibilities, or explanatory thinking, and scored accordingly. Analysis of the scores indicated that the Philemon questions were significantly more difficult than the others, and there was a significant difference between the two ability groups. No differences were found between the sexes or with age, nor in any interaction, although Bagshaw did not test the marked increase in scores between twelve and thirteen.

Richmond (1972) also used Peel's (1971) criteria to assess responses secured from the test he developed, scoring 0 for no response, 1 for a logically restricted response, 2 for circumstantial, 3 for logical possibilities, and 4 for logical deduction type responses. He took children aged thirteen to sixteen from a wide range of backgrounds in a secondary modern school, [1] in four experimental groups. The first part of the test consisted of a set of passages, such as an extract from the Sermon on the Mount in which each passage was followed by the questions: "What do you think this means?" and "Why do you think this?" The second part of the test used passages containing a key concept, but with the term coded, and for each passage respondents had to indicate what they considered the coded term to be and the reason for their judgment. The key concepts included the Bible, Jesus, love, and religion. Scores significantly increased for the coded judgment and free judgment tests with age, and unusually, also on Hyde's (1965) attitude to religion scale. Most pupils seemed to be at an intermediate level of thinking, at the circumstantial or the logical possibilities level, and there was a significant relationship between the scores for both the coded and the free passages with scores on the attitude to religion scale. The four coded passages proved to be less demanding than the free passages, of which Richmond stated that the subjects did not know where to locate the problem or its essential elements. It was rare to find a consistent level of response to these free passages, which was not surprising, bearing in mind their considerable differences in style and content.

Subsequently the work was carried further (Richmond, 1974) when a group of pupils aged fourteen to sixteen were subjected to eighteen separate tests, including those already used. These showed that religious judgment was most closely associated with intelligence and a range of other indicators of linguistic ability, such as the ability to make abstractions and to interpret figurative language. How-

1. See Glossary for nomenclature of English schools.

ever, the religious concept test of Hyde (1965) had no significant relationship with religious judgment measured by these means. The result is a striking indication of the difference between two styles of religious thinking, one a cognitive approach to religious narrative material, the other a knowledge of church doctrine. Richmond was critical of the level of abstraction required by the religious education provided in the early years of secondary schooling at that time.

Further confirmation of Goldman's work was secured in Indonesia by Tanuwidjaja (1974), with children (mainly of Chinese ancestry) aged six, nine, thirteen, and sixteen from Christian schools, using the biblical stories and the pictures adapted to depict local situations. The same stage-type development was recorded, but at a later age, a difference explained as due to the style of education. In Italy, another study pointed the same way; Mocciaro (1983), with a large sample of children from eight to fourteen, also demonstrated that there was a definite development in religious thinking and in the image of God as seen by levels of abstraction. Meanwhile, other relevant studies were in progress. Kousoulas (1973) tested Catholic, Protestant, and Jewish children about their ideas of God and of rain. As the children's scientific understanding of rain increased, so their concept of God became more abstract, with Jewish children displaying more abstract ideas about God than for rain, and the others the reverse. The Jewish children had significantly more abstract concepts of God than the Catholics and Protestants. Age was always a significant factor—older children explained rain more in natural terms than younger. Although the children had their own spontaneous religious ideas, external religious influences became integrated in their thoughts and affected their concrete or abstract idea of God.

In the United States a large-scale extension of Goldman's work was made. Peatling (1973) set out to produce a questionnaire type test based on Goldman's work that could be widely used. He took twelve questions from the biblical stories and set out four possible responses for each, at different levels which he called Very Concrete, Concrete, Abstract, and Very Abstract. His selection of these responses was theological and took no account of the psychological classification of Goldman's five key questions. The test was first used in Episcopalian schools (Peatling, 1974); a developmental process was established, with mental age, rather than chronological age, as the best predictor. Great stress was laid on the finding of plateau periods of apparent equilibrium followed by periods of apparent transition, in accord with Piagetian concepts of cognitive development. Middle adolescence was a period of considerable change in religious thinking; the development of abstract religious thinking in Episcopal schools was later than Goldman recorded. There was a marked preference for some concrete item responses among abstract religious thinkers. Later (Peatling, 1975) he identified the retarded or subnormal pupils among all those tested and noted that by age eight few gave Very Concrete responses, but most gave Concrete responses. A sizable proportion recorded Abstract responses, a result for which no adequate explanation was given.

Peatling's test was used with Lutheran pupils (Peatling and Laabs, 1975); there was sufficient difference between the findings to provoke discussion. The Lutheran pupils showed a later development than the Episcopalians and had no similar preference for abstract religious thinking; at the end of senior high school the Lutheran pupils were at about the same level as the Episcopalian pupils at the end of junior high school. The reasons for the differences did not seem clear to the authors. A further repetition with Methodist students and Bible class teachers (Peatling, Laabs, and Newton, 1975) added little of significance; only the mean scores of the entire samples were compared; predictably, the Lutherans, with the youngest sample, scored lowest, and the Methodists, with the oldest sample, scored highest. A similar pattern of development was found in schools and colleges in Finland, with an age-range of seven to twenty (Tamminen, 1976), but a group of theological students responded in terms of concrete religious thinking typical of seven-year-old children. Tamminen concluded that the Very Abstract Religious Thinking test was related, not only to concrete-abstract cognitive development, but also to belief and disbelief. To this suggestion of a theological bias in the test, Peatling (1976) responded by discussing cross-cultural differences in results from this type of testing. Subsequently Peatling (1977) traced development from nine to over fifty years of age using only the Religious Thinking Total Abstract Scale. He found two further plateaus, one extending from thirty to forty and a second from the mid-forties to the end of the fifties, suggesting a continuing cognitive development throughout life. The highest scores came from people with the highest educational achievements.

By testing Bible class members, aged from eight to eighteen, Miller (1976) demonstrated significant relationships between age and the developmental stages of moral and religious thinking. Webster (1975) interviewed subjects in four age groups between nine and eighteen about biblical stories and their own ideas, to investigate their perception of God as a judge. A developmental process operated, passing through an invariant sequence of stages, but at different rates, with the possibility of development ceasing at any particular stage. The stages were of individual recompense, followed by covenant relationships, leading to universal justice. It was related to the general development of cognitive ability, to interactions in the homes and the religious communities of the individuals in their acceptance of the concept of God as judge, and to their overall concept of God, with the beliefs and actions which sprang from their total religious understanding.

Gates (1976, 1977) interviewed primary- and secondary-school children about material related to different dimensions of religion and to levels of scientific and political understanding, supplementing it with written answers from larger groups. A mythical fairy tale from *Where the Wild Things Are* and the Buddhist story of the blind men and the elephant were used, and questions were asked about thunderstorms, space exploration, the importance of familiar people, such as their father, doctor, teacher, or member of Parliament, and other items. This secured an abundant response, and a selection of this material is given as a valuable appendix to his thesis. Responses confirmed a developmental sequence of stages with a shift from random, undifferentiated responses, through concrete and specific responses to those which were personally interpretive and objectively weighed. There was a consistency in the level of responses to the various questions. He found no difference between the fairy tale and the moral fable despite Godin's (1968b) criticism of Goldman that children's hermeneutical capacity would have been less limited if miracle stories had not been used. A great degree of individual consistency was found giving the impression of a general comprehension level arrived at by each child and exercised anew on each specific item. Extreme variation was relatively infrequent, the more usual variations were between two main levels, as might be expected if their thinking was in a process of development. Such fluctuations as there were between the two stages were more often found between separate religious items.

The evidence indicated a changing form of understanding as children grew older, consistent across political and scientific as well as religious spheres. The girls had a somewhat lower level of scientific and political understanding. Development did not detract from the importance of their comprehension at any age. There was evidence of differing degrees of belief within the same pupils; when asked whether everyone who was superstitious was religious, or vice versa, it became clear that they did not have to be connected. Although superstitious belief was associated with low-level scientific literacy, religious belief, belonging, and private prayer did not share this link, but neither were they linked with high-level political or scientific comprehension. The pictorial imagery used to represent God and religious belief again demonstrated coherence and consistency and could be accepted as representative expressions of children's understanding of religious language. Limits in theological comprehension were comparable to those in the political and scientific spheres; the assumption that secondary school pupils were well enough equipped to reject religious teaching as false was no more valid than the assertion that they were in a good position to reject science. More elaborated intellectual comprehension of the symbolism of ritual and story developed as the children grew older, but in the earlier responses there could be personal understanding of a different order, no less important for being intellectually naive.

Abraham (1979, 1981) argued that while Goldman's results could not be dismissed, his approach to religious education was unacceptable; a method was needed to bring improved understanding. She used Peatling's scales to compare the effects of teaching groups of children aged nine to ten in Sunday schools by a normal syllabus and a cognitive conflict syllabus. She found little difference except in the older group, where the girls, and to a lesser extent the boys, showed a somewhat greater movement toward abstract thinking when taught by the experimental method. Degelman, Mullen, and Mullen (1984) used the "Thinking about the Bible" test to compare the development of abstract religious concepts in two different denominational groups of children from eight to seventeen, and found that Catholic children, especially the older ones, used more abstract responses.

Nye, Keys, and Carlson (1981) (Nye and Carlson, 1984) asked pupils in private schools questions about God, such as: "Where does God live?" "What does God look like?" "Does God get mad?" "How old is God?" "Is God like a person?" "What are some things God cannot do?" Responses were categorized into two levels of abstraction and three age-groups were distinguished, five to eight, nine to twelve, and thirteen to sixteen. Every question showed a significant difference between the two levels with age in the Protestant group and all but one in the Catholic group. There was no significant denominational difference in the development in any age-group apart from a somewhat better insight among the youngest Jewish children and in the middle group Catholic children, who tended to give more level one responses. The lack of any substantial difference between the development of children nurtured in three quite separate traditions indicated that the development depended on general cognitive development and upheld the Piagetian view of cognitive development. Religious education could be effective only within these limits, which supported Goldman's contention that children under the age of ten or eleven were unable to formulate the abstract concepts needed for an adequate theological idea of God, and formal instruction about it was not advantageous.

Goldman's findings and the inferences he drew from them had an immediate and long-lasting effect; new styles of religious education, especially for younger children, appeared in revised agreed syllabuses and handbooks designed to support them, although it should be recognized that in this he had successfully popularized the progressive thinking of the time (Hyde, 1984). His stance continued to be influential for a long time (cf. Holm, 1973, 1975). Yet almost from the outset his conclusions were the object of criticism, even to the extent of his receiving abusive, anonymous letters. The next chapter deals first of all with the nature and substance of these criticisms, and it is important that they should be seen in their context.

For a long time there had been strong disagreement about biblical teaching for children. In the early days of the English Sunday school movement extensive use was made of the Bible even with the youngest children. A hundred years later, something of this tradition still survived among more conservative Sunday school teachers, although the materials provided for them both by the Church of England and the Free Churches had become much more selective in their biblical material. Alternative teaching materials with a much greater biblical emphasis were also available from other publishers, which were widely used by evangelicals–a situation which still prevails. Goldman was closely associated with those who guided the Free Churches in their syllabus making and who were looking for a greater emphasis on children's experience in their religious education.Their educational philosophy was that of Froebel–which then was by no means universally accepted. Already they were experimenting with the use of thematic materials with children, in attempts to convey Christian beliefs and values with greater relevance. At the same time, publishers of Sunday school teachers' handbooks were adapting this material for use in schools, where religious education had only recently been made mandatory, and was still almost entirely biblical. To many conservative evangelicals Goldman appeared to be attacking the very foundations of their religious education programs. Their assumption, never clearly spelled out but implicit in much of the controversy, was that by its very nature the Bible should not be treated as other literature. By virtue of its inspiration, its truth could be directly imparted to children of any age by the activity of the Holy Spirit, and any denial of this was blasphemous. Goldman became a scapegoat for them, and some of the criticism directed against him appears to have originated from those motivated by such a theological point of view.

Chapter 2

Religious Thinking—Criticisms and New Approaches

Although Elkind's studies had attracted no adverse criticism, those of Goldman immediately produced quite hostile reaction as well as more sober criticism. It is important to distinguish between the psychological and the theological arguments. It became clear that Goldman's test assumed a particular theological point of view, and it is quite proper for this to be challenged. But the developmental framework which had been established should not be rejected on theological grounds, as some attempted to do. This needs to be kept in mind as other studies of religious ideas, understanding, and development are reviewed.

More recently attention has been given to a much broader concept of religious development than regarding religious thinking in Piagetian terms. It partly depends on the studies of the development of moral ideas which originated with Piaget but was greatly extended by Lawrence Kohlberg. This large field of study is touched on only as it has some direct bearing on religion. It provides the model in America for James Fowler's approach to faith development and in Switzerland for the recent studies of religious judgment by Fritz Oser and his colleagues, with which the chapter concludes.

Despite the widespread favorable response to Goldman's work, and the stimulus it gave to new thinking about religious education, it attracted considerable criticism, almost from the beginning. One issue, which was to be frequently argued, was the miraculous element in each of the stories he used. It was first

35

raised by Salman (1965) who, in a highly favorable review, commented on the miraculous material used and suggested that it might have affected the results secured. Other critics included some reputable English academics. One of the first was Fleming (1966) who argued that only long-term, longitudinal studies could establish such conclusions and dismissed the work as anecdotal and confused, incapable of generalization, although it offered a challenge to improve the methods and content of teaching. In fact, her criticisms applied to the whole range of Piagetian studies then available; their replication and the magnitude of the work sustaining them has effectively removed the ground of such criticism. At the time, Goldman made a characteristically vigorous reply (Goldman, 1965c, 1967).

Hilliard (1965) recognized that most teachers would agree that children do not become capable of formal operational thinking before a mental age of thirteen or fourteen. Goldman's work gave substance to what many had accepted by an intuitive insight. He defended the sampling on the ground that quality, not quantity, mattered, and considered that the analysis was impeccable. (Few critics have realized how much time and effort are required to interview two hundred children, and no critic has replicated a similar extensive study.) Hilliard also wanted a long-term study which took into account the background of the children and the type of teaching they had experienced. One of his most pertinent criticisms was that in the story of Moses the important question, "Do you think this really happened?" was not asked until the end of the sequence. He suggested that if the children had known that their understanding was not supposed to be subordinate to an expectation of literal belief, their responses might have been different. This may have been true with younger children, but Miles (1971) has shown that miraculous elements do not affect the responses of adolescents.

Godin (1968b), who contributed to a symposium on "Ronald Goldman and Religious Education," wrote sympathetically about the results of the study. He considered that Goldman had not studied the awakening of religious symbolism but only the development of a hermeneutic capacity to interpret symbolic narratives. Describing Piaget's work on the formation of symbolism in childhood, Godin regarded the symbolic function as one of expressiveness. The problem for religious education was that symbols in myth or ritual were transmitted culturally, so that children first assimilated them passively; their understanding of a story such as that of Abraham and Isaac was influenced by their underlying anxieties or aggressiveness. This expressive aspect of religious symbolism and its consequent perceptive distortions had been ignored by Goldman. He wondered if a similar development would be observed with narratives of personal encounter, such as Zacchaeus' call or Peter's denial. To pass from a literal understanding of a story to understanding it as a spiritual event required formal operational thinking, but there was also a symbolic comprehension by which children found themselves to be vaguely related to such miracles, even if their interpretation remained bound to the concrete stage. Although Goldman reminded his readers that religious thinking was symbolic, he had made no effort to investigate the origins of religious symbolic thinking which Piaget had demonstrated to be of importance. To this Goldman replied (1969) that he did not question this aspect of the need for children to feel their way into religion and had in fact advanced this as part of the program of worship and exploration with young children, but the main difficulty was to communicate it at a verbal level. The reason why biblical stories were isolated in time by younger children was not because of place differences or miraculous elements, but because of a total misconception of the Bible. The same symposium carried half a dozen other articles evaluating the educational importance and significance of Goldman's work, including a critique of his methodology and current criticisms of it (Hyde, 1968).

Langdon (1969) considered Goldman's findings deserved neither uncritical acceptance nor unthinking rejection. He criticized the research structure and the absence of specific hypotheses to be tested and in particular the lack of attention to the variables regarding the children's background. It was open to the charge that presuppositions had biased the findings. The sample was not adequate to test religious conceptual development but only religious teaching in state schools. A method of dealing with several different theological stances should have been adopted, and analysis would then have made clear the effects of all the variables. Nor was the scalogram analysis sufficiently stringent. He approved the projective pictures used but expressed serious doubts about the biblical material. The data from the interviews was worthy of painstaking analysis by all concerned with children's religious concepts, without always agreeing with the suggested interpretation of it. Overall, the study was restricted to an intellectual factor, but this was of the utmost importance, and the research was a valuable contribution to the field.

Flavell's (1970) discussion of conceptual development in childhood noted that the studies in children's religious thinking well illustrated his theme that the overall level of intellectual development determined conceptual structuring in specific areas. He regarded the work of Goldman and of Elkind as demonstrating that the form of children's thinking at a given age or stage was remarkably consistent. The essential ingredient of religious identity was at first external, going to a certain church, and only later internal, possessing certain beliefs. Children's concepts of prayer exhibited the same development from outer to inner aspects.

Torrance, Goldman, and Torrance (1974) made another appraisal of learning readiness for curriculum construction in religious education, designed for the Southern Baptist Association of the United States. They offered much support for dealing with intellectual content without impeding a later, fuller understanding. They contested the attitude that religious education required acceptance and understanding of authoritarian teaching; creativity was the basic method of Jesus' teaching, and it should be so equally with children, arousing their curiosity and provoking their thought about old and new ideas. Children needed to learn to be sensitive and open to intellectual and emotional problems. Religious growth followed general experience, and experience of life was needed before religious language about it could be understood. Such language was the servant of religious experience, and its premature use could damage spiritual development.

Attfield (1974) accepted Goldman's findings but argued that conceptual development was not fixed but depended on an individual's environment and the teaching experienced. A logical understanding of specific concepts was first needed; if A depended on B, B did not need to be fully acquired before A was beginning to be picked up. To understand the concept of God as personal first needed some comprehension of a range of other concepts. He returned to this topic (Attfield, 1976a) with a fuller examination of the logical analysis needed before psychological study of conceptual development could be meaningfully undertaken. He then (Attfield 1976b) commented on the moral components of Goldman's test; children would not see what was involved in God being just and consistent before they could deal with moral principles, which required the stage of formal operations. Goldman's results on these items were implied by the autonomy of ethics, and the logic of morality would not be altered by enclosing it within a religious domain of thought. Only at the level of formal operations could children argue from premises to a conclusion and back again, and such thinking was required to hold a general concept that God loved all men alongside the Red Sea story. Attfield supported Goldman's argument that Old Testament teaching should be delayed, not however so that it could be considered from a New Testament standpoint, but rather to allow ethical thinking to develop sufficiently. He made a comparison with science teaching, which in many areas could not exceed the level of pupils' mathematical competence. Lupton (1974) was critical of Goldman for his lack of control of other variables and his use of scalogram analysis on a relatively small sample. He considered his results were not adequate to support such wide generalizations, and his items showed theological problems.

Murphy (1977a) contended that a major criticism of Goldman's and Peatling's work was that mature religious thinking was equated with an abstract, symbolic understanding, contrary to the view that a literal or historical interpretation of biblical stories was also possible. He made no reference to the responses of young children, but discussed the evidence regarding children's understanding of parables secured in Scotland by Ainsworth (1961) and in the United States by Beechick (1974). Despite their conclusion that the development of understanding was a stage process, Murphy considered their results indicated a gradual development toward understanding, reached by most children by the age of ten. In the light of his studies of the parables (discussed in chapter 6), he argued that the developmental trend was complex, and gave no support for a simple stage development theory, summarizing his criticism of the theory by tabulating the ages at which changes in the level of thinking had been suggested in eight different studies (Murphy, 1977b). These differences cast doubt on the validity of the theory, which should explain the results of a variety of studies and detect how movement through the stages took place in terms of the factors producing it. Without this, one could see no educational benefit but only an assortment of poorly supported and poorly constructed theories. Religious development was a complex process related to the ability to deal with abstract ideas, to conceptualize historical time so that different events could be seen in their sequential order, and to have a sufficient level of religious vocabulary and linguistic ability to deal with a variety of forms of language. No one doubts these criteria, but Murphy did not suggest an alternative basis on which the cognitive development of religious understanding could be considered.

In passing, it can be observed that alternative developmental theories have been put forward by European scholars which do not rely on Piaget. A review of some of them was made by Berger and Van Der Lans (1979), who described a premagical period from age two to four; a period in which God was regarded as a magician, from four to seven; and from six to seven, a time of simple, materialistic anthropomorphism. At eight to nine God was still regarded as human, but was now surrounded by angels and could not be touched. From twelve onward the concept of God was a spiritual one.

Greer (1980b) took Murphy to task on his criticisms. Three of the studies cited came from very different approaches to children's thinking and could not be expected to fit a theory they were not designed to investigate, whereas the remaining five not only displayed good consistency in the form in which they were tabulated by Murphy but were even more consistent when their authors' comments about the ages of change were noted. Far from demonstrating the weakness of stage theory, Greer regarded Murphy's study as supporting it—the children studied fell within the concrete operational stage of development and reflected maturation within that stage. The study could be taken as another step in the elaboration of a more precise theory of stage development. This criticism equally applies to the longer account (Murphy, 1979) with its fuller analysis of results showing that the allegorical understanding of the oldest age-group was significantly better than the remainder. However, Murphy interpreted it more tentatively; a variety of factors affected the way in which children responded to the questions which did not support an oversimplified view of the developmental process. A rigorist might complain that no clear hypothesis was set out, nor was one either proved or disproved.

An examination of Goldman's work from a theoretical perspective was undertaken by Roy (1979). He noted a number of matters not of fundamental importance. For example, the increase in the mean I.Q. from 105.6 at age fourteen to 119.1 at age fifteen in Goldman's sample could affect the results. He noted inconsistencies between the findings of Goldman and those of Peatling. Unlike previous critics, he discussed the validity of the Piagetian concept of stage, looking at studies which raised doubts about a simplistic account of it. He was aware of motivation in religious learning and made reference to studies of religious attitudes which had a bearing on understanding. He took up Goldman's phrase "Readiness for Religion," asking if it implied conceptual hurdles to be overcome at each stage level; he thought that it should be seen more in terms of attitudes than of cognitive structures. However, he had no quarrel with Goldman's insistence that children should have the potential to understand the material offered in their curriculum.

He asked if the theory was predictive for children in a given age-group and what were the determinants of concept formation. Citing Donaldson's (1978) account of Mc Garrigle and Donaldson's (1974) studies of young children's conservation insight, he asked if there was a possibility that answers were given showing misunderstandings and irrelevancies because the problem did not make sense within their experience. The question is indeed a good one, but Roy, like other critics, did not discuss how the logic of understanding conservation—which is based on observation—may be applicable to religious thinking about narrative material, nor indeed did Rowe (1981), who also cited Donaldson. In her book Donaldson acknowledged her indebtedness to Piaget, and she saw her work as extending the Genevan studies and not undermining them. Subsequent studies of similar problems have shown how complex the question is, and that responses of young children vary a great deal with quite small changes in conservation experiments, or with the wording of the questions asked about them. Roy argued that religious knowledge is not capable of being understood in a Piagetian sense at any level, which would seem to imply that the development of religious knowledge is not a rational or logical process. Not many would agree with this inference, and there is no evidence to support it.

Roy broke new ground in this appraisal by considering Piaget's approach to learning, and the distinction between logico-mathematical (LM) learning and physical (P) learning, which is discussed in Appendix 6. It is interesting that Roy based this discussion on Elkind's (1981) succinct summary of Piaget's theories but did not take up the other points Elkind raised about religious thinking, nor make reference to Elkind's own studies in the field. He also turned to Furth's (1977) discussion of figurative and operative knowledge; quoting Furth's illustration of a child's observation of a mail carrier delivering letters yet remaining unaware of the postal system of which he is part, so that good figurative knowledge was combined with inadequate operative knowledge. Again, Roy was not certain that operative knowledge was possible or even desirable in religion and contended that Goldman, by regarding religious truth as a cognitive construction, had failed to consider all that may legitimately qualify as religious knowledge. The theological stance of Goldman was thus held to invalidate his developmental view of religious education. He took no account of any of the other studies in the field, and on psychological grounds his rejection of the application of a developmental approach to religious thinking has not been upheld. Yet by using a more broadly based Piagetian rationale he brought a valuable new perspective to the discussion. A brief, but more fundamental criticism of Goldman's use of Piagetian theory came from Wilhoit (1982), who argued that the agreement between them was only superficial. In particular he cited the concept of memory; with Piaget this was seen as dynamic and reconstructive, whereas Goldman had treated it as static.

The most radical review of Goldman's work hitherto published is that of McGrady (1983). He noted, unlike his predecessors, that Goldman subjected only five questions to Piagetian analysis and that, while discussion of the operational characteristics of some concepts only occupied a few pages, no less than eight chapters were devoted to theological analysis. In simplifying the stories their religious significance was minimized, while elements suited to the analysis were stressed disproportionately. It followed that understanding of the stories themselves was not tested but only certain aspects which appeared to parallel Piagetian situations. Had Goldman rested his conclusions on his Piagetian analysis rather than on his theological analysis, the rigor of his testing would have provided stronger support for his findings. He took issue with Murphy's (1977b) criticism; while the curriculum applications Goldman made did not necessarily follow, he rebutted the suggestion that stage theory was inappropriate for the study of religious thinking and criticized his presentation of the data, some of which was inappropriate for the comparison, and for the lack of recognition of the two intermediate stages Goldman described in a five stage development, which was not one of "three easy stages." Nor was attention given to the difference between preoperational and concrete operational thinking, an error which also occurred in Peatling's work. "Prereligious thinking" was the phrase Goldman used in his more popular book (1965a), but in his thesis he consistently referred to intuitive religious thinking, which is preoperational and cannot be combined with concrete operational thinking. McGrady's research continues and none of it has so far been published.

The theology of Goldman's test came under strong criticism first from Hawes (1965) and then from Howkins (1966) in a booklet which became widely quoted among Conservative Evangelicals, the term which he favored to describe his own theological stance (Howkins, 1972). His detailed criticism of the form in which the biblical stories were adapted was similar to that made later by McGrady (1983) and Maas (1985a, b); it is now generally agreed that the tests of Goldman and Peatling reflect a theological position. Howkins wanted a longitudinal study to be made; he also objected to the use of the same questions for children of widely different ages. Those familiar with Piagetian methodology know that in practice children understand the questions, but at the level of their own thinking and not as adults, which is revealed by their answers. He did not discuss whether the styles of thinking Goldman disclosed would operate regardless of theological differences, and his contention that the children's answers were limited by their inability to express themselves rather than by their primitive ideas, still lacks support from research. Without empirical evidence such assertions cannot be seriously considered. Nor did he explain how his request for teaching on the children's level of understanding should be given or admit that Goldman had shown what these levels of understanding were.

Peatling's work passed without criticism for a long time; it is curious that there was no objective discussion of it in *Character Potential*, the journal which he edited and in which much of his work was published. Doubts about his test were first voiced by Greer (1983b), who submitted Peatling's list of responses to independent theological judges, all of whom agreed that it contained a theological element by which theologically conservative respondents might endorse concrete or very concrete responses. Such an explanation is given force when Tamminen's (1976) results are recalled—Finnish theological students' responses were similar to those of American junior age children. Greer then used the test with a small group of adolescents having first used the questions in an interview; although it appeared that scores secured by the two methods were related, closer study revealed interesting anomalies. In an interview, explanations of the bush burning but not being burnt ranged from concrete to abstract, yet in the written test most respondents endorsed the intuitive, very concrete reply, "God was protecting the bush." This, and other similar findings, confirmed Greer's judgment that the test was not fully reliable. He also doubted the validity of the plateau which Peatling identified, not only because a cross-sectional study was less reliable for this purpose, but also because the methodology was not adequate. Discussing the different ages recorded by Goldman and Peatling for adolescent development, he rejected Peatling's suggestion that the period of transition was longer and later than Goldman had suggested. Despite such reservations, Greer recognized the value of the test as a useful tool and used it to study religious thinking and religious attitudes among secondary school pupils in Belfast (Greer, 1980a). Religious thinking scores consistently lagged behind those in the United States, so that Belfast pupils remained in Peatling's intermediate stage. This Greer regarded as an effect of the theological bias in the test, and in a strongly religious country pupils were hindered from showing a preference for abstract religious thinking.

Miles (1983) also complained that Peatling, by failing to use the Piagetian method of interviewing, failed also to keep the Piagetian stages of thinking. (Bergline, 1974, showed that it was possible to make inferences from performance in multiple-choice items to the Piagetian thinking processes.) Miles considered that Peatling's criteria resulted in a large, unrealistic intermediate stage unsupported by Piagetian research, and his results did not relate to or throw light on serious Piagetian studies. He noted that Peatling depended on Piaget's (1969) monograph *The Psychology of the Child*, concerned with philosophical questions related to the origin, structure, and function of intelligence, whereas the basic text for his purpose should have been Inhelder and Piaget (1958) *The Growth of Logical Thinking from Childhood to Adolescence*. However, like Greer, he still regarded Peatling's test as a useful instrument in its own right.

One further point needs to be made. No critic has noted that the test fails to make each item of approximately the same length. In multiple-choice test construction if one item of a group is much shorter or longer than the others, respondents tend to endorse that item if they are uncertain about the correct response. The problem arose from turning oral questions into printed items without considering the consequences.

Kay (1981a) used Peatling's test with secondary school pupils in England, Ulster, and Eire, but not without criticism of it. In an earlier unpublished examination of its functioning he had found a linear relationship between the test scores and age, which would not be the case with a stage development. It must be noted that Peatling had found a number of plateaus which he cited as validating the test, and Kay was using a simplified system of scoring. This linearity was again found in Kay's main test with more than three thousand pupils. His other criticism was that when a small group of children were tested with it, and with a test for formal operational thinking, the "Thinking about the Bible" scores bore little relationship to those of the independent test. Kay also subjected thirty-six of forty-eight items to factor analysis and found that the Concrete and the Very Concrete items almost all loaded on the same factor; the Abstract items on a second factor; and the Very Abstract items on this and a third factor. The results indicated that the test distinguished mainly between Concrete and Abstract, and the Very Concrete and Very Abstract items did not appear to give valid distinctions. He regarded "Abstract" responses as indicating possible skepticism as well as a form of religious thinking. Among the many conclusions of his study, Kay found that in the first four grades of secondary schools, religious thinking scores related more to the school than to the home. Scores on Peatling's test also related strongly to ability among Church of England school pupils in England, to literalism among Ulster Protestant pupils, and to frequency of personal prayer among Ulster Roman Catholic school pupils. The highest literalism scores were found among Ulster Protestant pupils, while in Eire the Protestant pupils showed the most liberal or abstract thinking about the Bible of any group tested.

At this point it is appropriate to refer to the study of Hoge and Petrillo (1978a). Goldman had contended that a gap between concrete religious thinking and higher-level cognitive functioning in other areas tended to produce a rejection of religious belief. They used Peatling's RTTA scale with a group of high-school students. Included also were questions about their possible rejection of doctrine and about religion and science, as well as a test of logical reasoning and a range of questions regarding strongly held beliefs, religious behavior, religious attitudes of parents and friends, and their familiarity with religious material. Some refused to undergo the test, more boys than girls, more of those most alienated from the church. The results were confusing, but Goldman's assertion was not supported; apart from a group of students in a private Catholic school more abstract religious thinking was found to be associated with greater rejection of doctrine and of the church. It might be suggested that one reason for this finding is to be found in the different religious backgrounds of the American adolescents and of Goldman's in England, many of whom had little effective contact with any church, unlike the American group. However, a more likely explanation is that if, as Kay (1981a) suggested, Peatling's test of abstract religious thinking is equally a test of skepticism, then Hoge and Petrillo's results could not be other than this, and their difficulty in securing other significant results could well be due to the weakness of this particular test of religious thinking.

Maas (1985a, b) was another critic of Goldman. She took the stance of narrative theology as exemplified by Stroup (1981) and the viewpoint of church-based religious education. She described the wide-ranging influence of Goldman and Peatling, who were regarded as having provided scientific certainty for restricting the use of the Bible with children. Her extended theological discussion lies beyond the scope of the present review, although its basis is insecure, as Dillistone (1989) has shown. Not all books of the Bible could be called narrative, there appeared to be different types of narrative theology, and it was not clear what made a narrative theologically significant. Maas rightly set Goldman in the context of the British scene but seemed unaware of the problems of religious education with unchurched children in state schools. She misinterpreted Goldman's concern about adolescents rejecting Christian faith on the basis of a quasi-scientific way of thinking, as a desire to ensure that no adolescent underwent a world-shattering crisis of faith by replacing faith with gnosticism. His theological basis was an outmoded evolutionary developmentalism which had resulted in the loss of the Old Testament. He displayed a total lack of appreciation of the significance of narrative as a teaching tool. Further, his concept of religious thinking was entirely restricted to the cognitive so that his test was theologically invalidated, as was the concept of religious thinking he described. On the other hand, Robinson's (1977a) view of childhood provided an effective contrast to the assumption that children were incapable of experiencing, perceiving, or thinking as mature adults. Religious development was not the development of religious thinking but was faith development as postulated by Fowler (1981). Maas' discussion was limited to the Burning Bush material, with a well-documented argument against the adaptation and use of this passage and the underlying implications. At times the vigor of her writing leads to distortion, as for example Wilkinson's (1965a) comments about some of Goldman's remarks becomes a diatribe, and Priestly (1983) a "sworn enemy of Goldmanism." No reference was made to the material from the pictures used, nor to the material from the investigations undertaken by Elkind (1961); the problem of cognitive limitation in understanding religious material seemed irrelevant.

In her final chapter Maas described a test she constructed about the Burning Bush in which children could display their knowledge about the story; that God still heeded the cry of the suffering and sent people to carry out his purpose and that God's promise was alike applicable to the children—which incidentally Goldman (1963b) also required. The test was used with five boys and three girls between seven and seventeen, including a Catholic and an unchurched child. Very little information was given about their background. Their replies convinced her that concrete thinking was no obstacle to a theologically adequate understanding of Old Testament material, so that even children under seven should be exposed to such stories as these. Some of the children had a greater ability to interpret the biblical material than the two seventeen-year-old girls who, despite their adequate knowledge, had never before been asked how such material applied to them. Most of the children were familiar with the Moses narratives; they recognized that the story did not explain what "holy" meant, although the youngest guessed that it meant "good." Questions about Moses' fear showed that a sense of awe in the presence of God was found only among the older children and was entirely absent or only very partially discerned in the youngest; the other children explained Moses' fear in terms of his guilt for having killed an Egyptian. It emerged that regular Sunday school attendance appeared to be an important factor in bringing children to levels of operational thinking. The material recorded also showed that there was a growing insight with age, but no analysis of it was undertaken.

The study stands as a useful theological critique of a particular point of view; no doubt other critiques could be written from other points of view as fashions change in theology and biblical exegesis. Maas exposed much confused thought in many syllabuses regarding the use of the Bible and concluded that it was necessary to live with the tension created by the cognitive limitations of children and their need to learn the Bible. From a psychological viewpoint it provides little evidence concerning the way children actually develop religiously. Educationally it makes no contribution to the curriculum, lacking suggestions regarding biblical material. It could be used to justify a return to the materials and style of teaching found fifty years ago, which would meet the theological criteria suggested, although religious educators throughout the Western world were acutely aware that in practice it did not facilitate religious development. Older teachers can recall the satisfaction of telling stories to preadolescent children, which were inevitably well-received. But the problem is how, because of their cognitive limitations, they interpret them. We do not know how they come to sense their imagery, nor the ways by which in time they may discard false images. An earlier generation of children brought up on such storytelling have grown in understanding, but they were also immersed in the worship, liturgy, and symbolism of their church or synagogue, while adults lacking such experience seem also to lack this insight. Religious education in state schools in the pre-Goldman days did not produce any apparently different long-term result than it does today.

Lee (1988) had a better insight into the significance of Goldman's findings, regarding them as showing what for long had been known, that young children were not ready to learn higher-order cognitive material. But he was critical of making adult understanding the norm; he considered that children should gain familiarity with biblical passages, setting them in their own cognitive repertoire. A full understanding of them could not be achieved even by some adults. Krych (1985) also argued that the inability of children to think abstractly did not prevent them from being taught doctrine, and proceeded to teach justification by faith to Sunday school children aged nine to eleven, basing her approach on suggestions of Tillich and the use of transformational narrative by which both question and answer were communicated in the classroom. The doctrine was taught to her satisfaction to these children. The advice of Godin (1971) needs to be recalled about the late acquisition of historical consciousness and the slow development of symbolic functioning, so that there could be little understanding before the age of eleven or twelve of such ideas as the connection between the attributes of God and the historic facts of the life of Jesus.

Most American commentators welcomed Goldman's findings, and the limitations of children's thinking have been widely recognized. Fleck, Ballard, and Reilly (1975), (Ballard and Fleck, 1975) suggested that the three Piagetian stages could be used as a model for teaching religious concepts to children in Bible-centered religious education. They provided illustrative examples and stated that the biblical material had to be appropriate to the cognitive level of the children and related to their needs and experience. Spilka, Hood, and Gorsuch (1985) commented that the existence of cognitive stages was clearly established and the usefulness of Piagetian stages was also apparent, but they regretted the lack of experimental work on religious cognitive development. Foster and Moran (1985) argued that Piaget's basic structures of assimilation, accommodation, and disequilibration were evident in the parabolic method of teaching used by Jesus, and it was still necessary for an effective teacher to disequilibrate the learner, a method that could be used with success with a variety of experiences, a wide spectrum of ability, and a mixture of learning styles. Cole (1986) retorted that it was inappropriate to use the Bible to confirm psychological theory; rather there was need first to engage in a critical examination of a theory before looking for biblical convergences. To this Foster and Moran (1986) replied that the parables were recorded lessons and not the theological concepts that Cole had suggested, and the underlying structure of biblical lessons was related to modern learning theory.

George (1977) undertook a critical evaluation of stage theory as applied to religion, noting the extent to which it had long been assumed and the similarities between such studies as those of Harms (1944) and Piaget. Although sympathetic to Robinson's (1977a) point of view which stressed the validity of the religious experience of children as young as five, she regarded his approach as intuitive and based on self-reporting, unacceptable to psychological theory and lacking a scientific framework. Nevertheless, even affective development was by stages, and these she described first as nonverbal, aesthetic, and dominated by sense impressions, when knowledge was sensory rather than cognitive. From about seven to eleven it was experiential and concrete, with aspects of the first stage remaining, but fading in time, and dominated by verbal expression and concrete signs and symbols. After this an enlightened awareness and use of imagery developed. Robinson (1983) used stage theory as a framework for suggesting a model of personal development in which cognitive and affective elements interacted; this was illuminated by much autobiographical and anecdotal material and was used as the basis for the development of a comprehensive school curriculum for religious studies.

After George's study, the English translation of Piaget's (1981) discussion of intelligence and affectivity became available, in which he demonstrated the parallel between the cognitive and the affective, claiming that affective structures were not distinct from intellectual structures but had to do with cognitive reflection about our relationships with other people. Conflicts between affective and cognitive elements were due to feelings being at a lower developmental level. Feeling could advance or retard intellectual functioning, but it could not modify structures. He would not accept a dichotomy between intelligence and affectivity—behavior could not be classified under either; the true distinction was between behavior related to objects and behavior related to people.

Nipkow's (1986) extensive survey had shown that adolescents relinquished religious belief because they had not experienced divine help, they could not reconcile belief with undeserved suffering and death, they could find no reality corresponding to the idea of God other than its possible psychological value, and they did not find in their local churches the experience of the early church or the spirit of the Sermon on the Mount. Reich (1987, 1989) noted that the second of these was about difficulties in relating religious and scientific explanations of the world. Children developed a worldview in stages; up to about eight, children tended to regard God anthropomorphically, creating the flat earth as they knew it in a universe which had always existed. Between nine and twelve, scientific images grew to prominence, nature and God were seen as independent, with God seldom intervening, although enabling plants to grow and inspiring moral activity. In adolescence, with the advent of formal reasoning, rational explanation was sought, and inadequate religious worldviews were discarded, as Goldman (1964) had observed, although mature thinking could accommodate different perspectives by "complementarity." A small earlier study (Oser and Reich, 1987) of children and adults who were asked to solve nine problems in terms of two explanations for each showed five consecutive levels of thinking—between six and ten one or the other explanation was chosen; from eleven to fourteen some considered that both might be correct, and some that both explanations were needed; by twentyone most regarded the explanations as complementary, and finally a sophisticated synopsis of all possibilities was presented. The final problem had been about religious and scientific explanations of the origin of the universe, and a similar response pattern had been observed. Three respondents between thirteen and sixteen were interviewed two years later to see if they had progressed to complementarity in their thinking; one still regarded it as a matter of factual proof, another felt there was something beyond scientific explanation and had begun a reassessment of her views, and the third showed much greater awareness of the differences between religious and scientific knowledge. Although complementarity was by no means the only possible relationship between the theories, it was a mark of formal thinking which offered a means to clarify discussion and assist adolescents toward a more mature religious understanding.

Greer's (1984b) survey of fifty years of the psychology of religion in religious education objectively sets much of this argument in perspective, but the discussion is not yet ended. Slee (1986) reviewed Goldman's continuing influence, which had established Piagetian theory and method as an important model for subsequent research, citing the replications of the research and other independent studies which had investigated different levels of logical thinking about religious materials. This had resulted in concentrating on understanding biblical texts to the neglect of other more imaginative and creative aspects of thinking. She made the point, following Dittes (1971), that Goldman employed two different models of religion, the explicit content-defined model characterized by traditional patterns of belief and practice, and the implicit model, rooted in personal experience, to which all other knowledge could be related. These were contradictory rather than distinct yet partially related aspects of religion known to be multidimensional. This dualism was not noted by Goldman, and it obscured the relationship between his research findings of children's understanding of the material and the nature of the implicit religious education he proposed. Subsequently, Slee (1987) suggested that further research in religious thinking was needed based on a linguistic model of semantic, communal, convictional, and figurative usages of religious language.

Slee (1986) also critically examined the psychological scaling procedures Goldman had used with the five representative items. She was critical of the manner by which response categories had been combined for his purpose but made no reference to Goldman's (1965c) justification of this as a recognized procedure, nor to Peel's (1959) advocacy of the method, which Goldman had followed. Her conclusion was that the methodological grouping of Goldman's stage theory was extremely weak, if not spurious, and did not provide adequate grounds for a theory of stage development. Criticism of the scaling method is heightened in the light of more recent fundamental discussion regarding this technique. Moser and Kalton (1971) in their lucid style demonstrated the value of Guttman scales, especially when applied as originally intended. Scalogram analysis examines the responses of a group of individuals to a range of questions which should be in the same order of difficulty for all respondents. Goldman was not using scaling for this purpose; on the contrary, he wanted to establish an order of responses to a single item against the mental age of a group of children. His objective was not merely to demonstrate a developmental process but to show that the development was discontinuous; around particular mental ages Piagetian stage theory seemed to suggest there should be a marked change to a higher level of scoring, and the establishment of "cutting points" was used to indicate this development. Even on the basis of Goldman's own results, the changes from preoperational to concrete operational thinking disclosed by these five items ranged from mental age 6.6 to 8.10, and to formal operational thinking from 12.8 to 14.2. These bands, while supporting a discontinuous development, did not establish it as a rapid change specific to a particular mental age. (The absence of rapid change was noted in the tabulation of Elkind's responses in the previous chapter.) The nub of the criticism however lies in the concept of reproducibility. Moser and Kalton (1971) pointed out, with illustrations, that a scale could not be adequately assessed by a coefficient of reproducibility ranging from 0 to 1, since there never was a benchmark of zero. Valid reproducibility required a scale of not less than ten items with their endorsement ranging from 20 percent to 80 percent. Salomonsen (1972), when making an analysis of interviews about religious education and preparation for confirmation, had used the Rasch technique which deals in a more satisfactory manner than Guttman's method with the problems of responses which do not fall into place. Another theological assertion lacking empirical justification was made by Csanyi (1982). He contended that the distorted religious images of children between six and twelve were not permanently implanted in them but were stepping stones to a basis for a later adult understanding. While it is true that most children who grow up in the church community do outgrow the crude ideas acquired earlier, we do not know how many adults are still limited in their understanding by vestiges of such ideas. Without nurture many children do not outgrow these misunderstandings, which was the ground of Goldman's concern.

In view of the critical discussions of Goldman's work, and the ongoing reappraisal of Piagetian theory, a statistical reexamination of Goldman's data was made, with his permission, since it is still the best available about the topic. This is reproduced in Appendix F. It confirmed that there was no sex difference in the responses, it provided a detailed picture of the stage transitions of the five items analyzed, and demonstrated that the other variables measured—attendance at church or Sunday school, Bible reading, and private prayer—made little difference to the scores, which were dominated by the children's mental age. It shows that the cognitive dimension which Goldman set out to study shows clear developmental trends with mental age and is little affected by other variables.

Despite the criticisms, Goldman's work has been widely accepted and remains influential, even though less extreme applications of it are now frequent in religious education syllabuses. He has not returned to the topic but has continued to explore the development of children's thinking in other realms. It is now recognized that a stage development is not an abrupt process but produces quite different styles of thinking. This is universally true, not only about number and conservation—the areas of Piaget's early studies—but equally about history and geography, as is shown in chapter 7. Rosenberg (1989a, b) has pertinently commented that this universalism is a true test for religious thinking—thinking directed toward religion, as Goldman described it. There was no difference in the understanding of religious identity between Elkind's Catholic, Jewish, and Protestant children, and the same criteria apply to the children of any religion. No doubt in time there will be studies of children's understanding of the scriptures and the religious concepts of other great world faiths.

THE DEVELOPMENT OF FAITH AND RELIGIOUS JUDGMENT

If religious thinking was all that concerned religiousness the matter would rest here. But a cognitive grasp of concepts is only one part of religious activity; their application is also required, both by commitment to them in faith and by the application of them in religious judgments. The growth of faith with its cognitive and affective aspects of belief integrated into a unity is a more demanding study; this has received attention as the issue of faith development has been brought to the forefront by the work of James Fowler. Religious judgment has been brought to a sharp focus by Friz Oser.

One approach to long-term development was made by Riccards (1979). He surveyed a number of studies dealing with aspects of the development of religious ideas, referring to the work of Elkind and Goldman and their use of Piaget's developmental theory. He set out the limitations of stage theories as he saw them; maturation was highly individualized, producing almost imperceptible effects, and questions about the irreversibility of stages had not been satisfactorily answered. Even so, it seemed to him that there was a sufficient body of knowledge to provide at least a theoretical framework of a stage theory. He concluded that over the whole span of life eight stages would account for most research findings. These were 1) a familial stage in the first years of life, dominated by parents, with little consciousness of God, prayer, or denomination; 2) a fairy-tale period from three to six, when God was thought of as an old man, a father, or a child with magical powers; 3) institutionalism, from seven to eleven, in which preadolescents understood God in more spiritual terms and identified with the organization of the church, if supported by the family; 4) conceptual, from twelve to fifteen, when adolescents internalized religious concepts and perceived God in more abstract terms such as love and fatherhood; 5) a stage of conflict, from fifteen to nineteen, frequently described as a period of crisis or of problems in late adolescence; 6) reevaluation, from nineteen to thirty, with a reduced saliency of things religious in adult life, so that religion was either accepted not too intensely or neglected; 7) determination about the importance of individual religion, after thirty, so that it is either reintegrated into a personal philosophy or abandoned; 8) resignation after sixty, when for many religion became an important way to deal with death. These stages were related to those of Erikson and of Loevinger and to the development of political sensibility.

Fowler's faith development theory has largely centered on continuing adult development. A short summary cannot do justice to his work, which has attracted wide attention since it first appeared (Fowler and Keen, 1978). Six stages of faith development were described, with transitional phases between them; the development was regarded as parallel to seven other developmental processes, those of Piaget's logical thinking, Selman's role-taking, Kohlberg's moral judgment, the bounds of social awareness, the locus of authority, the form of world coherence, and the role of symbols. These were set out in tabular form (Fowler, 1980). Because of Fowler's dependence on Erikson, it is worth recalling this psychological model.

Erikson formulated a theory of psychological development which has attracted much interest in America. His ideas are readily available in such accounts as those of Maier (1978), Roazen (1976), or Stevens (1983). He described the development of personality from birth to old age by the realization of identity through eight successive stages, each of which had to be achieved by resolving inner tensions. The stages were reappraisals of those of Freud. First a newborn baby needed to acquire a basic sense of trust and overcome frustration, which provided the basis for hope. At two, when children were capable of independent action, they had to acquire a sense of autonomy and free will. At five they had to use initiative and overcome guilt, leading to a realization of purpose. At eight they had to achieve a sense of industry and overcome a sense of inferiority so that they gained a sense of competence. Adolescence was the time when identity had to be realized and confusion about it overcome. Young adult life saw the realization of love by developing the capacity for intimacy and avoiding isolation. In maturity secure adults grew to provide care for the next generation. Finally, in old age wisdom came as the product of a mature sense of identity which had overcome despair. These phases are described in great detail, but the vocabulary appears to be as much ethical as clinical. The stages of emotional development are remarkably parallel to Piaget's stages of cognitive development; Maier (1978) discussed this in some detail. But Erikson adhered to the basic ideas of Freud and paid no attention to other aspects of ego development, such as ego maturation or the place of self-esteem and self-criticism, and provided no empirical data to support his system.

Fowler's conception of faith included nonreligious as well as religious worldviews, whereby the self reacted to others and to what transcended them. In a more recent work (1981) he showed by a fictional dialogue his dependence on Piaget, Kohlberg, and Erikson to establish the relevant characteristics of the development, which he had identified from lengthy interviews. These semiclinical interviews, while having a common structure, were not concerned with specific details, tasks, or problems, as was the case with Piaget, Goldman, or Kohlberg, so that their evaluation was much more subjective. Fowler regarded his model as provisional, and the stage structure it described was a means of organizing responses to questions asked in the interview rather than a formal classification system.

At the start was undifferentiated faith, up to three, preconceptual and prelinguistic, when infants formed a disposition in which trust, courage, hope, and love together developed to form the basis of later faith development. This was followed by:

1. Intuitive-Projective faith, from three to seven, based on fantasy and imagination, without logic and dominated by perception. Deity as cause or creator was understood in magical terms. Children were influenced by adult attitudes, language, and example and by stories relived with lasting effects.

2. Mythic-Literal faith, from seven to eleven, when children began to think logically and concretely; beliefs and symbols were held literally and facts differentiated from fantasy. Other points of view were appreciated, cause and effect were understood, and earlier imagination was curbed. An anthropomorphic image of God was much more developed. Symbolic materials were deeply affecting, but reflecting on their meanings was not yet possible. Some adults retained much of their religion at this level.

3. Synthetic-Conventional faith arose at twelve or later from the acquisition of formal-operational thinking, distinguishing facts from values, and related to the range of personal involvements encountered. Many adults remained at this stage, which was conformist, accepting the judgments of significant people and lacking the security to construct their independent perspective. Strongly held beliefs and values were not viewed objectively.

4. Individuative-Reflective faith could arise after eighteen when adults accepted responsibility for their own beliefs and attitudes. Self-identity and an individual worldview became dominant. Symbols were translated into conceptual meanings with tensions between them and their group, and also between subjective feelings and objectivity, self-fulfillment and service to others, and between the relative and the absolute.

5. Conjunctive faith after thirty saw the reemergence of symbolism, appreciated because its reality was more fully comprehended. At mid-life, experience led to the acceptance of paradox and contradiction and an outgoing concern for the efforts of other people seeking to establish their identity and meaning in life.

6. Universalizing faith after forty was the final stage achieved by such people as Gandhi, Martin Luther King, or Mother Teresa, in whom the search for unity had been completed and for whom the present was enhanced by the transcendent. It was only once encountered in an interview.

By way of illustration, a case history was given of the tumultuous life of Mary, her unhappy marriage and her movement into and out of the charismatic movement, accompanied by changing religious stances which demonstrated the distinction between the structure and the content of faith; content was concerned with theological beliefs, whereas structure was concerned with the response made because of faith. This important distinction underlies much of the confusion noted about religious understanding in Appendix E.

Fowler undertook little statistical analysis of his material, and when he discussed the reasons for differences in stage development between men and women, he did not check the statistical significance of the small differences between their scores. Important differences could well be expected, since patterns of religious belief and behavior consistently differ between the sexes.

A limitation of the theory is that it ignores much recent work in the psychology of religion. Structure and content need to be related to the basic dimensions of religion now widely acknowledged. A study which Fowler quoted (Chirban, 1981, based on an examination of transcripts of Fowler's interviews) showed that extrinsically oriented religion was almost completely confined to the earlier stages of faith development. Beyond this, little other systematic investigation has been undertaken, which partly accounts for the limited enthusiasm that the theory has as yet engendered. Spilka, Hood, and Gorsuch (1985) dismissed it because of its abstruseness and complexity and lack of empirical research. Shulik (1979) regarded Fowler's approach as an extension of Kohlberg's understanding of moral development and confirmed this by a study of elderly people, for whom faith development was related to an awareness of changes brought by age. He regarded both theories as an adaptation of a common developmental process, but contrary to the expectations of Erikson's theory none of them was engaged in any life-review. Leean (1988) confirmed a relationship between Fowler's faith development and Erikson's life cycle. He drew a parallel with Kohlberg's scheme, noting the fundamental difference between the frequently held stage four moral development with its stress on the laws, rights, and duties of the social system and the next stages in which moral decisions were based on the principles which undergirded the social system. Power and Kohlberg (1980) showed that in terms of Fowler's Faith Development, moral development always equaled or preceded faith development but did not necessarily ensure it.

Fowler's definition of faith has also come in for a great deal of criticism. Thus, Moseley and Brockenbrough (1988) saw a tension between Fowler's ambiguous definition of faith, which he distinguished from religion, and his basic monotheism due to his dependence on the theology of Niebuhr. Loder (1980) discussed the experiences of violent or continuous negation and void which affect everyone and regarded Fowler's theory as flawed by its lack of reference to them. Conn (1981) noted the implications of affectivity in Kohlberg's approach to moral reasoning, and its absence in Fowler's theory, contending that it focused on knowing about faith, in a Piagetian way of thinking, and not on the content of faith. Miles (1983) was critical of the theory's unexamined assumptions and its lack of distinction between spiritual growth and the development of religious concepts. However, as a model of religious conceptual and intellectual development it was superior to the Piagetian model. The latter was concerned with operational ability to handle religious ideas irrespective of the religious quality of the judgments, whereas Fowler's was a model of conceptual and intellectual development based on religious norms appropriate to the stage.

Webster (1984) took note of the criticism that the theory lacked the normal procedure of psychological experiments using a statistical analysis of results designed to test stated hypotheses, was difficult to replicate, and was not based on proper sampling techniques. He questioned its dependence on Kohlberg's theory, which should require the invariance of faith development, and asked, as had been asserted of Kohlberg's theory, if it was Western rather than universal. Kohlberg had been criticized as only describing general cognitive development related to social relationships, and his higher stages were suspect, all of which could apply to Fowler. His claim to have extended the theories of Piaget, Kohlberg, and Selman lacked both substance and confirmation but rendered him open to any legitimate criticism made of any of them. Nor had he justified his integration of the stages of such disparate theories. Believers equally could contend that their experience of faith was little related to Fowler's search for meaning and Fowler's stages did not obviously correspond to their own spiritual progress—even more so for those of positions other than Christian. Fowler's warm concern had provided valuable insights and stimulated much thought. His work should not be seen as a scientific theory but as an exercise in practical theology about the way people construct meanings. Heywood (1985) was critical of Fowler's description of stages which were presumed to exist on the basis of Piagetian theory, and his contention that faith stages were a structural whole, without offering any independent empirical proof of such stages. The problems of stage theory itself and the philosophical basis on which the theory rested made it an uncertain foundation, and Fowler's "logic of conviction" was incompatible with Piaget's operational structures concerned with rational certainty. In a post-Piagetian period alternative developmental models should be used. Fowler's problem arose from his dependence on Kohlberg's understanding of Piaget, which erroneously led him to regard Piaget as offering an accepted theory of cognitive development that could be broadened into other areas, whereas the theory was not only suspect but could not be thus extended. Smith (1985) was more sympathetic to Fowler's intentions, indicating the modifications Kohlberg had made to his cognitive theory over the years and their consequence to Fowler, and contending that Piaget had not been wholly overthrown. Cognition remained important in human development, and the invariant sequence of stages held by Piaget, Kohlberg, and Selman on which Fowler rested had not been disproved. Moreover, there was much theological support for Fowler over a broad field, Catholic and Protestant.

The point that Fowler is open to criticisms made against Kohlberg soon becomes evident. Philibert (1988) regarded Kohlberg as proposing a system of moral structuralism, and this was true also of Fowler, who not only depended on Kohlberg but defined faith so that it was a moral response to God's initiative. Fowler made faith a kind of logic—for which there was plenty of prior support—and his stage theory was culture based, elitist, and compliant to forms of mass culture.

Gilligans' (1977, 1980) criticisms also apply. She asserted that Piaget, Freud, and Kohlberg had overlooked women; development was the development of boys. She was critical of some of Kohlberg's descriptions of moral judgments which did not adequately recognize the experience of women, and of Piaget (1932), who paid no attention to girls' responses about morality when they were different from those of boys. Her study of statements made by women contemplating an abortion showed a first transition from selfishness to responsibility, a second level of goodness seen as self-sacrifice, a second transition from goodness to truth, and a third level of the morality of nonviolence. She argued that a morality of responsibility needed to be integrated with a morality of rights, and the biblical picture of Abraham willing to sacrifice his son contrasted with the mother pleading for her child before Solomon, relinquishing the truth to secure her child's life. Friedman (1985) examined from a philosophical stance Gilligan's contention that women exhibited a different form of morality—the morality of care and of responsibility in contrast to Kohlberg's stage sequence. She did this first by a logical analysis of the stories of Abraham's willingness to sacrifice Isaac and Socrates' dialogue with Euthyphro. She then looked at the logical consequences of making a series of modifications to Kohlberg's Heinze dilemma by changing the sex and roles of the participants. She was critical of both Kohlberg and Gilligan; there was an absence of any real integration of moral considerations having to do with care and relationship and of an adequate account of how people reason about complex situations in terms of moral rules and principles. Like many others, she seemed unaware that Bull (1969) had recorded highly significant differences in moral development between boys and girls. Despite the almost universal finding of the greater religiousness of women, Fowler paid little more attention to it than any other. When Friedman, Robinson, and Friedman (1986) tested Gilligan's theory by using an appropriate measure of moral judgment in a mixed group of students they found no differences due to sex, or to any other personality measure used.

Ford-Grabowsky (1986, 1987, 1988) criticized Fowler's theory as being purely cognitive. It confused ego development and spiritual growth and their developmental trends that could not be logically combined. It also lacked data about a Christian understanding of faith. Jung had carefully distinguished between the ego and the self and held to the concept of the outer and inner self, designating the ego as the center of consciousness, but regarding the self as the totality of both the conscious and the unconscious. This mirrored the concept of the outer and inner person expounded by the mystic Hildegard in the twelfth century. There was an innate desire to know God, with a progression from sin to repentance to salvation that was not included in Fowler's faith development. Fowler's case study of Mary showed that Mary's first conversion to belief in God affected only her ego, but her subsequent conversion to full Christian faith with its profound effect was the conversion of her inner person. Thus diagnosed, Mary was at stage three in cognitive terms, as Fowler had stated, but her deeper religious development was more advanced and was at stage five, a situation impossible according to Fowler.

Raduka (1980) regarded Fowler's stages of faith development as corresponding to Jung's stages of personality development and from a study of five individuals was able to provide supportive evidence and psychological explanations of the apparent contradictions observed. These were due in part to the theological emphasis on transcendence and the psychological emphasis on immanence of the two systems. Bradley (1983) noted that Fowler's faith development theory was concerned with the process rather than the content of faith, and faith as a way of knowing and as a way of valuing seemed to have parallels with Jungian-based personality types. Evidence from testing tended to support the contention. The women tended to score lower on faith development than men.

Fowler's work quickly stimulated further studies, as well as attracting criticism. Grannell (1977) elaborated a related theory of faith development in which Kohlberg's and Erikson's influence were paramount. Gorman (1977, 1978) found that high-school students' level of Kohlberg's moral development and Fowler's faith development were both strongly associated with socio-economic status and mental ability, and faith development was also facilitated by the experience of the death of someone close, and by experience of lifestyles and perspectives different from those of the subjects. These fostered role-taking—an important element for both moral and faith development. Trevelyan (1978) made a substantial theoretical study by applying to adolescent development the psychological perspectives of Erikson, Jung, Kohlberg, and Tillich. He demonstrated their relevance to adolescent religious development in terms of peer groups, goals, moral principles, opportunities for creative expression, conscious self-development, and the examination of ultimate meanings. An experimental course in religious education which provided six very similar categories indicated that these provided a satisfactory basis for curriculum development. Vanden (1985) used Fowler's faith development interview in a series of family studies. Rigidity in the parents' faith structure, which was at Fowler's third stage, depending on external authority and deficient in abstract thinking, was associated with rigidity in family life, with authoritarian rules and predictable and repetitious patterns of communication. In a comparison of the faith development of two groups of Catholic students, men showed higher levels of faith development than women and affiliation was negatively associated with faith development, suggesting that the tendency of religious institutions to keep their members in an authoritarian mode of faith hindered its development (White, 1985). Adolescents from two different churches had different levels of faith development; one group was solidly in stage three, the others had moved to the transition to the next stage, which reflected the levels of faith development of the two communities, which in turn was influenced by their leaders (Simmonds, 1986).

Kalam (1981) worked with Kohlberg and Fowler to relate moral and religious development to cognitive development. In a town in South India where Christians, Hindus, and Muslims had long lived in harmony, and different religious factors would have the least effect, boys, adolescents, young, middle-aged, and old men from each religious group were interviewed. Three of Kohlberg's moral dilemmas and the cognitive aspects of Fowler's Faith Development Interview were used. A detailed examination was made of the psychological basis of both Kohlberg's and Fowler's stage structures, closely following Piaget. Fowler's stages were shown to consist of cognitive elements and affective and ego-developmental elements forming a tightly knit unit, theoretically depending much more on Kohlberg than Piaget, notably in the description of a sixth stage of adult development. The relationship between Kohlberg's and Fowler's stages should have been one of parallel development yet half the cases showed a larger or smaller degree of stage difference; this was contrary to both theories. Since earlier studies had shown much greater agreement, Kalam postulated that these were biased by their scoring being undertaken by the same individual and not externally collaborated, whereas his scores were confirmed by the authors of the two systems. In the absence of sufficient agreement, or a clear pattern of difference, the theoretical assumptions of the two authors had to be questioned, and this was undertaken in detail.

The main argument concentrated on Kohlberg's theory, but the findings were *a fortiori* also applicable to Fowler. They concluded that Kohlberg's stages were not content-free structures but specific descriptions of content development. They were subject to even more criticism, because they were based on Erikson's pattern of ego-development, and the structural properties of cognitive development could not be applied to them. It followed that what was required was the recognition that it was taxonomies of virtues and beliefs which were to be studied. So long as understanding was regarded as part of religious development, a study of their taxonomies was essential. The continuation of such Piagetian studies was preferable to Fowler's theories, described by one critic as a well-informed hunch, a library of *a priori's* articulated into a series of unproved assumptions that had not been deeply tested in any usual sense of that word (McBride, 1976). Kalam isolated a series of developments. The ideas of God and of life after death showed examples of syncretic thinking; concrete thinking and abstract thinking followed a developmental pattern with surprisingly little difference across the different religious groups. His subjects had dealt with hypothetical moral situations and religious issues using the same cognitive style, and in transitional stages, the issues showing vestiges of lower style thinking were the ones with which the individuals were not familiar; familiarity with an issue facilitated Piaget's cognitive décalage. Thus, many could deal with the idea of God at a formal operational level, but accepted or rejected ideas of the devil or evil spirits with concrete thinking—they had seen them, or not seen them, and their effects. It seemed likely that the presence of the contexts in individuals' environments and the freedom they had to interact with them without coercion or inhibition must be responsible for facilitating development.

Furushima (1983, 1985) undertook a cross-cultural research project on faith development, interviewing Hawaiian-born Buddhists. He concluded that the claim of universality for this developmental structure was partially substantiated, but further exploration was needed in areas where faith was affected by particular cultures, or where explicitly Christian concepts such as those of God or sin were involved. Fowler's theory did not account for all the data and could be criticized on a number of grounds, such as the social aspect of faith, assumptions about higher stages, the styles of faith expression, and the metaphoric dimension of faith and its cultural features.

Dowd (1985) proposed eight stages of Christian development, moving from faith through self-discipline to Christian love. They were related to Erikson's developmental stages but not to Fowler's stages. A test to identify them proved to have good statistical reliability. Christiano (1986) argued that Fowler's essential contribution was to include an affective element in faith development, having first secularized his theory, but it still lacked clarity. Broun (1984) made a comparison of ego development and Fowler's faith development among university students and staff. Age had no effect on either of the variables, which were found to be significantly associated, possibly due to a shared cognitive component. Faith development was also found in this sample to be unaffected by religious practice or specific doctrinal beliefs. Sweitzer (1984) studied the symbolic use of religious language among evangelicals from the perspective of Fowler's faith development theory, using eight important phrases to be defined. Higher scores were secured by older and better-educated subjects and corresponded to different levels of faith development. There was no difference between the sexes.

Borklund (1980) was also interested in the characteristics of the religion of maturity and studied four mature individuals in depth. For each of them, reflection on experience had added new dimensions to their original psychic positions leading to wholeness. The process was not linear, but cyclic—awareness, choice, and discipline were repeated in every aspect of experience, always opening doors to new opportunities for learning and growth. The precondition was a stance of openness—to God, to themselves, to others, and to change. This openness arose from an important internal sense of authority; childhood environment led to initial religious commitment, but their persistence with the process had proved to be the crucial element.

Since Rest's Defining Issues test had simplified the measurement of Kohlberg's levels of moral development, Barnes and Doyles (1989) set out to produce a similar scale to indicate the level of respondents' faith development as defined by Fowler. They used it with a group of Catholics and compared faith development with their religious orientations. Extrinsic religiousness was related to stage two faith development, intrinsic religiousness to stages three and four, and quest to stage five. Green and Hoffman (1989) assessed students' levels of faith development from their self-assessing responses to a single statement. When the students had also to evaluate the similarity or difference between themselves and the profiles of others, those in the earlier stages gave more positive ratings for the religiousness of those similar to themselves than those dissimilar, but in the higher stages this was not the case, and there were no significant differences in the ratings.

Kwilecki (1988a) was critical of theories of faith development, such as Fowler's, which did not allow for the great variety found in religious development. They were at fault because they did not recognize the strength of cultural influences or take account of them and were themselves Western and intellectual. These assertions and indications of a culture-based approach were illustrated from a case study. To this Barnes (1989) retorted that despite accepting some of her criticisms, her approach would validate the type of religious group loyalties that produced religious conflicts such as those in Northern Ireland or Lebanon. Fowler's theory was a hypothesis that was not invalidated if some development did not conform to it, to which Kwilecki replied in the same journal issue. Her position was clarified by her work (Kwilecki, 1988b) with black and white rural communities in Georgia among fundamentalist church members and illustrated by four more case studies. In these groups, those most capable of articulating a coherent and complex religious discussion regarded the Bible as inerrant, absolutely and exclusively authoritarian. This spiritual authoritarianism coincided with analytical ability and conflicted with all those from Allport to Fowler who regarded dogmatic conviction as immature. The discussion continues—Kwilecki (1989) and Kahoe (1989).

It does not follow that these articulate believers were necessarily at a high level of religious development. The four cases demonstrate clearly how cognitive development—in this case evidenced by their articulate responses—is not the same as faith development; it also shows that faith development measurements are bound by theological assumptions. It is possible to envisage distinguished scientists, eminent in their professions, renowned for the religious quality of lives which display Christian virtues to a high degree. Yet some of these believe in biblical inerancy and authority and propound their faith with clarity. Their theology may seem simplistic to those theologians they would regard as suspect, but does it diminish their faith? How is it inferior to that of middle-aged church members who never graduated but have learned to accept the paradoxes and contradictions of faith without great intellectual activity and show a simple understanding and warmth to other people?

Practical applications of the theory were soon suggested. Tulloch (1985) found that a sixteen-week cognitively oriented Bible-study program produced a small development in the faith stages of the six adult participants. S. Francis (1987) illustrated the use of faith development theory as a basis for religious education. It needed cautious use, since spiritual essence could not be explained in the materialistic terms of cognitive development and was something other than the sequential, linear and stage-related terms indicated. Schurter (1987) thought that Fowler's early stages offered a useful guide for ministering to the mentally retarded. Fowler (1984a) himself compared the faith which is believed—the Christian story and its narrative structure—with *paideia*, the gradual introduction into the faith. This he related to his developmental view of faith; it could be that *paideia* engendered specific virtues and clusters of life-saving emotions and the call to partnership with God. Liturgy and prayer provided the context in which imagination and emotion could be awakened within a community of hope in God as Lord of a future commonwealth of love.

While this critical discussion of Fowler's work was continuing, an important and extensive series of studies on religious judgment was being undertaken in Switzerland by Oser. Accounts of the reseach and its bearing on religious education, together with related studies by his colleagues, include Oser (1980, 1985, 1988), Oser and Gemünder (1988), Nipkow, Schweitzer, and Fowler (eds.) (1988), and Bucher and Reich (eds.) (1989).

Oser (1980) adapted Kohlberg's use of moral problems to develop a series of religious dilemmas—problem stories designed to elicit religious judgments indicating stages of religious thinking. One was the story of Paul, a young doctor who survived a plane crash in which he prayed, pledging his life for the poor of the third world and was then offered a lucrative position at home (Oser, 1985). The dilemmas have been adapted and used successfully in very different cultures. Oser regarded his cognitive stages as distinct from Fowler's, which he criticized as a conglomerate from various sources. They were dissimilar to the stages of the development of religious concepts but were about judging and valuing the meaning of events as people faced failure, incompetence, and death. A boy aged ten who described God as an old man with a white beard—the lowest of Goldman's stages—also asserted that if something bad happened to us, God could preserve us from a much larger evil—a higher cognitive level of judgment. When people made religious judgments they were about an understanding of divine-human relationships, and had to do with bi-polar elements such as the holy and the profane. These had their own developmental processes; for example, a mature understanding recognized that the holy is mediated by the profane, whereas a child would say "either it's holy or profane, but it can't be both." The other elements were freedom versus dependency, hope versus absurdity, the everlasting versus the temporary, trust versus anxiety, explanation versus mystery, and transcendence versus immanence. From his sample of subjects aged nine to seventy-five, Oser described (1980) the replies to one story made by five subjects, each of them representative of one of the stages.

The stages were again illustrated from typical replies which children and adolescents gave when asked why God allowed some other children to lose a parent through divorce or death (Oser, 1985). Before the first stage children could not differentiate between events due to human error and those of transcendental causality. In the first, "Deus ex machina" stage of determinism, reasons for the replies were found either in human inadequacy or in God's will. There were reasons for things happening, but subjects felt they were at the mercy of a God whose power was ultimate and whose interventions were regarded as a reward or a punishment, and they acted because of his compulsion. It was a unilateral situation, full of hope or despair. "It's a punishment, and God did it. He always does things like this with some people."

When this was seen to be too simplistic, the second "do ut des" stage of reciprocity was reached. Human activity was seen to win God's favor, bringing reward and preventing punishment. God sought the best for humans but only intervened in the world in certain circumstances; there was only a crude understanding of causation. It was a preventative, give-so-that-you-get concept; people were able to influence God so as to protect their own interests, but this made life more secure—"God wants it to be a lesson for them, and they will understand it later."

When critical thought arose, hidden causes were not regarded as adequate explanations, and the third stage of "deism" or voluntarism was reached. Now events were seen to be of a human causation for which God was not responsible. Man and God were independent of each other in a state of peaceful co-existence. Human autonomy was better appreciated, but somewhat ambivalently; free will and conformity with God were independent and in tension until the individual will was seen to be dependent on God. All existence was regarded as contingent; a relationship with God arose from an act of faith. "It is ridiculous to say that everything which does not work out in this world must be viewed as if there were a hidden reason for it."

Later, it could be realized that human existence was dependent on the ultimate; people were God's instrument in a plan by which the world moved toward goodness, although they could still direct their lives. This was the fourth, "correlational," stage "of the divine plan." The divine-human relationship was characterized by autonomy; responsibility for an individual's actions lay within God's unseen plan for everybody. It was seen as love and goodness, since individuals shared with God the idea of what is right in a relationship which is for the sake of his plan. "There is always a possibility of preventing divorce waifs." "This is exactly where the unseen, god-like call in us lies, to engage ourselves in activities which would benefit humankind, for example, to provide family therapy or financial support."

The fifth stage arose when the human and the divine aspects of stage four were bound together, and human reality was interpreted in the light of the existence or absence of communicative love. It was the stage of the perspective of religious autonomy and brought the self-fulfillment discovered when God was experienced as the reality which liberated and made human autonomy possible and meaningful. This understanding of God arose when the freedom of others was fully acknowledged. A sixth universal stage (Oser, 1980), not included in the later studies, saw a relationship with God as the reason for the whole of history and not only the basis for the existence of the subject and of other people.

This hierarchical structure, from stage two, also had the potential to contain an atheistic rejection of belief when other explanations of meaningfulness were advanced. It pointed to an educational need to go beyond acquiring religious knowledge and exploring religious experience creatively and, by social activity, to lead pupils to higher levels of religious judgment by the use of similar dilemmas.

Oser (1988) provided a summary of the statistical basis for the research derived from the fuller account (Oser and Gemünder, 1984), some of it presented graphically, and including the tabulated agreements found among eight different dilemmas. Stage one, which accounted for nearly half the responses at ages eight and nine, was found in only a tenth of those at eleven and twelve, and hardly at all at fourteen and fifteen. Stage two accounted for rather more than half of all responses between eight and fifteen, was less than a fifth at seventeen and eighteen, and was not found later. The third stage was first observed at ages eleven and twelve and dominated the responses at seventeen and older. Stage four was first observed at ages fourteen and made up a fifth of the twenty to twenty-five group. A fuller theological account of the stages was also provided, and finally a reply to a number of criticisms made against the theory and method, such as the Paul story being a moral and not a religious problem, the stage progressions not always corresponding to higher levels of judgment, the structural-cultural problem not being universally solved, together with questions about the theory of religious development and its presentation.

The debate about Fowler continues and is still unresolved, now made more complex by the similarities and differences between his stages of faith development and Oser's stages of religious judgment. The discussion lies outside the scope of this review. Mention can be made only of the most recent contributions about Fowler's concept of faith in Dykstra and Parks' (1988) symposium, with its severe criticisms, theologically, that Fowler gave no place to the redemptive activity of God, or of individual commitment, but saw faith only in terms of meaning. There were methodological problems, one of which concerned the lack of theistic commitment at the top of the scale. Nor had Fowler overcome all the problems of social-developmental research, allowed for psycho-dynamic aspects of faith, or dealt adequately with the first years of life. Against such strong criticisms Fowler defended himself in a final chapter. Fowler and Oser are considered in Nipkow, Schweitzer, and Fowler (1988) and in the brief report of the first symposium on religious development and education (Slee, 1988). Here, the considerable difference between Fowler's concept of faith and Oser's concept of religious development becomes apparent, as well as the difference in methodology of the two men. Unlike Fowler, Oser is free from theological dependency. Neither of them taps the religious experience and imagination of individuals. By dealing only with aspects of socialization through a cognitive developmental tradition, they cannot deal adequately with the symbolic aspects of religion such as play in childhood and ritual.

The situation today could not be better shown than by the contrast between two recent articles. Petrovich (1988) retrospectively reviewed Goldman's (1964) work. She complained that he and his critics had confused "thinking," which was a cognitive activity about forming concepts, making judgments, and drawing inferences with the affective nature of opinions, beliefs, and attitudes, while it was not clear how the rules of logical reasoning should apply to biblical narratives. The present-day relevance of Piaget was curtly dismissed; no alternatives were offered or positive suggestions made about how religious education should proceed in consequence of this. Readers must judge for themselves how relevant such criticism is in the light of the reviews of dimensions of religion and neo-Piagetian findings. A very different note was sounded by Gerber (1988) in his discussion of the continuing research and neo-Piagetian influence on it. Historically, the psychology of religion had three main areas. The first originated with Freud and was developed by Jung, Fromm, Erikson, Godin, and Vergote. James had initiated a fruitful descriptive area, and Elkind and Goldman were the founders of the application of genetic epistemology to religious psychology. This had been applied by Kolhberg to morality and then by Fowler to faith. Finally, Oser had overcome many difficulties in studying objectively the logical processes of making religious judgments, although he admitted the problems in distinguishing between what was moral and what was religious in this. Gerber gave an account of the work of these three, more extensively that of Oser, whom he regarded sympathetically.

Unlike the Piagetian-type studies of religious thinking, which indicate how intellectual development affects cognitive understanding of religious ideas, the stages of Fowler and Oser are specific to religion, and while mental development is necessary for their evolution it does not of itself bring it about. While the work of Fowler has tended to be descriptive, Oser as an educationist is concerned with the need to bring about development in religious judgment and has introduced the use of religious dilemmas into the classroom for this purpose. The wheel has turned full circle: twenty-five years after Goldman the emphasis in research is once more on the process of religious education.

Chapter 3

Children's Ideas of God

The first investigations into the religion of children were explorations of what they thought about God. It immediately became clear that the younger the children were, the more remote their ideas were from those of adults. Research was occasional and sporadic, with no continuous theme and has tended to remain so, following the varied interests of those undertaking it. No easy classification of it is possible, so it has been brought together in somewhat overlapping areas of age. The variety of ideas recorded reflects the different cultures and home backgrounds in which the children have grown, shown for example by the varying extent of their crude anthropomorphisms. Finally, attempts to explore children's understanding of the religious vocabulary used to describe God by adults are summarized.

What we think about God—our concept of God—is related to what we feel about God; while the cognitive and affective are related, affective religiousness is an independent dimension (Krull, 1984). Different belief systems give rise to different conceptual systems about God, as was shown by Sternberg (1979), who isolated eleven characteristics of God which could be organized into three groups—his perceived benevolence, eternality, vigor, and lenience; his perceived falsity, untrustworthiness, cruelty, and unknowableness; and his wrathfulness and severity. Such belief systems are related to the psychological needs of individuals (MacRae, 1977; Day, D. 1980), who regard humanity as endowed with similar qualities to God (Schoenfeld, 1987). The variety of ideas of God held by children must be set in the context of the great complexity and diversity of belief held by mature believers. Analysis of ratings by students of the extent that ninety-one adjectives were appropriate to describe God indicated not only traditional Christian concepts but such ideas described as deisticness, eternality, evaluative, kindliness, omni-ness, and wrathfulness (Gorsuch, 1967, 1968). Hammersla, Andrews-Quells, and Frease (1986) adapted this scale of adjectives for use with Evangelical students. Commitment was related to positive concepts, more strongly for the women than the men, but it had no relationship with "vindictive" and was inversely related to "irrelevant" and "distant." No differences were found for age. The findings confirmed Gorsuch's assertion that equally committed people may differ significantly in their concept of God. In its complexity, the image of God reflects affective influences. It will be seen that it is related to an individual's image of ideal parents and past upbringing, to personality traits (Neff, 1977), and to mental health (Rizzuto, 1974, 1979).

Studies of the idea of God in childhood and adolescence have a long history and have shown much consistency in spite of differences of approach and sampling. In one review of them, Wright and Koppe (1964) noted normal developmental sequences regarding the description of God and faith in God. The very simple ideas of children of two and three associated God with nature and living in churches or heaven, and with magic; they expressed little more than a simple belief in God and that he cared for them. These ideas were extended at four and five by the idea of God as powerful, watching over people, and punishing wrong-doing. They showed a real interest in knowing him and wanting to please him. Their ideas further developed in the next two years, when some of them felt close to God. Recognition of the orderliness of God's activity next emerged, and although still dominated by anthropomorphic terms, a few children showed the first traces of more abstract concepts, that God is spirit or is love and is not confined to one place. By eight or nine an understanding emerged of God's attributes as all-powerful and all-knowing, associated with nature, but also a loving father and seen to be spirit. A sense of responsibility emerged to work with God and participate in church activities and a strong sense of the dependability of God's universe, all combined with a growing sense of a personal relationship with God and responsibility for others close to them. At ten and eleven a sense of personal relationship became evident, and continuing questions about God's nature could now be linked with an element of doubt. Finally, at twelve or thirteen, anthropomorphism ended, God's relation to nature was seen as less important than his relationship with humanity, and he was described in terms of his attributes. Expressions of faith reflected the culture of their church. There was eagerness to participate in and contribute to the church, now seen as a place to learn about God. A search for meaning resulted in some blaming God for the troubles in the world, which others saw as the result of not cooperating with him. Participation and responsibility continued to grow in the last two years, some expressing an unquestioning faith, and others, doubts. While some questioning was theoretical or hypothetical, others thought of God as a guide for their actions.

The early studies

The first investigations began a century ago. They were unrelated and often bore the marks of their authors' interests. They brought to light children's spontaneous ideas of God, or else ideas they had been taught, modified by their limited understanding or imagination. They range over a wide area and show only limited continuity in their conceptual content, preventing a satisfactory classification of them.

Barnes (1892) found from six to twenty a wide range of descriptions of God including ideas of omnipresence, omniscience, and omnipotence, but with few references to Christ. Questioning was first detected at seven, but a fully critical spirit did not develop until fourteen, and by fifteen abstract ideas were expressed. Tanner (1906) asked children between eight and fifteen, mostly of Dutch Protestant origin, about God. Their answers reflected their conservative upbringing, independent of denomination or age. Better responses came from girls than from boys; half the children loved God because he was good to them, but many ideas were vague, especially in their understanding of Christ; half showed some sense of gratitude to him and some understanding of the nature of his mission. Mudge (1923) noted that the external world of sight and hearing was more immediate to a child and tested children from six to fourteen; 77 percent had a visual, anthropomorphic imagery of God which did not noticeably change until later adolescence. 72 percent of high-school students were still thinking anthropomorphically, as were 11 percent of college students, but no advanced students. Such thinking sprang from the pictorial images of God presented in childhood. Of greater importance was the growing ability to appreciate attitudes and relationships toward God. Bose (1929) included ideas of God in his test of religious concepts; these showed a marked developmental trend from eight to eighteen away from the ideas of fatherhood or spirit toward a more philosophical idea of a supreme being or the ethical idea of the highest ideal. Freeman (1931), in a conversation with five-year-old children, found that Christmas was seen as an occasion for getting with little consciousness of giving. Some children explained that it was about the birth of Jesus, which led to the expression of ideas such as "God gives us everything if we are good, when we are bad he takes it away and punishes us"; "once Jesus got killed and he got alive again and then he died again"; "the Jews did it, they are bad."

Ideas of young children

Some studies have concentrated on the ideas of younger children. Cavellett (1983) stated that children from three to six had a natural sense of God and his proximity; they were capable of appreciating those biblical and liturgical symbols which expressed God's presence in their lives. This assertion needs more precise accounts, such as that of Mailhiot (1962), who studied urban Canadian Catholic children aged four and five who had received religious teaching at home. Their prayers expressed requests, often nonsensical, in peremptory tones, or sought reprisals against those who had frustrated them; "I want some sweets, I want a lot of chocolate," "I want Peter to be smacked very hard." Such prayers were quite unlike the conventional prayers usually taught to small children. These children reacted positively to pictures of the child Jesus, but they did not recognize pictures of him as a youth or man, identify him as such, nor react to him religiously. Their ideas of God were similarly conditioned by egocentric thinking. They regarded adults as subordinate to themselves, of no consequence except as they affected their feelings. Similarly, God was thought of as the child Jesus, a child par excellence, a model admired, served, and worshiped by parents, just as each of them would like to be. Most regarded Jesus as protecting their parents from evil and explained this in terms of his magical powers. Jesus was a generic name, so that they spoke of Daddy Jesus, Mummy Jesus, and Baby Jesus, but Jesus' parents were regarded as subordinate to him and as being at his service. Because God was regarded as a child, ready to help them, sharing their joys and sorrows Mailhiot suggested that this should be made the focus of their spiritual development. Imagery of God is visual and anthropomorphic (Mudge, 1923). Before the age of eight ideas of God remain unsatisfactory (Graebner, 1964); even when a few children showed relatively mature insights, the ideas were those of adults to which the children had to learn to give "satisfactory" responses. Few studies have considered what children themselves spontaneously think God is like, and none of them is concerned with the youngest children.

Johnson (1955) asked girls and boys aged six about their ideas of God and of Jesus. Nearly all thought God was "in the sky" or "in heaven" and saw his role in terms of creator, protector, and moral judge, attributes also associated with their parents. These ideas were expressed in characteristic ways: "He makes flowers," "He tells you not to do bad things," "God has fairies—magic—to magic you." When asked, "Who is Jesus," most replied, "He's God," "He's the Son of God," or, "He's the King of Kings." Their assurance and ease appeared to indicate verbalism without understanding. Jesus was regarded as God, as a living person, and as a historical person. Stories of his birth, his death, his ability to cure illness and blindness and to raise the dead were outstanding. Descriptions of a superhuman being and spontaneous remarks showed confusion between someone living on earth and someone living in heaven. The inconsistencies of their preoperational thought were further complicated by their attempted use of a difficult adult vocabulary. Many were perplexed by the relationship between Joseph and God, both described as Jesus' father. Johnson reported a boy of four saying, "I did begin to say my prayers once, and then I got frightened and stopped in the middle." "Why?" "In case it was true, and God would appear." However, most children liked prayers at school. She considered that religious stories had only a limited use, since they were liable to produce only superficial learning at a purely verbal level; their value lay in their power to recall and reinterpret feelings which the children had experienced. The difficulties of presenting the story of Jesus to infants seemed to her to be insuperable, and because the idea of God was more easily accepted by children, since it fitted in with their normal development, she preferred to answer their questions with reference to God and not to Jesus. It will be seen that others, such as Berryman (1979), come to a very different conclusion.

Martyn (1967) interviewed children of seven and eight in inner-city Catholic schools about their ideas of God. Verbalism accounted for 31 percent of their replies and realism for 36 percent; the children showed no awareness of God as the Supreme Spirit but regarded him as tangible, able to be visualized, fitting into their experience, and showing the properties and behavior of a man. Their understanding of God was confused, limited to their essentially concrete level of thinking, displaying literalism, intuitive associations, and partial, fragmentary thinking. If God could not be fitted into these categories they regressed to the preoperational thinking of magic or fantasy, found in 10 percent of the responses; 22 percent attained the level of religious thinking indicated by showing a sense of wonder or awe, especially for God's omnipotence. There were significant relationships with intelligence and age and also significant differences between the schools.

Tamminen, Vianello, Jaspard, and Ratcliff (1988) reviewed recent European studies of the religious ideas of preschool children. A series of Scandinavian studies had shown that because they were not as literal as children of eight or more, they were able to grasp some religious concepts in biblical stories about people and their activities. Varied degrees of anthropomorphism were recorded; it was almost total in the drawings of children aged twelve, yet those aged seven and eight regarded God as helpful, good, kind, invisible, or a spirit (ideas unlikely to be expressed at this age in drawings). In one study children of four found it hard to describe what God looked like, but in another, anthropomorphic descriptions were forthcoming, which were supplemented at a slightly older age by superhuman features. Different questions elicited responses at different levels from the same child, and since "what does God look like?" prompts a different response from "what is God like?" findings do not necessarily contradict each other. Almost all believed God loved them and felt safe with him (Vaatainen, 1974), though some regarded this as depending on their belief or good behavior. Four-year-olds found it difficult to answer questions about Jesus, but as they grew older responses became more positive as the idea of God became more familiar. Because God lived in heaven, their sense of his closeness was a problem; he watched over them or came down to them or used angels as helpers or used some supernatural power to do it. God was seen as the creator of everything, although not until six did the idea become dominant.

Italian research (Tamminen, Vianello, Jaspard, and Ratcliff, 1988) similarly showed preschool children perceiving God in human terms as a special man, able to save a drowning man because he can swim, but unable to help endangered airline passengers because the aircraft is too heavy. God and Jesus were often confused; Jesus was good but a nun was even better. He was the hero of a sad story of long ago, he died, but is still alive in heaven. About six or seven less anthropomorphic ideas start to develop and the ideas of his omnipotence, omniscience, and omnipresence. Before this, few four-year-olds and only a third of the five-year-olds attributed some kind of omnipotence to God (Vianello, 1980). Magical thinking among these children was found to be due partly to adults encouraging it (Vianello and Marin-Zanovello, 1980) and some religious education reinforced it.

Three successive stages were found in Belgian Catholic preschool children's ideas of God. Up to three, children were interested in objects depicting the cross, called them "Jesus," enjoyed handling them and made crosses, and learned to make the sign of the cross. Before they were three, they had distinguished between Jesus (or God, depending on the family vocabulary) and the cross, learned that God lived in the church, and wondered what was his work and what were his feelings. Jesus was known as a human character. This "God as object/God as human" stage was followed by a "God as superhuman" stage. Jesus, though represented by a cross, lived in the church. The term "God" was used more often, with a growing interest in the divine, but it was hard to accept that he could not be seen, except by saints and people in heaven. God was there only to help children—their religion was inherently selfish—but they recognized that his power was different from that of humans. Their interest in religion was dependent on the mother's interest, especially for boys, who faithfully repeat their mother's gestures and enjoy the pleasure their praying gives to their mother. Girls of this age were more independent in their personal rituals and often had Jesus as an invisible companion. The masculine, father image of God made for greater differences between boys and girls at this age and for some girls presented a problem.

The third stage—God as Divinity—was from about four to six. God was now perceived in simple terms of transcendence and immanence; he existed in two realms, before life and after death, in heaven, and in the present, maintaining nature and family life, in an alliance with children. It was a time of questioning; he controlled the weather, gave life, knew everything, rewarded good behavior but denied benefits because of lack of prayer. Sex difference persisted. Girls were frequently disappointed that they did not perceive God directly and compensated for it in their imagination; an invisible Jesus was a problem, but by six the liturgy expressed their relationship to him. Boys identified themselves with the image of the limitless power of God and of Jesus but also were fascinated by the power of evil and the devil. Some boys joined forces with God to supplant the father from their mother's eyes. By six, however, the problem of evil was recognized since God's omnipotence often appeared to be ineffective, producing a crisis of faith which needed educating to greater understanding.

Young children's ideas are still very fluid and ill-formed and they are expressed with difficulty whether verbally or pictorially. They are much influenced by the style of the question or the person who asks it. Because there is no certainty that they have ever thought about it before they may make a quite spontaneous reply.

Yet they appear to have some understanding of God in ways that are not crudely anthropomorphic, with a positive attitude of trust in him. Much depends on what they have learned at home or in church, what pictures of God they have seen—if any at all, and what vocabulary they have come to use. Some children will have been taught to pray to God, some taught to pray to Jesus, some not taught to pray at all. It must not be forgotten that in the Old Testament some of the loftiest ideas about God are presented by pictorial imagery—Isaiah of Jerusalem saw the Lord sitting upon a throne, high and lifted up, and his train filled the temple. The real issue is what are the images that children use and how they are bound by them. To what extent do they indicate an idea of God that is egocentric or theocentric, and to what extent are their images only human or more than human?

Studies with school-age children

Investigations with somewhat older children have considered two separate issues; most investigated children's understanding of theological concepts, and a few probed the spontaneous religious ideas of children.

Swainson (1939) secured written ideas about God from children between seven and fourteen. God's goodness, kindness, and love appealed most to the young, the less able, and the girls; the boys, the more able, and the older children wrote about the objective ideas of God's power, greatness, and cleverness. Many described God as spirit, without defining the term, and some spoke of a spirit "dressed in a white robe." Understanding developed with age and ability, but younger and less able children showed a complete disregard of abstract and difficult ideas and tended to express subjective ideas. The idea that God was invisible appealed most to the boys; relatively few spoke of God as father, and of these most were girls. Older children regarded the function of God as helper and guide, the boys as a source of miracles, a king or a ruler and girls in terms of his relationship with individuals. A small group described his dwelling-place; very few spoke of the in-dwelling of God, half of them in the oldest age group. Unbelief was rare and found only in those after twelve. Mathias (1943) found no significant difference between ideas of God when they were related either to age or to Sunday school attendance; God was regarded as loving and omniscient and a source of justice, ideas which were expressed with much anthropomorphism. Many expressed dependence on him.

Ludwig, Weber, and Iben (1974) asked parochial school children aged six, nine, and twelve to write a letter to God. Detailed analysis of the letters showed four major categories—their areas of concern, their social awareness, their consciousness of time, and their image of God; and within these there were some significant age differences. Children aged six wrote about personal sustenance or physical needs, showing their religious perception to be external. (The authors refer to this as "abstract," which is confusing.) God was seen as a father, possibly remote. Children aged nine were becoming more reflective and physical concerns were of less importance; the perception of God was somewhat more remote, the object of religious doctrines, but meaningful in the personal experiences of daily life. Interest in doctrine was in accord with Piagetian descriptions of this stage as concerned with obeying rules and regarding authority as sacrosanct. At twelve emotional concerns sharply increased, while doctrinal and physical concerns decreased, as would be expected with the approach of adolescence. Religion pervaded all personal life in daily experiences and in respect of the ultimate questions now asked. God was no longer remote but was regarded as a friend and confidant, seen in more personal terms. Though many still thought of God as a father, the proportion was significantly less than that of the younger children. Thoughts were now expressed about the past and future, whereas before only the present was of concern. This ability to reflect on the whole of experience was regarded as a mark of maturity, although no indication was given as to how it involved more than a better developed concept of time.

Booth (1965) explored the ideas of ten-year-old children about the creation story and the parable of the unforgiving servant; many children held anthropomorphic ideas, and only a minority had an adequate conception of God as creator. Included in the studies of Nelsen, Potvin, and Shields (1977) responses from children were secured to items measuring support and power for each of five figures—God, clergy, mother, father, and the President. God was seen as the most powerful and the most supportive; of the remainder, the most supportive were seen to be the clergy, followed by mothers, fathers, and the President. On the power items the reverse order was found. The idealization of the clergy was surprising but regarded as an important diffuse support for religious institutions and religiousness.

Singer (1959) complained that earlier studies had not made provision for children to express their own ideas or areas of disbelief. He compared children aged eight, eleven, and fourteen and their parents in Jewish, Presbyterian, and Episcopalian Sunday schools in Chicago, using a test he devised to probe their understanding of concepts of God in relation to the ideas of my father, my mother, the President, love, sun, tree, my minister, teacher, and policeman. There was no difference between boys and girls, or between children and adults, but there was a significant difference between the ideas of Jewish and Protestant children, but not between Episcopalian and Presbyterian children. Children expressed a generalized attitude toward God which was broad and included widely separate attributes.

White (1970) considered that research had imposed a conformist theological appraisal on children's answers to questions about God. When they said he was big, orderly, overwhelming, or punishing it revealed nothing of their belief in him as gentle, fair, kind-hearted, or forgiving. He undertook relaxed discussions with Jewish and Roman Catholic boys aged seven, ten, and thirteen and made a phenomenological analysis of the data without the usual references to magical or anthropomorphic ideas. Four categories were identified—God's existence in time, in substantial form, in space, and in activity; in each category was a range of themes. God was perceived as a being with, or without, a beginning, who could, or could not, die, or who was dead. He was described as incarnate but invisible, or not incarnate; he was everywhere, somewhere in particular, or not in any place. He cared about man, communicated with man, intervened with man, and was involved with the creation of man. Thus he was regarded as a being who was incarnate, as a level of being which is immediate and as an idea that is insensible. There were remarkable similarities of beliefs with few differences due to age or denomination until adolescence, when perceptions of God began to differ considerably from those of childhood, and the two denominational groups also began to differ. Before this, some were found with very mature ideas, Jewish boys with Catholic ideas, and all manner of combinations, so that classification of ideas by age or by denomination seemed to be quite artificial. At seven, no single thought was characteristic, except for a Jewish concern that God was an invisible man who was everywhere. At ten, Catholics viewed God as the one who helped man and who created the world, and Jews emphasized that God was everywhere. At thirteen, Catholic boys showed interest in the Trinity and Jesus which had not appeared before, and Jewish boys questioned the existence of God and his role in creation, regarding God as an abstract or nonphysical being, if indeed there was a God.

Jewish and Catholic boys differed mainly in their perception of temporality and in Catholic boys' concern over the origin or death of God, a concern apparently related to the death of Jesus, since the two identities were never clearly distinguished. Catholic boys at this age saw God as the all-powerful, all-present creator whose Son was Christ. Jewish boys of all ages tended to emphasize that God was not an incarnate being; this in part seemed to explain their disavowal of the traditional role of God as creator. Conceptions of God were appropriate only to particular denominations; beliefs were diverse and about individual phenomena, since only symbols of God were visible in the world. Almost half the boys said either that God did not, or might not exist, or that he was dead, despite their ability to provide descriptions of God. Their cognitive knowledge about God did not guarantee conviction, since their exposure to "rote theology" resulted in their knowing about God, but not knowing God. They had an academical rather than an existential faith, and, as with adults, they practiced nominal theism. White considered that teaching about the Trinity, eternity, or immortality should be replaced with a humanized theology with its focus on moral criteria and an existential contract to life. Despite this criticism, studies of learning of "rote theology" continued and the means of facilitating it, such as that of Flynn and MacNamara (1975), who demonstrated that those who had been taught the Canadian catechism could express more acceptable ideas of God on the test used than those not taught it.

Heller (1986) investigated the ideas of God held by Catholic, Baptist, Hebrew, and Hindu children in Michigan by interviews, drawings of God, storytelling, letters to God, and drama. Jewish children regarded God as very active in history and the present and concerned for his chosen people and those who suffered. With

Catholic children, family images were prominent, and God was concerned about guilt, purity, and forgiveness. Baptist children stressed the nurture God provided but regarded God as emotionally distant, concerned about order and organization, which reflected a cognitive emphasis. The Ashram children had a very strong sense of community; God was close enough to be a real person, yet regarded as an abstract force or a form of energy. The children aged four to six already recognized leading religious concepts; playfulness entered into their concept of a God who made life happy, related to their pleasures, fantasies, and simple aspirations and was sometimes good, sometimes not so. Those aged seven to nine had increasing knowledge, but awareness and curiosity depended on individual experiences. God was related to a sense of being special and a yearning for self-importance; they questioned whether or not they were close to God and found a meeting-place with him in sleep and dreams. At ten to twelve came a sense of doubt and hesitation with greater formal knowledge, a concern with injury and pain showing a recognition that not everything was tailored to their needs, and curiosity about what God could and could not do.

There were marked sex differences. All saw God as a great father, but boys stressed God's rationality and his participation in events. He was at a great distance, even when involved in an individual's life, which made him hard to contact. Because he was a big man they could model themselves on him; they had no doubt that he was male—the idea of a feminine God gave rise to anxiety. Girls' God images had aesthetic facets (rationality versus the aesthetic is a recognized socialization difference between men and women). Their God was more passive, at times an observer rather than a participant. They felt close to God; he was male, but there were hints that he was more androgynous. Different attributes of God were related to their personalities; some saw him as friendly; to others he was an arbitrary judge; the lonely regarded him as something distant in the sky; and he was also the king, the inconstant, the heavenly lover, the therapist. These ideas arose from the influence of the religious community and the family. Maternal and paternal images were important, as were those of the couple and of the grandparent. Some topics were common to all children and arose from their perception of family interpretations of institutional religion, which otherwise was seen as an unpopular, dry, and obligatory activity, from their interaction with parents and siblings, projected on to their representation of God, and from their own self-awareness and perception of the world. Together, these contributed to their understanding of the power of the deity, to their experience of intimacy with God, his omnipresence, the recognition that the world and its events was connected with God, and a sense of anxiety, tension, or awe when formulating statements about God. Over-socialization by church and family inhibited many spontaneous religious ideas, and the effect of the media and television was very strong; high exposure to it brought very anthropomorphic imagery. Science and technology also had considerable socializing influence, but the influence of the family was primary, and in it the quality of relationships and the availability of solitude was fundamental.

Pictorial studies

Harms (1944) was the first to use pictures to probe religious understanding, arguing that children's verbal expression did not reveal their true ideas. Having previously devised nonverbal tests to explore humorous and aesthetic responses, he now secured pictures of God drawn by children and adolescents. From this material he showed that up to six the idea of God was one of fantasy; God was thought to be a king, often bearded, who lived in the sky. However, at this "fairy-tale" stage the concept was also associated with a sense of awe which distinguished it from fairy tales, so that even very young children had a deep and original religious experience. Children between seven and twelve were at a realistic stage—God was conceptualized in concrete, personal terms, and described by conventional religious symbols, such as the crucifix or Jewish star, or was depicted as a human figure or father helping or supervising people and no longer as a fantasy figure; many anthropomorphic ideas were expressed and an emotional element was also found. Finally in adolescence there came an individualistic stage of great diversity; some used conventional ideas, often with sensitivity; some used more original, unconventional symbolism, such as pictures of a sunrise or of light breaking through dark clouds to express the individualistic character of their own religious experience, and some depicted the imagery of religious cults quite outside their experience, similar to those from early Egypt, Persian mythology, or Chinese Buddhism. Clark (1958), in an extended account of Harms' work, thought that authoritarian influences had been strong in the first adolescent group, while the third group bore the mark of a more humanistic style; both supported Fromm's concepts of authoritarian and humanistic expressions of religion.

Other pictorial studies followed. De Valensart (1968) used three styles of pictures to illustrate gospel scenes and showed them to children aged five, seven, ten, and twelve. Three-quarters preferred the realistic pictures, and for the seven- and ten-year-old children their details seemed to correspond best to their understanding of the Bible. The five-year-old children made their choice on the strength of some attractive detail, whatever the style of the picture. Half the children noticed the symbolic signs, so that the symbolic sense of children could be educated through well-drawn pictures containing symbolic signs. Pitts (1976) asked children aged six to ten to draw a picture of God and of another person. Those under eight found it difficult, the pictures of God usually containing less detail than those of humans. Comparisons of the pairs of drawings showed that even the youngest children gave some sign of religious socialization. Significant denominational differences were found, so that the Catholic children used the most religious symbolism, and Mormon children more than all others represented God in terms of a robed figure, often accompanied by a wife and children. A lesser degree of anthropomorphism was found in Lutheran children, then Mennonite, Methodist, Catholic, Unitarian, and finally Jewish children, which indicated the theological characteristics of their denominations. Age development was explained by Piagetian theory. Pitts recognized that children might well have ideas which they could not reproduce in this representational way. That drawings of the human figure give reliable information regarding children's conceptual development has been established by such studies as those of Harris (1963), Goodnow (1977), or Kolls (1980), but their use to probe ideas of God assumes visual thinking in anthropomorphic terms.

Graebner (1964) also encouraged Lutheran children to express their own ideas by giving them pictures, including four religious ones, and asking them to write about them. The children first developed shadowy impressions about God arising from contact with parents, siblings, teachers, and other adults, and when one level of perception was reached it became the basis for a more objective and discriminating concept. A very wide range of ideas showed a remarkable similarity among all the children. They were not affected by the regularity or absence of prayer; Sunday school attendance, class, and age seemed to make little difference, but from age eight a fuller concept of God was found. By then there was knowledge about the essential distinction between God and man, yet once this was learned there was no difference between the age groups. Understanding was affected by length of attendance at a parochial school; many years attendance brought more mature theological ideas and after nine a greater insight into Christian ideas of God. A few younger children showed reasonably mature insight, but this was balanced by others quite the reverse. After four years attendance at a parochial school there seemed to be an element of stereotyped answers in children's written responses, with little difference between boys and girls, but better insights were related to higher intelligence. Graebner concluded that children saw God less in personal terms and more as the God of the Bible and the catechism—all knowing, all powerful, forgiving repentant sinners, but a watcher who was not too close to mankind. Theological qualities of God tended to be confused; ideas of God as eternal, all powerful, all knowing, or all present were confused with each other. It was the creative function of God that was most clearly and frequently identified; next he was seen as all-powerful and punishing evil, and a God of mercy and kindness.

Despite Graebner's assertion that there was little evidence for age development, Williams (1974) found a developmental sequence using the same test with children and adolescents from different religious backgrounds, although findings on a personality test he used at the same time were less clear. Sohn (1985) also used Graebner's test in a revised form with Lutheran children and demonstrated that growth in the comprehension of God improved with age.

Hindley (1965) regarded art work as a more reliable means of expressing religious concepts for less able children and asked boys aged eleven to fifteen to write an essay and draw a picture illustrating their ideas of God. After teaching about God, the study was repeated. There was a significant improvement between the tests in written and art work, and by twelve an ability was developing for analytical tasks. The art work showed a lower level of development than the written work, and it provided a better indicator of real understanding than the verbal evidence. Dawes' (1954) finding was confirmed that the dominant concepts of God were his power, his concern for the individual, and his role as creator. Many boys of eleven or twelve were still at Harm's realistic stage, but the individualistic stage was beginning with some of them, and its proportion increased with age.

Smith (1976) explored the God concepts of forty moderately retarded children and adolescents aged eleven to eighteen. God concepts were found to be similar to those they held of their mothers and fathers, with the maternal influence the stronger. There were no sex differences, and age did not affect the sample; this was expected, since their mental development had been arrested at a preoperational stage. There was no relationship with church attendance.

Adolescent ideas of God

Bradbury (1947) found that material conceptions of God tended to disappear about the age of fourteen, except with the less able; although references to a spiritual form were found as early as eleven, even by fifteen it was not certain that using the word "spirit" indicated an abstract form. The idea of God as someone who is loving and caring and possessing the attributes of an ideal parent was general. Bradshaw (1949) examined changes in adolescent belief; after fifteen or sixteen few boys spoke of God as a father, and this he saw as a strong argument against the classical psychoanalytic theory (discussed in the next chapter). The idea of God as a creator decreased with age, and similarly the idea that God was good. The belief that God heard prayer seemed to be consistent, but older adolescents were less willing to believe that he spoke to them in prayer or answered prayer. Disbelief in the divinity of Christ arose about fifteen or sixteen. At eleven most believed in God; the movement away from belief with growing age was toward agnosticism and not to atheism. It seemed that even if early belief was due to imitation and suggestion, such belief served an essential function when children asserted their right to independent judgment.

Dawes (1954) investigated the religious beliefs of secondary school boys. The little disbelief encountered was usually of intellectual origin. God's power, even if only conceived as that of a super-man, was the most prominent idea, followed by the idea of God as concerned for individuals as their helper, guide, or friend, and God as creator. He disputed Bradshaw's (1949) claim that the idea of God's goodness receded with age, finding that there was a slight increase in it. Differences in meaning of the items used in the two tests might account for it, and also the sampling, since Bradshaw's sample was restricted to more able boys and girls. Bradshaw had secured responses to given statements, while Dawes used a content analysis of unstructured essays, a difference of importance to the results. The dominant concepts—of God as power, father, and creator—were important in providing a basis for maturity by giving a sense of security, an object of authority, and meaning to the world. Many of the boys confused thought about God with thought about the historical Jesus. In adolescence, as boys grew away from their parents, it could be the sentiment for Jesus rather than for God which became dominant. Walker (1950) in a study of Scottish children aged eleven to fourteen found similar ideas prevalent, but these children also associated a sense of awe with God, who to them seemed also to be mysterious and fearful.

Bowden (1958) developed a test to measure anthropomorphic thinking among children; validating it showed considerable disagreement between the theological and the philosophical assessors about items which were not easy for children to understand—statements, such as "God created man in his own image, so he must be like us to look at," "God is more like a spirit than anything else we can think of," and "people who think clearly conclude that God has no form." From ten to thirteen there was a slight increase, without significance, in accepting the ideas that God possessed form, was concrete in form and was a person; beyond this age accepting such ideas declined. The concept "spirit" showed much confusion. No other study has suggested a peak of anthropomorphism at thirteen, so that the test and its results must remain suspect.

Rees (1967) compared older adolescents who were Catholics, Anglicans, Non-conformists, Quakers, Jews, and agnostics on a number of religious beliefs and personality traits. Catholics differed significantly from all other groups in the prominence they gave to Mary and to sacramentalism and were the most strongly authoritarian. Members of the Church of England came between Catholics and Nonconformists on most scales; and the latter, like the Quakers, were unsympathetic to the Mary concept and sacramentalism but gave greater support to the concept of God as judge. The Indwelling Spirit had the greatest prominence among the Quakers, who also displayed the greatest verbal ability. Jews rejected concepts of Jesus and Mary and regarded God as father and judge in transcendent terms. Agnostics were confused. All Christian groups regarded God primarily in terms of Jesus, favoring immanent rather than transcendent descriptions.

In France, Deconchy (1964, 1967) used a word-association method to categorize the ideas of Catholic children. Before eleven they thought of God mainly as creator, or of his greatness, goodness, justice, strength, and beauty; these were human attributes, so the descriptions were anthropomorphic. From eleven to fourteen God was seen in personal terms, such as father or sovereign; an emphasis on virtues indicated a refinement of what was still anthropomorphic thinking. There was an increasing tendency with age to think of God in parental terms; at nine fewer than one in ten of the children thought of God as father, but a quarter or more of boys aged thirteen and girls aged fifteen did so. This was followed by an interiorization, when God was conceived subjectively as love or trust; anthropomorphic ideas disappeared and the image of God became abstract and vague. The decline in thinking of God as creator continued through adolescence, but girls, unlike boys, continued to hold personalized ideas, linking Christ as Savior with attributes of greatness and goodness and an attitude of trust.

Emotionally disturbed children had ideas of God different from those of normal

Protestant children, but they all responded alike to some ideas, especially disso-
ciating God from punitive ideas. The disturbed children associated God with
authority figures, unlike the others, and had negative self-concepts, to which the
meaning of God was related (Price, 1970).

An extensive study of the growth of faith among young French Catholics was
carried out by Babin (1963, 1964, 1967). He described the characteristics of faith
development in adolescence and surveyed the beliefs and opinions of boys and
girls aged eleven to nineteen. A key question was, "What does God mean to you?"
which yielded much relevant information. Ideas which became stronger and dominant in late adolescence were of God as great and powerful, as guide, and as an
ideal. There was a smaller incidence of regarding him as a confidant, as mysterious, and as source of life and light. Ideas of God as creator, as spirit, as merciful,
and the seldom mentioned trinitarian ideas weakened in significance. Ideas of God
as a loving father, eternal, just, and perfect weakened temporarily during adolescence but subsequently recovered.

Babin described three major characteristics of the sense of God, the first, nat-
uration, a term recognizing a natural religious impulse, a relationship with God
motivated by experiences and needs. The second, egomorphism, regarded God
as a confidant, as pure or as an ideal; this was imbued with subjective factors so
that God was envisaged in the form of the individual ego. Fewer late adolescents
spoke of God as spirit, an indication that catechetical and objective formulas were
being discarded; on the other hand, more late adolescents spoke of God as confidant or friend—this was more marked with girls than boys, who were more likely to describe God in spiritual terms. Many showed a sense of divine immanence
in nature and envisaged God as they would wish him to be rather than as he is
revealed. The third characteristic was to see God in moral terms. There was now
a marked difference between the sexes in their apprehension of God. Girls, sensitive to personal relationships, displayed strong relationships with God, whom
they regarded as a protector and a consoling presence. Boys were more concerned
with the nature and order of things and envisaged God in terms of being and
action, the great explanation of the world. Girls saw God as one who watched over
them, a view more static than that of the boys, who saw God as a support in the
warfare they had to wage, helping them reach their goals and strengthening them
against temptation, a view which was also more utilitarian and egocentric than
that of the girls. One consequence of adolescent development was in the understanding of God as father; for many, father meant creator representing power or
ruler; such an image contrasted with father representing love. It was noticeable
that the love of God was perceived less among older adolescent boys but more
among older adolescent girls.

Various observers have recorded the conservative religious ideology found in
the Southern states. In a study of belief in Southern Appalachia, Nelsen (1972)
showed that adults regarded God more as a wrathful, righteous judge, than as a
loving savior. Subsequently (Nelsen, Waldron, and Stewart, 1973), two basic

images were found among students, the image of God as punishing, wrathful, and avenging and the image of God as loving, helping, kind, and forgiving; only the latter was associated with church attendance. Hunter (1982) looked at types of conservative belief from a different perspective, reviewing the sociological debate about it and defining American evangelical beliefs in terms of religious profession and personal adherence to doctrines of biblical inerrancy, the divinity of Christ and eternal salvation through the redemptive act of God through Christ, all measured attitudinally. Dobbins (1975) made the point that in his counseling experience the majority of his clients had come from Evangelical backgrounds and had held a punitive image of God in their childhood. The church did not create pleasurable associations for children, giving them a taste for spiritual things but overwhelmed them with its verbal content. Children under twelve could not usually understand eschatology, which they distorted into frightening ideas. Research was needed to establish levels of readiness for learning spiritual truths.

McDowell (1952) investigated children's and adolescents' understanding of theological terminology about God. He constructed a test from children's statements about the terms used to describe God in the Catholic catechism—such as divinity, providence, or omnipotence. He did not fully overcome the difficulty of deciding which immature statements were to be regarded as essentially true. A large number of American Catholic children were tested to discover the extent to which they understood this vocabulary, how their thinking conformed to the instruction they had received, and the extent to which they held crudely anthropomorphic ideas. Many misconceptions and erroneous ideas were revealed, which he described with considerable detail. These were not replaced by more mature ideas with increasing age, but rather the learning process ceased in the upper grades. He was puzzled by the fact that before learning was complete and at a time when increasing maturity might be expected to bring an improved rate of learning it seemed to stop, so that there was no significant increase in mean scores for boys after age thirteen or for girls after fifteen. His test was used again in several other studies.

Shuttleworth (1959) tested English children between nine and fifteen with thirty of McDowell's items and also secured their ideas expressed in free writing. There was a close similarity with McDowell's results, although the younger children obtained somewhat higher scores. Anthropomorphism decreased from 47 percent at nine to 7 percent at fourteen, but more abstract concepts did not develop very much in this period. Some confusion between God and Jesus was still found, most of all in the thirteen-year-old group. Few referred to an all-loving, all-knowing God, although more than half, greater with the girls, regarded God as beneficent, despite increasing skeptical comment from the older children, especially boys. Those with greater religiousness tended to secure higher scores on the test with age, but the scores of those with less religiousness fell with increasing age. The highest scores came from those with above average ability and religiousness, the lowest scores from those with above average ability and below average religiousness. Girls always tended to score higher than boys. The ideas expressed in essays tended to complement the results of the test, but with some divergence, so that few references to God as father were found in the essays, whereas more than half accepted the idea in the formal test.

Kuriakose (1960) repeated McDowell's test in an English Catholic school and two nondenominational schools, giving an extended account of the responses secured but without any analysis of them. The mean scores for each group calculated from his data show no significant differences between boys and girls, between pupils from Catholic and non-Catholic schools, nor any significant increase of score with age, although the Catholic boys approached it. Cerney (1965) also repeated McDowell's test in the United States, confirming his results, but a number of improvements in learning were noted, which continued for longer than previously recorded. Children attending public schools but receiving religious instruction in classes organized by the Confraternity of Christian Doctrine (CCD) did less well than those in parochial schools. A learning plateau was observed in the upper levels of the elementary schools, the high schools, and in a college sample. There was a significant drop in scores at fourteen, suggesting a "crisis of faith" or the result of the style or content of teaching. Unlike boys, girls in CCD classes compared favorably with those in parochial schools in some aspects of learning. The better performance of girls over boys narrowed in the high-school years, and little subsequent difference was found. A vocabulary test showed that there had been an improvement since 1952, but too many technical terms were still being taken for granted.

Hyde (1959, 1965) used a doctrinal test of the Image of God in his attitude study of secondary school pupils. Responses to the representative statements, which had been obtained from free writing, showed that a normal learning process took place among pupils in regular contact with a church, girls securing higher scores than boys. Those no longer in touch with a church displayed no significant learning at all. Religious learning, indicated by recognizing the best descriptions of God, was strongly associated with positive attitudes to religion and to the church. Among the many findings it was obvious that the decline of anthropomorphism with age was steady and not concentrated on any particular year. The acceptance of ideas of God as creator and as father showed a marked reduction with age, except for the church-going girls, nearly all of whom accepted these ideas at every age tested. Similarly, age brought a reduced acceptance of orthodox ideas of Christology, except among the church-going girls. The girls scored higher than boys in all the tests, and church-going pupils scored higher than nonattenders.

MacLean (1930), using a written questionnaire, concluded that teaching rather than age was responsible for the development of children's ideas; one well-taught group excelled all others. Children tended to accept both conservative and liberal ideas of God without recognizing any conflict. Many agreed with statements asserting God's omniscience, omnipresence, and immutability or asserting his nature to be that of a loving father, forgiving and protective. Fahs (1930) regarded such findings as a depressing list of superficial contradictions and preferred to regard religious growth in the affective terms of a developing maturity originating from children's satisfactory relationships with their family and their behavior patterns. She felt that adult ideas of God were not needed by children of three or four, for the emotional tone of their lives could be disturbed by the thought of a stern, autocratic God who punished naughty children, or one who failed to do what they had come to expect of him in their limited understanding.

Stubblefield and Richard (1965) investigated the concept of God among two groups of mentally retarded adolescents and adults. Their mental age significantly affected their conceptualization of God; the older and somewhat abler group with an age range from sixteen to thirty-seven, regarded God as involved in human life to a greater extent than the more retarded group aged thirteen to eighteen. These adolescents, with a mental age of five to seven, thought of God in universal rather than omnipotent terms and as very much available to them. They attributed human characteristics to him more than the older, less retarded group, although they were not very concerned about his physical appearance.

Stevens (1975) constructed a scale to measure belief in God by selecting forty statements of belief and unbelief from pupils' essays, typical of the categories suggested by Kirkpatric and Stone (1935), and used it in secondary schools with students aged fourteen to seventeen. About half the sample were identified as religious, more girls than boys; their least preferred category was cosmological, which was the most preferred with the quarter of the sample who were nonreligious. All placed the other categories in the same order—personal, epistemological, and social. All four types of statement were needed for an adequate measure of belief in God. Boys aged fifteen and sixteen displayed a lower level of belief than those who were older, presumably because this group was academically and socially selective. Beyond this validation, no further use was made of the test, nor comparisons made with other similar research.

Evans (1968) secured brief essays on God, sin, repentance, the Bible, and the church from first-year students at colleges of education and trained teams of assessors to categorize the concepts and to measure the extent of their acceptance or rejection. The complex structures revealed were used in a longitudinal study to chart changes in thinking by repeating the exercise at the end of the three-year course. A wide range of beliefs was discovered for each item; ten categories were needed to classify beliefs about God, which ranged from near anthropomorphic descriptions in terms of human personality to completely impersonal and formless concepts. Many students described God as a real person who was all-knowing, all-seeing, all-powerful, and a caring and punishing father in heaven. Other students described God in terms of a presence found in church and in worship, a mysterious being who heard and answered prayer, the source of life and help in trouble, and who was good and was perfect love. There was a marked movement by the end of the course away from personal concepts toward more abstract expressions. Although three-quarters still held to a belief in God, 15 percent of those who had formerly professed belief had by now rejected it, largely because they found it impossible to reconcile the idea of God with natural disasters and human suffering. Those who expressed doubts at the start of the course did so because of the lack of proof and inability to reconcile the idea of God with the world at large; only three of them changed their position during the course. The stronger the doubt expressed, the more abstract was the associated concept of God.

The general outline of children's descriptions of God is very similar to that suggested in the review of Wright and Koppe (1964) noted at the beginning of the chapter and need not be repeated. Often the ideas of children are only verbalisms, words repeated in a correct context without proper understanding. At first the ideas are often of fantasy, at a fairy-tale stage. During the school years thinking is largely in concrete terms, a realistic stage when God is envisaged anthropomorphically, in concrete human categories. But even by this age, considerable variations of the perception of God are to be found. From an early age, children may display reverence and awe at the thought of God. Adolescence brings the ability to think abstractly, and from the age of eleven children begin to think of God in terms of spirit. Differences of culture affect ideas of God; children used to symbolism in worship grow to make use of it in their thinking. Relatively few children at any age really understand the terms traditionally used to describe God in worship or in the catechism, and there is not a tendency for understanding to improve as adolescence proceeds unless there is some regular church contact. Adolescence brings some clear distinctions between the ideas of God held by the sexes. Boys tend to think in terms of God's power and authority and regard God as a spirit but tend not to envisage him as father except when it is a term of authority. Girls tend to think in terms of relationships and of his love.

Chapter 4

Parental Images and the Idea of God

Following the account of ideas of God held by children at different ages, this chapter describes a series of studies of the relationship between the image of God and the image of actual or ideal parents. For the most part, the research has been undertaken with adolescents and adults, but the evidence indicates the extent to which children's ideas about their parents are the basis of their ideas about God. These studies are not only of interest because of the bearing they have on the theories of Freud about the origin of the idea of God but because they also point to some fundamental differences between the sexes in the conception of God and thus indicate that there are maternal characteristics in the image of God which most individuals hold.

Freud, the controversial founder of the psychoanalytic school, was an atheist who regarded religion as a neurosis which needed to be cured; it was an illusion—which could be true or false—based on wish fulfillment. God was nothing other than an exalted father. Despite his secular Jewish background, his Catholic nannie took him to church up to the age of three, and he later gained knowledge of the Bible. His theory arose from the insights he gained in his work with clients suffering from obsessional neuroses, and his account of religion is contained in *Totem and Taboo* (1913), *The Future of an Illusion* (1927), and *Moses and Monotheism* (1939). According to these, religion, as well as morality and civilization, springs from the Oedipal conflict, a concept he based on what he believed were the practices of totem and taboo among primitive tribes. Sons, expelled by their jealous and tyrannical father, united to slay and eat him. Subsequently, they missed the security and control he provided and deified an animal, or totem, which they worshiped as their dead father. Motivated by these dynamic aspects of infantile sexuality, a small boy unconsciously becomes filled with a desire to possess his mother and in consequence hates his father. This hatred for one for whom he held tender feelings gives rise to a sense of guilt for the repressed wishes for incest and murder. It is resolved only by attempting to assimilate the father's qualities and do his bidding. Subsequently, the inability to overcome life's frustrations leads to regression to the time when he was dependent on his father. The result of this is a search for the father image, from which springs conscience and the concept of God, a substitute father figure of power and the source of all religion. Religion was thus a flight from the frustrations of life to an illusionary security of belief in a divine father. Mysticism was a regressive experience. Daughters were not similarly described, nor was the image of the mother significant.

Freud's theory has been contested and modified in varying degrees; at an early stage Jung and Adler broke away, going in such radically different directions as to call into question the possibility of any empirical support for psychoanalytic theory. Some faithful followers have taken strongly opposed positions on particular aspects of the theory, especially regarding child development, and others, notably Erikson, have substantially adapted Freudian theory. Recent positive accounts of religion from a Freudian perspective have been given by Rizzuto (1979) and Godin (1985), and its influence is evident in the Louvain studies to be described. Whatever the mechanisms, the importance of parents in the psychological development of children is undisputed. There must inevitably be a measure of ambivalence in their relationships, for both of the parents not only sustain and encourage their children but also withhold and restrain them. Nor can it be in dispute that the idea of God is closely associated with this relationship.

Some studies of parental images and the idea of God have been directly concerned with Freudian theory. Larson and Knapp (1964) used a projective technique to compare the responses of a Protestant group ranging from late adolescence to middle age and found that the fear of God was much more characteristic of men than of women, and this they considered gave support to Freud's theory. Deconchy (1968) reviewed previous studies of the concept of God and parental images, in which the relation God-Mother was preeminent in men, whereas in women the relation God-Father predominated. It emerged that the development of the idea of God in boys was more marked by the notion of the Virgin Mary, whereas the opposite happened in the case of girls. Cooper (1970) was interested in psychoanalytic theories of the image of God and interviewed able Scottish boys from five to nine using a projective test based on four pictures—a boy looking at a greenhouse with a broken pane of glass; a boy watching his father laying bricks; a boy with his parents entering the door of a church; and a boy kneeling in prayer at a bedside. Two pictures concerned the father-son relationship, and two an understanding of God. Three questions of particular interest were, for the first picture, "Will the father know what he has done?" and "Does the father always find out when the boy has done something wrong?" And for the second picture, "Are there any things the boy's father cannot do?" The results suggested that the boys were closer to their fathers than was believed and that discovery of the father's limitations would be earlier in life and without serious consequences. The third picture showed the difficulty younger boys had in understanding the omnipresence of God. More than half the boys attended church with their parents. Despite frequent anthropomorphism, examples of sophisticated spiritual thinking about God were also found, but the frequency of references to God in spiritual terms could have been due to the high levels of intelligence and church-going in the group. When Doerrer (1970) used projective techniques and pictures to investigate Lutheran school children's ideas about God as father he found that age brought greater maturity, especially after about eight or nine. The religious background of the children's families appeared to have no association with their developing concepts of God; many of them thought of God as harsh, and they tended not to relate this image to their daily lives.

Lewis (1956) described the development of religion from a psychiatric viewpoint as proceeding in three stages similar to those of Piaget. In infancy the relationship with the mother was of prime importance, experience of her goodness becoming in later life the basis of faith in God. If this was flawed it would subsequently give rise to problems of belief. In middle childhood the capacity for religious development was most easily lost. The bond with the mother was weakened, but magical ideas persisted so that children desired to work or experience miracles. The main consideration of their heroes was their power—even those who chose Jesus as their ideal person did so because he performed miracles and displayed his power in many ways. Play involving these ideas was concealed from adults. They were at an age in which gangs operated and their own rituals and rules were of great importance. Church attendance with parents was pleasurable if occasionally they had parts to play in its worship. The image of fatherhood now grew to importance and had consequences for later ideas about God. In adolescence, spiritual ideals were apprehended quite suddenly; just beforehand the magical became the mystical, and an awareness of the existence of God was to be found.

Nelson and Jones (1957) had examined how parental influence affected the image of God with a test in which emotional responses such as "I have a sense of being protected" were matched with key sentences such as "whenever I think of God. . ." using twenty adjectives in positive, neutral, and negative senses. Feelings for God were related more to those toward the father but with differences between men and women. Strunk (1959) had used the same technique. Godin and Hallez (1964) reviewed these studies and felt that the technique would be valuable in a better designed experiment. A sample of fervent French Catholic adults married and single, some members of religious orders, with an age range from late adolescence to middle life was tested, and the process repeated for ideas about mother and father. The results indicated an important tendency for the image of God to be influenced by the psychological image of the parent of the other sex—the God/father relationships were stronger for women than for men, and vice versa. This was enhanced when the preferred parent was of the opposite sex, and was less marked when the preferred parent was of the same sex. Parental influence tended to fade with age.

Nelson (1971) compared Freud's theory of the image of God as an exalted father with Adler's theory that it arises from the recognition of perfection. He repeated Nelson and Jones' (1957) test as used by Godin and Hallez (1964) with high-school students, college students, and adults. The image of God was found to be more closely related to that of the preferred parent, who was more often the mother, but it also had some reliance on the image of the parent of the opposite sex. There was a general tendency, greater for men, to prefer the mother, but about a third of the men and half the women had no preference for either parent; in this group the association with the image of God was not only about equal for both parents but was greater than when there was a preferred parent. If no preference indicated a more harmonious family, then both parents would be nearer to the ideal of perfection. This gave no support to Freudian assertions but was in accord with Adler's hypothesis. Rizzuto (1974, 1980) commented on this finding, arguing that Adler referred only to the subject's idea of perfection and not to the internalized parental image. Summarizing Freud's position, she observed that he was concerned only with the effect of the father and not other members of the family who also affected the image of God. She described two case studies showing how the image of the father affected the image of God; in one instance a warm image gave rise to an image of God that supported the warmth and belief of the subject; in the other, a dominant, remote father was associated with a latent belief in a remote and authoritarian God of a man who no longer practiced religion. Belief in God, which was never final, developed from relationships and inner convictions.

Spilka, Armatas, and Nussbaum (1964) took up earlier work on parental images of God. Responses from a very religious group of Catholic girls were compared with those from a general group of students. Analysis of responses gave surprisingly different results. The very religious group had most prominently a concept of a wrathful, avenging, and punishing God, whereas the general group saw many attributes such as comforting, patient, faithful, or kind, terms which are socially desirable qualities, even though the respondents' social desirability scores were not related to their concept scores. The general sample indicated what they thought God was like, or what they would like him to be, whereas the Catholic girls defined what God was not like. It proved difficult to reconcile the two sets of results, except as demonstrating that different groups possess varying God concepts, and even an apprently homogeneous group shows many different views to be prevalent. A further study (Spilka, Addison, and Rosensohn, 1975) gave little support for any of four main theories about the origin of the concept of God—the Freudian, Adlerian, social learning, and self–esteem theories. The complex relationships that were disclosed suggested some interaction between ideas of self, parents, and God. There was much similarity of imagery among adult Protestant believers of all theological opinions, but those most certain differed in their willingness to use anthropomorphisms and in their confidence that God could be experienced directly in a personal relationship (Broughton, 1975). The studies reviewed so far have originated mainly in the English-speaking world although another important group is predominantly Catholic and European in origin and ethos; together they show a considerable advance in understanding of the topic. A notable series has emanated from the Centre of Religious Psychology at the University of Louvain, headed by Antoine Vergote, undertaken variously with adolescents, students, and adults. Many have been deposited as masters' or doctoral theses, and some of them form the basis of a series of articles in a single issue of *Social Compass*, in which a major contribution is that of Vergote and Aubert (1972). The chief objective of these studies is about the parental figures and the representation of God. Some earlier accounts of them were given by Vergote et al. (1969), Vergote and Aubert (1972), and Vergote (1980), followed by the full report of Vergote and Tamayo (1981) which brought them to a conclusion; their range was such that more than a dozen different contributors were involved in describing them.

Hutsebaut (1972) reviewed the work of Vergote and his colleagues; in one extensive study the image of God was first investigated among Dutch Catholic adolescents aged fourteen to twenty. Boys scores on almost all items decreased with age, except for that of God as judge, but no clear pattern was found with the girls, who tended to score a little higher but with a similar response pattern. Then four responses were secured from adolescents to the question "What does God mean for you" followed by "Which of them do you prefer?" and "What is God definitely not for you?" Some aspects of the adolescent image of God showed stability and permanence; in particular God was conceived as the absolute. While God was viewed at every age in adolescence as father, friend, helper, or benefactor, this idea was primarily held by those in mid-adolescence seeking some degree of help or support. The view of God as creator or as providence again was found in all age-groups, but its significance tended to decrease with age, and the older group thought rather in such terms as "the meaning of life" or "the finality of life." Doubts and difficulties about religious faith were quite regular in later adolescence.

Jaspard (1972) found marked differences in the religious ideas of children from six to twelve. Boys had a more socialized religion, identified with relationships mediated by ritual activity; girls displayed a more loosely structured religion, with a close personal relationship with God. The differences sprang from different relationships with their mothers, but boys and girls alike regarded God and Jesus as strongly masculine (Jaspard, 1980). All children showed interest in the artifacts of the church, the priest and his actions and gestures. Boys of seven and eight showed as good an understanding of some of the rites as girls of ten. Vercruysse (1972) tested Dutch Catholic adolescents aged seventeen and eighteen and adults to determine what meaning they attached to God as a significant part of their lives. The adult responses disclosed four factors of which personal "presence" was the most important and included items displaying a sense of responsibility to God's authority. The adolescent responses gave six factors, and despite many differences she felt there was a fundamental compatibility among them. Adults tended to think of God in personal terms, while adolescents tended to think of him more as an impersonal, dynamic presence. Both groups equally accepted that God was the ultimate explanation and tended to reject the idea of a providential and helping God. The meaning assigned to God originated through active contact with the world and with people, or from asking large metaphysical questions, rather than from an experience of human need. Whether God was conceived in personal or impersonal terms, he was seen as the basis, guarantee, and goal of what man does rather than as taking care of, or comforting people.

Van Aerde (1972) gave a scale about perceptions of God to a group of Dutch-speaking Catholics. Women's responses were higher than the men's, especially in fear and respect for God, in thankfulness, and in the sense of his mystery. Those who most emphasized God's mercy were least affected by fear of him. Age, sex, and occupation affected the image of God; for example, farmers were less affected by the manifestation of God in creation but had a strong sense of his mystery and the awe-inspiring dimension of his nature. Laborers and farmers tended to rely on God's moral and material support, giving thanks when they received it and blaming God when they did not. Other nonmanual occupations differed little among themselves, stressing in particular God's mercy.

Early on in this group of studies a distinction was made between the idealized figures of the father and the mother and the images of the subject's own actual parents, based partly in visual memory. In one test of the Semantic Differential Parental Scale which was developed, Vannesse and De Neuter (1981) demonstrated from students' responses that their real parents were significantly different from their symbolic parental figures; to some extent everyone shares in the recognizably different perceptions of an individual who says "I never had a real father" or "a real mother." The authors asserted that it is these symbolic figures rather than the images of the actual parents which influence the psychological development of children, and in turn their representation of God. The concepts by which God is described, even the God of unbelievers, have this psychological significance. The earlier studies of Strunk (1959), Godin and Hallez (1964), and Nelson (1971) were criticized not only on the ground that they were inconsistent but that their items did not permit the full exploration of the parental functions other than in terms of affective proximity. They did not describe how young children's first under-standing of mother and father was modified to give rise to different idealized parental figures. Hutsebaut (1972) deduced from adolescent replies to the question "What does God mean for you?" that God was regarded as the absolute. They suf-fered some degree of doubt in later adolescence and envisaged God in relational terms such as father or friend as well as in terms of his qualities and characteristics.

The scale was developed (Vercruysse, 1972) from the experience of Spilka, Armatas, and Nussbaum (1964) and Gorsuch (1968), with half the items paternal, half maternal. Previous research had shown, and subsequent research confirmed, that while all items related to both parents, some related more strongly to the father and some more strongly to the mother. Subjects used the scale to assess their images of what an ideal father and a mother should be, the actual image of their parents, and their image of God; from their scores the semantic distances among the three figures could be ascertained for each respondent. Subsequent analysis demonstrated the reliability of the scale and confirmed that it functioned as intended. The validity of the scale is crucial to the considerable body of results accruing from its use, and some doubt must remain about it having a built-in cultural bias and about the selection of attributes to which responses are made. It was first used with Dutch Catholic adolescents (Hutsebaut, 1972), and then translations into French, English, Spanish, and Italian allowed its use with adolescents, students, and adults in many different cultures in Europe, North America, South America, Indonesia, and Africa. Since translations required some variation of phrasing and vocabulary, each translation was tested further with comparable groups of Catholic secondary school and university students.

Variations typical of particular cultures revealed that, with few exceptions, the figures of ideal mother, father, and God always had similar characteristics. The mother figure proved to be the simplest, with its maternal items showing the greatest saturation, from "who welcomes me with open arms" (5.59) to "who lets you be a child" (3.79), followed by its paternal items ranging from "the one who maintains order" (3.60) to "power" (1.57) (Vercruysse and de Neuter, 1981). In eight different tests in four different cultures the maternal items together secured mean scores ranging from 4.45 to 5.15, whereas the paternal items were much weaker, with mean scores ranging from 2.33 to 3.59. The mother figure was characterized by tenderness, patience, acceptance, and sympathetic concern and, to a lesser extent, always waiting, all-embracing, and always present. Of less consequence were the paternal items that referred to law and order, such as legislator, judge, power, and sternness. The mother figure's affective availability, providing security and care and typifying unconditional love, remained a stable symbol for both sexes throughout the years.

The item saturation was less extensive in the paternal figure, the paternal items ranging from "firmness" (5.22) to "stern" and "who examines things" (3.64). But the contrasting maternal items overlapped the paternal ones to an extent, ranging from "close to whom one feels at home" and "who welcomes me with open arms" (4.08) to "who is always waiting for me" (2.24). A complex structure was thus disclosed for these many adolescents and adults. The paternal items were much more strongly associated with the father figure than the maternal items were with the mother figure, and the maternal items contributed more to the father figure than the paternal items did to the mother figure, and so were relatively more important. Further, some maternal items proved to be at least as important to the father figure as did some of the paternal items. Hence the father was characterized by items that described initiative, action, dynamism, firmness, and authority; the core of the parental figure was constituted by law and availability, and the relative strengths of the associated items suggested that the father figure was not characterized as authoritarian. Rather, Vergote (1981) interpreted law as the stability which provides security in the context of a warm relationship. The maternal items expressing loving concern were also attributed to the father with a high degree of intensity. While the maternal image was relatively simple and attractive, the paternal image was much more complex; this complexity provided the basis for the greater symbolic power of the paternal image. Such a complexity of relational qualities could be conflicting, and since both sexes presented almost identical parental figures despite the tendency of women to score more highly, Freud's Oedipus complex as popularly understood was not supported.

Because of its greater complexity the father figure was a more adequate symbol for God, for whom both paternal and maternal dimensions are relevant. The paternal items in the representation of God had quite different strengths from those in either of the parental figures, so that God was viewed primarily as providing authority and justice by his knowledge and power; he was the giver and guardian of the law, characteristics much less strongly associated with either father or mother figures. Action and initiative were perceived as more important qualities in the parental figures than in God. Whereas the mother was seen primarily as one who is tender, patient, and accepting, God was perceived relatively less than either parent in terms of care but was most strongly characterized as ever-present and waiting, as self-giving love and as a safe refuge. In this respect God was perceived as more maternal than paternal, as essentially displaying availability and providing law. Thus, both parental figures were seen to symbolize God, but because his representation included paternal items not significantly attributed to the mother figure, and because the maternal items were similar to those integrated into the father figure, God was called father. Vergote and Aubert (1972) commented that while Freud regarded the father as the symbol for God as invented by the child's demand for protection, providence, and care, these were really maternal values. They noted that Jung's work allowed for such maternal ideas.

Tamayo and Desjardins (1976) distinguished between the structure of beliefs—the way by which concepts and values were organized and integrated, and the content of beliefs—the values and realities which are central or relevant to a particular structure. In a study of undergraduates they identified two groups. Abstract individuals were characterized by task orientation, rather than by dependence on rules and regulations, and were more innovative, capable of more complex patterns of integration, and more tolerant of ambiguity and uncertainty. Concrete individuals were influenced more by the source of information than by the information itself and showed a greater need for structure and order, were more dogmatic and resistant to change. The situation of a particular experience affected them more than the experience itself, so that they had difficulty in bypassing their immediate experience of the divine image so as to formulate and integrate its symbolic dimensions. They were more conditioned by stereotypes of divinity. In the structures of the image of God and of parents there was a larger semantic distance between the mother-father images and the parent-God images for boys and men than for girls and women, and the abstracts had a greater father-God distance than the concretes.

Tamayo and Dugas (1977) studied a group of French Canadian students aged twenty-one and found a difference between the sexes in the image of their parents, but not of God, the women displaying less contrast between their parents than the men. Unlike similar studies in America, the degree of faith and the level of the students' studies—possibly the effect of their cultural environment—affected their conceptual image of God, and this image was more adequately modeled by the mother image than by that of the father, despite the findings to the contrary of all previous studies.

When results from testing Catholic adolescents in different cultures were compared (Tamayo, 1981), it was found that characteristics of the parental figures, and more particularly those of the mother, varied from one culture to another. This was regarded as arising from cultural differences in the affective mother-child relationship. The symbolic power of the mother figure in understanding the representation of God was at its greatest in terms of availability in every culture, but because the law–related items were associated directly with the representation of God but were of low intensity in the mother figure, the overlapping of the law factors in the maternal figure and the representation of God was indistinct. God was as much paternal as maternal for the American and Colombian groups, he was more paternal for the Indonesian and Filipino groups and for males in Belgium and Zaire, and more maternal for females in Belgium. Many other cultural differences were recorded, for example, the American sample perceived God in terms of law more strongly than did the Filipino sample. Vergote (1981) concluded that it was the culture, and not individual psychology, that determined which components of the parental figures were attributed to God. Yet when believers were compared with men and women in religious orders, very personal factors seemed to affect their representation of God, so that they appropriated in their own individual manner the context of the name of father.

When American high-school and college students were compared with Dutch-speaking and French-speaking Belgian students (Vergote et al., 1969), the image of God was found to be more paternal than maternal, but in the American sample alone it became more maternal with increasing age. All Americans emphasized the paternal aspect of God, whereas for the Belgians parental qualities tended to correspond to the respondents' own sex. But older postadolescent Americans of both sexes integrated more intensely the maternal aspects of God. The American liberal arts students reported a more maternal mother and less paternal father than the science students, whereas the Belgian science students conceived of God more in maternal terms and literary students more in paternal terms.

The use of the scale with delinquents demonstrated marked deviations in the parental roles (Tamayo and St-Arnaud, 1981), and in particular the absence of the law or authority factor, as had been indicated by other research in the field. Its use with a small sample of schizophrenics confirmed that their mother figure was greatly distorted and impoverished and seen primarily as a judge, and, as if in compensation, the father figure was enriched. These abnormal perceptions, in which both groups displayed the absence of availability in the mother figure, resulted in corresponding differences in the representation of God, including a preference in the delinquent group to describe God in terms of the maternal values of intimacy and affectivity which were so strikingly absent from their own experience. To them, the name of father gave to God a different meaning from that found in normal Christian usage.

In the light of the cultural differences found between American, Dutch, and Belgian students, and the unusual profile of the delinquents, it is not surprising that more extreme differences were found among Hindus. When a group of Canadian students were compared with a group of Hindus from India (Desjardins and Tamayo, 1981) the parental figures of the Indian sample were found to have little similarity to those of the Christians. The Christians perceived divinity through affective values such as availability, proximity, and tenderness, but the Hindus did so through values such as authority and law and order, which, unlike the Christian perception, were only secondary to the description of the parental figures.

In a study of the spontaneous language about God used by seminarians, Vannesse (1977) found it corresponded more to a maternal than a paternal image, so that they stressed God's love, using language which conveyed the desire for a loving, caring, warm, reassuring presence, as first experienced in the infant's relationship with the mother, and relegating to the background the prophetic dimension of his word. The language of today's church resulted in the recruitment of young men who responded to it sensitively. Such language was ambiguous, since mystical union is oriented toward bliss and joy and as such is not specifically Christian. Genuinely Christian language must use equal references to paternal symbols. A further study of seminarians and nuns (Vannesse and Neff, 1981) disclosed that there was an unusually strong bond with the mother which influenced their representation of God, so that once more, while they emphasized the dimension of unconditional love, the corresponding dimension of the paternal items led to a reduced perception of the prophetic dimension of God, which the authors felt could lead to some passivity regarding the actual conditions of society.

Coster (1981) interviewed French-speaking Belgian children, looking for developmental characteristics. Children aged six to eight saw their parents as caring for them, protecting them, and near to them in their activities, guaranteeing their security, indicating that the essential components of the parental figures are formed early in childhood. The father was perceived as being more distant than the mother; the boys regarded this as arising from his absence because of his work, but with the girls it was related to his being of a different gender from themselves. Children nine to eleven perceived the father as a model to be imitated; the mother was seen similarly by the girls, and boys and girls both saw her in terms of relationships. These phases were reflected in their representation of God. The younger children regarded God as preoccupied with them, giving them what was requested, tolerant, kind, and protective—qualities desired of their parents—and they also saw him as creator and master of the whole earth. Boys understood this especially in terms of God's power, particularly in creation, just as the father was perceived in terms of his work; the younger girls saw this transcendence more in personal terms—because God was master of the world he was also their protector. Older children insisted on the educative aspect of God similar to the parental figures, showing them what to do, approving or punishing their behavior, but doing it in a way superior to that of their fathers. On the other hand they also saw God as being open to them, with the qualities found in the mother figure for children of this age—being available, comforting, trusting, and considerate. The analogous structures between the parental figures and the representation of God appeared not only in the structures themselves but also in their evolution and in the different perceptions of boys and girls.

The three figures of father, mother, and God which thus have fully developed by adolescence were shown in another study (Tamayo and Cooke, 1981) not to change in any fundamental way with age. A comparison made between adolescents and elderly French-speaking Catholic Canadians indicated a close similarity with each of the three figures, although the semantic distances were less for the elderly than for the younger.

Some support for this range of perception, and an indication of variations in its strength between individuals, was given by the small study of Godin (1975), who found that responses of French-Canadian Catholic adolescents to his questions "to what are you referring when you say Word of God?" could be classified into three groups. In the first, the dominant thought was of authority and competence, of giving direction, of being expert or father. The second group responded in terms of help, friendship, need, warmth, gentleness, brotherhood, intimacy, proximity, encounter, and feeling, while the third group used such terms as abstraction, conscience, doctrine, idea, question, and thought.

This series of coordinated studies, with little parallel elsewhere, has so far attracted little response. Fay (1983) used Vergote and Tamayo's scale with other tests for an in-depth study of five Christian women. They were found to include both paternal and maternal characteristics in their representation of God, but the emphasis was on the maternal. God was regarded as complex, powerful, and relational; primary attributes were availability and unconditional acceptance rather than law and authority. Justice and Lambert (1986) found an association among two adult groups between the personality of the father as perceived in childhood and adolescence and their image of God. This was also the case for the larger group alone of the mother's personality. They considered that this confirmed the findings of Tamayo and Desjardins (1976) but did not support the Freudian concept that the father alone contributed to the image of God. Roof and Roof (1984) found that women's response to suggested images of God were stronger than men's, older subjects more than younger, and less-educated more than well-educated. Conventionally religious groups responded most to both traditional and contemporary images of God. Contrary to the findings of Vergote and Tamayo (1981), mother images were most common among older, uneducated women in the South. There were marked denominational differences; Protestants gave the strongest responses, followed by Catholics, Jews, and "nones." According to Randour and Bondanze (1987) the cultural concept of God has a strong influence on the development of the representation of God among women and on their psychological development; a case study indicated the effects of changing this image.

Bulkeley (1981) was influenced by these studies, and undertook an independent investigation throughout childhood. He was critical of Vergote's instrument, not only because it was unsuitable for use with younger children, but because it was the product of a particular culture and had not given entirely consistent results when used in translation. Nor did the maternal items appear to give an adequate distinction between the paternal and maternal image. He used adjectives from Osgood's semantic differential, applying them to mother, father, and God. Younger children were able to complete the test satisfactorily, and he used it with boys and girls aged seven to fifteen in Glasgow, securing measures of the interdependence of each of the three images for each child. The image of God was like the image of both the mother and the father. Scores of the youngest children showed that their image of God was very dependent on their parental images. This similarity of the images decreased with age, consistent with children first modeling God on their parents and later modifying their ideas. The images of the boys and of the girls at all ages were significantly different, contrary to the findings of Deconchy; Bulkeley considered this could be due either to the different test instruments, or to the insufficient opportunity his own test gave for boys to register more severe or punitive aspects of the image of God. His results gave no indication of development beyond fifteen. On this test the image of God was closer to that of the father than of the mother; this in fact agreed with the findings of Vergote and Tamayo (1981). There were wide individual variations; some children even showed a negative relationship between parental and divine imagery or gave negative scores for one parent but not the other, which confirmed that the quality of family life affected the image of God. From this demonstration of the importance of the image of the mother in influencing children's images of God, he argued at length that it was necessary to broaden religious language to express more adequately maternal aspects of God, setting psychological and theological perspectives side by side.

McKenzie (1987) studied the differences between symbolic and actual parent concepts as they related to God concepts. He found mixed support for the theories that the God concept would be better predicted from the symbolic father rather than the symbolic mother concepts, or that it would be better predicted from the actual mother rather than the actual father concepts. He established that the God concept was similar to that of the preferred parent; it was more complex than had been usually acknowledged, and it had a more cognitive surface structure and a more emotional underlying structure.

A few independent studies raise related issues. Greeley (1981), in his extensive study of the religious imagination, found that ideas of God as loving and protecting, and an idea of God as a mother, were found in the adolescents and adults with the most advanced religious ideas. It was associated with an understanding of Jesus and Mary as warm and loving. The emergence of these "positive optimistic beliefs" was primarily related to the perceived quality of Catholic education and religious experience but also to the influence of friends and parents, church attendance and spiritual readings, as well as nature-oriented activities, retreats, and a happy marriage.

Other adult studies have also shown wide variations in the image of God, and factors associated with it. Neff (1977) compared active and contemplative French-speaking Belgian nuns by using their written answers to such questions as "For me, God is. . ." The God of the contemplative nuns was found to be more distant and more transcendent; they were of a more passive nature, marked by self-negation and self-distrust, with little desire for action. They had taken refuge in God as a mother par excellence and in an institutional structure which protected them against weakness and fostered a mother-daughter relationship to the detriment of brotherly relationships. The active nuns more frequently compared God to a person who was near to them or saw him in terms of immanence; they were full of devotion, of love for others, of desire to do good, and to be faithful to their ethical ideal. They liked their efforts to be noticed and appreciated but did not like to be challenged or to revise their opinions. Gender differences in the adult image of God were examined by Nelsen, Cheek, and Au (1985); analysis of their data revealed three closely related images—God as king, as healer, and as understood in relational terms. Women in the sample scored more highly than the men only on the image of God as healer. Their attraction to this supportive concept was regarded as partly due to the succor they received in their church participation, a suggestion supported by the fact that when church attendance was held constant, the gender difference was diminished.

Another study from a different culture was that of Kròl (1982). He tested Polish boys and girls aged fourteen to sixteen from working-class families with a scale about responses to father, ideal father, and God. He was able to distinguish two groups, one with "good" fathers and the other with "bad" fathers who, on the mothers' admission, were alcoholic to the extent that their children were adversely affected. The group with good fathers had a more positive image of God than the other group, and there was close connection between the image of God and the image of the real father. Boys had a more negative image of God than the girls in the group with bad fathers. It appeared that these boys, but not the girls, associated the image of their real father with their image of God.

Beit-Hallahmi and Argyle (1975) argued that the notion that God is modeled after the father is the most easily tested of Freudian hypotheses. They contended that belief systems are not created by particular individuals but are transmitted from generation to generation, being accepted because the private fantasies and images of individuals correspond to their cultural traditions. Similarities between the image of God and the father are to be expected, since they are openly expressed by many religions, and religious traditions themselves are learned in the first place through parents. Despite the limitations of the studies, it would appear that it is a general rather than a specific parental projection which operates. The exception, that of Vergote et al. (1969), demonstrated a stronger paternal than maternal image, but the paternal image often differed from that of the subject's own father. They regarded this study, unlike the others, as less affective and more cognitive, so that it seemed that the cognitive component was culturally transmitted, whereas the affective component was derived from the attitude to the parents. This last comment would probably be modified in the light of the more recent studies just reviewed; what is interesting is the extent of agreement between the authors and the main findings of Vergote and his colleagues. They also quoted the study of Spiro and D'Andrade (1958) in which, by comparing images of God in eleven primitive cultures, it was shown that a punitive image of God was found when the father was punitive, but a benevolent father was associated with a benevolent image of God. The conclusion they reached was that the more generally accepted, broader, interpretation of Freudian theory was substantiated, insofar that the deity could be regarded as a projected love-object in which positive qualities were projected more than negative ones. Freud was not able to account for the prevalence of maternal deities, and the connection between the mother image and that of the deity supported a Jungian interpretation of religion.

The image of God is thus seen to develop in early childhood from children's perceptions of their parents—what they are and what ideally they should be. Punitive or loving images of God are closely related to parental attitudes. Some evidence points to the importance of the preferred parent; some evidence points to the influence of the image held of the actual parents, but the great weight of the Louvain studies indicates the strength of the image of both of the ideal parents, as well as the rich variety of ideas to be found. Whether the details of these findings are applicable only in the Catholic cultures in which they were undertaken is not certain. Freud's emphasis on the father figure has to be extended to include that also of the mother, which contradicts Freudian theory.

This considerable body of research has not impressed all commentators, apart from the philosophical difficulty that it can be interpreted to imply that the image of God is nothing more than a projection of human images. Nor can it be extended to apply to religions which are not monotheistic. Gorsuch (1988) cited the criticisms of Kirkpatric (1986a) about the methodological and conceptual problems of projective studies of the image of God and his contention that such theories were so loosely defined that there was no adequate theoretical background for research. The basic difficulty was that there was a fundamental similarity between any concepts of goodness as applied to God or to parents. Any two elements that both met a criterion of good would show some positive association. Further, the correlations recorded in these studies, while significant, were nevertheless weak. These results were regarded by Spilka, Hood, and Gorsuch (1985) as only of philosophical interest and not worthy of further research. Despite fairly rigorous procedures in an extensive program of research, they had not been able to support Freudian theory and were unable to offer a psychological theory to explain them. There was an apparently insuperable research problem. An individual's religious heritage contributed to the image of God as did also the similarity arising from all highly valued objects. A means had to be found to remove the effects of these from the image of God and then identify any parental projection in the residual image.

The most fitting conclusion is to recall the comment of Piaget (1965)—"Our results entirely support those of M. Bovet according to which the child spontaneously attributes to his parents the perfections and abilities which he will later transfer to God if his religious education gives him the possibility."

Chapter 5

Religious Beliefs and their Development

While much research has concentrated on children's ideas of God, some has looked at a wider range of religious ideas, including prayer. The ideas of preschool children about religion are dominated by the phantasies and partial understandings which characterize much else of their thinking, ideas which are soon to be replaced by the concrete literalism most children achieve by the age of seven and by the emergence of more sophisticated concepts and judgments in adolescence. Surveys of religious beliefs and practices are reviewed in chapter 12.

Religious ideas of younger children

Although the early years of childhood have been the subject of intense psychological study, little research has been undertaken regarding the beginnings of religion. For more than a century, most studies have been about adolescents, and the younger the children, the fewer the studies, so that there are relatively few about preschool children. At no period of life can there be a complete separation of cognitive and affective aspects of mental activity, and this is most evident in the first years of life when understanding and feeling are so closely intertwined. Insight into early religious development has tended to depend on inferences from wider psychological knowledge. For a description of the place of feeling in the life of young children, arising from their vivid imagination, and the way that it leads from curiosity into the religious feelings of awe and worship, that of Yeaxlee (1939) could hardly be bettered. Although research has been limited in its extent, many descriptions of religion in early childhood are available, as they have been for a long time, e.g., Wilson (1928), Hunter (1956), Madge (1965), Berridge (1969), Ratcliff (1988), and the parents' guides of Brusselmans and Wakin (1977) and Barber (1978, 1981).

Some studies of the religious ideas of children of five and under have been made, which give a glimpse of the less-developed ideas of younger children. One of these was the review of Léonard (1957) and his account of prayer and piety in the first years of life. Four-year-old children born into a religious environment are intrigued by religious interests and ask many apparently profound questions (Britton and Winanc, 1958). Religious beliefs were meaningless to young children, even though they might learn to use religious words in context. Because their concepts were realistic, they interpreted what they heard in terms of what they knew, so that God became a man who wore clothes different from other people (Hurlock, 1969); this reflected the way in which ideas of God had been presented to them.

The way that young children used religious words superficially in the right context, but without any real understanding of their meaning, was noticed a long time ago; Brandenburg's (1915) record of the extensive vocabulary of a three-year-old girl included her attempt at twenty months to repeat the chorus of a hymn she had heard, in which "Leaning on Jesus' everlasting arms" became for her, "Leaning on Jes, I lost my arm." Such mismatches have provided insight into the way that young children learn the meaning of a new word which does not belong to their familiar world of objects, situations, and states; a hypothesis has to be made about its meaning which is tested the next time the word is heard. Their vocabulary grows from observing the conventions about the use of language and realizing that new meanings have to contrast with those already known (Clark 1983). Few religious words have to do with concrete objects, and most of its vocabulary has to be learned in this way. Words infrequently heard are not likely to be understood. Beiswanger (1930) and his team examined the use of Old Testament material with children and suggested that none of it was suitable for those under the age of nine, despite the use of some familiar stories from an early age. Even the Victorians had become aware of the problems of conceptual difficulty for very young children (Allery, 1985). By the age of six, children have learned to a limited extent the meaning of a number of religious concepts (Josephina, 1961), but up to the age of five understanding is very restricted. Religious perception is still external, related to personal sustenance or physical needs (Ludwig, Weber, and Iben, 1974).

Attitude to religion cannot be measured with confidence before the age of eight, according to Francis (1976), who failed to secure reliable responses from children of seven to his attitude scale. Harms' (1944) description of the early "fairy-tale state" was noted in the previous chapter. Moral judgments are acquired as a result of the influence of social factors, according to Ruffy (1981), who studied Swiss and American children aged four to nine. Ausubel, Sullivan, and Ives (1980) suggested that different religious environments may affect the rate of children's early moral development. Eisenberg-Berg and Roth (1980) tested children of four and five for their responses to pictures which required them to make a moral choice, such as helping an injured child or going to a party. When this was repeated after eighteen months much of their hedonistic orientation had been supplanted by a needs-oriented one. The authors argued that since much religious teaching at this age was about selfishness, it should encourage such reasoning and discourage hedonism.

Philibert (1985) contended that the early years provided not only an experience of the best of life, with a sense of loving parental care, but also moments of separation and frustration; this dependency provided the fundamental feelings of contentment or dissatisfaction with the prospect of life. A high degree of ambivalence between the two could be sustained when children were contented, but when mistrust dominated their feelings it gave rise to an infantile desire to dominate, resulting in a manipulativeness that disrupted social trust. These two orientations were the basis of the symbolic and diabolic images of God. Such ideas are basic to the theories of Erikson as interpreted by Fowler (1981) which were considered earlier.

The understanding of Catholic children of six was studied using four pictures for each concept chosen; one picture related to the question asked by a teacher. The great majority identified terms such as "church," "cross," "chapel," "St. Christopher," "altar," or "crucifix." Some terms, such as "Jesus' birthday," "Our Lord," or "My Body," proved to be more difficult for some children than for others. All of them found "Holy Ghost," "Good Shepherd," "Host," and "Easter" difficult to identify. This verbal identification suggested a background of religious concepts which had been absorbed from religious symbols such as pictures, statues, the Christmas crib, and stories, which they must have met in their homes, since they had not received any formal religious education (Josephina, 1961). In a different cultural setting, the ideas of French-speaking Catholic children aged five to seven have been investigated in Montreal. They had been taught the Canadian catechism and three quarters of them had correctly assimilated essential teaching about the resurrection but were confused about the meaning of hell. The fundamental difficulty sprang from the language used, which had become a source of confusion and misunderstanding for the children. Their anthropomorphic thought-forms and the misconceptions learned from adults made the problem more difficult (Darcy and Beniskos, 1971). Nordberg (1971) discussed the difficulty that children had in understanding the terminology of even a simple catechism. He contended that religious instruction was started at too early an age and it needed teachers who were knowledgeable about religious concepts. The production of conceptual belief was a false objective; instruction should begin in the context of the family and teaching should be for meaning.

In the face of cognitive limitations, Batson (1974) argued that religious growth in young children was prevented, not by their lack of cognitive development, but by their lack of experience without which they could not grasp symbolism. They needed to feel that they were loved and accepted by the church. They also needed the opportunity to develop the ability to use symbolic thought and use it to interpret their experience of life. Within a responsive environment they could find symbolic, pro-social means of expression and deal with conflicts with their family and friends. Berryman (1979) suggested that children should not be taught intellectually but should play with appropriate materials. This was supported by Elkind's (1980) suggestion that at every age play is an important means of expression in religious education. Both of them are emphasizing that the intellectual barriers to understanding require an approach that is also affective.

Elkind (1980) distinguished between recreational play and developmental play and also referred to Montessori, who regarded play as children's "work." Piaget regarded play as displaying a developmental structure and he distinguished between play as accommodation to social reality and play as assimilation of objects and activities to children's needs. Very young children indulged in practice play, as when a baby grasps an object and then drops it; from about two children engaged in symbolic play—playing house imitates adult roles without learning about them, although by endowing dolls with life play reflected personal needs for mastery and control, yet without social adaptation. When concrete operations were attained symbolic play was displaced by play with rules; children played together socially using socially constructed rules with a diminution of egocentricity. In religious education play had to be expressive, for it made a different contribution. Since religious education prepared children for adaptation to the spiritual world the value of play was that it provided them with an opportunity to express their understanding of religious ideas and thus to discover their own spiritual potential. In this context Elkind included in play such activities as written expression or the use of art, music, or drama, making suggestions very similar to those of Berryman from an allegedly contrary point of view. Hall (1988) gave a psychological perspective on the use of fantasy in religious education—one of a number of articles on play in religious education featured in that journal issue concluded by Huber's (1988) account of learning through fantasy games.

Ratcliff (1985a) described and assessed the use of play in religious education for preschool children, so that they acted the roles of praying, taking an offering, leading the singing, and preaching. He stressed the value of adults entering into it and taking on its roles; he regarded it as important for the children to act out selected biblical stories. These suggestions about playing with religious materials are by no means new; Loomba (1942), writing from a Hindu perspective, made the same point. He argued that children came to religion with a desire to find the cause of events, first endowing their parents with the causative power which they later transferred to God, and claiming that young children of the same age all showed the same type of religious beliefs. The idea of God was assimilated by play, and the religious objects used in play—a wax Lord Krishna with cows of clay and milkmaids of wood—had a reality to children distinct from that of the adult world. Mimicry was important, and the actions and attitudes of worshiping adults were reproduced with solemnity and attention to detail. At this preschool age God was still thought of as a strong man, with fear playing a part, since God could be the cause of punishment and misery. Such fear gave rise not to awe but rather to curiosity; where a religious system included Satan or a devil or some other evil spirit children had been observed to be greatly interested in him, feeling sorry for him, sympathizing, and inclined to be friendly with him.

Goldman also was at pains to make teachers aware of the difference between what they thought they were teaching and what the children actually learned and insisted (Goldman, 1963b) that intellectual teaching about religion had to be set alongside teaching children by a subjective, feeling approach which was allied to the world of poetry, music, and art. In this way intuitive or existentialist knowledge was acquired. Teaching biblical events only chronologically and historically would be defeated by the younger children's difficulties with the kind of thinking such a study required. Even at eight to ten children confused King Saul with the Apostle, Jesus was seen as living about the time of Moses, and Palestine was situated, according to one eight-year-old, just a few miles from Cardiff. Rather, he argued, children must be able to recognize in the material similar experiences to those which are normal for them. They will not memorize all the facts, but they may penetrate to the essence of what is taught, something which cannot be assessed, but which lies in a realm of feeling and an area of experience which young children understand but cannot express or explain in words. He described an experience of teaching the creation story with a class of eight-year-olds; they could not adequately understand it, but by music, movement, and painting, they expressed forcefully the darkness retreating before the light, and order springing out of chaos. We lack descriptive accounts of this type of activity, such as when a class of six-year-olds discovered what it meant to be lost and by this discovery came to some understanding of the parable of the Lost Coin (Wilkinson, 1965b).

Such an approach to young children contrasts with the suggestion of Dechambre (1983) that despite their cognitive limitations, nursery school children's hunger for stories can be met by Bible stories which are preceded by silence, given in front of a display of an open Bible and followed by appropriate prayers, so as to produce an appropriate response. Wills (1971) regarded the Bible as the source book for a teacher's self-preparation and inspiration, but she preferred to use general topic work to bring children to the experiences fundamental to religion. "Shelter" was found to be related to loving and caring, Christmas and Easter were times used for young children to re-create the experiences of self-giving, love, and new beginnings. Barber (1978) brought insights which sprang from many years association with the Union College Character Research Project to bear on the religious nurture of two-year-old children. She described their abilities and indicated how these could be used, especially by parents, to help them learn and develop attitudes basic to religiousness. Subsequently, she broadened her approach to include all preschool children (Barber, 1981). She saw a limited but important use of the Bible with them, preferably from selected picture books of Bible stories. But her main concern was to facilitate growth in faith, hope, and love by an "attitude education." The practical consequences of such an understanding provided the basis from which many authors, in the last twenty years, have developed approaches for religious education with young children, e.g., Bullen (1969), Cliff and Cliff (1966), and more recently Brandling (1980), the Schools Council Religious Education in Primary Schools Project (1977), Mumford (1982), and Ratcliff (1988).

Religious ideas in childhood and adolescence

With older children and adolescents more studies are available. Thouless (1935) found that statements such as, "Tigers are found in parts of China," secured responses from students with only a few showing high degrees of certainty or uncertainty, whereas statements such as, "There is a personal God," secured a polarized response, with large numbers expressing high levels of belief or disbelief. He concluded that individuals tended to hold or reject beliefs with very strong convictions, so that doubt and skepticism were unusual and represented an unstable attitude of mind. Brown (1962) used this study for a further examination of the strength of religious belief with Australian students and included personality and attitude scales in his test battery. Religious belief proved to be a relatively isolated cognitive system in which intensity of belief was independent of opinions about other matters but depended on strong social support; church membership and attitude to the church showed a strong relationship to the strength of belief but not to the personality variables, although strength of belief was associated with an authoritarian attitude. Smith (1941) argued that children's religious development was both intellectual and emotional. Preschool children had an emotional, imaginative enthusiasm with little basis in fact, followed by a period of hard realism with little emphasis on imagination. Then came a period of pre-adolescent doubt, in which there were fluctuations between idealism and realism and, finally, a more steady and practical type of idealism. However, most subsequent studies stressed cognitive development.

An early landmark was the work of Bose (1929), who tested children and adolescents from eight to eighteen. He was concerned to discover the actual meanings children gave to religious terms and how maturity brought better understanding. Since children could interpret them only through their limited experience, vagueness implied a poverty of experience as well as of understanding. While the children had formed few erroneous ideas, vagueness and confusion about the meanings was widespread. Names of special days or places were familiar, but terms such as conversion, Savior, or Christian were not properly comprehended. Eight-year-old children seemed to understand them almost as well as older children, and even teachers were only a little better. Attendance at church school had no relationship with learning but church membership did. There was only a weak association between scores and mental age, and religious education seemed unrelated to their life situations. A reexamination of his results shows more positive features than he claimed. By combining responses to all the ten concepts, a development with age is apparent, and by comparing higher and lower scoring groups a significant increase of score with age is shown:

SCORES ON TEN ITEMS BY PERCENTAGE OF TOTAL GROUP			
	Age		
Scores	8-12	13-15	16-18
0/1/2	11.78	6.90	5.59
4/5	15.88	16.76	21.36

Wheeler and Wheeler (1945) found church attendance to be related to religious knowledge. Church-going junior-high-school children showed a higher degree of factual knowledge than nonattenders. All scored highest about Christmas and lowest about Good Friday, Easter, and the Golden Rule. Non-church-going children showed more anthropomorphic thinking, regarding God as a king rather than a father, emphasizing his sovereignty and power rather than his love and compassion; he was regarded as unwilling to love the bad but only those who worshiped him and refusing to help those who failed to thank him. They were more confused about prayer but had greater tolerance of other religious faiths. Differences were smaller on questions about death and immortality, partly because church-going children were also confused. They regarded the chief purpose of religion as being to save them for a future life. The greatest difference concerned understanding of the church and its sacraments. There were also some denominational differences in children's knowledge. The Union College Character Research Project (1959) reproduced a substantial collection of the religious ideas of children from two to thirteen reported by their parents. They related to God, Jesus, the church, prayer, and the Bible but were presented without comment, leaving readers to make their own judgments. They support an effect of age on the development of ideas, in accord with much subsequent research.

A projection test based on five pictures was used to explore the psychiatric disorders and religious orientation of persistently delinquent adolescent boys (Gerkin and Weber, 1953). The same technique was used to evaluate an unspecified experimental program of religious education for emotionally disturbed and delinquent boys; increases in the references made to religious symbols in the pictures by the taught group suggested some success in the program (Gerkin and Cox, 1955).

Belgian adolescent girls with five years religious instruction regarded the resurrection as a proof of Christ's divinity, which 62 percent accepted. Private school pupils secured a higher proportion of favorable responses than state school pupils, but in both groups this declined with age (Dache, 1971). Also in Belgium, an important study of the symbolic perception of children aged six to twelve showed that insight into the sacramental nature of the eucharistic rite was reached about eleven or twelve, when it was understood symbolically. Girls were more sensitive to aspects of Christ's manifestation and boys to aspects of the covenant and the reconciliation between God and man. Younger children showed immature insight, regarding the host as Jesus, and its form, not its composition, was thought to be important. Between eight and nine the presence of Jesus was still seen without any reference to the rite; at this age the boys were beginning to understand the role of the priest, although he was regarded as a man endowed with sacred powers, which suggested that their thinking was still at the level of the magical (Jaspard, 1971; Dumoulin and Jaspard, 1973). Symbolic perception is of especial importance in religious traditions which make use of symbolism in their rituals and requires more than cognitive understanding; in this case, according to Rogers (1980) it needed a sense of affective presence, the beginning of effective action, the interiorization of ethical conscience, and the development of a sense of law and work. The study finds support from the finding of Godin and Marthe (1960) in which magical-type explanations of automatic efficacy of the sacrament were typical of children aged eight to eleven with traces of such thinking persisting until fourteen, comparable to Piaget's assertion that children up to twelve use magical modes of thought and confuse signs with what is signified until seven or eight.

Outside church schools difficulties arise. Research at the Stockholm School of Education (1977) looked at the ideological problems that teachers faced with preschool and junior-age children. Quite young children asked them questions about issues such as life and death, violence, war and oppression, belief and religion. These had become controversial to adults because they had been formulated in highly abstract ways, but children asked them out of their immediate experience and faced the issues at their own level with greater frankness. Teachers with a religious commitment regarded themselves as more able to deal with them, but most saw a problem in that everything could be explained to the children except the church, death, and sexuality. They lacked training in this area, and their philosophical outlook might conflict with that of the parents. Much needed to be discovered about the thoughts children really had, how they managed to follow a discussion of this type, and what influence their homes had.

Dahlin (1990) investigated the concepts of religion of Swedish adolescents aged fifteen and sixteen. Some described "our religion" in terms of nationally held beliefs and customs, regarding it as a social dimension, although some degree of personal religion was implicit in such ideas. Few of the remainder considered themselves to be religious. They expressed a belief in a higher power, or regarded religion as giving security to its adherents. Religion was seen in terms of secular humanism, reduced to the fear of punishment or the desire for security. At school they had gained toleerance for other cultures, but this was indifference rather than understanding.

Differences in concept scores between children aged eight to ten in two London schools could be attributed to difference in religiousness rather than environment, girls scoring higher than boys. Symbols, such as "soul" or "angel" and actions, such as "worship" or "love," were understood by about half of the children, but characteristics, such as "merciful" or "humble," were less well understood (Dennison, 1962); this might have been because of differences in the difficulty of the test items rather than to their conceptual content, a problem seldom recognized. Most ten-year-old children regarded the story of Adam and Eve as literally or partially true, but while some children had muddled ideas, others were moving toward symbolic thinking. Few of them could understand the petition about forgiveness in the Lord's Prayer, although almost all felt that prayer was of benefit to those who prayed (Booth, 1965).

Pupils from twelve to sixteen showed many orthodox ideas about the nature of God, miracles, heaven and hell, goodness and evil but often with little understanding. They displayed little hostility to religion, but despite goodwill much doubt and perplexity was found; attempts were being made to discover an adequate meaning of the word God. Many pupils seemed unhappy about many traditional religious statements especially of a more emotive kind. The general picture was one of imprecision, illogicality, and often sheer muddle. Boys proved to be more skeptical than girls (Daines, 1966). When Kuhlen and Arnold's (1944) test was adapted for a study of religious belief among pupils aged eleven to fifteen in a Welsh comprehensive school, age was found to bring increasing uncertainty, and while older girls showed much stronger belief than boys there was no difference between the younger pupils. Intelligence affected beliefs critically in varying degrees, and older boys tended to become increasingly critical and uncertain (Simon and Ward, 1975).

Lupton (1974) developed and validated three scales to measure religious awareness. The first required an understanding of brief New Testament passages, the second required subjects to select and evaluate pictures best suited to illustrate religious themes, and the third, a word test for religious awareness, required the choice of the least and the most religious out of five words in each of seventeen groups. Items in the scales had been subjected to rigorous scrutiny by informed assessors, and each scale showed good internal reliability. Yet results from pupils aged fourteen in six comprehensive schools proved to be surprisingly inconclusive. They showed no significant relationship to scores on Hyde's (1959) scales, which by now were less related to the changed emphasis in religious education. The first two scales did not show any effect due to either sex or church attendance, which the third scale did. Nor was there any regional effect on the scores, except that the Welsh-speaking pupils did less well in the first test with its greater English language dependency. Only scores on the first scale showed a significant association with those on the third scale; the picture test showed negative associations among the group of church-attending pupils. It would seem that individuals are much more strongly affected by nonreligious factors than by religious ones in picture tests, but the results from the other two tests were out of step with almost all other research findings for reasons apparently unknown. Did they unwittingly measure some other dimension of religion, or were they perhaps unexpectedly dominated in this sample by verbal ability? Or do tests of a different style inevitably produce different results? Lupton was not able to pursue these important questions.

Koppe (1973) undertook a four-year longitudinal study of Lutheran children and adolescents to investigate the effect the church congregation had on their religious learning. Religiousness was regarded as a perspective on life, and individual perspectives were established at an early age. Religious learning was the result of involvement in many pragmatic life perspectives. These were about relating to God and the church and being a Christian and they suggested ten principles for growth. From eight, children were at a perspective-building stage, concerned with learning the official sources of truth and more dependent on the authenticity of truth and authority. They were testing that these perspectives were adequate and could be accepted and thus internalizing them. Preschool children, early and late adolescents were at perspective-applying stages, and growth took place when it was realized that the perspectives no longer appeared to be satisfactory. Perspectives would not be enlarged without experiences which challenged them and a community which gave them the support needed when making changes. Some adolescents always depended on authority for their beliefs, especially that of the Bible, but others who were less troubled by inconsistencies showed individuality in their preference for a variety of interpretations.

All who were identified with the life of the church most readily accepted favorable ideas about God, Christ, Jesus, or the Holy Spirit, that God and Jesus were loving and forgiving, and that individuals should be responsible for their own behavior and its consequences. They gave a lower priority to ideas which restricted the activity or love of God, to accepting responsibilities within the church, and to help in maintaining its finances. They varied according to their local church in regarding God as a generous provider, a judge, a loving protector, or their personal creator. Girls were more biased than boys toward personal concern for people and for social aspects of life. Unlike boys, preschool girls preferred peer–group to adult-led activities, showing greater independence, although boys were more active physically. In early school years, girls were better in communication, social relationships, and accountability, boys tending to simplify their situations and deal with specifics. Subsequently, girls dealt intuitively with situations rather than analyzing them, whereas boys tended to evaluate and compare them.

In all the areas investigated, as they grew older children moved from a phase of building perspectives based on adult authority to one applying perspectives to particular situations. In this process, development arose not from the culmination of past experiences but rather from moving away from earlier experiences. By twelve, children had come to regard the church as a place of training for adult life; it was another institution alongside home and school, and they began to look for ways of expressing their membership. At puberty adolescents held varied opinions; social and emotional growth, rather than intellectual, was more significant in identifying with the church. God was regarded as important from very early in life, even though the concept was completely egocentric at first. From an awareness of God grew a desire to give him something or to do something for him. Later, anthropomorphic ideas faded, and children sought to discover how they could serve and obey God and find his will for themselves. Ultimately, identification with the church became identification with being a Christian, when congregational life became of less importance than relationship with God.

Murphy (1978), whose studies of parables will be considered later, suggested that even though children might use religious language which they did not understand, they might also have thoughts and experiences which they could not verbalize. He explored this by using groups of five words for a topic, giving three of them to a child and asking which pair best went together, such as good, bad, true, evil, wrong; hymn, church, Bible, cathedral, prayer; or God, Jesus, angel, Devil, man. A matrix of responses showed the extent to which meaningful words were chosen. The groups of words had sufficient meaning for children aged six to relate them to one another; at eight and ten there was some development in the ability to relate the words, as well as the degree to which particular groups or clusters of words were related to one another. He also used an opposites test which revealed that some pairs such as "good-bad" were better recognized than others such as "love-hate," and that eight-year-old children were better at the exercise than those a year or two younger. The results, though from small groups of children, suggested that the meaning of the words studied was developing with these children. Between six and ten there was a fair vocabulary of words with either a religious meaning or relevance to religious discourse. The development of religious thinking in children was a problem both of the meaning of religious words and of cognitive development. Some studies on the development of understanding of historical time indicated increasing insight with age, but only a few children aged eight could name an event before they were born, and none of them had any real conception of the time-span of biblical stories. They could all name an Old Testament character, but they could only guess if he lived before, during, or after the time of Jesus.

Turner (1970, 1978) developed a Religious Language Comprehension Test based on terms in common use. Subsequently (Turner, 1980a, b), he argued that religious ideas in childhood were circumscribed by the general characteristics of children's thinking and that in adolescence progress toward more general and abstract understanding was often partial and confused. The metaphors it employed demanded selective transfer to unusual contexts of some of the familiar association of words, and to do this, young readers could draw on only limited experience. The test was used in Northern Ireland to examine the relationship between intellectual ability and the comprehension of religious language, by comparing boys in four age-groups from two comparable controlled and maintained secondary schools. (The test was carried out in Belfast, so that the controlled school would be largely of Protestant pupils, likely to have a greater church involvement than would be the case in England, and the maintained school would be Catholic.) The mean mental ability scores of all groups showed no significant difference, but mean scores for religious language comprehension showed considerable variation. At each age level, the mean scores of the Catholic maintained school boys were significantly greater than those of the local authority controlled school and there was a significant improvement with age apart from the thirteen-year-olds in the maintained school (caused by a precocious high score in the previous year). A fair number of boys attained an understanding far beyond rote learning in a difficult test, showing facility with specific terms and expressions used by religion. Having also used the test program to study the pupils' attitude to religion (reported in chapter 8) Turner compared mental ability and religious attitudes, finding a significant negative association only in fourteen-year-old pupils in the controlled school; otherwise there was only a very slight association between the two, negative in the first two years of the maintained school and the third and fourth years of the controlled school, and positive in all others.

Johnson's (1973, 1974) Confirmation Progress Test about Christian living, doctrine, understanding religious words and biblical passages was used with other tests in five American Lutheran junior high schools. There was a slight relationship between religious knowledge, intelligence, and academic achievement, and better understanding was associated with an intrinsic religious orientation; the more children knew about religion the more they tended to be intrinsically oriented. Extrinsically oriented children showed a strong association between religious knowledge and approval-seeking, an association shown to be a desire to secure approval from God. The suggestion that the more that was known about religion, the more would responsibility be accepted for individual successes and failures in school, found no general support. The cognitive abilities related to religious knowledge were similar to those required for any cognitive activity, and theological issues could not be dealt with before formal operational thinking had developed. Johnson regarded the historical insight needed to deal with biblical chronology as being too advanced for junior-high-school students. His findings concerning intrinsic and extrinsic orientations in children and young adolescents are of particular interest; the intrinsic children scored significantly higher on his test than the others. They tended to bring their needs into harmony with their religion and were thus more motivated to learn about it, whereas extrinsic children were more interested in the social aspect of religion rather than in religious knowledge, selecting only the knowledge which was instrumental to their religion. Their God-approval motive indicated inadequate knowledge of the biblical notion of God as a God of love and of the distinction between the law and the gospel. Intrinsically oriented children tended to be internally controlled, especially in assuming responsibility for their failures, which suggested that they had a greater knowledge of the concepts of personal responsibility, sin, and forgiveness.

This finding, again relating religious learning to religious motivation, recalls the general observation of Musgrave (1973), who in his discussion of the curriculum, made a clear distinction between academic knowledge and the behavioral knowledge which is acquired only by access into the system from which it springs. The first religious ideas and feelings, like deeply rooted values such as the sanctity of human life, the toleration of religious beliefs, the pursuit of health, the condemnation of racism, or the care of the very poor, and some positive feeling for one's nationality, are learned in the family. They are learned in the same way as the knowledge that is used unthinkingly in daily life, such as the way that French children learn whom they should address as "tu" and whom as "vous." He observed that responsibility for such knowledge had been shifting from the family to the schools; educational organizations had to focus on the values which underlay such knowledge. The roles learned in the family created a version of social reality that governed the acceptance of any new version offered by a teacher. This meant that there might be a threshold beyond which learning did not take place because of what had already been learned outside the school. Only those with a certain level of value orientation might be motivated to learn a given type of knowledge. This has two important bearings on religious learning. Much religious knowledge is behavioral knowledge, acquired from within a religious institution, and such behavioral knowledge can only be acquired in this way. Logical understanding of religious texts is a normal cognitive process and requires academic knowledge only. Insight into religious concepts becomes increasingly behavioral knowledge, and has little or no relationship with the former. Behavioral knowledge is evidently the cognitive aspect of what is popularly called "lifestyle."

A number of other unrelated studies need mention. There was acceptance of the traditional biblical image of Jesus by almost all children between ten and sixteen at a youth camp, and although boys of fifteen and sixteen tended to express some doubt about it, girls showed more orthodoxy and devotion (Savin-Williams, 1977). Persistent cultural influence was evident in the religious beliefs and practices of Maroon children aged six to twelve in Jamaica, which reflected traditional ideas gathered from the study of church school materials and participation in Christmas and Easter celebrations. Some confusion between God and Jesus was observed. While most adults in the community denied holding an African belief in Obeah, the children had some knowledge of it. Some retention of African culture in the community was noted—the use of drums with concomitant dancing, hand-clapping and singing, and telling Anansi stories to children (Galloway, 1981).

Evans' (1968) investigation of the ideas of students about God was described in chapter 3. He also studied their concepts of sin, repentance, the Bible, and the church. All these concepts proved to be just as complex as that of God. Thus, seventeen categories were needed to accommodate beliefs about the church, and fourteen for beliefs about the Bible. The Bible was seen by many as full of contradictions and fairy tales, even though most were largely ignorant of it; threequarters thought it was unique, but this proportion dropped nearly to a half during the course. After three years sin was no longer regarded as personal by the majority but in more theoretical terms, and repentance was seen psychologically as therapeutic, without reference to belief, rather than having a spiritual value. The church was criticized because of the conduct of its members, who were seen as intolerant, ignorant, introverted, and failing to expound their beliefs, and for its clergy and their sermons, but the criticisms were reduced to some extent by the end of the course.

Very little attention has been given to the effects of physical disability on the development of religious belief, although the disabilities which retard all learning would appear to retard religious learning. The religious knowledge of adolescents in secondary schools and units for the hearing-impaired was retarded although it was better than that of normal nine-year-olds. Greater hearing impairment tended to reduce scores, and the profoundly deaf had the lowest scores. It appeared that to make something of a school assembly some degree of residual hearing was needed. Provision of religious education varied considerably in the schools; it was taught in only a minority of residential schools and further education establishments and was usually an option for a partially hearing unit in a comprehensive school. Asked what was the most important thing in life, no one gave a religious response, and only a quarter gave any type of positive response. No one gave religious education as a subject preference. About half of the sample expressed belief in God, and two-thirds never attended church (Sabell, 1983). This depression of religious knowledge has a parallel in the finding that congenitally blind children were seriously retarded in attaining Piagetian levels of concrete operational thought, although they were not retarded in tests of moral judgment (Stephens and Simpkins, 1974).

Prayer

To close the chapter, some studies about prayer need mention. Tamminen, Vianello, Jaspard, and Ratcliff (1988) described Scandinavian studies of prayer where children often have evening prayers with their mother. External behavior, such as folding the hands, was associated with prayer, but its basic purpose was known. Half the children from four to six knew that prayer was talking about anything to God; with age the proportion increased, as did the practice of praying for others. Prayers could be about anything, happy or sad. Prayer could be spontaneous, with strong feelings, in such times as illness; most of the time it was fun and nice. Prayers were usually addressed either to God or to Jesus, according to what they had been taught, but in illness more often it was to Jesus, who healed the sick. At this age it was almost impossible to distinguish between magical and religious elements in prayers, which were said ritually in the same manner, often asking God to provide some service. Magical explanations for saying prayers increased after this age but were not found at all in later years. God heard their prayers but did not necessarily answer them, and age brought a decline in their trust that they would be answered. Boys tended to pray with less regularity than girls, who were more likely to claim that their prayers had been answered.

Prayer and its vocabulary continues to be a problem for long after early childhood, as several descriptive studies have shown (Robinson, 1964; Madge, 1964). Mumford (1982) recalled Goldman's tape-recording of a child playing at school assembly, revealing many verbalisms but also a real sense of reverence. Childs (1983) noted that the psychological origins of prayer were associated with the social and cognitive development of young children, and the phenomenon of private speech in early childhood was related to adult prayer. Individuals' experience of prayer varied; it also was multidimensional. It could be meditative, ritualistic—relying on reciting prayers or using set prayers, petitionary, or coloquial—holding a conversation with the deity (Poloma and Pendelton, 1989). Such prayer experiences are influenced by an individual's religious orientation; intrinsics tend to score higher on Hood's Mysticism scale and extrinsics are less likely to reach a state of quiet contemplation, so that their prayer is more likely to be petitionary (Hood, Morris, and Watson, 1989).

In chapter 1 the developmental study of children's prayers by Long, Elkind, and Spilka (1967) was considered, and the changes which age brought in the understanding and content of their prayers. There were three stages of the content of prayer: undifferentiated, five to seven; concrete, seven to nine; and abstract differentiated, ten to twelve. Similar findings emerged from the study of Goldman (1964)—before nine, children thought prayer was answered automatically, unanswered prayer was due to naughtiness or praying too quietly, and they described it in terms of magic. After nine, they regarded unanswered prayer as due to an inappropriate request, and from thirteen, rational and spiritual explanations were common. There were also a few who reached an advanced stage.

Brown (1966a) investigated adolescents' beliefs about prayer in America, Australia, and New Zealand. He used a test about prayers for success in a football match, safety in a battle, avoidance of detection for a theft, repayment of a debt, fine weather for a church fete, survival in a shark-infested sea, and for a sick grandmother. Two key questions proved to be, "Is it right to pray in this situation?" and "Are prayers likely to have any effect?" There was no cultural difference between the nationalities. Belief in the causal efficacy of petitionary prayer declined with age, but the decentering process was not entirely completed. The level of belief varied according to the moral circumstances, so that those circumstances involving moral disapproval, intervention with natural processes, and trivial activities were thought to be relatively unsuited for prayer, but situations of personal danger were thought to be the most suited. The appropriateness of prayer did not relate to age but was influenced by adult attitudes conveyed in religious teaching. The results implied that this type of belief in the efficacy of prayer was a mode of egocentric thought.

The study was carried further (Brown, 1968) when boys aged twelve to seventeen, described as Catholic, Church of England, and Protestant, were given a questionnaire with seven possible prayers to be used before a football match, a battle, and an examination. They included petitions for success, qualified success, good performance, a simple offering, and a petition for blessing. Girls were not tested because it had been established that no sex difference was involved. All groups agreed that the battle was the most appropriate situation for prayer to be offered, with the football match next. Catholic boys showed the greatest belief in the efficacy and appropriateness of prayers, while the Anglican boys showed the highest belief in the nonspecific effects of prayer, with the Protestant group displaying a predominantly magical view. Increasing age brought a consistent decrease in those stating an unqualified belief in the material efficacy of prayer. The results showed that belief in the things prayer may achieve did not depend on the way in which the prayers should be expressed; direct petitions for success were infrequently chosen whereas prayers for a blessing or to receive "what is best" were the most frequently chosen. The relationships between belief, age, and religious training suggested that there was a complex integration of process. Belief in the efficiency of prayer was not fully freed from childish explanations even at eighteen. Because the development of belief needed to be directed toward the internalization of religious processes, it seemed that children should be taught how to pray rather than having prayer available as a means to gain benefit.

Rosenberg (1977, 1989a, 1989b) contrasted Elkind, Goldman, and their successors with Fowler and Oser. The former described the development of understanding biblical texts and religious concepts in Piagetian terms but failed to describe the essence of religious development. The latter adopted Kohlberg's model to describe unique religious stages which were not merely the reflection of general thinking applied to a religious content, although to call them universal stages seemed premature. She proceeded to explore the distinction in a study of children's prayers. These had shown weak developmental trends in earlier studies. Yet despite the marked decline in belief in the efficacy of prayer, most adolescents reported that they continued to pray, and Brown (1968) subsequently distinguished between direct causal efficacy, a physical change, and nonspecific efficacy, a spiritual influence on the person praying. To this issue Rosenberg addressed herself.

Jewish children from five to fifteen were interviewed in Israel; they came from religious state schools, that is, they were strongly orthodox, or from nonreligious state schools. The interview centered on an appropriate picture of a boy or girl praying at the Wailing Wall, and questions included, "Why do we pray?" "What do we pray for?" "Are prayers answered?" "What are the conditions necessary for a prayer to be answered?" From much data five content areas were identified relating to conditions for prayer to be answered: How? the behavior and stance of the person while praying; Who? the characteristics and deeds of the person praying; What? the moral and functional aspects of the prayer; The Receiver, the conception of God's will and judgment; Subjective-reflexive, prayer as a subjective matter referring back to the person praying. Each content area showed clear subdivisions, and these showed ages parallel to Goldman's findings as well as marked differences between the "religious" and "nonreligious" groups, notably that all the content areas tended to persist with the "religious" children.

A complex analysis of the scores assigned to the children's responses enabled Rosenberg to define four distinct age-related areas regarding the conditions required for prayer to be answered. The first group aged five to seven had a simple concept of prayer; how prayer was offered, such as wearing a skull-cap when praying, was important, and petitions were simple and the effect of content only distinguished between good and bad petitions. The greater the number praying, the quicker would be the answer. The "religious" children of the second group aged eight understood prayer as a religious act of thanksgiving and taking the place of Temple sacrifice; the "nonreligious" children aged eight to ten said people prayed because they believed in God and wanted to honor him. The first traces of doubt were found when prayer was not answered. Prayer was usually about a difficulty or problem; it showed a general stress on law and order as found by Piaget. Content was important if it was to be answered—it should not be silly. The final judgment was in the hand of God. These children believed in God, not as adults believe that he exists, but that by respecting God, God would respect them. Some children in the "nonreligious" group were polytheistic: "Each religion has its own God. . . . If (a man) is a Christian he should go to Holy Mary. . . ." The third group of "religious" children aged nine to twelve was the most heterogeneous, sensing, but unable to express, the abstract element of prayer. Petitions tended to be for the community or for all mankind. Almost all the content areas were thought to affect the efficacy of prayer. The children were juggling with the complications of the different categories in which God finally decided, with a preference for prayers from good people, for big things, and because he is compassionate. The fourth group of all adolescents aged thirteen to fifteen valued prayer as important in itself and affecting those who prayed for a variety of reasons, according to individual beliefs. Some saw it as a psychological need; nonconventional believers talked of a God who was a personal friend. Petitions were often very personal and mundane—for success in exams or romance. It was most important to the "religious" adolescents who saw it in terms of communication with God. They believed in the efficacy of prayer and saw some importance in other content areas; formal prayer was important, as was the praying community. The prayers of a great pious man were most likely to be answered, but ultimately the answer was part of the plan God had for the whole world which was beyond their comprehension.

Thus, there was a clear development of the prayer concept with age and a marked difference between the two groups, the "nonreligious" apparently having more in common with the other studies of prayer with non-Jewish children and adolescents and being closer to Western culture. They developed their concepts through substitution—former concepts disappeared to be replaced by others, whereas with the "religious" children concepts were developed by integration and were more specific to their particular culture. The earlier studies of cognitive development of prayer were not merely empirical but were meant to be epistemological. They showed, together with this study, that the strongest empirical support for the claim for stages was in the preformal level of lower stages. Here the similarity between cross-cultural groups was greatest. But when formal judgment is achieved and adolescents can understand and express abstract religious ideas, the psychological interpretation was more complicated and affected by theological considerations.

To conclude, while preschool children may exhibit feelings of reverence and awe, their religious ideas are as yet superficial and often the product of their fantasies. They learn to recognize some words as religious, and use them in a proper context, but with little or no understanding of their meaning. They are gaining a religious vocabulary which they learn from their homes and their churches. Despite its inadequacy, it becomes the basis of what will be better understood when they grow older, providing they receive satisfactory religious education. At first, this will be concerned about establishing an attitude of faith rather than with the rote learning of biblical or doctrinal material. The crudely anthropomorphic ideas of the youngest children start to be displaced about the age of six. Growth of understanding is facilitated by appropriate play and role-play, through which they can relate religious ideas to their growing experience of life. At this age prayer becomes more meaningful, but a mature understanding of it is not reached before adolescence, then doubt begins to arise about its efficacy. Throughout childhood there is a growing appreciation of the significance of the religious symbols regularly met in worship. Between six and ten children can acquire a useful vocabulary of words that are religious or relevant to religion, but many of them still lack the historical time-scale necessary to see Old Testament stories in a proper perspective. About the age of eleven insight into the sacramental nature of the eucharist develops, and magical explanations of the sacraments begin to fade. But confusion remains about many religious ideas and doctrines. For many adolescents this brings doubt about religion rather than clarity, a doubt which for some grows throughout their student years while others display a growing strength of belief.

One suggestion of Rosenberg seems of great importance. Religiously committed children develop from stage to stage by assimilating and integrating new insights as Piaget described, and the level of their conceptualization is raised. Those without such religiousness abandon one set of ideas and substitute another, so that disappearing concepts are replaced by other new concepts. One of the significant features of this review is that frequently, in broadly based samples, those with higher religiousness display very different insights from those with lower religiousness.

Chapter 6

Understanding Parables, Allegories, and Myths

There has been a growing interest among psychologists in metaphor.
Nothing about it is as simple as it first appears; if this is in doubt, a
good introduction to the subject is provided in the collection of essays
gathered together by Ortony (1979). At the same time biblical schol-
arship and religious education have found a parallel interest in nar-
rative and story, and the combination of the two draws attention to
children's understanding of the metaphoric material found in the
Bible, notably in the parables. Some research has been directed to
this, but not nearly enough, and so far more attention has been given
to the theological and linguistic than to the psychological aspects.
The research into metaphor comprehension, reviewed in Appendix
H, shows that the type of metaphor makes a considerable difference
to its understanding; its relationship to its context is of prime impor-
tance and children's familiarity with the context is almost essential
to their understanding. The results of the research reviewed need to
be appraised against this theoretical background. The later part of
the chapter looks at other related issues, in particular, understanding
symbolism, and concludes by considering some of the discussion
about symbolic thinking.

Soskis (1987), in her extensive study comparing the scientific and theological
use of metaphors, has shown that metaphor is the principal means by which Christians speak about God. Davies (1978) in a discussion about the nature of religious
language and its verifacation, argued that language when used in a religious context is like language used metaphorically. Although it was not immediately appar-

116

ent, on examination the term "God" also was used in a figurative sense. The recognition of the philosophical importance of metaphor in religious language is also matched in a psychological understanding.

The significance of metaphoric understanding in religious thinking has only lately begun to be recognized, as by McGrady (1987) who identified six necessary cognitive activities in understanding a metaphor as recognition, comprehension, production, extension, interaction, and evaluation. But how much children could understand the parables or the sayings of Jesus is a topic with a long history, going back to Franklin (1928), who made the first study, though earlier work had some concern for it. His test was concerned with sayings of Jesus and with a number of simplified and abbreviated parables. From the results he ranked both sayings and parables in an order of difficulty (apparently unaware that this required all questions to be of comparable difficulty); it was the Good Samaritan, the Rich Fool, the Talents, the Prodigal Son, the Two Foundations, the Pharisee and the Publican, the Widow's Mite, and the most difficult, the Sower. The developmental patterns for each of the parables and for the sayings were remarkably similar. The sayings of Jesus proved to be more difficult to understand; girls usually scored higher than boys, but the boys caught up at mental age sixteen. The finding which excited his greatest interest was the uneven rate at which comprehension improved; this was slower between eight to eleven and thirteen to sixteen, and he commented, "The strange consistency with which the eleven to thirteen increment in comprehension and other aspects of a growth curve repeat themselves in all the different combinations of uses would seem to indicate that the eccentricities of the curve are a function of internal ripening of native ability." At this time Piaget's work was only in its earliest stages and was almost unknown in the United States. Comprehension appeared to be relatively independent of environmental factors that were supposed to be important—their attendance at church or Sunday school or that of their parent. This appears to be the first study that shows that comprehension of some religious material is dependent on mental ability but independent of religious involvement.

It is sometimes mistakenly assumed that although children have difficulty in understanding such material, adults do not. How far this is from the truth was shown by Schroeder and Obenhaus (1964), who included biblical comprehension in their study of American religion. The Good Samaritan parable was scarcely understood by a fifth of the population with the lowest mental ability, and more than a third of those of average intelligence had not much more insight. There was only minimal understanding of the Bible in almost all of the churches, and neither preachers nor Sunday school teachers effectively communicated cognitive material, so the understanding of Christian tradition, the nature of God, or the meaning of Easter was much less than was generally supposed.

More recent studies mostly relate to the stage theory proposed by Goldman. Mention has already been made of Ainsworth's (1961) study of parable. Gregory (1966) undertook a simple test of the understanding of four parables by two groups of boys with average ages of thirteen and seventeen. Because they generally thought "prodigal" meant "pleasure-seeking" there was a general misunderstanding about the Prodigal Son. When the older boys showed greater insight, it was usually due to their greater maturity of experience rather than to better religious comprehension. This maturity sometimes inhibited understanding, because they were more down-to-earth than the younger boys; thus they showed less understanding of the significance of the Workmen in the Vineyard. Many boys did not fully appreciate the meaning of the Good Samaritan story because of their limited knowledge of its background. There was considerable evidence of a lack of comprehension of the nature of the parables, and they were more confusing to the younger boys tested. When questioned about the Bible, few boys agreed that every word of it was true, but the majority accepted that it contained a true message even though it was very hard to grasp. About half of them thought that archaeology had proved much of the Bible right rather than science had proved most of it wrong, but the older boys' responses suggested a shift of opinion toward the latter point of view.

An important series of Swedish studies, of which mention was made in chapter 3, has been described by Fagerlind (1974). Included in them were empirical studies of children's religious thinking (Westling, Pettersson, and Fagerlind, 1973). They found that children of ten to twelve thought in such a way as to make it impossible for them to interpret and explain the meaning of a parable directly. Yet when it was taught with a concrete illustration they could extract something meaningful from it. This was especially so if the teaching related to their own experiences, when they could understand the ethical content of some parables. They could not generalize about unfamiliar situations, but given something familiar to their experience, they could discover some general meaning which was applicable to themselves. (This appears to be a good illustration of the relationship of a metaphor to its context, discussed in Appendix H.) At a much later age, a group of college students best remembered religious messages that were familiar and acceptable to them, and they tended to distort the content to make it fit their own beliefs. Their memory was also affected by their interest and their verbal ability (Pargament and De Rosa, 1985).

The Swedish children were able to understand and use symbolic expressions about problems they had already met, even though they were not yet able to analyze them in logical terms. When a group of children aged ten were asked to express their ideas about God by drawings and writing, they produced material rich in symbolism. Thus, their understanding of the parable of the Lost Sheep was related to their own experiences of being isolated or ostracized just as the Lost Son related to their own experiences of justice. Teaching about parables at this age was viable providing the problems that emerged were familiar to the children and important to them. This did not imply that a full understanding was possible. The style of teaching encouraged by the project as a result of these inquiries was subsequently found to produce much more positive attitudes to the subject than was formerly the case. Before this, Wilkinson (1965b) had described a similar, successful approach used with young children.

To facilitate the religious education of maladjusted children, Debot-Sevrin (1968) used the parable of the Good Shepherd with normal and maladjusted children aged six and seven. Despite every effort to help them understand the symbolism of the shepherd and the sheep, neither group could recapitulate what they had been told if the teaching was purely oral, although the use of pictures and puppets as teaching aids helped a little. At this age metaphorical thinking in an unfamiliar context could not be induced, despite repeated and devoted attempts, but it is of value to have the failure of such a brave attempt on record. Later, Godin (1985) described the responses of a group of children aged eight to ten to the parable of the Good Shepherd. One child was reminded of his mother being worried that his brother had not returned home, and phoning round to make sure he was not lost, identifying himself, not with the lost sheep, but with the group deprived of their mother's attention. Such attachment, for the sake of the gratification it brought, was far removed from a Christian experience. Another child was reminded of going crazy when not being able to find a building block in its box and unable to play until he had found it; this child had adopted the point of view of the shepherd.

Working with a group of teachers, Hyde (1969) investigated the religious insight of less able secondary school children aged eleven to fourteen. They devised a simple test about short sayings of Jesus, such as that about the broad road and the narrow gate. Each saying was linked to a related event within the children's experience, and with five short statements about it which had to be endorsed as true or false. Correct responses required simple understanding of the implicit metaphors. There were also questions about the meaning of phrases in the Lord's Prayer. Their responses were compared with those of primary school children of all abilities aged seven to ten. The primary school children showed a consistent increase of scores with age. The less able secondary-school children showed a much smaller increase in scores. Only the pupils of fourteen achieved scores equal to those of the ten-year-old primary-school children, and their level of ability was somewhat higher than the other secondary pupils tested. One lively primary-school class achieved the highest scores of all. The results indicated the great difficulty that less able adolescents have in understanding even simple parables and metaphoric material. The results confirmed the similar findings of Hebron (1959) about less able secondary pupils. She found that they could deal with background and narrative material in the gospels, but a proper study of the historical Jesus could not succeed before they were thirteen. She also recorded the profound effect the passion story had on one boy with a history of being rejected. In an institutionalized retarded teenage group, Peterson (1960) found the educable could remember Bible stories and repeat them and remember the moral of a story after it had been explained. The severely retarded gave immediate responses to joy, stories, and class activities but retained little, and the retention of religious concepts for many of them was not possible.

Greenacre (1971) devised a simple test of understanding allegory based on a simplified version of the By-path Meadow episode in Bunyan's *Pilgrim's Progress*. Able children were interviewed, and their responses were scored on a thirteen point scale. There were three types of response, the literal; a partial transfer when children had some understanding of the story, but not of its symbolism; and a total transfer, which involved an understanding of the symbols found in the story. A girl of nine who was familiar with a hymn about "The King's Highway" achieved a high score for her age; this illustrated Beard's (1969) suggestion that special situations facilitated thinking at the level of formal operations in some limited field, or in easier and more familiar situations. Girls scored higher than boys, but were overtaken by fifteen or sixteen. In the older groups church influence had a marked effect on understanding. Some able children could understand the use of religious allegory before thirteen, and it was thus a means for such picture-language to assist religious understanding.

Beechick (1974) was a teacher who later became the editor of a theologically conservative religious education series. She came to her study of children's understanding of the parables with knowledge of Goldman's work and its antecedents and criticisms. She chose five groups of children from seven to eleven from a Baptist school with a known record of traditional teaching. They were given a Piagetian-style interview on three parables, the Two Houses, the Rich Farmer, and Jeremiah's story of the Potter. The story was revised after the questions had been asked, and then they were repeated. Then every child was asked, "What does Jesus/God want us to learn from this story?" Eight items were selected for study, concerned with the analogies of house and life, storm and hard times, the potter and God, clay and the nation, clay and you, the double analogy—built on rock (obey God's word) and built on sand (not obey God's word), why did God call the man a fool? and how would one not be a fool? The response scores showed a highly significant linear relationship with the children's ages. Beechick suggested that analogies of action were understood first, followed by analogies of actors, and finally by analogies of objects acted on. If children were egocentrically involved, and could see themselves as actors in one part of the analogy, it was easier for them to understand it. The three levels at which responses were given were equivalent to Piaget's stages, the first, the intuitive stage, attained about seven; the second level, the concrete operational stage, from approximately eight to ten; and the third level, the beginning of the formal operational stage. The overall response pattern shows a fairly sharp movement up to the first level and a somewhat less sharp movement into the third level between ages seven to eleven. However, it is evident that the first two levels represent a much more gradual developmental period.

Murphy (1977a, 1979) undertook a range of studies. He used six parables—the Rich Fool, the Good Samaritan, and the Pharisee and the Tax Collector in "modernized versions," and the Two Houses, the Sower, and the Lost Sheep and tested children aged six to eleven in East Scotland on any four of them. Some children were given verbally a multiple-choice test and the remainder interviewed in a less structured way. Replies were analyzed for three levels of understanding, the first reported facts only, the second showing a simple understanding, and the third an allegorical understanding of the material. There were differences in performance between different parables, so that the Good Samaritan was understood much better than the Rich Fool, although the latter was more comprehensible in a modern version. Multiple choice answers led to better responses about the Two Houses but had little effect on understanding the Pharisee and the Tax Collector. He concluded that while his study showed a developmental trend toward an allegorical understanding of parables, the development was not simple and was influenced by a variety of factors: the parable itself, the form in which it was told, and the method by which understanding was tested. He contended that it gave little support for a simple stage-development of the development of understanding of biblical parables, attempting to discredit a Piagetian stage interpretation without using Piagetian criteria to evaluate the responses. This is another study which relates closely to the problems of developing a metaphoric understanding which are discussed in Appendix H, where it is shown that not all such development is of a Piagetian type.

Schimpf (1972) identified eight types of biblical stories and regarded them as either symbolic, such as myths and parables, or as explaining or clarifying tradition, such as anecdotes and legends. They facilitated the discovery of a sense of individual and corporate identity, and could be used to that end in home, school, and church. Because they dealt with basic human needs they still effectively communicated religious meanings. The suggestion subsequently published by Slee (1983) that the different styles of figurative speech found in the parables could have an effect on children's understanding of them was taken up by Streeter (1981), who chose four parables, the literal illustration of the Friendly Stranger (the Good Samaritan), the similitude of the Lost Sheep, the parable proper of the Two Builders, and the allegory of the Sower. He used them in the simple translation by Dale (1966) to investigate how children aged six to twelve would understand them. He individually interviewed them about the tape-recorded stories and asked, "Did you understand that story? Tell me what it was about. Do you think anything like that could happen today? Do you think the story has any meaning for us? Tell me how and in what way." Responses were analyzed using the categories suggested by Peel (1971)—restricted, circumstantial, comprehensive circumstantial, and imaginative. There was a significant improvement in understanding with age; the Friendly Stranger was better understood than the other three stories, but contrary to expectations there was very little difference in the responses to the other stories. In the Friendly Stranger all children aged twelve and most children aged ten gave level four imaginative responses, whereas in the other three stories only one or two responses were secured at this level with almost half the children not reaching the third, comprehensive circumstantial, level. Further testing with older age-groups is needed to show if the complexity of the linguistic form of the material is reflected in a sequence of comprehension. Meanwhile, the literal illustration was shown to be more readily comprehended than the similitude, the parable proper, or the allegory tested. Yet general studies of children's understanding of metaphor show that other factors also operate, and one of them, the contextual, varies between the parables used.

Ratcliff (1987) cited Wilcox' continuing research and her findings about the parable of the Lost Sheep. Before five, children displayed an imaginative style, concentrating their thinking on actions and objects, and using body movements and egocentric speech in their thinking. At this age fact and fantasy were not clearly distinguished. Between five and eight the children showed a literal style, reasoning with concrete logic to classify, organize, and learn relationships, and to form simple concrete analogies. About ten, the third conventional style appeared, characteristic of adolescents and adults. These children looked for a deeper meaning to biblical accounts but tended still to accept conventional concepts uncritically; they often overlooked inconsistent thinking and seldom examined the validity of their conclusions. The reflective style was found toward the end of the high-school years; now consistency was sought between biblical content and its interpretation, and some accepted interpretations could be questioned. The students sought to develop criteria that would validate one of the several possible interpretations of a biblical passage; the stage was marked by intellectual struggle, and it was important to understand the meaning of abstract terms.

Slee (1983) criticized earlier studies because attention had not been given to the linguistic structure of those tested. Reviewing recent relevant scholarship, she cited Linnemann's (1966) suggestion of four linguistic types, as used by Streeter. Others had insisted that parables have a multiple meaning, part of which had to be supplied by the hearer. In teaching and in research, they should not be treated as though they were uniform in type or essentially allegories; beyond teaching they also challenged the existence of the hearer, operating independently of their original context and making affective as well as cognitive demands. Such understanding requires cognitive abilities well beyond those of younger children, and Slee gave no indication of how this might be achieved, although when she asked how children identify with characters in the parables the conclusions of Beechick are recalled; parables were better understood when children could identify themselves with one of the characters. Rowins (1987) considered preaching in parables was the most effective means of communicating with children from five to twelve, but when he reinforced his teaching of ten-year-old children with parables he found they had not learned more than those who had not received it. We still need to know how children might use the historical background of parables to understand them and, even more, how they assimilate and react to them. It must not be forgotten that Linnemann insisted that Jesus' parables were not for instruction, argument, or exhortation, but to win the agreement of his opponents in a genuine decision.

In the previous chapter mention was made of Berryman's (1979) approach to teaching. He suggested that children ought not to be taught the "meaning" of a parable. Conventional teaching treated knowledge as "I-it" when it could only be understood in terms of "I-Thou." Parables were metaphors extended to a narrative form, and children needed personal participation in the metaphors used. He illustrated this by reference to a child of three who walked up to a picture of the Good Shepherd, pointed to the lamb being carried, and said "Me." Children should play with materials related to a story so as to gain some experience of their underlying metaphors. For the Good Shepherd, figures such as grass, water, dangerous places, a lost sheep, and a wolf would be used, and afterwards the children would paint a picture of it, thus becoming familiar with the images of religious tradition. His account suggested the activity of a talented teacher—one can imagine a group of children fascinated by him; however, he gives no real indication of what actual learning takes place when this method is used, although he is certain that it is better than "writing answers in a word-book." In a later article (Berryman, 1980) he makes clear his indebtedness to the ideas of Montessori, explaining that her religious education curriculum employed a creative use of Christian symbols and concepts. Subsequently (Berryman, 1985), he stated that children's relationships with God depended on the way in which they learned religious language—either from fear, to please parents, or as an end in itself. The only satisfactory method was to learn it in a way that involved their spirituality, so that familiarity with Christian speech resulted in their becoming Christian. Since this involved the relationship between religious experience and religious language, he summarized seven major approaches, giving prominence to the Montessori tradition in which children worked with materials that made incarnate the images of religious language. The use of play in religious education was mentioned in chapter 5.

Symbolic understanding and biblical material

The question of understanding the parables raises the wider issue of biblical understanding. There are differences in comprehending various translations; Yeatts and Linden (1984) studied comprehension of six versions of the Bible in a Christian liberal arts college. Theologically liberal students could comprehend and recall material just as well as the theologically conservative. All modern versions were more comprehensible than the King James version, and the Living Bible and Today's English Version were judged more comprehensible than the Revised Standard Version or the New English Bible and were also preferred for poetic literature, for which the New International Version was recalled better than either the Revised Standard Version or the King James version. No differences were found for narrative literature. On proclamation literature, the Living Bible was more comprehensible than the King James version or the New English Bible. Yeatts (1988) returned to this study using a narrative passage, a poetic, and an expository one. Despite the popular belief that the resonant language of the King James Version made its recall simpler, this was not the case in this sample. The narrative passage was less well recalled from the New English Bible than from the other versions used. The expository passage was the most difficult of all the passages used and was more theological, although meaningfulness was not related to recall. It was better recalled from the New English Bible and Today's English Version.

In her study of the parables, TeSelle (1975) broadened the consideration of metaphorical thinking from its application to the parables to the whole range of biblical interpretation and theology, asserting that biblical language was metaphorical language and had to be regarded both as logical and highly conceptual and also as affective and expressive. There were no technical words with special meanings but only words which had been made to mean more than they usually meant. Metaphoric thinking was more than poetic thinking or primitive thinking but the way in which human beings moved in all areas of human discovery, so that even theology was parabolic. The parable arrested the listener by its vividness, leaving the mind in sufficient doubt about its precise application to tease it into active thought. It was not primarily knowing about the kingdom that appeared to be crucial, but rather deciding when confronted by it.

It is not parables themselves which have to be comprehended, but what they might imply. It has been suggested that this principle is true for all religious symbols; Linner (1979) gave a number of literary illustrations showing the same symbols used both for belief and nonbelief. In particular he cited a Swedish poet who recalled, in religious terms, his experience of being caught in the Agadir earthquake; an abbreviated version of the poem appeared in a recent hymnbook. But neither before nor after had the poet given any indication of religious belief, and Linner contended that his religious vocabulary was only a linguistic usage of what was prevalent in the poet's environment and proceeded to discuss how it was possible to determine an author's true position; it became clear that what was at issue was the attitude toward the truth of a symbol or statement of belief and not just the use of it, even in an understanding manner.

At this point mention must be made of Andrews' (1981) study of the use of metaphors as models in religious discourse and its implications for religious education. She examined the emergence of life themes, seeing them arising partly from the influence of Goldman. She compared a life theme which arose from the experience of children with a religious theme which used life experience as a form of methodology rather than an arbiter of content. Such themes were metaphoric models, similar to those used in science, and at times necessary for understanding. Models were needed to interpret experience and evoke insight and to express a sense of the Ultimate. They allowed articulation in areas of theological discourse, rendering intelligible what otherwise defied analysis. From this stance, which provided an analysis of theological metaphors, she looked at a number of agreed syllabuses, showing how such an analysis could be used to simplify teaching and enhance learning. It was possible to provide an approach to parables based solely on their content, e.g., parables of the Kingdom included parables of farming and agriculture, and in turn these included parables of wheat-farming, of which there were three.

Myth and biblical language

The nature of New Testament language and the effect of understanding it was the subject of an investigation by Palmer (1978), who insisted that the Jesus story must be categorized as myth. It had long been central in religious education, and it would remain so even if it had a different part to play in a pluralistic society. Children needed to learn to differentiate between mythical and other forms of understanding, such learning was bound to depend on the presentation of biblical material. Despite differences between authorities, there was sufficient agreement as to the kind of story which could properly be regarded as myth, myth being related to the meaning which men seek amid the contradictions of human experience. Myth offered society a means of social integration and ritual giving entrance to a higher level of reality. The mythical behavior of the Jesus story had been apparent from the first, and it still related to beliefs and ethics, remaining the formative and developmental experience of Christian communities and individual believers. Its role was educative, and its presentation expected to cause changes in, or stabilization of belief, values, and behavior. It offered a way of salvation for those who chose to "live in its story" (the phrase Berryman used of children and parables). Telling the story to older children as history and telling it to younger children alongside stories of fantasy and imagination or as a factual narrative which in many ways contradicted their experience was bound to be misleading and could lead to a total rejection of Christianity.

Teaching methods such as these were hardly likely to draw an affective response within which the myth could operate especially when it took place in circumstances where the story was totally removed from its religious context. Because this seemed to have been the normal situation of the past, Palmer asked if this was one factor which contributed to England's becoming less Christian than it was before. Even in a pluralistic situation at school the Jesus story was seldom treated in the same way as stories of other great religious founders and leaders. Because its truth did not necessarily depend on its historical accuracy, children should be able to come to a more mature reflection on the different narratives and recognize the Jesus story as myth in the full sense of an often misused word. The study of at least one myth in depth could lead to the skills of evaluation, in which myth would be seen as a synthesis of experience and not as an object of analysis. This would require more than discussing significances but also visits to places of worship and the use of play, dance, drama, and music—as Elkind suggested. Aylwin (1981) commented on the current lack of use of the classical myths and legends in British schools and, urging their value in aiding emotional development, offered a considerable range of appropriate teaching activities. What is needed for English teaching would seem to be even more needed for religious education.

Another study is that of Doran (1978). His consideration of the place of myth in the Bible and religious education included an empirical examination of children's understanding of myth. Children aged seven to fifteen were interviewed about five stories—the Egyptian creation story of Ra, the all-powerful; the Sudanese creation story of Juok creating men to be white, reddish-brown, or black; Adam and Eve in the Garden of Eden; the birth of Hercules to Zeus and Alkema, and the birth of Attis to Cymbele, his marriage, destruction, and resurrection. The children heard the stories from a recording, with the text before them, and were then questioned. Their responses were categorized into five groups:

a) Inadequate responses due to insufficient understanding, mostly from younger children who tended to focus on a single, often irrelevant, detail of little or no significance; many believed that a story was true if its source was the Bible.

b) Uncertainty was the reaction of a smaller group consisting mostly of younger children. Katherine, (8.0) sure about Genesis, was uncertain about believing the other stories since they were not brought about by God. Adrian (9.6) confused Ra with Jesus, and Richard (9.6) believed the Ra story "except when he made things by speaking." Nigel (10.0) was not sure if he could relate the Genesis story to evolution; the birth of Hercules reminded him of the story of Mary and Joseph, but he didn't believe there were gods or giants. Julie (13.10) could not believe that the infant Hercules was strong enough to strangle a serpent but saw parallels with the infant Jesus and remarked doubtfully, "If one's true, the other must be as well—they're both about the same sort of thing."

c) Disbelief was the characteristic of the largest group and it increased with age. These children rejected nonbiblical stories out of hand, and some would not believe anything. Paul (7.6) believed in Jesus but not the other one; Paul (7.10) said, "God could not walk in Eden, he was a tree of fire, like it says in the Moses story" and Ian (7.10) remarked, "Adam wasn't the first man, it was cave men." After eleven a scientific attitude came to the fore, there was skepticism about creation stories; Ra was thought to be just a good story, but stories about Jesus were "a load of rubbish." After thirteen skepticism was accompanied by a more mature attitude, e.g., rejecting the Greek idea of Zeus but not declaring another person's belief was wrong (a number of pupils also showed a tolerant attitude), dismissing nonbiblical stories, and regarding Jesus as son of Mary and Joseph, or taking a science fiction approach to Ra.

d) Literalism characterized the next largest group in which stories were accepted as literally true. Few believed all of them; literalism reached a peak at nine, but some believed all Bible stories literally. Adrian (8.0) oscillated between seeing Ra as a rival to Christ and as Christ himself. He accepted the Genesis story, but confused Eden with Golgotha, and rejected the idea of resurrection; when told it was true of Jesus he would not believe it, even when informed that it was in the Bible. Peter (7.11) thought the Ra story to be true, because Ra was God, yet would not make the same deduction about Juok. Many were put off by this unfamiliar name, even when they regarded it as a different version of the Genesis story. James (7.8) knew that if it was in the Bible it must be true but had difficulty over a talking snake. The older boys in the primary schools showed rather less credulity, although a few of them were more extreme than any of the girls. Andrew (10.3) believed in Hercules—he had heard of him before, but he didn't believe in the Christian God. Carl (8.9) believed stories about Jesus but was not sure about God. After eleven many similar remarks were made, but a greater emphasis was found on science which made some more skeptical but had little effect on those who believed Bible stories. Michael (12.4) said there was nothing to prove the other gods existed, "but with God scrolls have been found." Nicolla (11.8) believed in the divine creation of man, but not from clay, and was attempting to reconcile the view of her biology mistress and her parents biblical viewpoint. John (13.10) believed Christian stories because "you hear them more often." After fifteen most in this group believed the Genesis story but denied the others, and at after seventeen some could still take one or more of the stories literally.

e) Rational responses were given by a smaller group, nearly all of them secondary-school children. David (6.8) said, "God created the white people, Juok the black and brown." Deborah (11.9) was the first to mention the possibility of symbolism, suggesting that all religions were different expressions of the same basic beliefs. Nigel (17.0) said that details didn't matter, the mind "needed something to hang on to"; Delyth (17.2) saw the stories, especially the last two, in terms of analogy.

f) Affective responses characterized the final group. Garry (11.9) regarded the Ra story as "impossible—its more like a Greek myth. . . . It shows how the Egyptians thought about their world" giving a jumble of scientific and mythical images. Reginald (15.5) saw creation and resurrection themes as both true and comforting, while Susan (15.1) commented, "It looks after everything; it puts all the power man hasn't got into categories; it's a warm kind of feeling and is poetry as well. . . . It doesn't make us want to believe it, there are so many things to question." At seventeen they can speak of "the absolute beyond human understanding" or "unavoidable anthropomorphisms." Rachael (17.6) was religious and scientifically orthodox but believed in "the underlying factor," and Angela (17.0) spoke of a supreme power but not God as a person; she is described as thoughtful, intelligent, and essentially religious person who over a decade had not been convinced by her teachers at school and church of the credibility of the Christian faith.

Apart from those expressing disbelief, there were many in all the groups who relied on the authority of the Bible, but no evidence was found of any who had been taught how biblical stories could be true. Biblical authority was for many children a pivotal point; for some, if the Bible story was true, the others could not be; for others, because the biblical story was true, the others also could be. This was an important finding for teachers, whose own beliefs and attitudes were important. The scientific challenge arose for many because they felt that science had made religion untenable, yet the children were still capable of wonder and awe and intellectually needed help to recognize that science also provided mythopoetic thinking, as, for example, the concept of the "running down universe" that must come to an end, whereas, with religious mythology, a belief about what will happen in the future is given in the form of factual knowledge. One group, with their parents, would not tolerate the mildest critical consideration of the Bible or investigate the beliefs of other religions; such literalism seemed to them to be an essential part of Christian belief.

Despite parallels between some of his findings and those of Goldman, Doran was critical of Goldman's approach to teaching the Bible. Bible stories could be used with young children in a way that they could be experienced together with similar stories from other religious mythologies. In this context even young children could begin the process of experiencing the essential unity of the religious experience of mankind. Other creation myths should be used as well as those of Genesis; many children were greatly relieved to discover that there were other creation stories and that they were not expected to believe literally something which their own innate intelligence told them was not true in their sense of "being true."

The creation story was discussed by Greer (1972b) with groups of children from six to seventeen, and their difficulties in understanding showed three developmental stages. First, the younger children interpreted it literally, although many were dissatisfied with such an interpretation. Second, between nine and thirteen their understanding was dualistic—there was a scientific and a theological way of looking at creation in accord with Goldman's concept of the two worlds of childhood. Scientific understanding began among older primary school children, who then regarded the two ideas as conflicting. Finally, a few reached a simple understanding of the symbolism in the creation story, but most, even among the older children, were struggling with the problems raised by a literal interpretation of symbols. Those who achieved some understanding of the symbolic nature of the story did not believe it held any relevance for them.

Van Bunnen (1964) looked for the recognition of a sense of awe in children's responses to the story of Moses at the Burning Bush, and he questioned children from five to twelve in Catholic French-speaking schools in Brussels about it. A few gave an ambivalent answer, corresponding to Otto's (1950) idea that attraction and fear were simultaneously evoked by the sacred. The recognition of fear grew considerably with age; it brought an increasing awareness of a distance between man and God which was shown by increased reverence. Younger children reacted to the thought of God's presence as to a kindly, fatherly figure; the older children began to feel that it was awe-inspiring, so that fear as well as joy would be natural. This was demonstrated by the numbers who said they would kneel down before him; only one kindergarten child said this, but the majority of the older children did. The text described Moses as hiding his face but not falling on his knees; the association between kneeling and the sense of the sacred was the spontaneous response to such questions as, "What would you do if God suddenly appeared before you?" Many children spoke about the fear of being burnt by the fire, or being afraid of it, a response which decreased with age. As they grew older, the children's capacity to see the symbolic value of things and acts increased, so that they saw fire in symbolic terms. The awe felt in God's presence increased with age, and a growing proportion indicated a sense of the ground being holy, God being present, or close approach being wrong. Fear of burning which characterized children at five or six was largely replaced by a sense of reverence for the sacred between ten and twelve. The story of the Burning Bush could be grasped in its symbolic value by most children of eleven and twelve, provided that it was told so that the religious symbolism of the story was stressed and explained when being recounted.

The symbolism of fire was also used by Winand (1972), using free association and impromptu stories, in an investigation of French Catholic adolescents' understanding and use of biblical and liturgical symbolism. Biblical knowledge exceeded liturgical knowledge; boys, stimulated by the ideas of courage and strength, were attracted to power theophanies, whereas girls stressed the quality and depth of those theophanies perceived more in terms of the personal and intimate. The girls were more familiar with the liturgy and more responsive to its words than the boys, who responded more to the physical aspects of the rite itself. Catholic school pupils retained the influence of their primary-school level catechesis more than those from state schools, and religious influences tended to diminish differences between sexes or schools. They were alive to symbols, and the liturgy had a powerful and positive response, although this was affected by the individual's secular and religious context.

Passman (1980) made a very different type of study in this same area. He contended that children between eight and eleven were able to understand religious symbolism beyond the level indicated by their speech, and they could participate in what a symbol pointed to. Religious education should increase awareness and sensitivity to life's religious dimensions beyond knowing about religion. Words could be used so that an association of cognitive and aesthetic elements was quickened with a corresponding increase in understanding. To illustrate this approach, he produced a scheme of work based on the small town of Leominster which made use of such components as movement and dance and puppetry.

Symbols and religious knowledge

The relative dearth of research studies about children's understanding and use of religious symbolism is in contrast to discussion about the topic, and the chapter closes by reference to some of this. Hayes (1969) recorded his American evangelical opposition to a religious education which had grown out of late nineteenth-century liberal theology, claiming that it must be the servant and not the master of revelation. He recognized that in biblical interpretation it was necessary to distinguish between what was symbolical and poetical, doctrinal and practical, and he called for a second look at preconceived notions about teaching symbolism to very young children, stating that all communication dealt in symbols, and the real problem was to help learners understand very complex truth. He wanted to know the sequence in which the Bible should be taught and to have guidelines for teaching which recognized the psychology of human growth and learning. Two decades later a clear recognition of these issues has not received universal assent, but his insistence on the importance of symbolic thinking remains crucial.

Fawcett (1970) in his study of the symbolic language of religion carefully distinguished between signs, symbols, allegories, parables, similes, metaphors, and analogy, noting the importance of metaphors in this type of usage. There was a danger that a metaphor hid the analogy on which it was based, so that its comparison might be taken literally, especially when the allegorical character of the metaphor was no longer apparent as it was to those who heard it originally. A parable was made from a typically human situation and highlighted the existential character of life, the need for decision and compassion, and authenticated itself out of experience, opening up levels of experience otherwise locked away. Because men saw themselves faithfully reflected in Jesus' parables and began to see themselves as they were, they could turn away angrily. As with a joke, one either saw the point of a parable or failed to see it.

The French anthropologist Dan Sperber (1975) drew on his field experience to criticize theories of symbolism. Symbols were not a code to be cracked, nor were they signs or to be paired with interpretation; interpretations were not meanings. Symbolic thought should be seen as cognitive, but evolving in a different way from language and representing a different point of view from a linguistic stance, as when an individual emigrated to a new society and might still take as an insult what would have been such in his original milieu. Accordingly, Sperber developed his concept of semiology, which was symbol-based knowledge and learning, by which symbolic statements co-existed within statements about the world which would seem to contradict them. Thus, the Dorze knew that because the leopard was a Christian animal it must fast on Wednesdays and Fridays, so on these days domestic animals needed less guarding; they were not worried by the contradiction that leopards were dangerous every day. Symbolic knowledge was thus different from other forms of knowledge; it was not about words or things but about memories of words or things, as was shown by the mechanism of symbolic thought. People did not have a logical classification of smells; unlike color, a smell was rather described by the way that it evoked memory and by its other associations. Similarly, symbols evoked a picture of the world which, if it were made explicit, could only itself be put in quotation marks.

Davies (1985) took up this evocation of memory as a major activity of symbolic thought, comparing the relationship between semantic and symbolic knowledge. Just as the memory of a situation may give meaning to a particular smell, so particular Bible stories or hymns could act in the same way, recalling a significant occasion. He stressed that it was not the semantic knowledge of religion that was of importance to the worshiper, but the symbolic action through ritual and in life; theological knowledge and piety could exist in quite separate compartments. Symbolic thinking was intricate; to an extent, all individuals achieved their own symbolic systems and intuitions, just as every religious tradition had its own particular set of symbols which were guarded as metaphors for those ultimate experiences of its members. The biblical documents which formed the basis of highly semantic studies were also highly symbolic, the product of religious groups concerned not with literary production but with their relationship to Jesus. This created problems, not only for children with some sort of religious commitment, but also for those without it who might have little experience of symbolic activity to enable them to criticize or benefit from school religion. A child who had learned to use the Bible as a focus of religious activity found it difficult to turn to it as an object of rational study. Interfaith studies added to such difficulties; exposure to an unfamiliar faith and its buildings, scriptures, language, and music needed a memory of more familiar parallels to make sense of it.

From a theological perspective Heimbrock (1986) argued that mythical thinking was a half-way house; it was not consistent with developed formal operational thinking since it was not a purely rational and objective kind of thought about reality. Piaget's influential ideas of cognitive development and Freud's dealing with emotional aspects assumed the same developmental perspective. Piaget should be compared to Freud's writing about symbols, although he tended to deal with their emotional aspects and neglect the cognitive. They both regarded development as arising from necessary features of human thinking, and many had followed them in this respect. This model was not appropriate for the study of religious symbols if they were thought to represent a less mature kind of thinking than propositional logic. A new examination was required of how human subjectivity was treated in psychological approaches to religion if, as Tillich asserted, religion expressed ultimate personal concern. Measuring religious experiences solely by the level of formal operational thinking would by its impact on our understanding of the religions of the Far East demonstrate cultural imperialism. Fundamental concepts, models, and methods needed to be reformulated in a way which represented a less rigid view of reality to reach a genuinely postconventional level of research relevant to our own culture and to others. Heimbrock's critique of Piaget may not command general assent, and he overlooks Piaget's stress on the place of interaction with the environment as essential to development. But his basic contention that as yet there is lacking an adequate psychological account of the development of symbolic and mythical thinking is a point to be taken. Just as intense religious experience is seen and interpreted as religious only as its subjects are influenced by their social groups, so it would seem that religious symbolism requires this social interaction for its understanding. It is affective as well as cognitive, but its rationale, even if not formally logical, still needs mature thought forms for its full comprehension and expression.

It is interesting to set beside the theological considerations a more general approach to symbolism in books which have an established appeal to children. Jan (1973), reviewing their characteristics, stressed the folk tale in which identical themes were expressed in various forms, as myths, legends, or tales. Fairy tales no longer appealed to present-day children, but magic did. The important children's stories were essentially symbolic in character; they were not adult books on a reduced scale, and the problems of childhood played no part. Children could be drawn by curiosity to read and appreciate works considered too advanced for their age, since the main consideration was that of feeling. There were enchanted moments in literature, not only in children's books, available to all children.

Yet response to religious symbolism is not spontaneous among many English children. Martin and Pluck's (1977) survey, referred to in chapter 12, recorded the inability of adolescents in their sample to respond to any type of symbol. Suburban English children of nine or ten explored the symbols suggested to them by Christmas, starting from a New Zealand poem with the lines, "And robins I have never seen pipe out a Christmas call." At first, they recalled holly, robins, and bright colors, or a stagecoach traveling through snow; these were the sure signs of Christmas. When they remembered its religious significance they showed poor understanding of such words as frankinsence, myrrh, and manger. The images they knew—even the partridge (in a pear tree) they had never seen—were those that had been imposed on them (Hawkins and Pratt, 1988). Yet when Kukuyama (1963) asked American children aged eight to thirteen to write what they wondered about there was a marked increase with age of those who wondered about religion. There were more girls than boys among them, but the boys, almost all of whom came from evangelical or reformed traditions, wondered more about heaven and the after-life. Hardly any wondered about music or the fine arts.

Magee (1985) noted the changing attitudes to the use of story in religious education; after a period in which it had been questioned there was now a new recognition of its significance in the process of religious education. He made a detailed examination of its use in two series for children in Catholic schools in Ireland. Priestley (1983) insisted on the importance of story in religious education, regarding it as an art form which created images rather than concepts and required imagination rather than cognition to extract its meaning. Goldman's approach owed everything to the language of the objective sciences and nothing to the language of religion or the arts, so that what was measured was not the children's religion but rather their ability to do theology, a very different thing. Teachers should be concerned not with demythologizing but with recovering mythical thinking. Story conveyed truth not as sharp concepts but as images with blurred edges, and such truth was grasped imaginatively, with cognition coming later. He argued (Priestley, 1981) that restricting the use of the Bible with younger children was based on this fallacy and that imagination rather than cognition was the main truth concern. Christianity was understood by an act of imagination and not by a process of critical analysis. He did not want a return to former methods of biblical teaching, or to a confessional approach, but rather a new style and method based on these insights. It was wrong to demythologize; myth should not be deprecated but understood, so that the appearance of God in the Burning Bush did not cease to be a poignant reality. The importance of story to children, and its relevance to theology, is dealt with in a series of articles in the same journal issue. Long before this, Goodenough and Goodenough (1962) had argued that a symbol must first be meaningful for children at its concrete level and that it also needed to be associated by them with a moving experience. Such affective approaches to symbolic learning arise naturally in the context of worship and religious nurture but are limited in classroom situations, especially among older pupils, where many lack a religious background and confessional teaching must be avoided, except in church schools. Ability to deal with metaphor has once more emerged as an important element in understanding biblical material.

Two issues are clear. The first, which has to do with all the preceding developmental studies, concerns relating teaching content to the age of children taught. Age boundaries are not precise, but the three styles of understanding variously described by Piaget, Elkind, Goldman, and many others are established beyond any doubt. The many studies which contribute to this have had idiosyncratic origins, most of them arising from uncoordinated research for higher degrees—what Ratcliff (1987) called the shotgun approach. One can but echo his appeal for better, continuing, coordinated research bearing on specific problems of children's understanding faced constantly by teachers in school and church. The second is to accept that symbolic thinking is almost a novel concept and that it is deserving of much more attention than it has received hitherto. It is surprising that in the field of poetry and literature it has not engendered more research—or can it be that those who teach these subjects do not face a similar problem?

Chapter 7

Related Studies and Teaching Styles

*Children's understanding in many subject areas of the school cur-
riculum have been investigated, notably in science and mathematics.
A safe generalization is that they all show similar developmental
trends in line with the Piagetian studies. It was observed earlier that
historical insight was required for adequate biblical understanding.
This review of the development of cognitive aspects of religion concludes with reference to studies of understanding material from historical and other related subject areas which have some relation to
biblical narratives. The chapter concludes with a summary of the few
studies of the effects of teaching styles and methods on religious
understanding.*

In view of the interest that Goldman's work aroused and the controversy it
engendered, it is surprising that there was relatively little follow-up. The application of Piaget's theory to religion had its parallels in many other subject areas,
and because there is some similarity in teaching content between religious studies,
history, and geography, it is useful to consider some educational research in these
fields, since the results have a bearing both on religious thinking and on general
cognitive development in adolescence. The studies about history answer the questions raised by Murphy (1978).

Once Piaget's work became more widely known and applied it became clear
that while his account of the types of thought found from early childhood to adolescence illuminated much classroom activity, its application to adolescents in
secondary schools was less useful. There were great differences about the advent
of fully operational thinking both between individuals and subject areas. In England, Peel (1971), a leading exponent of Piaget, extended his work on the devel-

134

opment of adolescent thinking into a more descriptive approach and initiated a series of related studies by himself and some of his advanced students. Those of Bagshaw (1966) and Richmond (1972) about religious thinking have already been noted, but others with a bearing on the subject need mention.

Lodwick (1957), in an elegant small study which attracted much attention, tested children aged seven to fourteen with pictorially illustrated narrative material about Stonehenge, King Alfred and the cakes, and Florence Nightingale, assessing responses at one of five levels. Analysis of responses to individual questions was not satisfactory, but a better result was secured when all the material was grouped together. When the highest score for each child was taken, mental age was shown to be a better criterion than chronological age, and the results conformed to Piagetian stage theory, with transitions at about mental ages 6.9, 9.8, and 11.9. Stones (1965) made a similar study of the development of comprehension of historical narratives among pupils in a secondary girls school, using passages about Robert Owen, Joan of Arc, Charles the Great, and Prince Henry the Navigator. Three questions requiring written replies were set on each passage, the first needing only a factual answer, the second something more than a purely concrete reply, and the third a simple hypothesis. Replies were graded into categories of thinking. Development of understanding was related both to age and ability. The level of thinking of the less able pupils was the same as that of the abler group a year younger, but they never achieved a significant proportion of abstract explanatory responses. In all the groups aged twelve and thirteen concrete descriptions tied to the circumstantial details of the material predominated, but among abler pupils abstract, explanatory type responses began to appear in the fourteen-year-old group, and nearly all could respond at this level after this age.

Two important historical studies were undertaken by Hallam (1966, 1975). He first (Hallam, 1967, 1969, 1972) studied the historical thinking of children aged eleven to sixteen about three passages dealing with Mary Tudor, the Norman Conquest, and the Civil Wars, basing his method to some extent on that of Goldman. He graded replies to questions on each story according to Piagetian criteria for operational thinking. The subjects' levels of thinking across the stories and questions were found generally to remain the same. Scalogram analysis indicated the chronological and mental ages which distinguished the three stages with a better result than that of Goldman (1962), approaching the requirement of Peel (1959). Because of the weaknesses of scalogram analysis his findings were supported by the alternative method of examining the average scores of the subjects' answers. It seemed that concrete thinking in history began in the twelfth year and formal thinking began soon after sixteen (mental age 16.5 to 18.2). Although a few younger pupils were capable of formal operational thinking at times, it also appeared that even preoperational thinking occurred among the oldest pupils. However, overall there was a steady decline in preoperational thinking and a steady increase in formal thinking with increasing age, but at sixteen most historical reasoning was at the concrete operational level, even though one pupil aged

14.8 showed great maturity of thought. The low incidence of formal thinking in history was in keeping with the other comparable investigations he cited, and the generally recognized problem that before the age of sixteen it was difficult to teach history other than at the level of factual description; beyond this it was concerned with the inner motives of adults living in another century with a culture very different from that of contemporary society, as his test passages had shown.

Moral issues were raised in the test from questions about the belief that God helped one side to defeat the other. Hallam (1968) also analyzed the responses about this. Only two in his sample queried the existence of God, and most saw in New Testament terms that God would not wish anyone to be ill-treated or killed. The replies appeared to be somewhat superficial, since most failed to develop a cogent argument based on the promise of a loving God. In some instances the argument was weakened by Old Testament ideas. For the most part the group was not able to appreciate the moral situation of another age.

In the second study comparisons of teaching history by different methods were made with children aged nine to ten (Hallam, 1978) and thirteen to fourteen (Hallam, 1979a). In both the primary and the secondary schools he taught a year's syllabus on the Tudors and the Stuarts; one class was taught by a formal method, and in a similar class much individual and group work was used to present the children with contrasting points of view about people and events. He regarded the former method as encouraging figurative knowledge and the latter operative knowledge. A third class was taught the same syllabus by the normal school teachers the following year. All children completed a test at the beginning of the work and a year later, after a long school holiday. The younger children he had taught improved their test scores more than the control class, but those taught experimentally outstripped both of the other classes, and there was clear evidence that their historical reasoning had improved. The result with the secondary school children was not so clear. The results supported the Piagetian theory that true progressive development takes place only when children are in an intermediate stage, in this case, those aged nine and ten moving toward concrete operations. When the testing had taken place the children had also been given two Piagetian tasks (Hallam, 1979b) involving the chemical combination of two colorless liquids and the equilibrium of a balance. There was a reasonable agreement between all three tests regarding the children's levels of thinking, but historical thinking always lagged behind, and the evidence was not sufficiently convincing to support Piaget's concept of a *structure d'ensemble* operating.

De Silva (1969) studied understanding of historical concepts in a large suburban comprehensive school. He used ten artificial words, first in paragraphs and then in sentences progressively showing the significance of the word more obviously. Responses were related to four styles of thinking—logically restricted, circumscribed conceptual isolation, logical possibilities, and deductive conceptualization. There was no significant difference in the responses of the groups aged twelve to fourteen, but these differed significantly from the fifteen- and sixteen-year-old groups, which themselves were also different; there were evident changes in styles of thinking at about fourteen and at fifteen. With abler pupils, logically restricted thinking declined with age, so that a high proportion of deductive conceptualizations was found, whereas in the others, much less advanced thinking was found. A repetition of part of the test with a group of postgraduate students, including some historians, yielded far from impressive results, suggesting that the test was very demanding.

A similar study about geography was undertaken by Rhys (1966) who tested children aged nine to sixteen in a junior and a secondary modern school, using problems arising from texts, pictures, and maps. Below eleven the children could not reason realistically about the material; then from age twelve or over they gave descriptive replies which attempted an analysis of the problems based on a single piece of evidence. Beyond thirteen a realistic stage was reached when they offered more than one piece of evidence and began to relate cause and effect, but not until after fourteen was full hypothetico-deductive reasoning attained. In general, development was better related to chronological age rather than to mental age.

Best (1967), in a study of explanatory thought in adolescence, found that mature thinking was observed earliest when the material used was most closely related to the subject's experience. The problem of looking after a young child at home proved to be the easiest to understand of several passages about familiar social situations. School subjects remote from experience were the most difficult; these were history and religious education. A somewhat similar result was found by Ellis (1970) in the response of adolescents to literature about violence. Not only was there the expected improvement in understanding between the ages of thirteen and fifteen, but the pupils' reactions to violence depended on how near the particular passage came to their personal experience. Ellis also noticed that in teaching such material, particular help was needed to understand metaphorical language. Mason (1974) investigated adolescent judgments about poetry, using De Silva's (1969) extension of Peel's criteria. The development of an affective response was similar to the cognitive development; after fifteen the number of mature explanatory judgments was about equal to the number of partial responses, and not until seventeen was mature judgment finally reached. Kassim (1980) undertook a more theoretical study of the interrelationship of language, maturity of judgment, and the level of abstract thought in young adolescents, and in a sample of children aged nine to sixteen, found that cognitive maturity was related to the use of language.

Clarke (1974) made an extensive study of the development of adolescent judgment with a large sample. Nine passages were used as well as tests of conceptual development, attainment, and creativity. Once more the development of mature judgment was shown to involve a long process but was particularly marked between twelve and fourteen, supporting a Piagetian interpretation of the development. Age and ability were the main factors associated with the development, but the effects of creativity and of socio-economic status were not apparent. The lack of consistency in levels of judgment shown by the younger children showed regression to lower levels of judgment because of their lack of verbal repertoire and different levels of experience regarding the material.

These few studies show a surprising agreement with those of Goldman and Miles, when allowances are made for the differences in the materials that were used. The type of development that is disclosed is the same from study to study, and there is reasonable agreement about the ages at which different types of thinking emerge. It becomes evident that while mental ability is fundamental for the development, indicated by the relationship with mental age often recorded, chronological age is in some instances of equal or even greater importance. This is a measure of experience, so that experience as well as ability is an adjunct of understanding. There is confirmation that for narratives such as these, fully developed formal operational thinking is delayed until about seventeen. The findings about historical thinking have an added relevance to biblical understanding which frequently requires the appreciation of a historical perspective, as Murphy (1979) observed.

The impetus that Peel gave to determining the levels of understanding of narrative material has faded, nor has there been any further significant work on these lines in religious understanding. Yet Peel's demonstration that mature understanding is the result of a long process marked by identifiable periods has been carried further, especially by Biggs and Telfer (1987). The neo-Piagetian SOLO taxonomy (Biggs and Collis, 1982), describing the structure of learning outcomes, has become an increasingly used tool in the hands of many teachers. By examining and describing the consistency and extent of responses to a cue at different ages they have defined five developmental stages, the preoperational or prestructural (4-6), the early concrete or unistructural (7-9), the middle concrete or multistructural (10-12), the relational (13-16), and the formal operations or extended abstract (16+). Their approach is that of teachers, and the usefulness of their taxonomy in teaching is widely recognized, so that it is surprising that hitherto it has not been used in research about religious understanding, which still tends to be dominated by earlier work or theological fashions, rather than by the newer thinking of educational psychology.

To complete the discussion, a few other developmental studies need to be considered. Blair, McKee, and Jernigan (1980) made a study of children's beliefs in Santa Claus and other fantasy figures and found that they were related to age rather than stage development. In a statistical analysis of their results, when the effect of age was controlled there was no significant relationship between stage and belief. Disbelief was complete for both boys and girls by the age of eight, and belief was shown to be associated with the chronological age of the children but not with their developmental stage. A similar finding was made by Prentice (1978). Warren (1980) related beliefs in a range of such figures to children's age and sex; increasing age brought decreasing belief in Easter Bunny, elves, fairies, goblins, monsters, Santa Claus, and the tooth fairy but had no significant effect on belief in demons, the Devil, God, the Holy Spirit, Bible people, the Abominable Snowman, aliens, Bigfoot, ghosts, invisible people, the Loch Ness Monster, vampires, and witches. Belief in angels, Jesus, and Moses by children aged ten was significantly less than for any other age group. The only sex difference was that more girls than boys believed in the tooth fairy. Among British and Canadian children, older children were less superstitious than younger, boys less than girls, and those of greater mental ability less than the others. Science-based education had little effect on such beliefs (McLeish, 1984).

Griffiths (1977) studied the development of animistic ideas in young children drawn from rural, urban, and inner-city areas, the latter with Asian, West Indian, and white children in equal proportions. Animistic thinking was regarded as describing inanimate things as living. The children were asked about items which they could see, a stone, a branch of a tree, a woodlouse, a penknife, a tape-recorder, a stop clock, a pot plant, clouds, living mice, and a model car. Their replies were classified into conceptual levels. Animistic ideas about clouds were the last to be abandoned; a developmental continuum was found without precise age boundaries but with increasingly relevant answers related to chronological and mental age. The children were in their first term at school, and their language reflected the influence of their home environments. It showed a close similarity of ideas, even between the different racial groups. This Griffith regarded as indicating that early in life children's animistic thinking was universal. Over the whole sample, the Asian and West Indian children displayed more animistic thinking than the remainder, owing to the language and practice of their homes reflecting animistic concepts in their two communities. The rejection of animistic thinking was accelerated by a favorable environment, such as living in a house with a garden and having pets; this was not possible for the inner-city children, whose contact with living things was minimal. This contact was so closely associated with the environmental effect that no individual effect could be isolated. The impoverishment of life in inner-city areas resulted in reduced stimulation for the children, which appeared to have lasting effects. Teaching children about living things in no way helped them to understand the significance of living and not living; those who had been taught were more animistic in their responses, giving support to Piaget's contention that relevant knowledge is insufficient to develop children's concepts in the absence of the opportunity to perform the requisite intellectual operations.

Hacker (1984) was critical of Piagetian theory as applied to the development of scientific understanding and regarded the time-consuming method of clinical interviews as being inevitably selective and impossible to provide genuine replication, an ethnographic technique rather than a psychometric method of gathering data. He applied his system for analyzing science lessons to science teaching in primary and secondary schools in Western Australia and noted six levels of intellectual ability that were emphasized in the classroom. These he considered indicated gradual, quantitative changes in thinking rather than discrete qualitative stages with emergent intellectual functions. Some pupils as young as five or six were able to make hypotheses about scientific phenomena and to devise suitable tests for their ideas. He commented that Piaget was far too pessimistic regarding the abilities of younger children, who can and do engage in inferential thought processes.

A similar result was secured (Barnsley and Wilkinson, 1981) from a very different approach in a study of the development of moral judgment in children's writing—a much neglected field. They accepted that there was an overwhelming body of evidence for the age-related development of moral concepts, although there was disagreement about the number of appropriate stages. Results from an analysis of written work from children aged seven to thirteen showed that the optimum level of moral judgment followed Kohlberg's position, but within a single piece of work earlier levels of judgment might be embedded. This supported a cumulative stage hypothesis, as Bull (1969) had proposed when he observed that his four stages could survive into adult life. Both Piaget and Kohlberg had proposed a discrete stage theory, whereby a higher stage replaces a lower one.

TEACHING STYLES AND METHODS

The correct religious stance of teachers in English schools is under frequent discussion. The concept of neutrality, which is widely upheld, was rejected by Lloyd (1981), who argued that the religious neutrality demanded of teachers and pupils envisaged a rational child, detached from his roots, assessing the claims of different religions neutrally presented by an uncommitted teacher. This was impossible and undesirable, since children were supposed not only to study religion but as a result decide on their own commitment. Religious understanding could only be acquired fully where religion was being practiced and not where it was only spoken about. Certainly college students in California regarded their most effective teachers as being self-disclosing and, to a somewhat lesser extent, those who advocated a particular position (Kuiper, 1976).

Although various opinions have been expressed regarding a teacher's stance, no British studies have been made as to its effect. Teachers' attitudes and interest in religious education have been studied, as for example by May (1968), who undertook a widespread circulation of a questionnaire about religious and moral education to teachers in County Durham schools. The returns indicated that a substantial majority of teachers were at that time in favor of religious instruction and school worship, with a majority favoring moral education lessons distinct from religious education, even though the survey indicated overall a strong case against isolated moral education. However, Litherland (1969) was critical of these findings, regarding the issues as too complex and the survey lacking in clarity, so as to cast doubt on its reliability.

Little research has been undertaken to investigate the effects of teaching styles on pupil's learning, although some aspects of it are frequently discussed. Alves (1968) compared two groups of secondary schools with greater or smaller success rates in their religious education. The difference was related to the numbers of more experienced teachers, and it suggested there was a period of maximum teaching efficiency reached after fifteen years but falling off after another ten.

In his monumental trilogy on religious education, Lee (1973) suggested a taxonomy of the teaching act for religious education and complained of the lack of research into the teaching of religion. It must be observed that this is a particularly difficult field, as work in other subject areas indicates, since the effect of the particular approach and the style of the teacher are almost swamped by many other variables which bear on the students' learning. Even so, some attempts have recently been made.

Black (1968) was interested in developing young children's religious ideas by suitable teaching. She interviewed children aged six in groups of five before and after a nine-week thematic teaching program based on the first seven Beatitudes. The children were involved in a great deal of discussion about their experience. She then related these to topics intended to deepen their awareness of God. Content analysis of each child's responses showed that they had moved toward a more personal image of a loving and forgiving God who provided all their necessities but was not feared as a judge. Their social awareness had also been fostered. Although half the children displayed verbalisms, some of it was reduced by using a teaching vocabulary from the children's own experience. More than half showed egocentrism and almost as many showed anthropomorphism, but there was no evidence of animistic thinking in the group. Their thoughts and feelings revolved around their own needs and wants, and they showed confusion about the distinction between God and Jesus. The ideas of sorrow and forgiveness proved difficult for them to accept, although a few seemed to have grasped the idea of forgiving others. It was important to avoid using abstract ideas which lacked meaning for them, since this could retard future development. Moore (1976) described the problems of using the Old Testament with younger children, who asked such questions as, "How could God kill the Egyptian children in the plagues?" Goldman had shown we could not theologize; we had to tell, and not teach, Old Testament stories without concern for their being understood. Stuhlmueller (1976) argued that the Bible was a book for all, although adults understood it differently. Children needed the Old Testament and should come to it with attitudes of trust, love, and obedience.

The learning of eleven-year-old Methodist Sunday school children was most influenced by their sex (girls learning more than boys), the attitude of the teacher (women proving to be more successful than men), and classes with more homogeneous age-grouping. Six months later a significant retention of learning was also found (Sowell, 1977). When a group of Catholic high-school students were taught for a year by an interdisciplinary method related to Erikson's eight life stages, in which accepted truths were critically challenged, it proved to be very successful because of the students' positive response to it and the enhanced attitudes it engendered in terms of personal and family relationships, personal faith, and self-understanding (Culnane, 1978).

Heywood (1973) listed the skills pupils needed for their work in religious education lessons. He suggested a range of linguistic skills related to recognizing and using symbolic language, and the historical skills needed to distinguish between fact and interpretation and to form conclusions from an analysis of relevant factors. Whether teachers were aware of these issues remained in doubt. However, Barnes and Shemilt (1974) used a random sample of secondary schools for a study of teaching styles. They found that some teachers, especially in the sciences and languages, were largely concerned with the transmission of knowledge and used written work as a means for pupils to acquire information. Other teachers were concerned with interpretation, and pupils' writing was used as a means of helping them think about issues, which facilitated their cognitive development. This approach was particularly true of the religious education and English teachers in the sample. Lewis' (1982) study of the purposes of writing in five main subject areas was a follow-up of Barnes and Shemilt's work. A careful study of practice in the first year of secondary education clearly demonstrated that in the particular school used teachers tended to be either interpreters or transmitters. Although English and religious education seemed to have a near monopoly of the expressive and poetic forms of language, interpretive usage was found only in English teaching. This implied some criticism of the religious education teachers in the school. Other criticism came from Wall's (1983) examination of the assumptions made about religious education which were only inadequately achieved in practice. In the school he investigated it was not only that relatively few pupils thought that it helped them in self-understanding, or regarded it as a personal quest for values and meaning, but most saw it as concerned mainly with the transmission of knowledge, in which they were involved in a passive manner, reading, writing, and listening. Knowledge was indeed acquired, but few saw any use for it in the future. It is evident that teaching styles in religious education vary widely.

Kerry (1980) also studied the teaching procedures used in religious education. He analyzed the demand made on the thinking of pupils' from eleven to fourteen by three teachers, using the techniques developed for the Teacher Education Project. Important concepts or abstract ideas were omitted or simplified, most of the lessons being given to handling data, with little teacher talk at an abstract level. Verbal transmission was concerned with management of the class and with giving information, so that a surprisingly small amount of thinking at a cognitive level was required. This was rectified in the homework set by the head of department, which required pupils to apply knowledge and think out issues, but the other teachers only required information to be collected and recorded. The author made it plain that this was a study in a single school and that the findings could not be generalized, but it became apparent that some teachers might not sufficiently stretch their pupils in a subject in which an ability to handle abstract ideas is an essential teaching objective.

Poole (1986) investigated the effect of two teaching methods with pupils of fifteen. With considerable care she produced a biblical lesson and a thematic lesson about the same material from Jonah, which was not expected to be familiar to most of those tested. She used it with pupils from six different schools in a single lesson for each group. At the end of the lesson they were tested, as were a parallel untaught group from each school. The teaching method made no significant difference to the results from those she had taught, although the taught groups scored significantly better than the untaught groups. There was no significant difference between boys' and girls' results. The dominant learning factor was church attendance, followed by teaching, even though it was unaffected by its method, and then by a prior knowledge of the material. When allowance was made for these, no other variable was significantly related. The apparent differences due to school attended, denomination, or to parental social status apparently arose from these main factors. This result is in line with Francis (1979c) findings.

To conclude, it is appropriate to refer to the outstanding small study of Anderson (1967), who tested the levels of propositional thinking of girls aged eleven to thirteen about eight short comprehension passages. Half of each group had first been given four lessons about dealing with simple logical problems. The test was given in two stages five weeks apart; this was to show any lasting effect of this preliminary teaching. Responses were classified into the categories of Peel (1971). The teaching had a marked effect, greater than that of age, mental ability, or the form of test used. The results also suggested that when given a test using multiple-choice questions, pupils could operate at higher levels of thinking than they could reach unaided in free responses, so that this form of test was unsuitable for studying levels of thinking. Anderson's result is similar to that of Hallam (1978) on history teaching and leaves no doubt as to the lasting value of teaching designed to improve cognitive performance at this age. As Culnane (1978) has shown, such results call into question the value of religious teaching that is confined merely to passing on information. It remains to be seen what the effect will be of the recent emphasis on students' critical skills required by the new form of the English General Certificate of Education examination for pupils of sixteen and over. Press reports of the first examination results speak of generally improved levels of performance, but no real assessment of the religious studies papers is yet available.

Chapter 8

Studies of Religious Attitudes

Scales for measuring attitude to religion have become widely used to measure religiousness. The methods of their construction are described in many textbooks, and modern computing techniques have greatly facilitated what previously were the tedious statistical operations needed to secure their reliability. How attitudes should be defined, what it is an attitude scale measures, and how attitudes are related to belief or behavior, are technical issues that are discussed in Appendix I.

For almost fifty years school children's attitudes to religion and to related issues have been investigated, almost entirely in England and Wales. The studies have varied about types of school and their locations. Few of them took advantage of earlier work, and in most instances new scales were developed for the purpose. In consequence, caution is needed in comparing results, although there are a number of broad areas of agreement. Many interesting details emerge from these studies, but the dates at which they were undertaken need to be kept in mind because of the continuing decline in religiousness which many of them reveal. A good many have been presented as academic dissertations and theses which are not easily available to the general reader, and brief accounts of many of them are included. Because of their great variety and scope the account of them has been made chronologically, without any attempt to make any further classification. Some are included because they are predominantly interested in affective responses but properly deal with matters of belief as well as of attitude.

An attitude to religion scale gives a numerical value for the extent of an individual's feelings about religion. Religion is here a general term. A high score does not indicate saintliness, nor a low score sinfulness; they are only the more extreme scores observed in typical groups of respondents. Attitude scores say nothing about beliefs or religious behavior. A group of respondents with similar favorable scores might well include members of many different denominations, holding very varied beliefs and religious orientations. Their theology could range from strongly conservative to extremely liberal positions. Some could be most active in their churches, others have little or no such involvement. When results of attitude studies suggest other factors which have some relationship to religiousness, its wide boundaries must not be overlooked. Greer (1983a) warned about the problems caused by confusing the psychometric term attitude to religion with the more popular phrase religious attitude—attitude to religion was a measure of an affective dimension, but the underlying concepts were formative in the development of the attitude.

Since the first use of a scale to measure attitude to the church by Thurstone and Chave (1929) many scales for measuring attitude to religion have been developed. In the United States their use has often involved students, but seldom children; in England there has been a long history of their use with adolescents. With few exceptions, the results have shown that girls tend to score higher than boys, and with both sexes scores tend to fall with age. Interest in the studies then arises not from their repetitions or the diversity of scales used but from the other details which emerge. The research has tended to be unsystematic, especially in the earlier days. In the United States, a number of studies have been made about the religiousness of university students, some of them including tests of their attitude to religion. These are more appropriately described with other associated factors in chapter 12. Considerable variations were found between different student groups, the differences reflecting regional and denominational variations. Telford (1950) found in a study of the religious attitudes of church members that Mormons displayed the highest scores, followed in order by Catholics, Protestants, and finally the unaffiliated; women always scored higher than men.

In Britain sporadic interest in adolescents' religious attitudes was stimulated by the provisions for religious education in the 1944 Act. Grocock (1940) found that most of the grammar school[1] boys he studied had some church connections, and a third of them professed to be really interested in religion. Attitude scales were used for the first time in this field by Glassey (1945) who studied the attitudes of children and their parents to education, religion, and sport. Religion attracted the lowest attitude scores both with children and parents, but girls showed a more favorable attitude than boys. Conversely, boys' religious attitudes were more strongly related to those of their parents than were those of the girls. Moreton (1944) conducted a study in attitudes to religion among adolescents and adults.

---

1. For the significance of grammar and modern schools see the Glossary.

The adolescents were stated to be more favorable to religion than to the church. While most of their parents did not attend church the majority expressed the intention of doing so when they were older. He found little evidence of any attitude change with age.

The attitude of adolescents to their intellectual, social, and spiritual development was investigated by Forrester (1946). Home influence had most to do with their acceptance of a scale of values; they were attracted to practical religion rather than to mystical, and ethical teaching rather than doctrinal was held in esteem by them. This was subsequently confirmed by Hilliard (1959). Forrester found that there was little difference in attitude between the boys and the girls in her sample. To the same period belongs Bradbury's study of the religious development of the adolescent (1947). He had observed when teaching that interest in many religious questions developed earlier than was generally supposed. He found that the first incidence of religious doubt came in the fourteenth year with boys, and a year or two earlier with girls. He related this to the appearance of critical reasoning at about the age of eleven and to the onset of puberty. He found no significant difference between groups of higher or lower intelligence or between different types of school.

Daines (1949) made a detailed study of the attitude of adolescents to religion and religious instruction in grammar schools. He found a close relationship between attitude to religion and pupils' interest in art and poetry. His scores tended to give a bipolar distribution with separate groups of high-and low-scoring children, unlike scores on his other aesthetic tests, which were normally distributed. He demonstrated the presence of a religious factor which affected the aesthetic tests and urged that an increased use of aesthetic experience would help to deepen religious sensibility. Hughes (1953) investigated the effect of religious education on the moral attitudes of children in a secondary modern school with a test of attitudes about loyalty, friendship, and social responsibility and looked for differences arising from a year's teaching about the gospels. Two forms taught with an emphasis on its application to daily life showed a significant improvement in their moral attitudes as compared with the control group.

Rixon (1959) tested boys and girls in secondary modern and grammar schools on their attitude to scripture as a school subject, their perception of its usefulness, the time spent on it, the degree of interest felt toward it, and its helpfulness in giving meaning to life. The results from the modern schools showed higher scores than those from the grammar schools, a result which pointed to a more critical attitude among the abler grammar school pupils.

Varma (1959) tested children in three secondary modern schools, using a scale with the same responses to measure attitudes toward mathematics, history, geography, science, English, and religious education. Pupils were also asked which subjects they liked best and least, and reasons for their preference; preferences correlated significantly with attitude scores. Mathematics and English were liked best as being useful in later life, geography as giving knowledge of the world, and any subject if it was interesting. Those liked least were seen as "dull, boring, and silly." The attitude scores gave English and geography as the most popular subjects, followed in order by science, mathematics, history, and religious education. While religious education had the lowest vote for the "liked best" subject, history, science, and mathematics had more votes for being liked least.

Edwards (1959) used a moral attitude scale to test secondary modern school boys and found a decline in scores about honesty, responsibility, and moral rightness between eleven and fourteen but no change in the friendliness scale scores. Very few people of a moral or religious nature were chosen as an ideal person. There was only a slight association between moral attitudes and intelligence; many boys were confused over the definition of moral concepts and uncertain when presented with instances of moral conflict and asked to explain why they would act as they chose to.

In order to investigate the relationship between religious attitudes and religious learning, Hyde (1959, 1963, 1965) compiled and validated scales to measure religious behavior, attitudes to religion and to the church, and other tests to measure the image of God and a range of traditional religious concepts. They were used to test all the pupils in four single-sex secondary schools in the Midlands. Analysis of the responses to religious behavior items showed a regular step-wise progression of interest and activity, from being "a little religious" to going to church at least once a Sunday, with the great majority falling into this pattern. Bible reading was not related to any other variable. There were significant differences between those attending church once a month, or more often, and nonattenders. Churchgoing boys secured similar attitude scores on both scales at every age tested; those not attending church showed a marked decline with age. In every group, girls scored higher than boys, but the development was similar. In the whole sample attitude scores were strongly associated with religious behavior scores. There was little evidence of any sudden changes in religiousness taking place, as would be indicated by typical conversion experiences. Church-going and prayer were also related to the development of religious concepts, and in turn these were strongly related to positive religious attitudes and behavior.

James (1974) repeated Hyde's tests in a large Catholic comprehensive school in Birmingham. There was greater religiousness among the girls than the boys, but it declined with age, although in this denominational school, the levels of religious behavior were high. Because most pupils attended church, many of them compulsorily, she examined a group with greater religiousness shown by higher scores on the religious behavior and interest test, rather than by church attendance. This group showed a decline in religiousness between the first and third years, which was partly recovered in the fourth year. Analysis of the data showed interest to be the most significant factor, followed by age and by sex. The girls had a more developed idea of God as Father than the boys, regarding him as a benign being, whereas the boys thought more in terms of pure spirit and were less anthropomorphic than the girls. Concept scores declined with age, despite the increased mental maturity associated with growing older. The interested group scored considerably better than the lower interest group.

Garrity (1960) tested secondary modern school children about their attitude to religious instruction. Girls scored higher than boys, and a decline in scores was observed in the second and third years. Church-going made a considerable difference to the professed attitudes. Among children with unfavorable attitudes to the subject many claimed that their attitude arose from dull or bad teaching.

Patino (1961) used a scale based on statements about God made by French-speaking adolescents in Belgian state and denominational secondary schools. The items conveyed ideas such as "the justice of God is something which frightens me very much." Girls scored higher than boys; boys in denominational schools scored higher than those in state schools, but with the girls the reverse was true, so that overall state school students scored somewhat higher than those in denominational schools, except for items about the goodness of God. Scores increased with age, except for items about the fear of God, a feeling stronger with boys than with girls, and found more in the denominational schools than in the state schools. Higher attitude scores were also associated with higher social class groupings. A test on catechetical knowledge carried out at the same time showed that most students knew the doctrines of the nature and attributes of God quite well, but terms such as "the divine providence" or "the divine nature" were largely unknown or misunderstood. Scores increased with age, the denominational school students tended to score higher than those in state schools, and the boys higher than the girls. Scores on this test were almost entirely independent of those on the attitude scale. A simple test about choosing and explaining a gospel parable showed that the denominational school boys had the least grasp of its meaning; this test gave results the reverse of those on catechetical knowledge. It finally seemed that the adolescents who had biblical knowledge superior to catechetical knowledge also professed a better attitude to religion.

In the United States, Allen and Hites (1961) measured the attitude to religion of older Methodist adolescents, together with a test of biblical knowledge and other ratings. Analysis of the responses produced nine separate factors having different associations with religion; they were religion as man's relation to deity, traditional mores of the church, skepticism, striving for security, family religious life, security through religion, religion and science, secular religion, and humanism. The authors regarded this result from an apparently homogeneous culture as indicating the complexity of religion and its multidimensional nature.

Jones (1962) (Dale and Jones, 1964) tested the most able fourth-year pupils in mixed grammar schools in industrial South Wales on their attitude to scripture lessons, the Old Testament, the gospels, and the Acts of the Apostles. Questions about religious activity and parental occupation were also included. Social group differences were found, in which the girls' attitudes became more favorable and the boys' attitudes less favorable with lower socio-economic status. A small group of Welsh-speaking girls scored much higher on the attitude scale. The analysis of the results was directed almost entirely toward the differences between the sexes. The girls liked scripture and had a favorable attitude to it as a school subject; the boys had a moderate liking and a moderate attitude toward it. Very few expressed dislike for it. The differences between the sexes were significant overall but not in every school. Girls showed a more positive attitude to the gospels than the boys; this difference was not found for the Old Testament or the Acts of the Apostles, which was the topic least liked by both sexes. Boys and girls taught by women teachers had higher scores than those taught by men. Nonattendance or occasional Sunday school attendance were associated with lower scores, an effect enhanced by their socio-economic group. A similar result was found for church attendance. Attendance at church and Sunday school was unusually high, two-thirds of the girls and nearly half of the boys regularly attending both church and Sunday school.

Poppleton and Pilkington (1963) used their attitude to religion scale with students at Sheffield. There was a significant decline in belief among arts and science students in the early years at a university, a decline which continued only with science students. The highest scores were registered by final-year medical students and postgraduate students training for teaching. Denominational comparisons showed that Catholics and members of small evangelical sects scored highest. Women scored higher than men. Overall, final-year students, when compared with those in the first year showed a slight increase in scores for belief and private prayer and a slight reduction for church attendance and membership. Three-quarters held some form of religious belief, two-thirds prayed privately sometimes, a quarter attended church at least once a week. Eleven years later this was repeated (Pilkington, Poppleton, Gould, and McCourt, 1976). There had been a substantial shift away from religion on each of the eight measures used; there was now a sex difference on only five of the scales, and it was evident that the difference in religiousness between the men and the women was less than before.

Their scale was used by Fraser and Stacey (1973) to test theories about the effect of attitude on personal judgments. Their results indicated that the students tended to accept statements of opinions in accord with their own and reject those that were dissimilar. Those with more extreme attitudes grouped most of the statements near the two extremes, but those with less extreme attitudes spread the statements more evenly over the range.

Johnson (1966) tested pupils in secondary schools in Manchester. The pupils' self-assessment of their attitude to religion was consistent with their scale scores, which showed that older pupils had a significantly less favorable attitude to religion than the younger, and boys less than girls. Church and Sunday school attendance was found to have a significant relationship.

Walker (1966) adapted Moreton's (1944) scale to measure the attitude to religion and to religious education of students training to be teachers in five colleges of education. There were no significant differences between the three year-groups, but women had more favorable attitudes than men, and the first-year students more favorable attitudes than the remainder. In interviews she found most students regarded college as broadening their religious understanding, but small fundamentalist and antireligious groups were hostile to this influence. Parental religiousness, measured by frequency of church attendance of both parents, and the family attitude to the church, was strongly associated with the students' attitudes. Favorable attitudes to religion were also associated with an enjoyable association with a church. Unfavorable attitudes had been encouraged by disillusion with the behavior of so-called religious people, the narrowness of the church as it had been encountered, rival interests in sport which took up all available leisure, and the influence of friends not interested in religion or the church. At the time the students said that their sixth form religious education had been acceptable whereas that of earlier years had not. Discussion had been welcomed as were life-oriented studies or those of other world religions; they were critical of lessons that had been boring, insufficiently related to life, academic, and without spiritual value, seen to be secondary to other subjects or taught by teachers without adequate class-control.

Kesteven (1967) developed scales about religious education, school assembly, prayer, the Bible, the future life, and Jesus Christ and used them with youth club members aged thirteen to twenty. There was no difference between those still at school and those who had left, nor between those in grammar schools and modern schools, except for attitude to religious education, when the grammar school group was more favorable. The mean attitude scores of different youth clubs varied considerably and church youth club scores were similar to the others. Girls were more religious than boys, but this was significant only on the scale about prayer. Eighteen percent of the boys and 38 percent of the girls professed to attend church weekly, and a similar claim was made for 12 percent of their parents. Forty percent of the boys, 27 percent of the girls, and 47 percent of the parents attended hardly ever or never. Religious education was favored by many, who claimed to have learned much about God from it. Similarly, despite criticism of it, most felt school assembly to be worthwhile, but favorable attitudes appeared to be related to parental religiousness and not to the schools. Prayer also was favored by most, although practiced with regularity by few; it was strongly associated with belief in God but not with belief in the divinity of Jesus. The Bible was highly regarded, but it was an ambivalent reaction since for most it held no personal significance. Only a minority read it because it gave them strength; most found no dynamic quality in it. This was equally true for boys and girls. Most expressed belief in a future life, and this belief was strongly associated with other religious beliefs and attitudes. Much support was indicated for orthodox belief in Jesus Christ, and this was significantly associated with regular church attendance and other areas of religious belief. Doubt was more prevalent among boys than girls.

Alves (1968), surveying religious education in over five hundred schools, interpreted results from his attitude to religion scale as indicating the majority of respondents to be fairly favorable to Christianity, girls more than boys, and sixth form students less than those of the fourth forms. Scores for the attitude to the church were markedly less than those to Jesus, who was regarded by the majority as a savior, however defined. A bare majority were willing to be labeled as "Christian." Religious behavior scores, based on church attendance and private prayer, showed the same pattern of deterioration with age, girls scoring higher than boys. The majority apparently joined occasionally in worship and prayer, with slightly greater activity by the grammar school pupils.

There was an association between the mean attitude scores of pupils in a school and the teaching experience of the religious education teacher. In the majority of schools where the highest attitude scores were recorded the teacher had fifteen or more years experience. After twenty-five years teaching the position was reversed. Higher attitude scores were associated with the teacher's desire for their personal Christian commitment and for their sense of moral responsibility, with the status of the subject and its staff within each school and with external examinations being held in the subject. Items about moral judgment showed a growing permissiveness with age, but girls remained more authoritarian than boys. Those more likely to accept a Christian label tended to be authoritarian in their moral stance, but it was not clear whether this association had anything to do with the school, although in the few schools where pupils had high authoritarian scores the religious studies staff held strongly authoritarian views. In more general terms, while some schools showed a lively concern for Christian issues and had staff of high standing who cared for the spiritual development of their pupils, there was also evidence of a lack of rigor in student thinking essential for religious studies at a more advanced level beyond the age of sixteen.

Alatopoulous (1968) developed a scale about a range of moral issues and used it with the Sheffield Institute test of religious knowledge (1961) and the attitude to religion scale of Poppleton and Pilkington (1963) with sixth form students in four single-sex and two mixed grammar schools. Most girls scored similarly to the somewhat younger Sheffield girls; most boys did as well as the girls and better than the Sheffield boys. Two groups of apathetic boys from a poor socio-economic area had much lower scores. Girls scored higher than boys in the attitude to religion scores. It is of note that there was a great difference in mean scores between the groups; for the boys they were 57, 58, 74, and 79; for the girls 71, 83, 85, and 88. In the school where the boys scored 57, the girls scored 85. Such diversity shows the danger of making wide generalizations based on results gathered from only a few schools.

In a personal opinion test those with more conservative moral attitudes tended to obtain higher scores on the attitude to religion scale, confirming Cox's (1967) finding that religious adolescents took a more strict view on many moral ideas. Scores on the religious knowledge test were strongly associated with those on the attitude to religion test but quite insignificantly with scores on the personal opinion test. He concluded that in this sample, while attitude to religion was related to moral judgment, religious knowledge was not related. (However, his correlation coefficients between attitude and knowledge of 0.428 for the girls and 0.231 for the boys should be compared with 0.250 for boys found by Jordan (1941) between attitude and attainment in a range of subjects.) Boys were more lax than girls toward sex, drinking, honesty, and personal relationships, and more conservative moral attitudes were found in the higher socio-economic grades for boys and girls. Religion appeared to be an integrative force in their personality. There was support for Cox's finding that in a mixed school the girls were more likely to be assimilated to the boys' standards than the reverse.

Esawi (1968) investigated the relationship between religious attitudes, moral attitudes, emotional adjustment, and home adjustment in secondary school pupils, adapting the scale of Poppleton and Pilkington (1963) and constructing a similar scale to measure moral attitudes. A related series of essays disclosed a wide range of beliefs. The vast majority expressed favorable religious and moral attitudes, girls scoring higher than boys. Church attendance was significantly associated with religious belief. Grammar school pupils scored lower than those in the other schools, and Esawi regarded this as due to teaching which encouraged discussion and critical thinking. Differences in religious and moral attitudes were found to be associated with the type of school attended, and this was shown to be related to the school rather than to social class. Intellectual ability had a negative association with belief. Parental encouragement, when found, was strongly associated with favorable religious attitudes and more frequent church attendance. It did not vary between the sexes but was more prevalent with the younger pupils. The girls scored higher than the boys on the moral attitude scale; unlike them they did not show a significant increase with growing age. Although there was a strong association between religious and moral attitudes, there was no corresponding association between religious attitudes and emotional adjustment, but those with high attitude to religion scores had a slight tendency toward poorer emotional adjustment.

Hindley (1970) argued that a study by adolescents of their search for independence and identity should enhance their attitudes to themselves and to others, and their religious attitude, since religion satisfied psychological needs. After teaching a course on the significance of a liberal Christian belief to pupils of fourteen and fifteen, with some groups also undertaking studies of adolescence, he found that comments in essays showed that the course aroused interest and indicated that in some pupils the expected changes had taken place. But there was no indication of this in the test scores. In most groups girls scored higher than boys on the attitude to religion scale, and the fourth-year scores were less than the third year. Girls scored higher than boys on the attitude to self and others test, in which responses showed that the pupils identified most with their parents, and the preferred parent was usually of the same sex. The pupils consistently gave low rankings to themselves; parents, followed by teachers, always ranked higher.

Hepburn (1971) reviewed American studies of adolescent attitude to religion in relation to religious education, noting the problems of definition as well as the legality of attempting to change religious attitudes in schools. He complained that there was a dearth of information about the development of religious attitudes in adolescence (that is, apart from the measurement of them), regarding this as one of the least researched areas of contemporary religious life. He observed that there was a high level of interest in religion among adolescents, but some studies had shown that the more intelligent of them had begun to question religious belief.

Povall (1971) used Garrity's (1960) attitude to religion scale and other tests with pupils aged twelve and fourteen. Age and sex had significant effects on attitude scores, but not verbal ability or the social class of the pupils. In single-sex schools the older boys had less favorable attitudes than the younger boys, but the position with the girls was reversed. In coeducational schools the younger girls had the most favorable attitudes of any group tested, and boys taught with them had higher scores than those taught in boys' schools. Older girls in coeducational schools had less favorable attitudes than older girls taught in girls' schools. This finding about the girls is in agreement with the results of Wright and Cox (1967a) about students over sixteen. Teachers' attitudes to religious education indicated that most of them agreed that pupils should be given standards of morality and behavior, many thinking this could be achieved by Christian teaching, and that schools could compensate for its omission in home life. The subject was found to have a poor image, which Povall thought arose from a lack of specialist teachers.

Atkins (1972) found no hostility to religion or religious education among pupils aged fifteen in the East Midlands but much interest in religious issues, despite boredom with what was taught; teaching the Bible seemed to have the opposite effect of what was intended. Boys were much less interested than girls; very few boys engaged in private prayer and none attended church any longer, nor did their parents. Almost half the boys and two-thirds of the girls professed to believe in God, but far fewer boys believed that prayer was answered. Sunday school was dismissed as childish, and religion was regarded as irrelevant to life. The majority believed that Jesus had lived, only 40 percent were certain of his resurrection, and many unformulated ideas were held about him. Atkins regarded the subject's low esteem as being due to restricted time-table provisions made for it, and to the unfamiliarity of religious language.

Hinchcliffe (1973) tested boys and girls in two single-sex grammar schools and a comprehensive school. The boys showed a greater interest in moral than religious issues and were bored by religion. Girls scored higher than boys on both; they tended to regard themselves as Christian and considered this to be important, whereas the boys tended to the contrary point of view. Girls showed slight support for the morning assembly, the boys were slightly more opposed to it; many did not feel that worship was appropriate for school. Girls regarded prayer as important, but not the boys, and were more frequent in church attendance. Analysis of the data showed a strong, antireligious factor and a second factor apparently related to underlying ideals. Whereas Cox (1967) had found only 44 percent of his large sample interested in life after death, 85 percent of this younger sample professed such an interest.

Students at a college of education were tested on their attitudes to the Bible and to teaching it at the beginning and at the end of their three-year course by Jones (1974). He divided them into high, middle, and low religiousness groups according to their ranking of religious values in Richardson's (1965) scale of six values and tested their opinions about the religious significance of the Old and New Testament, the Bible as literature and as a historical document. He also used nine biblical verses in a belief scale. All responses were associated with religiousness and sex, as might be expected, but not with socio-economic status. The sex difference was not significant in a group of mature students. Attitudes were generally more favorable than unfavorable but tended to decline during the course. The high religiousness group was more favorable to the New than to the Old Testament and had become more conservative in their biblical interpretation during their course. The low religiousness group was less favorable to both Testaments and became more critical of them by the end of their course. Decreasing religiousness was progressively associated with a less favorable and a more critical attitude to the Bible. Overall, men changed little during the course, regarding the religious aspects of the Bible less favorably than its literary and especially its historical aspects; they showed a more critical approach to the Old Testament than to the New Testament. Women moved toward the more critical position of the male students during the course, and scores on their religious values scales declined. Although overall there was no significant change of certainty about religious belief, about a quarter of the students, predominantly women, always indicated complete certainty of belief, while the smaller group indicating complete certainty of disbelief doubled in size over the period. Many students showed only a limited understanding of the religious significance of three well-known biblical stories. The students were much more favorable to teaching the Bible in primary than in secondary schools, but by the end of their course they had grown somewhat more critical of their own experience of secondary school religious education and a little less favorable to primary school religious education.

Cove (1975) studied developmental trends in religious beliefs, attitudes, and values among adolescents in two Catholic high schools, testing them in 1970 and again in 1974. Over the period there was a deterioration of scores on the scales of God awareness, moral responsibility, and religious participation and no change in scores on God relationship, meaningful life, and biblical concepts. However, Blum (1976) undertook a four-year longitudinal study of Catholic high-school students aged thirteen to sixteen. He found no change in their religiousness over the period, although there were indications that among the older students some religious values became associated with a more mature outlook. The results are not necessarily in conflict—different scales were used with different students in different schools, and aspects of individual religiousness had been modified, whether or not there was an overall change in it.

In some West German schools Miller (1977) studied the attitudes of pupils in the religion class, with the help of teachers of varied backgrounds. Pupils expressed a hostile attitude to the church, but it appeared that they were really indifferent to it. Despite this attitude, it was possible to interest them in religion. In contrast to his general findings he noted a very positive response from a group of 34 girls of fourteen and fifteen in a denominational school taught very competently by a nun; this he regarded as related to the school's educational style and its taking the subject very seriously.

Mitchell (1977) compared boys' attitudes to English, history, science, mathematics, geography, and woodworking. A number of significant differences were found between their attitudes to the subjects and interest in them. These were found both in the first and fifth years but not in the third year, a time of attitude formation. There were also differences between the schools. Grammar school boys, with lower attitude scores, exhibited a great stability of attitude toward the institutional variables, yet showed a greater independence of thought toward the curriculum; the global effect of the school proved to be greater in the modern school. Growing maturity tended to reduce school differences at the end of the fifth year, after disenchanted modern school pupils had left. Although the tests did not include any about religion, the patterns disclosed show once again the complex factors involved in the formation of pupils' attitudes. Jordan (1941) had found that it was "useful" subjects such as English and mathematics which retained boys' interest, and French and history witnessed a decline in interest in the older age-groups.

Mark (1979, 1982a, b) examined the relationship between Yinger's functional understanding of religion—"how is a man religious?" and traditional religiousness in two Sheffield comprehensive schools, similar in size and social background and differing in pastoral and academic concerns. His scales measured attitudes to others, using statements such as "friends should not argue with each other." Results disclosed a religious factor, a compassionate factor, and a cognitive factor associated with religious knowledge. A compassionate attitude was unrelated to conventional religiousness. In the more academic school, with a strong cognitive element in religious education, scores on religious thinking increased with age. In the more pastoral school, with an emphasis on moral education and attitudes, there was little development of religious thinking after the second year. In both schools, scores on attitude to religion, attitude to others, and religious behavior declined with age; girls always scored higher than boys, and the academic school produced higher scores than the pastoral school, a result regarded as inexplicable. Attitude to religion was not important for religious understanding. 48 percent never went to church, 39 percent never read the Bible, 34 percent never prayed; conversely 9 percent attended church every week, 16 percent prayed every day, 2 percent read the Bible daily, while 43 percent read it sometimes, and 35 percent prayed sometimes. The majority had little contact with the church, but there was no widespread atheism or lack of interest in religious issues.

Mark also questioned individually a smaller group about two prose passages, a creation story from *Zorba the Greek*, and a passion story, *The Long Silence*. Responses to aspects of the interview were scored and scores were significantly associated with intelligence and religious knowledge. The first story was negatively associated with religiousness, and neither showed any significant relationship with a compassionate attitude or helpfulness. Much valuable information derived from the interviews was recorded, demonstrating that the pupils could discuss religious issues intelligently and at times offer insights indicating depth and maturity; these came mostly, but not entirely, from those of greater mental ability.

The result indicated the need for research into the effects of religious education curriculum materials. Other possible factors which might have accounted for the difference between the two schools in their religious outcomes were not known. It could be that parental choice influenced the academic school entry and created a social difference between the schools. No English studies have been undertaken on the religious effects of the general ethos of a school, although apparently similar schools can have a very different ethos.

Other studies of a compassionate attitude have been undertaken in the United States. When Cline and Richards (1965) studied religious dimensions a compassionate attitude proved to be relatively independent of conventional religious beliefs, and the irreligious rated just as well for love and compassion for their fellowmen, so that the authors commented that religious commitment was extremely complex and there were many ways to be religious and to express it in behavior. Rokeach (1969) also found that frequent church-attenders were somewhat less compassionate than infrequent attenders. He argued that the most distinctive Christian values were about concepts of salvation and forgiveness and that there were different value systems for the religious, the less religious, and the nonreligious. Only a third of church-goers had become truly religious and another third were hypocritical. Christianity had been more successful in teaching the proscriptive "thou shalt nots" than the prescriptive "thou shalts" of the Sermon on the Mount. A shift of focus was needed to teach that salvation was the reward for obeying the Sermon on the Mount rather than the Ten Commandments. Salvation was highly valued by people who were conservative, anxious to maintain the status quo and unsympathetic to the plight of the poor, while the value of forgiving was not related one way or another to these issues. Nelsen, Everett, Mader, and Hamby (1976) tested Yinger's measure of nondoctrinal religion on students and found little internal reliability between the items. It was not a unitary system—factor analysis indicated one factor about belief and order, similar to Yinger's concept of nondoctrinal religion, and another about the value of suffering. Both of these related to items about traditional institutional religion, the first very strongly, and this result challenged the idea that nondoctrinal religion was quite distinct from denominationally based religion. A related topic is that of "helpfulness," which has often been shown to be related to religious orientation; studies about it are recorded in Appendix D.

Russell (1978) noted a deterioration in attitudes among his former primary school pupils after two years of secondary school education and set out to investigate the attitude to religious education of children aged eleven in their last year at a primary school. He constructed a projective picture test with drawings of a nativity play, a school assembly, the Bible used in class, a visiting minister, and classroom prayers at the end of the day. When interviewed, children had to select an appropriate drawing of a child's face to match the picture; full-face and profile drawings of boys and girls had been developed to suggest favorable, unfavorable, and neutral attitudes. The test was used in five schools. Very few children gave markedly unfavorable responses, some were very favorable, but most were neutral. Subsequently the children were interviewed about their responses and then completed an attitude to religious education scale. The follow-up test gave similar results, with some shift from neutral to favorable responses, especially among his own class, so that he regarded the projective test as a better indicator than a scale open to giving socially desirable responses. Neutrality was found to be difficult for children to describe. A comparison of favorable and unfavorable responses showed that a nativity play would be well-received, as would a visit from a minister. School assembly and the use of the Bible were the least popular activities; apparently assembly was disliked for its nonreligious elements and lack of participation. Schools with the greatest religious education activity had the largest numbers of favorable responses, and the Catholic school far exceeded the others. (Apparently, the activity, and not the syllabus, affected pupils' attitudes.) It was evident from the children that their neutral position was not one of indifference but rather an uncommitted, open-minded stance with a potential for interest to be stimulated.

A substantial study of attitude to Christianity has been undertaken by Francis (1976) who has given a number of accounts of this extensive project (e.g., Francis, 1977a, 1978a,b, 1980a,b,c, 1984a; Francis, Wesley, and Rust, 1978; Kay and Francis, 1983). His objective was to secure accurate information about the Christian development of children and variations of this development between different groups of children. He assumed that an attitude score was a better indicator of development than a behavioral score such as church attendance and abandoned attempts to measure accurately cognitive development. With great skill he developed an attitude scale for use in primary and secondary schools; it included items about the Bible, the church, God, Jesus, prayer, and school religion and showed a high degree of statistical reliability. The four factors disclosed by factor analysis did not clearly relate to these topics, and in the absence of a meaningful pattern Francis concluded that this demonstrated the homogeneity of the whole scale. A somewhat different result was secured in a factor analysis of responses of children aged ten (Francis, 1977b). He also examined possible effects of testing; he included a lie detection test in his scale—that is, a few items which were known to attract more extreme responses from those eager to score highly. Anonymity or lack of it appeared not to affect test scores of ten- and eleven-year-old children (Francis, 1981); children's responses were significantly affected only if the test was administered by a priest rather than by a known or unknown teacher, and even then it was only the lie-detecting scores which so increased, not the attitude test scores proper (Francis, 1979b; Francis, Pearson, and Kay 1983a).

Hunsberger and Ennis (1982) reviewed this last result, along with other studies, in the light of the known difficulty of interpreting negative results. They concluded that although no experimenter effects had yet been demonstrated, it was better to remain skeptical about the issue. Saigh (1986) used an intelligence test in a Catholic high school to investigate possible test administrator influence. Three groups were compared; the examiner of the first group prominently wore a cross, the second examiner wore a star of David, and the third examiner wore no religious symbol. The first group scored significantly better than the second, suggesting that the second group was to some extent inhibited by an examiner from another faith. Saigh, O'Keefe, and Antoun (1984) replicated this experiment with pupils aged ten to twelve, with a similar result.

Francis developed Hyde's (1965) religious behavior scale to measure religious behavior and religious involvement separately. The complete test instrument was first used in two junior schools and two secondary schools. The result indicated a steady decline in attitude scores from children of eight in primary schools to adolescents of fifteen in secondary schools. No age proved to be of special significance in this change, but there seemed to be a growing disenchantment with Christianity. On each of the three variables, attitude, involvement, and behavior, girls scored higher than boys; involvement declined in the same way as attitude, but religious behavior scores showed some increase between eight and eleven before a subsequent decline. Goldman's observation that a deterioration in attitude begins in the primary school was confirmed, and also Hyde's finding that where high religious behavior and involvement scores were maintained, attitude to religion did not deteriorate with age. The primary school results are similar to the observations of Gesell, Ilg, and Ames (1977) who asserted that by the age of seven children began to distinguish religiously between what they knew and what they had been told, and by nine their interest in God and religion was not strong.

Care is needed in the interpretation of children's attitude scores following the demonstration by Vaillancourt (1973) of the instability of the responses of a thousand children aged nine to fifteen to attitude questions dealing with political socialization. Over six months, less than three-quarters confirmed their religious allegiance as Catholic, Protestant, Jewish, or none. They showed much instability over their attitude to the President, but this decreased with age. Such instability might be due to their having to think about the topic for the first time and to its remoteness from their normal experience. Both of these issues are relevant to the attitude to religion responses of children lacking regular contact with religious ideas and religious observance. Comparable scores over a period for groups of children may conceal many individual changes which, if in opposite directions, would not show in group scores nor in the range of scores if it was a continuing process.

Francis (1979c) used path analysis to examine the relationship between school influence and pupil attitude, a technique in which assumptions are made about the direction of causality of some of the variables in their relationships. In this case, it was assumed at the start that the children's religious behavior and attitude toward religion was dependent on their parents' religious behavior and not the other way around. From this assumption he demonstrated that religious behavior, influenced by parental example, was the most powerful predictor of the attitude scores. Only the Catholic schools exerted a significant positive influence. It followed that improvement in attitude to religion required religious behavior to be fostered, a goal acceptable in denominational schools but not in others. The study led to four important conclusions (Francis, 1978a)—there was a constant deterioration in children's attitude to religion; the roots of this were to be found in the primary schools; there was a more hostile attitude found among secondary school pupils of fifteen; and maintenance of favorable attitudes was associated with the extracurricular influence of the church. Subsequently, the scale was used in an eight-year study of the effects of church schools on primary school pupils' attitudes to Christianity, described in chapter 14. When later the test was repeated (Francis, 1978b) the trends were confirmed but with a marked increase of alienation from Christianity at about fourteen rather than fifteen. A still further decline in attitude to religion scores was found in further replications in 1982 (Francis 1984a,b) and again in 1986 (Francis, 1989b).

In another study (Francis and Carter, 1980) the attitude to religion scores of pupils entered for public examinations in religious studies was compared with those not entered in county and voluntary aided secondary schools; twenty-one schools took part in the test. Within county schools a minority opted for the examination; in the Church of England schools only a minority did not take it, and in the Roman Catholic schools all students took it. The results will not surprise those familiar with these examinations; examination results consistently show that students opting for religious studies achieve better grades than those compelled to take it. So it proved with their attitude to religion scores. When allowance had been made for external variables, no significant difference was found between any of the school groupings, apart from the minority of county school students who took the subject as an option, and these had a significantly more favorable attitude to religion. No investigation was made of the association between attitude scores and the results the students secured.

Next, Francis (1984c) turned his attention to the difficulty of measuring Christian belief, since most tests had been formulated in traditional terms unsuited to the modern range of beliefs. He compiled a questionnaire related to conservative, liberal, and dogmatic beliefs, unbelief, uncertainty of belief, and dogmatic rejection of belief, and also about religious education. This was administered to ordinands and to postgraduate students pursuing an education course. Methodist, conservative Anglican, and liberal Anglican traditions were represented. Analysis indicated four dimensions of belief—belief, uncertainty of belief, dogmatic belief, and dogmatic rejection of belief. The unbelief items made no additional contribution to the scale, and responses to liberal and to conservative belief items were not independent. A higher level of belief was found among the ordinands where two styles of belief were found. Dogmatic belief was characteristic of the Methodist and conservative Anglican groups, whereas the liberal Anglicans displayed the more open mind that "liberal" implies. Discussing the items about religious education, Francis (1984d) noted that they were heavily loaded on a single isolated factor, which seemed to show that beliefs about religious education were autonomous and unrelated to other forms of Christian belief. This was consistent with current trends in the philosophy of religious education.

There remained the possibility that the decline in religiousness shown by this testing might be due to some flaw in the test instrument itself or to a general adolescent discontent. Francis and Stubbs (1987) modified Francis' attitude scale by a slight rewording to remove references to school. When used with adults it showed great reliability and their scores were strongly related to church attendance, personal prayer, Bible reading, religious beliefs, and religious self-assessment. Factor analysis on this occasion suggested that the scale was of a unidimensional nature. Francis (1987b) developed a general attitude scale to school subjects. Pupils from eight to fifteen, from a comprehensive school and three feeder primary schools, were tested. At eight, games was the most popular subject, but there was little difference between religion, English, history, the school, mathematics, and music—in that order. Five of these hardly changed order through the school years, and at fourteen and fifteen English, the school, mathematics, and history showed some modest improvement in the score. Games fell back a little but still remained in the lead. Religion fell from second place and with music showed a steady decline through the years, finishing as the least popular subject. Since a decline in attitude to religion had been recorded in many other results, it could not be something unique to the schools involved. That music became unpopular in the secondary school could be unique to the school, unless confirmed by other research.

The availability of this simple reliable attitude to religion scale has led to its widespread use in further studies to be described later. In Kenya, its use in a study of the effect of scientific thinking showed that the idea that science achieved absolute truth had an adverse influence on the religiousness of students aged seventeen and eighteen (Fulljames and Francis, 1988).

Kay (1981a, b) was primarily concerned with the religious thinking of secondary school pupils in England, Northern Ireland, and the Irish Republic, but he also made use of Francis' scale. A more favorable attitude to religion was found in the denominational schools tested than in the others; Ulster Catholic schools yielded the most favorable scores; there was no significant difference between English Catholic and Church of England mean scores, but English state schools gave the lowest scores. Kay noted that this result was at variance with Francis' finding about Church of England junior schools.[1] He also noted that the study of world religions tended to be associated with somewhat lower attitude to Christianity scores. In the Church of England schools teaching about the Bible was associated with more favorable attitudes; it appeared that it was the way lessons were taught rather than the content which influenced the outcome. Greer (1983a) did not think the data justified this conclusion and that if World Religions had been taught to classes which included non-Christian pupils then lower scores on Francis' scale would be expected. Kay noted the result that pupils' positive attitudes to religion were associated with frequent parental church attendance, and concluded that the schools were more likely than the homes to influence religious thinking. Study of the physical sciences had a deleterious effect on attitude scores only with Ulster Catholic girls. The variation of scores according to social classes was not consistent in the different cultures; the children from professional classes in England tended to score highest, but among Catholics in Northern Ireland lowest of all. However, individual characteristics such as sex, age, or personality proved to be more closely associated with attitude to religion than those of school or home. It would seem that one of the important findings of Kay's extensive study is the insight it provides into the great variations that exist between different religious cultures; the responses even of the Catholic children differ significantly between church schools in England, Northern Ireland, and the Irish Republic, and this can only be due to the result of the perception of religion as found in the different societies at large.

Further confirmation of adolescent religious apathy disclosed by much of this research is to be found in the popularity of the subject. Francis (1979c) referred to a number of studies of this over a long period of time, all of which showed that religious education was usually held in low esteem by pupils. Its popularity as a subject for public examinations is also an indicator. Keys and Ormerod (1976) found that it occupied a low place in pupils' esteem, boys ranking it last of all subjects, at fifteenth, and girls at twelfth. They also found that subject choice by examination candidates was complex and involved the perceived easiness of the subject as well as liking for the teacher. Religious education was regarded as relatively easy, ranked fourth by boys and fifth by girls. Roke (1985) made a study of examination subject options in three schools and found that only in the single-sex girls school was religious studies an option, and then with a smaller entry and a lower rating as to its relative subject value. The preference recorded for religious studies in the statistics of public examinations, which are available over many years, shows that the subject is well down in the order of popularity; its rank was fourteenth out of twenty-four in 1989.

While much of this research has recorded a decline in attitude to religion with increasing age, a decline which has become greater with the passing of time, very little attention has been given to means of enhancing attitudes. Many years ago

1. See chapter 14.

an experienced teacher told the author that when groups of older adolescents were able to discuss religious issues at length with recognized exponents of Christianity, they adopted critical stances, whereas when confronted with critics of Christianity, they adopted believing stances. Such an insight received support from Batson (1975); having persuaded a church group of students to affirm their belief in the divinity of Jesus, he produced evidence which denied the resurrection and which identified leading churchmen who had discarded their faith. Some of the students dismissed such evidence, but there was an intensified belief recorded among those who accepted it. This is in line with the well-known study of dissonance by Festinger, Riecken, and Schachter (1956) mentioned in chapter 11.

These studies, ranging over a period of nearly sixty years, using many different tests and sampling techniques, do not bear close comparison but still show some striking agreements, best set out in a tabulated form:

FACTORS RELATED TO RELIGIOUSNESS

		Gender	Age	I.Q.	Moral Devt.	Church	Parent	School	Social Class	Sample Size	No. Schools
Glassey	1943	Yes	Yes	No			Yes			300	
Moreton	1944						Yes			354	
Forrester	1946	Little					Yes			639	
Bradbury	1947		Yes	No				No		1800	
Daines	1949	Little	No							1090	
Hughes	1953				Yes					367	1
Bowden	1958		Yes								410
Wright	1958						Yes			343	6
Davies	1959	Yes								1090	
Hyde	1959	Yes	Yes	Some		Yes				1977	4
Rixon	1959							Yes		500	4+
Garrity	1960	Yes	Yes	No		Yes				4000	
Patino	1961	Yes	Yes					Yes	Yes	1000	4+
Jones	1962	Yes				Yes			Yes	290	10
Johnson	1966	Yes	Yes			Yes				1440	
Walker	1966	Yes	Yes				Yes			421	5
Kestevem	1967	Yes				Yes		No		100	10
Alves	1968	Yes	Yes					Yes	Yes	1360	60
Antopolous	1968	Yes			Yes			Yes	Yes	335	6
Esawi	1968	Yes	Yes		Yes	Yes		Yes	No	400+	3
Hindley	1970	(Yes)	(Yes)							92	1
Turner	1970		Yes							400	2
Povall	1971	Yes	Yes				No		No	960	12
Atkins	1972	Yes								200	3
Hinchcliffe	1973	Yes								82	3
James	1974	Yes	Yes			Yes	Yes	Yes		341	1
Miller	1977							Yes			
Mark	1979	Yes	Yes	Yes				Yes		2096	2
Francis	1976	Yes	Yes	Yes						900	4
	1979	Yes	Yes	Yes		Yes	Yes	Yes	(Yes)	2272	30
	1984	Yes	Yes	Yes		Yes	Yes	Yes	(Yes)	2388	30
	1986	Yes	Yes	Yes		Yes	Yes	Yes	(Yes)	2295	30
Kay	1981	Yes	Yes	Yes			Yes	Yes	Yes	3116	7

Francis (1979a) briefly reviewed most of these studies of children's attitude toward religion and pointed out cautiously a number of findings which appeared to stand despite the differences in the scales and the approaches of the various authors.

Nearly all the studies showed that the younger children displayed more positive attitudes than older children and girls more positive attitudes than boys. Age brought doubt and a more critical attitude. There was no peak age for conversion. Several studies reported a significant relationship between intelligence and attitude scores, with a few deviations from this finding. Church attendance had a significant relationship with attitude scores, and there was a strong relationship between the attitude scores of children and the religious behavior of their parents. Church attendance, favorable attitudes, and religious understanding went hand in hand. Apathy rather than hostility was frequently reported: there was still a latent interest in religious issues but not in religious institutions. A compassionate attitude was not associated with a positive religious attitude but more strict moral codes were. Regional differences persisted in England but were much more marked among England, Northern Ireland, and Eire.

Some studies have investigated variations in pupils' attitudes and behavior in different schools; there were marked differences between apparently similar schools, between single-sex schools and coeducational schools, between grammar schools and other secondary schools, and between local authority schools and church schools.

Chapter 9

Religious Experience

Religious experience is a term that has been used to describe a variety of affective religious happenings. These include conversion, vocation, penitence, charismatic experiences, glossolalia—speaking with tongues—and much else. It has often been used in psychological studies as the name given to such states as peak experiences or transcendental experiences. They are experiences of wonder, of awareness of an absolute, or of trance states; it is claimed that they have their origins in the experiences of childhood, sexuality, or the expectation of the subject's group. Because these have been the topic of much recent study, the present chapter is mainly concerned with them. In England, research has often been based on the analysis of descriptions of such experiences given sometimes by students or more frequently by adults of all ages. Some of them recall events of childhood or adolescence, and a few come from adolescents themselves. Because they allege that such experiences have occurred at an early age, they are described here, despite their adult origin. Similar studies have been made in America and elsewhere, and experimental work has also been undertaken to investigate something of the external and psychological circumstances which may trigger such states. The chapter concludes by looking at some recent studies of conversion.

Religion begins with religious experience and is sustained by it. It is nourished by liturgy, music, art, and architecture. The significance of scripture is more than cognitive, for it carries also an affective response from believers. When the familiar sounding words of the Bible are replaced in a new translation there is protest at the loss. Otto's *Idea of the Holy*, more than any other work before, offered a guide to the feelings of reverence and awe encountered in worship; the numinous could not be grasped by the senses but was induced by an absolute which fascinated and terrified. Schleiermacher's *Addresses on Religion* laid the ground theologically for claiming, among other things, that feelings were an essential aspect of religion. Yet the psychological study of the affective aspect of religion has often been neglected.

The nature of religious experience

There is a great deal of confusion regarding religious experience. This is at once evident from its definition and its relation to other types of experience. The problem becomes apparent in the vocabulary used to describe it—religious experience, intense religious experience, mystical experience, ecstasy, peak experience, nature experience, transcendental experience. These are terms variously used to denote states which may or may not be psychologically comparable. Some people describe such experiences as profoundly religious, but others describe them as having no religious reference. For many believers, worship lacks the ecstatic element which others sometimes insist is an essential element of religious experience.

What makes an experience religious? Reid (1961) spoke of basic experiences which he regarded as essentially religious, bringing with them a sense of the mystery of being. This interpretation could be religious, but it was not inevitably so. Clark (1964) considered that there must be something unique in the quality of the experience itself that made it religious and that quality was the mystical. Hausner (1973) compared the religious and psychological stances typified by Maslow and Thomas Merton and disputed that peak experiences were religious. Astey (1984) insisted that worship contained elements of mysticism, and its language was not cognitive; "Holy, holy, holy. . ." was not a description of God but an expression of praise. At the heart of worship was a numinous sense of the presence of God. Religious attitudes were learned from such experiences, and the learning of doctrine and the formation of Christian attitudes took place together. Despite these difficulties there appears to be an underlying psychological state common to all of them.

Clarke (1981) set out a philosophical argument that the natural roots of religious experience were common to all men, and Hay (1986a) argued that the different world religions were expressions of a common core of experience and not the social construct of a reality which was derived from a language which expressed it—the more complex the language, the more complex the experience. The common core was subject to cultural interpretation, so that in a Californian study 37 percent of Protestants and only 26 percent of Catholics responded positively to a question about their having had a sense of being saved in Christ. Religious experience (Hay, 1986b) tended to be seen either as numinous, after the account of Otto, or as mystical, following Smart. Features common to the majority of them were that many came in times of great distress, or a minority in times of great gladness; they frequently occurred in loneliness; they brought a sense of intense reality; they carried the perceptual quality of seeing and hearing; and they were of long-term benefit to their subjects. There appeared to be some personality or genetic factor which prevented them from being universal. Robinson (1984) regarded religion as man's response to his experience of the transcendent and defined religious experience as an awareness, however momentary or imperfect, of an order of reality both beyond and yet capable of permeating the rest of life. Recent research had emphasized that the capacity for such experiences was universal, although often weakened by social or psychological factors, but having its full flowering only within a community, not in isolation, nor sought as an end in itself. Stark (1965) sought to find an adequate definition of religious experience, limiting it to a sense of contact with a supernatural agency. An analysis of replies to a questionnaire led him to suggest four main types of experience, either divine or diabolic, which were confirming the specific awareness of a presence; responsive to the presence; ecstatic by contact with the presence; and revelational, becoming a confidant of that presence.

Another classification of religious experience was made by Margolis and Elfinson (1979) on the grounds that previous attempts had introduced a bias by the use of structured questions. Analysis of responses to an open-ended interview identified four types: transcendental experiences, including a sense of relatedness to God; temporary disorientations which they called vertigo experiences; life change experiences, a sense of unity marking the beginning of a change of life; and visionary experiences perceived as a genuine contact with a divine presence. This was claimed to be an accurate representation of the characteristics of a religious experience and confirmed the multidimensionality of religious experiences.

Fahs (1950) gave many illustrations of the momentary wonder common among young children which provided a basis for reverence and could lead to communion with God. Smith (1985) argued in both psychoanalytic and theological terms that in infancy children began to experience the existence of a transcendental reality; its image was confirmed or altered by their mother. It was the development of faith at this early stage which led later to a religious development of the committed, intrinsic style.

Clark (1968), following William James' assertion that personal religious experience arose from mystical states of consciousness, regarded such states as different from any other but validated by the profound changes of personality which followed them. He contended that psychedelic drugs could induce mystical states, citing instances of their use with alcoholics and criminals with positive consequences. Overall (1982) argued that mystical experience was like the exercise of a special skill, such as art, and different people had differing degrees of skill in it. Kristo (1982) considered that, despite Stace's (1960) characterization of it, mystical experience was still interpreted with much diversity regarding its ultimate significance. He argued that as a human experience, its interpretation depended on the social context of its subjects, and it represented a growth in certainty that what men lived by was indeed true, so that it was more a knowledge of certainty about oneself. It was the beginning of a new story the mystic wanted to live.

Surveying the incidence of ecstasy, Ennis (1967) noted the lack of any study linking it with everyday life, despite the fact that it could become an agent for social change. But Robertson (1975), in a long discussion of aspects of mysticism from a Weberian point of view, concluded that it was of no sociological significance.

Trance states are associated with some forms of religious experience. Winkelman (1986) described them in terms of brain activity, characterized by a type of slow wave ECG activity which imposed a synchronous pattern on the frontal lobes. These trance states could be induced by many means, including fasting, isolation, sensory deprivation, meditation, sleep, dream states, extensive motor behavior, drug and alcohol use. They could be associated with magic or religious practice.

Munkachy (1974) described peak experiences as a generalization for the best and happiest moments of human life and for experiences of ecstasy, rapture, bliss, and of the greatest joy. Clippinger (1973) suggested that peak experience was the realization that what ought to be, is. All people had such experiences, but many found it difficult to admit. They did not take place in some remote realm called the sacred, but in daily life, with friends or family, where the sacred was apprehended. He did not regard the withdrawal from institutional religion by the young as being withdrawal from the ideals of love and brotherhood, and he gave an account of the uninhibited worship of an impoverished rural community in which the worshipers found a sense of reassurance and joy.

Dittes (1969) observed that intense religious experience was often associated with a reduction of normal patterns of judgment, perception, and control of behavior, as was the case with mystical experience, trance-like experiences, glossolalia, and sudden conversion. These states had their parallels in hypnosis, hysteria, and psychoses and could be induced by drugs or by sensory deprivation. Individuals undergoing them were particularly open to the suggestions and expectations of the social group in which they took place, and they were more likely to occur among people with weak egos—those who depend on others, had inner conflicts, were low in self-esteem, subject to guilt, or showed some deficiency in identity. Johnson (1984) argued that intense religious experience was a creative and revelatory event depending on the psychological resolution of inner conflicts and stresses. Depending on its interpretation and the response to it, it could result in a transformation of the symbolic representation of God. Such a transformation process should be seen as fundamental for Christian nurture. Vergote (1964) saw religious experience as immediate contact with the divine; a sense of the divine in nature was remote from city life but was related to the individual's religious background and culture; in the world of today, nature had been secularized. Liege (1968) distinguished theologically four kinds of religious needs—a need for security from a divine if impersonal transcendence; a fear of sacredness experienced in the presence of the divine; an obligation to pay homage to the divine, without any emphasis on benefits to be obtained; and a need for union and mystical aspirations. Loder (1981) regarded the essence of religious experience not merely as affective or ecstatic, although these might have some place in it, but as convictional knowing, which produced a fundamental Christocentric transformation of the ego arising from its interpretation of some highly significant event. Such transformations, of which the conversion of Paul was characteristic, were illustrated from his personal experience and from those whom he had counseled and were analyzed in terms of analytic psychology. In common with recent existential philosophy, there is an emphasis on "the void"—known by absence, loss, shame, guilt, hatred, loneliness, and death—which is transformed by the holy.

Martin (1972) regarded aesthetic experience as religious experience, with no dichotomy between the sacred and the profane. Aesthetic experience was life enhancing because it perceived the depth of reality in forms least reducible to the categories and functions of being. Muyskens (1982) also was interested in a possible relationship between religious belief and aesthetic preferences in the visual arts and found in a student group that there was an association between religious belief and a preference for realistic rather than impressionist or abstract paintings. Daines (1949) also found a relationship between pupils' attitude to religion and their interest in art and poetry. But Borowitz (1980), in his discussion of the concept of spirituality in Judaism, regarded aesthetic experience as limited since it did not provide any ground of values; spirituality had to be sought in worship, observances, and a traditional way of life, and even so genuine spiritual experiences were sporadic, often unexpected. Beit-Hallahmi (1986) considered that religion could be understood as a form of art that interpreted reality and expressed both individual and group identity. To regard religion as an art form was an advance in developing a psychology of religion which helped the understanding of the basic processes, functions, and consequences of religion.

Some deny any religious interpretation of such experiences. Melchert (1977) was skeptical about the claims of mystical experience, contending that their value could be understood and their occurrence explained in terms of physical realism. Bourque (1969) found in adults that ecstatic or transcendental types of experience were to be observed in both religious and secular conditions and that the differences were not so much qualitative in nature but rather a product of the subject's environment. From an archeological perspective Hayden (1987) contended that in times of scarce resources, alliances between groups were needed for survival. They depended on emotional bonds between different groups, generated through ecstatic states induced by rituals, which led to the transcendental concepts shared by all religions. From the earliest times, the core of religious experience was ecstatic. Knowles (1975) noted how much fear and anxiety were emphasized in the literature about mystical experience and showed how their symbols and phantasms could be related to the psychology of Jung. Rosolato (1980) traced the history of mysticism and the lack of interest in it among French psychologists and concluded that it showed that humans had an extraordinary propensity to construct myths and ideals to overcome anxiety about the unknown. However, Douglas-Smith (1971) demonstrated that genuine mysticism was unrelated to neurotic or psychotic states and did not arise from suggestibility, hysteria, pathological lying, paranoia, or other such aberrations but stood in its own right. Meissner (1984), from a psychoanalytic stance, commented that psychologically, mystical states could be regarded as embodiments of the highest, most differentiated, and integrated attainment of any religious capacity or, alternatively, as regressive phenomena arising from a fixation at infantile levels of development. He argued for a new examination of how human subjectivity was treated in psychological approaches to religion. There were three levels of understanding: things were first understood as facts, next as representations, and then by constructing experience by means of a concept of the transcendent. It was the construction of both our relationships and our world in reference to a conceptualization of alternative possibilities. When we attempted to measure religious experiences solely by the level of formal operational thinking we might well be depending on our own cultural assumptions. We had to reformulate our fundamental concepts, models, and methods in a way which represented a less rigid view of reality in order to reach a genuinely postconventional level of research relevant to all cultures.

Straus (1981) looked for a naturalistic explanation of religious experience. It was important to distinguish between the experience and its interpretation. Interpretation was affected by the culture, situation, and previous history of the subjects. Ideas met frequently in their childhood gave rise to the symbols by which they subsequently interpreted and organized their life. Vocabulary had a very symbolic affect. They came to accept a point of view which depended on their background culture, and then they assumed the perspectives and enacted the roles considered desirable in their group. In this way conceptual interpretation was affected by the way they interpreted life. This gave them a social context with suggestions affecting their programing of a religious experience, and provided its triggering. It was most likely to occur when they interpreted life with religious symbolism and were at the time under some degree of stress or crisis. When normal consciousness was disrupted it brought a reliance on the interpretation of the group. The group recognized that such an experience was plausible and personally desirable, and they had guides to facilitate a response to the ecstatic event. This readiness allowed for triggering to happen, but while triggering was usually embedded in a social group, its mechanism was not fully understood. Individuals could have different religious experiences at different times in their lives, and when their social contexts had changed the experiences themselves could differ in their interpretations. It followed that while an individual might seem to experience an absolute reality transcending the material world, that experience was intimately related to much of the context and history of the subject. Franks Davis (1986) argued against such points of view. There were two basic criticisms that had been advanced; the reductionist regarded such experiences as religious only when they were given a religious interpretation while other critics complained that subjects could give no consistent account of them. Against this, he contended that there was a cumulative argument in favor of their religious interpretation, and the intrinsically religious experience of a holy presence was good evidence for a broad theistic hypothesis.

Yinger (1970) regarded religious experience as a response to what was seen as ultimate reality; it ranged from the reaffirmation coming from performing an accustomed rite to the loss or the heightening of self in a trance or ecstasy. He approved Stark's (1965) taxonomy and thought that the most common and most neglected experiences were those affirming contemporary religious views. Going to church was a religious experience, possibly of a low level of intensity. Hearing the story of the Prodigal Son or attending a revival meeting could renew and confirm again a former faith. People might relate to the social order by withdrawing from it in pietism or attacking it by prophecy, whereas mysticism accepted it. He proposed a ninefold classification of experience; it could be oriented to the past by revival, to the present by affirmation, or to the future by conversion; its attitude to the social order could be of escape through pietism, of acceptance in mysticism, or of opposition through prophecy. The intensity of the experience could be low, when it was confirming; it could be medium, when it was responsive; or it could be high, when it was ecstatic. On the basis of this analysis he could evaluate different types of religious experience.

Godin (1985) provided a valuable psychological analysis of religious experience written from the point of view of European Catholicism. He placed religious experience in a wider context which included sudden conversion and what he called the fusional joy of the pentecostal and charismatic groups(described by Harrison, 1974), which he valued rather than deprecated. A fourth type of experience arose from the excitement of conflict and was most evident in the sociopolitical religious groups of Latin America. In this context he discussed the application of liberation theology to social and political ends and the excitement of a messianic conflict in fighting for justice. The final thrust of his argument looked at psychological aspects of normal Christian experience and the eucharist. Holm (1982) also included detailed accounts of such experiences as trance, ecstasy, or glossolalia in his account of religious experience.

Pearce (1979) related aspects of emotion to Bloom's taxonomy to suggest teaching procedures about the emotions of religion, religious experience, ecstasy, and peak experience, with a bibliography of source material for teaching. Minney and Potter (1984) looked at the educational aspects of religious experience from both a philosophical and a teaching stance, including in their pamphlet a valuable account of such work with secondary school pupils and some of their responses to it.

American studies of religious experience

The contrast in ethos between American and English studies of religious experience is another result of their research perspectives; many American studies are oriented toward the psychology of religion, whereas the English studies often have an educational background.

Lukoff and Lu (1988) discussed the problems of research into mystical experience in their review of its methods and results and the relationship between the findings of qualitative and quantitative studies.

An early study of religious experience was carried out by the Elkinds (1963), who analyzed responses by young adolescents to questions about feeling close to God. The six situations most frequently cited were in church or synagogue, times of solitude, anxiety, worry, prayer, and of moral action. Five types of experience were recorded—appreciation of divine intervention, meditation bringing a heightened awareness, grief over bereavement, religious initiation, and revelation experiences of direct communication. Girls displayed more experiences than boys, although the boys reported more church experience. The most intelligent, who conceived the deity in broader terms and were less conformist, were most likely to feel close to God in solitude. Little reference was made to prayer; since at a later age this was important to students, it appeared that growing maturity brought some change. Although traditional forms of religiousness were resisted, the group regarded religious experience as a significant part of their lives.

There are some accounts of experiences of elation or ecstasy in early childhood recalled in adult life by those who underwent them. Ranwez (1964) described the accounts of these given by a number of authors; it was difficult to discern what at the time was a child's authentic religious experience, rather than a colored account of it given later in life. Darcy-Berube (1974) contended that there was a capacity for religious experience in young children and an intuitive acceptance of God's revelation; by identification with significant adults they became sensitive to God's presence, and in this process the family was of importance. Luber (1986) studied peak experiences recounted by children of five to sixteen. Out of 432 incidents, only thirteen were genuine peak experiences; most were of pride and happiness, and some older children recounted themes of identity. When Farmer (1988) interviewed adults about the religious experiences of their early childhood, many complained that their validity had been denied by their education. Involvement in imaginative activies was the primary means of their interpretation. An early spiritual awareness was the beginning of a lifelong development, and developmental models should recognize this.

Breed and Fagan (1972) found that undergraduates without strong orthodox belief were more likely to have had some form of peak experience than those with a moderate or strong belief. Munkachy (1974) described peak experiences in terms of the best and happiest moments of life for experiences of ecstasy, rapture, bliss and joy. He used a questionnaire to investigate the extent of their occurrence among students. Two-thirds of the students he questioned remembered having such experiences before they were seventeen, and of these a half were between the age of six and eleven at the time. Students at traditional schools, colleges, and adult schools had fewer such experiences than those in alternative educational settings. Gilkey (1977) considered peak experiences as a break in normal consciousness allowing other modes of awareness. This was a form of adaptive regression, a temporary lifting of the ego control and a basis for artistic activity. Because of this, they should thus be related to creativity, and he demonstrated it by his studies of the peak experiences of forty university students, although it emerged that peak experiences were not associated with scores on a test for the imaginative use of words. McCready and Greeley (1976) found much that bore upon mystical experience between people of different types of ultimate values and between different denominations; they tended to be over age forty, male, college-educated, not poor, black, Protestant, with a childhood in a supportive, religious, and joyful family. Such experiences were far more common than had been generally realized.

Goodman et al. (1974) described three different anthropological studies of possession-trance in St Vincents in the Caribbean, Brazil, and Mexico in which more extreme behavior was associated with religious experience. The Mexican group had learned trance behavior and used it to combat severe stress in a healthy process of adaptive behavior; on St Vincent's lower-class shakers engaged in a ritual of rebellion, finding a spiritual status to compensate for their economic situation.

Mathes (1982) found with 125 undergraduates that the tendency to have a mystical experience was associated with romantic love and hypnotic susceptibility, which he regarded as indicating an ability to suspend contact with objective reality. Subsequently Mathes, Zevon, Michael, Roter, and Joerger (1982) developed a scale to measure peak experiences and used it in five separate undergraduate studies. Those who had peak experiences were also likely to report experiences involving intense happiness and even more, "cognitive experiences of a transcendental and mystical nature." Peak experiences were thus shown to be primarily transcendent and mystical cognitive events.

With the growing use of psychedelic drugs to stimulate visionary experiences, Havens (1963) contended that these were often described in religious terms by subjects who were not believers, although their greatest religious effect was on those who were prepared for a spiritual encounter. He found evidence of the formation of redemptive groups based on drug mediated transcendental experiences.

A long-term study was started by Hood (1970), who noted an upsurge of interest in the various forms of altered consciousness and suggested that these were common among people who did not use religious language to describe them. He (Hood, 1971, 1972) produced empirical data supporting the theory that intrinsically oriented people would derive special experienced meanings from religion denied to extrinsically oriented contemporaries. His test for religious experience was a questionnaire, the Religious Experience Episodes Measure, derived from descriptions in James' *The Varieties of Religious Experience*; his tests were mainly with groups of students. He also interviewed (Hood 1973a) two contrasted groups of intrinsic or extrinsic students and confirmed the result, using five criteria of personal experience based on Stace (1960): ego, noetic (i.e. purely intellectual), communicable, affective, and religious qualities.

He established (Hood, 1973b) that high scores on his REEM scale were associated with hypnotic susceptibility, implying that such experiences were due in part to suggestibility and then (Hood, 1973c, 1974) considered the psychoanalytic view that an "oceanic feeling" which many regarded as the basis of a religious mystical experience was a characteristic of a primary ego state that was only later associated with religion. First tests were inconclusive, but since the test of ego-strength used contained some religious items, in a further study, using a test of psychological adequacy devoid of religious items, the REEM scores of a high psychological strength group were significantly larger than those of a low psychological strength group, indicating the need to use tests free from religious dimensions. With such a test there were grounds for believing that states of intense experience were a source of psychological strength; only a strong ego could be relinquished nonpathologically and was likely to be associated with mystical, peak, or ecstatic experiences. His finding conflicts with Dittes' (1969) observation that they were likely to be associated with people with weak egos.

This was followed by the construction of a test of mystical experience (Hood, 1975) based on Stace's (1960) analysis. Analysis of its use with a large group indicated a first factor of intense experience, not necessarily religious, and a second factor of religious interpretation, regarded as an expression of traditional religious experience which might or might not be mystical. Intrinsically religious subjects scored more highly on this new M scale; they were more open to experience, ego permissiveness being related to the psychoanalytic notion of regression in the service of the ego. Such openness was indicated by belief in the supernatural, ecstatic emotion, and alternations of consciousness. The results demonstrated that empirical research on mystical experience was possible, which should be studied in the same way as other human experiences. Further use of this scale with undergraduates (Hood, 1976) showed effects due to denomination, church attendance, and decisions to change, abandon, or accept church membership. Those with no denominational allegiance scored highest on both factors, with frequent church attenders next. It appeared that those who were moving into or between the churches, but not out of them, were most likely to report some form of mystical experience; that is, it was associated with dissatisfaction with a particular church membership. (It could also be related to the novelty of a new situation!) In a mainly Southern Baptist group, students who were intrinsically or indiscriminately favorably oriented were more likely to interpret their experiences during prayer in relevant religious terms than the others (Hood, Morris, and Watson, 1987). Caird (1988), in a factor-analytic study of Hood's mysticism scale, found a unifying and an interpretive factor; the latter, on further analysis, yielded noetic and religious factors.

Next Hood (1977a, 1977b) found that persons of relatively high self-actualization were more likely to have mystical experiences triggered by drugs, whereas those of lower self-actualization were more likely to have them triggered in religious or nature settings. This culminated in a practical experiment over several days (Hood, 1978b) in which older male high-school students were sent in solitude into woodland conditions for a day and a night. Beforehand, after explanation of what to expect, their expectation of a mystical experience was measured. Stressful conditions caused by bad weather and heavy rain affected some groups. Subsequent testing using Rosengrant's (1976) adaptation of Hood's REEM test, showed that when there was incongruity between the expectation and the actual setting encountered mystical experience was heightened, although setting stress itself had no significant effect. No explanation for this result could be offered, but it did suggest a nonpathological orientation to mystical experience. This experiment might be compared with another of the same period. Smith (1977) examined the effects on religious orientation of different religious activities in a group attending a three-day retreat, a group who accepted an eight-week daily prayer schedule, and a control group. Those attending the retreat became significantly more intrinsic, maintaining the change over a two-month period, but only slight changes were found in the other two groups. Men changed more than women, but there were no subjects who made a significant change in the image of God. It appeared that the differences observed between the men and the women were related to differences in their religious socialization.

Hood, Hall, Watson, and Biderman (1977) investigated cultural differences affecting the incidence of intense religious experience by comparing four matched samples; in the American Indian and the Mexican samples the incidence was significantly higher than in the Caucasian and Mexican-American samples. Conditions under which intense experiences, aesthetic, religious, or mystical could be triggered and evaluated were studied further (Hood, 1980), using drugs, prayer, or no trigger. The social legitimacy of the trigger was found to be a factor which affected the evaluation of the experiences and of their trigger. Dogmatism, which was strongly associated with social acquiescence, operated in the reverse direction. Social acquiescence generally was associated with a positive evaluation; when it was held constant, dogmatism tended to be associated with a negative evaluation.

Because mystical experiences are at times described with erotic language, Hood and Hall (1980) compared the language used by men and by women to describe mystical and erotic experiences. Women described both using receptive language, but men used agentive language to describe the erotic but not the mystical. This result was seen to be related to the known difficulty of males to experience union, agentively expressed, with a masculine conceptualized image of God. Lewis (1974), in an analysis of the ecstatic experiences of students, had found that the common trigger events included not only natural scenery but heterosexual interaction and orgasm. De Neuter (1972) had investigated the nature of religious experience, studying aspects of it among a group of students. It was evident that a relationship with God could be described in sexual terms, but these took many forms and there was a marked contrast between the accounts of students with high levels of belief and those with low levels.

Further studies continued in association with other colleagues. Hood, Hall, Watson, and Biderman (1979) showed that undergraduates reporting mystical experiences showed stable personalities, but it was necessary to use a personality inventory that was not pathologically oriented for this to be evident. Morris and Hood (1980) found religious membership did not affect the incidence of mystical experience, but a Baptist group gave it a more religious interpretation. All who reported it described it in religious terms. Hood and Morris (1981a) found in a group of mystical, nonmystical, and uncertain students experience but not knowledge was associated with the outcome, demonstrating the strongly affective nature of mystical experiences. Undergoing sensory deprivation (Hood and Morris, 1981b) intrinsic and extrinsic subjects displayed significantly different outcomes for the effects of religious imagery but showed no different reaction to other images.

Thomas and Cooper (1978) examined the types and incidence of religious experiences among respondents aged from seventeen to twenty-nine. About a third responded positively to a question about the feeling of being close to a powerful spiritual force—a result similar to Greeley's (1974) and confirmed by a recent Gallup poll (Gallup and Jones, 1989). Further analysis showed that only 2 percent of the whole sample had undergone a classical mystical experience; 12 percent had an experience of faith and consolation devoid of the extraordinary, and 12 percent described a psychic experience involving extrasensory perception, telepathy, or other such events. This convinced the authors of the need of careful attention to the content of reported experiences; the descriptions encountered were very similar to the classifications of Stace (1960) and Hood (1975). Subsequently (Thomas and Cooper, 1980), they recorded that among college, civic, and religious groups, 34 percent reported some degree of mystical or spiritual experiences; when these were related to personality scales it was found that such experiences tended to be reported by those more open to new experiences and less intolerant of ambiguous statements. There was no indication that such experiences gave rise to any permanent personality changes.

Glock and Wuthno (1979), surveying religious beliefs in San Francisco, asked if respondents had ever had the feeling that they were in close contact with something holy or sacred. Fifty-two percent of adolescents and 49 percent of adults said they had not, half of these saying that they would like to have such an experience. Of those reporting an experience many said it had produced a lasting influence on their lives. A large proportion reported having experienced the beauty of nature in a deeply moving way, but only a third reported having had the feeling that they were in harmony with the universe. The results suggested that people may be coming to regard conventional religion with skepticism or apathy; there was no suggestion that religious sentiments were dying out; they remained pervasive although taking different forms. The experiential component of conventional religion had been subordinate for a long time, but its status could be starting to change, and a sign that it was doing so was the emergence of the Catholic charismatic renewal. Thomas, Cooper, and Suscovich (1982) questioned a group of subjects from seventeen upwards. 34 percent reported an intense spiritual experience and 28 percent had undergone a "near-death" experience, unaffected by age, with fewer older than younger subjects. There was a significant association between the two types of experience. Currie, Klug, and McCombs (1980) found some support for Stark and Glock's (1968) taxonomy but suggested that the saliency of an experience should be based on the number of experiences reported rather than on their meaning. The explanation of an experience was not to be found in its set but rather in the cumulative effect of having a series of minor experiences.

Moehle (1983) used a multidimensional scaling technique with groups of students and adults, first to secure their definition and account of religious experience and then to sort and classify each others' accounts, eliminating the experimenter effects due to providing limiting definitions in a test. Almost three-quarters of all subjects reported such experiences, a high proportion which she regarded as due to the openness of definition permitted. There were four major factors in the students' responses and three in those of the adults. The two held in common were a spiritual-temporal dimension related to the extent to which the experience involved other people who shared in it. Students also displayed a factor related to experiences of awe, or natural beauty, music, or art forms, and a factor related to the extent that the experience was perceived as religious, or bringing salvation, commitment, or rededication and a social-interactive dimension related to whether the experience was a single event or a continuous or long-term event. Adults did not show these two factors.

Hoge and Smith (1982) distinguished between normative religious experiences, such as sudden conversion or a gradual awakening to religious commitment, which were expected and encouraged by Protestant churches, and nonnormative experiences, due to personal psychological factors affected by a range of interpersonal relationships, following Stark (1965). They tested a representative sample of adolescents aged sixteen from Catholic, Baptist, and Methodist churches. Fifty-eight percent recorded many types of experiences which were best categorized by the Elkinds' (1963) classification with an added category called salvation or inspiration; this was the most frequent, especially among the Protestants. Few in the sample spoke of ecstatic or revelatory experiences. Both normative and nonnormative experiences were found, with the salvation-inspiration experience seen as normative for adolescents in the Protestant churches. In the sample, this type of experience, more frequent among girls, occurred disproportionately at eleven or twelve, possibly due to the churches programing for it, whereas the nonnormative experiences were diverse and varied and could not be associated with particular styles of church involvement or personal relationships. It was more frequent among Catholic adolescents. Nonnormative experiences were idiosyncratic and unpatterned. In no case was cognitive ability associated with religious experience, nor was family influence very predictive of it.

British studies of religious experience

British psychological studies of religious experience have almost entirely been concerned with students and the adult population. They began with the first report of Paffard's (1970) study and quite independently with the widely advertised requests for accounts of a certain type of religious experience by Hardy (1970), who regarded them as being fundamental to human nature (Hardy, 1975). He considered the need for contact with a power thought to be sacred arose from the evolutionary process; submission to God was similar to submissive animal behavior apart from human conscience, which was due to social tradition. He stressed the solitary aspect of religion, in which awe and fascination gave rise to emotions which were not natural. Stevens (1986) also regarded religious belief and ritual as encoded in the genetic structure, and he suggested that this did not explain away religious insights into the essential oneness of all experience but rather corroborated them.

Beardsworth (1977) undertook an analytical description of the first 1,000 responses to Hardy's request. Many of them were visual, with accounts of visions, illumination, or transformation of surroundings, a feeling of unity with the surroundings or "out of body" experiences. Some were auditory, with comforting or guiding voices; some involved inward sensations, and many concerned a sense of presence. Some descriptions were in orthodox religious terms but by no means all. One description was in terms of Buddhist meditation, another as psychic; for one agnostic it was nevertheless a "real" experience. One recognized the experience as signaling the recurrence of mental illness; another described the results of using drugs. Only one individual cited an experience of childhood. The similarity of affective and cognitive states was examined, the duration and after-effects of the experience, with considerable similarities found between comparable groups. Common to many was the sense of a presence, not necessarily divine, experienced in an individual, highly personal manner which gave rise to a strong emotional response of warmth, comfort, support, or of shame or terror, causing the respondents to relax, uncoil, expand, or blush, tremble, or sink to their knees. The experience was not of sensation but of a meeting; someone was seen, heard, touched, or felt to be present. Strong emotion tended to color the experience and the situation leading up to it, with often a strong reversal of feeling from depth of despair to unbounded joy.

Gates (1976), in planning the interviews described in chapter 1, held the possibility of detecting "signals of transcendence" within the secular expression of children. From time to time children spoke specifically of their own religious experiences, and there was ample evidence that religion came to them in many different guises, in explicit institutional terms, from family attitudes, beliefs, and degrees of religious belonging and from formal teaching in religious communities or schools. It also came from friends and relatives, from the neighborhood, and the media. More implicitly, it could also be provoked by personal reflection in any context in which children were quite simply aware of being. Religion thus was part of every child's experience even before beginning school, as they endeavored to make sense of what they found in the world. All of them, even the youngest, were engaged in constructing their individual loyalties and beliefs. Beliefs mattered to them and were being formed into a distinctly personal equation.

Paffard (1970, 1973) recalled his earlier experiences of almost painful intensity, which suddenly took him into another dimension; these rare moments, familiar to Wordsworth, associated with the idea of beauty and the divine, he called "transcendental." C. S. Lewis's *Surprised by Joy* and A. L. Rowse's *A Cornish Childhood* both described somewhat similar experiences, but while they led Lewis into religious belief, Rowse, finding that his churchmanship had nothing in common with such moments of ecstasy, regretfully rejected his belief. Believing that such experiences were widespread, Paffard sought the help of senior pupils and undergraduates with a questionnaire. More than half reported some kind of experience, girls and women more than boys and men, undergraduates more than sixth-form students. (Wright (1962) had found one in five professed to have had an experience of "the presence of God.") About three-quarters of them practiced a religion. Nearly all those reporting transcendental experiences had attempted some creative art, compared with little more than half of the others, and were more interested in reading poetry. A great variety of experiences were recorded, many of them reproduced and discussed. Most had occurred in adolescence, especially between twelve and seventeen. They were associated with the feelings of (in descending order) the awesome, serene, lonely, frightening, mysterious, exciting, joyful, ecstatic, melancholy, sacred, sad, joyful, and sensual. They were more commonly associated with solitude, with evening or night, and with being outdoors in the country. Among the arts, music had a considerable predominance in inducing such experiences. A great deal of what had been written could be placed under one of ten headings, or a combination of two of them—awe, joy, fear, enhancement, calm, trance, pleasure, melancholy, longing, and pain. He concluded that a person calls his experience religious or aesthetic or describes it in some other way according to his basic beliefs. Dundas-Grant (1975) discussed Paffard's work, claiming that it was easy for the believer to say that in these moments God was revealing something of his nature directly to someone ready to listen. To some, such experiences were to lead to a full experience of Christian faith, but for others they seemed to indicate something far greater than the religion presented to them in church, chapel, or school.

Robinson (1977a) sent a questionnaire to many of Hardy's respondents who had mentioned some childhood experience, asking for greater detail. The respondents covered a wide age range, with nearly a third of them over sixty. Unlike Ranwez (1964), he did not regard the recollection of distant childhood experiences as being colored or modified with the passing of time as a serious criticism of the reliability of the material. Rather, he judged his respondents to be people in whom the original vision of childhood had never wholly faded. He took issue with Goldman's statement that religious insight (a cognitive activity) generally began to appear between twelve and thirteen, contrasting it with statements about the profound experiences of very young children (which were affective), and contended that Piaget denigrated children who failed to achieve adult norms and obscured the power of their memories to retain significance in later life. In a later discussion (Robinson, 1977b) he argued that the recollections of childhood experiences were of great reality to their subjects, making the point that if it was difficult to distinguish what was actually experienced from what a lifetime's reflection had drawn from it, this did not detract from the power and authenticity of the original impulse, but rather confirmed it as a perception of reality which had stood the test of time.

Some descriptions were designated nature mysticism, others a recovery of sensed truths once known and long forgotten. Parental influences were prominent for many but for others entirely lacking, for one the idea of a loving father in contrast to known, unloving fathers grew to become God before the age of seven. Some recalled words used in church and its rituals as a great stimulus; for others, they were dull, to be endured as a duty, and ultimately to be rejected. A sense of identity was the hallmark of experience in some cases, or a sense of timelessness. An awareness of death proved to be momentous for some; with others it was a sense of morality and rightness. For some these experiences were obviously intense but not for all; peak experiences were extreme instances of a capacity that is normally much more ordinary.

As in Paffard's accounts, there is a great deal that is not specifically religious. Paffard regarded the description as reflecting the individual's basic beliefs, so that the emotional state existed in its own right, but Robinson asserted that every childhood feeling of wonder, joy, or awe was an insight into a transcendental dimension which could develop into an articulated religious experience. Earlier, Robinson (1971) had given citations from the Religious Experience Research Unit file, favorable, neutral, and hostile to traditional religion, arguing that although there might be doubt about the place of spiritual experiences as part of the educational process, unless children were taught to recognize such experiences in others, and even more to cope with them in themselves, little would have been accomplished. This educational objective he elaborated (Robinson, 1975) in a discussion about the importance of myths, legends, and sagas learned in childhood, suggesting means to stimulate the imagination of children so that they gained valuable insights from their spontaneous moments of wonder.

Subsequently, Robinson (1982) contended that learning to understand life spiritually started with nourishing the imaginative life, more particularly guiding the imagination into creative forms of activity. While it was not religious, it could be moved to ask questions which later could be recognized as religious. Scholarship and theology were needed to keep Christian tradition alive, but they did not necessarily make any demands on the imagination at all. With these issues in mind he set out (Robinson and Jackson, 1987) to use a questionnaire technique to ascertain the extent to which adolescent religiousness was associated with a creative imagination. Scales were developed to measure explicit and implicit religion, numinous and mystical experience, religious practice, artistic activities, social service, skepticism, the (materialistic) good life, and alternative lifestyles. No attempt was made to relate these scales to other similar instruments, such as comparing numinous and mystical experience with Hood's REEM and M scales. The questionnaire was very widely used, but since more than half of the respondents professed to go to church often (how often is not stated) the sample appears to be unrepresentative.

An extended analysis of responses showed girls scored higher than boys, and fewer were disillusioned with education. In rural areas there was a greater sense of community, less materialism, and less questioning of traditional values. The group who had found school religious education helpful were not less skeptical than the remainder and indicated less implicit religion and mystical experience than those preferring English or Art, which suggested that they were pious and conventional. The theistic numinous experience was associated with religious activity; its relationship with the broader mystical experience was complex, since the latter was unrelated to religious activity. Those with numinous experience tended also to have mystical experience, but the converse was not true. Evidence was found to suggest that the experiential element in religion was related to arts which stimulated the imagination. Scientific interest, which also did this, did not lead to a growth in religious awareness, but active involvement in social responsibility programs did. Those who participated in religious activities tended to have greater religious awareness and religious experiences, mostly of the theistic type. They tended to be satisfied with the language and beliefs of their church, to be less cynical about morality and less concerned with the materialistic values of the good life. Many of those unresponsive to established forms of religion showed a positive interest in intrinsically religious questions, and nearly four-fifths of the whole sample said they had had an experience which could be described by the authors as mystical.

Doubts about the reliability of recollections of past experiences have been raised by the Swedish study of Pettersson (1975). He developed a procedure whereby personal or imaginary representations of the crucifixion and two artistic portrayals of it were the basis of a study. A comparison made after intervals of between two days and a week demonstrated a marked tendency for past religious experiences—in this case related to the choices about the picture of the crucifixion—to undergo distortion in the direction of what was anticipated and away from what was actual. The time interval, in this case never more than a few days, did not affect the general tendency but only the extent of it.

Following the studies of Paffard and Robinson, Tickner (1981) used a range of evocative material without any specific religious reference to secure oral and written responses from children of six to fourteen and from some of their parents.

These were found to relate to many different circumstances such as family life, school, nature, new experiences or height, and described feelings of contentment, happiness, security, achievement, concern, distress, fear, anxiety, frustration, trauma, and the transcendental or paranormal. In some cases the children appeared to fantasize, identifying themselves with a character in the story given to them, and many experienced difficulties in recounting their experiences. Very few used specifically religious terms in their statements, except when there was an implicit religious reference in the guidelines provided. From the considerable body of material obtained and reproduced many elementary transcendental experiences could be deduced comparable to those of more mature individuals. The accounts indicate the problem of describing an affective experience without an appropriate vocabulary.

Hay (1977) was concerned about religious experience and education, giving a popular summary of his earlier work (Hay, 1979a). Although he chose to follow Smart's six dimensions of religion, it was only to the experiential that he devoted his attention. He argued that the work of the great founders of religion all sprang from profound religious experiences, in which their followers might be expected to participate and concluded that there was a common core to religious experience which knew no religious or cultural boundaries. His research interest was stimulated by asking postgraduate students about their religious experiences and finding some extraordinary accounts among them (Hay, 1979b). Subsequently, (Hay, 1982) he used a National Opinion Poll to pose the question, "Have you ever been aware of or influenced by a presence or power, whether you call it God or not, which is different from your everyday self?" and made (Hay and Morisy, 1985) a survey by direct interview of a random sample. Finally, Hay (1988) reviewed the history of investigations of religious experience. He considered that religious education should give priority to the experiential dimension of religion using aspects of this.

A number of conclusions emerged; of those who attended church with some regularity 56 percent occasionally recorded such experiences; 26 percent of those who never attended church services recorded them, showing that they were not necessarily connected with traditional religious institutions. Forty-one percent of the women and 31 percent of the men in the NOP sample said they had at some time been aware of or influenced by a presence or a power, 18 percent once or twice, 10 percent several times, 6 percent often, 2 percent all the time. There was also an increase with age; 29 percent of those in the sixteen to twenty-four age group responded positively, increasing to 47 percent of those over sixty-five. Since during their lifetime there had been a marked decline in religious observance, older people were more likely to have come across religious ideas and values as children than those born later. Similar studies in the United States, where there was much less decline in church-going, showed little or no link with age. Positive responses were associated with those having a longer education and with those of middle- and upper-middle classes. Regular church-goers most commonly experienced the presence of God, but 90 percent of the reports relating to prayer, premonitions, or a presence not labeled came from those who seldom or never went to church. Examples of contact with the dead came from working-class women with a minimum of education, and working-class people in general reported a range of experiences including witchcraft and the influence of flying saucers, which had little to do with Christianity.

From the Nottingham survey came many descriptions of experiences of the divine, of answered prayer, of an unnamed presence, of the presence of the dead, of nature-mysticism, and of premonitions. A few spoke of conversion experiences, some of fate, some of evil powers. Half lasted for not more than ten minutes, often only a few seconds. Half also occurred when people were distressed or ill at ease. A small group said their experience was more or less continuous. Two-thirds occurred in solitude. Most were left with more positive feelings—peace, restoration, happiness, elation, uplifted, or awestruck. Most regarded it as a religious experience, using the term in a broad way. Three-quarters felt that it had changed their outlook to some degree; those without such feeling usually did not define their experience as religious. Many had not told anyone else about it because of their fear of ridicule. The extent to which religious experience was a feature of childhood was not explored, although some spoke of adolescent experiences. For some of the undergraduates it seemed the experience they described belonged to their adolescence. Educationally it seemed important that children should explore what it meant to be religious rather than simply to be a member of a religious institution.

In a comparison with American studies, Hay and Morrisy (1978) observed that the response (36 percent) in this country fell about the middle of the range of a number of American surveys (20 percent to 50 percent) and was close to that of Greeley (1975). Female predominance was more marked in England; in both countries responses were related to age, social class, and years of education; differences with other findings might be due to differently worded questions. In a further discussion regarding the frequency of numinous experiences, Hay (1983) noted that Jung had used the numinous as an important concept. He had defined these experiences as rare events, but he had described them as frequent; everyone, he had stated, had for much of the time the possibility of being seized by a force deserving the most careful consideration. Since this was not a general experience, Hay considered their absence to be due to the power of religious rituals to control them, holding numinous experiences in check, so that properly performed religious rites rendered them rare, bringing under control the suggestive power of numinous primordial imagery. He did not explain how these rites inhibited the religious experience of the majority who seldom or never take part in them.

Main Mein (1982) used material drawn from Robinson's *Living the Question*, and found little difference between the responses of religious adherents, older pupils, and a group of teachers, lecturers, and workers in the Samaritan organization. She reproduced many descriptions of their transcendental experiences, comparable to those of previous studies. The context of the experiences ranged from natural beauty—the most frequent—to state of mind, religion, relationships, and achievements. The elements of the experiences were predominantly of joy, but also of peace, awe, trance, heightened perception, enlightenment, and some negative elements. Their significance was seen primarily as noetic, as a cherished memory, or as inspiring. Almost a third of the respondents claimed to have had such experiences often or very often, adults more than the students, and the great majority recalled them frequently.

Main Mein regarded this area as important for religious education, not because it offered a proof of religious faith, which it did not, but because it was a common experience in childhood, adolescence, and adult life and could be a step toward the growth of spiritual awareness. However, Greenwood (1984) differed, contending that while some children had experiences of the numinous, the holy, or the transcendent, or experiences of a prophetic or conversion type, it was equally true that many did not, and many adults who considered themselves religious did not have them either. Children's religious experiences could be of four different types; there were peak experiences; the puzzling meaning-of-life type experiences; the advanced experiences of the holy, mystical union, vocation, or conversion; and experiences connected with their inner life and emotions. In a teaching context what was meant by religious experiences were the inescapable experiences which they all had to deal with—fear, loneliness, despair, aggression, anger, boredom, bewilderment, or remorse. Having such experiences did not constitute religion, but there were techniques to deal with them which could be called religious, and she proceeded to suggest methods and materials suitable for such a study by secondary-school pupils.

In Northern Ireland, Greer (1981a,b) asked senior pupils in Protestant schools, "Have you ever had an experience of God—his presence or his help or anything else?" A third of the boys and half the girls replied affirmatively. The largest group were concerned with guidance and help, couched in terms of assurance. The second largest group spoke of God's presence, in terms of a constant awareness rather than of moments of special illumination. A number mentioned prayer as their occasion of experiencing God, prayers about choice of friends, overcoming theft, for parents facing illness, or for a lost dog, all matters of great practical concern. Others referred to a conversion experience in traditional evangelical terms. In a minority of cases there were clear examples of transcendental experiences—when climbing a mountain, at a scenic view, in a church building, or at a service of holy communion. Greer commented that an experience and its interpretation are so closely interwoven as to be virtually inseparable and noted that the claim of many students to have direct experience of God gave support to the theory that religious experience is relatively common. Although more than half were regular church attenders, few had a sense of the church as a building or community mediating the presence of God, rather it was the place where the gospel was proclaimed. This theological framework provided a means of interpreting their experiences. The study is important because it sheds light on a strong evangelical tradition, and it may well be that similar findings would be secured from other evangelical adolescents in Britain or America.

Greer (1982a) made a further study of Catholic and Protestant pupils aged twelve to seventeen in Northern Ireland schools, using the same question. Marked differences between the sexes and the denominations were found. Thirty-five percent Catholic boys reported an experience, 64 percent Catholic girls, 31 percent Protestant boys, and 40 percent Protestant girls. There was little difference between the age groups; the high percentage of Catholic girls was striking. The most frequent experiences were again of guidance and help, followed by experiences of answered prayer, some trivial, others profound. Next, examination stress stimulated prayer and some form of experience of God, and then death, depression, and illness. Apart from God's presence experienced in these categories, others described situations when this sense of presence became very real to them, as in solitude or in the celebration of the sacraments. Other experiences came from dreams, deliverances, or the papal visit. Catholic pupils were more inclined to report religious experiences, consonant with their greater religiousness compared with Protestants; conversion experiences were not found among them. There was no means by which the authenticity of these experiences could be tested, many were related to the normal experiences of adolescence, but that did not necessarily exclude their authenticity.

Miles (1983), after making a comprehensive survey of transcendental experience and mysticism, tested a group of senior secondary-school students who were being taught a course about it. He compared them with an untaught control group, using attitude tests, changes in levels of understanding, mental ability, and student characteristics. Approximately 55 percent of the students reported transcendental experiences; they were more likely to be creative, to spend time alone, to practice religion, and to read poetry for pleasure. Surprisingly, there was no significant difference between the sexes; the students of English working for advanced examinations were more likely than the other students of English to have had transcendental experience. The taught group of students had no greater interest in it at the beginning than the control group. For most who claimed to have had a transcendental experience, it had been in adolescence; only 20 percent had an experience before eleven. About 55 percent reported ten such experiences or fewer and about 75 percent remembered their experiences afterwards. About 55 percent were alone when such experiences occurred; about 60 percent reported they took place in the evening or night; and for about 80 percent they occurred out of doors. They were best described as mysterious, lonely, serene, awesome, exciting, or frightening. The course proved to be a significant factor in developing the students' understanding of the philosophical description of transcendental experience; it did not induce it. No sex difference was recorded, but mental ability was significantly related. Miles finally surveyed eight types of transcendental experience, concluding that while it could simply be a monumental event, for many it had been a means of either personal enrichment or personal transformation and conversions.

European and New Zealand studies

A Swedish study about religious experience in children from nine to thirteen was described by Klinberg (1959). Essays entitled "Once when I thought about God. . ." showed the most common factors producing a religious response were distress at illness, their own or of someone close to them (more for girls than boys), misfortune, and loneliness, especially in the dark or in isolation. Few referred to worship, to nature, or to feelings of guilt. Their experiences were similar to those of adults. Their writing indicated a rich inner life with a strong sense of serenity, security and trust, longing for purity, receiving forgiveness and answers to prayer, a sense of thankfulness, joy and certainty and of the presence of God. A few had experienced a mystical sense of the presence of God. Conversion experiences were described by children belonging to churches emphasizing such experiences; they appeared to be serious, despite the children's limited ability to deal with the emotions that might arise. Some cases of doubt were revealed, possibly due to conflict between anthropomorphic ideas of God and a scientific world-view. A few unusual concepts of God were also disclosed, when ideas of justice, devoid of love and forgiveness, produced an evil image. There was no significant difference between boys and girls.

Holm (1982) set out to replicate the major aspects of Hood's work in Finland and Sweden. He found he needed a major reconstruction of the REEM scale because of linguistic and cultural differences, but the M scale could be used with the omission of two items. He was able to confirm the major findings and noted that the two types of mysticism which the M scale measured appeared to conform very closely to two types of mysticism described intuitively by a Scandinavian scholar—personality mysticism with characteristics of an encounter with a personal God, and "infinity mysticism" characterized by merging into a superterrestrial or eternal principal.

In Finland, Tamminen (1981) secured responses about the sense of God's presence and guidance in various situations from a large group aged seven to twenty. Positive responses came from 90 percent of those between nine and ten but only from 55 percent of those fifteen or sixteen. A sense of God's nearness was associated with situations related to prayer, loneliness, and fear, as well as the emergencies they encountered. Tamminen, Vianello, Jaspard, and Ratcliff (1988) reported Finnish studies of children aged six to eight who described God as being very close to them at times; these experiences were often at evening or at night, when they were alone, but very few had found them through nature. They were also associated with difficult situations—of danger, or being in hospital, or with being forgiven after wrong-doing.

In New Zealand, Holt (1986) made a press appeal for accounts of religious experience; an analysis of the replies and of interviews of six of the respondents disclosed eighty-four elements which were grouped in the themes of light, acknowledgement, being filled, mystery, judgment, love, encounter, death and rebirth, quest, and unity. These themes were related to the psychoanalytic theory of the development of the self, by which religious experiences such as those of goodness, safety, and love recapitulated the experiences of early infancy. They contributed to psychological growth by supporting inner reality and strengthening the self and by deepening the individual's relation to outer reality.

One conclusion from the range of studies reviewed is that the various experiences that have been described are not uniquely religious. They may be found in all human experience, but they can be interpreted as religious by those who have a religious perspective to life. Godin (1985) was clear that intense religious experience is an experience that has been interpreted in a religious manner and inevitably bears the impress of its subject's culture and education, since there is an essential ambiguity about it. In any realm, experience is always gained and interpreted in relation to the individual's attitudes; response to nature will be interpreted as aesthetic or as religious or as both according to the individual's perspectives. Experience gains its meaning from the total philosophy of the subject.

There is some agreement between the various descriptions of the experiences in the accounts given of them. They were mysterious (Miles, Paffard), awesome (Main Mein, Paffard), joyful (Main Mein, Munkachy, Paffard), frightening (Miles, Paffard), calm (Paffard), serene (Miles), of peace (Main Mein), lonely (Miles, Paffard), and exciting (Miles, Paffard). In addition, they were also of enhancement, pleasure, melancholy, sad, longing, pain, ecstasy, sacred, and sensual (Paffard), auditory or visionary (Beardsworth), and of trance, heightened perception, enlightenment, and with negative elements (Main Mein). They were associated with solitude (Elkind, Hay, Paffard), with evening or night, and with being outdoors in the country (Greer, Paffard), in church (Greer) or synagogue, and in times of anxiety, worry, prayer and of moral action (Elkind), and with natural beauty (Beardsworth, Glock and Wuthnow, Hay, Main Mein, Robinson), state of mind, religion, relationships, and achievements (Main Mein). As with mystical experience, they may have sexual overtones (De Neuter, 1972, Hood and Hall, 1980).

Four factor analyses of responses from studies varying in their subjects and contents showed more agreement than might be expected, which suggests that there is a measure of common ground measured in all of them. This is shown by the table opposite:

Conversion

To conclude this chapter, the topic of conversion needs to be considered. Conversion is not restricted to adolescence, but adolescence is frequently the time when some form of religious commitment takes place. Conversion studies have not been restricted to adolescents, but the results point to the processes by which commitment is made. At times, the samples have been biased, for example by including only theological students. Earlier studies were summarized by Beit-Hallahmi and Argyle (1975), and recently by Silverstein (1988). Once prolific, they

FACTORS RELATING TO RELIGIOUS EXPERIENCE

Moehble (1983)	Stark (1965)	Margolis and Elfinson (1979)	Hood (1972)
	specific awareness of a divine or diabolic presence	transcendental, including a sense of relatedness to God	noetic
a factor related to experience of awe, or natural beauty, music or art forms	ecstatic by contact with the divine or diabolic presence	vertigo experience, a temporary disorientation;	affective
	responsive to the divine or diabolic presence	life change sense of unity beginning a change of life	ego
a spiritual-temporal dimension —the extent that it was perceived as religious	revelational, becoming a confidant of that divine or diabolic presence	experiences perceived as a genuine contact with a divine presence	religious
a social-interactive dimension—the extent to which the experience involved others sharing it			communicable
a factor related to whether the experience was a single event or a continuous or long-term event			

now have become fewer. The debate about the age of conversion has been resolved by the recognition that better religious education brought an earlier commitment, and the age of conversion was affected by children's anticipation of being converted in those churches where it is a social expectation. According to the Southern Baptist Convention, many are now converted at nine or ten, which is a time of increased social conformity. There is such variety in religious experience that inevitably a great range of conversion experiences has been recorded, both sudden and gradual. In consequence, it is not surprising that it has proved difficult to make satisfactory psychological theories about it.

More recently psychological models of conversion have been proposed and sociological perspectives explored. Stark and Lofland (1965) suggested a model for conversion made from observations of a millenarian cult; there were four requirements: Converts needed to experience acute tension within a religious problem-solving perspective so that they regarded themselves as religious seekers; they encountered the cult at a turning point in their lives; they formed an affective bond within the cult and relinquished attachments outside it; and if then they were exposed to intensive interaction they became effective members. This was followed by a fuller study (Lofland 1966). However, Snow and Philips (1980) found only limited support for the model when applied to a study of the Nichiren Shashu Buddhist movement for Japanese Americans. Then Lofland and Skonovd (1981) identified six basic motifs for conversion—the intellectual, mystical, experimental, affectional, revivalist, and coercive. They compared their operation under belief participation, the extent of social pressure, the length of time, the level of affective arousal, and affective content. When this model was used some aspects of it did not apply, some functioned in some groups but not in others, and the only two indispensable factors were those whereby the interaction with members of the group resulted in conversion (Greil and Ruddy, 1984). The model led to a conversion theory of rational choice, regarding it as due to the convert's evaluation of the social and cognitive outcomes of converting relative to not converting, and explaining the motives of conversion in terms of social and cognitive rewards and the beliefs accepted by converts as due to participation; their decision depended also on the evaluation of these beliefs by other people they regarded as significant (Gartrell and Shannon, 1985).

Robinson (1979) regarded religious belief as being predominantly cognitive, and accordingly studied the communication process in conversion. Converts with high cognitive complexity reported greater dispositional changes in themselves and an increased likelihood to be influenced by people with whom they were not well acquainted. A prototype conversion would be when a friend or minister lovingly communicated, particularly by example, a message which emphasized God's love and that a new life was possible by conversion. While the communication process in conversion was shown to be related to information processing, the pervasiveness of the conversion experience, especially in affective areas, resulted in a number of inconsistencies. Downton (1980) regarded conversion as a ten-stage process that was started by personal unhappiness, leading to an awareness of religious responses and then to a religious initiation that could be gradual or sudden. The individual was then identified with the new cause and its values, so that further positive experiences led to increased commitment. Rambo (1982) regarded conversion as representing three different psychological mechanisms: those of identification, with a sense of joining oneself to a powerful leader or God; of introjection, by incorporating the attributes of the leader into ones own personality, and of displacement, transferring negative emotions from one's own person to another. Balch (1980) observed the dramatic changes in people who became members of a millennial cult. He concluded that these were not transformations of their personalities, values or beliefs, as was commonly supposed in studies of conversion, but rather were due to their rapid learning of the roles now required of them.

Snow and Machalek (1983) argued that the radical change in a conversion experience was the means whereby people orient themselves to the world by a set of assumptions they take for granted, their "universe of discourse." For converts, four indicators of this were their biographical reconstruction, by which they recreated their past from their new perspective; their adoption of a master attribution scheme which informed all their experience; the suspension of analogical reasoning—avoiding the use of analogy to describe their experience; and the new role by which converts saw themselves as members of a particular group. Staples and Mauss (1987) found that the last three were all found in evangelical Christians and were general indicators of religious commitment; only biographical reconstruction was unique to converts.

Scobie (1973, 1975) distinguished between sudden, gradual, and unconscious conversion among students in several theological colleges and described three forms it might take. Sudden converts scored significantly higher on religious conservatism than the others, were more authoritarian, and showed less personality control and intellectual efficiency. Sudden conversion had a strong emotional element and took place in less than a few months. It was unexpected—the subjects had not given any prior consideration to religious belief. Gradual conversion was a slower process in which particular aspects of religious beliefs were slowly adopted as the subjects changed from rejecting Christianity to accepting it. The gradual converts were more conservative than the unconscious converts. These had never rejected belief, but acquired it in the same way as other attitudes from parents and peers throughout the process of childhood development. Many of them were introverted, which meant that they could be rapidly conditioned but would take a long time to relinquish previously held beliefs, which made them prone to derive their religious beliefs from their parents; most were found to hold similar beliefs to their mother or father. However, 16 percent of them were extreme extraverts, and this group was extrinsically oriented and displayed conventional religious values, making them less likely to choose the ministry as a vocation. Sudden converts tended to choose a theological college more sympathetic to their experience, but these differences were only partly attributable to differences in their theological courses. It did not logically follow that a group of believing laymen would record the same experiences. A Gallup poll has shown that gradual conversion is twice as frequent for American evangelicals and other Protestants and even more frequent for Catholics (Gallup and Jones, 1989).

Parker (1977) also identified different types of conversion; in all of them influence of peer groups and the congregation played an important role. In a gradual conversion involving a lengthy intellectual process, the convert was less neurotic and more mature and tended to have a religious home background. Converts to sectarian religious groups tended also to be less neurotic and more mature but came from homes without a religious background. Charney's (1986) longitudinal study in the Church of Jesus Christ of Latter Day Saints showed that those who accepted the faith were of a more seeking disposition than those rejecting it and had more intimate and meaningful relationships with the Mormon missionaries, whose skills in making relationships and in instruction were of great importance.

Among conservative evangelical theological students those suddenly converted to the faith of their parents had high neuroticism scores and were described as a regressive group who demonstrated their conformity by this dramatic capitulation. The remainder were regarded as able to emancipate themselves without difficulty, and for them conversion was a progressive and a maturing process (Roberts, 1965). But among Australian theological students, when no distinction was made as to the type of conversion experience there was a negative association between religious conversion and neuroticism and a positive association with extraversion. Parental religious belief was negatively associated with conversion, but it was positively associated with dogmatism and with fundamentalism (Stanley, 1965). Sudden converts tended to be less intelligent than those with a gradual religious development and to fall into a hysteric type of personality—there was a negative association between intelligence and hysteria. There were benefits as well as dangers in such an experience; the convert found better relationships with accepting people and a relief of guilt and anxiety but tended also to make a naive acceptance of a whole theological and social system (Kildahl, 1965).

Allison (1968, 1969) looked at the controversy regarding sudden conversion from the perspective of psychoanalytic ego psychology. While it was generally agreed that gradual conversion was a progressive, integrating development, it had been asserted that sudden conversion was a form of psychosis, a disruptive, disintegrating and pathological, regressive condition. He interviewed and tested theological students, some with a sudden conversion experience, using Rorschach test material to indicate the extent to which they used more primitive, illogical modes of unconscious thinking, and the adaptiveness of their thought processes. The sudden converts were more likely to employ such thought forms but they also showed better integration. This indicated that their conversion was an adaptive and integrative experience. The result of a selective sample could not be widely generalized, but it demonstrated that conversion could occur in individuals with adaptive and not pathological traits.

"Born again" Christians, and those with a sudden conversion experience, had stronger religious beliefs and social interests than ethical Christians lacking such experience; their deep religious commitment gave them a sense of meaning in life, great concern for the welfare of others and more dogmatic thinking (Paloutzian, Jackson, and Crandall, 1978). Conversion brought an enhanced sense of purpose in life which, after a few weeks of reassessment when the novelty of the experience had worn off, became fully established. The reorganization of values following conversion needed greater clarification (Paloutzian, 1981). Converts or penitents who had undergone rapid religious change secured lower scores for self-esteem than long-term religious individuals, but their religious ego-identity scores were higher; otherwise conflicting results were obtained, except that all groups showed high intrinsic religiousness. Sudden converts were not different from long-term religious individuals on the measures used (Rothenberg, 1986). Converts were shown not to be more committed to their religious group than those brought up in it, nor to be less likely to defect from it. Differences in commitment and defection were found among both types and depended on interactions with other members of the church (Barker and Currie 1985). Those most favorable to evangelism were, in descending order, the relatively young, Protestants, non-Catholics, members of a high-outreach Protestant denomination, those of any religion rather than those of none, and those active in religion (Seyfarth et al., 1984).

Gibbons and De Jarnette (1972) found high hypnotic susceptibility was associated with conversion experiences having strong emotional responses. Subjects of low susceptibility were more likely to emphasize cognitive aspects of their conversion, describing the group constraints associated with it, and to perceive their mother as only slightly or not at all religious. Such mothers would have been less likely to have encouraged ideas lacking objective reality. Gillespie (1973, 1979) applied Erikson's concepts of identity to the phenomenon of conversion in a theoretical study. Conversion was a decisive change, whether gradual or sudden, identified by unification of the self, a positive resultant function, and an intensity of commitment to new ideas. Since Erikson regarded these as affecting ego strength and identity, conversion could be seen as an identity experience.

Reese (1988) regarded conversion as one example only of religious change and described three fundamental categories of these: Radical conversion, which brought a significant change of identity and life style and involved mystical elements, high internal stress, and little social influence; regeneration, which resulted in significant changes within an existing religious system with little seeking and moderate social influence; and attenuation, which was a calm deepening of values already held, with a high level of seeking but little stress or social influence.

Heirich (1977) considered three sociological explanations of conversion which regarded it as the consequence of stress—an explanation offensive to converts themselves; the product of parental influence, or the result of an interaction making a different assessment of personal experience possible. By comparing gradual

converts to the Catholic pentecostal movement with other Catholics, the explanations could be supported. However, they left key issues unresolved, since they
applied only to those already oriented toward this quest and gave no reason for
their prior orientation. For converts religion was not so much a truth system as
a ground of being that ordered and oriented their experience, and it was brought
about by a conscious shift in their sense of grounding. We needed to know what
circumstances brought such changes in perceptions of ultimate reality. If stress
was to be related to mystical or ecstatic religious experience, a much more precise
definition of it was required. Further, observers had to take seriously converts'
altered sense of ultimate reality when they asserted that it was unknowable and
nonrational; many religious movements called into question the sociological sup-
position that individuals always moved from the nonrational to a commitment to
rational perspectives. Sophisticated analysis showed that quite mundane interpersonal factors were important in this sample—infrequent Mass attendance
together with Pentecostal friends, one of whom introduced the convert to the
group, or not being an eldest or only child.

Silverstein (1988) was critical of many attempts at a psychological analysis
of conversion, based on superficially delineating conversion types and ignoring
basic similarities. The different types were often basically therapeutic, but modified by social and historical factors, while conversion was essentially heterogeneous. Not all conversions were fundamentally the same, the result of brain-wash-
ing or of a search for social experiment. The motivations, psychodynamics, and
social contexts often differed greatly. He considered that there were four areas
affecting all types of conversion—its outward form, experience, motivation, and
psychodynamics. Conversions could be very similar in some of these areas and
quite different in others. Merely comparing sudden with gradual conversion disguised many effects, as did the assumption that the convert was always active in
seeking for change. The outward form of conversion should be as it appeared to
an observer. The experience of the convert could be active or passive; at times,
unconscious motivation accounted for a convert's passive role. Personality factors
also affected the form of conversion. The capacity for transcendence or the desire
for release from inner stress was affected by the social conventions of Western
society.

Yet conversion remains unpredictable. Wilson (1976) made a very thorough
longitudinal study of urban and rural teenage converts in a southern state, comparing them with unbelieving peers. No characteristics were found that gave a
predisposition to conversion, nor was any radical personality change involved,
although subsequently the converts increased in self-sufficiency, introversion, optimism, dogmatism, and mental health. The rural adolescents showed greater social
distance, were more tough-minded and practical than their urban counterparts.
The results were related to several relevant psychological theories and were
regarded as countering ideas that conversion was associated with mental illness
or was related to a reduction of dissonance.

The emergence of new religious movements in recent years, and the methods they have employed to attract followers, have brought new attention to studies of conversion. It is clear that gradual conversion represents a continuous religious development, whereas sudden conversion is associated with some form of problem which it resolves. The studies show that the research emphasis is now upon the process of conversion, assisted by current statistical techniques. The new perspective adopted by a convert provides significant new meanings to life and offers a useful field for further research based on atribution theory.

Chapter 10

Personality and Religion

Many attempts have been made to relate religiousness to particular personality traits. Although these studies are almost entirely concerned with students and adults, they have a bearing on children's religious development since it is in childhood and adolescence that personality is formed. What becomes apparent from the studies reviewed is that while no particular personality trait is associated with religiousness in general, individuals' personalities often affect the form which specific aspects of their religiousness takes.

There have been many assertions that religion appeals to people with particular personality traits, so that they have variously been described as introverted, neurotic or mentally ill, over-anxious, personally inadequate, authoritarian, motivated by a need for social conformity, dependent, or overtly suggestible. Such assertions have often been based on arguments from psychological theory and inadequately tested with empirical studies. Many such studies have been made since this criticism of Dittes (1969), but their results have been inconclusive. This is not surprising when the variety of measures used to define religiousness is considered—behavioral, belief, attitudinal—as though there had been no study of the dimensions of religion. The substantial differences between intrinsically and extrinsically oriented people, described in Appendix D, are a pointer to the need for better definition, and research continues into orientations and the types of religion associated with them. Differences are found between religions, as might be expected. While there was a great similarity between Catholics and Protestants, they differed significantly from Jews and nonaffiliates. High scores for religiousness were associated with the most frequent church attendance (Gladding and Clayton, 1986).

194

Another problem arises from the many approaches to the measurement of personality. Different personality inventories, using different questions, have produced different personality profiles, and each inventory has its own particular vocabulary to describe personality traits. Similar traits measured by different tests are far from identical. To avoid misunderstanding in the review which follows, the technical vocabulary of the personality tests has been retained, even when it appears somewhat obscure.

These, and other difficulties, become apparent in some studies. A number of investigations had shown an apparent association between introversion and religiousness; a study of alcohol and drug use among Christian and Jewish adolescents showed a relationship between introversion and religiousness and that introverts with high religiousness had the least drug dependency (Aiken, 1979). The greater religiousness of introverts was found in Poland by Chlewinski (1981). Kay (1981a) also found extraversion in secondary-school pupils to be associated with lower scores on Francis' Attitude to Religion scale. Francis, Pearson, Carter, and Kay (1981a) made a study of the effects of extraversion and neuroticism on attitude to religion scores using the Eysenck Junior Personality Inventory, but since Eysenck's personality theory did not provide a clear rationale for presuming such a relationship, the question was not as straightforward as had been at first supposed (Francis, Pearson, Carter, and Kay 1981b; Francis, Pearson, and Kay, 1982). Subsequently (Francis, Pearson, and Kay, 1983c) they returned to the topic, and introverts scored higher than extraverts, a result which added substance to the relationship between introversion and religiousness. Then Francis and Pearson (1985), following changes in the most recent edition of the personality inventory, repeated the test and found no difference in attitude scores between introverts and extraverts. They commented that a complex problem had been further complicated by this change in the definition of the theoretical postulates of the personality theory, and the results from the series of tests showed the danger of making generalizations across different editions of the same scale. Cronbach (1984), in his review of ten personality inventories, was somewhat dismissive of the Eysenck test, commenting that its three dimensions, psychoticism, extraversion, and neuroticism, played a central role in his neo-Pavlovian theory of normal and abnormal personality. On a different personality scale, neither introversion nor extraversion had any association with religiousness (Lee, 1985). A comparison of responses about introversion and extraversion to both the Myers-Briggs Type Indicator and the Esenck Personality Inventory showed how complex the construct was (Sipps and Alexander, 1987).

A number of studies have concluded that there are no personality effects on religiousness. There was no significant association between students' religious belief and personality but only with their religious background and denomination (Martin and Nichols, 1962). Personality measures were poor predictors of attitude to religion, whereas attitude to science was significantly related to such traits as self-sufficiency and emotional stability (Barton, Modgil, and Cattell, 1973). In a test for temperament with Christian and secular undergraduates, the small differences between them could have been due to other factors, and it seemed that there were no fundamental personality differences associated with Christian belief (Dodrill, 1976). In an extensive survey of religion in the Midwest no psychological differences were found which related to the theological stances of Protestants or Catholics; there were no basic personality differences between them and no distinctive denominational cognitive structures. It seemed they were much more influenced by the general Midwest culture than by their religion (Schroeder and Obenhaus, 1964). Data from adolescents would not support the theories that regarded religion as a neurosis, that better mental health was associated with stronger religious belief, that people with doubtful religious beliefs were necessarily emotionally unstable, nor that strongly held belief or disbelief was a mark of instability; but it seemed that religious belief offered support to those with emotional difficulties (Esawi, 1968). Personality had no association with concepts of God nor with religious education, or even the lack of it (Ahrendt, 1975).

Other studies have found some association between personality and religiousness. In Poland those with greater religiousness tended to record greater emotional maturity, more superego control, greater self-control, and higher sensitivity (Prezyna, 1969). Religious students were usually conventional, but they were not maladjusted or personally inadequate, as would be expected from Dittes' (1971) review of the topic. Religiousness did not vary with low self-esteem, but tended toward a positive relation with internal control. Preschool children with experience of religious education showed greater self-reliance, feelings of personal worth and of belonging, freedom from nervous symptoms, better personal and social adjustment, and better social skills; but there was no indication that the result was due either to the educational program, or to other factors (Wingert, 1973). Students holding supernatural beliefs just starting their university course tended to be of lower intelligence (Salter and Routledge, 1974), and fundamentalist beliefs were associated with conservatism in politics and theology, and also with lower grades, more authoritarianism and dogmatism, but not with believing in ancient astronauts, lost tribes, sunken continents, monsters, and the like (Eve and Harrold, 1986). The length of education of sociology students had no effect on their religiousness, but when it was combined with achievement, higher scores were associated with decreased religiousness (Witt and Smith, 1978). Otwell (1988) also noted that students' levels of religious belief were associated with their academic achievement. However, Zern (1987a) found religiousness was negatively associated with students' ability and had no relationship with their achievement, but it was strongly associated with the capacity to maximize their potential. High-school students in New Zealand who were church members were more tender-minded, higher in superego strength, lower in dominance, and more conservative than others, a difference persisting over five years; they also showed a significant decline over the period in guilt proneness and anxiety (Barton and Vaughan, 1976). In adolescence empathy was indirectly related to religiousness; when differences in levels of religiousness were controlled, there was a significant association, empathy increasing with age (Francis and Pearson, 1987). Undergraduate and graduate students who were intrinsically religious scored higher on self-control, personal and social adequacy, and on stereotyped femininity, and the nonreligious on egocentric sexuality and restlessness (McClain, 1978). Differences in cognitive style were associated with differences on a number of religious issues, particularly about reincarnation (Evans, 1985). Lenient Seventh-Day Adventists tended to be more expedient, assertive, experimenting, and happy-go-lucky, while strict adherents tended to be more conscientious, submissive, conservative, and serious. Increasing age was associated with greater strictness (Walker, 1985).

Francis, Pearson, and Kay (1988) used the Junior Eysenck Personality Questionnaire and Francis' attitude to religion scale with a large group of adolescents aged eleven to sixteen and discovered a positive association between religiousness and the lie score. The authors considered that unless they were bigger liars, this might be because the more religious pupils were less mature or more socially conforming. Gorsuch (1988) discussed this issue, observing the need to use threshold scores with a lie scale, and suggested that religious people who had higher standards of personal morality were more likely to admit using the peccadillos which everyone did.

Shackle (1974) regarded the differences between the religiously interested and distinctively Christian profiles described by Richardson and Chapman (1973) as due to differences in the cognitive style of thinking. One was a convergent, observer type and the other a divergent, participant type. The two types also related to the personality functions of either sensing-feeling or intuitive-thinking, according to the Jungian Type Survey Manual. She tested two groups of students, one in the third year at a Catholic college of education, mostly of women, with a range of ages, subject interests, and abilities; the other of religious studies students in all three years of a women's nondenominational college. In both groups conservatism in religious education was associated with salience in religion, and progressiveness with nonsalience. Orthodoxy was also associated with salience and with conservatism in the first group. Only the first group showed the expected association between divergent thinking and conservatism about religious education and between convergent thinking and progressiveness about religious education. Both groups showed the salience of religion in divergent thinkers and the lack of it in convergent thinkers. A further test showed conservatism in religious education to be associated with intuitive and thinking personality functions and progressiveness associated with the sensing and feeling functions. There was no association between introversion or extraversion with religious involvement. The results supported the argument that differences in religious stance were associated with personality functions, and that teachers with religious commitment would prefer to teach from their own stance. It also appeared that a progressive approach to religious education came from those who were interested in religion but not committed to it. This finding for a student sample is not borne out by knowledge of mature, experienced teachers most active to further progressive objectives.

The Myers-Briggs Type Indicator (Myers, 1962) has been used with tests of religiousness. Mystical experience of undergraduate students measured by the Hood mysticism scales was associated with intuition and feeling scores on the personality scale whereas there was no association with either sex or introversion-extraversion (Campbell, 1983). In a comparison of two of the personality types described in the Indicator, among Catholics and Episcopalians the intuitive feelers had mystical experiences significantly more often than the nonintuitive feelers (Dendinger, 1983). Among high-school students differences in belief were associated with personality types; the more concrete, literal, and definitive nature of traditional orthodox beliefs tended to be those of the sensing and judging types, whereas intuiting or perceiving types tended to be less orthodox, with beliefs that were more figurative and flexible. Extraversion or introversion made no difference, neither did the school attended or age, but greater orthodoxy was associated with more frequent church attendance (Lee, 1985). Personality contributed to the ideological commitment of undergraduates from conservative Bible colleges, the sensing and judging personality types showing strong associations between conservative theology and conventional moral judgment (Childerston, 1985). The different psychological types identified by the Myers-Briggs Type Indicator tended to be associated with particular spiritual gifts among students and church members (Phoon, 1987). When undergraduates interested in religion were placed in high and low groups according to their self-righteousness and self-esteem scores, the broad-minded subjects, who were low in self-righteousness and high in self-esteem, gave high scores for objectivism, intrinsic and quest religious orientations, and were the least concerned about other people dominating them. The insecure subjects, who were high in self-righteousness and low in self-esteem, exhibited a marked preference for strong power structures and gave high scores for extrinsic religious orientation. The other two groups were less differentiated; the arrogant—high in both self-righteousness and self-esteem—were more like the insecure group, and the meek—low in both measures—were more like the broad-minded (Falbo and Shepperd, 1986).

Sex differences

The widely observed greater religiousness of women has led to some studies of underlying religious differences between the sexes. They were noted as giving marked differences in religious development between the sexes by Gruber (1957), and implications of the difference for religious education were noted by Hyde (1965). An investigation by Cline and Richards (1965) demonstrated differences in patterns of religious belief and behavior. The authors commented that their conclusions were strengthened by the close agreement among the three different types of test they used—a questionnaire, a projective test, and an interview. Joubert (1978) investigated the tendency of those attending church to accept more irrational beliefs than their nonattending peers; the association was significant among men students but not among the women. In a study of belief in the supernatural, Randall and Desrosiers (1980) found that while it was independent of orthodox religious beliefs, it had a significantly greater acceptance by women. Among Israeli high-school students, Florian and Har-Even (1983) showed that girls feared death because it brought the loss of identity, whereas boys were fearful of its consequences to their family and friends and of punishment in the hereafter. Nelsen and Potvin (1981) demonstrated from a national sample of adolescents that the sex difference in religiousness varied from region to region and according to denominational differences about sex-role definitions; it was also affected by parent-child relationships.

Some commentators look for sociological rather than psychological reasons for the behavioral differences. Yinger (1970) was concerned to explain why in American society women were more religious than men. He thought this was due to a number of social influences; women occupied a more important place in the socialization of the young and were therefore expected to keep the traditional standards of society more than men. In general they had narrower contacts and had therefore experienced less secularization than men. In American society they wielded less power than men and had fewer secular-group contacts; religious associations and interests therefore seemed to fill a more important base in their lives, even though this was manifestly not true of all women. He compared this with the fact that men were predominant in public acts of worship among Jews, Muslims, and Buddhists. De Vaus (1982b), discussing the lack of empirical data explaining the sex difference in religiousness, refuted the argument that the child-bearing role of women accounted for their greater commitment to institutional religion in the United States by an analysis of data from National Opinion Poll surveys between 1972 and 1980. Then (De Vaus, 1984) he similarly showed from the same data that it was not explicable by the lower proportion of women at work but rather was accentuated by the low church attendance of men not fully employed. Finally (De Vaus and McAllister, 1987), women's child-rearing role and differing attitudes to work was not found to account for their greater religiousness, whereas their lower rate of employment was an important explanatory factor.

Greer (1972a), in his study of the religion of adolescents of sixteen to eighteen in Northern Ireland noted that the ratios given by Argyle (1958) for an index to compare the greater religiousness of women with that of men when applied to the English sample of Cox (1967) showed a persistently smaller ratio for the Northern Irish sample on twelve different criteria. He argued that this could not be due to some of the factors put forward to account for this sex difference—the girls were still at school and not exposed to work and the conflicts of industry, nor involved with the church through the crises of birth, marriage, and death. But the difference in their socialization was seen in that fewer girls than boys remained at school at this age, and then fewer undertook scientific studies. In Northern Ireland religious belief and practice characterized a large proportion of the population. In

England, with a more secular climate, boys were not encouraged to the same extent; the beliefs and practice of girls, who were motivated internally, were less affected by the climate of opinion. In a strongly religious community the environment encouraged adolescents to become religious, whereas in a more secular community boys were more likely than girls to move away from religiousness. The sex difference was apparent in that the English girls were significantly more religious than the Northern Ireland boys.

Because Smith (1982) was concerned that Christianity and the image of God had been distorted by a sexist emphasis on masculinity, she studied the responses of Protestant men and women to scales measuring sex role, social behavior, self-esteem, and religious experience but found no significant associations between them. Although God was perceived as predominantly masculine, but with feminine traits, there were no grounds for feminist criticisms of Christianity. Sex-role identification with God did not appear generally to predict self- esteem or religious experience. Bayer (1982) was also interested in the relationship between religiousness and sex-role identity. He developed his own scale of religious orientation to distinguish evangelical, nonevangelical, and non-Christian. Among students, evangelical women had more traditional sex-role expectations compared to nonevangelical women, but there was no difference between the men's groups.

It is surprising that no other aspects of sex in adolescent religiousness have been investigated apart from the gender difference. All schools of psychology recognize how important is the emergence of sexuality in adolescence. Suggestions have been made to relate this to enhanced adolescent religiousness, thus associating conversion with puberty. It is in adolescence that sexual attitudes and stances are established, and these undoubtedly have significant effects on religiousness. Yet sex seems to be a "no-go" area in empirical research on religion. Wright (1972) refers to the substantial evidence that religious people are less permissive than others about a range of sexual ethics and activities and often extend this to questions of pornography, abortion, birth control, and divorce; this attitude persists, despite a trend to greater permissiveness in society. Many of the world religions have similarly adopted a restrictive attitude to sex. Yoga permits only limited sexual activity, although some aspects of Hinduism are characterized by much more sexually explicit imagery. The enlightened Buddhist must remain continent. The Catholic priest must be celibate, as also must monks and nuns. Taylor (1953) made a distinction between two types of Christian attitudes to sex, contrasting opposing stances. The patrists took a restrictive attitude, limiting the freedom of women, who were seen as inferior, and valuing chastity more than welfare. They were authoritarian and conservative, opposed to innovation and distrusting research and enquiry, inhibited and fearful of spontaneity, with a deep fear of homosexuality, maximizing sex differences, ascetic and afraid of pleasure. The matrist attitude was in every instance the converse. Historically, one or other attitude seemed to dominate for long periods, but in a time of change they were confused. Before the Christian era, religious and sexual experience were the two roads to emotional satisfaction, and were often combined. The Christian church closed the road of sex to traffic, and heavily policed the road of religion. Protestantism had shorn religious ceremonies of their unconscious appeal, and today many had abandoned the pursuit of religious experience. Taylor's two stances have central features in common with the extrinsic and intrinsic religious orientations, but to regard them as paternal or maternal seems an over-simplification of the parental images. Yet they shed light on the trend to greater sexual permissiveness that is well established, when society has emerged from the harsh and hypocritical repressive nature of the Victorian era. Hardin and Gold (1988), in a study of sex, sex guilt, and experience, found that students who defined themselves as nonreligious had more explicit and richer sexual fantasies, which implies that religiousness has an inhibiting influence.

Does Christianity still regard sex as a rival to be contained, as if the satisfaction of sexual experience removed any desire for religious experience? Attitudes to sexuality have religious consequences. There is little sympathy for homosexuality in the churches, and in Britain the Church of England suffers divisive controversy about the ordination of women. Those most opposed to it appear in many ways to be "patrists," and in the press allegations are made that they are the most ready to accept homosexuals as priests. There remains an urgent psychological need to know how religiousness and sexuality interact, and what is the religious consequence of a well-adjusted sexual life, how such an adjustment is made in adolescence, and how a healthy adjustment can be fostered. Adolescence is marked by the emergence of sexuality, a topic treated extensively in the textbooks, but how sexual stances are formed, and how they affect religiousness remains unknown.

Religiousness and mental health

Becker (1971) reviewed the evidence for associating religion with psychological health and found it fragmentary and inconclusive. In consequence he suggested holistic research models which would clarify the concepts of psychological health and mature religion. This required a description of superior religious commitment and personality in concrete, living terms, but needed to be used in conjunction with empirical measures of development. According to Levin and Schiller (1987) data from 200 studies showed religion had been a major focus of epidemiological research for two centuries, and there was an important association between religion and health.

Male evangelical theological students were more worried about their physical and mental health than nuns and university graduates and had greater difficulty in achieving emotional control. In contrast to the better adjustment of the Catholic nuns they were more prone to morbid thinking, depression, and pessimism; they displayed a tendency to narcissism and to exhibitionism, which could be gratified in the pulpit. In view of the claim that evangelical religion brought inner joy and peace, it appeared that the theological students were under greater social stress and suffered from poverty and from earlier childhood deprivation (Goring, 1980).

In an attempt to relate religiousness to mental health, Batson and Ventis (1982) tabulated sixty-seven investigations, showing fifteen giving a positive association, fifteen giving no association, and thirty-seven giving a negative association. Further examination showed that whenever religious orientation was considered, in all but one instance, extrinsically oriented subjects tended to have lower levels of mental health, while intrinsically oriented subjects showed a variety of negative or positive associations according to the criteria being considered.

A nonreligious group of students and adolescents were more self-actualizing than any other group, and the Catholics the least. The results invalidated the theory that good mental health was associated with an intrinsic religious orientation in any faith; the extrinsic could be more healthy because a separation between the self and the belief system allowed for values to be lived instrumentally in a rapidly changing social environment, and the content of a belief system could open or close an individual to a healthy response to living (Brown, 1974). No association was found between students' degree of religious experience and measures of psychopathology or maladjustment, but the result was questioned since the test used (Hood, 1970) was found to be insufficiently discriminating or applicable to those lacking unusual or extreme religious experience (Fay, 1977). It was the hopefuls—the highest of four levels of religiousness—that achieved the best psychological well-being and satisfaction with life; religious optimists—the next level—like all the others, showed little deviation from the average and no greater happiness in life (McCready and Greeley, 1976). People reporting religious experience had a higher measure of well-being, contrary to the theory that religion was a form of neurosis; if mystical experience was produced by regression to an infantile state, those who reported it should be more unhappy and anxious than those who did not (Hay, 1982). Yet students from the Church of Jesus Christ of Latter Day Saints with continuous religious development and mild religious experience had better mental health than those with discontinuous development and intense experience, although the latter enhanced adjustment. Mental health was not significantly associated with religiousness, although some particular aspects of religiousness might show positive or negative associations with it (Bergin, 1983).

Religious behavior was a better predictor of psychological well-being than professed attitudes, especially among black men and women (St. George and McNamara, 1984). Gorsuch (1988) cited studies which indicated that religious people were healthier and less likely to commit suicide than the nonreligious. When discussing their mental health is was necessary to keep in mind how this was defined; if it meant fewer guilt feelings, this was psychologically satisfactory, but if it was a question of openness, this was not satisfactory as it was a philosophical matter. Bergin, Stinchfield et al. (1988) found no association between religiousness and mental health in a group of students, but those whose religious development had been continuous, with mild religious experience, were more healthy than those with a discontinuous development and intense religious experience, although the latter had enhanced their adjustment. Weis (1987) found in a group of Hare Krishnas that the men, but not the women, showed above normal well-being, although on all other tests they were normal.

Important events in life affected people in different ways, but overall positive happenings tended to make a strong religious belief even stronger, while negative events had the reverse effect (Albrecht and Cornwall, 1989). Women who were very religious suffered less distress and displayed better psychological adjustment than others; this was probably also true for men (Crawford, Handel, and Wiener, 1989). Intrinsically religious Bible college students had low manifest anxiety, high self-esteem, and experienced few daily hussles and uplifts (Robertson, 1989).

There is evidence to show that it is not religiousness which makes people neurotic, but that the mentally unstable can find support in religious belief. Personality tests of members of the Jesus movement indicated a pattern of maladjustment which was shown by subsequent retesting to have remained stable. Before their conversion the majority had reported unhappiness, difficulties in life, and heavy use of drugs; it appeared that they had switched their dependency successfully to a rigid belief system but still could be described in terms of addiction (Simmonds, 1977). Detailed interviews of one hundred members of religious fringe groups indicated that they were not suffering from psychotic illness, but rather they were struggling with developmental problems and had found their needs were met by the beliefs, mysticism, community, and structure of their fringe group. Frequently they were also attracted to a charismatic leader. In consequence, many reported that painful psychological symptoms had been relieved and their personal happiness had increased (Levine, 1978). A comparison of the best and the most poorly adjusted male students showed the well-adjusted group was significantly different from the poorly adjusted group on a ways to live scale, on a ten commandments scale, and on a values scale, a result denying the association of religiousness with mental illness (Berger, 1978). The mental health of members of the Unification Church proved to be below the norm for psychological well-being, but they also reported significantly greater neurotic distress before conversion; attribution theory[1] could account for their improved emotional state (Galanter, Rabkin, Rabkin, and Deutsch, 1979). Different religions could have different deleterious effects—a depressive personality was associated with membership of Hare Krishna or the Inter-Varsity Fellowship; a catatonic personality was associated with membership of International Meditation or the Divine Life Mission; and a compulsive personality was associated with the Unitarians (Margaro et al., 1984). The time spent on religious activities was positively associated with happiness with the subject's religion and with life satisfaction but not with perceived stress (McClure and Lodea, 1982). Religiousness facilitated the formation of mental health as was shown by the association between intrinsic religiousness, personality integration, and purpose in life; a male Muslim group secured higher scores on

---

1. Attribution theory is discussed in the next chapter.

all these measures than a Christian group (Jalali-Tehrani, 1985).

Problems are not solved when different dimensions of religiousness are considered. Hunt (1972) had regarded the mythological dimension as the most mature, but Hopson (1982) found the only group vulnerable to life stress were males with this outlook. However they obtained higher scores on some other measures, showing that they relied more on their own inner values than on doctrines, unlike literal subjects, and their inner-directed qualities seemed to generate conflict with theological perspectives. The other-directed outlook of the literal group blended better with a religious perspective but formed a dependency which hindered growth and personal freedom. In general terms, Bergin (1983) stated that his analysis of twenty-four students revealed no support for the theory that religiousness was associated with psychopathology and that better specifications and measures of religion were needed if progress was to be made because religion reflected a multidimensional phenomenon that had both positive and negative aspects.

The relationship between neuroticism and religiousness has also been investigated. Pruyser (1977) argued that religion could produce neurotic constructs by its distorting reality, motivating the regression from rational to archaic thought patterns, failing to deal constructively with aggression, condoning infantile wishes, and encouraging feelings of helplessness by encouraging a surrender to authoritarian demands. There were no significant differences among groups of Catholics, Anglicans, nonconformists, Quakers, Jews, and agnostics in scores on neuroticism or on introversion-extraversion, but nonconformists and Quakers had the greatest difference on both scales (Rees, 1967). Caird (1987) found no association between reported mystical experience and Eysenck's personality factors of introversion/extraversion, neuroticism and psychoticism, and Francis and Pearson (1988) found no association between religiousness and either neuroticism or extraversion with the short-scale Eysenck Personality Questionnaire. Watson, Hood, Foster, and Morris (1988) examined the contention that the concept of sin and prayers of confession led to neuroticism and loss of self-esteem but found to the contrary that sin-related beliefs were not maladaptive and promoted healthy self-development. There was no difference in the neuroticism scores of university students with high or with low religiousness, which showed that religiousness and emotional stability were not related (Choudary, 1989), and the religiousness of eleven-year old children had an inverse relationship with psychoticism and no relationship with neuroticism (Francis, Lankshear, and Pearson, 1989).

Among adolescents at school, psychoticism in boys had a marked negative association with their attitude to religion, an association not found with girls (Kay, 1981c; Francis, Pearson, and Kay, 1983b). In a church-controlled residential school for mentally subnormal children religiousness was associated with neuroticism and the children's scores were well above normal. Religiousness decreased with age, but contrary to previous findings with children of normal intelligence the religiousness of these children was also related to their intelligence. Their neuroticism scores reflected a high level of anxiety which predisposed them to conform to the social norms of the environment; it was this which led to their high level of religiousness (Francis, Pearson, and Stubbs, 1985). Among atheists, Catholics, Jews, and Protestants, irrational beliefs, religiousness, and religious affiliation were all associated with a sense of guilt, which with different emphases tended to be higher in Catholics and Jews (Demaria, 1986).

Some professionals concerned with mental illness have also given the problem sympathetic attention but others show bias. Some mental health professionals showed a diagnostic bias against patients who were traditionally religious and still more against those charismatically religious (Rhoades, 1979), and this could affect investigations into religion and mental health (Sweigart, 1986). Records of institutionalized patients showed that there were no proportional differences between the denominations in the number of patients but that denominations had significant differences in the types of disorder (Buckalew, 1978). Over a three- year period in a psychiatric clinic the religious affiliation and psychiatric diagnosis of over 7000 patients indicated that neither religious affiliation or a lack of it was a guarantee against mental illness, but under psychic stress members of particular religious denominations tended to have particular psychiatric disorders; such people might associate with particular religious groups in order to meet particular psychological needs. Mental illness did not relate to general religiousness, but specific forms of mental illness did relate to specific forms of religiousness and religious orientation was one factor (MacDonald and Luckett, 1983). No difference was found between the emotional problems of patients undergoing therapy with different types of religiousness (Sharkey and Maloney, 1986).

In a Norwegin hospital, no difference was found between the religiousness of psychiatric and surgical patients, but the group with medium religiousness was not as emotionally healthy as the highly religious group. As religious integrity and stability increased, so psychiatric morbidity decreased; it appeared that religiousness brought an increased psychological stress for some people while serving as a means of self-actualization for others (Heskested, 1984). Psychiatric patients were more extrinsically oriented and significantly lower in faith than normal people (VanderPlate, 1973). The pattern of mystical experiences reported by schizophrenic individuals differed in identifiable ways from the experiences of other schizophrenics, even though they differed from the descriptions of traditional mystical experiences (Siglag, 1986).

Purpose in life has interested some researchers. Crandell and Rasmussen (1975), in two studies involving students, found a significant relationship between lower scores on a purpose-in-life test and higher scores in a value survey for pleasure, excitement, and comfort, suggesting to them that a hedonistic philosophy contributed to an existential vacuum. Higher scores on the purpose-in-life test were also associated with students displaying an intrinsic religious orientation but not with those with an extrinsic orientation, a result confirmed by Bolt (1975) for both intrinsic and indiscriminately proreligious orientations. Dufton and Perlman

(1986) analyzed responses to the purpose-in-life test from conservative, nonconservative, and unbelieving students. The test was shown to have two main factors, one reflecting purpose in life but the stronger factor reflecting satisfaction with life. The conservative believers tended to secure high scores on both factors of the test.

Anxiety and religiousness

Anxiety and dogmatism have often been associated with religiousness, but contradictory findings have been recorded, and in some instances it has been shown that religious orientation is a decisive factor. Among undergraduates religiousness was associated with fearfulness and anxiety, and the nonreligious tended to give healthier scores (Wilson and Miller, 1968). Sudden adult converts showed significantly more anxiety than other people, suggesting that their higher level of anxiety indicated a less well-adjusted state of being (Spellman, Baskett, and Byrne, 1971). Women students from highly orthodox denominations—notably Baptists—were the most dogmatic, in contrast to the gospel teaching about concern, compassion and respect for others, but they also showed a lower level of anxiety apart from Episcopalian students, who had the lowest scores on belief and anxiety. The most anxious were the Catholic students. Adherence to practices whose roots were in values internalized in childhood gave rise to the least anxiety (Glass, 1971). In a different context, religiousness in male graduate students in India was associated with rigidity and anxiety (Ahmad, 1973), and religiousness was greater among Muslim undergraduates than among Hindus and was not influenced by caste status in either religion; it was associated with anxiety, authoritarianism, rigidity, and intolerance of ambiguity (Hassan and Khalique, 1981).

Some contrary findings have also been recorded. Hauser's (1981) review of adolescents and religion noted that those who were religious had less worry and anomie and were more secure. Anxiety did not affect religiousness in Swickard's (1963) study. It showed a strong negative correlation with self-esteem, so that low self-esteem was associated with high anxiety (Hart, 1985), but, as will be shown, religiousness is normally associated with higher self-esteem. Religiousness in students, especially when measured by a sense of nearness to God, was associated with lowered anxiety and heightened repression; the association was stronger in men than in women (Richek, 1971). The Christian experience could best be described as attachment to the Heavenly Father, and within this attachment was a secure versus anxious dimension (Washburn, 1982). A reason for these contradictory results is suggested by the finding of Sturgeon and Hamley (1979) that intrinsically oriented parochial college students had less anxiety and greater internal locus of control than those extrinsically oriented. The result shows the need for distinguishing different styles of religiousness when looking for other associated nonreligious influences, as by Mostul (1980), who recorded that tolerance of ambiguity was associated with trait anxiety and an extrinsic religious orientation. In turn, trait anxiety was associated with lower self-esteem, and negatively, with purpose in life. Purpose in life, self-esteem, and intrinsic religiousness were positively related. Intrinsically oriented undergraduates showed less anxiety and the extrinsically oriented showed greater anxiety on some aspects of the anxiety scale. Testing religiousness without distinguishing its orientation would give differing results depending on the numbers of intrinsic and extrinsic subjects in the sample (Baker and Gorsuch, 1982). Intrinsically oriented students were negatively related to anxiety but positively to self-control (Bergin, Masters, and Richards, 1987). Among a group of Catholic charismatics, their conversion experience brought a decrease in anxiety and an increase in intrinsic religiousness (Johnsen, 1986).

Another finding about academic stress came from McCall (1981); a fifth of the fundamentalist freshmen tested were suffering from strong religious conflict, mainly arising from the classroom and resulting in such symptoms as inability to sleep, eat, concentrate, or study. Religious fundamentalism was not associated with anxiety but was negatively associated with religious conflict, which was always associated with anxiety. An anxious temperament was a factor associated with superstitious habits noted by Marsh (1981) in his study of superstition, which he found to be strongly related to religious belief. Both were seen to be striving to overcome the stresses and uncertainties of life, and both were usually to be found in the same individual rather than existing as alternatives. Superstition depended most on age, then on having one or both parents superstitious, and then on religious belief.

Authoritarianism, dogmatism, and religiousness

Rokeach (1956) considered that the concept of the authoritarian personality was a very specific factor and devised scales to measure political and religious dogmatism; he noted that while political opinions might be polarized between Catholics and Communists, both displayed considerable dogmatism, and religious dogmatism involved prejudiced knowledge about faiths other than one's own. A closed belief system warded off conflicting aspects of reality and gave rise to a feeling of satisfaction and security. Spilka and Reynold (1965) found that among women college students authoritarian subjects were threatened by ideas of a considerate, kind God, involved and interested in people's affairs but saw him as unreal, impersonal, abstract, distant, and inaccessible. Some studies also concerned with authoritarianism and dogmatism have already been noted, e.g., Glass (1971), Hassan and Khalique (1981). Higher attitude to religion and fundamentalist attitude inventory scores were associated with greater dogmatism (Swindell and L'Abate, 1970). However, when a previously noted dramatic increase in religious orthodoxy among Mormon university students was examined, Mormon affiliation so dominated the responses that more detailed analysis was inhibited. Such conformity might be desirable for an institution, but it increased the difficulty individuals faced in exploring and challenging the culture, and distorted their sense of reality (Rytting and Christensen, 1980).

The relationship between religion and prejudice was not strong, but religious orthodoxy was strongly associated with authoritarianism which in turn was strongly associated with prejudice. Religious orthodoxy apparently encouraged authoritarianism which in turn gave rise to prejudice (Thompson, Michel, and Alexander, 1970). Dogmatism was most strongly associated with religious conservatism (De Giuseppe, 1971). There was a negative association between religious conservatism and social status measures, and since the latter were associated with intelligence, the link between conservatism and intelligence may be due to social status (Scobie, 1975). Those most certain of their beliefs were less differentiated in their self-concepts, described their mothers in a less differentiated way, and used repression as a mechanism of control to a greater extent than those who experienced some religious doubts (Turner, 1963). Religious orthodoxy was significantly associated with authoritarianism and religious values with humanitarianism (Fehr and Heintselman, 1977). In evangelical groups people with more relationships outside their religious circle tended to be less dogmatic than the remainder (Wilson, 1984). Among high-school students and undergraduates in Israel, the religious sons of religious families were more authoritarian than the nonreligious sons of religious families but not more than the religious sons of nonreligious families. The result supported the theory that authoritarian people are attracted to orthodox doctrine (Weller et al., 1975). Urban middle-class adolescents were religiously more liberal and less authoritarian than working-class adolescents and those with middle-class expectations. Upward social-class mobility showed a positive relationship with liberal religiousness, but those with marked authoritarian attitudes were more resistant to change (Baggot, 1978). In England and the United States strong religious commitment heightened a sense of social compassion and concern for equality and reduced prejudice, in contrast to those of only a nominal religious identification (Perkins, 1985). The nominally religious were less humanitarian, less egalitarian, and more racist than those with no religion. Among orthodox and liberal Catholic and Jewish and nondogmatic students, religious affiliation, church attendance, and years of religious education did not affect moral development, but they were associated with dogmatism, and greater dogmatism produced a lower level of moral judgment (Wahrman, 1981). In Iran, where other environmental factors were similar for the Muslim, Jewish, and Christian students examined, the personality differences due to the effect of different religions by their impact on the socialization and culture were studied. No great difference was found between the Jews and Christians, but the Islamic students were affected by an authoritarian, rigid, punitive, and guilt-inducing culture so that they were significantly more religious, politically minded, prejudiced, and inclined toward supernaturalism and institutionalized religion. In the same way, they judged their parents as more authoritarian, dogmatic, punitive, demanding, conservative, fear-inducing, superstitious, and moralistic than the others (Nowparast, 1980).

Adorno's authoritarianism-dogmatism scales showed an association with the extrinsically but not with the intrinsically oriented students. Those with an intrinsic orientation were associated with the socially desirable traits of responsibility and internal locus of control; extrinsically oriented students tended to be negatively associated with these (Kahoe, 1974). There was no association between dogmatism and intrinsic religiousness among adolescents (Strickland and Shaffer, 1971). Contrary to expectations, extrinsic and nonreligious students and adult groups of church members were less dogmatic than the indiscriminately proreligious (Brown, 1974). Consensually religious students were strongly associated with dogmatism. A dogmatic system was developed in childhood as a defense against the anxiety caused by a stern father who did not understand and a rigid, rather than a loving, mother (Raschke, 1973). Intrinsically oriented Baptist students showed authoritarianism, but it was differentiated into specific aspects of prejudice relating to particular aspects of Baptist beliefs (Kahoe, 1977). Catholic undergraduates holding beliefs not accepted by rationalists tended to be dogmatic and extrinsically religiously oriented (Primaveia, Tantillo, and DeLisio, 1980). When people with dogmatic personalities are religious, then they express their religious beliefs dogmatically. The relationship between a religion that is not dogmatic and intrinsic religiousness, to which these studies point, is less obvious.

Self-esteem and religiousness

Different aspects of ego-psychology have emerged in the study of religiousness, and these must next be considered. Studies concerned with self-esteem have shown conflicting results. Self-esteem came from children being loved and accepted by their parents, love which reflected the love of God (Saussy, 1988). It also arose from an authoritarian religiousness—and the more dogmatic was religious belief, the more it satisfied the need for a sense of importance, identity, and security (Oswald, 1970). Yet people holding orthodox religious beliefs were more submissive and dependent in interpersonal relations (Dreger, 1952). Adolescents' self-rating had a negative association with attitude to religion and church attendance (Strunk, 1958). High-school students at a Lutheran youth camp with images of a loving God tended to have high self-esteem, but those with images of a stern and controlling God tended to have low self-esteem and signs of maladjustment or personality disorders. Low self-esteem appeared to inhibit religious ideals (Flakoll, 1974).

Among undergraduates, religious values and religious orthodoxy showed no relationship with self-esteem (Fehr and Heintselman, 1977). Because previous findings had been inconsistent, Bahr and Martin (1983) tested high-school students with a number of instruments and showed there was little relationship between self-esteem and religiousness. They argued that religiousness should not be associated with self-esteem because of evidence that religion was associated with deficiencies in the personality; if "the sick" whom Jesus called found religion to be efficacious they would tend to display the self-image of "the well" who did not need religious activity to strengthen their self-esteem. But in a group of Catholic sisters there was no relationship between religiousness and ego-strength, although greater religious conservatism was associated with lower ego strength (Marron, 1984). Catholic high-school girls showed an association between self-esteem and an image of a loving God, and negatively, with an image of a rejecting, punitive God (Benson and Spilka, 1973). In a study relating cognitive and affective concepts of God to psychological maturity, self-actualization did not unequivocally relate to loving and kindly concepts of God as was anticipated; "born-again" Christians were found to be less self-actualizing, and those whose affective experience of God was less in terms of traditional Christian ideas proved to be more self-actualizing (L. Day, 1980).

Among high-school juniors there was a significant association between self-esteem and religiousness for boys but not for girls (Moore and Stoner, 1977), a finding confirmed among adolescents by Potvin (1977). Catholic adolescents with marked religiousness had a positive sense of self-esteem in the United States, Latin America, Puerto Rico, Spain, and West Germany. It was greater among girls than boys but was negatively associated with religious knowledge (Smith, Weigert, and Thomas, 1979). Among Latin American males, for whom the masculine concept of "machismo" was dominant, self-esteem was related to religiousness only among those who failed to maintain "machismo" according to accepted standards. In Montreal, the self-actualization provided by the church was unrelated to some students' personal religious experience but came rather through their opposition to the church, or by secular channels. They were disaffected with the church and their religion was centered on God rather than Christ; it was individualistic, rational, and moralizing, imposed by their education rather than freely chosen; some had become submissive to it, others were on the point of rebellion (Sevigny, 1971). The more religious were students from two universities in Cairo, the higher was their self-concept (Habib, 1988).

Carter (1979) made an extended philosophical and psychological review of the literature concerned with the development of the self and self-esteem, subjecting her conclusions to a sophisticated test of pupils aged sixteen. The scales were about self-esteem, dogmatism, personality traits, attitude to religion, religious behavior, and intelligence; the subjects were undertaking intensive religious education as an examination subject. All the religious education groups showed significantly better scores for Coopersmith's self-esteem inventory, the Lipsitt's self-concept, and the Francis attitude to religion scales than the control groups, and they were less dogmatic. Their better scores on Rosenberg's self-esteem scale were not significant, neither were indications that they were more extravert and less neurotic. Analysis showed that the Lipsitt self-concept score, with the greatest group effect, was affected by attitude to religion and by sex. In turn, attitude to religion, here uninfluenced by intelligence, social class, or parental church attendance, was related to sex, personal prayer, and church attendance, and to religious education in the county schools. The somewhat lower attitude scores of the Church of England schools group was thought to be due to the fact that these students were compelled to take the examination; this was also true in the Catholic schools. (Francis and Carter (1980) reported the same result.) In the Catholic schools parental religious practice enhanced their children's religiousness. Carter concluded that county school religious education, together with religious behavior and sex, was a predictor of religious attitude, and this had a highly significant effect on self-concept. The study leaves unresolved the question whether the personal religiousness of the county school pupils who chose to take the examination was further enhanced by the religious education, as their religious knowledge probably was.

Marthai (1980) developed scales to measure religious maturity, indicated by such factors as intrinsic motivation, behavior change, growth, and satisfaction. Among adolescents of twelve to sixteen in Christian schools it was associated with self-esteem and intrinsic religiousness and negatively with anxiety and extrinsic religiousness. Religiousness, which was socially desirable, related to self-esteem for all boys and intrinsically oriented girls among adolescents in Catholic parochial schools. Aspects of the stereotyped male role were incompatible with aspects of religiousness, so that religious training influenced boys' sex-role identity, tending to affect their social development. In girls it reinforced the communal orientation, adding little to their social development. In consequence, sex-role identity proved to be less related to religiousness in women than in men (Suziedelis and Potvin, 1981). There was no relationship between the self-concept of eight-year-old Sunday school children and their learning during a sixteen-week period (Ashby, 1968). Spirituality among postgraduate conservative Baptist theological students was related to a healthy self-concept, although intrinsic religious orientation was only associated with two of the measures of spirituality; it seemed that a positive self-concept was developed in the context of caring relationships with acceptance, forgiveness, and encouragement, and biblical teaching regarding living and conduct (Colwell, 1986). There was a significant association between self-esteem and several measures of Jewish identity (Tabachnik, 1986). Self-esteem was shown to relate negatively to dogmatism and to irrational beliefs (Daly, 1982), but no association between them and religiousness was sought. Hoelter (1980) asserted on theological grounds that religiousness would have a positive effect on self-stability and on self-esteem, whereas religious hostility would have an adverse effect; his data supported this model but the weak relationships indicated that it was more complex.

Watson, Morris, and Hood (1987) found that the inverse relationship between belief in sin and self-esteem only operated when belief was expressed in traditional language about guilt. When explicitly humanistic self-esteem scales were used the negative association was more prominent, and some self-esteem items were in opposition to a conservative religion scale. Positive self-esteem was associated with an intrinsic orientation.

Locus of control and religiousness

Locus of control is the extent to which individuals regard what happens to them as due to their own internal control of events or due to such external forces as chance, luck, fate, the system, or powerful other affecting their rewards. Deconchy, (1978) in his brief summary of existing references to it, considered that it was worth further study for its association with religiousness. Investigations about whether faith related to oneself or to some other source showed four types of faith—faith in God, faith in people, faith in oneself, and faith in technology. There was a general basic trust underlying the different dimensions of faith, and a highly significant association was found between faith in oneself—that individuals control life in a positive direction, and internal locus of control—that individuals can affect what happens to them (Tipton, Harrison, and Mahoney, 1980). Protestant students showed the greatest internal control, followed by Catholics, and then by Jews, and it was strongly related to the frequency of religious participation (Shrauger and Silverman, 1971). Stark (1963) found among almost 3,000 graduate university students that church attendance was negatively associated with their self-assessment as being intellectual, their desire for future employment to be creative and original, and their desire to be respected in their own field outside their institution. In a group of psychology students, Catholics displayed greater externality than Protestants (Geist and Bangham, 1980).

Religious students were in general conventional, and there was no indication that they were maladjusted or personally inadequate, as would be expected from Dittes (1971) review of the topic. Religiousness did not vary with low self-esteem but tended toward a positive relation with internal control (Rohrbaugh and Jessor, 1975). Locus of control had no effect on the image of God held by Catholic high-school girls (Benson and Spilka, 1973). A more thorough study showed that locus of control scales were inadequate without responses reflecting belief in God, and a scale extended in this way was used with different Protestant denominations. Four locus of control factors were identified, and that about God discriminated very significantly among the denominations, although further research was needed to ascertain if religiousness was an antecedent of locus of control (Gaskins, 1978). Students who called themselves religious had higher locus of control (Gladding, et al., 1981). Evangelicals were less internally oriented (Gabbard, 1986), and internal locus of control was not associated with committed-intrinsic religiousness among students, but chance locus of control was associated with extrinsic-self-serving religiousness (Hanson, 1987). Jackson and Coursey (1988) studied a sample of black adult church members with very fundamentalist beliefs; their strong belief that God controlled their lives did not inhibit their belief in their personal, internal control of their lives. Their effective coping was achieved through God by their personal control. Intrinsic religiousness and God control were related, but the belief that God controlled the world did not ensure a sense of meaning and purpose in life. In a study of a group of cancer patients aged from ten to twenty-three, half claimed that their religion gave them security in the face of death and helped them to understand and accept their illness, although they were not more religious than the others. There were no significant age differences in their locus of control scores, which suggested that their condition had accelerated the development of internality among the younger patients (Tebbi et al., 1987).

Identity status and religiousness

Marcia (1966) sought empirical support for Erikson's concept of adolescent identity achievement in his eight life stages. He studied how college students coped with the psychological task of achieving their identity and classified male undergraduates in four groups representing achievement with a relative freedom from authoritarian values; a moretorium, in which achievement was delayed; foreclosure, in which authoritarian values were endorsed, and identity confusion, illustrated in the continuum from the playboy to the schizoid personality. The first group of students had shown the best performance and perseverance on a stressful concept attainment task, and the second were similar; the other groups were less successful and their self-esteem had been found to be vulnerable. The four ways by which adolescents resolve their identity have suggested that conventional faith and conventional morality are associated with a foreclosed identity status. In this, an apparent stability disguises the need for values to be rearranged if their external reference group changes its position; if the values are long-standing, the individual's identity is threatened. Although previous studies had proved inconclusive, a significant relationship between cognitive development and diffusion, foreclosure and moratorium was demonstrated by Skinner (1983); achievement scores increased as cognitive scores increased.

Hill (1986) complained that there was a paucity of research concerned with theories of the development of religiousness in adolescence. A cognitive, Piagetian-type development, in which formal operations combined with a mature intrinsic orientation should represent the culmination of the process. Comparison of Fowler's faith development with Kohlberg's moral development and the relationship established between identity status and moral development pointed to useful conclusions. Conventional faith and conventional moral reasoning appeared to be parallel, and conventional faith was inflexible and stereotyped. It contrasted with an internalized committed postconventional faith, which a number of studies had shown to be positively related to identity resolution. There was a body of evidence suggesting that conservative churches tended to encourage the maintenance of conventional morality and conventional faith. Meissner (1984) regarded this as the result of a critical superego, and the feelings of guilt it produced led to a legalistic type faith which was immature and unbiblical.

Before adolescence a conventional faith was normal, and in early adolescence this usually developed without difficulty into a faith which was concrete, related to other people, and was conventionally socialized. A lack of formal operational thinking could inhibit this development, but the achievement of formal operations did not necessarily result in further progress to postconventional faith. Most adults remained at the conventional levels both of faith and morality, which meant that in adolescence the transition to postconventional faith did not take place. Fowler (1984b) had stressed that transactions were often accompanied by struggle and even guilt and grief. Young (1981) regarded stage four as primarily an inner acceptance of the community's values, and this acceptance did not come about without initial dissonance, be it cognitive, affective, or behavioral. There were five ways to resolve this dissonance. Four of them were defensive—individuals could refuse to recognize the dissonance, repress it, discount its source and render it invalid, or castigate themselves, regarding it as resulting from their own failure, and reaffim their own system of values. Such reaffirmation produced the legalism found in the evangelical churches. The other way to resolve the dissonance was to challenge the validity of one's own individual values. Adolescents who did this, rejecting for the time being parental and religious values, were often regarded as rebellious. They became alienated, angry, confused, moody, and in conflict with authority—the classical description of identity confusion. Most of those who reached this stage passed through it to reestablish their values, values appropriate for postconventional faith and morality, retaining many of those that had been temporarily rejected.

The plausibility of Young's suggestion depends on whether religious and moral development are associated,[1] regarding which opinions differ, although, as will be seen later, Getz (1984) concluded that the relationship was established within narrow boundaries. This is an area where research continues. In some families and churches, adolescent questioning may lead to a forced compliance so that they adopt a defensive mechanism to quell their doubts and remain entrenched in a highly structured society that consistently reinforces its own traditional values. Alternatively, adolescents may heighten their rebellion into a permanent attitude and never resolve their doubts, unless such questioning is seen as experimentation and recognized as holding the potential for growth. While there are other possible causes of adolescent rebellion, this model explains why for some, but only some, adolescence is a time of storm and stress. It warns that compliance may not indicate development, but should rather be seen to indicate a foreclosed identity status associated with a less mature, conventional level of faith. Hill (1986) considered that adolescent rebellion and its satisfactory resolution was well illustrated in the parable of the Prodigal Son. However, Martin (1985) thought that a continuous, stable growth of the self-concept of adolescents had been observed, providing no evidence for a period of storm and stress, and boys tended to hold a more favorable self-concept than girls.

In considering the educational implications of adolescent development Hayes (1982) noted that it was the time when the self was discovered as something

1. Morality and religiousness is discussed in chapter 13.

unique, uncertain, and questioning. Moral judgment moved from the preconventional to the conventional level. Ego-development proceeded from a conformist to a conscientious stage through a transitional stage; individual acceptance of the rules of the group moved to a stage characterized by a conscious preoccupation with obligations, ideals, traits, and achievements measured by inner standards. This development came about through social interaction; not all people developed into adolescence, and not all adolescents became adults, for most adults were in the conformist stage. Adolescents needed to be involved in the examination of their personal conflicts and actively practice using their judgment. They were most powerfully affected by the influence of their peers, and the interactions of any peer group were related to changes in self-development. The integration of every new generation of adolescents into society required some change on the part of the adolescents but some change also on the part of society.

Adolescents tended to be diffuse, but this was largely due to inexperience, uncertainty, and hesitation (McCready and Greeley, 1976). Adolescent girls with the lowest ego-identity status also had the lowest religious values (St. Clair and Day, 1979). Although individuals with low identity status were associated with lower levels of moral reasoning, the converse was not established (Mischley, 1976). Because concepts of faith and morality were chronologically related, faith development preceded moral development so that religious education was important for moral development. Faith provided the milieu in which cognitive ability to reason at a higher moral stage could develop, and an autonomous faith might be a necessary condition for the higher types of morality (Mischey, 1976, 1981). Identity achievement among some adolescents in a private girls high school was marked by their having faced doubts about beliefs and values and after considering alternatives, making commitment to a definite position. Others who had similarly questioned goals and values but were still doubtful were at moratorium. Both the groups were academic high achievers. Foreclosure represented those who had doubted values without appraising alternatives, and their choices frequently reflected parental preferences. Identity diffusion subjects might or might not have experienced such doubts, but they had no serious intention to examine alternatives and expressed no commitment to an ideology. These groups were low-achieving academically, and also lacked the flexibility and purposefulness of those with stronger self-esteem (Hummel and Roselli, 1983). An investigation of the lower age boundaries of identity development with children from ten to sixteen showed almost all of them to be in more than one identity status, depending on the context, and there was a significant development of identity status with age. The negative association with parental socio-economic status suggested that better educated parents gave their children greater freedom of choice and in consequence they came later to making firm choices. Religious belief always had the second largest number of children at each of the four identity states, showing great variations between individuals in coming to firm conclusions (Archer, 1982). Students at Christian colleges tended to differ on their religious orientation and moral development according to their identity status (De Witt, 1987). A comparison which related the religious ideas of adolescents and adults to one of three levels of religious complexity showed that the adolescent group had significantly lower scores for complexity, and in all the sample complexity was related to levels of ego development (Nieratka, 1984). Intrinsic, committed religiousness was significantly associated with ego development and tolerance. It appeared that each ego stage was associated with qualitatively different forms of religiousness (Terrance, 1987). A study of the ego-identity status of high-school pupils showed that a Mexican-American group were more likely to adopt their parents' commitment to religious and political beliefs (Abraham, 1986). Because adolescence was the period when identity is resolved, Hill (1986) contended that it was the ideal time to make the transition from a consensual, extrinsic, conventional faith to an intrinsic, committed, postconventional faith.

MacMain (1980) used different terms to describe the faith development of young adults involved in local churches. A few were confused, some still embraced the experienced faith of their parents, some clung to the faith of the church to which they were affiliated, some raised doubts and questions and moved into a searching faith, while a few had worked through their commitment to an owned faith. The description fits closely the classification of Marcia (1966).

The empirical evidence gives support to the suggestions made about the religious consequences of adolescent identity achievement and offers an explanation of why adolescent storm and stress is an occasional and not a regular feature of development. In strict terms, identity achievement is not a personality trait. None of these traits, however they are described, is related to religiousness, although, as was said at the outset, in a number of instances they affect individual religiousness. The important distinction lies between the religious orientations. Introversion and extraversion prove to be unrelated to religiousness. Authoritarian students are not necessarily religious, but when they are they have an authoritarian form of religion. The greater religious involvement of women owes much to social expectations, but whether this accounts entirely for it is uncertain. Religiousness appears to be associated with mental health, especially among intrinsically oriented people, but because it can also provide support for the mentally unstable, their presence clouds the result. Anxiety appears to be enhanced by some forms of religion, notably the authoritarian, but it is reduced by others, and similarly locus of control appears to differ according to the form of belief. So it becomes apparent that as personality develops in childhood and adolescence, it will affect the style of religiousness that they adopt, but it does not predispose them either to accept or to reject a religious outlook.

Chapter 11

The Development of Religiousness

The chapter opens by looking at some psychological theories of religion, such as the recent consideration of attribution theory and cognitive aspects of the origins of religion. Sociological theories that bear upon it are also mentioned. Some aspects of religious development have already been considered—conversion in chapter 9 and the effects of ego-development in chapter 10. The present chapter continues by looking at the social influences of the family, the peer group, and society at large. Religiousness, which depends on an individual's membership of a religious group, is influenced by many social pressures. In the first years of life the family strongly affects young children's growing knowledge and attitudes, and this continues for many years. As children grow older they become aware of alternative attitudes and values, and in adolescence parental influence will almost certainly be challenged, and possibly rejected to a smaller or greater degree. Parental attitudes and religiousness strongly influence their growing children. How much influence a school has, independent of the family or reinforcing family attitudes, forms the subject matter of the final chapter. As adolescents begin to take their place in wider society, they are much more open to its influence than before. They are now fully exposed to ideas, often claiming to be scientific, which regard religion as irrelevant to modern life, or are strongly opposed to it. Secularization permeates contemporary society throughout the Western world, affecting even the patterns and extent of church life.

Argyle (1964) enumerated seven psychological roots of religious belief. It provided a direct need reduction, so that the minor Protestant sects flourished among the economically underprivileged with their belief that the world would soon end. The Cargo Cults provided a good example of this. Religion reduced anxiety, so that older people were more likely to be religious and hold a belief in an afterlife; it was possible that the medical students in Poppleton and Pilkington's (1963) study were more religious than other students because of their contact with death and concern about it. Religion resolved internal conflict; Protestant doctrine and practice tended to arouse and then relieve guilt feelings, and it had been shown that such feelings were related to the attitude to the church in adolescence. Similarly, Baptist ordinands had been shown to have more guilt feelings than Catholic ordinands, even though there was no difference among their laity. The gods were perceived as fantasy parental figures, malevolent when child-rearing was primitive, but benevolent when children were nurtured. Children of punitive Christian parents believed in a sterner, more punitive God. Religion also provided an ego-identity, in particular in the sects for those who had been uprooted socially, such as American or African country people coming to live in cities. Religion provided cognitive clarity, satisfying the need for understanding the world, as when primitive people postulated a thunder god when puzzled by thunder, or when adolescents sought a purpose in life. Anxious people proved to be the most dogmatic about their belief. The least acceptable basis to theologians was the biochemical, although it was known that LSD could produce the mystical states of religious experience.

Spilka, Addison, and Rosensohn (1975) sought experimental justification for theories about the origin of the concept of God. They used a substantial battery of tests with sixteen-year-old high-school Catholics, but they found little support for the theory that self-esteem gave rise to the concept, or for Adlerian theory, and no evidence to support either the Freudian theory or that of social learning. The degree of overlap in the theories was considered in practical terms and the problems of analyzing such data. In consequence, they had no confidence to assert the superiority of any theory. They recognized the complexity of the relationships involved in the semantic similarity between ideas of self, parents, and God.

Attribution theory

Attribution theory is an area of psychology that has recently come into prominence and is of importance because of its bearing on religion. People need to explain what happens to them by attributing events to causes, and interpreting them in terms of their accepted meanings and values. New experiences, frustrations or failures, the loss of personal control or freedom, and the threat of fear or pain all require explanation. This causal attribution is most important when some event challenges the meaning system. When this system is strongly held, people tend to behave in terms of it. There are very many instances when inferences have to be made, often with considerable confidence, about the perceived causes of behavior and events as being due to oneself, to other people, to chance, or to God.

The study of such perceived causation has come to be known as attribution theory, and it has extended in a somewhat ill-defined manner to examine the processes by which causes are attributed to events in an attempt to understand them. It has been subjected to an increasing volume of research, and some now regard it as likely to displace the study of attitudes as a major interest of social psychology. It has an important bearing on the explanation of religious behavior and the strength of the beliefs and behavior children and adults hold. Individuals tend to think that more people agree with their opinions than is usually the case and explain events on the basis of their own presuppositions; such attributions tend to be self-confirming and thus grow in strength. Although psychologists are aware that the attributor's beliefs and motives may give rise to errors in the attribution, there is as yet only a partial understanding of the processes by which this happens, or by which beliefs may or may not come to be modified in the light of subsequent events. An introduction to the topic and a bibliography is given by Kelly and Michela (1980). Spilka, Hood, and Gorsuch (1985) make it the basis for their account of the psychology of religion and use it to provide insights into a wide range of topics, including religious experience, mysticism, conversion, moral behavior, and religious development. Preston (1987) discussed the concept of personal constructs, by which individuals explain the meaning of events and anticipate future events, noting that some such constructs were subordinate to others. When he examined how constructs were organized from adolescence to old age he concluded that the study of constructs was a useful method of studying religious experience, and the differences found between the denominations indicated a social process in construct formation.

Proudfoot and Shaver (1975) appear to be the first to relate attribution psychology to the psychology of religion; they limited it to explaining emotional states but saw it as a useful means of explaining how experiences are interpreted on the basis of religious beliefs. This suggestion was subsequently extended (Spilka, Shaver, and Kirkpatrick, 1985). They contended that an attribution system provided a single conceptual framework which embraced a broad range of attitudes, beliefs, and behavior. Thus, intrinsically oriented people who regarded God as beneficent, tolerant, and available came from supportive family backgrounds and were high in self-esteem. Social influence was important in establishing such a system; most religious experience occurred in conditions which the subjects regarded as having high religious salience. Slocumb (1981) tested the extent to which attribution theory affected religious explanations. When students were read stories that were toned religiously or nonreligiously and then questioned about the causality in them, there was a major difference between the more and the less religious; the less religious students made a significantly greater number of attributions to physical causation than the more religious group, who made more attributions to supernatural causes. The effect was equally true for the less religiously toned material. Gorsuch and Smith (1983) found that among evangelical undergraduates increasing religiousness was associated with a greater tendency to attribute responsibility for events to God rather than to chance, especially when they had a good outcome; fundamentalists were not more likely to do this than other conservative believers. Other people involved were also held to be responsible. Religious faith acted as a perceptual set, pervading cognition and providing a framework from which all reality was viewed. Because of this, religious subjects felt themselves to be in control of their situation with the help of God and proved to be more optimistic than the less religious. Pargment and Hahn (1986) studied causal and coping attribution to God in health situations and found different reactions. Some regarded God as angry, giving just punishment for sin, and others as benevolent, whose will accounted for situations that were not easily understood.

Spilka and Schmidt (1983) noted a number of studies which suggested that attributions to God tended to be made by individuals when a situation was both important and personal or was affected by illness or injury. They read short stories about these things to young people and asked them questions about the role of chance, religious faith, and God in the stories. Whether God or chance was thought to be involved in the events varied according to the situations depicted; God was more often thought to be involved in the events when the stories were about personal rather than impersonal circumstances. Smith (1983) demonstrated that there were two types of attribution to God. People without any theology, or with a theology that was not conservative, attributed greater responsibility to God when events appeared puzzling, than did the theological conservatives, who did not attribute a causal inference to God but only a sanctioning of the event.

Although attribution psychology is a recent development, the tendency of religious people to attribute events to divine intervention is an aspect of the earlier studies of cognitive dissonance. This research began when a research team infiltrated a group who were anticipating an imminent visit from extraterrestrial beings. The adjustments to this belief made by its members when it failed to take place provided the basis of Festinger, Riecken, and Schachter's (1956) well-known study. For belief to persist in the face of contradictory evidence a supporting group is needed, and a few studies of such persistence continue. Wilson (1978) studied the effect on Jehovah's Witnesses of the failure of their prediction of the Second Coming in 1975; abandonment of belief was too traumatic an outcome for those dominated by their beliefs, and in consequence there were calls for greater faith and a reinterpretation of prophecy by enhanced Bible study, leading to a new devotion to the cause. In contrast, when an earthquake prophesied by its founder did not occur, a Japanese sect disintegrated (Sonada and Norbeck, 1975).

Cognitive development and the origin of religion

Elkind (1970) regarded religion as having an individual as well as a social origin and saw it as meeting cognitive needs. He cited Piaget's suggestion that new mental capacities need to be realized through action. Thus the development of conservation brought an understanding of permanence, and with the discovery of death, the need for the conservation of one's own life, an issue which fully arose only in adolescence, and for which a religious solution was possible. Similarly, the growth of language and symbolic play brought an ability to use signs and symbols, and a lifelong search for personal representation. This could be satisfied by religious representations of the transcendent, signifying what is neither spatial, temporal, nor corporeal. When an ability to make logical deductions arose, then children tried to relate things to one another with respect to time, space, causality, and origin; this search for relations, if the idea of God had been accepted, required a religious means of establishing a relationship with the transcendent. The similarity of this observation with attribution theory cannot escape notice. Finally, in adolescence arose the introspective ability to examine objectively one's own thoughts and feelings and to make overriding theories as to the underlying reasons for things. This search for comprehension never met with complete success, but religion, by its body of myth and system of theology, provided a solution to the problem of comprehension. In such a way there was a close fit between basic cognitive need capacities and the major elements of institutional religion. If religion had evolved so as to meet these needs, we could speak of its origins in childhood. There were no unique religious elements—no inherently religious drives, sentiments, emotions, or mental categories. There could be uniquely religious adaptations, such as the concept of God or the transcendent; such concepts, once accepted, entailed genuinely religious problems, but such a concept, whether a personal construction or acquired from institutional religion, was superordinate, transcending the particular individual or social needs as well as the phenomenological factors out of which it arose.

Youniss (1978) argued that socialization began by the age of two. Piaget had spoken of empathy, sympathy, sharing of perspective, and affection; it followed that individuals did not construct social knowledge on their own, but such knowledge involved contributions from other people as well. Over time social relationships changed, so that an acquaintance could become a friend, then an intimate; or alternatively, it could suffer estrangement. Parents and children constantly changed their relationships as children grew out of infancy and parents reached old age. By defining the construction of social knowledge in terms of practical action, Piaget's theory was open to dialectical theorists who usually emphasized their difference from Piaget. Santilli and Meacham (1982) supported the contention that individual knowledge was constructed through collaborative actions with other people, so that adolescents were not logicians attempting to understand the social world but were actively participating in it and through this were able to build structures of knowledge. The development of formal thought proceeded at different rates in different domains, so that when formal thought was not apparent in one particular domain this could be the result of a lack of interest and experience.

Brown (1965b) used Rosenzweig aggression scores to provide evidence for the sociological basis of eight Australian denominations. Strength of belief was due to membership and acceptance of the church, unlike Argyle's (1958) theories of religion, which were all reductionist apart from those of cognitive need and social learning. He regarded belief (Brown, 1966b) as a relatively independent predominately cognitive activity, acquired and sustained by social influences within a supportive and believing context. It was due to social learning rather than to emotional factors, even though metaphysical questions were asked and religious answers to them might show an emotional dependence and willingness to accept nonrational interpretations. The affective concomitants were probably not specific to religion, although they influenced the way individuals expressed their beliefs. He noted his findings that there was a single factor to which a variety of religious variables were related, and this factor was independent of a general response set, opinion strength and certainty about matters of fact and opinion; it was very similar to the "religionism" factor extracted from studies of social attitudes. When he repeated tests of political, religious, and social attitudes after thirty years (Brown, 1981b) the Australian university students showed that religiousness remained a stable factor almost identically structured in both tests. It was an underlying ideology rather than a deep psychological structure confirming that religion should be seen as a relatively isolated cognitive system. It apparently involved a conservative form of belief which related to social and sexual control, shown by responses to items about birth control, premarital sex, and abortion and was oriented toward a consensual religiousness rather than representing a personally committed stance.

Sociological aspects of religious development

Yinger (1970) asserted that a functional theory of religion explained the phenomena by its consequences. Social learning was a source of religious need, and people who were most interested in religion and expressed the strongest need for it were almost entirely drawn from groups that were most concerned about training their members to be religious. These included a family tradition of churchgoing, the social support provided by a religious denomination, and acceptance of the church as a significant institution. This was not inconsistent with the idea that individual needs were among the sources of religion, but what was learned, and the intensity of religious interest, were carried along on a social stream. There would appear to be little difference in character between liberal and conservative Christians, it seemed probable they were simply taught different religious beliefs.

In his study of the social psychology of social movements, Toch (1966) had relatively little to say about religious movements, but his broad conclusions are relevant to them. Those holding unpopular beliefs, such as the Spacecraft Convention of UFO enthusiasts, argued that it was the very validity of those beliefs which made them unpopular—a result similar to Festinger's theory of cognitive dissonance (Festinger, Riecken, and Schachter, 1956). This study of how members were recruited had many parallels to the methods of religious institutions and evangelists, and he described situations in which the new members, having "seen the light," made their commitment, sacrificed their autonomy, and accepted authority, rejecting incompatible ideas or facts by a process of selective perception, as in becoming a member of the Communist party or an order of Trappist monks. Increasing commitment brought a greater relevance of functional autonomy; instrumental believers belonged only because their personal needs were satisfied, whereas dedicated members were belief-centered, belonging primarily because they agreed with what the movement stood for. This division was comparable to Allport's intrinsic and extrinsic religion or to Almond's (1954) esoteric and exoteric membership of the communist party.

The dynamics of disaffection were also discussed. When dissent grew among some members then their latent perceptual discrepancies emerged and their latent reservations became manifest, giving rise to various types of crisis situations. When such members overcame the impediments to defection, then they faced the difficulty of establishing new identities with the consequent cognitive reorganization involved. Return to a former commitment could achieve this, but more often it had to be by slowly discarding beliefs and attitudes as new ones became available. As in all social movements, independent observers had to evaluate the effect of membership, and weigh the security provided by faith in the movement against the blindness and poverty of the closed mind it might bring. It was necessary to evaluate a movement not only by the extent to which its members were satisfied but also by its consequences, as with the Nazis.

Finney (1978) discussed theories of how people become religious, noting that most studies were concerned with religious socialization in childhood and adolescence. He approached the topic by considering five dimensions of religious commitment, those of ritual practice, knowledge, experience, belief, and devotional practice and by analyzing responses from a telephone survey. Membership of a religious group had important consequences for an individual's religious knowledge, experience, belief, and devotional practice. These could be interpreted in sociological terms of group norm conformity and of cognitive and behavioral consistency. The level of individuals' education was inversely related to their experience and belief but positively with their religious knowledge. Experience was adversely associated with higher levels of income, confirming a deprivation hypothesis. Knowledge, belief, and devotion were stronger in women than men, and older people scored highly on devotional practice; age also tended to enhance knowledge but had a negative effect on experience.

Greeley (1982b) gathered together a number of his previous research studies in support of a theory of religion which he called secular because he regarded religion as springing from a human predisposition to hope which it constantly renewed in the face of continued disappointments, a development of Berger's (1969) argument from hope. In this hope-renewing situation the unnamed force encountered was depicted in the idea of God and captured in a range of symbols which in turn were organized into religious stories, explaining the situation of individuals in the world, pointing out good and evil, prescribing right action, and giving an assurance of ultimate purpose. The social forces underlying this process he had described in his previous book (Greeley, 1981).

Mol (1983) regarded religion not only as providing an identity for individuals and groups but also for societies, offering stability in the tension between change and the need for stability or integration. Religion could be seen as the sacralization of identity, modifying the conflicts between incongruent identities. Its rituals and myths gave individuals and groups a transcendental ordering and an emotional anchorage which enhanced their identity, while social integration and differentiation were simultaneously at work. There was a basic human need for religion, and its function was seen neither in terms of the cult of the individual nor of social solidarity but in a compromise between them.

Roberts and Davidson (1984) sought to clarify differences between the Weberian approach to religious involvement which stressed the meaning religion had for an individual and that of Durkheim, where the emphasis was on the importance of the group. Responses from Methodist and Baptist churches demonstrated that an individual's meaning system had a strong influence, while belonging was the most important source of religious involvement. The effect of socio-demographic characteristics was indirect, and particular religious beliefs had the least effect. The strong involvement of members of conservative denominations was due to their allegiance rather than to their beliefs. This finding from a group of adults supports Potvin and Lee's (1982) conclusion that by the end of adolescence religious practice was the strongest source of religiousness.

Parental Influence

Parental influence is a topic that has been under scrutiny for a long time. Most textbooks on the psychology of adolescent development refer to the many studies which bear on parental effects on the personal development of their children; a useful survey slanted to religious interests is provided by Lee (1973). In the account of the studies about religiousness which follows, it must not be overlooked that correlation does not imply a causative relationship. In the press a finding that there was a tendency for criminals to have been smacked when young by their parents more than other children was given the headline, "Smacking Makes Criminals." Yet their more frequent punishment may have been the result of more frequent delinquency arising from quite different causes. Toch (1966) stressed that children were indoctrinated by their parents, whether intentionally or not. Their first view of society was seen as that of the parents, and their dependence on them brought a measure of conformity, especially when expressions of like-mindedness were rewarded. The home was restricted in its sources of information, and small children were unaware of this, nor could they rectify it.

At birth children are entirely dependent on their parents, and their first contacts with society are mediated by their parents. Dependence brings conformity, especially when conformist opinions are rewarded. Only slowly are children influenced by other people and later by school; parents are the primary agents for their socialization and for transmitting to them the cultural norms of racial, ethnic, moral, and religious attitudes. Sociological evidence for this is well-documented, but usually little attention is given to religious aspects of it. Fowlkes (1988) gave a well-documented description of religion and socialization in early childhood, reviewing relevant sociological theories. Simmons (1983) contended that foundational attitudes toward life and existence were one aspect of religion, and the fundamental attitude of trust and happiness learned in early childhood within the family led in later years to personal religious commitment. The religious symbols, traditions and practices of parental belief were learned in the most enduring way through normal religious practices within the home. Moseley and Brockenbrough (1988) discussed the beginnings of faith development in early childhood and pointed out the importance of family religious rituals to young children who have to come to terms with the imagery which they are acquiring. Among others, they described a girl of five who was well on her way to Fowler's second stage.

Clauser (1966), in an extended review, noted the consequences of different aspects of family structure and parental personality, although his references to religion were limited to the differences between Catholics and Protestants. First-born children tended to be more religious than their siblings (MacDonald, 1969), and parental religious influence was stronger when both parents held the same beliefs (Middleton and Putney, 1962). In the final chapter, parental influence will be shown to be associated more strongly than schools with fostering the religiousness of children. The real issue is the extent to which home influence is lasting, for in adolescence it may be rejected. It is equally necessary to know how it varies with different types of religious belief and behavior. Few studies deal with young children. Some conflict in results seems attributable to different measures of religiousness used, whether of belief, behavior, or of attitude.

When home and church reinforce the same points of view, the influence is strong; a two-year analysis of the religious teaching given to young children in a fundamentalist church showed that the children were socialized by the cultural forces of their families and the church community into learning patterns that preceded those which arose from normal schooling. They were taught to obey authority and to adopt a particular attitude to the Bible and its interpretation, memorizing and reciting it. The beliefs and practices of their teachers were in contrast to those of the general culture (Zinsser, 1985). Age may bring changes in these effects. When the spiritual growth and development of evangelical high-school students from Christian high schools and public schools was compared, it proved not to be affected by attendance at a Christian school or by its form of biblical teaching but by parental church attendance (White, 1985). Protestant adolescents had great similarity to their parents' understanding of the meaning of classical religious symbols, and partial consistency over religious belief, but in their attitudes to the church there was a significant discontinuity (Wieting, 1975). For Christians in a Catholic school in Pakistan parental religiousness was predictive of the religiousness of boys and parental support was predictive for girls. Both were predictive for boys in American schools but only parental religiousness for girls. Parental religion rather than parental support was predictive for all American Protestant children and was the better predictor for Catholic children in state schools (Nelsen and Rizvi, 1984).

Between age thirteen and fourteen adolescent religious practice was strongly related to parental religiousness and, to a lesser degree, to their own internal religiousness. Between age fifteen and sixteen they began to construct with their peers their own worldview; this affected their own internal religiousness, and it became the dominant influence on their religious practice. Parents again became influential between age seventeen and eighteen, but now adolescents tended to reconcile their early religiousness, reached from this parental authoritarian basis, with the modifications they had made to it by their interactions with their peers (Potvin and Lee, 1981). University students showed only moderate levels of agreement with their parents on a number of issues, but a greater tendency for agreement on religious issues. Parents who shared similar religious orientations with their children were in greater agreement with their children's attitudes (Hunsberger, 1985). Parental age can also make some difference. In Baptist, Catholic, and Methodist families, the transmission of religious values to adolescents of sixteen was enhanced when the age of the parents was relatively young, when they agreed about religion and sustained good relationships with their children.

Harvey and Felknor (1970) studied the effect of parent-child relationships on the development of students' belief systems; four different types of belief were discovered. In the first system students depended on external authority, preferring structured situations, intolerant of ambiguity, and unwilling to consider new information. Their parents had stressed agreement, fairness, the family reputation, and religious observance. Fathers were strict, frequently punishing their sons without explanation, and mothers, while offering warmth and approval, allowed little freedom, so that their children were very dependent on them. Sons were more critical of parents than daughters. The second system was characterized by negativism; its members rebelled against authority yet were anxious without guidelines. In their homes they had experienced much disagreement, especially about the fathers' lack of religious observance. Parents were regarded as arbitrary, unfair, and lacking in warmth. The fathers were not strict, the freedom they allowed was seen as due to indifference; the mothers often punished their children. The third system comprised those wanting to be liked and accepted, depending on individuals in power and manipulating others of lower status to be dependent on them, which led to a better conceptual organization. Their mother provided much warmth and approval but had sought their dependence; their fathers were less fair and more distant. The fourth system was the most abstract, with a highly developed cognitive structure; its members showed high task orientation, independence, internal standards of conduct, and the ability to consider many points of view so that new information was easily assimilated. Parents were not strict or arbitrary but were fair, warm, approving, and giving independence. There was little disagreement between them, both being interested and involved with their children and more concerned with their accomplishments than with social criteria.

This account of the effects of parental disposition has some similarity with the discussion of Vergote (1980) based on clinical observations related to the identification of parental images. When these were not adequately formed, moral development was disturbed. Inadequate affective bonding with the mother produced demanding, distrustful, and unsympathetic individuals, with feelings of hate and revenge stronger than those of love. The demands of the father were needed for law and authority to be established and balanced by the sense of his love. Hoffman (1971), in a review article, argued that children's moral structures were largely shaped by the way parents interacted with them. Their approach to discipline affected the extent to which their children would adopt their values and attitudes. He discussed this with reference to features of moral development, such as the internalization of values, guilt over transgressions, resistance to temptation, acceptance of blame, and considerations for others—all of which have religious overtones.

The continuing church participation of recently confirmed Lutheran adolescents was associated with a high level of parental activity, consistency, and education and with good family relationships. It was also associated with worship and religious teaching related to daily life, a sense of belonging to a congregation which provided meaningful social experiences, an approachable minister, a view of religion as being practical, and feeling of personal relationship with Christ (Jarvis 1967). The religious beliefs and practices of Catholic students were due to a strong family influence (Montgomery and Montgomery, 1975), and family support was a strong factor in distinguishing between Catholic altar boys committed to the priesthood and those undecided or uncommitted (Curcione, 1973). Parental belief and church attendance were found to be strongly associated with the religiousness of senior school students, especially girls (Cox, 1967). The religious thinking and concepts of young Seventh-Day Adventist children was influenced not only by their age but by their families' religious practices (Davis, 1978). Hoge and Petrillo (1978b) cited previous studies showing that parental religious values were a strong influence on adolescent church attitudes, whereas there was little effect from socio-economic factors, from type of school attended, from years of formal religious training, either in Sunday school or Catholic school, or from religious education programs. Religious knowledge had little effect, and cognitive development had none; the level of activity in clubs or organizations in the school or community was irrelevant. The main factors were the types of relationships with other people. The very strong influence of parents was mostly through their behavior, not through a conscious effort to socialize their children into the church. Parental religious practice was a major determinant of adolescent religiousness among Catholics, even more with girls than with boys, and their church attendance was related to many aspects of their children's religiousness (Suziedelis and Potvin, 1981). McCready (1979) showed that the religious socialization of Catholic adolescents was primarily influenced by the quality of the parent's relationship. Parental religiousness and parental support were the significant predictors of the children's religiousness, even though there was no significant relationship between the two factors (Nelsen, 1980).

Among a group of Danish adolescents and young adults parental influence, with reasoning, was the strongest influence in the formation of religious attitudes but was of much less consequence in the formation of political attitudes (Iisagar, 1949). Yet to the contrary, parent's political opinions influenced their children but not their religious attitude, except for Catholic children (Hirschberg and Gilliard, 1942); their stated opinions on politics and religion had little effect on their children, except as they were perceived by them, and such perceptions tended to be more traditional or conservative than was actually the case, with agreement between parents greatly exaggerated. This "polarized misattribution" was independent of sex and possibly reflected the position of the generations in the interactions of socialization (Acock and Bengtson, 1980).

Between 1963-1974 the frequency of children's prayer when compared with their parents showed a decline for mothers and daughters and to a smaller extent for fathers and sons; parental practice influenced the children (Morgan, 1981). The importance of family worship was demonstrated by comparing two groups of elementary school children; the children in a group engaged in an eight-week period of frequent family worship made a significant advance in religiousness (Perry, 1979).

Denominational differences in parental influence have been recorded. There was a growing strength in family attitudes to the church from Protestants to Catholics, then to Jews; the strongest relationship between parental and children's attitudes was in the lower socio-economic groups. Protestant children tended to diverge more from parental conservatism toward change than did Catholic children (Newcomb and Svehla, 1937). On the other hand, a study of the persistence of differences in religious outlook, apparently due to the influence of social and theological factors, showed that parental orthodoxy was the strongest factor, and when allowance was made for it denominational influence retained no significant effect (Nelsen, 1982). But a contrary finding was that membership of a church predicted adolescent values better than those of the parents, so that it appeared that socialization in religious values took place in cultural subgroups more than in nuclear families (Hoge and Petrillo, 1982). Adolescent alienation was associated with the quality of relationships with their parents and other authority figures, peer groups, their own self-concepts, the influence of the media, and negative influences from the church such as uninteresting sermons, restrictions on lifestyle, and deficient devotional life (Laurent, 1986). The religiousness of high-school students in Evangelical Free Churches was significantly less than that of their parents, although they shared the same beliefs, behaviors, and outlooks. In religious development, parental influence was the major factor in a Presbyterian group, whereas in the Evangelical church groups, church and parents were both influential. Christian schools had no influence, despite popular expectation (Inskeep, 1986).

The influence of peers was important for adolescents' self concept, but there was no evidence that adolescent religion was a product of a distinctive youth subculture. A youth subculture was a matter of ritualistic conformity, but it was not important in the maintenance of ideals, values, and religion. These owed much more to the home where the mother and her close friends were a strong influence. Parental support appeared to be more important for religious belief than for religious activity. As adolescents moved into adult life, while they still regarded religion as being of importance, they engaged in less overt religious activity in line with what they perceived as an adult model (De Vaus, 1983).

University and college life does not undermine early parental influence, although there are denominational differences. Mennonite students in a Canadian university and three church-related colleges showed a greater agreement with their parents' religious ideas than Catholic or United Church students, even when allowance was made for the reported emphasis on religion in the childhood home. Over the three years of university education there was a persistence of religiousness and no move toward more liberal beliefs. The students in the church-related colleges showed a limited tendency for greater agreement with parental belief than the others, but there was no relationship between this and years spent earlier at parochial schools. There was no support for the idea that conservative Protestants had the greatest reaction against religious teaching (Hunsberger, 1973). Liberal Protestants showed least agreement with parental religious ideas, and the emphasis placed on religion by the family in the students' childhood was only partly related to these differences (Hunsberger, 1976). Peer influence on the religious and sexual behavior of freshmen at Church of Christ colleges was so strong that, despite their former influence, parents no longer constituted an effective reference group for these new college students (Woodroof, 1986).

In early and middle adolescence, religiousness was associated with that of parents, but at college age it was most strongly related to attitudes of peers, although former pratice remained as an anchor while beliefs were evolving. Adolescence brought a greater capacity to reason and question, and it increased the opportunities to share the experiences of others. Attitudes were polarized, and the increase of religiousness among the more religious matched the decrease of religiousness of the moderately religious.When college culture encouraged questioning, such a set of mind led to academic success, but also it was a catalyst for those already primed for it (Ozorak, 1989).

The educational level of the family is also a factor. The attitude to religion of educated parents showed a stronger attitude toward religion than their student children (Kirkpatric and Stone, 1935). Better educated people displayed less hostility toward minority groups, a consequence of their greater cognitive flexibility, and a liberal, open-minded climate in a family, whatever its social background, exposed children to information that was conducive to the development of friendly attitudes toward various outgroups. On the other hand, low self-esteem in poorly educated people was associated with persistent negative attitudes (Schönbach et al., 1981). In the intellectual culture of university teachers there was little evidence of a "religion of science," but the strongest predictors of religiousness were childhood religion and home culture; religious commitments had strong noncognitive sources which were little affected by intellectual training (Hoge and Keeter, 1976).

Increased family size tended to bring increased family affection and activities in Mormon families, and since frequency of attendance at the Mormon Temple was a key factor affecting religiousness, when account was taken of this, other factors ceased to be significant. The influence of the mother, rather than the father, was of greater importance (Wilkinson and Tanner, 1980).

Some indication of sex differences appeared in a study of Australian Catholic adolescents; girls were significantly more favorable toward institutional authority than boys. Acceptance of authority was associated with belief in God in both sexes but with church attendance only among the boys. This difference between the sexes could be explained by the assumption that boys tend to be hostile to authority and become defiant of parents and teachers who try to coerce them into church attendance, whereas girls, who tend to avoid conflict, react differently (Rigby and Densley, 1985).

Can children influence parents? Pinkenson (1987) recorded that Jewish parents with children in Jewish day care centers when compared with similar parents whose children attended secular centers, showed increased Jewish friendships, home ritual observances, and holiday celebrations and increased contributions to Jewish organizations. He concluded that day care of a high quality which included religious education and stressed the development of Jewish identity for its young children also increased the parents' Jewish identity and brought them to a stronger affiliation with the Jewish community. He did not consider the possibility that parents with the greatest Jewish involvement were more likely to send their children to a Jewish day care center.

Perhaps the more extreme parental attitudes were lacking in a Baptist, Catholic, and Methodist sample which showed that it was parents' attendance at church rather than a conscious effort to socialize their fourteen-year-old children's attendance that had a strong influence on them. Otherwise, they had little influence on their attitudes toward the church and church youth programs. Despite the strength of parental influence, the amount of parent-child tension turned out to be quite unimportant, and church rejection as a psychological extension of parent rejection was only weakly supported. For some it was largely due to a dislike of past religious training and to perceptions of church leaders as unapproachable, insincere, or uncertain about their beliefs. Rejection of church youth groups was mostly due to being snubbed or rejected by the others, to pressures from peers against church youth programs, and to unpleasant experiences in past religious training (Hoge and Petrillo, 1978b).

When a group of lapsed adolescents were compared with a matched sample, the groups differed only in their responses to parental religious teaching and the emphasis placed on religion in childhood (Hunsberger, 1980). Another study of lapsed students showed that the degree to which freedom of thought was encouraged and religion emphasized in their homes in childhood were the two best predictors of their retention or rejection of religious involvement (Hunsberger and Brown, 1984).

Parents and teachers no longer influenced the moral judgments of boys at Kohlberg's postconventional stage of moral development but had been replaced by peers. Girls at the same stage were still influenced by their parents to some extent, but there was an indication that they rejected their father's influence. The ambivalence and hostility of a conservative, authoritarian family structure was associated with conventional morality. Postconventional morality altogether rejected such values, and this represented a legitimate expression of resentment against the authority of a parent who was perceived as unjust (Henry, 1987).

Parental control and nurture

The style of parents' control of their children arises from their attitudes, which profoundly affect children's development. So it is not surprising that parental control often has a religious outcome for children. Hirschberg (1955) commented that children's ideas of God, sin, guilt, and forgiveness grew out of their experiences of parental love and authority and their parents' reaction to their successes and failures, accomplishments and mistakes, and their joys and sorrows. Harsher parental discipline with a rigorous religious training motivated children to present themselves in a favorable light, even if it meant reporting things of doubtful truthfulness (Crandall and Gozali, 1969). A parental threat to withdraw affection was a powerful means of securing conformity, although it was weakened if other sources of affection were available, as from the other parent; this combination of affection and discipline resulted in the development of strong guilt reactions (Moulton et al., 1971). Muslim and Hindu adolescents of fourteen and fifteen had prejudiced parents who used a retributive, authoritarian control (Hassan and Khalique, 1987). In Christian high schools, adolescents' concepts of God were affected by authoritarianism in the family, which was associated with an extrinsic religious orientation, and appeared to impair their spiritual growth. It induced a closed cognitive style and a degree of over-dependency (Ernest, 1982). Authoritarian child-rearing attitudes were related to some of the ideas of God of first-year students (Swickard, 1963). Previous studies of Zern (1987b) had shown that obedience to parents in early and later childhood was associated with higher levels of cognitive functioning; it followed that since religion promoted obedience among children it was a valuable trait, and the criticism should be rejected that it fostered obedience without understanding. An unhappy childhood was associated with the rejection of religious belief (Vetter and Green, 1932), and students who rebelled against their parents tended to be less authoritarian and conservative. This was less likely if the parents held the same faith (Putney and Middleton, 1961b). Students with less religious belief and devotion reported low parental control and nurturing, whereas those with greater religiousness reported high mother control and good communication or high control and high nurture (Luft and Sorell 1987). Church attendance, prayer, respect for clergy, and belief in God had an association with obedience to parents and to unjust laws, and with patriotism and disapproval of illicit sexual behavior (Black and London, 1966).

Only ineffectual parents used the strategy of children being threatened with punishment by God for bad behavior to enhance their power to control their children. Its effect was to produce compliance rather than an internalization of values, and God was seen as a threatening surveillance force unless compensated by the idea of God benevolently rewarding good behavior. The children of these families exhibited a high level of self-blame, and their parents tended to be of low income, belonging to sect-type churches (Nunn, 1964). Participation in religious activities at school had a socializing effect on adolescent drinking behavior, those who came from a strong anti-alcohol family background tended to drink more frequently than those from a background which was more tolerant but did not encourage alcohol use (Preston, 1969). A replication of Nunn's study showed that such parental control was less frequently encountered. It still produced in children the image of a benevolent God who rewarded good behavior; the malevolent view was associated with a lower level of internalization (Nelsen and Kroliczak, 1984). An extrinsic religious orientation was found in students whose childhood had been marked by suspicion, distrust, insecurity, and feelings of inferiority; because of this, they tended to belong to a church because it offered them a safe and powerful in-group (Tisdale, 1966). Yet strong parental control and support brought increased adolescent acceptance of traditional religion.

Catholics were more likely than Protestants to use corporal punishment (Lenski, 1961). Parental control and support affected religiousness not only among Catholic adolescents but also among Mormons of twelve to eighteen (Weigert and Thomas, 1972). Adolescent dogmatism and religious beliefs were associated with those of their parents. Adolescent dogmatism was also associated with their own anxiety and anomia and with an extrinsic orientation, though not with orthodoxy (Thompson, 1973).

Protestant adolescent religiousness related positively with parental acceptance and negatively with rejection and power control. The intrinsically oriented were associated with parental empathy and acceptance and psychological control. Extrinsic religiousness was associated with an uncontrolled environment in which parents were perceived as distant, whereas an atmosphere of acceptance where parental demands were clearly stated and internalized fostered an intrinsic orientation (Lindquist, 1980). Parental indifference gave rise to feelings of insecurity and a craving for recognition, as did an overstrict or inconsistent discipline. Unsatisfactory relationships between parents and children were a significant cause of delinquency (Thilagaraj, 1983). Parental methods of control and influence directly affected the belief systems of their student children. Practices that made use of fear and shame were associated with the highest scores on religiousness and family closeness, while denigration and fear were associated with the lowest scores on self-esteem (Batres, 1984). Both commitment to a church and to religion by children from eight to thirteen involved in youth organizations was associated with social influences and nurturing family practices with democratic control. Antisocial behavior, alcohol use, racism and sexism were related to restrictive parental regimes, and inadequate parental support was also associated with drug use and sexual activity (Forliti and Benson, 1986). Parental religiousness and adolescent religious belief were strongly related to religious practice in Catholic and Protestant groups, but neither affected the decline in practice with age, although the decline varied with different categories of religious experience and parental control (Potvin and Sloane, 1985). Yet in Antigua and Barbuda religious affiliation was the best predictor of adolescents' religiousness; their perception of parental support or control and their demanding or punishing behavior had no effect on it, although the mother's demanding and punishing behavior did affect some aspects of it. In this culture there was minimal support for generally accepted theories depending on parent-child interaction (Sheppard, 1986).

The alienation of Seventh-Day Adventist adolescents from their parents' beliefs was associated with the quality of the relationship with parents and other religious authority figures, especially when it was about religious matters, and also with the perceived inconsistency between profession and practice in the lives of their religious teachers. If they attended an Adventist school, then the deleterious effect of the school could exceed that of the home. There was also some association between alienation and belief in a stern, judging God rather than a God of love (Dudley, 1978). Adventist adolescents misattributed their parents' beliefs and values, but not their behavior; this supported the role of cognitive attribution with its cognitively oriented aspects in the transmission of values (Villeneuve, 1984).

Parental praise had no effect on improving the rate of high-school students' Bible reading, or improving attitudes to it, but a monetary reward had a positive influence on both. The movement toward independence in adolescence confounded the effect of parental praise, whereas there was no such adverse effect on money as a reinforcer (Captain, 1975).

Paternal and maternal influences

Differing conclusions have been reached regarding the relative religious influence of mothers and fathers. When reviewing a number of studies Hoge and Petrillo (1978b, 1979) noted the conclusion that fathers were more influential than mothers on adolescent religiousness. Each religious dimension of a student sample could be predicted from that of their fathers, despite the observed generation gap between them. The fathers perceived their student children to be more orthodox than they really were, and the students perceived their fathers to be less orthodox then they were (Williams, 1972). A crucial aspect of handing on Christian faith to Catholic children was the amount of God-talk in their homes, and the involvement of the fathers in this was of particular importance (Chesto, 1987). Catholic children's self-esteem proved to be significantly related to that of their father, except for first-born sons (Marto, 1984). Students who perceived their own roles as similar to those of their fathers showed higher scores for religious belief than other students; the absence of any significant sex difference gave no support to Freudian theory (Tobacyk, 1983). Catholics were more likely than Protestants to see one parent dominant—usually the father (Hess and Terney, 1962). In a study of a broad range of adolescent religious activities, Kieren and Munro (1987) found that girls were influenced by their fathers and not their mothers, whereas boys were influenced by both parents. Is paternal religious influence similar to moral influence? The father's influence on his adolescent sons' moral judgment showed a complex influence; his self-esteem predicted paternal warmth which was positively related to their level of moral development by enhancing congruity between them, but the fathers' encouragement of autonomy had a negative effect on it (Oliker, 1979). Just before adolescence it was the mother's nurturing of children's faith rather than the father's which was effective; fathers were only influential when they talked with their children about faith and their children asked them questions about it (Dry, 1989).

However, stronger maternal influence has also been recorded. In the substantial parental influence on adolescents, that of the mother was the stronger, and there was no evidence for any sex-linked effects (Acock and Bengtson, 1978). Mothers were perceived as more religious than fathers (Wright, 1962), and both parents had similar effects on their children, but maternal religion was an especially strong influence on daughters. When mothers had low levels of religiousness, their sons were adversely affected to a marked degree (Nelsen, 1980). The parents' belief systems influenced their children, and the mother and her general attitude influenced them more than their father (Schmidt, 1981). The mother's influence in the home was the dominant one (Hunsberger and Brown, 1984). In Seventh-Day Adventist churches, mothers tended to have the most traditional religiousness, followed by fathers and then adolescents. Children's religious values were significantly related to those of their parents, with the mother's influence the stronger, but their church membership also had an effect (Dudley and Dudley, 1986). The religiousness of young adult sons and daughters was associated with that of the mother, and the religiousness of sons was also associated with that of the father, when the relationship with the parent of the same gender was a strong one (Philben, 1988). A different perspective between the sexes was that girls perceived the parental power structure as more equalitarian than did boys, since the mother was regarded as more powerful by girls than by boys (McDonald, 1980). The studies take little account of age; it is possible that growing maturity brings greater insight and a different perspective to these relationships of parental personalities and abilities.

The two groups of studies supporting the stronger influence of both the father and the mother are not necessarily in conflict if the area of their influences is more carefully defined. The relationships of adolescent sons with their fathers and mothers were different from that of adolescent daughters, and relationships with friends of the same sex were again quite different (Youniss and Smoller, 1985). In the transmission of religious beliefs and practices by parents to their first-born adolescent sons, mothers and fathers had different roles. Adolescent church attendance was associated with that of the father, but their religious experience and practical application of religion was associated with the mother (Clark, Worthington, and Danser, 1988).

Abusive and divorced parents

Parental discord can affect the religiousness of children; Nelsen (1981) found that the decline in religiousness of children from intact families was significantly greater when there was fighting or frequent argument between the parents. It was most marked with boys from such homes who were also subjected to corporal punishment at home. Girls were not similarly affected. This could be due to boys seeing the father as an authority figure, and the mother as an affectionate figure, whereas girls see the father both as an authority and as an affectionate figure, and with growing maturity perceive their parents to be less religious.

The attitude to religion of adolescents from intact families did not differ significantly from a smaller number with a single parent. Those from homes where the parents were happily married had a significantly higher score than those whose parents were divorced, but those with separated parents had an even higher score. It was not the actual break-up of the family but the subsequent desolation that brought a change, so that children from separated homes found some consolation in God, or transferred their fantasies about the missing parent into a favorable attitude to God (Kay, 1981c). The study did not indicate if there were long-term differences between children of divorced and of separated parents. When religious behavior was taken as the measure, a different result was secured, for adolescents from separated and divorced families had the lowest rate of church attendance, those from intact families the highest, and those from families where one parent had died were intermediate. It appeared that religiousness was related to family cohesion (Ambert and Saucier, 1986). Silverstein (1988) reviewed a number of studies indicating that converts and cult members were often characterized by a history of poor relationships with both parents and peers, and their parents often suffered from a degree of mental illness and were not happily married. Their change in lifestyle could be a rebellion against their upbringing which brought a submissive attitude toward God and a new authority figure who compensated for an inadequate father.

In a study of parental attitudes to child rearing, Neufeld (1979) studied child-abusing parents, some of whom had a religious affiliation, and other parents in various religious groups. Abusive parents who were religious had a more positive attitude to child rearing than the other abusing parents; their scores were almost equal to those of fundamentalist parents. There was a significant difference between abusive parents and religious nonabusing parents, although not between abusive and fundamentalist parents. No significant difference was found between men and women. In the religious groups the Jewish group had the most positive attitudes, and the fundamentalist group the most negative; their attitude to their children was affected by their idea of God as being punitive and their children often being regarded as bad, selfish, or demanding.

Parental attitudes to religious education

Many British parents regard religious education as a necessary subject for study at school. When a Gallup poll had indicated that only 4 percent thought it should not be provided, a survey of parental attitude was undertaken. More than three-quarters wanted religious education retained as a compulsory school subject, and 90 percent thought that if there was no legal requirement schools should continue to provide it (May and Johnston, 1967). But the questionnaire was alleged to be biased in favor of religion, so that given a neutral set of criteria parents would have indicated only that they wanted moral teaching for their children and some knowledge of their cultural background. Children needed to know about and understand Christianity but not so as to lead to Christian faith—an objective which was widely recorded in the agreed syllabuses of the period (Hill, 1968).

Musgrave (1971) in a historical review of family influence in education in England, suggested that the original church school movement channeled the charity of the wealthy into schools for the poor in order to provide a minimum Christian education to keep these children in the station for which they were destined. Since then, the schools had been compelled more and more to exert the social control which economic circumstances had taken from the family. From a very different, theological, stance Fishburn (1983) also argued that twentieth-century parents had been deprived of much control over their children.

When these studies are considered alongside those on parental images and the idea of God it is apparent that parental influence on childrens' religiousness is both strong and complex. In some instances the association may be due to some other factor—it could be argued that if parents attend church, this encourages their children to attend also, and both parents and children derive religious beliefs and experience from church attendance. However, the cumulative impact of the research is that the strong associations between parental religiousness and that of their children is causal. Within this influence, many factors are at work. The relationships between parents and children are complex; they are different for fathers and mothers and sons and daughters and are affected if one parent is preferred. Much less attention has been given to the influence of older or younger brothers or sisters and other members of the family. In a period when women's role in society is changing, some religious beliefs encourage equality between parents, other beliefs still support the dominance of the father. Their roles vary in different cultures, and within families, the personalities of both parents differ greatly. It is in their homes that children first learn about religion, or are taught unconsciously not to be religious, and their religious beliefs and behavior are encouraged or discouraged by their parents throughout childhood. What is not known are the more precise details of how these influences operate, and without such knowledge, attempts to help parents bring up their children in a religious faith are bound to be haphazard.

Peer group effects

Peer group influence in adolescence is a strong social constraint. Membership of a religious group brings with it strong social pressure from the norms of that group. Its influence on the verbal expression of moral and religious belief was demonstrated when three separate groups were asked questions about controversial moral issues; one group first heard the tough responses of two older students, the second group heard tender responses, and the control group was uninfluenced. Results showed that group pressure clearly operated, but did so equally for the tough and tender influences; there was some evidence that the effect decreased with age (Davies, 1971). Among students, the Protestant ethic was significantly related to membership of a group holding conventional religious beliefs and political conservatism. It was not related to socio-economic status, nor to personality variables but was due to this social and cultural background (Beit-Hallahmi, 1979). In chapter 12 there is reference to adolescent participation in a church or its youth programs having little relationship to their religiousness. What was of paramount importance was the nature of the relationships they had with other people (Hoge and Petrillo, 1979). Clique structures tended to interfere with the religious goals of Sunday evening youth groups meeting on church premises. The cliques that formed in them tended to be of the same sex; they were held together by a common interest, such as athletic interest or college grade, and sports figures dominated the larger groups (Shippey, 1970).

The religious attitudes and practices of a sample of New York Catholic adolescents aged sixteen were shown to be more strongly related to those of their peers than of their parents, and even less related to possible school influence, yet they perceived their parents to hold more positive attitudes than they held themselves, but their peers to hold less positive attitudes (Pazhayapurakal, 1989). Parental influence decreases as adolescents grow into adult life. After ten years the beliefs about God of former seventeen-year-old adolescents had changed and their attitudes were less positive. Parental influence had weakened, and now its effect was indirect through the persistence of earlier beliefs and attitudes, so that former frequent church attenders tended still to be the most regular. Now the strongest influence was that of the spouse; wives had more positive attitudes and higher levels of traditional beliefs than their husbands, and when these were strong, their husbands also tended to be like their wives (Willits and Crider, 1989).

Potvin and Lee (1982) undertook a significant study of how the relationships between religious belief, experience, and practice changed with age among adolescents. It showed considerable denominational variations. The highest scores for religious practice were achieved by the sects, followed in order by Baptists, Catholics, mainline Protestants, Jews, and others, with those of no religion scoring least. The younger adolescents, who had practicing parents and came from more conservative denominations, had their religion strongly influenced by their own continuing religious involvement and appeared still to be submissive to religious authority and to the norms of their parents. At fifteen or sixteen a Piagetian-style development of differentiation and decentration took place, and belief proved to have a greater influence than practice. Peers began to influence directly adolescent religion and beliefs. From fifteen to seventeen they were constructing their own worldview, and former religious beliefs and practice were affected when they proved to be in conflict with their newly formulated philosophy. At seventeen or eighteen religious practice had become autonomous and an individual religious lifestyle had been formed, so that now the greater influence of religious practice was reestablished, and either traditional beliefs were confirmed or new beliefs and experiences generated. Age itself did not cause the development, and the term stage was inappropriate. Not all adolescents developed to the point of constructing religious meanings, nor did they do so at the same age, although at fifteen or sixteen the process appeared more salient.

When Scandinavian boys were questioned about the religious attitudes of their friends, every boy believed all the others to be less religious than himself. Because each of them perceived the expectation of the peer group for him to be a little less of a Christian than he actually was, each of them thought himself to be the most religious. Such an expectation must have sprung from a fictional social pressure (Rommertviet, 1953).

When all these influences have been considered, the comment of Rosenblatt (1984) might be recalled: In many countries, children who have known nothing but war have two things in common, an absence of revenge and a belief in God, and in this they differ from older generations.

Social influences on religiousness

There has been a great deal of research into the extent that social forces affect religiousness, and some of it has a bearing on this review. When the religious nurture of children is seen as a process of socialization, as by Fowlkes (1988), the significance of social influence becomes apparent. By the time that school starts, children have become aware of other people with other ideas and attitudes. Parental omniscience is now challenged, if only in trivial matters, by that of their teachers. For the rest of their lives they will be affected by external social pressures, not only the general trend of attitudes, such as secularization, but the pressure of the groups to which they belong, at work, in leisure, and for religious activities. Churches, like schools, have a hidden curriculum teaching the values of their culture by their use of time and space, furniture arrangement, and social habits. Within this, there was a reaction between the church and the cultural expression of youth which hitherto had not been considered (Neville, 1982). Religiousness was associated with having friends in a local congregation; in a Mormon sample it was shown that it could be strengthened or weakened by other strong external friendships (Cornwall, 1987). The significance of church friendships varies. Newcomers felt churches where members had large numbers of church friends were cliquish, and they were not easily absorbed into them; here membership was either static or declining. In two growing churches members had far fewer church friends and a strong desire to add to them (Olson, 1989).

Jahoda (1951) regarded the abandonment of belief as due to social and emotional, rather than to intellectual factors—the reasons given for unbelief were usually inadequate and were sometimes irrational. In early childhood the content of religion was often meaningless; religious belief had given rise to guilt and fear by the age of eight or nine with nonbelievers from a strongly religious background. Schooldays brought a general decline in the emotional significance of religion, and with adolescence came a widening of interests not necessarily religious. To this period belonged the real decline in religious interest, which was thus associated with the reduction of home influence and the effects of starting work or going to college. It seemed that belief itself faded before church-going habits were finally abandoned. Earlier, Rosander (1939) regarded this decline as related to the increasing social and economic obligations of adolescents and the changes in interest this produced. It was not possible to say how much was due to a breaking away from parental control, or from finding other ways of securing the social and emotional benefits formerly provided by the church. A study reported in the final chapter asserts that well-intentioned teachers in English primary schools confuse their pupils about religion and sow the seeds of later disaffection.

Radke, Trager, and Bavis (1949) used a projective picture test to explore the social perceptions and attitudes of children from five to eight. Contrary to usual expectations, they found that the children were already showing much awareness of their racial and religious groupings, and were all learning the expectations of their group and its stereotypes and prejudices. The black-white racial division was the most marked and the Jewish-Christian division next, with much less reaction as yet between Catholic and Protestant—the latter a term not understood by many. Age increased prejudice without improving knowledge of other groups, and there were no apparent sex differences. Another study of children from nine to sixteen showed that the majority of them had a low level of understanding of cultural similarities and differences; they had learned prejudices against minority groups without any personal experience of them (Radke and Sutherland, 1949). Powell and Stewart (1978) showed that with children and adolescents religiousness had a significant negative correlation with ethnocentrism. The decline in religiousness with age was not unique; it was true also of ethnocentricism and punitiveness. It was evident that by eight these children had learned to hold society's traditional beliefs, but thereafter they proceeded to unlearn orthodox social values and become gradually liberalized. The children seemed to have copied the authoritarian behavior and attitudes of their parents but gradually have become aware of alternative models. Personality also had an effect, since extraverts were more sociable in their behavior. Support for the early learning of social attitudes came also from Smidt (1980). Social factors were shown to influence the social judgments of Swiss and American children from four to ten. They were presented with stories of moral dilemmas, classified in three Piagetian stages, and the results indicated the role of social factors—such as dynamic exchanges, discussions, and opposition—in the development of moral values. Cognitive conflict was seen as aiding the achievement of high-level responses (Ruffy, 1981).

Nias (1972) developed a conservatism scale applicable to children. Boys and girls of eleven and twelve gave very similar responses, and analysis of them showed four major factors, with ethnocentrism and punitiveness loading negatively on religion and sexual morality. This was in contrast to the adult pattern where the religious factor loaded positively on a conservatism or authoritarian factor. The result demonstrated that children had developed consistently organized sets of attitudes in these four areas by this age, with a close similarity between the sexes. Religious attitudes were noticeably different from the pattern of adult attitudes, the latter appeared to develop as the result of a complex interaction of personality and various learning factors. The attitudes of children were determined by simpler social processes and particularly by the influence of parents and teachers; at this age religiousness retained the original Christian ethic of loving one's neighbor.

Scobie (1978) regarded the development of attitudes as a complex process. Genetic factors and environmental influences gave rise to an individual's personality traits, and these shaped the ways of thinking about a topic which he termed the ideology level. This included such broad social orientations as conservatism, authoritarianism, or tender-mindedness. By adolescence personality was well-established and ideological structures were developing; it was these, in their interplay with parents, peers, and society, that gave rise to a wide range of attitudes which tended to be resistant to change. Thus, a conservative ideology would produce a conservative attitude to religion, to politics, to child-rearing, or to whatever was appropriate. The complexity of this attitude development was due to the interplay of these factors; an individual's specific social attitudes might be consistent or inconsistent; environmental pressures might or might not support them or themselves prove to be inconsistent, some supporting and others opposing the attitude.

Potvin (1977) in his study of God images of adolescents concluded that the image of God was due to socialization and the projection of parental images, an issue discussed in chapter 4. Nelsen and Potvin (1977) compared information about children and adolescents with other studies of religiousness in rural and urban situations, noting among much else that the relationship between socio-economic status and fundamentalism almost disappeared in rural situations, although elsewhere there was a high incidence of it among Protestants. Roberts and Davidson (1984) regarded social relationships as the strongest factor in maintaining religious involvement, with an individual meaning system compatible with such membership as its main adjunct.

The religious beliefs of religious groups may strongly influence aspects of their members' behavior. Mormon students who were the most favorable to the church indicated strong sympathy with traditional Mormon attitudes about avoiding the use of alcohol, tobacco, tea, and coffee. This attitude was also found in a nonaffiliated group who were apparently of Mormon background, but it was not found among the Catholics (Telford, 1950). In the West Midlands, West Indian adolescents who were Seventh-Day Adventists were found to have more positive attitudes to school, teachers, parents, and policemen than Rastafarians and were more tolerant of the British way of life. This was explicable by the religious presuppositions of the two groups. Adventist theology required obedience to parents and those in authority, and, looking for the transformation of the present order, enabled it to be tolerated in hope. Rastafarians considered themselves as possessing the knowledge, wisdom, and goodness of God and were thus less tolerant. In this instance it seemed that social attitudes were dependent on religion (Barnes, 1983).

Undergraduates in India indicated a desire for social distance from Sindhis, Christians, and Muslims but a closer relation with Brahmins and Hindus. There was a significant association between high religiousness and a reduced feeling of social distance, so that the students with the highest religiousness were significantly less likely to express a desire for social distance with any ethnic group (Verma and Upadhyay, 1984). Among high and low caste boys in India from four to fourteen their religious preferences and prejudices proved to be socially learned attitudes. They developed with age, emerging early in childhood and crystallizing about eight or nine. Prejudice against other religions was fully internalized by fourteen or fifteen; the main traget of prejudice for Hindu children was Muslims. Prejudice was positively associated with religiousness, with pro-caste attitudes and with such personality traits as anxiety, authoritarianism, conformity, and rigidity (Mukhopadhyay, 1986). Rather different were the Greek Orthodox junior highschool students in Australia. Most had been born there, but almost all had one parent born overseas. They had all attended a Greek Orthodox school at some time. Some of their religious practices arose from individual religious commitment, others, such as attendance at Orthodox celebrations of Holy Communion, were strongly associated with Greek rituals, and this was the strongest of the influences isolated (Athanasou, 1984). Another Australian study showed how children may be disadvantaged when the religious values of their group conflict with those of society. An Orthodox Jewish day school in Australia had a strong Chassidic culture at variance with the secular academic tradition. The interaction of these two cultures frustrated the boys attending the school. They faced a cultural dissonance which affected their relationships and produced hyperactivity, anxiety, tension, conflict, and even aggression among them (Bullivant, 1976).

Deconchy (1984) maintained that while the conformity inherent in an orthodox system could not be explained entirely in terms of psychosocial processes, social control not only maintained the ideological conformity of members but also prevented them from realizing the gap that existed between their beliefs and what was usually accepted as rational. Loewenthal (1985) shed light on this; religious students, when asked to explain their religiousness, accepted the situational rather than the dispositional explanation to a greater extent. They seemed to be more aware than the nonreligious of external causes of their religiousness. They were also more likely to agree with favorable items in the test instrument. Subjects tended to see their own behavior more as externally motivated, whereas observers saw the reverse. Fuller analysis of the responses indicated that they preferred to explain religiousness in terms of a purpose in life, a need for security, and of their upbringing. While the nonreligious used explanations such as brainwashing, an unquestioning attitude, and a need for security, the religious preferred the explanation of an inspirational experience (Loewenthal, 1986).

The manner in which social factors operate is complex. Bronfenbrenner (1974) observed that many American young people failed to integrate into society and often displayed signs of social alienation. This was primarily due to problems in family life arising from such factors as mothers at work or broken homes. These factors could be traced back to the underlying social problems which gave rise to them and to the social attitudes which isolated the young from the world of adults. He commended the Russian system, whereby groups of workers made regular contact with groups of children—usually a class at school—introducing them to the world of industry or commerce. He contended that without responsibility and involvement, young people were bound to be alienated. The same could well be true of religious attitudes and involvement in the church.

Lemon (1973) considered that attitude was often regarded as a mediating construct which related responses and social situations but as such was ill-defined. He warned that individual differences interacting with social aspects provided an immense number of relationships to be considered. Even so, social attitudes persisted, so that although attitudes seemed to be the product of social structures, changes in these structures did not necessarily change attitudes. He cited the stability of the Indian caste system, unaffected by changed economic circumstances and the Japanese attitude to kinsmen unaffected by industrialization. The same is apparently true of religious attitudes; Alves (1968) found marked regional variations in children's attitude to religion ranging from the least favorable in London and the South East, through those of the Northern Industrial areas, the Midlands, the South West, and the North, to Wales, where the most favorable attitudes were found. This finding was very similar to the church attendance proportions gathered in the census count of 1851, noted by McLeod (1973).

A number of other studies have also indicated marked regional differences in religiousness, even if cautiously. Rural and small-town residents were not more religious than urban residents but were more conservative in outlook (Nelsen, Yokely, and Madron, 1971). There were significant differences between the geographical regions in the United States which proved to be more effective determinants than education, occupation, or income (Alston and McIntosh, 1979). Shortridge (1977) used four different categories to examine American regional differences in religiousness and found substantial agreement between the regions disclosed and those of earlier studies in his review. He described and mapped five regional types—traditional, intense conservative Protestant, diverse liberal Protestant, Catholic, and super-Catholic. It appeared that some new regions were emerging as a result of possible mass changes in patterns of religiousness. Despite the decline in many regional differences in the United States, religious differences were unchanged, so that migrants from another region tended to adopt the level of religious commitment found in their new region (Hill, 1985). This finding confirms that of Stump (1984) that when people move between regions their religious commitment tends to change in the direction of that of their new area, increasing in the South or decreasing in the West, so that migration may contribute to the persistence of regional religious differences. Later, Stump (1986) found continued regional variations in religious participation over an eight-year period, using a large sample of white Catholics and Protestants. When students in Southern and Northern American universities were compared for dogmatism, there was no significant difference in Catholic scores from either region, but Southern Protestants were much more dogmatic than those in the North, reflecting the greater theological conservatism of the denominations strong in the Southern states. In this continuing cultural situation it seems that religious dogmatism generates a more general dogmatic attitude (Kilpatrick, Sutker, and Sutker, 1970). Geographical location had significant positive effects on four measures of religious belief—the nature of God, the divinity of Jesus, the meaning of the words "heaven" and "hell," and the Bible. It also played a limited role in mediating some other effects (Petersen and Takayama, 1984). The cohesion of West Midland immigrant communities had a religious association which varied with their geographical origin. Participation in religious activities was important to such communities, and it appeared to be more from religious than social reasons. Religion was an under-researched aspect of ethnic identity and community understanding (Johnson, 1985). A similar persistence of religious cultural regions and the stability of their borders over long periods has also been recorded in France (Gellard, 1978).

Secularization

Secularization is a mark of contemporary Western society, but caution is needed when comparing studies of it. In England, as in many European countries, there has been a decline in the membership of the mainstream churches since the beginning of the century, and less than 10 percent of the population now regularly attend church. McLeod (1973) described how the churches had very little contact with the working classes in the East End of London, where church attendance was a mark of respectability required of shopkeepers rather than a habit of devotion. Cox (1982) made a detailed study of the churches of Lambeth in South London and demonstrated that despite the importance of church attendance in Victorian times it had started to decline before 1880. The reason for this appeared to be that local and central governments were starting to provide a range of social services previously undertaken by the churches which kept them in touch with families with a diffusive Christianity who otherwise would only use them for the rites of passage. This contrasts with the high level of religiousness found in America. Toch (1966) suggested that for some religious beliefs and practices alone were no longer sufficiently appealing, and because the churches still wanted to retain their membership they had come to be concerned with nonreligious functions, even to the extent of becoming community churches.

Young and old alike are exposed to the social climate, which continues to erode religious belief and practice. This process of secularization is too well-known and documented to merit general discussion except where studies have some bearing on religious development. Its effects have often been recorded, as when Alston and Hollinger (1972) compared responses to the questions about religion in surveys of 1957 and 1969 and noted that in the interval most of the population had become much more pessimistic about the influence of religion on American society; only 14 percent thought its influence was increasing, whereas 76 percent did so previously. However, Deshen (1972) used a study of a particular Israeli synagogue to discuss secularization. He distinguished between the eradication of religious rituals, symbols and belief arising from a loss of faith, which he termed abandonment, and effacement, in which although the rituals and symbols were abandoned, there was not a loss of faith in underlying religious values. Another Israeli study (Liebman, 1983) of antinationalist and ultranationalist organizations suggested that extremism was the religious norm, and religious moderation was a strategy of individuals or groups to find protection against a hostile environment; when the secular culture declined, extremist tendencies proliferated. Krausz (1977) considered that throughout the Western world Jewishness was finding secular ways to express itself because of its loss of religious identity.

In Australia, McAllister (1988) investigated three theories which explained secularization in terms of modernization, which had brought more education, employment status, and income; in terms of life cycle effects, which were changing the habits of young parents who used to return to religious activities to set a good example for their children, and in terms of a generation change arising from modifications of the social climate. Since the beginning of the century, religious affiliation had dropped from 96 percent to 76 percent and those saying they had no religion had risen from 2 percent to 11 percent. Catholic affiliation had remained stable, but Anglican affiliation had declined, and a growing number of their members no longer attended church. Modernization appeared to offer the best explanation of the trend.

Weigert and Thomas (1970a) first studied the effect of secularization on Catholic adolescents in Merida, San Juan, St. Paul, and New York. They noted that secularization affected several dimensions of religion to reduce their importance, but religious knowledge was enhanced since increased information about a culture was part of the process of increasing secularization. They also observed (Weigert and Thomas, 1970b) that while in Merida there was apparently no parental effect on adolescent religiousness, elsewhere high parental control and support brought increased adolescent acceptance of traditional religion. It looked as if the Anglo-Saxons attended church because of parental expectation, whereas the Latins did so for their own individual reasons. Subsequently, Weigert and Thomas (1974) used four measures of religiousness to compare Catholic students in cities in America, Germany, Puerto Rico, Yucatan, and Spain. The more urbanized and industrialized the society and the lower the cultural recognition of religion, the lower was the degree of individual members' religiousness, except for religious knowledge. Despite the differences found there was a consistency across the cultures which suggested a common religious structure in which belief and interiorized religion was the keystone. When this research was extended to Germany and Spain the findings were confirmed; religiousness, but not religious knowledge, was consistently associated with conformity to the expectations of parents and priests, though not to that of friends. The degrees of religiousness varied in different cultural contexts; it was high when parental support was combined with cultural expectation, and in all five cultures adolescent conformity and religiousness was always strongly associated with parental support (Weigert and Thomas, 1979).

The educational, counseling and rehabilitation functions, once the exclusive responsibility of the clergy, were now undertaken by other agencies, and at the same time the media had eclipsed the church as a source of information and guidance and the character of England had become multiracial. When the social order no longer required a religious legitimation for its actions and individuals no longer sought religious justification for their behavior, religion would be reduced to the level of a social option (Wilson, 1977). In the gains and losses of English Protestant churches over twenty-five years, against a general background of decline in membership, some more conservative denominations showed a marked increase, and identifiable evangelical groups within the larger denominations also showed growth. This was not due to mass evangelism but because conservative Protestantism had been more successful in nurturing children in a belief system which proved to be well-designed for transmission to children (Bruce, 1983).

Donnelly (1979) regarded secularization as describing the decline of the church. The residual or invisible religion often encountered was not an unnecessary, leftover fossil, but the persistence of an innate tendency to belief that was a predisposition and underlying orientation of all individuals. In his survey of adolescents and young adults in an inner-city situation he found little traditional religion, rather more nominal religion, much belief in luck, horoscopes, ghosts, and an afterlife, and only a few examples of "secular man" when all such beliefs were repudiated outright. He accepted Martin and Pluck's (1977) conclusion that young people lacked an adequate vocabulary to explain and justify their own symbolic behavior and that the world of imagination and of the affections was expressed, if at all, only with difficulty and with labored, limping speech. Picture language, imagery, parable and parody, metaphor and simile, which poetry shared with religion, appeared to have been replaced by a wooden literalness which was death to the imagination; something was lost to culture when the distinctive content of religious language modulated through Bible-reading, prayers, sermons, hymns, and discussion was no longer a familiar part of modern speech. Yet he also found that although the present was not an age of faith and ecclesiastical thinking was losing social control, there remained an openness to reinterpret experience and a willingness to learn in which God was regarded as a strong possibility. There was no indication of a permanent and irreversible demise of religion; the decline of the church appeared to be part of a wider decline of arbitrary rule.

Secularization also affects the status of religious groups. The religious curricula of Roman Catholic colleges showed a movement from the theology of a subsociety to that of a body accepted by American society and was accompanied by less reliance on authority and more submission to secular academic disciplines. The dichotomy of Weber and Durkheim which regarded Catholicism and Protestantism as separate and indentifiably sacred orders within society could no longer be upheld (Schubert, 1987).

Chapter 12

Surveys of Religious Beliefs and Practices

Research into the religious beliefs and behavior of adolescents has been spasmodic and uncoordinated. In England it often has an educational background and includes pupils with few or no links with the churches and who have vague and poorly formulated beliefs. There is a marked decline in belief and church attendance as adolescence proceeds, and this continues after school leaving into working or student life.

In the United States, research has often examined the beliefs of the committed and the reasons for alienation. Many adolescents are involved in church life, but their belief may be superficial. Doubts are often unexpressed and may increase until belief is discarded. Involvement in church activities is influenced by parental example and by the warmth of relationships with church members and leaders.

Surveys of students have shown marked changes in their religiousness over the years; a period of decline has been followed by a return to more traditional beliefs and values but not by a return to the churches. Often during student life beliefs are questioned and then discarded by some, amended by others, or held steadfastly by yet others. While orthodoxy tends to decline with age, some church colleges sustain it.

Surveys of adolescent religious beliefs and behavior abound, both in the United States and in England. It is commonplace to compare surveys to establish trends over a period of time or between one group and another, but caution in interpreting

247

results from such an exercise is needed unless the trends are persistent. There are continuing regional differences in religiousness,[1] apart from the major differences between the nations. Any study of religious behavior needs to take account of the class structure of institutional religion and the long-term decline in church attendance. McLeod (1974) showed that English church-going in the Victorian period was partly a mark of respectability, and in areas such as the East End of London it had always been low. The decline from 1886 to 1903 was part of a pattern throughout the West, related to the liberalization of religious thought and the largely unchurched working classes were taken up with the socialist ethic of the growing labor movement. This decline has continued throughout the century, and affects all society. It is well-documented (e.g. Argyle and Beit-Hallahmi, 1975), but there is less information regarding children and adolescents. The retreat from the churches has not been limited to any one country; it has occurred in varying degrees throughout the Western world but least in America, where 25 percent engaged in some kind of religious activity at weekends, while only between 5 and 8 percent of Europeans did so (Caplow, 1985).

Some relevant issues may not necessarily be brought to light by a survey. Piazza and Glock (1979) explored the differences in belief among adults who said that they definitely believed in God. There were substantial variations, not just among Protestant, Catholic, or Jewish believers, but also in the kind of God in which people believed. There was an association between traditional religion and conservative politics—the social order should not be changed because God had ordained it. There were other traditionally religious people who did not regard God as regulating the social order but saw him as influencing their own lives and were relatively liberal on political and social issues. Adolescents probably develop in the same way.

ADOLESCENT RELIGIOUS BEHAVIOR

English and Irish studies

Martin (1980), in a general discussion about church attendance in England, pointed out the marked denominational differences in the affiliation of young people. He distinguished between the more liberal denominations—the Methodist and the United Reformed Church—and the evangelical Baptists, pentecostal, and independent churches. The former were poorly supported between the teens and the mid-forties. Otherwise the attendance of those under fifteen was above average in all the churches, especially the evangelical. The Church of England was somewhat below average with young adults, the time when their families were being set up. Migration had given the Roman Catholic Church a more youthful age profile which was wearing off with time, so that above forty-five attendance was

---

1. Regional differences in religiousness are summarized in chapter 10.

below the national average; at this age liberal Protestants were strongest. The imbalance due to sex was a worldwide phenomenon, but it was less than common observation suggested; it was greatest with the Free Churches, and especially with those over sixty-five. In a relatively secular situation it was easier for adolescents to leave the church than to bring peers into it, a problem which was accentuated when there was a missing young-adult generation and was even more acute in smaller churches. Young men were under pressure from their peers about their leisure pursuits and activities and often were also concerned with their family and career, and the church had little to offer them specifically. It had long been known that there was a decline in religious belief and behavior during adolescence, even though for some this was a time of conversion or heightened religious experience; after the age of thirty this could be reversed (Argyle, 1958).

A recent Church of England survey (General Synod Board of Education, 1989) showed that on a normal Sunday the church made contact with less than 2 percent of children from two to five, less than 7 percent of those from six to nine, and 6 percent of those from ten to thirteen, to total of 393,000. Sunday schools tend to lose their members after the age of nine and the higher proportion of girls increases after this age. Yet about a third of the child population, almost three million children, have been baptized in the church. The church also has contact with children through a number of children's and youth organizations, youth clubs, and choirs. The Free Churches have similar contacts; they have more Sunday school and Bible class scholars, but their numbers are declining. This decline is in step with the defection of adults. Numbers of Easter Communicants in the Church of England and their percentage of the adult population and the recorded membership of the Free Churches and their Sunday school scholars and Bible class members are given in the following table:

	Year						
	1950	1960	1970	1976	1980	1984	1987
Infant Baptisms+	672	554	466	428	365	309	289
Easter Communicants*	62	70	51	47	47	43	42
Free Church members*	52	46	38	34	30	26	26
Confirmation candidates•	142	191	113	94	98	80	66
Free Church S.S. scholars•	1542	1224	999	718	633	491	496

+ rate per thousand live births.
*rate per thousand of population aged 15 and over.
• totals in thousands.

The figures can be compared with the mean scores of secondary school pupils on Francis' (1989b) Attitude to Christianity scale:

Secondary school pupils' attitude to Chrisitanity scores			
1974	1978	1982	1986
77.8	74.9	70.4	68.4

The Bible Society (1978) survey of religious attitudes of young people in England and Scotland compared those at school with readers of the Buzz magazine, directed to committed Christian young people, and with Youth Club members. Four out of five of the boys and two-thirds of the girls in the school sample never went to church, yet half of them claimed to "belong" to Christianity. More than half regarded church services as boring, especially boys without religious affiliation. Nonattenders said they did not want to go, they would feel out of place, it had nothing to do with daily life, or they didn't understand what was said or done. More aged sixteen than aged fourteen regarded it as irrelevant to daily life.

Sunday school attendance was investigated at two Yorkshire comprehensive schools. Only 3 percent of those aged fourteen and fifteen still attended Sunday school and 40 percent had never attended. From the age of eleven attendance was related to parental church attendance. Boys who had attended earlier had higher religious attitude scale scores. This was not so with the girls, something which could be due to their greater religiousness. Scores on a Bible knowledge test were related to Sunday school attendance, but the length of time attended did not significantly affect the scores. Six percent professed to attend church weekly, and a further 4 percent monthly. Nine percent of the boys and 13 percent of the girls regarded themselves as definitely Christian, and a further 18 percent of the boys and 27 percent of the girls as on the whole Christian (Reid, 1977, 1980).

In three other comprehensive schools the religious knowledge of pupils was enhanced by attending church or Sunday school. Strength of belief was not related to mental ability, although in two schools it related to biblical and church knowledge. The results suggested that religious knowledge was not due to church or Sunday school attendance but to their parents being supportive of religious education in school. Those who attended appeared to know more about their faith than the politically committed did about their politics. Nonattenders showed little knowledge of basic Christian beliefs and facts, and the authors doubted whether Sunday school teachers were succeeding where professional teachers were failing. They did not test knowledge not taught at school to see if the attenders had learned any extracurricular material (Homan and Youngman, 1982).

May (1977, 1979) investigated the religious beliefs and behavior of secondary-school children, giving a detailed analysis of their responses which showed boys to be more skeptical than girls and pupils in the South of England more skeptical than those in the North. Ideas about prayer were centered, in belief or disbelief, on the self, on others, or on God. There was a decreasing concern for others as age increased but a growing concern for personal improvement. Age also brought a decrease in the belief that everyone should pray, attend church, or read the Bible but some reduction of disbelief in life after death. At every age a wide variety of religious opinions and styles of judgment was found, and different styles could be found simultaneously in the same individual.

The Youth Department of the British Council of Churches (1981) surveyed adolescents in Lancashire attending church on a particular Sunday. The majority were in regular attendance with 93 percent of the Catholics, 80 percent of the Free Church adherents, and 69 percent of the Anglicans having attended at least three times in the previous four weeks. Ninety-two percent of the Catholics and 31 percent of the Anglicans attended a denominational school, as did 12 percent of the Free Church adolescents. Half of them had at least 5 "O" levels,[1] and more than half over sixteen were still in full-time education. By their thirteenth birthday, 73 percent Catholic, 52 percent Anglican and 13 percent of the Free Church adherents had been confirmed or admitted to church membership. Most professed to believe in God, with only 11 percent uncertain. Smaller proportions of Anglicans endorsed statements of orthodox belief than did Catholic or Free Church members. There was much uncertainty or disagreement about God having made the world in six days. Only a quarter regarded politics as important, and few had confidence in the political parties. There was much concern about homelessness, unemployment, crime, and third world poverty; two-thirds were worried about the risk of nuclear war. Four in five regarded moral issues as being personally important, but half of those aged sixteen to twenty did not regard extramarital sex as wrong. Seventy percent of the Catholics opposed abortion, and there was also strong Free Church opposition to it. The report concluded that there was little sign of a delinquent subculture, but there were signs of violent activity in urban areas where young people felt alienated from the mainstream of society.

Francis (1984a) was involved in much of this research and subsequently provided a detailed analysis of the data, providing a wealth of detail about membership, worship, beliefs, moral attitudes, and much else, concluding with several character sketches. No attempt was made to relate the results to other surveys, although the sample appears to demonstrate greater religiousness than that recorded by Argyle and Beit-Hallahmi (1975). Nor is it clear to what extent differences were due to variations in socio-economic status. The relatively high involvement in further education suggests that the sample reflects the middle-class values with which English churches are often associated.

The members of the Central Y.M.C.A. in London who had recently come from

---

1. Five subjects passed in the Ordinary Level of the General Certificate of Education is often regarded as a hallmark of ability.

abroad had much greater religiousness than either those established here or the British. There was more church involvement among members living on their own; graduates showed lower religiousness and more hostile attitudes to the church and the Bible but were just as likely to have attended church in the previous year, suggesting that they had more strongly structured beliefs. There was a good deal of religious interest and goodwill to the church found among some of the unchurched group who did not seem to have made up their minds about religious issues (Francis, 1982). While the group was not representative it reflected frequently held points of view which were described in great detail.

Conway (1979) investigated the religiousness of eleven- to fourteen-year-old pupils in a coeducational Catholic school in Dublin. Ninety-eight percent professed to be Catholic, 74 percent saw their churchmanship as important, more girls than boys, more younger than older pupils. High levels of religious activity were recorded; 85 percent attended Mass weekly or more often, 67 percent receiving communion. Only 10 percent attended Mass more often than the required minimum, a quarter for spiritual reasons but another quarter because their parents insisted; half went because they wanted to. Forty-nine percent rarely or never went to confession, seven times the percentage that never went to Mass. Seventy-two percent went to confession less than they used to, a decline related to age among the girls. Frequent attendance at Mass was associated with acceptance of many Catholic beliefs, 80 percent prayed frequently, 19 percent read the Bible, and 11 percent said the Rosary at least weekly. Religious practice related to the practice of both parents and to the perception of the father's religiousness. At Mass 91 percent of them had experienced feelings of joy, but 77 percent of them had also felt boredom. A somewhat stronger belief in Jesus Christ and Our Lady than in God was recorded; full belief in God: 62 percent, in Jesus Christ: 69 percent, in Our Lady: 68 percent, belief with difficulty in God: 20 percent, in Jesus Christ: 14 percent, in Our Lady: 13 percent. This indicated a high level of belief, although 25 percent disbelieved in Hell and 31 percent did not believe in the Devil. Questions about the Holy Spirit showed much less insight. MacMahon's (1981) longitudinal study of Irish Catholic adolescents recorded a decline in religiousness with age. Weekly Mass attendance dropped from 78 percent to 64 percent by seventeen, many regarding Mass as irrelevant to life or boring.

American studies

Studies of adolescent church attendance need to be related to the pattern of adult attendance, which has many variations. Wingrove and Alston (1974) used data covering a period of thirty years to study patterns of church attendance among white Americans. A comparison of five cohorts[1] showed that each of them had its own characteristics, and although always more women attended than men,

---

1. The cohorts were defined by the decade in which their members were born.

they followed the same trends. All cohorts were affected by the same social pressures, so that attendance increased between 1950 and 1960 and declined after 1965, but otherwise there were inexplicable differences, such as those born between 1925 and 1934 showing increasing attendance until age twenty-five, followed by a growing rate of decline, whereas those born between 1915 and 1924 showed an almost opposite trend. Each generation establishes its own pattern; children's church attendance will follow the pattern of their parents, but adolescents form their own habits and possibly start a new trend. At any one time there are also persistent regional differences. Even so, church attendance in the United States has shown a steady increase over a long period. In their examination of statistics and estimates for American church membership, Finker and Stark (1986) gave the percentage of population regularly attending church as follows:

YEAR	1850	1860	1870	1890	1906	1916	1926	1952	1980
RATE OF ATTENDANCE	34%	37	35	45	51	53	58	59	62

Glen (1987) noted a growing trend in "no religion" respondents to United States national surveys between the late 1950s and the early 1980s. Because this had now leveled off it suggested a change in the degree of secularization in society.

Williams (1989) made a brief review of research data on adolescent religiousness, complaining of its scarcity. Extensive surveys had shown that while the church attendance of more than ten thousand pupils markedly declined between twelve and sixteen, there was only a slight decline in assent to the importance of religion. The attendance and interest of high-school seniors had increased a little from 1978 to 1980, but then declined, so that 35 percent reported weekly attendance, and 27 percent regarded religion as very important. Many more black students and Hispanics than white regarded religion as important. White boys tended to an extrinsic orientation, regarding religion as a set of rules, a means to the rewards of conformity, whereas girls saw belief as an end in itself, giving them a sense of relationship with God and with others. Education, age, sex, marital status, denomination, income, and urbanicity were factors that influenced the variety of religious participation found in black Americans (Taylor, 1988). A Gallup poll indicated that two-thirds of American adolescents claimed membership of a church or synagogue, and among these half the Protestants and a third of the Catholics attended church the previous week—more blacks than whites, with only a small sex difference. Attendance was greater in the South than elsewhere and lowest in central cities. While 51 percent adolescents stressed the importance of personal faith in 1984, by 1987 this had dropped to 44 percent—more among Protestants than Catholics. They saw religious belief as less important than did their parents, yet only one in five regarded belief as unimportant. Its importance was stressed most in the South, more by young women and by students of above average ability. Almost nine out of ten regarded honesty, responsibility, and self-respect as very important. Three-quarters of the Protestants valued hard work, as did two-thirds of the Catholics. Those from white-collar backgrounds were little more likely to attend church than others (Gallup and Jones, 1989).

Formerly, church attendance was erratic among adolescents, with no consistent age change. The churches with a formal youth program gained increased support; girls attended more than boys at every age; there was a greater decrease with age when the father's education had ended early. Adolescent boys with older brothers exhibited lower church-attendance rates, and those with older sisters the highest rates (DeBord, 1969). Age differences in religious behavior among Lutheran adolescents and adults did not show a great gap, and the youngest age group was the most heterogeneous in beliefs, attitudes, and lifestyle (Johnson, Brekke, Strommen, and Underwager, 1974). Often adult Mormons who had ceased to attend church did so because they did not believe some doctrines or accepted secular ideas. They also left because of the disintegration of their social bonds, the irrelevancy of social opinions, the formation of new bonds outside the church, or because they were unhappy or emotionally deprived or had a rigid family environment (Mauss, 1969).

An extensive research program was undertaken into the priorities and outcomes of the religious education programs of Catholic, Southern Baptist, United Methodist, Episcopal, and Presbyterian churches and the Church of God (Hoge and Petrillo, 1978b, 1979, Hoge and Smith, 1982, Hoge et al., 1982). From this a clear picture of adolescent involvement in religious activity emerged and the intentions of their leaders to help them to handle the moral problems of sex, drugs, and the popular culture. The principal determinant for church attendance was parental attendance and parental religious values. Peer pressures and types of leadership determined youth group participation; attitudes toward the church depended on past religious education, types of leaders, and beliefs. In fostering church commitment among the young, personal relationships with parents, peers, and church leaders were foremost. Baptists had stronger church commitment and involvement than the others because the Baptist system was stronger on these crucial variables, so that they liked their past religious training more than the others, described their leaders as more sincerely religious, and scored higher on credal assent. Liberal influences, which often induced attitudes of individualism, relativism, and doubt about some types of religious training, had some impact. Cognitive and intellectual factors were not strong determinants of church participation and attitudes, and a large range of factors proved to have little effect. Scores on a Bible knowledge test had little relation to other variables, and factual knowledge had little relation to church commitments. Support for some of these findings came from the study Dudley and Laurent (1984) undertook of almost four-hundred church-related high-school students at a youth conference. Religious alientation was strongly related to the quality of their relationships with pastors and parents as well as to their opportunities for involvement in their church. It was also less strongly related to their self-concept, to peer group influence, and to the influence of the media.

A national sample of adolescents showed that contrary to previous findings, outside the Southern States, affluent young adults showed low levels of church involvement and on three other measures of religiousness white-collar adolescents gave low scores. Among the Protestants in the sample there was a growing loss of interest (Nelsen and Potvin, 1980). Religious practices and orthodoxy were both affected by age and denominational allegiance; the analysis demonstrated that the decline in religiousness in adolescence was a more complex process than the previous literature had suggested (Sloane and Potvin, 1983).

The traditional picture of apostates, who reject the faith in which they were reared, is that they are young, highly educated, and hold liberal values about sexual activity and drug use. A study of a group of white apostates differentiated between five distinct types: those with successful swinging styles and financial success; the pessimistic side-tracked singles who had missed out on the good life; the young settled liberals, dissatisfied with traditional values; the young libertarians who negated religious belief but not its attitudes; and the irreligious traditionalists who were disbelievers disaffected by church affiliation but retaining its moral traditions (Hadaway, 1989).

ADOLESCENT RELIGIOUS KNOWLEDGE

Research studies of religious knowledge, as distinct from religious belief, are infrequent and for the most part have been carried out in the United Kingdom. A group of Sheffield teachers tested the religious knowledge of secondary school pupils aged fourteen and fifteen (Sheffield University, 1961). Technical school pupils[1] scored higher than modern school pupils and grammar school pupils highest of all, but differences were not large. Girls always scored higher than boys. The results showed a great lack of knowledge. Nearly three quarters did not know why Whitsum was celebrated; most could name two miracles and two parables of Jesus, but some confused parables and miracles. Only a few could name two Old Testament prophets, explain their importance, or put five events of the period in historical order. New Testament knowledge, although better, was still very limited. Most pupils reported only occasional religious activity, girls showed higher levels than boys; it was greatest among grammar school pupils and least among secondary modern school pupils.

Loukes (1961) sought to discover how far Christianity made sense to fourteen-year-old pupils. He produced with penetrating insight a descriptive account of their ideas and difficulties which created widespread interest and quickly became a classic in the field. Because no attempt had been made to secure any statistical data,

---

1. See the Glossary for the nomenclature of English schools.

he subsequently (Loukes, 1965) used the Sheffield tests in some schools regarded as having successful religious education. The results were similar. About two-thirds of the boys and three-quarters of the girls agreed that there was a great deal of truth in the Bible, and one in twenty regarded every word in it as true. The remainder thought it a hopeless tangle of fact and fiction, or disproved by science. The pupils' attitude to Jesus showed generally a more favorable response, but there was much inconsistency in their expressions of belief. Even in these "good" schools church attendance, which was more frequent among girls and the more intelligent, also showed a decline with age so that most fourteen-year-olds were on their way out of the church. But there was evidence of their personal quest and sense of morality. One piece of work which Loukes reproduced without comment as a cry *de profundis* well conveys the nature of such findings:

The Bible	there is a lot of rubis in it techers admit there is so I do not think that it is true.
Creation	I thin that it is a lot of Hill Billi nonsence that is no true.
Jesus Christ	I bont think Jesus heuled eney boby.
God	I carnt amagin anibody in the sky.
Sacrifice	I wood not dye for christianity its just Daft dyeing for Christianity.
Boring to be Good	Yes and No.
Heaven	How Do I now theres a heaven or you I Dot think there a heaven.
Suffering	('God couldn't care for us') God Daft I think that has one is true.
Prayer	Just a wast of time Prayer.
Church-going	I Dont go to Church Dont like Church.
Scripture Lessons	Lessons on the Bible are the same all your life Verey Bul.

Alves (1968) also used the test when surveying religious education in secondary schools known to have an interest in the subject. Grammar schools had higher scores for religious knowledge than modern schools, although most students over sixteen scored less than those aged fourteen, at an unsatisfactory level. A third of the modern schools did not reach this level of knowledge, unlike the great majority of the grammar schools. Although the modern schools pupils showed less ability to retain biblical knowledge than those of the grammar schools, they had almost the same ability to gain an insight into its meaning.

ADOLESCENT RELIGIOUS BELIEF

Studies of adolescent religious belief reflect the cultural differences of the countries in which they were carried out. In England, with its highly secularized society, where paradoxically religious education is a legal obligation in state schools, research has indicated widespread ignorance and apathy among adolescents. In the United States, where much higher levels of church attendance and church-related activities prevail, the picture is very different. Some care is needed in contrasting the two; American research is often church-based and reflects the points of view of adolescents with varying degrees of contact with the churches, and English research shows little of the thinking of religiously committed adolescents. In Ireland, and elsewhere, adolescents reflect their cultural background. For these reasons, the studies have again been grouped under national headings.

English studies

The erosion of belief and the incidence of skepticism and doubt are recorded in varying degrees in many surveys. Adolescence brought increased questioning of religious belief, and in middle and late adolescence the idea that God rewarded good behavior and punished wrong-doing was generally rejected (Hilliard, 1959). The problems of belief that arose with English Catholic children as they grew to maturity were carefully recorded by Berridge (1969) on the basis of her own investigations.

Martin and Pluck (1977) used group and individual interviews to discover what young people believed. Few clearly defined patterns of belief emerged, and few practicing members of any church were found. No spiritual questing was observed but rather a widespread hedonism in which nothing was wrong unless it had an obvious victim. Neighborly helpfulness, with a desire for a good job and happiness, summarized their values. Politics was even more boring than religion. Attending Sunday school was remembered as a pleasant experience before the age of eight, but after ten there was pressure against it, both to join in other peer group activities and to avoid being teased. Church-going, if it had begun, ceased usually about twelve to fourteen. There was wide agreement that adolescent church-goers were abnormal and would be ridiculed—this despite the feeling that individuals had the right to their own beliefs. Nearly all wanted to use the church for the rites of passage and many claimed adherence to the Church of England, "We're born C. of E." was a comment that encapsulated the feeling of many.

They held an extremely amorphous version of Christianity, with widespread assent to the vaguest belief in a God with neither power nor attributes, benevolent, never punishing but always forgiving. Belief in Jesus as divine was most restricted. It was generally held that all religions must be addressing the same God. A mostly male section had no belief in an afterlife, but death was still too remote to cause any qualm. There was a sliding scale of belief from the existence of God, the divinity of Jesus, the hope of immortality, the existence of the devil, fear of hell, and the infallibility of the Bible. Between 10 and 15 percent attended church each Sunday, and another 4 percent at least once a year. Adherence was not incompatible with nonpractice and near atheism, and this inconsistency was seen by the easy breach of childhood belief by a simplistic scientism which still allowed them to believe in superstitions, exorcism, and horoscopes; the difficulty of religious believing seemed to be more of vocabulary than of credibility. School religious education was largely dismissed as irrelevant and an excuse for misbehavior; there was a strong objection to "just being told." They said that their study of world religions had been enjoyed (despite their woeful ignorance of them), as had topical discussions, but they regarded neither as proper religious education. Yet they wanted their own children to be taught about religion by the schools so that they would know about it and could make up their own minds about it.

Minney (1979) considered these group interviews were of dubious value, because group pressure would have inhibited fully personal disclosures. Since religion had its own deadening myth among the young it required correction by greater emphasis in religious education on the social and ritual dimensions of religion and studies of the ideals and motivations of religious people. Crossan (1979) considered the report's emphasis on the privatization of belief indicated a need for more stress in religious education on its relevance, as well as a more critical approach to the claims of science and interpretations of biblical stories.

In the Bible Society survey (1978) nearly a third of the boys and half of the girls said that religion was important to them, but this did not result in their attending church. A few believed in God but felt religion was not important. Unlike the committed Buzz group, of whom most definitely believed in God, the majority of the schools' sample indicated uncertainty about belief, and not all of the quarter who definitely believed were committed to traditional religious practice. Believers tended to regard God as personal, but a quarter of the school sample regarded God as a force for good. As they grew older, it appeared that they tended to talk more about God—a quarter of those of fourteen and a third of those of fifteen had talked about God in the previous week. Three-quarters of the Buzz group regarded Jesus as God in human form, but only a third of the school group, with more girls than boys, and more among those professing religious belief; half those attending church at least once a month shared this belief. A half regarded the Bible as having something worthwhile to say for their lives, by providing a moral code and being relevant, in contrast with the remainder who regarded it as out of date, irrelevant, untrue, or difficult to understand. Both samples were critical of the way religion was taught at school, but the majority wanted it retained on the curriculum, although not restricted to Christianity.

The findings of these broader surveys are supported by more detailed studies in specific schools. In a comprehensive school in East London, Westbury (1975) showed the continuing alienation of the working-class population from the churches after more than a century. About a half of the pupils indicated that they had a religious outlook, believed in God, and religion had an attraction for them, despite the lack of parental support. Nearly a third of them had attended Sunday school but had given it up by the time they were twelve. Eighteen percent claimed to have made a profession of faith, but as the proportion decreased with age it seemed to have less significance for them as they grew older. Sixteen percent claimed to attend church weekly and 49 percent at least once a month, but no more than 10 percent had attended the previous Sunday, mostly younger pupils. Only 9 percent were associated with any uniformed youth organization and very few with one linked to a church. Fifteen percent attended a church youth club—most of them the younger pupils; and another 26 percent a club not connected with a church. Forty-one percent said they had been taught to say their prayers when young, usually by their mothers, but this meant little more than being encouraged to pray, and only one in five of them now prayed every day, although prayer was taken seriously by all. Similarly, very few read the Bible daily, but many showed great respect for it. When their replies were compared with their perceptions of their parents' religion it was evident that when both parents held the same beliefs or disbelief it was a strong influence on their children. Otherwise it was much less, with the mother's influence slightly greater than the father's. When strong religiousness was recorded by pupils or their parents it was mostly found in a small group of families of West Indian origin. The study showed that traditional religious education faced the difficulty that few of the pupils had any experience of a believing community; religious language was poorly comprehended and the parents, while not hostile, gave little positive support to it.

Among pupils from thirteen to fifteen in a comprehensive and a girls' grammar school in Yorkshire, girls showed higher levels of belief than boys, and certainty of belief among boys showed a considerable decline with age. The uncertain boys gave signs of a sincere search for truth but lacked understanding and were confused, and the older group gave more personal reasons. In all the sample, personal belief seemed to account for individual attitudes to the Bible. God appeared to be on trial with the evidence stacked against him. Evil, hunger, war, science, the lack of real proof, and much arguing otherwise meant that the Bible had been found wanting. God had not been seen but remained the most convenient answer to the deeper questions of man. That some unbelievers still had credence in a powerful supernatural force appeared to be due to the effects of science fiction and stories of UFOs, which were more powerful than biblical evidence (Kibble, Parker, and Price, 1982).

Irish studies

A notable contribution about religious education in Northern Ireland has been made in a series of well over fifty articles spread over the past two decades by Greer, starting with his thesis (1970a) on the religious beliefs, practices, attitudes, and moral judgments of Protestant students over sixteen and their parents, secured by adapting Cox's (1967) questionnaire. Most parents agreed with the provision of religious education (Greer, 1970b), although a third of the girls and a half of the boys did not. Because the sons of those parents who returned the questionnaire were significantly more religious than the other boys, it appeared that the responding parents were inclined to orthodox belief. The students were much more likely

to complain about forcing religion on those who did not want it. Those who supported religious education said school was the only place where they received it;
it helped them to make up their minds about belief and provided a sense of values.
Others regarded it as indoctrination, as boring or badly taught, and as the province
of the church. They were more likely to disagree with religious provision than
Cox's (1967) English sample and also rated it as less important, less interesting,
less relevant, and less useful, differences which were highly significant.

Responses to questions about belief in God (Greer, 1971) showed that 77 percent of the responding parents were completely confident, compared with 50 percent of the girls and 38 percent of the boys. The children of believing parents were
significantly more inclined to believe than their peers. Parents were also more likely to attend church than their sons, though not than their daughters; the level of
church attendance was high with 70 percent parents, 76 percent girls, and 65 percent boys attending weekly, and only 21 percent parents, 19 percent girls, and 26
percent boys attending only occasionally or never. Parental practice had a marked
effect on the religiousness of their children, more on daughters than on sons, and,
perhaps not surprisingly, those who compelled their children's attendance at
church or Sunday school had the largest percentage of them actually attending.
It was found that among the students attending church regularly there was a significant proportion of those uncertain about or disbelieving in the existence of
God. Comparison with Cox's (1967) figures showed greater church attendance
for every category of belief. It appeared that many students were in conflict with
parental religious belief and practice and, under pressure to attend church, developed resentment and critical attitudes both to the church and to individual members of it.

In a more detailed discussion, Greer (1972a) gave a further comparison with
Cox's (1967) English figures, showing that the greater religiousness of the Northern Ireland students was particularly marked for the boys, who were more likely
to believe in God, in the divinity of Jesus, to agree that life after death was an
important issue, to attend church, to pray privately, and to read the Bible. On moral
issues, they were more likely to judge gambling, drunkenness, smoking, lying,
stealing, and suicide to be wrong but less inclined to judge war or premarital sexual intercourse to be wrong, the latter being confined to the girls. The differences
were regarded as being in part due to Northern Ireland being predominantly rural,
a claim supported by some analysis of the Irish figures into urban and rural groups.
It was also noted that while they were more religious than the English students,
they were also more inclined to believe that the church had political influence,
a bad moral influence, and was not active in dealing with social problems—again
suggesting a critical attitude to the church. While they read the Bible more than
the English sample, they were less likely to find it helpful, and many were uncertain about its inspiration. Together, these results suggested a reaction against their
orthodox religious environment.

Denominational differences were also found in the sample between the main

Protestant churches, so that Church of Ireland students were less inclined to believe in God, to attend church, or to judge gambling, drunkenness, smoking, lying, stealing, and premarital sexual intercourse as wrong, perhaps because this church tended to be less evangelical than the Presbyterian and Methodist churches, or because its members tended to come from lower income groups.

In 1978, after a decade, Greer (1980a) repeated his survey in most of the same schools to study the effects of ten years of communal troubles on young people. There was a consistent trend for a small increase in the proportions professing traditional religious beliefs. Religious practice showed a slight decline, with marked reduction in church attendance; attitudes to the teaching of religion in school appeared to be less committed and polarized. Moral judgments showed a similar degree of stability; smoking was regarded with greater severity, but in other instances any slight movement was toward permissiveness, especially about premarital sexual intercourse. Greer regarded these results as indicating the persistence of religious belief at a time when there was also growing disenchantment with worship at church or school. Comparison with the repetition of Cox's (1967) study made by Wright and Cox (1971) showed less movement from established attitudes among the Northern Ireland pupils than among the English, and a remarkable similarity in the pattern of responses after a decade. This persistence of religious belief and the moral judgments associated with it appeared to differ from the evident secularization recorded in the English result. In Northern Ireland, violence seemed to turn many of those affected by it to religious belief rather than away from it, providing social support in addition to a sense of purpose and inner strength.

Next, Greer (1984a) looked at differences in moral attitudes between Catholic and Protestant pupils from fourteen to sixteen. There was no significant difference between the group opinions on drinking alcohol, drunkenness, lying, stealing, and taking drugs; Protestants were more severe on gambling and smoking—showing a puritanical strand—and Catholics were more severe on questions related to sexual morality and the sacredness of life, reflecting the teaching of their church. The results were similar in many ways to those of Wright and Cox, including the greater severity always displayed by girls compared with boys.

Finally, Greer (1988) asked Catholic and Protestant pupils from fifteen to seventeen in twenty schools in Northern Ireland to complete an open-ended sentence: "The thing I find hardest to accept about religion is . . ." Replies were classified into groups about God, creation, miracles, suffering, life after death, the Church, authority, morality, conflict, Jesus, the Bible, and other faiths. More boys than girls commented about morality; more girls than boys about suffering. More Catholics than Protestants commented about life after death and miracles; more Protestants than Catholics commented about the Bible. Their statements indicated a great variety of opinions that defeated any attempt to make generalized statements about adolescents' questions or difficulties. Many had looked in vain for tangible evidence to support their beliefs in God, Jesus, the afterlife, or the miraculous. Without this, the Bible lacked a sense of reality and could only be accepted by the credulous. If what was asserted to have occurred in the past did not happen now, it could not be believed; people were not cured by the touch of a hand, and it was bad weather and bad government which caused people to suffer, not God punishing sin. Orthodox doctrines such as his almighty power, his willingness to answer prayer, or the ressurection and the life to come were often questioned. Insincerity was condemned as hypocritical; they recognized standards of behavior not always practiced by adults and ideals which the church should embody. They resented authority figures who attempted to enforce religion and valued their freedom of choice. Greer considered that the data gave support to the view that many adolescents discarded religious belief as childish and not to be reconciled with a scientific worldview.

In Conway's (1979) study of pupils in a Dublin Catholic school, she found that a majority disagreed that a good Christian needed to attend church; a person was regarded as religious, not in terms of practice, but as displaying qualities such as love. In these statements much uncertainty was found. Most saw killing as always wrong, but only half regarded abortion as always wrong. A third regarded sex outside marriage as always wrong but a quarter justified it. Almost a half thought one religion was as good as another. This uncertainty was related to age, and adolescence was a time of increased doubt, when ideas of a vengeful God were discarded and greater independence to religious practice and ideas was emerging; increasing tolerance was found, so that a significant number believed that churchgoers were not necessarily superior to non-church-goers. At Mass there was a lack of appreciation of its real meaning. Although most of them had a good relationship with their parents, less than a third felt able to discuss problems with their father.

MacMahon (1981) undertook a two-year longitudinal study of fifteen-year-old pupils in Catholic secondary schools in Dublin and again two years later. Girls always scored higher than boys, the younger group higher than the older group. At seventeen pupils still at school scored higher than those who had left at fifteen. The difference had to do with the importance they gave to religious belief and their basic religious knowledge and to how articulate they were religious. The secondary school pupils also scored higher than those at vocational and comprehensive schools; no explanation for this was forthcoming, although there were large variations in the proportions of boys and girls in the schools. There was a decline in religiousness with age. Weekly Mass attendance dropped from 78 percent to 64 percent, many regarding it as irrelevant to life or boring. Their limited conceptual knowledge was a serious weakness. Although there was a high degree of acceptance of traditional Catholic beliefs, most respondents could not give a positive and meaningful statement of them. There was a widespread absence of a Christological religious conviction. Questions relating to the social dimension of religion produced more positive responses; the older respondents had grown more hopeful and displayed a higher level of moral reasoning. Home background provided the essential climate for fostering religious devotion; only half the fathers involved were seen to be certain about their faith, but mothers were regarded as having a stronger influence.

The majority claimed to have had a religious experience at least once in their lives, more at seventeen. More than a third said it was related to the beauties of nature, and it had to do with being alone in a church. The Mass was the other most important trigger when they were younger, and experience of death when older. Fowler's (1981) Faith Development Interview was used with a sample of them and most pupils of fifteen were found to be at the third synthetic-conventional stage. The interviews confirmed the importance of parental influence and indicated that cognitive development was significant in determining attitude to religion. A literal interpretation of religious concepts was inevitably accompanied by an inability to see the role or viewpoint of others. There was little indication that challenges about suffering, death, or economic conditions were integrated into a faith structure. The years fifteen to seventeen were not a period of religious development, but neither were they a time of alienation. A greater integration of religion and life at seventeen had to be set against a decline in knowledge, belief, and religious practice.

European studies

In Belgium, secondary schools students were asked what Christ represented. In the first year they saw him as a living example; the younger they were, the more were Christ's divinity and humility seen as opposed, especially in respect of his miraculous powers. This gave rise to a conflict, most acute for pupils in the fifth year. Eighty-nine percent believed in Christ's divinity, and many saw no practical difference between God and Christ. Neither age nor sex discriminated significantly, but those studying the social sciences claimed to experience Christ as a unique manifestation of God more than those studying natural science (De Blauwe-Plomteux, 1972). Young people from fourteen to twenty-one who identified themselves as Christian had received a Christian upbringing at home and at school, although this appeared to be more ethical than doctrinal. Their religion was Christ-centered, their belief structured in secular terms, and the church was largely irrelevant to them. Four major differences were observed in interviews of Christians and non-Christians—inwardness and personal experience versus the need for moral authority; community versus hierarchical structures; individual ethics versus social ethics; and rationality versus ritual. These were related to the nature of Christian identity (Voye and Remy, 1986).

In Spain a recent movement among young people has been from traditional religion to more flexible and value-oriented beliefs opposed to authoritarian, rationalist, and institutional attitudes, but maintaining a nominal affiliation with the church. This had its roots in the student protest movements of the 1960s, but it indicated that the liberalization of religious attitudes among adolescents was international and not the product of a particular culture (Gonzalez-Anleo, 1987).

Fagerlind (1974) has provided a useful summary of several Swedish studies arising from investigation of the best means to implement the goals of religious education. A preliminary study of the religious interests of children between the ages of ten and twelve, undertaken by Hartman (1971) showed a low level of interest in the current form of religious education. A subsequent study of spontaneous interests was generated by pictures of children accompanied by short unfinished stories; children had to state what they thought the child depicted was thinking. Two-thirds wrote about the problems of loneliness, being rejected, feeling inferior, and especially about being teased or beaten up. A third were also concerned about violence and war, some seeing war as frightening and terrible, others as unnecessary and unwise. Other important issues were ethical and existential questions. Only a few replies were directly about God and his existence or other religious topics (Hartman, Pettersson, and Westling, 1973).

A somewhat similar survey in Finland regarding children's and adolescents' questions and religious interests used written responses to open-ended questions about pictures of children, evocative statements, and a questionnaire. Speculations about the future, problems about society and the world, and problems about parental relationships all showed a marked increase with age, which was not true of speculations about the purpose of life or the mystery of death. A variety of fears tended to decline with age, as did stated religious problems, where the decline between nine and twelve was most marked. Early fears of ghosts and robbers gave place to fears of being ostracized or mocked. Age brought increased concern about war, peace, and disarmament as well as about pollution. Religious problems concerned the existence of God, which for some was certain, for others a problem; others included life after death and the end of the world. Boys expressed more problems than girls, although older girls were concerned about the suffering and death of Jesus—a possible consequence of the testing following closely on school-based studies of the Passion. Although in many ways the results were similar to those of the Swedish study, there was a striking difference in the much lower level of concern about personal relationships when the Finnish and Swedish children were compared (Tamminen, 1977, 1979).

A study of Swedish students in their last term at school isolated a progression of six types of religious belief. Only a few regarded themselves as religious and their ideas had been influenced by secular humanism, except for those belonging to the final category. First, religion was understood in terms of an unreflective belief about God and other related criteria; it was external and impersonal and focused on social dimensions. Next came belief in a higher power that was either traditional or arose from personal reflection. Third, religion was seen as giving security, with its belief and worship defined traditionally. Next, religion was regarded as a way of life regulated by belief in a body of doctrine that had been personally modified. The fifth category was purely subjective and regarded religion as personally defined. Finally, all the positive elements of these categories were combined to show the characteristics of true faith (Dahlin, 1988).

American Studies

Bealer and Willits (1967) commented that while much research had been undertaken with college students, relatively little attention had been given to adolescents' religious interests, and the studies were mostly unsystematic and frequently lacked an adequate definition of the religiousness they set out to study. Much research had failed to distinguish between the different dimensions of religiousness. Taking Glock and Stark's (1965) five dimensions of religion as a model, they summarized under each heading the findings of more than forty different studies. On the ritualistic dimension, a number of studies indicated a high level of church attendance and daily prayer. For the experiential dimension, most adolescents were concerned about religion but were unsure about faith. Many professed belief in God, but few felt close to God. With the ideological dimension, almost all accepted doctrine in general terms or, at the most, expressed some doubts about it. The intellectual dimension—knowledge about dogma, doctrine, and history—had few studies, but factual knowledge of the Bible among adolescents was low. The consequential dimension—the effect of religion on behavior—was poorly researched. Most American adolescents embraced a traditional belief system with a reasonable degree of participation; the level of religious knowledge was low, but interest was quite high, even though the development of this into faith was not typical. They were reluctant to deny the supernatural, yet unwilling to commit themselves firmly, so that their religious position was one of hedging. Some adolescents held strong religious commitments and acted on them. This religious variety was similar to that of adults; what was characteristic was that in their search for self-identity they would not risk social rejection by making religious doubts public.

It is interesting to compare this review with another publication of the same period, the report of the tenth annual meeting of The Academy of Religion and Mental Health (1969). Contributors offered perceptive comments arising from their own involvement with adolescents, not as reliable research findings, but as stimulating speculations—as for example, the assertion that in America adolescents were becoming isolated from each other, with fewer friendships and growing alienation.

While the strong religiousness of Catholics is well-established, there are not marked patterns of religious belief defined in terms of denominational affiliation; denominational labels were misleading (Toch and Anderson, 1960). Older Catholic high-school students tended to be more liberal in their beliefs than the younger, and at every age tested, girls more liberal than boys. There was also some association between academic ability and liberal thinking, which continued through adult life, when religious conservatism tended to increase with age (Coursey, 1971).

High-school students' attitudes showed a trend to greater maturity and tolerance between 1945, 1953, and 1959. While many girls always scored higher than boys on religiousness, there was a marked increase between 1945 and 1953 in positive responses to talking about religion and reading the Bible. Sunday school attendance similarly increased for girls but not for boys, and church attendance increased for girls by 1953 but not for boys until the 1959 count (Jones, 1960). Between 1964 and 1974 the religious involvement of black and white high-school adolescents was declining, especially among boys (Dickinson, 1976). By 1979, some reversal was seen, especially among the boys. The smaller decline recorded for girls in the first period still continued to an extent, so that the difference between the sexes had narrowed (Dickinson, 1982).

If adolescents take their beliefs from those of adults, some note should be taken of the comments of Hertel and Nelsen (1974) that despite the apparent decline of religious belief in America, Gallup Poll data about belief in the afterlife showed little change between 1957 and 1968; the difference was that fewer expressed doubts and more expressed disbelief, showing the need to distinguish between a decline in belief and an increase in disbelief. Roof (1978) studied religious defection among youth between 1972 and 1976, especially among those from affluent middle-class backgrounds. It appeared to be part of a larger syndrome of reaction against institutions and disaffiliation from society. The fact that the values and cultural styles which originated with youth spread throughout society meant that an increased defection from institutional religion was to be expected in the future.

A considerable research project by Strommen (1974) identified the effects of Christian faith in over 7,000 adolescents from ten denominations. Some were marked by low self-regard, self-criticism, lack of self-confidence and anxiety about academic problems, religion, their families, and the opposite sex. Others participated regularly in church activities, in prayer for others, in seeking divine guidance and responding to help made available by the church; these were marked by their optimism, their high self-regard, and their hope of greater church involvement in the future. Other factors were related to parental conflict, to concerns for social action and change, and to prejudice. There was such diversity of attitudes found that it was dangerous to make sweeping generalizations. The study provided a wealth of detail on such issues as the opposition found in significant numbers to traditional Christian sexual values.

Another extensive survey of religious belief in the thirteen to seventeen age group in three communities was repeated in one of them three years later. In this period an increase in orthodoxy was found in each age group, and although the girls were scoring higher, the boys showed the greater increase of belief. This increase did not extend to belief in God as a heavenly father watching over and protecting people; a general belief in God was apparently stable over a long period of time (Zaenglein, Vener, and Stewart, 1975). Many adolescents professed a religious faith and believed in the necessity of religion in life, with a high level of church attendance. However, this was less with the student population than with adolescents of high-school age (Jersild, Brook, and Brook, 1978). There were inconsistencies of belief among Catholic high-school girls—religious beliefs did not differ between those who believed in astrology or reincarnation and those who did not, although believers in astrology were significantly more likely to believe in reincarnation (Brink, 1978). High-school pupils showed greater disbelief in the paranormal than college students, with significant association between disbelief and the study of science, which was also found to be associated with less superstitious belief (Tobacyk, Miller, and Jones, 1984).

Hauser's (1981) review of relevant research indicated that many adolescents suffered doubt. Despite the decline of church attendance with age, lapsed attenders usually professed belief. The better educated tended to reject traditional beliefs, but those in the churches were more involved. Cults such as the Jesus Movement appealed to those who clung to a childhood moraltiy, seeking the security of definitive and complete answers. Parental influence in nonthreatening households was strong, giving the understanding and guidance needed when there was disillusionment with traditional church life. For many adolescents, belief had to be literal and simplistic.

If some beliefs are under criticism in adolescence, it is partly because they may have been acquired early in life. Smidt (1980) asserted that the traditional place given to religion was learned early in life by elementary-school children and was associated with attitudes of acquiescence to civil laws and political leaders, as well as with attitudes of support for the American political system. In adolescence these come under review. The theory that adolescent cognitive development brought religious belief under critical pressure was investigated by Ozorak (1987); existential questioning was often associated with changes away from orthodox belief, but it was not the cause of it. Beliefs of the strongly committed were strengthened by it; those whose belief changed had been affected by bereavement or disappointment with religious rites or leaders. In early and middle adolescence, belief was related to parental religiousness but not to peer group influence.

Most Mormon adolescents believed literally the stories of the Garden of Eden and the destruction of the earth by flood in Noah's time and also believed in original sin. However, only the most orthodox of them still accepted the Mormon teaching that the dark skin of some races was caused by God's curse on sinful man. Such literalism was a product of incomplete cognitive development in adolescence, expressed by restriction in levels of moral and religious reasoning, but it remained open to the possibility of further development in adult life (Keown, 1986).

Tests in a New York high school showed church attendance was not positively associated with academic achievement among Catholics and Protestants, and even less among Jews. It was parental education and the father's occupation, not church influence, which produced higher achievement (Oh, 1984). But among pupils of thirteen in a junior high school, the church-goers tended to have higher grades, fewer absences from school, better behavior, and more involvement in out-of-class activities (Gruis, 1979).

RELIGIOUS BELIEFS OF OLDER ADOLESCENTS

English studies

Wright (1962) studied the religious beliefs of boys at school over sixteen. Three-quarters professed belief in God; one group was involved in prayer and church attendance, mostly regarding Christ as God become man; the others regarded God as impersonal, an abstract principle of goodness. Science students displayed lower attitude scores, even though the majority of them professed belief. Nearly all were critical of school assembly, but showed goodwill toward it. More were favorably disposed to religious education than opposed to it, but discussion was regarded as preferable to Bible-study. Some of them had been strongly influenced religiously by particular teachers, otherwise schools had little influence on religious belief, whereas parental influence was admitted to be strong.

Cox (1967) tested students of seventeen and their parents from a random sample of ninety-six grammar schools. Half of the boys and three-quarters of the girls professed belief in God, somewhat less than the adult population of the time, with a strong emphasis by the boys on ideas of God as creator and by the girls as a loving father and a friend. Belief was strongly related to church-going, but differences in belief between church-goers and non-church-goers were not very marked; church-goers tended to give fuller comments on their answers, being more concerned about theological ideas. Almost all the small group of disbelievers who attended church did so for other than religious reasons.

Girls saw Jesus in terms of personal relationship, boys as a teacher associated with miracle stories. 44 percent of the boys and 68 percent of the girls believed in his divinity. While most regarded him as a good, wise, and great teacher, they were more interested in the nature of God; it seemed that a devotional Christ-centered approach was outside their interest. The miraculous element in the gospels caused much confusion and hindered belief in Jesus' divinity. Jesus was regarded as a Savior by a quarter of the Baptist and other evangelical church-goers, much less by Catholics and hardly at all by other adherents. Many were exercised by the problem of evil. Belief in life after death was rejected outright by a quarter of them. Of the rest, many were uncertain as to its nature. This reflected a more general uncertainty, since half of those doubtful about survival were also doubtful about God's existence. (It is interesting to note that Richardson and Weatherby (1983) found belief in an afterlife was strongly associated with religious affiliation and church attendance, and because of this, also with a prohibitive attitude toward premarital sex, abortion, and divorce.) Both sexes regarded the New Testament as historically more reliable than the Old Testament, more relevant and a more helpful guide to conduct but with a lower interest rating. More regarded the New Testament as inspired and girls always had a higher evaluation of both Old and New Testaments than the boys. Parental belief and church attendance were strong influences, especially on the girls. No relationship could be found with parental occupation, or with geographical region. Those attending a coeducational school were found to have a lower incidence of belief than those at single-sex schools; this was most marked in the case of the girls.

After four years the study was replicated (Wright and Cox, 1971). In the interval a considerable decline in support for religious education had taken place, and there was much less acceptance of the authority of the Bible. Girls remained more favorable than boys, but they had changed even more than the boys, and this extended to areas of religious and moral belief. Favorable attitudes were strongly associated with religious belief and practice. Arts students were more likely to believe that the Bible was inspired, and to read it, but not to find it more helpful than others.

Taylor (1970), with a major interest in church school effects, used similar material to survey the religious behavior of students over sixteen and their parents in single-sex church and county grammar schools. Girls always showed greater religious interest than boys, even in examination choices. Two in three expressed some belief in God, girls more than boys; one in eight were uncertain. Catholic schools showed a positive relationship with belief. The divinity of Christ was accepted more readily by Catholic school students and by girls more than by boys. The possibility of a future life was accepted by seven out of ten, and girls were the more likely to believe in it. Church attendance was closely related to belief in God and also to the practice of private prayer, which was the regular or occasional habit of three in four of the sample and was most common among Catholic school girls. Interest in religion had increased in the previous year for two in three of all students, and decreased for only one in five of them. It was greater among the girls; it was not related to the type of school but appeared as a characteristic of this age; three in four of all students described themselves as religious, and only 3 percent were hostile. Three in four found the Old Testament interesting, two in three doubted its relevance. The New Testament, which was seen as historically more reliable, was more highly regarded for its relevance and seen by most as interesting. The importance, interest, and relevance given to religious education was similar to that of the Old and New Testaments. Girls regarded it with higher esteem than boys, Catholic school students more than Anglican school students, and the latter more than those of county schools. Church-going was strongly related to the importance assigned to religious education, and compulsory religious education was approved by seven in ten of the students, with more girls than boys approving, and the same order of school preference. School worship was generally held in low esteem, three in five saw no value in it. More girls than boys approved of it, and two in three of the girls at Anglican schools found it helpful; four in five of the state school boys thought it to be valueless.

Rees (1967) studied the effect of religious education on pupils of sixteen to eighteen by asking third-year university students at Bangor, Cambridge, and Oxford about their beliefs. Many believed in the virgin birth and the resurrection in a very literal manner; others who had turned from Christianity said it was because they had assumed that such literalism was a prerequisite of belief. The strongest and most literal belief was among science and medicine students, where attitudes tended to be more polarized. The Cambridge group showed stronger belief and, because almost all of them had been at a boarding school, this might have been related to school influence. However, no significant difference was found between former boarding-school and day-school pupils, although private prayer was more frequent among former day-school pupils. More science students claimed to pray regularly, or not at all, than arts students.

Richardson and Chapman (1973)[1] investigated the religious beliefs of nearly 3,000 sixth-form students in thirty-nine schools, most of them fee-paying schools of a religious foundation. They provided much information from their interviews and the responses to their attitude scale. Students from single-sex schools tended to have greater religiousness than those from mixed schools, and the least religious were from the mixed comprehensive schools. A notable feature of the study was the classification of four religious stances: the distinctively Christian, the generally religious, the agnostic, and the positively atheist—all amply illustrated by students' statements and statistical data from the attitude scale. While providing many valuable insights for teaching staff and chaplains, no attempt was made to relate the results to other research, nor were standard questions asked about religious behavior. Religiousness was shown to be associated with parental church attendance, and students' religious practice was shown to affect their use of religious language and their satisfaction with their school, but religious practice was not defined. For most boarders, attendance at school chapel was apparently obligatory, but no account was taken of the usual measures of church attendance, private prayer, and Bible reading.

RELIGIOUSNESS IN STUDENT LIFE

Feldman (1969) reviewed more than 150 studies of religiousness among American students, giving a valuable summary of their conclusions. Most students attributed a relatively low level of importance to religion. The many reported changes in religious belief and practice were irregular from year to year, without any particular pattern and not like the usual trend away from authoritarianism and toward greater political liberality. Slight differences in attitude and belief between groups concealed much greater changes by individuals; since these individual changes occurred in both directions, their effect was largely disguised. Similar, but lesser, changes had also been observed among those of the same age not attending college, and a tendency had also been found for belief to be consolidated in the ensuing years, with some movement toward a more religious position. No studies had been undertaken to ascertain what conditions led to reduced orthodoxy or a decline in attitude in some students, nor whether such effects persisted or

---

1. The work was first published by the Bloxham Project Research Unit, Oxford.

increased after college. Nor had any account been taken of the multidimensional nature of religion.

Parker (1971) gave an extensive study of changes in the religious beliefs of college students, noting denominational difference and the effects of college life on their religious belief and behavior. At this time in their lives when intellectual development was reaching its peak, religious changes were small in stable environments, but the impact of the new environment of college in their first year brought about rapid changes. The evidence came from research that was simplistic in design, nonexperimental and cross-sectional, but the author's hope that improved research would enable conclusions to be reached about specific effects of particular forces has not been fulfilled. Similar research has continued, both in the United States and elsewhere, which has largely confirmed the trends already noted.

Longitudinal studies of student religiousness

While most investigations have looked at the beliefs, behavior, or opinions of one group of students at a time, others have explored trends in the climate of religiousness over the years by repeating similar tests in similar situations. Although college or university students are not a representative sample of their age-group, well-established trends in their habits are likely to reflect more general trends, and there have been significant changes in their religiousness over the years.

Between 1939 and 1955 increased religiousness among former students was comparable to that of contemporary students in the same college and was strongly associated with church attendance (Bender, 1958). Between 1961 and 1971 there was a decreasing frequency of Mass attendance and deteriorating attitudes about personal honesty, personal morality, and dating among Catholic students; nevertheless, they showed an increased concern for others, which meant that a reduced compliance with traditional church mores was found alongside an increasing conformity to the values of American society in concern for others (Moberg and McEnery, 1976). During this period students also showed a decline in their religious and moral attitudes and an increase in humanistic orientations. Yet on such items as "God is working through his church" the later group secured higher scores, suggesting that despite less participation in institutional religion there had been a strengthening of some broader Christian criteria (Moberg, Zylak, and Robzien, 1972). Over a shorter period, students of all the denominations represented during their three years residence showed little change in religious practice but a shift in belief to a less orthodox position (Dempsey 1966; Dempsey and Poole, 1970).

A comparison of surveys of the religious beliefs and behavior of students at Williams College over more than thirty years (Hastings and Hoge, 1976, 1981, 1986) showed that 1948 to 1967 was a period when their ideas became more liberal and they became less involved in church life. An increasing proportion stated that they had reacted against the beliefs once taught them. It was followed from 1967 to 1974 by a period of little change, although the proportion of those reacting against former beliefs still showed some increase. The last period, 1974 to 1979, showed a slight trend toward greater conservative belief and church participation. It was evident that the years 1972-1975 were a low point for traditional religiousness among students. A repetition confirmed these trends, showing a return to the attitudes of the 1950s, with the movement toward more liberal religious attitudes reversed, a heightened privatism and with greater conservatism on several moral topics, especially about the use of marijuana but with less concern about broader social and political issues. The nonlinear trends over the whole period showed that they could not be accounted for solely by a simple secularization theory but represented shifts in a larger value structure.

Hunsberger (1978) noted the frequency with which it was reported that students became less orthodox in their religious beliefs and practices during their years at university and made a two-year longitudinal study. He found a decline in church attendance but only limited evidence for a movement from orthodox beliefs and practices or for reactions against parental religious teaching. He concluded that if such changes took place, they occurred during the high-school years and that adolescents had their minds made up about religion before they reached university.

McAllister (1981) showed that the movement of students from traditional orthodox beliefs toward more liberal attitudes might have ended; this was in step with a somewhat reduced drop-out rate from the churches and a marked increase in reentry rates. Subsequently the women students of the 1980s were found to be more religious than the previous sample in terms of attitudes and beliefs but showed lower levels of religious behavior (McAllister, 1985). In a four-year study there was again a tendency for students to move away from orthodox belief; members of campus religious organizations tended to be more orthodox believers, and participants in these groups tended to become more religious during their student days, especially when personal friendships were also involved (Madsen and Vernon, 1983). In freshmen at the same college there was a decline in orthodoxy between 1973 and 1983 (Maneso and Sedlacek, 1985).

When the present-day attitudes of students who had graduated in 1969 were compared with those recorded in 1969 and 1971 in a small, religiously oriented college, the decrease in dogmatism that had been observed during the college course was maintained during the following eleven years, but increased religiousness and more liberal social attitudes were also recorded (Barnes, 1984). Identical questionnaires used with Catholic freshmen in 1961, 1971, and 1982 showed that in the first period there had been immense changes toward more liberal doctrines with demands for intellectual freedom and less concern about avoiding sin. There was more emphasis on God as living and working in human beings but less on God as a judge of behavior. There was also more tolerance in personal morality. All this was coupled with reduced religious practices. In the more recent period there had been much less change, and it was now toward more conservative doctrine, with less insistence on intellectual freedom and a movement back toward traditional moral attitudes. The liberalizing trend in sexual freedom continued, and Mass attendance remained at the lower level (Moberg and Hoge, 1986). Yet college appeared to have a delayed effect on some students. When tests on high-school students were repeated after ten years, their sex role attitudes had shifted away from traditional mores and, to a lesser degree, their religious attitudes from sacred to secular. These changes were greatest for those who had subsequently graduated at college, less for those who had attended college but not graduated, and least for those with further education (Funk and Willits, 1987). In a group of mostly Catholic students there was a swing away from conservative values during their four-year course at an English Catholic college of education but a return to them by the end of the course. Apart from such basic religious activities as going to Mass, personal attitudes were increasingly more highly rated than religious or moral attitudes. Interviews confirmed Francis's (1982) finding that these attitudes were established in the final years at school, rather than at college (Sutherland, 1988).

The cumulative effect of these studies provides evidence of some return to more traditional religious beliefs and morality in America after a long period of movement away from them, but the level of reduced religious behavior continues unchanged, as does the more liberal attitude toward sexual ethics. Adolescent and student trends need to be seen against the wider background of national trends, where moderate and liberal churchmanship appears to be in decline, whereas conservative churches and fringe groups grow stronger. Conservative belief is strongly linked to traditional value and lifestyles, and all religious groups are affected by an ongoing cultural polarization (Roof, 1984).

Religious belief and practice among students and young adults

De Vaus (1982a, 1985) used several measures of religious behavior in a longitudinal study of Australian adolescents. He doubted whether the decline in the religiousness of college students could be attributed to educational factors. He tested school students, subsequently repeating the test a year later when some were still at school and others had entered college or university or had started work. Overall there was a decline, which apparently had begun earlier. It was less among college students, and it concealed marked increases in belief, church attendance, and the frequency of prayer by smaller numbers. The changes in religiousness seemed to be due to people changing their reference groups. Even those who had left a Catholic school for tertiary education were not more adversely affected by the lack of the religious ethos previously experienced. It appeared that in college or university students still retained many of their previous social contacts and tended to move in similar social groups, and it was this which influenced their religiousness, not what they studied or the new ideas they encountered. De Vaus was critical of previous studies which had not used control groups (Feldman (1969) cited only two); their absence concealed the origins of religious change and made it appear, erroneously, that it was due to the effect of higher education. Previously, Gilliland (1940) had recorded that the attitude of students toward God and the church showed little change during their years of study, and it seemed that they came to college with their views more or less definitely made up. The results were said to be similar to others in the field. This idea that religious belief had been established by the age of eighteen was also supported by Hastings and Hoge (1976), although Parker's (1971) review pointed to the first year at college as a time of reappraisal. In Australia, Watkins (1979) compared students at the University of New England in 1977 with those of 1965. There had been a movement of 30 percent away from religious practice, but only of 10 percent in the proportion of those claiming religious belief, in contrast to England where the decline had been both in practice and belief. It appeared that students' attitudes to religion were largely formed before university entrance.

Relatively few students were troubled by religious problems; 12 percent had experienced a conflict, mostly in the last two years of college. The changes were due to a liberalization of belief rather than a rejection of it. The more orthodox tended to deny that their religious views conflicted with what they were formerly, but the more liberal students faced their differences and were less prone to deny the existence of contradictions (Havens, 1964). Church attendance, Bible reading, and an anthropomorphic view of God were most associated with the salience of religion among undergraduates (Schoenfeld, 1984). But Bible reading habits were found by Edwards (1984) to be most strongly related to reading attitude, and then to religious experience, followed by church participation and home background. Individual commitment was more important than home background or attending a church college. Students with church affiliations tended to find their friends within the church and had significantly fewer friendships than those without such an attachment (Bonney, 1949). In a study of racial attitudes, no difference was found between a group of non-black teacher education students and all other undergraduates, but the nonfundamentalist teacher education students had more positive racial attitudes than any other group, whether they were fundamentalists or nonfundamentalists from the general student body (Byrnes and Kiger, 1988).

When students were asked to indicate which of eleven areas gave rise to problems, religious items were chosen by less than a third. Religious problems were more frequent with women, and most were related to a loss of faith; they were not associated with leaving the family, exposure to scientific theories, or academic achievement (Beit-Hallahmi, 1974). It seems that in the present climate beliefs are more likely to be discarded than allowed to trouble those who hold them; cognitive dissonance results in belief being rejected, rather than being rationalized.

A trend away from orthodoxy with age seems well-established. The religious values and practices of students did not greatly change in their first year, when they were subjected to examination and clarification, except when the exploration of new social opportunities became a greater priority (Devolder, 1979). Students with religious commitment showed some decrease in religiousness after a semester at college, and formal training in logic dampened the effects of religious belief on religious arguments, although it did not affect their attitude to religion (Watkins, 1977). It was the influence of peers that caused changes in student religious beliefs and behavior; they first changed their behavior because of their new associations, and this led to changes in the way they thought about themselves and in their religious beliefs. There were no similar changes in other beliefs and values while they were on the campus (Becker, 1977). A comparison of freshmen and graduates showed that changes in religious loyalty and defection were influenced by their growth of autonomous thinking (Harriman, 1978). The present religiousness of Catholic students regularly worshiping at a university church was not related to their previous education or home influence but rather to religious influences on the campus and closeness to religious personnel (Spatti, 1978). However, the extent to which this heightened religiousness in church colleges exists is not clear; it could be due either to the selection of more religious students or the result of college life.The traits specific to religious groups of college graduates did not vary with individual religiousness, which suggested that the norms and role images of the religious groups did not necessarily arise from religious ideas but could be due to past cultural experience. All the differences between minority and mainstream religious groups could be explained in terms of the immigration experiences of Catholics and Jews (Greeley, 1964).

When the religiousness of first-year Catholic women students on a secular university campus was compared with those on a large and a small religiously oriented campus, very little difference was found, except that students on the secular campus tended to score lower on a scale about the effect of belief on conduct (Kanger, 1972). In three church-related colleges one college attracted distinctly liberal students. While freshmen changed little in religious knowledge, the Lutheran college students showed increased religiousness without gaining in the consequential dimension which indicates the personal and social effects of religious belief. They also found it difficult to express their convictions. As in the other colleges, belief in a personal God was reduced, as was church attendance, but there was also a greater concern to explore religious values, which, even though the college put them to question, were better retained with the knowledge that they had been compelled to refine their thinking and their feelings about them (Stanger, 1978).

Small changes in students' intellectual development, as it affected moral insight, could be attributed to college impact, but membership in a church college made no difference (Meyer, 1975). At a large public university fundamentalist beliefs were associated with conservatism in politics and theology and also with lower grades, less outside reading, more authoritarianism and dogmatism, and acceptance of the "Moral Majority." In a denominational evangelical college students of the college denomination gained greater achievement in their work; they tended to make better adjustments in a familiar cultural environment (Hoult and Peckham, 1957).

When an exploration of belief was carried out with English students there was an evident continuity with the style of belief found in the schools. Gray (1963) developed a scale to measure beliefs about God, Jesus, the Holy Spirit, prayer, the church, the Bible, man, life after death, religion, and behavior, and she tested first-year students training to be teachers in colleges of education. From responses to the items and free comments, a detailed picture emerged. Women always gave a higher proportion of positive responses; men in colleges of a religious foundation showed greater religiousness than women in the other colleges. There were pronounced differences between the colleges, even of the same type. Most students professed to believe in God and only 16 percent of the men and 13 percent of the women were agnostic; about a third claimed their experience of God had helped them to a better life. The same proportion stated that Jesus was their personal Savior, although almost three-quarters believed Jesus had died that mankind might be forgiven. Only a third showed knowledge of the Holy Spirit. Three-quarters thought prayer to be a source of help in trouble and that it was answered; almost as many considered the church to be doing good work. Fewer than a half regarded the Bible as relevant, or as helping them to believe in God; rather more would have liked to believe in life after death or thought there need be no conflict between science and religion.

There was much discussion about religion and behavior. Few claimed never to attend church, but weekly attendance was less than a third in the local authority colleges and twice that in those of a religious foundation. Similar but smaller proportions claimed to pray every day, but to some extent prayer appeared to be a reality to most students. Daily Bible reading was much less popular, and more claimed never to read it. It seemed that a majority had some interest in religion despite much ignorance, doubt, and confusion, but a substantial minority were indifferent. In one of the colleges, tests over three years showed marked variations between the years, but there was apparently some convergence between the sexes, the men becoming more favorable to religion and the women less favorable. In two other colleges, students studying religion showed more favorable attitudes, although their studies had revealed new problems of belief to them. To what extent this pattern is unaltered a generation later is not known, but there are some indicators that despite decreased church attendance basic religious beliefs are still held by many.

Theological colleges tend to attract students favorable to their theological position; students at conservative colleges become more conservative during their course, and students at liberal colleges become less conservative during their course (Scobie, 1975).

Francis (1982) undertook a survey of the opinions of members of the London Central Y.M.C.A aged sixteen to twenty-five. A third had been born outside the United Kingdom, so that it was by no means representative, but its detailed findings on beliefs and opinions in a pluralistic setting are of interest. Almost a half regarded themselves as Christian, but only a quarter claimed to belong to any denomination. One in four was agnostic; one in three denied the divinity of Jesus. Attending a place of worship, engaging in prayer, or reading the Bible were not held in high esteem. While the women were more religious than the men, there was no difference between the sexes active in the church. Students in the group showed a little less agnosticism than the worker group but a lower acceptance of the divinity of Jesus—differences more marked than social group differences and possibly related to the relatively younger age of the student group.

Wadsworth and Freeman (1983) made an analysis of statements about religious beliefs and upbringing made at twenty-six by the cohort of people born in one week in March 1946 who provide the data for the Medical Research Council National Survey. Fifty-seven percent called themselves Church of England, 30 percent had some kind of faith, and 13 percent were without religious belief. There was a marked change in belief between the generations apart from those classified as "other nonconformists"; 67 percent were believers, as against 87 percent of their parents. Higher educational achievement was the variable most strongly associated with change of belief, followed by an expectation of social mobility. The third, affecting only the women, was a previous emotional disturbance which often affected belief, either greatly strengthening or weakening it. The relationship with higher education could arise from the independence found by students away from home, which made it easier for them to change or drop their religious practices.

Hornsby-Smith, Lee, and Reilly (1985) in a survey of adult Catholics noted that they no longer exhibited the uniformity of belief and practice previously observed. The variety of unorthodox beliefs discovered was not properly described as common religion, a term which they restricted to beliefs and practices lacking any institutional context. The unstructured, heterodox variations of Catholic belief due to trivialization, convention, apathy, convenience, and self-interest they preferred to call customary religion. It is clear from the studies reviewed that both these variants of belief are often to be found; presumably, the further individuals are from their source of belief, the more likely it is that their beliefs are reduced to magic and superstition, lacking any coherent theological basis. Such beliefs, when held by parents, will almost certainly be passed on to their children.

Chapter 13

Religion and Morality
in Adolescence

It will have been noticed that from time to time accounts of adolescent religious beliefs have also included statements about values, which were regarded as a consequence of being religious. The chapter provides some account of more general adolescent values on which religiousness has a bearing, and of the relationship between religiousness and morality in adolescence. It leaves unresolved the questions regarding the appropriate systems of values which should be related to religiousness, and the effect on adolescents of the unagreed agenda of the churches on such major issues as contraception and population growth, abortion and deformity, war, pacifism, and unilateral nuclear disarmament. Popular evangelism presents a gospel which does not require any radical change in lifestyle, unlike the New Testament, but offers sacralization in return for church affiliation.

Adolescent values

In a group of youth club members from schools, further education, industry, and commerce, only a quarter took a favorable view of their own generation; they showed much awareness of social issues, and condemned irresponsibility. Their greatest concern was to make good social relationships, and they were willing, if necessary, to make a sacrifice for their families or their friends. Boys were more ready to accept responsibility in facing problems, girls to seek help from their families. They held respect for authority but were determined to assert their individ-

278

uality, which was usually the root of any conflict with an older generation seen to be reluctant to accept change (Holland 1968).

Kitwood (1978, 1980) undertook informal interviews, inviting older adolescents to give accounts of their experiences. They described situations which gave information about their family life, relationships, work, and personal values. Some spoke of a religious involvement, but even those committed regarded religion mainly as a way of living and a style of relationship; religious issues did not significantly emerge. Adolescence was not a time of intense interest in ideals, a philosophy by which to live, or an intellectual quest. To the contrary, there was an overwhelmingly negative portrayal of the educational process, even by those using it for their own ends. Most showed sensitivity about the feelings of their peers, an insight which indicated how they were appraised by others. From this arose a "perspective morality" with an emphasis on feelings, tending to be specific rather than general, with variations between persons. Because many were denied the opportunity of constructive involvement with the material world, and finding the intellectual realm unattractive, they became almost obsessive about their social world. They were characterized not by a search for identity, for which no evidence was found, but by living in conditions where generally the formation of a strong identity was not possible, so that their greatest need was for conditions to be provided for them where it could be attained.

Simmons and Wade (1982) gave adolescents of fifteen a sentence to complete to indicate the sort of person they would like to be. Many boys subscribed to materialistic values and many girls to social values. A second sentence about what mattered most to them reduced this tendency and the objection of some of them to the form of the question. One in five rejected the idea of an ideal person, preferring to remain themselves. The results contested the depressing finding of Martin and Pluck (1977) who found in group interviews that subjects were mostly at a loss for words.

Miller (1981) regarded American adolescent lifestyles as being related to religious commitment. He considered them to be complex symbols in motion, and a new concern with individuals' identity and uniqueness was emerging. In many of the new religious movements there were striking stylistic affinities, from clothing to living arrangements, which distinguished the groups from the rest of society. The groups which were weakest also lacked an identifying lifestyle, and identity was increasingly a function of style; the authority of tradition, law, or of a charismatic personality was being overtaken by taste as the hallmark of personal choice. Religiousness could be but one choice of personal taste, but alternatively it could give direction to all choices. In a Canadian survey of adolescent values and hopes, friendship, love, freedom, and honesty were among the most highly regarded values; relationships and music were seen as very important. Eighty-five percent claimed to believe in God, but only a quarter attended church with any regularity, even though they held positive views regarding organized religion (Ban, 1986).

Adolescent religion and morals

While it is often assumed in the churches that religiousness will be associated with enhanced moral judgment and behavior, evidence for this is not always forthcoming. In a number of studies a strong association between religiousness and acceptable moral behavior or the absence of deviance and delinquency is assumed to demonstrate a causal relationship. Usually there is no evidence for an actual causative effect; independent variables, such as parental and peer influence and personality traits, may simultaneously influence both religiousness, morality, and delinquency. Statistical techniques, such as path analysis, in which the assumptions regarding the direction of cause have to be indicted, seem to have been overlooked when religiousness is involved. The association of religion and morality is not a simple one, possibly because many accepted moral ideas are humanistic rather than exclusively religious. The relationship between religion and morality is partly one of stance; religion is primarily concerned with a relationship with God, morality with relationships with other people; while theologians affirm that the ultimate values of morality are rooted in the being of God, psychologists point out individual differences in the image of God, and moral philosophy seeks other foundations for morality than religion. Moral development has been studied from different but not necessarily exclusive perspectives; it can be regarded as social learning or seen in psychoanalytic terms as arising from parental interaction. Following Piaget and Kohlberg, its development has been measured as a cognitive understanding of justice - although in traditional philosophy, justice is only one aspect of morality, and in Christian living, love more than justice is the mark of a virtuous life.

Following the study of the independence of four dimensions of religion (Putney and Middleton, 1961a), noted in Appendix C, Middleton and Putney (1962) looked at the relationship between students' religious belief and moral values. They distinguished between social morality, where actions such as stealing or lying affect other people, and ascetic morality, where actions such as drinking or smoking affect the subject. The values of social morality were held with equal strength by believers and nonbelievers, but ascetic moral precepts were more strongly upheld by believers.

Similar questions about different moral issues were also investigated by Wright (1965) and Wright and Cox (1967b) among senior school students. Racism and stealing were most condemned, smoking and gambling least. Girls were more severe in their judgments than boys. Those professing religious belief were found to have a more exacting moral standard in some areas than the remainder. Severity of judgment was related to the indices of religiousness, a relationship which was stronger with more ascetic moral issues and with Catholics more advanced in particular issues. Age, subjects studied, or coeducation were not related to moral judgments. Two small extreme groups were identified, one highly religious, absolute in many moral judgments, and tending to express views in stereotyped phrases;

the other, usually boys who could not care less about what others did or thought, who saw no point in belief and emphasized the pursuit of enjoyment in life. Over a period of seven years their successors shifted to a more tolerant position on the ascetic issues, but there was no significant change on general moral values (Wright and Cox, 1971).

Nucci (1985) followed Middleton and Putney (1962) and Wright and Cox (1967b, 1971) in distinguishing between social and ascetic morality. He confirmed that when religious precepts opposed breaches of ascetic morality, believers opposed them more than nonbelievers, but that in areas of social morality believers and unbelievers alike would similarly condemn acts which resulted in harm or injustice to others. This was in accord with the philosophical theories which regarded morality as independent of religion. An overwhelming majority of Catholic students at high school or university thought it would be wrong if church authorities permitted such actions as hitting or stealing, but rather less than half of them thought it would be wrong for the pope to remove church rules about fasting before taking communion, ordaining women, using contraceptives, or engaging in premarital sex. A similar study was made with a group of children aged ten to seventeen of Amish-Mennonite parents who accepted biblical rules very literally, dressed very simply, and would not have radio or television in their homes. In interviews they were asked to justify their judgments about issues such as working on Sunday and women preaching, as well as stealing and hitting. They did not regard God's law as extending to members of other religions, and nearly all were prepared to accept changes in their religious rules if the Bible had not given directions about them. But most or all of them still regarded a breach of the moral code as wrong even it there was no biblical prohibition of it. Similarly, Dutch Reformed children in Chicago said they would not steal even if God had written in the Bible that Christians should steal. God would not command stealing because it was not the right thing to do—they appealed to a morality external to God.

The issue then is not whether religion, apart from specific religious prohibitions, provides a higher level of morality but whether religious people are more likely to behave morally.

The degree to which children are exposed to religious precepts about morality varies considerably, so that no direct religious association can be observed, and it does not follow that satisfactory moral judgment necessarily gives rise to comparable moral behavior. No attempt is made here to enter the vast field of research in moral thinking but only to indicate studies that are concerned with the relationship between religion and morality. The development of moral understanding, as distinct from moral behavior, has undergone scrutiny since the early work of Piaget (1932) and the considerable activity of Kohlberg, whose approach was the basis of Rest's (1979a, b) Defining Issues Test, used in some recent surveys about morality and religiousness. Some studies of religiousness and morality are concerned with possible parallels in conceptual development, others look for moral behavioral relationships with religious commitment, and some fudge the issue.

Religious orientation affects moral development. In different denominations intrinsically oriented adult members tended to observe the moral teachings of their denominations more than those extrinsically oriented, with significant differences between individual Protestant congregations and between individuals according to their religious seriousness. Moral development depended not only on the cognitive development of logical thinking but also on theological support for particular belief systems (Ernsberger and Manaster, 1981). The relationship is not a simple one. In a student sample, out of Batson's means, end, and quest orientations, only quest had a significant moral association, and of Allport's intrinsic, indiscriminately proreligious and indiscriminately antireligious orientations, only the indiscriminately antireligious was significantly associated (Sapp and Jones, 1986). When the relationship between religiousness and moral development was studied among adult Catholics, Jews, and Protestants, all of whom had been identified as "observant" in Fromm's use of the term, ten dimensions of religiousness were used, and all of them proved to be components of a single general orientation associated with moral development. Religious orientation was the manifestation in behavior of a thought process that affected diverse areas of life (Borenstein, 1982).

Ausubel, Sullivan, and Ives (1980) observed that most children were influenced indirectly by religious ideas, acquired by many means if not formally, and while for some religious observance was perfunctory, for others, it was important in determining their moral choices and regulating their relationships. Because religion was bound up with environmental factors, it was difficult to isolate its impact on children's moral development. Yet despite the complexity, attempts to find how being religious affects moral development have been made.

Hilliard (1959) extracted data from four other investigations to demonstrate that while younger children might hold a belief that God punished wrong-doing but rewarded the good, most adolescents rejected the idea of a punitive God, yet still regarded him as upholding the moral law. It therefore appeared that religious belief should facilitate the development of moral ideas. Catholic and Jewish school pupils could distinguish between the motivation and the result of actions earlier than other children (Boehm, 1962, 1963). Attendance at Sunday school had no significant relationship with children's powers of moral reasoning (Whiteman and Kosier, 1964); again, it seemed that it was religious belief rather than religious observance which had a moral outcome.

The Bible Society (1978) survey showed that differences on moral issues between the two main groups were marked. Only 13 percent of the school sample thought that sex without marriage was definitely wrong compared with 59 percent of the more religious Buzz group. Forty-three percent of the schools group regarded homosexual practice as definitely wrong, compared with 69 percent of the Buzz group. It appeared that many young people were not prepared to commit themselves to moral absolutes but regarded conscience as a guide to conduct; religious belief determined many moral views. Francis (1978c) studied moral and religious attitudes among pupils of fourteen and fifteen in schools in England,

Scotland, and Wales; they held permissive attitudes toward extramarital sex and abortion, but were conservative about homosexuality. Only 8 percent of them claimed to base their moral attitude on religious beliefs, and when compared with an earlier survey a significant movement away from Christianity was indicated.

Wolf (1979) found, against his expectations, that religious education had a negative effect on moral development, apparently because those most exposed to it either accepted its teaching as introjected values or rejected it in favor of an experimental set of values. Maturity, however, was strongly related to the amount of religious education received and to pupils' response to it. Kedem and Cohen (1987) found with Jewish children aged six that attending a Jewish school had no effect on their level of moral judgment, yet by age ten they achieved a higher level than that of Jewish children attending a secular school.

The higher the stage of moral development defined by Rest's (1979a, b) Defining Issues Test, the greater was the likelihood of students rejecting right-wing politics and orthodox religion; there was a marked difference between the levels of conventional and principled moral thinking. This suggested that religious and political belief systems were superimpositions of cognitive and moral content on categories of cognitive and moral structure (Sanderson, 1973). No significant difference was found in the moral development of junior high school pupils at a church school with others in a state school, although the church school pupils had relatively fewer lower scores and relatively more higher scores. In both schools, girls tended to score more than boys (Hardin, 1978). Graduate students of religion and of education in Calvinistic, Wesleyan, and varied theological environments differed significantly on tests of morality and religious orientations (Luther, 1979). When the levels of moral judgment were compared between three distinct groups, the scores of the doctoral students and the high-school students were typical, but those of the students in a fundamentalist seminary were low. They understood statements of principled moral judgments, but responded in terms of their churches' teachings (Lawrence, 1979). Similarly, scores on this test were low in groups with a literal belief in the Bible and high in groups with more liberal beliefs. Other studies supported this association, which was not affected by intrinsic or extrinsic orientations. It should not be overlooked that the evangelical emphasis on Jesus as Lord is often interpreted in submissive terms indicative of conventional moral reasoning (Brown and Annis, 1978). Undergraduates from conservative Bible colleges showed a strong association between conservative theology and the conventional level of moral judgment (Childerston, 1985). Evangelical students scored below average on moral development; this could be related to a lack of reflection on the content of their faith, weakness in an evangelical educational process lacking cognitive disequilibrium, evangelical orientation toward biblical care and concern rather than toward justice, or the manner by which the institution communicated its standards of conduct to its students (Dirks, 1988). Differences in moral development among religious students at a university, a state college, and a church college which persisted through their course showed that different types of students were recruited by the different institutions (Moore, 1979). Among three student groups classified as holding a liberal, a centrist, or a conservative religious ideology, the last had significantly lower scores for moral development (Kane, 1988). By testing the moral development of two groups of students at the start and the end of a four-year course, Shaver (1987) found a normal development among those who had attended a liberal arts college but not among those who had attended a Bible college. While there was no overall association between college students' moral reasoning and their religious orientation, those with high scores for an intrinsic orientation had higher scores on the Defining Issues Test, and those with a low extrinsic religious orientation had higher scores on this test than those with a high extrinsic orientation (Ang, 1989). Bouhmama (1990) developed an attitude to religion scale relating to belief in the Koran, God, the after-life, and the necessity of religion for meaningful life. When it was administered with Rest's Defining Issues Test to Algerian university students, no association was found between moral development and attitude to religion; the author considered that this result might have been affected by Rest's test being inappropriate for Algerian students holding strong religious beliefs.

Religion played a major role for many adolescents in their moral development, giving them greater security and more freedom from worry (Hauser, 1981). The effect of religious education on the development of moral judgment apparently depends on its nature. Among pupils aged thirteen to sixteen in Catholic, conservative Christian, Lutheran, and public high schools, church school students had higher scores than public school students, and those from the conservative Christian schools had a higher mean score than either the Catholic or Lutheran school students. The highest scores of all were secured by the oldest Lutheran school students (Stoop, 1979). The association of higher scores for both moral judgment and religious knowledge found by O'Gorman (1979) among Catholic boys in parochial and public schools could be due to mental ability affecting both of them. A similar result was secured by Harris (1981), who also found no association between scores for moral judgment and those for religious belief or religious practice. Among younger and older students in Seventh-Day Adventist high schools there was no association between moral judgment and any measure of religiousness, except length of time as a church member, which would appear to be a function of age rather than religiousness (Dunn, 1984). In a group of twelve-year-old children there was no significant association between moral development and religiousness, except for self-ratings of religiousness (Cranford, 1984). Sex, different types of religious education, and religious conservatism had no effect on the moral reasoning of Jewish high-school students, but for boys, the study of traditional orthodox Yeshiva based mainly on Talmudic texts was associated with greater social interest. Moral reasoning appeared to be a cognitive skill, whereas social interest was related to attitudes and was affective (Friedman, 1983).

Conservative believers tended to make judgments on the level of conventional moral reasoning, and there was a significant negative association between postconventional reasoning and nearly all the measures of religiousness used. Atheists and some liberal believers tended to make moral judgments at the higher post-conventional level. The differences were affected by demographic variables and by mental ability (Hoagland, 1984). There was significant associations between the level of moral development and grade level, Bible class grade, frequency of family worship, and prayer meeting attendance among students in a black Seventh-Day Adventist school. The years of religious education and attendance at Sunday school had no effect. The mean score on Rest's test was lower than the national high-school average, which could be the result of religious conservatism or of bias in the test (Brantley, 1986). People believing in an abstract rather than a personal concept of God, and who had an internal source of authority and a humanitarian rather than an evangelical social perspective, tended to use principled moral reasoning. The relationships were not strong enough to support the theory that the cognitive structure of religious belief influenced the development of moral reasoning. It also appeared that the beliefs in a particular denomination were related to the extent of opportunities available for discussing moral issues and viewpoints, since these also affected the development of moral reasoning (Blizard, 1980). It is obvious that levels of logical thinking can affect both moral and religious judgments, but a causal relationship between them is far from certain.

The literature regarding the general association of moral judgment with religious dimensions and orientations was reviewed by Getz (1984). She observed that there were a growing number of studies on morality and religion, due partly to the availability of Rest's Defining Issues Test. She drew attention to some of these, commenting that the complexity of religiousness accounted for the inconsistencies found between them, although some results appeared to be well founded. Other studies indicated a negative association with religious education or no association. There were evidently differences in other variables, such as the mental ability and the socio-economic status of the school samples, which while sometimes acknowledged were not considered in the research.

Oser and Reich (1990) reviewed the conflicting findings regarding the possible relationship between the development of moral and religious judgment. They compared the different conclusions with their own findings about the relationship between Kohlberg's moral judgment and religious judgment as defined by Oser and Gmünder (1988). Their data did not support the view that moral development was a necessary but insufficient condition for religious development. Rather, it appeared that a dynamic model was necessary, which varied according to stage, and was also affected by socialization and individual experiences.

From these diverse studies some firm conclusions can be drawn. Religiousness tends to bring adherence to religious prohibitions, but otherwise morality does not depend upon religion. There is no empirical evidence to suggest that religious people are more moral than similar nonreligious people. A legalistic form of religious belief seems often to be associated with conventional moral reasoning and would seem to have an adverse effect on the development of higher levels of moral judgment.

Religiousness and deviance in adolescence

The alienation and delinquency of a significant minory of adolescents is a problem throughout the Western world. There have been periods of significant increases in juvenile crime, although statistics about increased delinquency may only indicate an increased reporting of it or some change of police procedures. There are those who regard this as the inevitable consequence of a loss of religious faith by adolescents and by their society. The question is thus raised as to the extent that religiously minded adolescents are not involved in deviant behavior. Tittle and Welch (1983) affirmed that individual religiousness was the most effective constraint of deviant behavior in adolescents and adults when the conformity required by the appropriate religious community was not reproduced in the larger community, and religious constraint increased when secular controls were either weak or absent.

Psychologists look for the origins of this behavior in earlier life. Ausubel, Montemajor, and Svajian (1977) considered that the roots of emotional instability arose in early childhood through nonsatellizing. Satellizing occurs when children first become aware of their dependence on their parents and find their self-esteem in being accepted and valued for their own sakes as satellites of their parents. Conger and Petersen (1984) concluded that while some aspects of alienation were widespread in particular cultures, others were limited to smaller sub-groups, and the reasons for the feeling of rejection which led to deviant behavior differed greatly—it was imposed upon the poor, whereas the privileged rejected apparently inadequate social values. Higher levels of delinquency are associated with the disruption of community and family life, usually in inner-city areas. Delinquents have often been identified as being poorly adapted to society and maladjusted, finding it difficult to establish good personal relationships. Many studies indicated that early in life they were subjected to unsatisfactory parental discipline—erratic, too lax or too strict, with frequent recourse to physical punishment and seldom to reason.

Recent interest in the relationship between adolescent religiousness and moral development has focused on its effect in inhibiting delinquency. Neither of the surveys of adolescents in the United States (Middleton and Putney, 1962) and in England (MacDonald 1969) found any link between levels of antisocial behavior and church attendance, yet Nye (1958) had found a negative association between regular church attendance and more serious delinquency, a finding confirmed by Glueck and Glueck (1968) and by Ferguson (1952). Insofar as delinquency is an adolescent phenomenon, it tends to end by the mid-twenties, yet this is an age of minimum religiousness.

Albrecht, Chadwick, and Alcorn (1977) were critical of the inconsistency in measures of deviance found in many studies, and of the samples used. Adolescents in detention were likely to exaggerate their church allegiance in the hope of an earlier release, and data from them would give rise to an unfounded association between delinquency and religiousness. Their own investigations with Mormon adolescents showed that religiousness had a negative association with deviance; this was particularly true with self-reported deviance not involving a victim. Parental influence was another factor, and the strongest was the perception of the deviance of their peers (especially with boys). These three factors together gave reliable prediction of deviant behavior.

Rohrbaugh and Jessor (1975) considered that holding conventional or unconventional religious beliefs and participating in their rituals should restrain adolescent deviant behavior, and they investigated this among high-school and college students in a longitudinal study. Religiousness was measured in terms of its ritual, consequential, ideological, and experiential dimensions without reference to any specific religion. It was associated with intolerance of deviance, with conformity, and with conventional behavior concerning drug use and premarital sex; the association of religiousness with personal control was stronger with high-school than with college students and weakest with male college students. Those with more conservative beliefs did not differ from those with liberal beliefs.

A study of the self-reported delinquent offences of high-school students in different situations on issues such as drinking, smoking, vandalism, taking drugs, and theft suggested that inconsistencies in similar research could be explained because it had been largely carried out in metropolitan settings. There were groups for whom religious involvement and belief were significantly associated with a lack of delinquency, and there were social settings where there were denominational differences in the extent of delinquency. These denominational differences were most prominent for those who regularly participated in church, especially when there was a clear moral message from the denomination (Jensen and Maynard, 1979).

Shields (1984) contested the assumption by criminologists that religiousness was irrelevant to adolescent delinquency. He analyzed data from a national random sample of adolescents on five measures of delinquency used and contended that religiousness had a strong deterrent effect, and for four of the measures it was even stronger for the older group. It was also true about theft when parental harmony was high. Religiousness had a negative association with self-reported delinquent conduct among white high-school students, and while age brought decreased religiousness, it also brought increased delinquency (Peek et al., 1985). Yet religious commitment was only associated with the avoidance of delinquency in areas where religious commitment was the norm, while in secularized societies no such association was observed. In most schools where students with a religious background were in a majority there was a very substantial negative relationship between religiousness and delinquency, but this disappeared in the highly secularized schools of the West coast (Stark, Kent, and Doyle, 1982). The relationship between adolescent religiousness and deviance varied widely according to the form of deviance, as for example between the use of alcohol or marijuana (Cochran, 1987). Conflicting evidence could be due to the variety of statistical methods used in different investigations; when methods and tests of significance were sufficiently sensitive, religiousness had a strong negative association with all offenses (Sloane and Potvin, 1986). In all these studies a strong negative association between religiousness and delinquency is assumed to be the simple direct deterrent effect of a morality based on religious teaching, yet none provides any evidence to support the simple contention. Both are related to parental attitudes.

Ellis and Thompson (1989) noted that the inverse relationship between crime and religiousness was stronger when measured by church attendance than by other measures and argued that, far from this being a causal relationship, the operative factor was boredom. Boredom was tolerated by those who found comfort in the church, but it led to deviant behavior in others, and their research among college students showed that those who were bored with the church were more likely to offend. (Boredom with the church, which indicates a negative attitude to the church, is a mark of lower religiousness, so this argument is tautologous.)

Adolescent religiousness and drug use

The use of drugs by adolescents and its marked increase in recent years has cause worldwide concern. It is part of a general trend not limited to adolescence, but affecting large numbers of them to some extent. Many authors deal with the issue; a well-documented study dealing with the problem is included in Conger and Petersen's (1984) textbook. They show the extent of the problem, ranging from the very small use of heroin to the widespread use of alcohol and discuss the psychological motives which lead to these different forms of abuse, such as to reduce anxiety or tension. Only in a relatively few studies is the relationship between religiousness and drug use considered. Conflicting results appear at times to be the result of inadequate definition; drug use can cover several forms of drug abuse each of which has different characteristic behavior patterns. Rohrbaugh and Jessor (1975) showed that religiousness was associated with an intolerance of deviance, with conformity and conventional behavior regarding drugs and premarital sex. A decline in religiousness with age was associated with greater unconventional behavior regarding sex and drugs. Similarly, Kharari and Harmon (1982) found in an all-age sample that religiousness militated against the use of drugs. McIntosh, Fitch, Wilson, and Myberg (1981) studied the effect of religious controls on adolescent drug use in rural areas. Gorsuch (1988) stated that religiousness related consistently to a reduction in the use of illegal drugs and nonmarital sexual behavior and was often the most consistent predictor of drug nonabuse, although this was frequently overlooked in abstracts of such studies.

Hadaway, Elifson, and Peterson (1984) showed that religiousness in a group of urban adolescents aged thirteen to sixteen had a strong negative relationship with their attitudes to drugs and drug use, depending on the degree to which society regarded drug use as deviant—it was strong for marijuana and weak for alcohol, and it was also affected by such other factors as parental church attendance or church opposition to alcohol use. Lorch and Hughes (1985) used six different measures of religiousness in testing a very large sample of adolescents from eleven to sixteen. Religion itself was not a strong predictor of drug use, but it was more strongly related to alcohol use. The importance of religion was the strongest predictor, followed by church membership. It seemed that drug use or avoidance was due to internalized values rather then church ideology or peer pressures. This conclusion supported the finding of Burkett (1977) that church attendance was inversely associated with the use of alcohol and marijuana by white high-school students; many thought it to be wrong, whatever their parent's religiousness, which was less influential than their own personal asceticism. It appears that it is actual religious practice, rather than a more general expression of religious attitude, which is related to drug avoidance.

Dudley, Mutch, and Cruise (1987) studied religion, faith, and drug use among Seventh-Day Adventist youth aged twelve to twenty-four in North America. Very little use was found; most wanted to be in control of their lives and health. Regular participation in family worship and Sunday school attendance were the best predictors for alcohol avoidance and personal prayer for tobacco avoidance. More frequent use was found among those who disregarded such church rules about not listening to heavy metal rock music. Their membership status and the extent of parental education had little effect. Kent (1987) found that the extent of adolescents' substance abuse was inversely related to their religious practice, companionship with their mother, their perception of the consistency of their father's control, religious practice, and disapproval of the use of tobacco, alcohol, marijuana, and drugs. Koplin (1987) found in a large sample of high-school students that religiousness and all family variables tested were directly or indirectely inversely associated with drug use.

When over two thousand boys from eleven to twenty were tested on six measures of drug use, their religious affiliation was insignificant, apart from Catholics showing greater alcohol use than Protestants. Church attendance showed a stronger negative relationship, more for girls than boys, and this increased with illicit drug use (Adulf and Smart, 1985). Drug abuse was a minimal problem among a group of young Jewish adults (Davids, 1982), but a review of the relevant literature showed that drug use among Jewish youth was consistently higher than a generation ago and that it was inversely related to religiousness (Eckstein, 1978). When religiousness showed no relationship with drug use, then the practice appeared to be one aspect of a broader pattern of deviance. It was associated with sexual behavior, general delinquency, and social behavior and weakly related to school achievement and domestic behavior (Hundelby, Carpenter, Ross, and Mercer, 1982).

The use of drugs such as LSD to stimulate ecstatic states has been mentioned in the studies of religious experience in chapter 9. An important study was that of Clark (1958) and his more recent contributions (Clark 1969, 1973). Bron (1975) made the interesting observation that throughout history drug-induced ecstasy had been one aspect of religious practice. It followed that the present-day use of drugs rather than religion to solve personal conflicts and secure a transcendental experience of happiness was related to the breakdown of religion. The hypothesis is consistent with the findings reviewed.

Burkett (1980) studied the association of religious belief and adolescent drinking, and Perkins (1987) found students were at greater risk of problem drinking if they did not have a strong attachment to a particular faith or were children of an alcohol abuser. The characteristics of parental faith affected students' drinking experience in many ways, and their religious traditions were strongly associated with their children's behavior. Wilson (1988) observed that adult children of alcoholics were liable to be distressed, depressed, and feel guilty, and it made no difference if the alcoholic parent was also an evangelical Christian.

Adolescent sexuality

Many religious people hold strong views about maintaining traditional sexual morality. The sexual behavior of young people associated with the church is bound to be under scrutiny. According to Hoge and De Zulveta (1985), religiousness was only associated with the values and attitudes of American Christians about the church, family life, sexuality, and personal honesty, and also among Protestants with the use of alcohol. There were only weak relationships between religiousness and their attitudes to patriotism, government involvement with the poor, the equality of women, and marijuana use. Most values were not related to religious belief; its influence was always in a conservative direction. Only among the better educated, who were less conformist, did religious salience have some political association.

Once more, there are a number of accounts of sexual behavior in adolescence. Francis (1978c) noted among adolescents a movement away from traditional Christian morality toward more liberal attitudes to extramarital sex and abortion, but with conservative attitudes to homosexuality. Hopkins (1977) reviewed surveys of the topic made over nearly fifty years; despite the difficulties of comparison, it was evident that more college students were now sexually experienced than formerly, and while this was always true more of men than of women, the difference was now less than it used to be. Conger and Petersen (1984) also described with much detail the diversity of adolescent sexual attitudes and behavior. They pointed out many cultural differences and the effects of more recent permissiveness and of sex education programs. Almost all adolescents were less conservative in their attitudes than their parents and were greatly influenced by their peers. Among nonvirgins there were sexual monogamists and sexual adventurers; contraception and pregnancy were then relevant issues.

As with drug use, religious practice rather than religious attitude has the stronger relationship with sexual behavior. On two campuses between 10 percent and 15 percent of the students were cohabiting, more men then women, more Jewish than Catholic or Protestant students, and more who did not attend church than who did (Silverman, 1977). Premarital relationships had increased between 1972 and 1978 and the differences between various groups in attitudes toward permissiveness had narrowed; age and church attendance were the most constant predictors of these attitudes (Singh, 1980). Among a group of women students, religiousness was related to sexual activity and to the use or nonuse of contraceptives (Young, 1982). Woodroof (1984) found in a sample of adolescents aged seventeen to nineteen who were very active religiously that their religious belief and behavior was strongly associated with traditional avoidance of premarital sexual behavior. Belonging to a religious group provided role models and a sanctioning system for adolescents that operated to discourage sexual activity. The lower use of contraception by religious adolescents might be due to their lacking open dialogue, information, and support for contraceptive use from parents, peers, and others with whom they strongly identified (Strader and Thornton, 1987). In mixed black and white groups, church attendance was inversely related to promiscuity; sexual attitudes were moderately related to behavior, and the white men were the most promiscuous (Robinson and Calhoun, 1983). A group of black adolescent fathers were more likely not to be church-goers than comparable nonfathers (Hendricks and Fullilove, 1983). However, religiousness was not related to the sexual behavior and use of contraception by high-school students in rural New York (McCormick, Izzo, and Folcik, 1985).

Other studies have been about sexual attitudes and indicate that theological stances create much variety of sexual attitudes and behavior. The attitude to premarital sex of university students was associated with their religiousness as measured by a religious fundamentalism scale, but not their actual sexual behavior (King, Abernathy, Robinson, and Balswick, 1976). Fundamentalists were less accepting of premarital and extramarital sexual relationships than nonfundamentalists, and the men of both groups were more approving than the women (Maret and Maret, 1982). The negative relationship between conservative religious attitudes and permissive sexual attitudes outweighed the positive relationship between higher socio-economic status and permissive attitudes, but this was not the case with liberal religious attitudes (Bock, Beeghley, and Mixon, 1983). Among theologically conservative students in church colleges, religiousness was strongly associated with the rejection of premarital sexual behavior, but lack of strong religiousness did not predict the sexual activity found among many in this group (Woodroof 1984). A survey of nearly two thousand students, confirmed by a repetition, indicated that both love and sex attitudes were related to strength of religious belief (Hendrick and Hendrick, 1987). Many Spanish students were not opposed to abortion, masturbation, premarital sex, or homosexuality. There were no differences between the sexes, but their attitudes showed a strong relationship with their age and their religiousness (Lafuente Benaches and Valcarcel Gonzalez,

1984). Adult evangelical Christians viewed sex education in public schools more harshly than the population as a whole, and those who were the most anti-intellectual were the most opposed to it (Ostron, Larzelere, and Reed, 1982). Sexual liberation was fairly evenly distributed among a group of young Jewish adults; men tended to be more liberal than women, and those who had attended a Jewish school tended to be more traditional. Religiousness was negatively related to liberal attitudes (Davids, 1982).

Peer group influence is strong in this area. In a group of undergraduates, the attitude to sexuality and sexual behavior of the women was related to the perceived attitudes of their peers rather than of the church or their parents. For the men it was their parents, rather than the church or their peers. The lack of attention to the church was surprising in a private college with strong ties with a Baptist church (Daugherty and Burger, 1984). A comparison of black and white students revealed differences in attitudes to premarital cohabitation between the groups; their attitudes were strongly related to those of their peers, but parental attitudes were the best predictor of their behavior. Religious commitment and strong parental attitudes discriminated between those who cohabitated and those who did not (Jacques and Chason, 1978). Among nearly five hundred students neither age nor conventional religiousness was associated with sexual behavior. The greater the number of close friends thought to be nonvirgins by women, the greater the probability that either was also a nonvirgin (Seck, Keller, and Hinkle, 1984). Among almost five hundred Israeli university freshmen, those of strong orthodox religion left questions about sex unanswered. The women's sexual activity related inversely to their religiousness, but this did not apply to the men, although for both sexes the extent of religiousness was related to attitudes toward premarital sex. The highly religious students considered sex was less important in a relationship (Notzer, Levran, Mashiach, and Soffer, 1984).

These studies bring to light fundamental problems encountered in any study of religiousness and morality. Adolescent religiousness has been shown in many circumstances to have a positive association with acceptable adolescent behavior. It frequently is inversely associated with delinquency and on the use of drugs and traditional sexual attitudes. Moral ideas (as distinct from moral behavior) are related to some extent to those of the church, so that, for example, Catholics tend to hold moral positions defined by their church but not necessarily accepted by other denominations. In this way there is a theological perspective to moral concepts. But there is a developmental effect on moral insight and on religious understanding, as has been seen in earlier chapters. Some association would be expected between the level of cognitive religious development and that of morality, and to test the latter without reference to the former is bound to give rise to anomalies.

Chapter 14

The Religious Influence of Schools

Criticism of academic standards in American parochial schools led to research on their effectiveness, but this was soon broadened to evaluate their effect on the religiousness of their pupils. Weaknesses in basic research design resulted in conflicting conclusions, since allowance was seldom made for other influences, especially that of parents and differences between the schools themselves, so it was frequently assumed that the schools alone were responsible for differences in the religiousness of present and former students. Similar studies were made to a lesser extent in Great Britain and Europe, but it was in Australia that the nature and extent of school influence was finally disclosed. Because the style of research varies to some extent between the different countries, it is described for convenience under national headings.

It is surprising that relatively little research has been instigated by the church authorities into the effectiveness of their schools. They provided a considerable capital outlay in the first place to build them and face ongoing costs for building repairs (in the United Kingdom a high proportion of the cost of building is borne by the government). In the United States, as in Canada and Australia, there is no financial assistance toward the cost of educating the pupils, so that the church and the parents spend a very great deal to educate their children. The schools continue because all involved are convinced of their value, but they have had little empirical evidence to support their claims. Others have been very critical of the church schools, again with little support for the criticisms. Against this background, until recently only sporadic research has been undertaken to investigate the truth of the matter.

293

Sadly, much of the research has been flawed by its inadequate design. The approach often used was to compare the religiousness of former Catholic parochial school students with other Catholics who did not attend a parochial school. If the former showed greater religiousness, then it was assumed that this was due to parochial school influence. Such a simplistic approach overlooked many important criteria. School effect is only one of many possible influences, and in practice it can be confounded in several ways. Account needs to be taken of parental religious influence and the parent's choice of a particular school when more than one is available. The schools themselves are bound to differ in a number of ways. The admissions policy will affect the religiousness of their pupils. In the United Kingdom church schools are not fee-paying, since all the cost of educating the children is paid for by the local educational authority. Because of this, a Church of England primary school may often be the local community school, with pupils coming from many religious backgrounds or none. The church secondary schools give priority to admit those of their faith, but frequently they cannot achieve such a recruitment so that Church of England secondary schools will admit, with large variations, pupils from non-Anglican homes, and Catholic secondary schools admit some or many pupils from homes with little or no links with the church. This is particularly the case in Wales. Nor do all church primary school pupils transfer to the related church secondary school; many parents elect for their children to enter a nearby state school, perhaps for its convenience or because it offers facilities lacking in the church school. In inner-city areas faced with falling school rolls, where the church schools must keep their numbers up to avoid closure, the situation is even more complicated. Such situations must have parallels in other countries.

Church schools vary from school to school, just as state schools do. There are socio-economic differences in their catchment area which will affect the general level of ability of the pupils and add to the variations of religiousness on admission. Some pupils will be at a church school because, like their family, they are committed to their church and want to attend it; some will be there under duress—the school was chosen for them by their parents for reasons of convenience or family tradition but against their own desire to go to another school, perhaps with their former primary school friends. Every school has its own particular ethos, and research needs to allow for this as yet another among the many school differences.

Some or all of these issues were overlooked in much of the research to be described, so that reported differences in pupils' beliefs, knowledge, and attitudes may not be influenced by the school at all but by other factors. The weakness of this type of analysis is discussed in Appendix B; nowhere is it more evident than here, where only proper experimental design and analysis of data has been able to untangle the knot. This needs to be kept in mind in the accounts which follow; allowances were not made for extraneous factors in the research described except where it is stated.

AMERICAN STUDIES OF PAROCHIAL SCHOOLS

Studies of Catholic schools

In the United States there has been great interest in what constitutes an effective school and the criteria by which different schools should be compared. Purkey and Smith (1982) concluded that an effective school was characterized by order, structure, purposefulness, a humane atmosphere, and the use of appropriate teaching techniques; what was lacking were suggestions as to how schools could develop these qualities. Catholics have for long discussed the effects of their parochial schools; Veverka (1984) showed how in the 1920s Catholic education moved away from providing education for the children of an immigrant church, and because of widespread criticism of the schools and internal disagreement over the direction of policy, ideological criteria were replaced by a pragmatic concern for the schools' survival. During the late 1950s Catholic schools and colleges were alleged to be academically inferior, supposedly other-worldly, and rating obedience above intellectual autonomy. The general educational effects of church schools was criticized, as in the study of Quin (1965) who compared Catholic high-school students with Catholic, Protestant, and Jewish students in public schools and found that the parochial schools had a disproportionate number of closed-minded students, due, he suggested, to closed-minded staff. (Did the schools produce such students, or attract them from parents with closed minds in the first place? Such comparisons cannot prove causation.) He used this finding to explain the fact that fewer Catholics were to be found in the world of scholarship and research. Before this, Hirschberg and Gilliard (1942) had found that if Catholic children also attended a Catholic school, the religious influence of the home was stronger (or did they attend a Catholic school because their strongly religious parents had sent them to one?).

Rossi and Rossi (1957, 1961) also thought the formation of Catholic schools was owing to the pressure of immigrants to maintain a link with the country of their origin. Although the number of schools had grown considerably there appeared to be little difference between Catholics who had attended parochial schools and those who had not. Their former attendance was associated to some extent with their higher occupational status and also with a degree of their greater religious observance. This was overshadowed by much greater differences associated with their sex, the extent of their education, or ethnic effects. Former attenders were more likely to look to religious leaders as guides in public affairs, but all Catholics were more open to their leaders' influence than Protestants. The withdrawal of a significant proportion of the child population, often with higher ability and greater motivation, into church schools, had increased the proportion of disadvantaged children in the public schools, and this had resulted in the greater popularity of private, nondenominational schools. Lenski (1961) confirmed that Catholic parents who had themselves attended Catholic schools were more likely to send their children to them, to attend Mass and to pray more frequently, to hold orthodox religious beliefs, and to have few social contacts with non-Catholics. Compared with Protestants, Catholic parents valued obedience more strongly, put less emphasis on children thinking for themselves, and used more physical punishment. (This difference has now considerably diminished according to Alwin [1986].)

Other differences began to be observed. Boehm (1962), while studying the development of conscience, compared children in Catholic schools with those in public schools and found that, regardless of class or ability, the Catholic children were more advanced in distinguishing between motivation and the results of an action. Although the Catholic children were subjected to a great deal of authority and were used to authority figures such as nuns and priests, they did not show any greater dependence on adult authority in making moral judgments. Subsequently, Boehm (1963) compared small groups of gifted children aged nine to twelve in Catholic, Jewish, and public schools; in a story the Jewish children showed stronger empathy with an injured peer than the other groups and were more independent of adult authority, but the situation was reversed with a story of peer reciprocity involving no pain. Larvière (1964) found boys and girls of thirteen in Catholic schools in Montreal taught by nuns or priests had greater religious knowledge than those taught by secular teachers, and the difference in the girls' scores was highly significant. In a survey of Catholic parents, Fay (1974) found that those in the middle and upper classes, despite their weaker religiousness, showed religious motives for sending their children to parochial schools, even though they held a good opinion of the public schools. Some children attended a church school because of their parents' religiousness, others because of their social mobility.

The Notre Dame study of American Catholic schools (Neuwien, 1966) secured a great quantity of relevant data, but was disappointing in its superficial and unimaginative analysis of it. Thus, it concluded as a matter of satisfaction that the levels of ability in Catholic schools were above the national norms, but it did not relate this to the finding that the pupils tended to come from homes where both parents were Catholics and one or both had a good educational background. An inventory of Catholic School Outcomes was devised to test the achievements of students aged twelve and sixteen about Catholic rules, doctrines, and liturgy; results were regarded as being generally satisfactory. There were no important differences in the response patterns to the three different areas investigated; difference in performance due to age were not large and the best results came from girls in single-sex high schools. A Student Attitude Index was also devised; girls showed better attitudes than boys, and often elementary school children showed better attitudes than high-school students. The schools were seen to be the most fruitful source of religious vocations. The students from upper classes were more frequent in Mass attendance and showed less racial prejudice. Variations in the styles of religiousness found between boys and girls suggested that different approaches to their religious education were needed. Students' opinions about their religious development placed parental influence first, school religious education second, and teachers' example a close third; parish church instruction was fourth and classmates' example well down at fifth.

Before long research focused on the religiousness of former parochial school pupils, with an expectation that their education would be associated with greater religiousness. The first major study, carried out by Greeley and Rossi (1966) has by the care with which it was pursued become a definitive work. Their results showed a significant association between Catholic education and adult religious behavior, an association which survived under a wide variety of conditions. It was strongest for those who came from very religious family backgrounds; there were significant differences which distinguished in particular those who had all their schooling in parochial schools from those who did not, especially in matters pertaining directly to church attendance and doctrine. It was very strong for those, especially men, who went to Catholic colleges. There was a strong relationship between Catholic education and religious behavior for adolescents who were currently at school. They emphasized the interdependence of Catholic schooling and the religiousness of parents, operating with multiplier effect. They found no confirmation for the notion that Catholic schools were divisive, but there was only a weak link between religious education and the social attitudes it was generally thought to nurture; this was slightly stronger for those who went to Catholic high schools and stronger still for those in their twenties and those who went to college. There was a direct relationship between social class and sending ones children to Catholic schools, at least for families where both parents were Catholic.

They concluded that there was no evidence that Catholic schools were necessary for the survival of American Catholicism; three-fifths of those who went to public school and whose parents had gone to public schools went to Mass every Sunday. Catholic schools apparently made the elite more elite, but their absence did not lead to a decline in minimal allegiance. Even so, the average differences between Catholics who went to Catholic schools and those who did not were quite impressive and would lead most researchers to say that the relationship was very powerful; they expressed surprise at the strength of the association of Catholic college attendance with adult religious behavior and social attitudes. The authors felt at the end of their task that Catholic schools were neither as bad as their most severe critics would portray them nor as good as they might be—like all other schools. It seemed that the controversy about Catholic education would continue, and it needed to be directed to make education as good as possible.

It also emerged that for those not attending Catholic schools there was very little relationship between religious behavior and attendance at the religious instruction classes. These were usually organized by the Confraternity of Christian Doctrine (CCD). The data suggested that CCD programs would need major improvements before they could be seriously considered a suitable alternative to Catholic schools. On this point Moriarty (1972) compared the effects of parochial school religious instruction with CCD instruction of Catholic children in public schools. Those from parochial schools showed better religious knowledge than the CCD students; the difference was small but significant. The CCD students from public schools proved to be more community-oriented, more tolerant and open-minded, although once more the differences were not large. The parochial school children did not show any greater self-esteem. Girls performed better than the boys. Neither group displayed the propositional thought required to understand the doctrines of the church, which Moriarty regarded as a failure of both methods of instruction; he did not consider the possibility that such understanding might require the greater mental maturity which only age can bring. He concluded that there were doubts as to the value of parochial schools and suggested that there was no justification for building any new ones if improved religious understanding was their only objective.

Subsequently, Greeley (1969) studied students who had graduated seven years earlier; for them attending a Catholic college had brought no economic, educational, or individual handicap. It became evident that compared with Catholic graduates from non-Catholic colleges, they were politically and socially more liberal. This was interpreted as springing from the influence in Catholic colleges of the members of religious orders who were committed to social action.

When Greeley and Gockel (1971) reviewed the literature describing the impact of parochial schooling on the religious development of young people they were critical both of the extravagant claims made in favor of parochial schools and of the excessive criticism of them. There was need for more research on the relationship of religious education to the total process of religious socialization. The church had not set out to find why Catholic schools were much more effective with German and Irish ethnic groups than with Polish and Italian. They suggested comparing the relative effectiveness of various parochial schools, where experimental controls were easier to achieve.

Greeley, McCready, and McCourt (1976) replicated the Greeley and Rossi (1966) study eleven years later with added scales and variables. At a time when religious observance was generally decreasing, the decline for those who had attended Catholic schools was much less. This they interpreted as indicating that the schools appeared to have increased their influence and in a time of change were of greater importance than in a time of stability. Only the religiousness of the spouse was of greater influence in predicting the religious behavior of former pupils, and the level of parental religiousness and education was of less importance than previously. The apparent influence of Catholic education was especially strong for those under thirty, for men from very religious backgrounds, and from southern European ethnic groups. (Hornsby-Smith, 1978, gives a detailed review of their studies.)

In South America, Benoit (1969) concluded that secondary schools tended to transmit traditional conservative values regardless of their affiliation. However, some students accepted more liberal or radical ideologies, so that four main categories could be described—those that accepted traditional values, typical of Catholic schools in small towns; those that accepted an ideology seeking a break with tradition, typical of schools in large cities; a minority with an ideology of rebellion, mostly found in state schools; and those who accepted a new religious ideology, found in all types of schools but especially the Protestant.

Yinger (1970), reviewing studies of parochial education, concluded that most of the differences between Catholics and Protestants about scientific and educational attainments were due to variations in class and ethnic background and other nonreligious issues. With the passing of time there had been a narrowing of the gap between the two bodies so that most of the educational difference had disappeared. Yet not all was well in the schools. In Canada, Lemieux (1970) concluded from a survey of teachers of religion in Quebec Catholic primary schools that only a half of them were satisfied with their work. Two-thirds regarded it as the most difficult subject and one-third as the least preferred. The pupils' lack of interest was seen as a major difficulty.

Fox and Jackson (1973) used data from a 1957 national survey to examine differences in educational attainment and persistence between Protestant and Catholic school pupils. No differences were found until allowance was made for such factors as race, the region of birth, social status, and the size of the community. Then it was found that Protestants were a little more likely to achieve a college degree and much more likely to persist in college. The differences were most marked among men from the higher social classes. Another study of Catholic education was undertaken by McCready and Greeley (1976). They had defined four ultimate value stances, the most positive of which they called religious hopefuls. Catholics in this category were much more likely to have been to a Catholic school. Since religion was greatest among the better educated, there would appear to be a strong college relationship with it.

Nelsen, Potvin, and Shields (1977) compared children from nine to fifteen attending Catholic parochial schools and public schools, testing their religiousness by the frequency of their church attendance, prayer, Bible reading, acceptance of biblical rules, and biblical literalism. All five measures showed a significant decrease of response with increasing age. Protestant children in the sample read the Bible slightly more than parochial school Catholics and were much more literal in their approach to it, but on the other items the Catholics attending a church school scored highest, followed by Catholics at a public school, with the Protestant children scoring least. The children's assessment of their parents' religiousness followed the same pattern and also declined according to the age of the children. The authors demonstrated that perceived parental religiousness was strongly associated with their children's own religion and that the schools were also related to it. According to Ridder (1985) Catholic schools provided more religious education, but on many issues those who had attended them did not differ from those who had not, although they did show greater Mass attendance and private prayer. Those who left school more recently showed greater religiousness than those leaving earlier. Their respondents also questioned church doctrine about Mass attendance, confession, birth control, divorce, married priests and the ordination of women, the leadership of the pope, and papal infallibility.

Coleman, Toomey, and Woodland (1975) regarded commitment as comprising the willingness to continue in a system, to accept its beliefs and values, and to practice the behavior deemed desirable. They applied these criteria to Catholic students in a Catholic and a state university. Despite the significant relationship between the criteria, much inconsistency was disclosed; many students had abandoned religious practices. Belief and behavior were significantly related to intentions about continuing in active membership of the church, as was parental religious influence and Catholic university influence. A comparison with results from Greeley and Rossi's (1966) survey of former parochial school pupils showed a marked decline in religiousness on every issue. In this Catholic student sample 95 percent professed belief in God, 79 percent in the divinity of Christ, 80 percent in the resurrection, 69 percent in life after death, 67 percent in the Trinity, 61 percent attended Mass weekly, only 35 percent accepted the inspiration of the Bible, 21 percent papal infallibility, and 14 percent accepted remarriage after divorce.

Greeley (1979) found the question "Do you believe in life after death?" to be of particular significance to Catholic school and college attendance; belief was entirely specified by Catholic school attendance. He regarded this as another proof that Catholic elementary schools had a lasting effect on their pupils. He also noted a considerable difference in the rate of church attendance by different ethnic groups, varying from 40 percent to 63 percent. All groups showed the same characteristic that the over thirties recorded higher proportions attending than the under thirties.

Fee, Greeley, McCready, and Sullivan (1981) undertook an extensive survey of Catholics in the United States and Canada and claimed that Catholic education was positively associated with religiousness when other variables such as parental influence were controlled. On this basis they argued that the building of Catholic schools should be given a higher priority. Convey (1984) also recorded greater church attendance and higher self-ratings of religiousness among students at Catholic high schools, as did Benson, Donahue, and Guerra (1989), who assumed that this was due to school influence.

Greeley (1982a) made a study of Catholic schools with significant black or Hispanic enrollments, comparing them with public schools. Attendance at a Catholic school was most rewarding academically for students disadvantaged by their racial background, the educational background of their family, and their own prior lack of educational achievement. For these students academic rather than religious attainment was most evident. Since many Catholic schools had been established for the poor children of Polish, Italian, and Irish immigrants, they were still doing successfully what they had always done. The schools had superior teaching, better discipline, and in many of them the influence of teachers in religious orders. Religiousness was not associated with academic performance, although some results from former studies were confirmed; white Catholics in parochial schools were more likely to attend church than those in public schools, but the difference was less with the Hispanics, and nonexistent for the blacks, half of whom were not Catholics. Greater religious devotion, especially among whites, was not associated with any greater acceptance of the church teaching on birth control; church school attendance did not produce more conservative political attitudes, nor affect feminist attitudes.

Bryk and Holland (1982) were cautious about making generalizations from Greeley's findings but welcomed them as offering further support for Catholic education. Greeley's results were in line with the finding of Hunt and Hunt (1975) that a secular orientation among Catholic urban black adolescents produced high educational and occupational aspirations and an attenuation of black identity. Although not found in the lowest class, it was present in the working class and was most apparent among those with the greatest religiousness; black Catholics tended to be of higher educational, income, and occupational levels compared with non-Catholic blacks. This found support from Curtis (1987), who investigated several aspects of a black Baptist elementary school in New York for children from low- and middle-income families. Their performance, when related to state school pupils, compared favorably with white children and was better than most minority group children.

Mueller (1980) was critical of previous research regarding educational differences between Catholics and Protestants. His thorough analysis used data drawn from national social surveys of ten five-year cohorts and showed the differences to be due to inadequate control of other variables such as family background. There was no significant difference between the two groups, although there was some Jewish educational advantage. This could be due to higher socio-economic factors and the greater emphasis on education Jews displayed. The discussion regarding the academic status of Catholic schools still continues, as is evidenced by the study of public and private schools by Coleman, Hoffer, and Kilgore (1981a,b). Alexander and Pallas (1985) looked again at the claim that Catholic schools produced greater learning in their pupils than the public schools. By taking into account the relative abilities of entrants it was shown that the differences between the two school systems were only trivial. But in the same journal issue Jencks (1985) contended that in the last two years at school Catholic students made much greater progress, although over twelve years of schooling the gains were much smaller, and, as with any instance of educational intervention, were likely only to be temporary, changing with time.

Studies in Protestant schools

A few studies in other church schools have produced similar results. Erickson (1964) compared the religiousness of secondary school pupils in five fundamentalist schools with fundamentalist pupils in public schools and found no difference between the two groups. Their religiousness was related to that of their parents, their relationships with their parents, and to their church training.

Johnstone's (1966) extensive study of the effectiveness of Lutheran schools as agencies of Christian education produced much detailed evidence about the religiousness and opinions of their adolescent pupils but concluded that it produced no significant difference in attitudes toward many social and political issues. They were more involved in many church-based activities and were more regular in church attendance, but this was because of family influence, apart from pupils from homes only marginally associated with the church. In this group alone were found significant numbers who regarded the school as providing the best knowledge of the Christian faith. There was no evidence to support the contention that Lutheran schools had a beneficial influence, mediated by the pupils, on their family life. In tests of biblical knowledge and understanding of Lutheran doctrine, parochial school pupils secured significantly better scores than those attending public schools, although their level of achievement was not considered satisfactory. Family influence accounted for doctrinal insight except for the marginal families. It was not surprising that parochial school pupils had more Lutheran friends than those from state schools and hoped to marry a partner of the same faith. The results were seen as casting doubt on many basic assumptions regarding the value of the system. It took no account of the quality of individual schools, even though some appeared to be superior to others.

Mueller (1967) compared a sample of students who had made a substantial attendance at a Lutheran school with other Lutheran students without such attendance, finding significant differences in both groups between those of higher and of lower religiousness. But when religiousness was held constant, school attendance made no significant difference. High scores on orthodoxy were due to a strong religious background rather than to attendance at a parochial school.

Kaiser (1978) found students in a hundred Lutheran schools had a deep commitment to their faith, with high scores for religious belief but not for religious knowledge. Their religiousness was related to a number of factors including race, sex, home, environment, parental church membership, their own church attendance, the length of their Lutheran education, the religious curriculum studied, and their general mental ability. Father's occupation and school size had no apparent effect.

Crandall and Gozali (1969) studied four groups of children from American public schools, Catholic schools, Norwegian Lutheran schools, and from a Norwegian fundamentalist sect. The Catholic and fundamentalist children showed greater religiousness and higher social desirability scores, that is, they had a greater tendency to present themselves in a more favorable light, even when it meant reporting things that were not likely to be true. Their defensive attitude, disclosed by this test, indicated their use of denial or repression defense mechanisms; this was seen as related to harsher parental discipline and more rigorous religious training.

Wiebe and Vraa (1976) compared the religious values of Mennonite high-school students in a denominational school with Mennonites and non-Mennonites in a public school. Attendance at the private school made no difference to the religious values held by the Mennonite students, which were significantly higher than those of the non-Mennonites. Tjart and Boersma (1978) compared the religiousness of pupils of twelve in a Christian school with those in a public school without reference to school and family influences. The Christian school pupils were more positive in their concepts of God and of prayer, had a greater intrinsic religious orientation and a higher moral concept of interpersonal behavior.

White (1985) used scores from the *Survey of the Spirit* to investigate the spiritual growth and development of evangelical high-school students. Spiritual growth was not affected by attendance at a Christian school or by its form of biblical teaching; it was affected by parental church attendance. In the test used, the mean score for all the boys was higher than that for the girls, which White regarded as unexpected; such a rare reversal of scores on a test of religiousness between the sexes without explanation must cast doubt on the construction of the test used.

There have been a few studies of Seventh-Day Adventist schools. Meltz (1980) found no difference in academic achievement or doctrinal commitment between students in Adventist or in state schools. In Brazil, Menegusso (1980) found Adventist secondary schools had significant relationships with their students' religiousness; the longer their attendance the more they tended to know religious facts and appreciate religious belief but the less they tended to translate them into their devotional life and lifestyle. Of all schools, the boarding schools proved to be the more strongly associated with all aspects of students' religiousness. Minder (1985) showed that students who had attended all grades of an Adventist school were much more likely to join and stay in the Adventist church. The length of time spent in an Adventist school did not relate to joining the church, but it did relate to remaining in the church, if it was joined. Graduates from a church college were more likely to stay in the church than other graduates.

Studies of Jewish schools

There have also been some Jewish studies of Jewish schools and adolescent religiousness and identity. Ash (1969) found only a minority of Jewish adolescents had an interest in Jewish rituals and festivals, and some struggled with their ideas about God, but for most of them religion contributed to their sense of identity. The relationship between Jews and Gentiles was a prominent theme, and their Jewish solidarity was enhanced by a sense of isolation, uniqueness, and persecution, even their sense of separateness from those who no longer practiced their religion. Jewishness was thus seen by them not only to be religiously, but culturally distinctive. Shapiro and Dashefsky (1974) made a study of Jewish men in their twenties and found that Jewish education had a mild but lasting effect on Jewish identification, which was enhanced by synagogue attendance and involvement in Jewish organizations. Advanced college education, which was secular, also enhanced a sense of Jewish identity.

Research comparable to the Catholic studies was carried out by Himmelfarb (1974, 1975a, b, 1977). Of all Jews who had received any religious education, 80 percent had received supplementary education in some type of Sabbath school, but this had no lasting relationship with their adult religious involvement, apparently due to the lack of time given to it. The amount of time given to Jewish schooling only began to have an effect after 2,000 hours, but 4,000 hours were needed for a significant effect. Still greater time had no effect until 10,000 hours. Only with sufficient time were curriculum revision and better teaching methods able to make a better contribution. Overall, four agents of religious socialization were identified; the religiousness of parents, the time spent on Jewish studies in Jewish schools, participation in Jewish organizations, and, most important of all, marriage to a Jewish spouse. When compared to Catholic studies Jewish schooling alone, without parental support, had a stronger association, probably due to more time being spent on religious studies in Jewish schools than in Catholic schools. Fuchs (1978) studied the Jewish identity of pupils from nine to sixteen receiving Jewish education of various forms. A sense of Jewish identity increased with the intensity of Jewish education and was at a maximum with the day school students. Other influential factors were involvement in Jewish rituals, parental involvement in Jewish communal activities, and their own self-concept. Jewish education was also associated with a number of other relevant issues, including intermarriage, support for the synagogue and rituals, and pride in being a Jew.

Bock (1976) supported these findings by his investigation of the roots of Jewish identification. Jewish schools were by then securing longer attendance but providing less Jewish classroom instruction. The total time spent on this was the best predictor of Jewish identification, with 1,000 hours as the necessary minimum and a leveling out between 4,000 and 6,000 hours before an increased effect up to 10,000 hours. Supplemental schooling, taking much longer to achieve this length of instruction, was less efficient rather than ineffectual. With personal values and beliefs, the home background was much more formative than the school. There was less identification among more recent generations of Jews, but there were pointers to this being now reversed. School and home had comparable effects on Jewish public behavior, which was related to Jewish self-esteem, and Jewish schooling had little effect on this, influencing specific aspects of behavior rather than feelings about Jewish self-esteem. Reliance on formal education for passing on identification emphasized public behavior rather than personal beliefs and values.

Goodman (1978) found that the religious attitudes of orthodox Jewish students were associated primarily with religious observance but to a lesser extent with Jewish education. Increased Jewish education was related to a greater acceptance of the orthodox Jewish faith and supported suggestions for extending Jewish day schools. Religiously motivated students who began their Jewish education later in life after some years in state schools attained attitude scores equal to those of the advanced Rabbinic students. Wallin (1978) noted in a study of learning by Jewish high-school boys with learning difficulties that those taught in Jewish schools showed more advanced moral development than those taught in secular schools, although attendance at denominational schools was not related to religious learning. Ness (1980) studied the religious and other related attitudes of students completing their studies at fourteen conservative Jewish afternoon religious schools. Girls were found to be more identified as Jewish than the boys; the father's Jewish education had a stronger association with their children's religiousness than the mother's. A Jewish home was strongly associated with student's Jewish attitudes, as also were some schools, irrespective of home practices. Parker and Gaier (1980) studied the religious beliefs and practices of conservative Jewish adolescents aged thirteen to seventeen, finding little relationship between their beliefs and practice. They were hardly related to attendance at Hebrew school or membership of a youth group, but they were associated with parental practice.

The different ethos of Judaism was shown in a study of moral development undertaken by Selig and Teller (1975) who commented that Kohlberg's description of his highest, sixth stage was unsatisfactory from a Jewish point of view. Kohlberg's highest value lay in individual conscience, but in Judaism it was for individuals to see themselves as part of the committed community, which Kohlberg would not regard as the highest level of moral thinking. For Jews autonomy was not found in individual conscience but in a living relationship with the Haladic community.

BRITISH STUDIES OF SCHOOL INFLUENCE

Church schools have an important place in British education; the controversies about them which once divided Anglicans and Free Churchmen have long been forgotten. They are almost all Catholic or Church of England schools, apart from a few Anglican/Methodist and Anglican/Catholic ecumenical schools and a small number of Jewish and Methodist schools. In England and Wales there are 19,426 primary schools, of which 4,797 are Church of England schools and 1,877 Catholic schools, and the 4,226 secondary schools include 233 Church of England schools and 439 Catholic schools (Department of Education and Science, 1988). In all primary schools, 17.5 percent of pupils attend a Church of England school and 9.4 percent of pupils attend a Catholic school. In secondary schools 4.1 percent attend a Church of England School and 8.9 percent a Catholic school. The involvement of the Church of England is much more at the primary level, whereas Catholic policy is to provide all education for most of its children in its schools. With a single exception, Catholic schools are always voluntary aided, whereas 41 percent of the Church of England schools are voluntary controlled.[1] The

---

1. See the Glossary for the distinction between these schools.

Catholic church carried a great financial burden when it extended these provisions in the postwar years, but the need for its educational activity has not been seriously questioned as in America. Consequently, there has been only a little interest in the religious effectiveness of any type of school.

Moreton (1944) had noted that in one Free Church public school included in his sample, where religious education was regarded with great seriousness, there was a steady growth of more favorable attitudes to religion throughout the school course. Alves (1968) had observed that it appeared that the character of a school was the most propitious when it was a stable and lively community in which the religious studies department was active in local schemes of social service and where a voluntary religious group was present. Some insight into the religious effectiveness of schools came from students' recollection of their former religious education secured by Daines (1962). He studied this among students from three colleges of education drawn from many schools. A third felt it had not been taken seriously and the time could have been better employed; only a half had discussed current problems or found the work of interest. Many had not been able to express their own views, discuss personal difficulties, and had felt their teacher was unsympathetic. College had partly rectified this, bringing a wider perspective, although it had added to the difficulties of belief of half of them. As many had maintained or increased their religious practice and prayer as those who had reduced it or who had no such activity. It seemed that while some students had received much appreciated help from their religious education, most were left with a conviction of its irrelevance and an unsatisfied desire to understand what religion was about or to have been helped in their personal problems.

The first serious British study of school religious influence was that of Taylor (1970), whose survey of senior students in church schools was noted in chapter 12; his findings also concerned school differences. Except with Catholic families, the lower the socio-economic group, the more attenuated was a pupil's religious practice. Students in Catholic schools showed much higher levels of belief than those of the other schools. School influence was always associated with that of the parents, and they had least influence when parental influences was weakest. There was a tendency to follow the example of the more religious parent, usually the mother. Parental example was more strongly associated with religiousness than the school, especially with Catholic girls. The mother was most likely to be seen to be religious by Catholic students, less by Church of England school students, and least by state school students. The father was also most likely to be seen to be religious by Catholic school pupils. The divinity of Christ was accepted more readily by Catholic school students; church attendance was much more regular among them and was very strongly related to parental example. When there was little or no parental support Anglican school boys attended more than state school boys, indicating that a school relationship was then observed. Pupils from homes with high levels of church attendance and also attending a Catholic school had higher attendance levels themselves than those not at a Catholic school. Private prayer was most common among Catholic school girls. Private Bible reading, undertaken regularly by only 7 percent of the sample, was much more frequent among the Anglican school students, especially the girls, which suggested a higher quality of Bible teaching in Church of England schools.

Students in the Catholic schools saw themselves as more religious than did those in the other schools; although the students ascribed their greater interest in religion to school influence, the evidence suggested that the greatest influence came from the home. The highest proportion accepting the inspired status of the Bible were Catholic school students, followed by Church of England school students; the proportion was either similar or higher than that of county school students. Religious education had more time given to it in the Catholic schools and least in the county schools, where few boys took religious knowledge in public examinations. Only in Catholic schools was there significant attention to doctrine. Church-going was strongly related to the importance assigned to religious education; denominational education was not in itself effective in encouraging more favorable estimates of the subject's importance.

Marchant (1970), investigating moral, religious, and sex education in schools, gave a questionnaire to students of sixteen and over in three schools and two colleges of further education in rural mid-Wales. Replies indicated that there was much antipathy to religious education; boys favored it less than girls, were divided as to its necessity, and were opposed to its compulsory nature. Most students regarded it as irrelevant to their lives and problems, and a substantial number complained that it was indoctrination and already taught by the churches. Moral education was seen as something desirable which was not provided by their religious education. Most thought the schools should give sex education and before puberty, somewhat earlier than their own; more than a half had received none at school, while more than half the boys had not received any from their parents. Parental advice, usually regarded as inadequate, was more available to the senior pupils than to those in further education, who were less able. Many requested a form of moral education about behavior, sexual conduct and values, living together peacefully, and understanding themselves and others.

Brimer (1972) made a survey of the attitudes of ten-year-old children in junior schools to school worship. They did not regard it as important, but their head teachers did. The more able of them were more critical of it, and those with regular church attendance were the most critical, apparently comparing it unfavorably with church worship. But this experience had facilitated their ability to worship, so that they were the most likely to claim to worship in a school assembly, a quarter of them always, and another quarter often, with few saying seldom or never.

Jarvis (1972, 1974) surveyed the opinions of junior school teachers about the secularization of children in their schools. He contended that there were three strands to the socialization process, the cognitive, the implicit, and the explicit. The cognitive arose from religious education, and a high proportion of teachers were using biblical material unaware of the conceptual level needed to understand it. Consequently children had to interpret it in their own immature way and rejected these interpretations as inadequate when they grew older, carrying confusion about religion into adolescence. This confusion, originating in junior schools, was perpetuated throughout secondary school life. In the socialization process, the junior children were complying but not internalizing. At the same time, there was much implicit and explicit religious socializing arising from the school culture and classroom activity. The daily act of worship, classroom prayers, religious themes in art and drama, hymn singing in music lessons, special activities at Christmas and other seasons, all exerted a considerable social and emotional pressure on children and became a value-shaping process, so that they acquired an affective affinity to Christianity. The national culture did not conflict with the children's feelings toward the Christian faith, but neither did it strongly reinforce them. In this way a great ambivalence was produced by the schools, which were fostering positive attitudes toward Christianity alongside great cognitive confusion. Because of this, children came to hold a residual sympathy for Christianity but rarely had a rational comprehension of it. The teachers' role was important, and they became significant others for the children in their classes. There seemed to be no difference in teachers' activities and attitudes between church schools and the remainder. Older teachers were more likely to show greater religiousness and use traditional biblical teaching, as were most women teachers. Overall, nearly three-quarters of the teachers regarded themselves as Christian, and 29 percent attended church with some regularity. It was ironic that those teachers who were less religious and less favorably disposed to religious education appeared less likely to be the cause of cognitive confusion, whereas those who were older, more religious, and favoring the retention of the status quo in religious education were more likely to cause confusion about Christianity as the culturally accepted religion.

A major project concerned with the religious influence of primary schools was undertaken by Francis, who first investigated if deterioration in attitude to Christianity was related to the syllabus material used. Detailed accounts of this work are available, some of them descriptive (Francis, 1980a, 1983a, 1984b), and one giving a summary of the relevant statistical analysis (Francis, 1979c). Thirty schools were used in East Anglia, five Catholic voluntary aided primary schools which used a Catholic syllabus of religious education; ten Church of England voluntary aided schools, five using a traditional syllabus and five using a modern syllabus and fifteen county primary schools, five giving traditional religious education, five giving it from a modern syllabus, and five not giving any religious education at all. The children were in their last two years at junior school. Results from path analysis indicated that social class influenced parental religious behavior, and in turn this influenced the children's religious behavior so that the religious influence of social class on children was indirect. Similarly, because social class influenced children's mental ability, this explained the association between mental ability and religious behavior. Children's religious behavior was a strong influence on their attitude toward religion. The Catholic primary school children scored five points higher on the 96-point scale than the county schools, whereas the Church of England primary schools using a modern syllabus scored four points lower. Similar results were secured when the tests were repeated four years later, but the differences between the groups were reduced, so that the Roman Catholic schools scored about three points higher and the Church of England schools about 2.5 points lower than the county schools. In all groups there was a reduction in religious behavior scores of both pupils and their parents. The findings were related to the type of religious education provided; less favorable religious attitudes among the children were associated more with schools using the newer syllabuses than with those using traditional ones, although there was no indication as to the type of material used in the Catholic schools.

The tests were repeated in the same schools after four years (Francis, 1983a) and again after four more (Francis, 1986a). This confirmed the first results; increasing age significantly predicted pupils' reduced religious behavior and attitude toward Christianity; being a girl predicted a higher score. Parental occupation, an index of social class, was a predictor of their own church attendance and of childrens' mental ability, so that social class indirectly affected children's attitudes. The children's religious behavior was the strongest predictor of their attitude toward Christianity. The decline in religious behavior and attitude between 1974 and 1978 was continued further in 1982, and was highly significant. Once more, Roman Catholic voluntary aided school pupils displayed a stronger attitude to Christianity than those of the county schools, and the Church of England school pupils showed a slightly weaker attitude. These school influences were constant over the eight-year period, and were exerted independently of parental influence. The religious objectives of Catholic education appeared to be achieved, since the Roman Catholic aided primary schools, even allowing for the influence of church attendance and parental attitude to religion, contributed greatly to favorable attitudes to religion among their pupils. Despite the hopes of the Church of England that by its primary school activity children would develop favorable attitudes to religion, unfavorable attitudes were more associated with pupils taught in some Church of England aided primary schools than in the county schools.

Francis' attempt to judge the effectiveness of a teaching syllabus by the pupils' attitudes to religion was later dropped; its effectiveness is determined by learning and knowledge and not by affective results. The influence of a school on pupils' religious attitudes involves also the quality of school worship and such sensitive issues as the children's perceptions of visiting clergy. Other variables still need to be explored to explain the lower attitude to religion scores of Church of England primary school pupils. In a dissimilar context Greer and Brown (1973) responded to criticisms voiced by Irish Baptists of the type of religious education introduced as a result of Goldman's suggestions. They compared two matched primary school groups of children aged eight and ten, one taught for a year the traditional Northern Ireland agreed syllabus, the other the West Riding syllabus, influenced by Goldman. The newer style syllabus provoked much more interest from the children, but the older syllabus gave better biblical knowledge. There was little difference in the attitude to the Bible of the two groups, although the authors observed that this was probably due less to the absence of any deleterious influence of the newer syllabus and more to attitudes formed over many more years.

Francis (1989a,b) also tested pupils in two secondary schools in East Anglia in 1974, 1978, 1982, and 1986. Responses to every item of his scale showed with remarkable consistency not only the greater religiousness of girls over boys and of younger pupils over older pupils, but a marked decline between each test. Thus, "God is very real to me" secured an overall positive response of 41 percent in 1974, falling to 33, 26, and 22 percent in the subsequent years. About one in ten attended church at least weekly, and although these gave many more positive responses, some of them appeared to be uncertain about their involvement. A third of the church-goers did not regard the church as very important or God as very real to them. One in six found services and listening to the Bible boring (and half of these, a waste of time); one in eight found it hard to believe in God, and one in ten thought the Bible was out of date. A third of all pupils professed to pray regularly and also showed much greater religiousness, although they gave fewer positive responses to the items than the church-goers, except for prayer. Again in this group many indicators of disaffection were found. Although the study was restricted to only two schools and a single test instrument, Francis considered the findings to be indicative of what seemed to be a much wider, continuing drift from the churches.

It should be argued that generalizations based on a small sample of schools in one area of the country are not valid. But the findings do not stand in isolation. Again and again, in previous chapters, the evidence of religiousness declining with age has been presented. The drift from the churches has continued throughout the century, and the decreasing number of adolescents attending the churches is not only a matter of common observation, but is borne out by the statistics given at the beginning of chapter 12. The greater religiousness of Catholic school pupils is not surprising; studies of Roman Catholic affiliation, in Britain, in the United States, and in Australia, consistently disclose higher levels of religiousness associated with their adherents. Australian studies have also shown that private Protestant schools (which by their fees introduce an element of social class selection) are frequently associated with lower levels of religious behavior among their pupils than state schools but even so have other advantages.

Finally, further confirmation of Francis' results came from his very thorough study of religion in Gloucestershire primary schools—a county without any large industrial cities (Francis, 1987b). Building on the previous studies of children's attitudes and of head teachers' comments, his method gave insight into the immediate process of religious socialization. Data from head teachers and children permitted a close examination of the religious partnership between church and state.

Detailed profiles of typical schools gave substance to the wealth of information secured, much beyond the scope of this survey. It emerged that there were no significant religious differences between schools situated in towns, suburbs, or villages. About two head teachers in three were church-goers, (similar to Jarvis' [1972] finding in the West Midlands) and they were influenced professionally by their belief; the extent of their church attendance was a highly significant indicator of the religious influence of their schools.

Once more, the religiousness of parents was the crucial influence on that of their children, and again their social status affected their church attendance, which in turn affected their children. The schools, with their range of provisions for religious education and worship and their contacts with local churches and clergy, also had a direct religious effect on their pupils, with results very similar to those secured and confirmed in East Anglia, Catholic primary schools having a much greater influence. Whereas in the earlier studies Church of England schools had the least influence, in Gloucestershire this was true only of the voluntary controlled schools. They achieved a stronger relation with the churches than did the county schools but had less influence on their children's attitudes to religion. The Church of England voluntary aided schools showed somewhat greater religious influence, but less than that of the Catholic schools. The same order was true of the religiousness of the head teachers of the schools in these four groupings, and it was this which affected the extent of their school's relationship with the church and with the clergy. Overall, many schools were in touch with the churches, fostering a Christian perspective as envisaged by the Education Acts, but when older head teachers retired there would be a reduction of school religious influence since younger head teachers were less religious. This study adds considerable weight to the East Anglian studies, although hitherto school effects in urban areas have not been similarly investigated. Such studies led Francis (1979d) to discuss the relationship between educational research and theology, not only the lack of insight shown in some research studies into theology and biblical scholarship, but the scant attention given to it by theologians.

Russell (1978) found that in primary schools, the extent of the religious education provided was associated with the children's attitude to it. He did not consider how the style of the syllabus might also influence it. Jarvis (1972), reported above, indicated how religious socialization takes place in all schools to varying degrees. Roman Catholic schools have a religious ethos permeating many school activities, apart from their religious teaching, which is often influenced by the newer approaches. When Seppo (1971) undertook a study of attitudes toward religion and religious education among high-school pupils in Finland he concluded that generally there was no link between religiousness and interest in religious education as a subject, although he noted some undesirable features among those with a strong interest in both. Later in this chapter it will be shown that some Australian studies convincingly demonstrate that it is not the content or the quality of the religious education lessons which influence pupils but the overall school

climate.
A study of multifaith schools

Marvell (1973, 1974a, 1975) studied the religiousness of multiracial groups of boys and girls aged eleven to fourteen from two mixed comprehensive schools with forty English children and groups of twenty Greek Cypriot, Turkish Cypriot, Indian, and West Indian children. Most of them wanted their religious education lessons to continue but on a broader basis. Life in England and attendance at English schools raised questions about the validity of religious belief in all the pupils, rather than reinforcing belief, and also introduced alternative ideas to them, in consequence the children either questioned the faith of their upbringing or accepted that the religious beliefs of other people were valid. The schools were less important religiously than the homes. Pupils first met a pluralistic society in personal terms at their school, and this broadened the basis of their peer groups with a racial mix of friendships. Whereas immigrant parents, and to a lesser extent English parents, had retained religious beliefs but abandoned religious practice, their children were abandoning belief as well. The English proved to be the most secular group, most of them being either agnostic or atheistic, although 92 percent attended Sunday school when younger; they either adopted a practicing religious role, or a secular alternative, much more than their parents. The West Indians displayed greater religiousness, and the Greek Cypriots more, with the Indians giving the most positive responses. A parallel study of morality (Marvell, 1974b) disclosed that all the parents sought to instill honesty into their children; next in order of importance for immigrant parents was obedience and for English parents, caring. The family had the greatest moral influence on the children, followed, some way behind, by the school.

Studies of Church of England schools

The recent study of Church of England schools by O'Keefe (1986) used schools in Inner London, the West Midlands, and the North West. It provided much detailed information regarding their policy and pupils at a time when their concern for religion was affected by the cultural diversity of society and the presence of non-Christian pupils in some of their schools. Admissions policies resulted in some secondary schools becoming almost entirely white schools in ethnically mixed areas, and because of a former grammar school image they attracted a disproportionate number of able pupils, to the disadvantage of county schools. Similarly, some primary schools drew the most able pupils away from county schools, even from a distance, although others, as neighborhood schools, enrolled considerable numbers of children of other faiths. In consequence much ambiguity of policy and practice was recorded, so that the historic policy of Church of England schools was frequently compromised. But while the practice of religion and the place of religious education in the schools was scrutinized, no attempt was made to evaluate its outcome. So far their effectiveness has not been examined with the detail awarded to Catholic schools in America and elsewhere. The great variations noted in ethnic and social composition would be likely to be associated with equally great differences in pupils' attitudes to religion. Even so, some studies look at aspects of this problem. The more broadly based work of Francis described earlier cast doubt on their effectiveness in nurturing more favorable pupil attitudes to Christianity than found in state schools.

Palmer (1965) compared the religiousness of children aged ten at Church of England and county primary schools. While results from one county primary school were very good, due to the interest of the head teacher, in general children from church schools were more likely to have contact with a church or Sunday school, to say their prayers, regard school prayers favorably, to have a better understanding of the nature of prayer and of the meaning of the Lord's Prayer. Their prayers were about securing some benefit such as help with their work, protection, the restoration of those ill, or for confession and forgiveness. They were more aware of the significance of the Christian festivals and of the nature of God and less likely to regard Jesus as an ordinary man. Their counterparts considered school prayers more as thanksgiving, praise, and worship. All the children tended to think of God as both "living but invisible" and "having a body." In all schools only a few thought they had been taught more about religion by their parents than by their school, and all were more influenced by their teacher than by what was taught. Children from the church schools left with greater religious knowledge, and they came from homes which, by supporting the religious activities of the schools, reinforced their religious education. These results arising from simple cognitive and behavioral assessments in Midland schools stand in some contrast to Francis's ongoing results from sophisticated attitude tests in East Anglia. There is no ground for doubting the validity of either nor for making wide generalizations from them.

Briscoe (1969) ascertained that while most officers of local education authorities were by no means convinced that Church of England aided primary schools made any special contribution to children's development, the great majority of diocesan directors of education considered that they made a contribution to their children's religious and moral development, and many of them also thought that they facilitated social development. In the light of these contrasting opinions he undertook a survey of head teachers and staff in primary schools in forty-five different areas. The head teachers of the church schools were practicing Christians, active in the school parishes, and maintaining good relations with the parish priests, who, for the most part, were in regular contact with the schools. The staff of the church schools were not involved to the same extent, and a smaller proportion of them were qualified to teach religious education than in the county primary schools. Because the church schools had this potential to achieve diocesan expectations, he tested children in their last year at church and county schools in two different areas with a test of understanding and of moral insight. The result was in accord with Francis' finding that church school pupils had not achieved any greater religious understanding or moral insight than those from the county schools, but to the contrary, a slightly lower score on the religious test and a tendency to seek the opinions of an authority figure in morality. These ten-year-old children were influenced by their level of cognitive development, irrespective of the type of school.

Many Church of England schools were included in Francis' studies described earlier in the chapter. In a study of teacher attitudes in Church of England schools in Suffolk, Francis (1983b, 1986b) noted that teachers in these rural schools were more concerned to introduce children to religious ideas than to religious practices. Teachers in the voluntary aided schools were even more concerned than those in the voluntary controlled schools to give priority to Christianity, with teaching about Jesus, the Bible, and the church. The younger teachers were less likely to attend church and were less favorably disposed to the church-school system. Only a minority of them had a preference to work in such a school, which indicated that teachers' goodwill for the system would decline as they took the places of their seniors. More than one in ten of the teachers believed the church schools often alienated their pupils from the church or from Christianity itself—a point of view repudiated by the majority. Half the teaching force argued that it was not the task of a Church of England school to initiate children into a religious faith; 30 percent of those in controlled schools and 55 percent of those in aided schools felt that such an initiation was right. Yet asked a similar question on a different topic 66 percent of the teachers in controlled schools and 88 percent of those in aided schools agreed that their schools should encourage their pupils to accept and practice the Christian faith. If these church-school teachers lack a consensus about the religious aims of their schools it is perhaps not surprising that pupils do not record attitudes to religion substantially different from those in county schools.

Francis (1983c) examined the possibility that a church school provided a more effective means of the church making contact with the children of the parish. He secured data from almost all Anglican clergy in a rural diocese about their contacts with children of six to nine, both in church and in voluntary aided primary schools. Those whose parish included a church school had, because of their initiative, much more contact in the week with children than those in parishes without church schools. However, children's church attendance on Sunday was unaffected by the provision of a church school; it was related to the size of the local population and the consequent size of the parochial church roll.

Studies of Catholic schools

Hornsby-Smith and Petit (1975) studied the social, moral, and religious attitudes of fifth-form pupils drawn from Catholic comprehensive schools and a local authority school. Catholic pupils professed much higher levels of belief in God (63 percent) compared with the other school pupils (30 percent) and in the divinity of Jesus (55 percent compared with 25 percent). Yet on the salience of Christian morality there was no significant difference, nor in scores on deference to parents and teachers, sexual morality, anti-intellectualism and rejection of contraceptive morality. Only on "independence within a framework" were the Catholic school pupils' scores significantly higher than the others. While the Catholic schools differed significantly in some respects from the comprehensive school, there was also a large measure of overlap in the beliefs and values of the students. The data also showed that the high levels of anti-intellectualism and acceptance of the traditional role of women as house-bound in their homes, which the authors had found in a previous study in a convent girls school, were not present in these schools and thus were not features common to all Catholic secondary schools. The authors pointed to the wide variations found between the schools on the Christian morality scores and observed that only one in five of the pupils agreed with the condemnation of premarital sex. Many pupils, even Catholics, stated that religion had no relevance for their lives, even though overall the difference between Catholic and comprehensive school pupils' opinions indicated very significantly the traditional morality of the Catholics. For these pupils, religion did not contribute to the formation of their social values and beliefs. The authors concluded that Catholic schools were a sufficiently powerful agency of socialization to generate some distinct clusters of social, moral, and religious attitudes on the part of their senior students, but large differences occurred within the Catholic schools themselves.

Hornsby-Smith (1978) provided a detailed account of studies of Catholic education in England and Wales, including his own considerable contributions. There were marked differences between Catholic schools and state schools. The strong religiousness and morality of adolescent girls found particularly in convent schools subsequently tended to wear off in a nonsupportive adult environment, and even before then some pupils had begun to doubt the relevance of religion. There were large differences in the Catholic schools themselves. Pupils' personal religious orientation was highest when both parents were Catholics, the mother having the stronger example. In a survey of pupils in schools in Southwark, weekly Mass attendance at eleven was found to be 83 percent for boys and 87 percent for girls, but at fifteen it was only 56 percent and 63 percent respectively. In every age group the less able showed a smaller percentage of attendance than the more able. More Inner London pupils attended Mass than those in the outer London boroughs, and lower attendance was found in Kent. But within the schools themselves there were significant differences in their pupils' attendance. In another study of disaffection among Catholic adolescents there were marked differences between the three schools studied, although parental influence, especially that of the mother, was important. Most disaffected young Catholics seemed to come from middle-class homes. Children of Anglo-Irish marriages tended to record lower religiousness, but lower parental activity rather than ethnicity accounted for this. Family influence was always more important than that of the school. Disaffection was shown to be mainly expressed by a rejection of authority, by the acceptance of the pervasive scientific spirit demanding proof and by childish ideas of God and religion.

Brothers (1964) interviewed young men and women in their early twenties who had earlier been educated in Catholic grammar schools in Liverpool; almost a half were university students or had just completed university studies, and a further quarter were women who had attended Catholic teacher training colleges. They came from a wide range of socio-economic backgrounds and demonstrated the considerable differences that had developed between former church school pupils. Fifty-seven percent reported their beliefs as unchanged, some with reservations; a quarter referred to Catholics becoming more critically disposed as a result of contact with non-Catholics, showing the impact of the environment on beliefs. They valued highly people who had experienced doubts but had overcome them. Twelve percent had become more tolerant of, and 13 percent more critical of Catholic beliefs. Although many had experienced doubts and hesitations, these were for the most part overcome. Those who had stopped going to church gave laziness as the main reason, but many also referred to the attitude of the milieu in which they lived or worked, where it was hard to maintain minority beliefs. Friendship patterns showed how closely they associated with other Catholics of a similar education, and for many marriage followed, a high proportion not merely being married in a Catholic church but marrying someone belonging to the same community or to a similar one.

Spencer (1968) studied the consequences of Catholic education in England, using the criteria of Mass attendance to gather data from thirteen parish censuses, the best evidence he could secure. There was a marked difference in Mass attendance between those who had never attended a Catholic school and those who had been partly or completely educated in such a school. The differences observed over a wide range of age reflected social changes during the long period which had altered the status of Catholics in the community, so that while Catholic education was not necessary as a means of religious socialization at the time of the 1902 Education Act, it had become so by the time of the 1944 Act. He noted the relationship with social class, and the type of educational institution last attended as a full-time student, which was strong, and with sex, which was weak. When he compared the relationships between parental religiousness and schooling with Mass attendance, it was the parents who were found to be the more important, leading to the conclusion that the empirical basis of the strategy of providing a place in a Catholic school for all Catholic children was doubtful.

After the survey had been completed the work of Greeley and Rossi (1966) came to hand, which gave further support to his findings; in particular he noted their conclusion that in the absence of reinforcement from the family, there was no reason to expect that the school would modify values and value-oriented behavior. Subsequently (Spencer, 1971), he suggested that the evidence available indicated that the situation in England and Wales was little different from that in the United States. However, he was critical of Greeley and Rossi's conclusions regarding religious education outside school; their analysis in this area lacked any indication of the consequence of parental religiousness, and the data regarding adolescents still attending public secondary schools suggested that their attendance at catechism classes appeared to relate strongly to earlier attendance at a Catholic primary school. Nor was there any distinction in the main adult sample between those who had received no religious education at all and those who had received it while attending public elementary and high schools.

In a different vein, Murray (1978) developed scales to measure the moral and religious belief of Catholic adolescents in English secondary schools. He compared two groups of pupils selected by school staff to represent more extreme orthodox or liberal views. The groups showed marked differences on all the scales except for that on abortion, with two factors operating, the first about religious life, religious conviction, and marriage and the second about permissiveness, abortion, and birth control. These provided a description of individual beliefs in terms of moral conservatism and moral liberalism. It was apparent that despite expressing orthodox religious views, many in the sample held views about birth control contrary to those upheld by the church.

Stratton (1981) made a study of pupils' moral and religious beliefs in Catholic schools in Shrewsbury. He found few clear-cut distinctions. Girls were more favorable than boys to religious education and the need for prayer; boys were more favorable to the need for religion, confession, the importance of Mass and of Mary, and were more opposed to abortion; they also held a higher expectation of marriage as being a life-long partnership. This response gave no grounds for regarding girls as generally more religious than boys. (Presumably Stratton refers to the content of belief and its outcome rather than external religious behavior or attitudes to religion.) Age differences showed a clearer pattern; at thirteen they tended to regard religious education more favorably than at fifteen, and to give more assent to the moral teaching of the church. The older pupils showed greater uncertainty about such issues as birth control and abortion. They displayed a more critical discrimination about the religious life and the religious practices involved in being a Catholic, and they placed a greater emphasis on personal choice and a recognition of the conflict of values in many moral issues. Mass attendance was associated with responses to almost every item, apart from a few about abortion and mixed marriages. Much church teaching and dogma was accepted, regardless of regular religious practice. Some differences were found between grammar and modern schools; the grammar school pupils showed a more positive approach to religion and its values, and a greater questioning of church teaching on birth control and abortion; the modern school pupils gave stronger assent to a traditional authoritarian stance. Grammar schools apparently included convent schools organized by an order of nuns. Schools with a better provision of qualified religious education staff, resources, and capitation secured a more positive response to religion and to moral decision making. Pupils in the schools with a greater proportion of Catholic staff tended to respond more positively to items about marriage, life values, abortion, and religious education.

Hanlon (1989) surveyed the provisions made for religious education in Catholic schools in England and Wales. Only 11 percent of the 614 schools approached responded, and these gave a somewhat depressing picture. In most schools the financial allocation for religious education was ranked below third (although Hanlon did not discuss the necessarily high cost of the science departments). Much religious education was taught by nonspecialists from other disciplines. A third of all who taught it lacked even the basic Catholic Certificate of Religious Education. One in six only had this certificate, so that a half of all teaching religious education lacked any academic qualification to do so. A minority held a specific academic qualification for religious education, 72 percent of heads of department and 90 percent of the other full-time religious education teachers. More than five hundred qualified specialists were needed immediately.

Francis' attitude scale was used in studies about specific organizational problems in Catholic schools. With the trend to end the school organization of first, middle, and secondary schools in the few areas where it had been established, some church schools faced reorganization into primary and secondary schools. The attitude to religion of pupils aged twelve and thirteen in Roman Catholic middle and secondary voluntary aided schools was related to their sex, age, and church attendance but not to the type of school attended (Boyle, 1984; Boyle and Francis, 1986, 1987a). It could be deduced that there was no argument from pupils' religiousness for or against a middle-school type organization. The problem of declining numbers due to a fall in the birth rate had brought a widespread need for much secondary school reorganization and amalgamation to Catholic secondary schools. Francis (1986c) was able to demonstrate that in the Midlands the distance traveled to school did not affect pupils' attitude to Christianity, so that longer travel to fewer schools would not matter. It emerged in this study that church attendance of parents and children was directly associated with their baptismal status, and there was a strong parental association; it was the strongest predictor of attitude to Christianity, which was also affected by age and sex. The attitude scores of the pupils were the highest among those with both parents baptized Catholics, followed by those with one parent a baptized Catholic—it made no difference if it was the father or the mother. Non-Catholics showed less favorable attitudes but with a greater range of scores.

Egan and Francis (1986) analyzed the factors associated with positive attitudes to school and to Christianity among pupils in Catholic secondary schools in Wales, where these schools include almost a fifth of non-Catholic pupils. Scales had been developed to measure pupils attitudes toward the traditional view of the Catholic school system, to religious education in their school, and to their school itself. Mass attendance proved to be the key factor, and this was related in a complex way to parental religiousness, in which the father's attendance was related to that of the mother. Mass attendance was strongly associated with favorable attitudes to school and to religious education. Pupils whose parents had ceased to attend Mass were less favorable to their Catholic school than pupils whose parents were not Catholic, and non-Mass-attending Catholic pupils were less favorable than non-Catholic pupils. They were a significant group within the schools, since less than half the girls and even fewer boys were weekly Mass attenders. Francis (1986d) had suggested that there was an incompatibility between the religious background of church-going non-Catholics attending Catholic schools and the religious assumptions of the schools. In Wales this was even greater with the non-practicing Catholic pupils of nonpracticing parents. The schools needed to make different provisions for these pupils if their religious influence was to be effective. Similar results were found both in America and in Australia (Francis and Egan, 1987).

Hartley (1984) was concerned with the objectives of Catholic schools and, following the Report on Christian Education of the First National Pastoral Congress, argued that schools should play an important if partial role in the relationship among parents, priests, pupils, teachers, and catechists, providing an experience of living Christian community. The need of such a partnership was made evident by the apparent futility of teaching pupils to appreciate the liturgy of the church if at home they found a lack of interest in it and in the parish a badly prepared liturgy which said little or nothing to them.

A Jewish study

Prais (1974) investigated the religious education of a representative sample of Jewish adolescents of fifteen and sixteen in London schools. They had received on average four periods a week, but for those not in specifically Jewish schools it was only two and a half periods a week. Boys had significantly more instruction than girls, especially in preparation for Bar Mitzvah. The findings stressed the problem facing part-time classes, but did not attempt any evaluation of the relative success of the different systems.

Studies of Scottish schools

Rhymer (1984) (Rhymer and Francis, 1985) used Francis' scale to test representative Catholic secondary school pupils in Scotland. Pupils from church schools had a more positive attitude to religion, and those in the nondenominational schools who received Catholic religious education scored higher than those who did not. In all schools religious education lessons were disliked, a matter seen to reflect the lack of a national syllabus at the time of testing and the insecurity felt by many nonspecialist teachers of the subject. Since adolescence is a time when some might turn from religion it was reassuring that the responses generally indicated a positive attitude to religion. A great majority had a high regard for personal religion and the importance of prayer and rejected the suggestion that the

Bible was out of date. The church was important to them, even though they found
its services boring; school religion was met with less enthusiasm. The result
showed girls had more positive attitudes than boys, attitudes to religion tended
to become less positive with age, and the extent of religious practice was partly
dependent on social class. A nondenominational school that made no provision
for Catholic religious education also had a small but significant deleterious effect
on Catholic pupils' attitudes. Rhymer used the results as a base for a wide-ranging
review of the school situation in Scotland, and the consequences of implementing
the recommendations of the *Declaration on Christian Eduction* made by Vatican
II. Later, Gibson and Francis (1989) tested a substantial sample of pupils in Scottish Catholic secondary schools; there was a normal deterioration of attitude scores
between the ages of eleven and fifteen. The sixteen-year-old sample scored higher
than anticipated, which could indicate that a disproportionate number of pupils
leaving school at sixteen were unsympathetic to a Catholic school. Overall, the
mean scores were lower in Scotland than they were for comparable Catholic secondary school pupils in England.

Studies of schools in Northern Ireland

In Northern Ireland, where polarization between Catholics and Protestants produces extreme political and social consequences, there has not been much research
concerned with school effectiveness. Even so, some studies look at aspects of this
problem, especially that of Greer about senior students in Protestant schools, to
which reference was made earlier. His detailed comparison with Cox's (1967)
English figures (Greer, 1972a) had shown the greater religiousness of Northern
Ireland students, particularly the boys, who were more likely to believe in God,
in the divinity of Jesus, to agree that life after death was an important issue, to
attend church, to pray privately, and to read the Bible. No association was found
between belief in God and school subjects studied, contrary to the finding that
boys in mixed schools who studied science were less religious than those studying
arts subjects (Wright and Cox, 1967a). This questioned the explanation that in
coeducational schools science had a masculine connotation which attracted less
religious boys to it. Similarly, the earlier finding that boys and girls in English
coeducational schools were less religious than those in single-sex schools was
now countered by the finding that girls in Northern Ireland coeducational schools
were more likely to believe in God and in the divinity of Jesus than those in single-
sex schools. This showed that when taught religious education together, the doubts
of the boys did not affect the girls in Northern Ireland. Greer was unable to explain
these different findings, which did not arise from sampling differences. The difference between Irish girls in mixed schools being more religious and more severe
in moral judgments than those in single-sex schools, could be related to their social
situation, since most rural schools were coeducational. This would be in accord
with Cox's (1967) suggestion that social factors might account for the differences

between girls in the two types of schools. Comparison with the repetition of Cox's study (Wright and Cox, 1971) showed less movement from established attitudes among the Northern Ireland pupils than among the English and a remarkable similarity in the pattern of responses after a decade. This persistence of religious belief and moral judgments differed from the secularization in England. In Northern Ireland, violence seemed to turn many of those affected by it to religious belief, which provided social support in addition to a sense of purpose and inner strength.

Despite the polarization between the communities there appeared to be some evidence for tolerant attitudes, especially among Catholics. Accordingly Greer (1985) constructed a scale to indicate the willingness of adolescents to value members of the other tradition as a measure of acceptance and nondiscrimination. It was administered to pupils of twelve to sixteen in secondary schools as was Francis' (1979c) attitude to religion scale. The openness scale showed significantly higher scores for Catholics than Protestants for the girls but not for the boys, and in each group acceptance scores increased with age. Attitude to religion scores decreased with age; girls tended to score higher than boys and Catholics higher than Protestants. When the effects of age, sex, and denomination were controlled, it became clear that there was a strong association between the two attitudes, so that contrary to popular assumptions, adolescents most favorably disposed toward religion were also most open to members of other religious groups. (It would be of great interest to know if this is affected by styles of religious orientation—is it true only for the intrinsically oriented?) Greer commented that it was not known if this openness continued in secular situations after school. It appeared that adolescence brought a growth in independence from family attachment to a particular church, so that while religious ties were loosened, community relations were potentially improved. The finding gave support to the conclusions of Powell and Stewart (1978) that in adolescence, individuals moved away from the religion and orthodox values of parents to a greater degree of liberalization.

Turner, Turner, and Reid (1980) (Turner, 1980a) argued that in the complicated and confused picture of adolescent religiousness, adolescents in Northern Ireland were likely to be different. They repeated the test carried out ten years before in the same two secondary schools, with boys of thirteen to sixteen. In one school all the boys said they were Protestant, and in the other Catholic. The test used Turner's (1970) attitude scale. A significant difference was found between the Protestant and the Catholic groups on each comparison; decade-by-school differences were also found. Scores on the attitude to religion scale became less favorable with age, and on both occasions the mean scores of boys attending the Catholic school were significantly higher than those attending the Protestant school. While the trends had encouragement for the Catholic school, even here there had been a decline during the decade. Scores were encouraging in showing positive attitudes, without evidence of the hostile attitude among older adolescents reported by Francis (1978a).

Finally, Turner and Davies (1982) studied a denominationally integrated primary school first established by a mill-owner for his workers' children and tested pupils in the final two years with Turner's (1970) attitude to religion scale. The results showed no significant difference between the girls and the boys but a significant denominational difference, Catholics scoring more than Protestants, but the highest scores coming from children of "other" Protestant sects. All Catholic children attended church with their families, but only some Protestants. The results supported findings on the primacy of the home in the development of religious attitudes. The authors regarded the school as responsible for the positive attitudes of those Protestant children having no family involvement in a Church.

AUSTRALIAN STUDIES OF CHURCH SCHOOLS

In Australia, as elsewhere, the effect of church schools has been under scrutiny. Mobbs (1981) argued that the distinctive characteristic of a Catholic school was the specific aim of producing Catholics. Rossiter's (1983) monumental thesis was primarily concerned with reconciling education in faith and education in religion by seeking a rapprochement between the curriculum of state schools and Catholic schools, but in the course of this he made a detailed survey of the Australian situation and research into the effectiveness of Catholic education. He drew attention to some findings previously unreported outside Australia, which, with others, are described in the pages that follow.

A number of attempts have been made to evaluate the degree of success of Australian denominational schools in fostering religious attitudes and the extent to which their pupils are found to be more religious than those from other schools. Roman Catholic schools have much in common with those of Britain or the United States, but other Australian denominational schools draw pupils not only from parents with denominational allegiances but also from parents who regard the schools as a better alternative to the state schools. Morrison (1985) investigated the reasons why parents sent their children to Australian Anglican secondary schools, since most of them transferred from government primary schools. Government secondary schools were not chosen because of some specific negative event or assessment of a school. Anglican schools were chosen because a place was available, it became possible to pay the fees, the parents were impressed by the school organization, teaching standards, student appearance and behavior, and because the school met their child's needs. Such a choice was financially expensive for parents and meant that their children lost their former friends. There was no consideration of the schools' religious affiliation.

Formerly religious education in state schools was given by voluntary denominational visitors, but the decline of this practice resulted in a reappraisal of its value. Plans were made for a form of religious education to become part of the school curriculum in Victoria (Howells, 1978). A similar situation in South Australia was described by Waters (1974), Ninnes, (1978), and Crotty (1986), with the development of syllabuses and the provision of in-service training for teachers unaccustomed to it. Mavor (1987) described the syllabus of religious studies that was being taught in Queensland government secondary schools. A full account of religious education in Australian schools can be found in Rossiter (1981), who also discussed at length the religious education issues in government and church-related schools, and the relationship between the two types of school when it was seen as an academic subject (Rossiter, 1985).

Dempsey and Pandey (1967) tested first-year university students to look for the effects of their schooling and claimed that former Catholic school students had a significantly higher level of religiousness than those from state or Protestant schools. Catholic students' scores were significantly higher on an attitude to religion scale, on questions about religious beliefs, and on religious behavior. There was not a significant sex difference in the Catholic group, but in the remainder women tended to show greater religiousness. Dempsey (1966) showed that in this same sample there was no significant difference between the Anglican, Methodist, and Presbyterian groups that comprised the Protestants. The only difference between former students of Protestant and government schools was that a higher proportion of the latter attended church weekly. However, the authors recognized that this result might well be related to other external influences, such as that of the home, and commented that while Catholic parents sent their children to a Catholic school to receive a religious education, Protestant parents tended to regard independent schools as prestige institutions conferring social status on their children, schools which rarely formed part of a particular church's total structure.

Ray and Doratis (1971) measured the religiousness and racial prejudice of Australian students of fifteen in Catholic and Protestant schools. Catholic and Protestant students did not differ significantly in either their religiousness or their racial prejudice, nor did social class affect religiousness. Religiousness, religious conservatism, and racial prejudice proved to be three independent factors, despite some complex interactions, whereby the more religious tended to be more conservative and more prejudiced, while the more conservative tended to be slightly less prejudiced. It appeared that in these Catholic schools attitudes were related to the general secular culture rather than to religious education.

Mol (1971a) provided an extensive sociological review of religion in Australia including material about Catholic school education, which appeared first as an exploratory study (Mol, 1968), subsequently summarized (Mol, 1972). He observed that Catholic adults who had attended Catholic schools scored much higher on the religious variables than any other group, and Catholics who had attended government schools scored more highly than Protestants, who seemed unaffected by former attendance at a Protestant school. Catholics went to church more regularly, prayed more regularly, believed in God more strongly, were more of the opinion that the church was appointed by God, and were more likely to have had religious experiences. Those who had not attended a Catholic school did not score as high, but even so, they scored more highly than the Protestants. Those with at least some Catholic school education tended to disapprove more strongly of premarital sex and of contraception than Catholics who had attended a state school. Catholics, irrespective of their type of education, showed significantly less disagreement with the statement that the most important thing for children to learn was to obey rather than to think for themselves. Former Protestant school students did not differ religiously from Protestants who had been to state schools, but politically were more in favor of the Liberal Country party, more had completed a secondary education, and more had fathers in the professional, managerial, or grazing circles. Catholics more than Protestants, and Catholic-school Catholics more than state-school Catholics, tended to have the majority of their closest friends in the local parish. It appeared that the more private, devotional experiences were more common among the older Catholics, but that public religious practices were largely independent of age. Mol regarded Catholic schools as reinforcing the religious influence of the home, and substantially reinforcing the church's hold on its membership—a point overlooked by much previous research. Protestant schools in Australia had no such effect on loyalty to the denomination, except for some minority groups.

Anderson (1971) criticized Mol, claiming that statistical correlations did not establish that religious practice was causally influenced by the school, and he drew attention to the fact that while there was a significant difference between the larger proportion attending church schools than state schools who had both parents attending church regularly, the difference was not significant when both parents were irregular church-goers. He saw the effect as due to home influence, and disputed the suggestion that Catholic schools had any independent influence. To this, Mol (1971b) made a spirited rejoinder. However, the other similar studies by Anderson and Western (1972) and Dempsey and Pandey (1967) supported Mol's finding that patterns of religiousness were related to the former type of schooling. Anderson and Western analyzed the data on religiousness from a broader, longitudinal study of attitudes and opinions of undergraduate students in six Australian universities. Once more, Catholics who had attended Catholic schools were more religious than those who had attended state schools, and Protestants from state or Protestant schools did not significantly differ. This was true not only of church attendance but also of strength of belief in God. On a measure of social liberation, there was a negative association with church attendance, and the former Protestant school students showed a somewhat higher score than those from state schools. But Catholics from state schools recorded much higher scores than those from Catholic schools. The authors still expressed some reservations about distinguishing between the relative influences of home and school. The particular value of these earlier studies lies in the way in which they focused attention on the religious influences affecting church-school pupils; of greater interest were the subsequent studies based on measures of the religiousness of the pupils.

Hansen (1986, 1971) concluded that religion was not very important in the life of the Protestant schools but was more prominent in Catholic schools. Scott and

Orr (1967a, b) compared the religiousness of pupils of thirteen to sixteen from single-sex Anglican boarding schools with pupils in coeducational state high schools. They used an Adolescent Values Inventory and also tests of religious knowledge, intelligence, personality adjustment, and questions about general background. In the state schools only a third of the Anglicans had been confirmed, whereas in the Anglican schools almost all had been. The state school pupils had a somewhat higher level of church attendance, and it appeared that a boarding-school pattern did not persist outside the schools. Anglican school pupils tended to conform more to the value-orientations of their homes than did their state schools peers, and they tended to display a higher level of religious knowledge. The boarding school chaplain was a major source of religious knowledge in the independent schools; in the state schools the source of religious knowledge was attributed in somewhat smaller proportions to the home, the local minister, and the schools' visiting clergy. When personality traits were examined, state school pupils were found as a group to be more mature emotionally and more outgoing. State school pupils were also found to be more assiduous Bible readers, whereas the Anglican school pupils tended to have a greater moral sensivity in practical morality, and although they disliked compulsory prayers they had a higher level of private prayer. Yet on the Adolescent Values Inventory they showed less religious zeal, more self-abnegation, humility, "timid followership," faction, and argument than those in the state schools. Thus, while the independent Anglican schools were less effective in promoting churchmanship and the acquisition of spiritual values, they were more effective in fostering the development of moral and social responsibility.

Two of these results are of some considerable importance, although standing in relative isolation. Much attention has been given to examining school effects in terms of students' religious behavior or attitude to religion but little to the overall effects on students' development of personality and value systems. There is clearly a need for further research and for discussion about precise objectives—which ranks higher, to parents and to church leaders, churchmanship or social morality? Second, no consideration was given to social class differences between state and independent schools. The finding that independent school pupils had a higher standard of religious knowledge but a lower standard of religious belief and practice than those in state schools was seen to be important. The authors regarded this as evidence for the principle that knowledge about religion had no necessary connection with zeal for religion and attitudes toward religious faith and practice. These results give a clear demonstration that religiousness is not a valid measure of religious education; the two are concerned with quite different dimensions of religion.

Another comparison of the religiousness of church and state school pupils, using a different test, was made by Prince (1972) in Western Australia, which confirmed Scott and Orr's findings that government school pupils scored more highly in religiousness than did Protestant school pupils. He tested pupils at a city and at a country high school and two single-sex church schools; girls scored higher than boys, and the attitude of church school students was less positive toward Christianity than that of the state school students. Some sexual permissiveness was expressed in all the sample, but more in the single-sex church schools; this he regarded as a product of the single-sex nature of the schools. He made no attempt to look at social class consequences, but he noted that the state school students were not only more religious, but also more diligent, self-sufficient, vigorous, and tolerant. He also indicated the counterproductive effect of regular compulsory worship in church schools, even though classroom religious instruction was by and large acceptable to them. His conclusions led him to question the possibility of developing a single overall program of religious education for a spectrum of students whose religious needs varied so greatly, so that he suggested a differentiation between the evangelizing and educating structures in church schools.

A similar result was secured by Poole (1983), who reported a comparison between students' religiousness in Catholic and other private church schools and in state high schools and secondary technical schools. They were asked about considerations when choosing a job, including serving God. By this measure, students at Catholic and technical schools were the most religious, while those at other church schools and secular schools were the least religious. Hyde (1977) questioned the grounds for Catholic education because of the similarity of attitudes to social issues between senior pupils from a Catholic girls' school and those in government high schools. Although the religiousness of the Catholic girls was much higher, this alone distinguished them from their peers. The general levels of religiousness were less than those found by Mol (1971a) four years before.

McSweeney (1971a, b), studying Catholic, Protestant, and state school students from twelve to fifteen in both urban and rural situations, found Catholic school pupils held significantly higher traditional, moral, and ethical standards and held in higher esteem ideas of thrift, self-denial, and sexual restraint. They were more oriented to the future, prepared on occasions to defer present gratification for future rewards. Among state school students there was much less agreement that abortion was always wrong, and shame rather than guilt tended to be the accepted concept of morality. No significant differences were found between pupils from government and Protestant schools, but rather a pattern similar to that found by the studies of religiousness of former pupils by Mol, Anderson and Western, and Hyde. Rural schools tended to score higher than other comparable schools, Catholic or non-Catholic. Social or economic variables were important in giving rise to these differentiations.

In studies of attitudes of pupils, parents, and teachers, Black (1970) and Roulston (1971, 1975) found that religious education was regarded as important but not satisfying. Black showed that pupils' attitudes to religion and to religious instruction declined from the first to the fourth form, and girls tended to have more positive attitudes than boys. Roulston found that although there was a great deal of interest in religious education, and students of sixteen still regarded it as important for providing a framework for guidance in life, it was ineffective and did not meet their personal needs. He concluded that it would be better to replace denominational instruction by specialist teaching and discussion about social and moral issues, and noted that many wanted to study world religions. The importance of religious education in the eyes of the general public was subsequently confirmed in a series of government reports.

Attempts to discover what was relevant to this age-group, by investigating the religious questions, problems, and issues vital to them, were made by Wiltshire (1973), by Bambach (1973), and by Nowotny (1978). Wiltshire surveyed adolescents mostly aged fourteen to nineteen from the Churches of Christ. They showed high levels of church attendance; liberal social attitudes were associated with liberal theological outlooks, found predominantly among those who were younger. The most conservative were in their early twenties, suggesting that becoming an adult brought a more conservative attitude. Liberal social attitudes tended to be associated with longer education. All who were interviewed showed strong opposition to gambling—an important issue in the denomination—but less support for total abstinence or the prohibition of dancing. Most were tolerant of abortion in some circumstances and very much opposed to the segregation of Aborigines. A substantial minority always disapproved of extramarital sex. Bambach (1973) recorded students' interests and questions at two English schools, and an analysis of it, supplemented by information from schools in Canada, showed that adolescents were concerned with broad, basic religious and social problems which related to their conflicts and tasks and their search for a practical, meaningful, relevant faith.

Although three Australian Catholics undertook their research in this field at the University of Notre Dame in the United States, it is better described here. Treston (1973), Whiteman (1973), and Burgess (1975) investigated the effects of a range of psychological and sociological variables on the religiousness of Catholic pupils. Treston (1973) (Treston, Whiteman, and Florent, 1975) distinguished two contrasting groups. The adult-oriented adolescents showed a higher degree of awareness of God and of relationship with God, participated more in worship, and had a higher regard for ethical principles. But the peer-oriented group showed a better understanding of Christianity as a unique religion.

Whiteman (1973) compared Catholics with different religious education backgrounds from parochial schools, public schools and CCD classes, public schools and Sunday school attendance, and public schools alone. These different backgrounds were not related to their religiousness; it was the students who experienced warm interpersonal relationship with others who had significantly developed a better sense of the awareness of God, maturity of values, self-regard, and a lifestyle that had meaning and purpose. But Sunday school rather than parochial school attendance significantly affected scores dealing with religious participation and awareness of God. Burgess (1975) undertook a longitudinal study of high-school students over four years; in the period their perception of adult caring had significantly decreased, but there was no significant change in their church attendance or in their social orientation, two factors which were obviously compatible for them. All three studies established a relationship between religiousness and adolescent attitudes; it was the hope of the authors that better understanding of adolescent development would make for more effective religious education. Rossiter (1983) thought that this relationship was not realized because they did not distinguish between the specific influence of formal religious education and the overall influence of the school itself. Religious education was complementary to the social environment of the school, but the two needed to be seen as making separate contributions to the religious development of pupils.

De Vaus (1980, 1981a, b) conducted a two-year longitudinal study of the religiousness of senior secondary school students. Social factors were an important cause of religious change, and not intellectual, academic or educational factors. He disputed the assumption (Glock and Stark, 1965) that people tended to be either scientific or religious. In support he cited Martin (1967) that it was absurd to suggest that the New Testament was an intellectual insult or Thomism was not compatible with modern logic. In his sample it was the most religious who most valued a scientific approach, and the perception of a conflict between science and religion was due to their religious outlook, not the cause of it. Young people tended to adopt the points of view of those with whom they most strongly identified. The personal and social environment of the school was more significant than formal religious education. In terms of religiousness, Catholic boys in Catholic schools were significantly more believing, devotional, and church-attending than Catholic boys in state schools; this difference was not found with Catholic girls, who in both types of school displayed high levels of religiousness. De Vaus suggested that because religiousness is regarded as compatible with feminism, Catholic girls did not need the support of a Catholic school in the same way as the boys, since a secular school did not appear to desacralize their religiousness.

Hickman (1971) claimed that the Greeley and Rossi (1966) survey of the impact of Catholic schooling in the United States was definitive, and he regarded the main religious influence as coming from the home, so that church schooling had little impact except on pupils whose parents were regular church-goers. This claim was soon to be disputed, and the controversy regarding the effects on religiousness of school and home resolved. Leavey's study (1972a, b) of sixth-form girls in nine Catholic girls high schools broke new ground, for she not only confirmed that the major religious influence on these students was parental but also demonstrated that a Catholic school could also have an independent influence, depending on the school climate.

School climate had previously been explored in the United States by McDill, Meyers, and Rigsby (1967) who devised a measure to study it in high schools and showed that certain types of school climate were conducive to higher academic achievement. Later Vick (1975) found a strong association between the managerial style of a school principal and the school climate, but Cuttance's (1981) review of research into school effects had no reference to the climate of schools; the nearest approach were studies of the effect of peer-group influences on academic achievement. He commented that studies of teacher effectiveness remained inconsistent. Hickey (1977) found significant relationships between staff perceptions of religious dimensions and the consideration, esprit, and thrust elements of a school climate; the religious dimensions were inversely related to disengagement and hindrance in the climate test. Faculty perceptions of each school's religiousness were significantly greater than those of the students themselves.

Leavey selected five variables and studied their operation in six areas of the students' activities, attitudes, and achievements to evaluate the religious effectiveness of the schools. She explored the extent to which Christian belief and secular subjects were integrated, the extent to which the students' worldview was religious, the effect of post-Vatican theology, the extent to which church-based religious and moral values were internalized, and religious practice and responses to an Ideal Religious Education Goals scale. Her scales, related to Glock and Stark's dimensions of religion, were developed with great sophistication. A comparison between high and low achieving students indicated that results were hardly affected by different methods of identifying the groups' religiousness. Comparisons were also made on parental religiousness, socio-economic status of the home, socio-economic status of the school, school religious achievement, and students' examination successes—the many variables so frequently overlooked, as was remarked at the outset. The most successful girls were the type of students which the schools hoped to produce, holding highly internalized beliefs, Catholic values and morality. They tended to come from professional and managerial homes, not only from religiously high-achieving homes but also from the religiously high-achieving schools. They also tended to include the high-achieving examination group.

Students from similar religious and social backgrounds responded differently in both religious and academic outcomes to schools with different climates—some schools tended to be high-achieving and others low-achieving on all religious outcomes. All schools tended to have a stronger effect than parents on cognitive areas such as integration or post-Vatican theology. In a small group of students, science was alleged to contradict Christian faith, but for the majority a post-Vatican understanding of doctrine was recorded. Students from more affluent homes were likely to condone abortion in some circumstances. The students regarded religious education as the least important goal of their schools, although their religious teachers considered it the most important. Students from high-achieving religious homes tended to be more critical of the actual religious education which they encountered, regarding it as below their expectations; the Sisters who taught it on the other hand regarded it as satisfactory. Some students with low religious behavior levels complained that there was too much religious education. In other respects the differences between the two types of schools were marked. Students from high-religious homes did less well in a low-achieving school, and students from low-religious homes did much better in a high-achieving school than the total sample, as Leavey's tables vividly show. Her conclusion was quite clear—the schools were having an impact on the students independent of their homes. Unless the students experienced the school as a Christian environment, they were not open to the Christian message; in other words, unless their experience of the procedures of the school in some way reinforced the Christian content of the school, then the Christian content was not mediated, and religious education was not successful. The success of Leavey's research came from her recognition that it required a range of different scales related to several dimensions of religion and a number of external variables to investigate so complex a situation, and more than a simplistic analysis of the data was needed. It is important to notice that it was the school climate and not the classroom climate which she found to be of prime importance. An Australian discussion of classroom climate was provided by Slattery (1974, 1979), who regarded the maintenance of a good climate in the classroom as an important contribution to the school climate. Leavey recognized it as having to do with peer-group influences and the personal relationships between staff and students in the school. Her study makes the religious influence of the schools she identified highly probable, but does not finally prove it, since it is possible that other influences, not identified in the analysis, may have been active in the apparent school effects.

Leavey's study was followed by those of Flynn (1974, 1985) and Fahy (1976, 1978, 1980a,b). Flynn undertook a similar study of students over sixteen in twenty-one Catholic boys' schools, finding a network of relationships between home background and school climate with academic achievement, religious behavior, and the religious attitudes of pupils. This confirmed Leavey's conclusions. A religious school had its best effect when it reinforced and supported a good religious atmosphere at home, and a good religious school had a better influence on students from homes with low religious influence than poor religious schools. Again, the school was shown to have an influence independent of that of the home. The climate of the school was the key factor in its religious influence; students' morale, their attitude to the principal, and adolescent freedom had an important role in producing this climate, as did the school procedures in its day-to-day administration, the style of life it valued, and what it celebrated or rewarded.

Fahy (1978) extended Leavey's work and developed new scales, using them over a three-year period. From sixteen to eighteen there was a marked decline in agreement that Christ was experienced as a real person, which had been found by Leavey (1972a), Flynn (1974), and Fahy (1978) to be a key predictor. A similar decline was also observed about a Christian lifestyle. Loss of confidence in the reality of Christ was associated with disinclination to follow his teaching. More than half would not accept that Christ had no relevance for them, although one in ten totally rejected his relevance, and four in ten wanted to know more about him and his teaching. Among the students of fourteen, three in ten sensed that Christ had some effect on the lives of people around them, but a similar proportion found it hard to believe in the resurrection or that Christ was present in Holy Communion. At eighteen, 70 percent of the students professed belief in God, compared with 57 percent of those of sixteen. Illogically, a rather greater percentage of both groups believed that God forgave them, although little over a half thought of God as a loving Father. Human suffering and war made belief difficult for three in ten, and increasing age brought a decrease of belief that the Holy Spirit influenced their lives. A positive finding was that the experience of a Christian living camp or weekend had a significant religious impact for 60 percent of the oldest students.

Fahy (1980a, b) used new scales for measuring Catholic faith and practice and the sense of social issues in seventeen Catholic boys' high schools. Students' religiousness was most strongly related to parental religiousness, but other outcomes—Christian faith and sensitivity to issues of social justice and a sense of Christian community in the staff—were related to the boys' perception of the social environment of the school. School-related factors were positively and uniquely associated with students' religious faith and awareness of social justice independent of their home, peer group, or personality. In the light of his results, Fahy criticized the methodology of the study of American Catholic schools by Greeley, McCready, and McCourt (1976), which had concluded that the school had no influence independent of the home background.

Subsequently, Fahy (1982) surveyed over 3,000 Catholic school students aged sixteen and eighteen, using the same test instruments with additional items about a religious vocation. Two-thirds regarded it as worthwhile, a third would be happy to see a friend enter one, and a tenth had thought seriously about it themselves. The same was true of boys and girls in mixed schools. Increased interest was found among older students, when decisions regarding work and careers were near. The proportion of the school staff who were members of religious orders was unrelated—it was the quality of their contribution which provided a stimulus to the students to contemplate a similar calling. Those interested in a religious vocation were not influenced by their peers but by a happy Christian home and a school environment which sought to develop a truly Christian community. Vocational attitudes were affected by the religious goals of the schools and their formal religious education. Once again a positive influence from the schools was identified, although this time no attempt was made to compare individual schools. Older adolescents sympathetic to a religious vocation must have very positive attitudes toward religion, and it is interesting to notice yet again in such a group religious interest increases with age.

Rossiter (1983) regarded these studies as the most comprehensive and sophisticated sociological work in this area that is available in English-speaking countries and noted that the study of public and Catholic schooling in the United States by Coleman, Hoffer, and Kilgore (1982) focused on scholastic achievement and discipline and not on religious variables. They had found that private schools, with a more academic climate and orderly atmosphere, provided a better education than public schools; they defended this (1981b) in a symposium based on their first draft report (1981a), but there was no discussion of religious influence. It brought into prominence the important issue of school climate, which has wider implications than that of religious influence.

Independently of these series of studies Francis and Egan (1987) repeated in nine Catholic schools in Sydney the study they had first carried out in Wales with pupils aged sixteen. Very similar results were secured. Once more path analysis showed that Mass attendance was the key issue, and again the pupils received more support in this from mothers, of whom half were weekly attenders, than fathers, of whom two-fifths were weekly attenders. The most satisfied pupils considered their parents had made the right choice in sending them to their school, whose friendly relationships between staff and pupils arose from their shared faith. To a lesser degree, they felt that their religious education had deepened their religious life and helped them deal with life's important problems. Pupils whose father alone was a Catholic tended to hold less positive attitudes than those whose mother alone was a Catholic. As in the Welsh study, there was a strong negative influence from parents who had ceased to practice their faith, more than when one parent was not a Catholic. The presence in the school of so many pupils from such homes prevented the full cooperation of home, school, and church that was the basis of Catholic education, and their different religious needs ought also to be recognized.

Athanasou (1984) studied the religious practices and knowledge of Greek Orthodox students of twelve to seventeen. Analysis of responses to his questionnaire showed there was a strong religious cultural factor affecting attendance at Communion and prayer and, distinct from this, separate religious and cultural factors related to church attendance and confession and reading Greek newspapers and books.

The unmistakable religious influence which some schools have been shown to exert cannot be a general one, as Anderson's (1988) research shows. He undertook a longitudinal study to explore the associations between the type of school attended and the political, religious, and social values of their students, as well as the schools to which they subsequently sent their children. There was a strong association between religious background and choice of a Catholic school, but when allowance was made for family and social influences there was no evidence of a Catholic school effect on religious behavior or belief, not even on social liberalism. Among Catholics, the mother's church attendance was directly related to the likelihood of their children attending a Catholic school, a link which was observed for three generations. Non-Catholic private schools, mostly Church of England or other Protestant church schools, added to the politically conservative attitudes of their students but had no religious effects. Their students tended to come from wealthy homes and have well-educated parents, who chose the school partly for intellectual interests. These students looked for high financial rewards in their choice of career and regarded their school as enhancing their career prospects. Those who had attended any type of private school were very likely to send their children to a similar one, and a growing proportion of professional people were sending their children to private schools. The greater the extent of the parents' education, the more likely were they to opt for a private school for their children. So it is that when former pupils are studied, no school influence on their religiousness independent of that of their parents' can be established. Yet when pupils in specific schools are studied, then school influence is found. We need to know from longitudinal studies whether this influence lasts beyond school days, or whether, as with the very religious English convent school girls described by Hornsby-Smith (1978), it fades when exposed to the secular adult world. Brothers (1964) showed how great were the secularizing pressures on educated young Catholics; could it be that just as some schools by their overall life have a positive religious influence, and others, for all their attempts, do not, so some parishes are effective in supporting the faith of their parishioners and others are not. The principal proved to be the key person in the schools; the parish priest must assuredly have a similar role.

The cumulative effect of these studies in the United States, the United Kingdom, and Australia shows that while parents have the strongest influence on their children's religiousness, the school also has an independent influence which arises from the school climate. It is not the result of formal religious education but is due to the attitudes that are fostered and the effectiveness of pastoral care. It can be negative, even in a church school. The outcome in Australia was to focus attention on the climate of Catholic schools, and a considerable number of studies followed concerned with staff morale, organizational climate, and the ideology of pupil control. For example, Ross and McTaggart (1983) found widespread agreement from Catholic teachers who had previously taught in public schools that essential factors were staff relationships, goal orientation, the religious dimension, student behavior, the principal's style of leadership, the number of students, and working conditions, and the majority agreed that Catholic schools were as good as or better than state schools.

Some details have emerged from a few studies which should not be overlooked. It was claimed that Church of England schools in Australia produced a sense of social morality in their students, rather than a sense of churchmanship—a result which must take account of the socially selective nature of the schools which appears to be of greater importance than their religious foundation. In the United States, Catholic children attending public schools with their religious education coming from CCD classes had less religious knowledge but a higher social morality than parochial school children. School climate may account for Francis' findings that Church of England schools in East Anglia do not greatly differ from state schools in their religious effects, when the churchmanship of all the head teachers is taken into consideration. Students at colleges with a church foundation, on both sides of the Atlantic, tend to display strong religiousness, but this would seem to be due to the religious convictions of the students who elected to attend such colleges. Yet the staff of these colleges can also have a liberalizing influence on their students.

What should be the objectives of a church school? The opinions of one broadly based group is known. Welch (1988) investigated what principals, teachers, parents, and board members regarded as the desirable results of Catholic elementary school education. They all wanted the children to develop a healthy self-concept and to live their religion as well as to learn about it. The Catholic educational background of the mother had a more important bearing on these issues than that of the father. There was no difference between the social classes. Rural residents rated family and community relationships higher than any other residents, and those in small towns similarly rated personal and academic items more highly.

However, most of these studies had little or no direct concern with religious education but instead raised the question whether formal religious education should be directed to areas of personal relationships and psychological development, to the detriment of religious studies. Since the home remains the strongest religious influence, Rossiter (1983) believed that the role of religious education in a church school should be about a cognitive grasp of religion, rather than personal faith and religious behavior. This plea was reinforced by the number of instances when pupils held religious education lessons in low esteem, despite the school's positive religious influence. So far there has been no detailed study of the comparative effectiveness of different approaches to religious education, which Elias (1979) stated has resisted serious evaluative research and testing so that its effectiveness is seen in different lights from different theological perspectives.

Elias also noted that recent studies in the United States had indicated a general decline in church participation, religious knowledge, and acceptance of the moral teaching of the church. The same trends seem to be at work throughout the Western world. The general unpopularity of religious education as a school subject, noted earlier, is not merely a British phenomenon; it is also found in Germany, according to Havers (1972), who described it as the unloved branch of learning, despite the immense effort of catechetical renewal and one of the best school organizations. In France the same is true, as Cousin (1985) showed in his study of nearly 5,000 pupils in Catholic schools, whose approach to belief was dilettante. To them the most important values were to set up a happy home and start a family, to have a good job, and to get the best out of life. The family was important to them and also the desire to be independent; they wanted to have experiences other than those generally favored by society.

On this note the survey ends. A minority of adolescents are strongly committed to their faith, whatever form it takes, and owe it in no small measure to the example of their parents, the influence of their church, and possibly to their school. Religious attitudes inform their decisions, and the church or synagogue is at the center of their social life. Mental development has brought for them a knowledge of the scriptures and the doctrine on which their faith is founded. In contrast, for many others, a majority in England, religion is not merely secondary, but it often has no place at all in their lives. It is not the basis of their values, it offers no hope for their future, nor does it provide them with a social focus. As G. K. Chesterton wrote in *What's Wrong with the World*, "The Christian ideal has not been tried and found wanting. It has been found difficult, and left untried."

Appendices

Appendix A

The Definition of Religion in Psychology

Religion is not a simple concept; many fundamental differences are to be found regarding it even in a single religion. There are not merely varieties of doctrinal emphasis but contrasting styles believers adopt about their beliefs and what is required or prohibited by them. The theological opposition between transcendental and immanental understandings of God are in some ways related to such matters as these.

Definitions of religion vary considerably, depending on their origin; theologians, philosophers, psychologists, and sociologists all have different perspectives. The pragmatic stance of Alatas (1977) is a useful guide: He regarded religion as necessary for integrating meaning systems for individuals and society, quite independent of its claim to ultimate truth. Its main characteristics did not apply equally to all religions (e.g., there is no idea of priesthood in Islam), but this did not prevent the study of religious phenomena, whether or not religion was regarded as desirable for human life. Nor did they apply to such questions as whether its emotional aspects were embedded in specific religious feelings qualitatively different from other feelings, or whether religion was primarily a social or an individual phenomenon. Alston (1977) also considered that the concept of religion had often been inflated to include phenomena normally classified as nonreligious; systems of belief which excluded the supernatural, the sacred, or prayer could not be bound together as religious without distorting its objective reality.

It is still a matter of dispute whether religion has elements distinguishing it from everything else which gives rise to unique psychological states. It is often assumed, perhaps implicitly, that religion is unique and its psychological manifestations differ from any others. But similar feelings and states to those of religious experience are felt in nonreligious circumstances; it does not follow that

336

they are religious although not recognized as such by their subjects. Feelings such as awe or reverence which are fundamental to religion are also felt by nonreligious people in nonreligious contexts. Membership of a church has similar group effects as membership of a tennis club or college, in which members share in group life and accept its rules and norms. The burden of proof still rests on those who claim that while the psychological variables found in religion are the same as those found in many other situations, within religion itself there is something unique with which they react. Whatever stance is taken, an investigator needs to remain aware of these uncertainties, otherwise the interpretation of data must remain tentative.

Yinger (1969, 1970) argued that religion required a functional definition that looked at its consequences; it was about the way an individual dealt with the threat of chaos in personal life and in society, so one should not ask if people were religious but how they were religious. Thus regarded, religion was about the values and meanings of fundamental concerns and there should be a sociology of quite specific religious areas, even though it was complex. When measured in this way it was largely independent of normal religious traditions. But Berger (1974), reviewing a number of functional definitions, doubted their usefulness if they avoided any reference to transcendence, which was of the very essence of religion; an understanding of religion from within was necessary. To this Grossman (1975) replied that such fears of secularized definitions were unfounded, and functional definitions were essential for any empirical study. Nevertheless, the complexity of the problem becomes clear if the differences are considered between those for whom religion is a thoughtful commitment and those for whom it is an extreme, fanatical response. Both may hold the same beliefs and engage in the same religious practices, yet these affect their lives in quite different ways. It is evident that these are not extremes on a single continuum called "religion," but, rather, religion involves more than one element, however it may be defined. There is a great difference between religious systems that give only broad moral guidelines and those that are prescriptive, with detailed moral codes for all particular activities. Beliefs can profoundly affect individual and social attitudes, and what is perennial has to be distinguished from culturally conditioned changes in the structure of the church and society. It is essential that factual and theoretical assumptions should be critically examined, clarified, and stated explicitly. McCready and Greeley (1976) were unwilling to limit religion to religious rites or beliefs but regarded functional definitions as often arbitrary in deciding what were ultimate concerns. They described five stances toward ultimate values as religious optimism, hopeful, secular optimism, pessimism, and diffusion.

There is also a large area of nontraditional religion defined in a variety of ways —the religion of those who answer "none" when questioned about their religion (Vernon, 1968), the religion of those who hold some form of belief in God but never engage in any form of religious activity except perhaps for weddings and funerals, as well as the religion of the house-group movement largely separated from the mainstream churches and sects, as discussed by Towler and Chamberlain (1973) or Hornsby-Smith, Lee, and Reilly (1985). Lemert (1975) reviewed the ethical stances of such quasi-religious individuals, noting their transcendental overtones. He preferred to use "cosmization" for the cosmic idea by which the content of religion was formed and made a case that religion was found whenever meaning was framed in terms of the general order of existence. There are radical differences regarding religion in both outlook and methods of studying it and confusion between religion, creeds, and the church. Ploch (1987) wanted religion to be seen as a way of being in the world.

Sociologists have tended to use two distinct approaches to religion; one tradition, following Durkheim, stresses the function of religion in producing social integration and is inclined to define religion in terms of the transcendent; the other, following Weber, regards religion as a cultural system, an interpretive scheme offering explanation and meaning for society and individuals and tends not to expect the demise of traditional religious systems. McCready and Greeley (1976) described four research models in current sociology of religion—a secularization model concerned with the decline in religious observance, a social class model regarding religion as cultural behavior, a church sect model dominated by religious organizational structures, and a Protestant ethic model relating need achievements to Protestant church affiliation, which was now becoming outdated by full acceptance of Catholics in society. Gannon (1972) argued that despite the sophisticated methods of contemporary research, the implications of religion in present-day society remained obscure. The products of elaborate statistical analysis of data from religious questionnaires and tests often gave a false assurance about the nature of the concepts they claimed to measure. A so-called measure of religiousness might only measure a feeling of security about the divine.

Studies of religion have usually been made in terms of traditional religious beliefs, behavior, and attitudes. One area has been concerned with an apparent decline in adolescent religiousness, with the questioning of many beliefs and the partial or complete abandonment of the church. In the light of these issues the question often needs to be asked whether such observations may not rather point to a change in religiousness, away from the traditional toward newer stances. Both interpretations are possible according to the definition of religion.

Appendix B

Problems in the Measurement of Religion

For a long time measurments about religion have been made from questionnaires with numerical values given to responses to their items. Yet such categories do not have a precise mathematical relationship. For example, when in an item scores of 1 to 5 are given to responses for "disagree strongly," "disagree," "don't know," "agree," and "agree strongly" it does not follow that there is the same semantic difference between each of the categories. The difference in strength of feeling between those who strongly agree and those who agree may be much greater than between those who agree and those who don't know, and it may vary between item and item. Nor should it be accepted that "don't know" represents the same neutral position for every item in a scale. Adolescents with a positive attitude to their church could still respond "not certain" to the item "My church is the best influence in my life," as did those with a negative attitude to the item "Church services always bore me, and are difficult to follow" (Hyde, 1965).

The effect of different influences on religiousness is often examined by using correlation techniques, which measure the extent to which the different variables are associated. One problem is that there is no way of deciding which is the cause and which the effect, or whether both are due to some other external variable. Height and reading ability in a group of school children would show a strong association of high statistical significance. In such an instance, there can be no doubt that the variables are independent of each other, although both are dependent on children's age. It is also true that in any test program, the larger the sample, the smaller is the difference needed between results for them to be statistically significant. Kish (1978) complained that too much attention was paid to results from tests of significance, and too little to the magnitude of the effects in the case being investigated. The sum of the effects of all variables, whether measured or not, is called the variance of the sample. The results of correlation analysis alone do not clearly point to how much of this is due to other variables not included in the tests.

Vegelius and Bäckström (1981) discussed the correlation issue, indicating a little used statistical solution, which did not use correlation techniques. Cohen (1968) demonstrated the value of multiple regression as a general system for the analysis of data of this nature. The problem of isolating the effect of one of many variables operating in a classroom situation is a common one. School policies, resources, organization and management need to be considered, as do teacher characteristics, teaching styles, teacher-student interaction and classroom organization. Pupils differ in their motivation and learning strategies, their socio-economic status, sex, and race, apart from their overall ability. The literature concerned with these varied levels of interaction has recently been summarized by Raudenbush and Bryk (1989) in their account of multilevel statistical techniques available to analyze the effects of schools and classrooms on student learning. The use of hierarchical linear model analysis is a highly technical area which cannot be pursued here. But the fact remains that frequently statistical methods have been used which are not suitable for the data investigated, and this can undermine confidence in the results secured.

An extension of correlation techniques is factor analysis. Gorsuch (1984) remarked that it was not a widely accepted psychological method except in the study of intelligence. Its use in religious research indicated a broad construct of general religiousness which could be subdivided into a set of more specific factors. Yeatts and Asher (1982) stressed the need for care when factor analysis was applied to religious variables; adequate sampling required at least one-hundred subjects, with greater numbers for more complex analysis and sufficient items in the test to guarantee reliability. When information was secured only from questionnaires returned out of a larger group, it should be recognized that the sample was self-selective and not typical. Roof (1979) drew attention to the limitations of factor analysis, which is sensitive both to the population examined and to the number and composition of items included in the analysis. Further, there were alternative methods for exploring the factors, and varying degrees of statistical rigor were used in making judgments, so that the results of any given analysis needed to be scrutinized carefully to establish the degree that one research study could be compared to another. He pointed out that researchers have come to be more and more concerned about how captive their findings and interpretations are to the methods they employ.

Warren (1970) was very critical of some aspects of experimental design, in particular the absence of proper random sampling in many studies. He also noted the radical changes of religiousness observed when a student group was followed for a further period; these showed that information from student surveys should not be generalized for an adult population. He was critical of the use of volunteers drawn from churches or colleges, since sampling bias was inherent in such groups. Frequently there was an absence of information regarding extraneous variables which should be controlled, and, while statistical analysis frequently resorted to correlation and factor analysis techniques, more sophisticated use of variance analysis in carefully designed experiments was rare. Yet, despite such weakness, there was often an over-enthusiastic generalization of findings, so that a study of a particular group of students was soon generalized and applied first to all students and then to the whole population. These warnings are applicable to many studies of children and adolescents.

Great caution is needed before accepting generalizations made from the results of a single study based on a small sample of children, groups, or schools. A few schools in one area of the country are in no way a random sample; it needs a much larger random sample to be representative and achieve results in which significant differences can be confidently generalized, as reference to Hinkle and Oliver's (1983) discussion shows. Tables of the size of sample needed to secure the required level of confidence can be found in such textbooks as Lin (1976); for the number of primary and secondary schools in England and Wales, a random sample of about 350 is needed if generalizations based on the results are to be reliable. A simple illustration of the wide differences that can be found between schools is seen in the mean scores for attitude to religion Alatopoulous (1968) found in just six secondary schools, ranging from 57 to 88; in the mixed school where the boys' score of 57 was the lowest of all, the girls' score of 85 was almost the highest. Only Cox (1967) tested a random sample of one hundred schools independently selected. Even testing several thousand children is not adequate for valid generalizations unless it is a proper random sample fully representing all the variables likely to affect the issues being investigated. Large numbers of subjects should not disguise the fact that a sample, far from being large, really comprises only a small group of schools and cannot provide a reliable basis for generalizations. Generalizations are really predictions, and, while most research studies are concerned to show that significant differences have been secured in the areas studied, it is almost unknown for this to be used to predict the probable range of results when the project is repeated.

Proper experimental design is seldom met in religious research. Comparisons are too often made between groups that come readily to hand, without regard to the influences that remain concealed, such as differences in religiousness that are due to sex, age, denomination, socio-economic status, or to regional variations.

The plant breeder, concerned to compare the performance of two similar varieties, knows that many factors influence plant growth—rainfall, sunshine, temperature, the soil and its fertility are only the more obvious. For an adequate trial he needs to grow both species in many different conditions, and only a proper statistical design enables this to be done reliably, with the greatest efficiency for the least effort. Experimental design is dealt with in many textbooks of statistics. Religiousness is affected by many different variables, but because it is difficult to design experiments to overcome their influence unrecognized effects may produce unreliable results without it being at first apparent.

If results from the United States and Britain are compared, it is important to remember the considerable differences in religious affiliation and church attendance; religion is one of the greater cultural divides between the two countries. For example, church attendance is much greater in America, and Alston (1975) showed that according to which measure was used, between a quarter and a half of the population of the United States could be considered actively religious. (In Great Britain regular church attendance is less than 10 percent of the population). Catholics were always significantly more religious than Protestants, who were always significantly more religious than Jews; women were always more religious than men.

Hansford (1975) was concerned because empirical and phenomenological approaches to the psychology of religion appeared to be mutually exclusive, and a synoptic approach based on them both was desirable. Wuthnow (1979) pointed out that since 1970 research into religion using quantitative data and methods had been more responsive to broader concepts of religion, giving attention to ultimate concerns, questions of meaning and purpose, and to the idea of studying the different ways that individuals coped with these questions. He observed that there were new concepts of religion in the literature, such as "invisible religion," and "civil religion," and there had been a growth of nontraditional religious movements. (Civil religion is not the traditional religion of a church or denomination, but represents the transcendental communal religion of the nation, giving approval to the current social order. The term has also been used to embrace such things as folk religion, a form of democracy, or the potential of civic policy.) Vernon (1968) observed that little attention had been given to the people who gave negative responses to questions about their religion. Among them groups could be identified such as those who rejected membership of religious organizations but attended formal services and those who had experiences involving the supernatural but who offered humanistic explanations for them; the "nones" were ethical and moral, but they did not relate their morality to church teachings. These should be classified as religious alongside those affiliated with church groups. Vernon (1962) also identified another problem; people gave different answers to direct and indirect questions about the importance of religion, so that there was a marked difference between an individual's private religiousness and his public religiousness which required socially acceptable answers.

It must also be remembered that the questions asked in a survey may have the result—intentional or not—of soliciting the responses the inquirer wishes to receive. Martell (1972) commented on a number of surveys of parental opinions about religious education in English schools that to some extent they all seemed to prove what their authors wanted.

Another problem, pointed out by Godin (1962), is that when research is direct-ed toward religious education there is confusion as to how success is measured. Not only were adequate tests needed of cognitive aspects of religious learning and affective aspects of motivation, but also a firm agreement between psychological and theological perspectives about the issues involved. His own attempt (Godin and Coopez, 1957) to develop a series of pictures for a religious projection test was not followed by any subsequent published report of their use.

The tension between what can be measured and what defies measurement remains. Empirical findings shed much light on the development of religion in childhood, but some regard must be given to the warning of McFarland (1984) who thought that the scientific view currently pervading the psychology of religion was limited, preventing the personal and comparative approaches from assuming their proper complementary roles.

Appendix C

Dimensions of Religion

In making an appraisal of psychological studies of religion a knowledge of the dimensions and the orientations of religion is essential. Research in this area has usually employed groups of students and church members, and not representative samples. Because they seldom involved children or younger adolescents, the find-ings cannot be applied as if they came directly from children. However, the knowl-edge that religiousness has psychologically different aspects and orientations affects the critical interpretation of many results about them. The nature of the religion that has become established by the end of adolescence must have been developing earlier. The interaction of the cognitive and affective aspects of religion is often concealed in apparently simple test material in which different dimensions of religion can be confused and the religious orientation of the respondents over-looked. As will be seen, there is far from a constant and close relationship between them; religiousness does not depend directly on religious knowledge and may take different forms. As a school subject, cognitive aspects are prominent, whereas those concerned for the religious nurture of the young are primarily looking to affective responses. Religious knowledge is the end product of classroom teaching in English schools, whereas positive religious attitudes are the objective of the churches. Both are but a part of the total structure of religiousness.

The emergence of the concept

Different psychological aspects of religiousness have long been recognized. Clark (1968) described a rational aspect, typified by the stance of Allport, and an affective aspect, as exemplified by James. Earlier, he had described personal religion as being either optimistic or as being associated with suffering (Clark 1958). There are many phenomena which can be called religious, varying greatly from one culture to another, but few to be found in all manifestations of religion. Even within Christianity, to which most attention has been directed, there is great diversity. Is there one single underlying psychological factor, a limited number of factors which explain most of the diversity, or no recognizable unifying pattern which can be perceived? Attempts to establish a group of basic components are not new; Murray (1953) described five objectives of religious education as something to know, to feel, to choose, to do, and to belong to, objectives which were to become important in psychological studies which followed later.

An important landmark were the studies of Glock and Stark (1965), on which they based five religious dimensions—ideological, intellectual, ritualistic, experiential, and consequential, which proved to be a stimulus for many more studies, with great variations in the dimensions described.

English teachers of religious studies are familiar with the analysis of Smart (1969) which became an important element in the influential Schools' Council Working Paper on Religious Studies (1971). He described six dimensions of religion, similar to those of Glock and Stark, as ritual, mythological, doctrinal, ethical, social, and experiential, indicating that religion always included each of them. Later, he offered a definition of religion based on them (Smart, 1973). His analysis won widespread support; Capps (1974) for example, comparing theories of religion, observed that many problems could be resolved by a multidimensional theory, and he regarded Smart's six dimensions as applicable to virtually all current concerns. Smart's approach came from a logical analysis. Psychological studies on the other hand rely on the statistical analysis of empirical data secured from responses given by individuals to questionnaires or interviews, often using factor analysis. Inevitably, the structure revealed depends on the tests and on the subjects responding to them, and even small changes in the test, or its use with another group of subjects, can sometimes produce quite different results. It should be seen as an exploratory technique, and wide convergence of results over a broad area are needed to accept results with full confidence. Very many studies have been carried out, and in what follows only brief reference can be made to major findings. A parallel is found in the studies of the nature of intelligence; in both sets of studies there is disagreement as to whether there is a single, unitary factor underlying all others.

Dittes' (1969) thorough review of religious dimensions still remains the best available account of the work at the time and the underlying theory. He examined the debate as to whether religion was a discrete, unitary variable or an area of research within which various variables could be identified. He contrasted studies of religion from the outside, which tended to produce a single factor, with those that viewed religion from the inside and produced multiple factors. He concluded that in tests that included many topics, religion was seen by the general population as a highly visible institution and could be measured as a single factor. But when predominantly religious groups were asked more sophisticated questions, then the diversity and complexity of religion was revealed, and Glock and Stark's (1965) five dimensions were an important guideline. An important distinction was also required between conservatism, a religion of the superego with an emphasis on guilt and authority, and liberalism, a religion of the ego supporting broad personal and interpersonal values. Dittes (1971) again concluded that the arguments for a multidimensional understanding of religion were compelling, even though a single strong religious factor was often indicated in broadly based studies. This common factor was closely associated with affiliation to a church and acceptance of its norms.

How many dimensions?

Over the years, various tests have disclosed up to thirteen dimensions, and where more than one test shows the same number of dimensions they are by no means similar. Two dimensions were isolated by Lindsey, Sirotnik, and Heeren (1986); three dimensions by Brown (1966b), Hunt (1972), Brown and Forges (1980); four dimensions by Cardwell (1972), Hertel (1973), Himmelfarb (1975a); five dimensions by Weigert and Thomas (1969), Miller (1974), Finney (1978), Caird and Law (1982), Hilty and Stockman (1986); six dimensions by Crocket (1972), De Jong, Faulkner, and Warland (1976), Gronblom (1984); seven dimensions by O'Connell (1975), Hilty, Morgan, and Burns (1984), Cornwall, Albrecht, Cunningham, and Pitcher (1986); eight dimensions by Malony (1985); nine dimensions by King (1967, 1969); ten dimensions by Meadow (1976); eleven dimensions by Webb (1965), King and Hunt (1973); twelve dimensions by Cline and Richards (1965), and thirteen dimensions by King and Hunt (1975).

Webb (1965) related his eleven factors to needs for peace of mind, for reverence, for explanation, and for love. Cline and Richards (1965) found different structures for the sexes. Fichter (1969) argued that there were many dimensions of religiousness and that different combinations of them were useful for different studies. Of special use was his fourfold scale of creed, code, cult, and communion. King (1967, 1969) had identified nine dimensions, which Dittes (1969) regarded as the most thorough mapping of religious space then achieved. Subsequently, Hunt worked with King, who had proposed nine dimensions of religion (King, 1967); they first proposed eleven dimensions (King and Hunt, 1973), but after a series of joint studies (King and Hunt, 1975) their scale included thirteen dimensions with six basic scales similar to the dimensions suggested by Glock and Stark (1965). When Hilty, Morgan, and Burns (1984) used this scale the result was different—there were now seven dimensions, a result confirmed by Hilty and Morgan (1985); the seven scales were more parsimonious than those of King and Hunt (1973).

Any study using factor analysis on a wide range of items about an apparently simple concept is likely to show a number of factors, for example, Furnham (1985) found five factors in an analysis of people's attitudes toward saving money. The statistical independence of the factors depends ultimately on the mathematical basis of the analysis and the extent to which subjective decisions are made in their interpretation. Inevitably the factors found relate to the nature and scope of the questions used. Graham (1978) found a relationship between religiousness and blood pressure. Zimmerman (1977) showed that religious motivation was multidimensional; Finney (1978), that religious commitment showed five dimensions, and Wimberley (1978), close parallels between the structures of religious and political commitment. Fehr and Heintzelman (1977) showed that different tests of religiousness could not be used interchangeably; two different tests of religiousness gave two different personality profiles of their subjects.

There has been little discussion about the reliability of such measures of religiousness. Clayton (1968) found a high degree of reliability in Glock's scales, and Lewis and Gladding (1983) claimed good reliability for the Gladding, Lewis, Adkins scale based on a retest of twenty-three high-school students after two years. But although the mean score of the groups was almost identical in the two tests, the two sets of responses gave an association which was barely significant, suggesting that within the group some members had changed their position in the interval.

Classifying dimensions

When these various dimensions are listed, it is evident that many of them represent particular aspects of one or other of the five basic dimensions of Glock and Stark (1965).

In some studies dimensions appear to represent distinctions in the formulation of beliefs, as with Filsinger, Faulkner, and Warland (1979) who applied them to seven types of believers—outsiders, rejectors, conservatives, modern religion, marginally religious, orthodoxy religious, and culturally religious. Miller (1974) indicated five unrelated belief factors—Judeo-Christian, astrology, lack of formalized religion, personal theistic religion, and Eastern religions. Meadow (1976) found ten dimensions associated with belief—Christian God, truth-seeker, church traditionalism, deterministic fatalism, sacred monism, stoic will, human goodness, sick soul, authoritarian control, and moral autonomy.

One or more belief-type dimensions appear in most of the studies. Usually the description appears to indicate either a traditional or a conservative form of belief—personal faith (Hilty, Morgan, and Burns, 1984), belief (De Jong, Faulkner, and Warland, 1976; Gronblom, 1984), traditional religion (Broughton, 1975), religious belief (Cardwell 1972), orthodoxy (Hilty, Morgan, and Burns, 1984; and O'Connell, 1975), doctrinal (Himmelfarb, 1975a, b), conservative-liberal beliefs (Crockett, 1972), fundamentalist-humanist (Broen, 1957). Other belief-type dimension are man as agent or object of redemption (Crockett, 1972) and cognitive sophistication (Broughton, 1975).

Religious practices are similarly variously described—religious participation (De Jong, Faulkner, and Warland, 1976), church involvement (Hilty, Morgan, and Burns, 1984), religious affiliation (Himmelfarb, 1975a, b), religious activity (Gronblom, 1984), communal participation (O'Connell, 1975), and ritualism (Cardwell, 1972).

Religious feelings underlie another group of recorded dimensions—religious experience (De Jong, Faulkner, and Warland, 1976; Gronblom, 1984), devotionalism (O'Connell, 1975), devotional, experiential, affectional (Himmelfarb, 1975a), communion, nearness to God (Broen, 1957), dependence on or independence of God, open or resistant to social change, certainty or uncertainty of belief (Crockett, 1972), God experienced personally versus vague impersonal relationship (Broughton, 1975), intolerance of ambiguity (Hilty, Morgan, and Burns 1984), attitude to church authority (O'Connell, 1975), comfort as a motive for religiousness (O'Connell, 1975), religious opinions about morality and institutional religiousness (Gronblom, 1984), and a compassionate factor (Cline and Richards, 1965).

Religious knowledge is less easy to distinguish from belief, but some of the dimensions clearly belong to this cognitive group—religious knowledge (De Jong, Faulkner, and Warland, 1976; Gronblom, 1984), knowledge of religious history (Hilty, Morgan, and Burns, 1984), ideological (Himmelfarb, 1975a, b).

The effects of religiousness again broadly contain a number of dimensions—religious effects (Cardwell, 1972), social consequences (De Jong, Faulkner, and Warland 1976; O'Connell, 1975), social conscience (Hilty, Morgan, and Burns, 1984), ethical and moral (Himmelfarb, 1975a), individual moral consequences (De Jong, Faulkner, and Warland 1976), life purpose (Hilty, Morgan, and Burns 1984), and sexual morality (O'Connell, 1975).

Varieties of dimensions

Other features emerged from the studies. Hunt's (1972) scales allowed a literal position which accepted religious statements at their face value, an antiliteral position which rejected a literal interpretation of religion, and a mythological position in which religious statements were interpreted symbolically; this distinction was necessary for a true understanding of religious commitment. Orlowski (1979) supported Hunt's distinction, based on his use of these tests and other scales.

Nudelman (1971) demonstrated a common devotion among Catholics, Protestants, and Christian Scientists. Such large denominational differences were recorded by Cardwell (1972) that despite common features, the structure of religious commitment seemed problematic. Even Catholic students in a liberal arts college and in a seminary showed marked differences (Burger and Allen, 1973). This could be due to differences associated with conservative or liberal religious ideas, as Crockett (1972) found when he explored the distinctions, finding that more than one factor was involved in distinguishing between them. Broen (1957) had found a fundamentalist-humanist continuum, ranging from man as sinful to man as having the potentiality of goodness, with significant denominational differences. In a sociological study Putney and Middleton (1961a) showed three types of respondents—believers, conservatives with high orthodoxy and missionary zeal, and skeptics who were more ambivalent about belief. Davidson (1975), by imposing a liberal-conservative dichotomy on Glock and Stark's five dimensions, showed that the ideological and intellectual dimensions contained some negatively related elements, the ritualistic and experiential dimensions contained associated but distinct elements and the consequential dimension separate but unrelated elements. Ritzema (1979), using Hunt and King's scales, found that the tendency to invoke supernatural explanations of events was associated with the measures of belief and practice. Fullerton and Hunsberger (1982) found that Christian orthodoxy was unidimensional, but when their study was repeated with a group of university students by Lindsey, Sirotnik, and Heeren (1986) they found it measured two dimensions, one of traditional orthodoxy, the second a rationalized form of modern religious orthodoxy. They saw this as evidence for a widespread development of a liberal, neo-orthodox belief. Hunsberger (1987) questioned this result, based on a single sample, unlike the original study, but they defended their procedures and reasserted the finding of two dimensions.

Gibbs, Mueller, and Wood (1973) found the relationship between the creedal and consequential dimensions was only significant when belief was strongly held. Cornwall, Albrecht, Cunningham, and Pitcher (1986) argued that belief, commitment, and behavior, functioning personally and institutionally, should give six dimensions, but their Mormon sample gave seven dimensions—traditional orthodoxy, Mormon beliefs, spiritual commitment, church commitment, religious behavior, Christian behavior, and home religious belief. The emergence of Christian behavior was regarded as important—it had to do with being a Christian in all aspects of life. In Finland and Denmark, Gronblom (1984) identified six dimensions, distinguishing different styles of religiousness. Another indication of the necessity of distinguishing the dimensional character of religion was provided by Cygnar, Jacobson, and Noel (1977), using scales which distinguished eight dimensions of religion and four dimensions of prejudice. The ritual and orthodoxy scales gave no association with any of the prejudice dimensions, but the religious dimensions of consequence, fanaticism and importance were significantly associated with them all. O'Connell (1975) found a negative association between individual consequences and social consequences, indicating a difference between social ethics and personal morality. Faulkner and De Jong (1966) found that the consequential dimension was less strongly associated with other dimensions and seemed to be different in kind from them.

To avoid ideas limited by institutional Christianity, Brown and Forges (1980) secured the basic religious concepts and characteristics of psychology students. These, when evaluated by the same group, showed three main factors, an institutional versus individual religious factor; a positive, humane, and unorthodox versus a negative, punitive, and orthodox factor; and a tangible, known versus an intangible, unknown factor. The result proved to be similar to that secured by Muthén, Olsson, Pettersson, and Stahlberg (1977) and earlier by Brown (1965a). An Australian study of nonconventional beliefs (Caird and Law, 1982) established a structure of belief quite different from traditional beliefs, Eastern (e.g., Buddhist, Hindu), theosophical, spiritualistic, an alternative lifestyle, and interest in psychic development.

Yinger (1970) produced material to demonstrate his functional approach related to a nondoctrinal religion without external religious indicators but concerned with ultimate questions. Machalek and Martin (1976) extended this and showed that the perception of life's ultimate concerns and strategies for coping with them were not limited to institutional religion. Roof et al., (1977) concluded that this nondoctrinal religion lacked internal consistency. It did not form a unitary scale but was also multidimensional. Chao (1980) replicated Yinger's study in Taiwan with groups of Japanese, Korean, Thai, New Zealand, and Australian students. Most were concerned about questions of meaning, suffering and injustice but felt that people could cope with these by their beliefs. The students' attitudes were similar despite differences in background. Brown (1981a) used Yinger's material with Australian students; his results suggested that many items related to political rather than to religious ideologies and were not strongly associated with conventional Christian items. In Canadian studies, Stack (1983) showed that any increase in invisible religion had not been sufficient to offset the decrease in traditional religion, and Bibby (1983) identified themes which might characterize meaning systems. He found that while some people developed these on the basis of unconventional ideas, there were many who had no such system at all but selected religious practices as they required them, as for the rites of passage. For such people religion was not unimportant, but it was only used when needed. This usage, and the result that many people claimed some sort of religious affiliation, indicated the difficulty in establishing identifiable invisible religions. Godin (1985) reviewed a number of studies describing functional religion; it filled voids, calmed fears, gratified wishes, reinforced beliefs, and at the same time strengthened group cohesion. It responded to culturally conditioned attitudes, conscious or unconscious.

One or many dimensions?

Is there a case for regarding religion as having a single dimension? Marvell (1976) argued on a theological basis that Smart's experiential dimension originated in revelation. It was the central feature of religion integral to all his other dimensions, and response to it had more in common with a sociological analysis of religion. Mueller (1980) contended that faith, related to the transcendental, was the sole religious dimension. Doctrine was only an aspect of it that had been modified by logic. Ritual was due to general aesthetic responses arising from education, and religion was a cultural system which followed its own rationale, e.g., there were two fundamentally different concepts of faith, one transcending the finite and liberating the believer from worry, the other binding and appropriating the believer through its requirements of unconditional commitment.

Fukuyama (1961) had concluded from his study of dimensions that religion could mean quite different things to different people and Kuhre (1971) demonstrated that different people expressed their religiousness in significantly different ways. There were bound to be inconsistencies between studies using different measures of religiousness. Filsinger, Faulkner, and Warland (1979) argued that individuals were religious in different ways, and each had a unique combination of high or low values on a range of religious variables; experimentally, seven types of religiousness were observed. Terry (1983) showed that psychology students and student Christian fellowship members differed on every religious measure used, so that the dimensions of the psychology group were very different from those of the believers. Hilty (1988) also contended that religion was multidimensional, on the basis of his testing Mennonites, Presbyterians, and Catholics.

Brown (1962) first considered that religious belief constituted a single dimension unrelated to a number of personality traits, and it behaved as an independent cognitive system requiring strong social support for its maintenance. Subsequently (Brown 1965a), he proposed three types of religious orientation—a single intrinsic-extrinsic dimension, a second concerned with institutionalism and individualism and the manner of accepting beliefs, and the third a belief-disbelief continuum. He thought that other dimensions might also be necessary. When his earlier test was repeated (Brown, 1966b) the number of personality scales used was increased, but again religious belief emerged as a single factor. Wearing and Brown (1972) found that a single religious score sufficed when their sample was heterogeneous, but with a homogeneously religious sample a number of religious factors were found. However, Clayton and Gladden (1973) subsequently found that a first ideological factor accounted for almost all effects and concluded that religion was not multidimensional. Ludwig and Blank (1969) considered that the multidimensional nature of religion was well-established and argued that faith should be understood as a perceptual set—a way of looking at things and responding in terms of an interpretation which pervaded many levels of behavior.

Poythress (1975) reported that underlying Glock's five dimensions was a single general religious factor. He continued to study Hunt's orientations and confirmed that nonliteral, proreligious people might be wrongly classified by traditional measures of religiousness. Weigert and Thomas (1969) compared Faulkner and De Jong's (1966) scale of five religious dimensions with those of Glock and Stark (1965) and Stark and Glock (1968), complaining that semantically similar structures were mixed up, a criticism that produced in the same journal issue a strong rejoinder. Clayton (1970) subjected the scale to scalogram analysis; the minimum criteria were met, suggesting that religiousness was more than a composite abstract concept but could be empirically unidimensional.

De Jong, Faulkner, and Warland (1976) found strikingly similar results among German and American students and identified six dimensions similar to those both of Glock and of Smart. Religious knowledge and social consequences proved to be quite separate dimensions, but the remainder, especially beliefs, religious experience, and religious practice represented a second-order general religious factor. They argued that it was not illogical to secure a result that was both unidimensional and multidimensional, since they represented different levels of abstraction. When religiousness was being investigated as one of a number of distinct variables, it was advantageous to regard it in a generalized manner; however, in theoretical studies or those concerned with cognitive, affective, or behavioral phenomena, more specific measures of religiousness were appropriate. They regarded the social consequences dimension, not as integral to religiousness, but rather as the result of it and noted that religious knowledge varied greatly in different cultural contexts. Their study was repeated by Hilty and Stockman (1986), who found a high degree of fit among adults for five dimensions of belief, experience, individual moral consequences, religious knowledge, and social consequences. The complementary nature of unidimensional and multidimensional theories is an important suggestion about an understanding of their practical use.

Dimensions in many faiths

The psychological complexity of religion so far disclosed is not restricted to Christianity; Hertel's (1973) study of religion in South India demonstrated that Sanskritization was also multidimensional, with dimensions related to worldview, worship practices, and attitudes toward low castes and toward women. As in the West, those of lower caste and poorly educated were less active in worship but held fatalistic or supernatural worldviews suggesting that differences in social status were as important in accounting for variations in religious expression as cultural differences. Miller (1974) found five major dimensions over a wide range of religions. Himmelfarb's (1975a) Jewish data indicated that religious involvement was much more associated with the behavioral than the ideational. It had four general orientations—supernatural, communal, cultural, and interpersonal.

Dimensions in childhood

Religious development in childhood and adolescence covers the time when traditional beliefs are learned and individual beliefs formulated, individual and group religious practices and rituals meaningfully established, feelings such as awareness, trust, and awe developed, relevant religious knowledge acquired, and the individual and social effects of religious commitment worked out. In each of these five areas there are many legitimate differences; they are only partially dependent on each other, if at all. It does not follow that if some children at a relatively young age are found to be capable of genuine religious experience they must also have overcome cognitive limitations in their theological understanding, nor that because such experience is possible, there is no need to consider the maturity of their religious thinking.

Appendix D

Religious Orientations

Another important distinction is that of religious orientation—the way in which an individual is religious. The distinction is important for understanding adolescent religiousness, but the studies have again used samples mainly of students and church members, so the results need to be projected backwards; the orientations begin to develop in childhood and become established in adolescence.

Argyle (1958), discussing measures of religiousness, noted the problems arising when using church membership or church attendance, since these did not necessarily relate to other religious activities, e.g., private prayer or belief. People might only observe an outward form of religion to keep up appearances or to avoid distress to relatives. Important differences in religious style first became evident when attention was turned to the relation between religiousness and racial prejudice. Monaghan (1967) had observed that the religious orientations of members of a fundamentalist church showed different stances—the authority seeker who wanted the church so as to be told what to do; the comfort seeker who looked to the church to reduce fears of death, illness, and age; and the social participant who found in the church a social home.

The study of the authoritarian personality by Adorno et al. (1950) had indicated that authoritarian and racially prejudiced people showed a high incidence of a "neutralized" religion, which preserved its doctrines in a rigid and haphazard manner and was used for self-centered aims to gain practical advantages or to help manipulate other people. Authoritarianism and ethnocentrism were found to be higher among church attenders. Investigation then revealed that extrinsic values were always associated with antisemitism (Wilson, 1960); more frequent church attenders showed less social compassion and were preoccupied with their own souls' salvation, while their other-worldly orientation and indifference to the social system implied endorsement of inequality and injustice (Rokeach, 1970). A similar association of racial prejudice and religion was found to exist in England and Holland, although there were significant sub-groups strongly committed to church values and to racial tolerance (Bayley, 1970).

Allport (1950) had described mature and immature religion. He was concerned that church-goers harbored racial, ethnic, and religious prejudice and came to distinguish two types, the extrinsic who used religion and the intrinsic who lived it in personal and individualistic terms and by regular church attendance. Intrinsically motivated churchgoers were significantly less prejudiced. Religion did not instill prejudice, but some prejudiced people also needed to be religious (Allport, 1966). Further study followed, e.g., Vanecko (1966). Allport and Ross (1967) took as intrinsic subjects those who not only agreed with intrinsic items on their scale but disagreed with extrinsic items, and similarly defined extrinsic subjects. From the remainder they isolated a group they called indiscriminately proreligious, and found that their indiscriminateness tended to relate directly to their prejudice, so that "religious muddle-headedness" was related to antagonism toward ethnic groups. Thus, it emerged that while intrinsically motivated church-goers were significantly less prejudiced than the extrinsically motivated, those who were indiscriminately proreligious were more prejudiced than the consistently extrinsic. The authors regarded it of great importance that measures of religiousness should be defined in such a way as to distinguish between these three different attitudes. They also noted that in a number of situations people with more extreme religious or antireligious measurements behaved in a very different manner from those less extreme. (This type of relationship is not infrequent in studies of religiousness and may lurk unsuspected in many studies.)

A similar approach was made by Allen and Spilka (1967), who distinguished between consensual and committed religion and defined them in terms reminiscent of Allport's mature and immature religion. They found a clear distinction between the two groups but only in respect of the prejudice associated with consensual religion and its absence from those with committed religion. Because the scoring of the test was difficult, an instrument was developed simpler to score but which incorporated some items from the Allport and Ross scale. These scales were comparable to some extent, whereas their original scale showed little relationship to extrinsic and intrinsic religion, which has precluded its wider use and its nomenclature. Committed and consensual are terms clearly defined, whereas a problem with intrinsic and extrinsic is that their definition lacks precision and descriptions of them vary. Hood (1971) showed that the two orientations were distinct and did not combine to give a single unidimensional scale. Hunt and King (1971) asserted that there was more than a single, bi-polar, intrinsic-extrinsic orientation, and they were not opposites. Amon and Yela (1968) identified two extrinsic orientations, one concerned with economic and social power and the other as a style of living. Since then it has come to be widely accepted that the two orientations are different, so that to some degree both orientations are found in all manifestations of religiousness. The terms have not been abandoned but have become the subject of many more studies, and it has been shown that both of them are associated with particular personality traits. Dittes (1969) provided a valuable review of the earlier studies, regarding them as contrasting an explicit and differentiated religion with a subjective and diffused one, as old as the distinction of the Old Testament prophets between the outward forms of worship and sacrifice and the inner commitment to righteousness and love of God. For research purposes institutional religion is much easier to assess.

Hoge (1972) followed suggestions that more specific definitions of religious orientation were needed and developed a scale to measure ultimate versus instrumental religion, the Intrinsic Religious Motivation Scale. Gorsuch and McFarland (1972) concluded that single-item scales, such as a simple Christological confession of the rated importance of religion, were good measures of an intrinsic proreligious position. Often single-item scales were useful when only a few items about religion could be included in a study. When some measure of traditional orthodoxy was required, then a multiple-item scale was a better measure. Weddell (1972) questioned the usefulness of the religious orientation measure among members of nontraditional religious groups when, unlike Baptists, Unitarians proved to be more extrinsic but less dogmatic and less prejudiced. McConahay and Hough (1973) found that intrinsic and extrinsic orientations were not related to love and guilt-oriented dimensions of Christian belief and concluded that the theological content of belief was an important factor in its measurement. Knight and Sedlacek (1981a) stated that the scales had only a limited use with non-Christian groups, and the disagreement of Jewish students with items on the intrinsic scale reflected a Christian bias in it. It has not been established whether personality traits produce a religious orientation, or whether religiousness affects personality, or indeed, whether both are the result of some other extraneous influence (Wiebe and Fleck, 1980). Gorsuch and Venable (1983) developed an age-universal, intrinsic-extrinsic scale that, with no loss of quality, could be used with children from the age of nine. Despite its promise, there appears to be no record of its use.

In the many studies about these orientations, a range of characteristics associated with each of them have been described. The extrinsic orientation is a selfish, instrumental approach to religion (Hunt and King, 1971) but lacked precise definition and could be the product of more general personality variables. Extrinsically oriented people tend to be prejudiced (Ponton and Gorsuch, 1988) or prejudiced and authoritarian (Meyer, 1974; Kahoe, 1974), and associated with theological conservatism (Donahue, 1985a). They often come from families lacking in personal warmth and have little desire for independence and freedom (Tisdale, 1967). They tend to be suspicious, evasive of responsibility, low in self-confidence, competitive, and assertive (Hamby, 1973; Kahoe 1974). They carry their narrow, self-seeking attitude to religion into their interpersonal relations (Dicker, 1975), although they have a small inverse association with assertiveness (Kraft, Litwin, and Barber, 1986). They display greater self-indulgence, indolence, and undeveloped ability but are also more flexible, self-reliant, skeptical, pragmatic, and more innovative, analytical, and less rigid (Wiebe and Fleck, 1980). They show little deviant behavior and are characterized by patience, humility, and nonerotic personal relationships, since they emulate a puritanical stereotype (Tisdale, 1967) and also are associated with concepts of success and achievement (Spilka, 1977). Extrinsically oriented subjects are more likely to be intellectually, emotionally, and spiritually restricted or conforming to less favorable psychological attitudes (Spilka and Mullin, 1976). Proportionally more of them believe in spiritual forces outside the individual, although not affirming traditional concepts (Hood, 1978a), and are less rational than those intrinsically oriented (Baither and Salzberg, 1978). They tend to have inaccurate self-perceptions that affect their behavior to other people and God (Spilka, 1976). They contemplate death in terms of loneliness, pain, of forsaking dependents, and as a natural end (Hood and Morris, 1983). They are associated with open-mindedness more than any other orientation (Thompson, 1974). Extrinsically oriented children were more interested in social aspects of religion rather than religious knowledge (Johnson, 1973, 1974). Popular devotional books emphasize such values as an ability to make personal decisions, attain success, gain wealth, and achieve security, which are attitudes consistent with an extrinsic orientation (Hoge, 1976).

The intrinsic orientation displays a very different profile; intrinsically oriented people are not associated with prejudice (Ponton and Gorsuch, 1988) or authoritarianism (Strickland and Shaffer, 1971; Kahoe, 1974), but with the socially desirable traits of responsibility and internal locus of control (Kahoe, 1974) and are inversely related to narcissism and high scoring on self-actualization (Watson, Hood, and Morris, 1984) and positive self-esteem (Watson, Morris, and Hood, 1987). They hold a more positive view of human nature and are more trustworthy of others (Maddock and Kenny, 1972) and have a greater concern for moral standards, discipline, conscientiousness, responsibility, and consistency, but they also reflect more conservative and traditional attitudes which, despite their positive features, could degenerate into rigidity (Wiebe and Fleck, 1980). They treat people as ends and not as means (Dicker, 1975); they tend to be trusting, holding positive concepts about themselves and others, intelligent and insightful, accepting responsibility, concerned with relationships, socially conformist, controlling their impulses, and are the most mature (Hamby, 1973). They are tolerant, less prejudiced, nonfundamentalist and theologically discriminating (Gorsuch and Aleshire, 1974). Their religion is that of a complete person who has internalized views of self, others, and God in line with classical theological thinking regarding the goals of the spiritual life; they possess stronger and more positive views of God, higher self-esteem, and a greater nearness to others (Spilka and Mullin, 1976). Their favorable psychological orientations toward the self (Daniel, 1980) are negatively associated with some aspects of narcissism (Watson, Hood, and Hall, 1987). They have a purposeful plan for life (Spilka, 1976; Soderstrom and Wright, 1977) and are associated with positive mental health (Entner, 1976; Donahue, 1985b) and with more positive attitudes to death and an afterlife (Spilka, Minton, Sizemore, and Stout, 1977; Hood and Morris, 1983). They include older, politically conservative, well-educated church leaders (Meyer, 1974). The orientation is not affected by age, sex, earlier nurture, or the lack of it (Daniel, 1980). Nor is its strength related to age in adolescents (Venable, 1984). They are more traditional than the extrinsically oriented, (Knight and Sedlacek, 1981b) and tend to be more observant of the moral teachings of their denominations (Ernsberger and Manaster, 1981). They have a compelling sense of helpfulness, giving it when it was not wanted, because it sprang from their own need to appear to be helpful rather than from true altruism (Batson and Gray, 1981). Intrinsically oriented children had better religious knowledge and understanding (Johnson, 1973, 1974).

The profiles suggest the greatest possible contrast between the two styles of religiousness, but while it may not be difficult to call to mind particular individuals who appear to be typical of one or the other, common observation suggests that the majority of religious people do not fall into either category. It must be remembered that in the research studies these characteristics were observed as trends, and in most instances the trend would not be large, indicating a slight though statistically significant association. The somewhat stark dichotomy is a good example of the need to look for the magnitude of an effect, even when it has been shown to be significant and indicates the danger of exaggerating results.

Nor may the dichotomy be as absolute as it appears. There was no difference in racial prejudice between two groups of students who showed marked differences on scales of religiousness, which suggested that religiousness and prejudice were independent (Boivin, Darling, and Darling, 1987). In Venezuela, nationality and not religiousness was the factor most strongly associated with prejudice (Ponton and Gorsuch, 1988). While extrinsically oriented students displayed racial prejudice, unlike those intrinsically oriented, the latter proved to be more prejudiced against homosexuals, so that in reality they were not free from prejudice but had accepted religious teaching which made them more tolerant of certain specific groups. Attitudes to other groups seemed to serve different psychological functions in the two orientations (Herek, 1987). Adventist church members on the Caribbean island of St. Croix were tested for prejudice against Rastafarians—an attitude that was not socially undesirable there. The intrinsic group were prejudiced more than the general population but not the extrinsic or quest group. This suggested that the relationship between religion and prejudice was not simple but depended on particular religious and social norms and that intrinsicness really represented an acceptance of the values of the group (Griffin, Gorsuch, and Davis, 1987). In a study of discrimination, McFarland (1989) found it was associated with the intrinsic orientation in women and the extrinsic orientation in men. Personally extrinsically orientated men had a general positive association with discrimination, and socially extrinsically orientated men had discriminating attitudes toward women and nondiscriminating attitudes to homosexual persons.

Since there is often opposition between the traits associated with the two orientations, it seen probable that they represent the personality traits of individuals who select elements of religion which sustain these attitudes. Kahoe (1985) considered that religious orientations were related to personality structures. The extrinsic orientation was associated with practical, careful, conventional, and proper traits and the intrinsic orientation with being tender minded, dependent, and sensitive in men, and with being conscientious and persevering in women, and in both sexes, with radicalism. Although they could be found simultaneously in a person, they were basically opposed. Morris and Hood (1981) compared work orientations with religious orientations; it was found that they were associated with each other in women but not in men. Wright (1972) observed that different

Christian traditions could support an "us-them" dichotomy—in which the saved, the baptized, the faithful, saw themselves as separate from the rest and sought to extend the separation to education, marriage, friendship, or even work. Authoritarian and dogmatic people can find religious hierarchies of status which appeal to them; religious conservatism and dogmatism find plenty of supporters. This topic is dealt with in chapter 10. In spite of the marked differences between these two stances, it is remarkable that relatively little attention has been paid to them in research about religious behavior, religious knowledge, religious experience, and other religious attitudes, and least of all in religious learning and religious education.

Meyer (1976) regarded religiousness as more complex than the intrinsic and extrinsic scales indicated and explored committed and nominal religious attitudes further, finding six clearly identified religious factors—general religion, closed-mindedness, situation religion, utilitarian nominalism, an anticlerical personal commitment factor, and true commitment. Hood (1978a) split the intrinsic and extrinsic scales at the median to create four categories—intrinsic, indiscriminately proreligious, extrinsic, and indiscriminately antireligious. The new categories represented inconsistent and conflicting stances which were commonly found, and the indiscriminately-anti category accounted for people who were ambivalent to religion but described themselves as not religious.

The indiscriminately proreligious and the indiscriminately antireligious groups differed significantly from each other and from the other orientations and were lacking in feelings of belonging and social competency (Bradford, 1978). Many of the indiscriminately antireligious professed belief in a personal God or a supreme being (Knight and Sedlacek, 1981b) and they tended to be trusting, conforming, cooperative, and conscientious, but bound by rules, lacking in self-confidence, and not given to an abstract approach to experience; they had not matured beyond levels of dependency. The nonreligious tended to be suspicious, autonomous, unconventional, aggressive, and competitive, acting on impulse and disregarding rules. Their lack of regard for responsibility to others and their self-centeredness implied a degree of alienation (Hamby, 1973). There was a great similarity of personality characteristics between extrinsic and nonreligiously oriented people, but both differed significantly from the intrinsically oriented (Wiebe and Fleck, 1980). Like the extrinsically oriented they displayed greater self-indulgence, indolence, and undeveloped ability but also were more flexible, self-reliant, skeptical, pragmatic, and more innovative, analytical, and less rigid (Wiebe and Fleck, 1980). Further examination indicated that those with the indiscriminate antireligious orientation were the most open-minded, more than those of the intrinsic and indiscriminately proreligious orientations (Thompson, 1974). However, like the intrinsics, they score highly on self-actualization (Watson, Hood, and Morris, 1984). Intrinsic and indiscriminately antireligious undergraduates had less prejudice than those who were extrinsic or intrinsically proreligious. Neither pair differed from each other, and the relationship was independent of sex and social desirability, even though it seemed that intrinsics were more socially desirable (Morris, Hood, and Watson, 1989).

A research team (Pargament et al., 1987) considered the problem of measuring the indiscriminate proreligious orientation, which hitherto had been done by calculating it from separate intrinsic and extrinsic scores. They devised and validated a new test for the purpose, which measured the orientation both individually and congregationally. It indicated great plausibility about religious material from religious people—thus, two-thirds of those tested agreed that "differences of opinion are always welcome in this church." The orientation was distinct from social desirability and appeared to be found most among members of strict churches. More research about it was needed. At the same time Kirkpatric (1986b) independently demonstrated by the use of factor analysis that the extrinsic scale had two major components, one of them personal and the other social. Both aspects of this orientation needed to be kept in mind when it was used. Donahue (1985a) noted that intrinsic and extrinsic orientations were associated with individuals' theological orientations, and the possibility of a curvilinear relationship should be considered, since this was not unusual in measures of religion. Dogmatism was not associated with either the intrinsic or the nonreligious orientation, but it was related to the extrinsic orientation and even more strongly to the indiscriminately proreligious orientation. While the intrinsic orientation was a good unidimensional nondoctrinal indicator, the extrinsic orientation was a mark of the sort of religion which gave it a bad name, prejudiced and dogmatic. There seemed to be three orientations, the intrinsic, the indiscriminately proreligious and the nonreligious. Gorsuch adn McPherson (1989) identified extrinsic items concerned with social relationships and with personal benefits.

Chalfant and Peek (1983) made a critical review of the methods and sampling used in these studies; investigations of racial prejudice seldom used representative samples, and other key variables, especially social status, were ignored. Their results, using independent representative samples, supported these reservations.

The nature of intrinsic and extrinsic religion was critically reviewed by Batson and Ventis (1982), who cited evidence that the intrinsic scale was also associated with some aspects of authoritarianism and orthodoxy and negatively with open-mindedness. They were not extremes of a single orientation but two independent dimensions, one which measured adherence to religion and the other the willingness to admit the personal and social gains it brought. They were certain that the intrinsic scale did not measure Allport's mature religion. Intrinsics, because of their need for social desirability rather than religious motivation, presented themselves as the reverse of prejudice or lacking in compassion, a conclusion based on an earlier study (Batson, Naifeh, and Pate, 1978). When the effect of social desirability was eliminated it was found that the negative association between racial prejudice and intrinsic religion was reduced, and it disappeared when measured by a behavioral test. Social preference was the active factor. However, a third orientation to religion, which the authors named "quest," still had a negative association with racial prejudice, even when social desirability was controlled.

They set out to demonstrate that "religion as a quest" was a third orientation (Batson and Ventis, 1982). They developed scales to measure specific aspects of extrinsic and intrinsic orientations, and a scale concerned with quest, the extent to which religion was concerned with an open-ended approach to existential questions. They called these three orientations means, end, and quest. In a subsequent study (Batson and Raynor-Prince, 1983) it was found that the quest orientation correlated positively with greater cognitive complexity in dealing with issues about existential concerns, whereas the intrinsic orientation did not. They noted that both the quest and the intrinsic orientations included characteristics of mature religion, but neither included all, so that the intrinsic orientation provided possibly more benefits, such as personal direction and peace of mind. However, Donahue (1985a) contended that Batson's means orientation proved to be almost identical with extrinsic religiousness, the end orientation was very similar to intrinsic religiousness, but quest did not relate to other measures of religiousness. Ponton and Gorsuch (1988), in a cross-cultural investigation of the association of prejudice with religion, used a Venezualian student sample; those with an extrinsic orientation were prejudiced but not those with an intrinsic or quest orientation.

Hood (1985) argued that Allport saw the intrinsic orientation as an indictor of religious purity, while Batson's quest orientation was based on a doubting aspect in Allport's concept of intrinsic faith. Doubting arose when an extrinsic orientation was abandoned in the hope of achieving an intrinsic orientation. Hood and Morris (1985) were critical of the quest orientation and its alleged superiority to the intrinsic, on purely conceptual grounds. Batson and Ventis (1985) rebutted this criticism, contending that the critics had failed to recognize that each of their three dimensions were simultaneously applicable to every individual. Hilty, Morgan, and Hartman (1985) undertook an extensive analysis of Batson's three orientations. Their results gave no clear answer, but while they did not overthrow Batson's paradigm, they indicated a preference for Allport's. Spilka, Kojetin, and McIntosh (1985) concluded that Batson had used samples with poorly defined religiousness. Individuals who were anxious and religious tended to have high quest scores, so quest measured religious conflict with anxiety. Despite Batson's assertion, quest was associated with social desirability, and also inversely with verbal originality and to some extent the intrinsic orientation, so it was not the case that quest was creative in a cognitive manner not true of the end, intrinsic orientation. Later, Kojetin, McIntosh, Bridges, and Spilka (1987) again found Batson's quest to be significantly associated with conflict and anxiety, although when the authors developed an alternative form of the test to give greater test reliability, the amended test behaved more as Batson had intended. It appeared that quest represented a form of intellectual deviance, associated with conflict and anxiety as well as intrinsic faith. Sapp and Jones (1986) found that quest, which assumed openness and flexibility, was associated with principled moral reasoning, requiring the same personal characteristics. The intrinsic orientation, which had more in conformity and orthodoxy, was not associated with this level of moral judgment. Sapp and Gladding (1989) confirmed the association of quest with levels of moral reasoning, showing that quest was a psychologically adaptive form of religion. Warren (1988) examined a number of personality traits and their association with religious orientations. Means and end were both associated with a dogmatic trait, but means had more conventional characteristics. End was associated with conservatism and acceptance of traditional beliefs, with a preference for structure, and displayed high religious salience and church attendance. Quest was associated with artistic characteristics and a more liberal outlook, and with a tendency to reject traditional beliefs.

Watson, Hood, and Morris (1985), in a study of religiousness and empathy with students, demonstrated that there was a direct relation between the end orientation and feelings of empathy and between the quest orientation and the cognitive perspectives associated with empathy; both were inversely related to the means orientation. Then Watson, Howard, Hood, and Morris (1988) looked at the association of intrinsic religiousness with conservatism. In an all-age sample quest was an intermediate form of religiousness found in late adolescence and early adulthood and seemed to be a precursor to an intrinsic commitment. Means also appeared to be an age-related orientation. Marron (1984) observed that Batson's quest orientation was significantly and inversely related to his internal and external measures. Donahue (1985a) was critical of its derivation from small student samples and its use of a complex scoring procedure and contended that Batson's understanding of intrinsic religion was faulty. Quest appeared never to be associated with any other measure of religiousness and seemed to be an agnosticism scale. Finney and Malony (1985) found that scores on a general measure of religiousness were positively associated with those on the end orientation but negatively with those of the means and quest orientations. It appeared that they were not three independent and unrelated dimensions but should be seen as typologies. Acklin (1984) found that the means and end orientations proved to be very similar to the extrinsic and intrinsic orientations, and quest was a matter of tentativeness rather than of maturity in religion. In general, religiousness was neither linear nor unidimensional but varied between individuals according to their particular situations. Walley (1984), using Batson's orientations, suggested that different orientations could be associated with different philosophies of life. Then an investigation into the independence of quest showed it to be an amalgamation of the means and end orientations (Watson, Morris, and Hood, 1989).

A further criticism is that the items on the scale of doctrinal orthodoxy which is part of the test instrument are all cast in terms of a conservative terminology, difficult to interpret by those with more sophisticated theologies, and it is hard to see how it can measure a broad theological spectrum. It is curious that nowhere do the authors mention the studies of religious dimensions which have indicated many aspects of belief—orthodox, conservative, liberal to name but a few. It would have been of no little interest to learn if there was any relationship between the belief structure and the religious orientation of particular individuals. Doctrinal, ideological, and intellectual dimensions cannot be unrelated. Similarly, the experiential dimension, with its affective content, could well have some associated with extrinsic and intrinsic orientations. This remains an area where as yet our knowledge is far from complete. It could be added that no account was available about the procedures used for the selection of items for the scales or of tests of their reliability.

A study of the helpful responses of undergraduates of known religiousness when presented with a "lady in distress" situation was undertaken by Annis (1976). Helpfulness was unrelated to church attendance, frequency of prayer, or literal belief in the Bible, a finding which the author claimed supported the contention that moral behavior developed independently of religious belief. Whether it was related to any of the religious orientations was not examined. In a similar study, Darley and Batson (1973), and later Batson (1976), studied student reactions to a confederate in distress. Those demonstrating the quest orientation showed a situational helping response; those with the end or intrinsic orientation also showed a helping response but less attuned to the expressed needs of the person seeking aid. Batson and Gray (1981) explored the idea that intrinsically oriented people might have a compelling sense of helpfulness, giving it when it was not wanted, because it sprang from their own need to appear to be helpful rather than from true altruism. They had already demonstrated that a sense of empathy led to an altruistic response rather than to the egoistically motivated help that was characteristic of some intrinsically oriented religious people. Marsh (1986) found in a group of theological students that prior training in helping only had a limited effect in a situation where the victim declined all offers of help; what was significant was the extent to which the victim's perception of concern was appreciated. However, Nelson and Dynes (1976) by an analysis of replies to questions about donations or service given for victims of an emergency on a regular basis showed that involvement in a religious organization was strongly associated with three of the four types of help described. Hunsberger and Platonow (1986) observed that religiously orthodox students were more likely to help religiously related charitable causes, but less religious students were just as likely to help nonreligious causes. The intrinsically religious were more likely to help than the extrinsically religious. Watson, Hood, Morris, and Hall (1984) demonstrated that empathy was a component of religiousness, intrinsic religiousness was directly related to it, and extrinsic religiousness was inversely related to it. The difference was not due to social desirability effects. The motivation of empathy was complex, with some dimensions of it reflecting a need to relieve the distress caused by the suffering of others for one's own satisfaction, but other dimensions related to a truly compassionate and unselfish desire to help victims. Wilson, Morris, Foster, and Hood (1986) undertook a series of studies concerned with the relationship between the end orientation and the social desirability scale but did not find any. Neither of the two scales were related to any psychological instability. Since the social desirability scale was confounded by religiousness, its use was inappropriate with measures of religiousness. Gorsuch (1988) in his review of studies of helpfulness commented that there was an implicit problem in defining what was socially desirable. There had been no change in data about it over a long period and across different regions, despite large shifts and regional differences in public opinion on some issues as to what was desirable. In a mostly Catholic student group, those with a high level of involvement in voluntary service displayed high intrinsic religiousness, and those who had applied for postgraduate voluntary service showed high quest and low extrinsic religious orientations. Altruism, often regarded as a religious value, was a function of religious orientation when it was expressed as helping behavior (Bernt, 1989).

Roof (1979) gave a valuable review of studies of religious commitment over twenty years, observing that increasingly it was agreed that religion was so complex that not only multiple dimensions, but also multiple approaches were needed for its analysis. He noted the development of "church-type" religious commitment in which Lenski (1961) had identified four dimensions made up of two types of religious group involvement, associational versus communal, and two types of religious orientation, doctrinal orthodoxy and devotionalism. Glock and Stark (1965) who suggested five religious dimensions, were elaborating earlier work in the field with other similar suggestions and their work had been carried a deal further, notably by King and Hunt (1975). Roof (1979) also observed that many other studies bore upon an individual's awareness of the permanent problem of human existence and tested this in deliberately nondoctrinal ways so that alternative systems for expressing meaning in life were found to be emerging. When considering the problems of measurement, he also noted that different aspects of religiousness were often confused in composite measures—the content, frequency, intensity, and centrality of religion to an individual. Gorsuch (1984) commented that while many scales were of a high quality, the dimensionality of religion remained a major problem, so that, for example, a single bifocal factor had not been found involving both intrinsic and extrinsic religion.

A recent critical review of intrinsic and extrinsic religiousness has been given by Donahue (1985a), based on an analysis of published studies, which concluded that intrinsic religiousness remained an excellent measure of religious commitment, as distinct from belief, and its nondoctrinal open-endedness enabled it to be used widely, even outside the Christian religion. Extrinsic religion, by its association with prejudice, dogmatism, anxiety, and fear of death, and its lack of association with altruism, was useful in measuring the sort of religion that gives religion a bad name. When the two variables were used together they provided a powerful instrument, whether the use was of the two main scales, or of the fourfold classification. Failure to measure religiousness is this way had led to many inconclusive or contradictory results which would be explicable in terms of the fourfold classification.

In an educational context other understandings of religion are to be encountered which offer a quite different orientation. Baxter (1977) considered that teachers in English schools, confronting responses from their students, were aware of a number of different stances—an antireligious attitude, a sophisticated symbolic understanding of religion, a historical, scholarly understanding of scripture, an occult, supernatural understanding, and a transcendental understanding. The occult was rarely met, the antireligious attitude was more common, but most frequent were the transcendentalists and those who held jointly a symbolic and historical understanding.

Appendix E

Religious Knowledge and Religious Understanding

The study of religious dimensions and religious orientations sheds some light on the complex structure of religiousness. When this is recognized then several problems fall into place, such as the confusion regarding religious knowledge and religious understanding. "Knowledge" and "understanding" are not themselves such simple terms as at first appears. There is an ambiguity in the term "know," and a distinction has to be made between knowledge as a disposition and knowledge as a process. Knowledge as a disposition means "I can say it"—the subject "can repeat the alphabet." But if one says "I know you are faithful," "know" means something arising from previous experience as the result of a process. Thus there is a difference between religious knowledge which is "knowledge about," e.g., scriptures, doctrines, and festivals and process knowledge arising from experience. Learning to be a Christian requires learning relevant information, understanding Christian discourse, acquiring skills, such as of worship, adopting attitudes, and learning to know God, something that cannot be taught. Learning about Christianity is concerned with gaining information and, to some extent, understanding Christian discourse. It needs information about its skills and attitudes from the stance of an observer but not participation in them. (Holley, 1971). Further, it is necessary to contrast the scholarly understanding of religion—i.e., knowledge as disposition, and religious faith—i.e., knowledge as process (Holley, 1978).

This distinction about forms of knowledge is complicated when related to the term "understanding." "Although he understands music he cannot play any instrument"—"understanding" compared with "can play" seems passive; nevertheless, it represents a mental reaction (Beethoven understood music, even when he could not hear a single note). In this sense one understands what is said or written; understanding a sentence means knowing what is expressed, an ability to answer questions about it; it represents a disposition, even though it may require considerable ability to translate it from one symbolism into another. "Religious language" as Ian Ramsey used it in a familiar language game, is understood in the first place in this sense. Its "oddity" can be interpreted or expressed in alternative forms, as part of a linguistic exercise. It is quite different when one speaks of understanding another person's behavior; such understanding implies putting oneself in the place of the person who is understood, sympathizing, perhaps even having been in a similar situation. Psychologically there is a much stronger effective element in such understanding. Understanding another language is primarily a cognitive activity; understanding another person is primarily an affective activity—the same distinction as between the scholarly understanding of religion and religious faith.

However, it must not be assumed that dispositional understanding is devoid of affective elements. Learning another language, a new physical skill, appreciation of twentieth-century music, all of which are the precondition of dispositional understanding of such fields of knowledge, require the active interest of the learner. Without the motivation of interest, learning is at first retarded, and finally inhibited.

Such considerations as these need to be kept in mind, as well as of the multidimensional nature of religion itself, when discussing the nature of religious language, knowledge, and understanding. Binkley (1963) suggested a sevenfold classification of religious language—empirical, of factual and historical claims; tautological, such as definitions of God; emotive, such as being at peace with God; performatory, in rituals and ceremonies; prescriptive, to enforce morality; mythical, which conveyed truth more adequately than much description; and paradoxical, the odd or extraordinary use of ordinary language. Hick (1963) considered that this classification evaded truth claims and could not deal with such a statement as "God loves the world"; he wanted to add a further category of metaphysical use.

Such diverse categories of linguistic usage, with the difference between knowledge as a disposition or as a process, underlies the suggestion that a distinction has to be made between thinking about religion, thinking religiously, and thinking in a religious language (Francis, 1979e). Thinking religiously, whereby a religious person brings a range of beliefs, attitudes, and practices to bear upon a particular topic, uses knowledge as a process; thinking about religion uses dispositional knowledge, as does thinking in religious language, but in a more advanced manner with the use of paradoxical language.

Diorio (1978) looked at the issue from the perspective of religious development, which he regarded as unlike normal development, since people who had acquired religious beliefs could subsequently discard them as of little value or replace them with quite different beliefs. When children acquired religious concepts they were integrated into their cognitive system just as other concepts were. This in itself did not indicate a positive development in human life, or show that religion could be justified from a developmental point of view. Some types of religious experience appeared to be questionable objectives for the attention of the young—many parents would object to the promotion of mystical experiences in children or adolescents, regarding it as peculiar. Because religion was contentious, neutrality became an educational problem, but children ought to gain objective knowledge about it and find a position of their own. However, Kibble (1980) argued at length that knowledge could be said to exist where 1) something was accepted as true, where 2) we accepted it, and 3) we had adequate evidence for it, even though we might not be able to articulate that evidence. On this ground an aim of religious education would be the attainment of such religious knowledge by individual students, not just knowledge about religion, but rather knowledge of religion in its fullest and deepest sense.

Melchert (1981) also considered the place of understanding in religious education which he related to four basic modes of understanding: sensory-motor understanding, which arose from physical manipulation; emotional understanding, such as that of a baby for the mother; analytic understanding, the ability to discriminate, the basis of scientific method; and synthetic understanding, a mode which developed often through the use of images or metaphoric devices. He contended that the objective of religious education must not be restricted to the analytical but should include all forms of understanding. To this Dykstra (1981) responded, welcoming the paper but urging that educators needed greater knowledge of the dynamics of understanding. The problem remained that religion was concerned with a reality that could not be comprehended but had to be lived in terms of faith in a God who could not be understood but had to be obeyed.

Cox (1983) discussed the ambiguity of the phrase "religious understanding" which could mean either understanding in the field of religion or a special type of understanding. He regarded understanding as a slippery concept that varied according to what was being understood and who was doing the understanding. Understanding religion could be a relatively superficial activity available to anyone prepared to devote time to its study, or it could imply experience of the beliefs and practices of a faith available only to those who had made a commitment to it. A phenomenological study of religion required pupils to put themselves into a believer's shoes, and there was no agreement that this could be done. At best, giving an onlooker's understanding of religion might possibly result in religious understanding emerging from it. In the present cultural climate four questions required answers—Was religious understanding a unique form of understanding? Could that understanding be studied objectively without personal commitment? Was such commitment confined to people with a conscious religious stance? and Was such religious understanding an appropriate educational objective? Ouellet (1983) insisted that religious education must include a phenomenological, an explanatory and a critical component. He regarded religious understanding to be defective without the insight that came from personal commitment and saw this as something to be gained by pupils, not from their schools, but from their families and religious communities. By narrowing his definition of religious understanding, he disputed that religious understanding was a proper educational objective. But if the result of classroom learning is not a form of religious understanding, the question remains as to what it does constitute.

Phillips-Bell (1983) was concerned with religious knowledge and argued that religion did not consist of one common essence but rather was the consequence of a number of religion-making characteristics—belief in supernatural beings, a distinction between the sacred and the profane, a moral code believed to be divinely sanctioned, ritual acts focused on sacred objects, feelings of awe, mystery, and guilt, prayer and communication with the divine, a particular worldview and the place of individuals in it, an organization of life based on that worldview, and a social group bonded by all of these. Against the claim that religious education was part of the education of the emotions, she contended that the emotions were a species of cognition, since the question "Is X an appropriate object of awe?" needed first an answer to "Is there an X?" If it was argued that religious belief was expressed in performative language which was concerned with such matters as trust in God and initiation into devotion, then, since this required an affective commitment, it was not appropriate to education. To argue from religious experience faced the problem that such experience was irreducibly personal and could not be publicly shown to exist. Hirst had included religion as one of the distinctive forms of knowledge, and if this was the case for all religion, then one world religion at least should be included in the curriculum to study the religious form of knowledge more fully.

The issue as to whether religious understanding can be purely objective or must require a degree of commitment, and whether such commitment must be to the particular faith of which understanding is sought, remains unresolved. In the context of English classroom neutrality, objectivity is often regarded as essential, but this does not prevent students from grasping complex doctrinal issues and gaining a scholarly knowledge of scriptures. In the context of church, mosque, synagogue, or temple the first requirement is commitment. Ryle's distinction between knowing how and knowing that is relevant, but it would seem that an element of both types of knowledge is needed for any religious understanding, the emphasis varying according to the context. However, the question remains as to whether any commitment to a desired object, such as a football club or a pop star, gives sufficient insight into a committed stance to enable religious commitment to be appreciated by the irreligious.

Since the question here has to do with children and adolescents, there is also a developmental aspect to it. Howe (1978) adopted a Piagetian perspective for his discussion of religious understanding, starting from the developmental process in which, first of all, things came to be understood in their context, then a representation of things was achieved so that objects experienced were preserved when not immediately present. In this, it was very important to grasp that representation was representative of something else; in biblical understanding, the context had to be perceived as a set of representations expressing or pointing to truths transcending the finite world. The third level focused not on things and representations of things but on the idealization of reality—defining, valuing, relating, and idealizing. Thus regarded, religious understanding was more than an apprehending relationship but was the construction of idealizations so that it could grasp, utilize, and reformulate idealizations which had peculiar significance as constitutive for religious communities and individuals. His treatment recalls the words of Inhelder and Sinclair (1969)—"understanding does not consist in simply incorporating ready-made and readily available data but rather in rediscovering them or reinventing them by one's own activity. Rediscovery is certainly facilitated by using a system of symbolization, but language as such a system is but an instrument and a child must learn to use it. This learning capacity is not provided by the instrument but by the subject." In such terms, adequate religious learning in childhood arises only from the spontaneous religion which children create for themselves out of the religious material which they are taught, and only by their own religious activity can full religious understanding be achieved.

Appendix F

A New Analysis of Goldman's Findings

In view of the critical discussions of Goldman's work and the ongoing reappraisal of Piagetian theory, a statistical reexamination was made of the data available in his thesis. This consists of a tabulation by mental age of all the responses to the five questions subjected to Piagetian assessment, and these can be related to the other variables—sex, parental support, social class, and behavioral scores on attendance at church or Sunday school, frequency of Bible reading and of private prayer. As was anticipated, the individual item scores had highly significant intercorrelations with each other, with the total score derived from the five items and with mental age. The result is reproduced in Table F 1.

Goldman's result that there was little difference between the sexes was also confirmed (boys = 1, girls = 2 for this purpose, r = -.033).

It is self-evident that for any particular child, the response to a particular item must be at one, and only one, level of operational thinking. Goldman showed that the cutting points determined by scalogram analysis on mental age varied from

TABLE F 1 CORRELATION MATRIX OF FIVE GOLDMAN ITEMS					
	MENTAL AGE	S1.Q2	S1.Q4	S1.Q5	S2.Q5	S3.Q5
S1.Q2	.760				
S1.Q4	.668	.611			
S1.Q5	.600	.466	.452		
S2.Q5	.700	.604	.562	.500	
S3.Q5	.732	.700	.619	.540	.613
total	.855	.847	.793	.713	.809	.874

item to item with a larger range among younger children; these are reproduced in Table F 2. It might be assumed that at about these ages there would be, for the whole group, a steep incline in the learning curve, and the inclines would be separated by almost level plateaus, indicating periods of no significant increase in group levels of operational thinking. This is not the case. In every instance, and in the total (five-item) score, the learning curve is linear and the linearity is very highly significant. S1, Q5 gives the lowest F value when the regression is compared with the residual, but even here it is 111.546. (At $p<.01$, F 1,200 = 6.76). The regression equation for this item is: score = 1.94 + 0.162 x m.a.

TABLE F 2		
GOLDMAN'S CUTTING POINTS FOR FIVE ITEMS		
MENTAL AGE		
S1.Q5	6-6	13-5
S2.Q5	7-10	13-6
S1.Q2	7-11	14-2
S1.Q4	8-2	12-8
S3.Q5	8-10	14-2

The responses for this item are reproduced as Table F 3. The tabulations for the other items and for the total score are similar. Goldman's cutting points indicate the mental age after which most children begin to achieve the higher levels of concrete operational thinking or formal operational thinking indicated by scores of 3 and 5, which are in fact intermediate levels.

The continuity of this development for each item, but at somewhat different levels, can be also seen by comparing the mean scores of the stage responses at each mental age. This is reproduced as Table F 4.

TABLE F 3
RESPONSES TO S3.Q5

Mental Age	Stage response							n
	0	1	2	3	4	5	6	
6	2	7	2	1	0	0	0	12
7	1	2	6	2	0	0	0	11
8	2	3	6	8	1	0	0	20
9	0	1	6	10	1	0	1	19
10	0	1	5	5	6	0	0	17
11	0	2	0	8	9	3	0	22
12	0	0	2	4	9	4	0	19
13	0	0	2	4	6	5	1	18
14	0	0	1	3	4	5	1	14
15	0	0	0	1	4	6	1	12
16	0	0	0	0	3	4	0	7
17	0	0	0	1	1	6	0	8
18+	0	0	0	1	5	10	5	21

TABLE F 4
MEAN SCORES OF STAGE RESPONSES

M.A.	S1.Q2	S1.Q4	S1.Q5	S2.Q5	S3.Q5	mean	n
6	1.67	1.50	2.50	2.25	1.17	1.83	12
7	2.27	1.82	3.27	2.27	1.82	2.27	11
8	2.55	2.70	3.35	2.85	2.15	2.70	20
9	3.00	2.74	3.84	2.84	2.79	3.05	19
10	3.35	3.12	3.18	3.24	2.94	3.18	17
11	3.68	3.41	3.73	3.50	3.50	3.59	22
12	4.00	3.37	3.89	3.79	3.79	3.74	19
13	3.89	3.44	4.11	3.89	3.94	3.94	18
14	4.30	3.64	4.14	4.29	4.14	4.14	14
15	4.67	3.75	4.50	4.67	4.58	4.42	12
16	4.86	4.14	4.43	4.43	4.57	4.57	7
17	4.63	4.50	4.50	4.75	4.63	4.50	8
18+	5.38	4.24	5.05	5.00	4.90	4.95	21

Another way of dealing with the data is to follow the method of Kurtines and Pimm (1983), who developed a Moral Development Scale and validated it, comparing the percentage responses for each stage at every age-group of their 270 children age 5 - 11 with Piaget's (1932) data calculated in the same way. Goldman's data was grouped into three main stages (0,1,2; 3,4; 5,6;) and analyzed in the same way. This was undertaken for each item and for the mean level of response recorded for all five items. The latter is reproduced as Table F 5. The same response pattern is secured if either the highest or the lowest response is chosen for each child from all five items, except for the obvious displacement toward higher or lower mental ages at which it is observed. The table also indicates the linearity of the change in response pattern, which was found to be highly significant. As a check, this pattern was compared with what would be expected from a perfect Guttman scale and the "errors" subjected to a Chi square test; the result again indicated a highly significant rejection of the expected smiliarity. The implications of this will be considered in Appendix G.

TABLE F 5

PERCENTAGE OF RESPONSES BY STAGES FROM MEAN OF FIVE ITEMS

metal age	stage			n
	1	2	3	
6	100%	0	0	12
7	73	27	0	11
8	30	70	0	20
9	11	89	0	19
10	0	100	0	17
11	0	100	0	22
12	5	90	5	19
13	0	89	11	18
14	0	86	14	14
15	0	67	33	12
16	0	43	57	7
17	0	50	50	8
18+	0	24	76	21

There remains the question of the extent to which the behavioral factors affect performance in this test. Some indication of this effect is given in the correlation matrix in Table F 6, which shows the highly significant correlation between total score and mental age and correlations of more than borderline significance with some of the other factors:

To examine these effects more adequately, a step-wise multivariate analysis of variance was carried out on the total (five-item) score, which shows how relatively small are the effects of the other factors, apart from mental age. Total score

TABLE F 6

CORRELATION MATRIX OF TOTAL SCORE AND BEHAVIORAL VARIABLES

	total score	mental age	church/SS attendance	Bible reading	private prayer
Mental age	.855**				
Attendance	.232**	.214**			
Bible	.355**	.331**	.215**		
Prayer	.175*	.171*	.342**	.334**	
Class	-.193*	-.345**	-.213**	-.113	-.046

** p<.01   * p<.05

was regressed on mental age, and one by one the remaining factors were added in the order of the most significant factor remaining at each operation. Table F 7 shows the result.

Table F 7

MULTIVARIATE REGRESSION ANALYSIS OF TOTAL SCORE ON FIVE VARIABLES

	MULTIPLE R	R SQUARE	F
Mental age	.85324	.72802	530.006
Bible	.85521	.73139	268.202
Attendance	.85619	.73306	179.412
Social class	.85700	.73445	134.834
Prayer	.85701	.73446	107.320

It is evident that mental age is highly significant, and the other factors make little practical difference; multiple r increases from 0.85324 to 0.85701; the sum

TABLE F 8

BETA VALUES IN MULTIVARIATE REGRESSION ANALYSIS

	Step 1	Step 2	Step 3	Step 4	Step 5
Mental age	.85324	.83308	.82618	.83931	.83947
Bible reading		.06141	.05458	.05355	.05449
Attendance			.04233	.04830	.04933
Social class				.04037	.04059
Private prayer					-.00358

of the squares from 3455.113 to 3485.676. The associated beta values are similarly dominated by mental age, and the other variables make little difference, as is shown in Table F 8.

Goldman set out to study cognitive aspects of religious thinking, and this result shows very clearly how successful he was in isolating the developmental from the affective aspects, which other studies cited earlier have shown to be so greatly dependent on religious behavior.

Appendix G

The Cognitive Basis of Religion

Religious thinking: the relevance of Piaget

Religious insight and understanding cannot be analyzed neatly into cognitive and affective domains; religion is holistic, and intrinsic, extrinsic, or irreligious stances provide different perspectives from which individuals evaluate it. The feelings, attitudes, and habits of thought acquired at an emotional level provide motives for thinking which help initiate and determine its direction. Even so, the ability of children to come to a rational appreciation of religious ideas is subject to the constraints of normal mental development. Because the pioneers in the field, Elkind and Goldman, related their findings to Piagetian theory, some attempt must be made to examine its relevance, both as Piaget propounded it and as it has been subsequently amended.

Piaget's enormous output and his insistence that attention should be paid to the way children think and express themselves has affected profoundly our understanding of children's mental development. It was inevitable that sooner or later children's thinking about religion would be examined from this perspective and surprising that this was not undertaken by Piaget himself, since some of his earliest writing was religious, as for example his Genevan lecture on philosophical and psychological aspects of immanence and transcendence (Piaget, 1930). For a long time he was unchallenged, but when *The Times Educational Supplement* of 18 March 1977 carried a special section with the title "Piaget in the Dock" it brought to the attention of the public the fact that his theories were now being questioned. Since his death in 1980 the reappraisal of his work has gathered momentum, making more intricate the already complex theories he had advanced. For our purpose it must not be forgotten that much of this theory is about genetic epistemology, concerned with aspects of mental structures and the biological basis of their growth. It is the observed consequences of the theory, rather than the theory itself, which has been applied by practicing teachers to an understanding of the development of thinking, be it about religion or any other topic.

One aspect of his theory is that mental capacity evolves through a number of stages in a fixed hierarchical order, as described at the beginning of chapter 1, and another aspect was the description of the more advanced stages in terms of logic. The age at which children pass from one stage to the next varies both with individuals and with their culture. Each of the stages—separated by intermediate stages—has its own characteristic way of thinking, differing fundamentally from those of earlier stages. Straightforward accounts of this are readily available, e.g., Cohen (1983), Elkind (1981), Ginsburg and Opper (1979), or a full account of the earlier fundamental work in Flavell (1963). Cohen (1983) gave an account of more recent criticisms of Piaget as restricted only to the logical solution of problems and disregarding differences of children's personality, sex, or emotional life. These are similarly stressed by Hamlyn (1978) in a more philosophical critique of Piaget, to whom he is sympathetic, but insistent that even cognitive development requires a social context of relationships with others which go beyond the cognitive. Even the logical basis of Piaget's work has come under criticism, and Ennis (1978) suggested that simple deductive logic was a better basis for assessing competence than the operational logic he used. Similarly, some of his long-accepted concepts have been challenged. Holland and Rohrman (1979) concluded that animistic thinking was not a genuine phenomenon but was due to linguistic confusion elicited by novel objects and by unfamiliar words.

A well-known issue is that the ability of children from four to six to comprehend a conservation problem is related to their familiarity with the test materials and the language used. When a "naughty teddy" instead of a sober psychologist pours water from one container to another the children's attention is focused on the water, since teddy is familiar and does not distract their attention, as a psychologist would. By this means McGarrigle and Donaldson (1974) demonstrated that a significant proportion of them had some understanding of conservation. But a result like this does not support the assertion that if Goldman had phrased his questions differently the children he tested would have shown better understanding; his questions were not about conservation, and no actual testing with recast questions has yielded such a result. Unlike critics of Piaget, those of Goldman have not produced findings in support of their criticism. When this conservation experiment was repeated in a modified manner to meet the criticism that ability to conserve had not really been tested, conservation responses decreased, although they were still found to some extent (Dockrell, Campbell, and Neilson, 1980). A range of studies have only served to indicate the complexity of such mental developments. But Donaldson (1978), in a review of experiments about children's logical thinking using as apparatus familiar toys and dolls, made it clear that children were not as egocentric or as limited in deductive reasoning as Piaget had claimed. Hacker (1984), in his extensive survey of understanding in science, found children of five or six able to make hypotheses about scientific phenomena and devise tests for their ideas and remarked that Piaget was too pessimistic about the abilities of young children.

Critics of stage theory

There has been a considerable debate about stages. Piaget himself allowed for an intermediate period between two successive stages, and it was never his suggestion that almost overnight children jumped from one stage to the next. He was however insistent that once the threshold had been passed, children's thinking was dominated by the logical level of that particular stage, and he went to great lengths to define the structure of each stage. Quite early on it became apparent that children's modes of thinking were not as precise as this; Flavell (1963) observed that there was "a somewhat less strong and less neat system than Piaget's grouping theory postulates," and later (1977) observed that cognitive development appeared to proceed slowly and gradually, rather than abruptly. Children might continue to perfect a grasp of weight conservation throughout most of middle childhood and into adolescence, so that the concrete operational stage itself, and not the transition to it, became the period of continuous growth and change. Piaget allowed for some irregularity by his account of *horizontal décalage*, in which children displayed different levels of thinking about problems involving similar mental operations, as when they can conserve substance but not number. Nor did he overlook the fact that children could be in different stages for different types of thinking, although extreme discrepancies were infrequent (Piaget, 1974). Critics of stage theory see *décalage* as introducing ambiguity, since the subject is not thinking as would be expected from the appropriate stage; the concept of an intellectual structure which varies in its nature according to the material to which it is applied was regarded as very confusing by Boyle (1982), who rejected even a competence model of stage theory.

In their detailed examination of Piaget's theory and its structuralist nature, Brown and Desforges (1979) criticized it especially for its validation. In almost all cases, they asserted, Piaget's critics accepted his observations and did not contest the phenomenon but rather said that other psychological explanations were available which fitted the data better. This would mean accepting the findings of Elkind and Goldman without casting them into the Piagetian mould to which Murphy (1977a) objected. Brown (1983) in a further discussion about weaknesses in stage theory accepted that the evidence for the invariant order of stages was strong but suggested that stage may reflect the logical structure of the tasks rather than some basic principle. Such theories should be used for practical purposes rather than being made the basis for statements about some ultimate reality. The worthy successor to this influential theory would be one which could capitalize upon the abstract descriptions of operations employed by the Genevans and marry them with task variables, and possibly with organismic variables in the learner too.

In a study of formal operational thinking, Wason (1977) investigated the problem intelligent adults had in solving a logical puzzle presented in different forms; the first consisted of four cards labeled A, D, 4, 7; subjects knew that each card had a letter on one side and a number on the other and had to name which cards needed to be turned over to prove, or disprove: "If there is a vowel on one side there is an even number on the other." The same problem using other materials showed that successful responses increased systematically as the content of the task became more familiar. Thus the Piagetian understanding that in formal operations the content of a problem was subordinated to the form of relations in it did not hold in this instance. Such criticism rejects the theory as one of performance but is deflected if the theory is seen as one of competence, in which the stages mark an upper limit which individuals can be expected to attain only under ideal conditions. The distinction between performance and competence theories was discussed by Stone and Day (1980), who regarded a competence model as constituting a statement about the types of knowledge generated by psychological structures, whatever they were. Miles (1983), in his thorough review of Piagetian theory and its application to religious thinking, supported a performance rather than a competence model because of the contribution now made by information theory. The difference is important when explaining mental functions but does not really affect educational practice; what children can understand rather than why they understand it is what matters in the classroom. Berzonski (1978) observed that not all adults developed complete formal reasoning and that those who reasoned formally might do so in come situations but not in others. On the other hand, Commons, Richards, and Kuhn (1982) used test results to support their theory that systematic and metasystematic reasoning existed as cognitive modes more complex and powerful than formal operational thinking, and it was found more among graduates than undergraduates in their sample.

The debate about stages continues, as yet unresolved, some regarding the concept of stage as a descriptive tool and not central to Piaget's theory (e.g., Mogdil and Mogdil, 1982), others seeing it as a basic tenet of Piaget's broad theory of cognitive development. Siegal and Hodkin (1982) took this position in order to criticize stage theory, asserting that in young children cognitive skills develop gradually. Siegal (1982), who favored an information-processing theory, compared linguistic and perceptual factors associated with the development of various quantity concepts, concluding that in young children language and thought function independently, only becoming related as concepts develop, so that their abilities are underestimated by tests depending extensively on language. But while the debate about stages is fundamentally concerned with the relationship between stage and structure, the concept of stage has been defended by a wide range of those concerned with education.

Gelman and Baillargeon (1983) also reviewed at length recent research on cognitive development bearing on Piagetian theory, and while they found themselves sympathetic to many of Piaget's fundamental ideas, they found little evidence to support his concept of major stages of development. In some instances the reasoning of young children about a problem, despite their limitations, could be similar to that even of adults. Within some domains of cognitive development there could be stages, and these could then be characterized by dominant levels of competence in dealing with a hierarchy of related concepts—which is what research in a religious cognitive domain has been attempting. Similarly, in a stimulating discussion about the relatively new study of children's understanding of stories, Mandler (1983) noted major shifts in functioning in early childhood, then between five and seven, and about the start of adolescence. General stage theory found it difficult to explain the adult problems encountered in transferring a particular principle to a new context. There were many objections to the belief that with maturity there was a final shift to formal operations; truly abstract thought was a rarity dependent on specialist training, and people solved problems on the basis of familiar routines. Domain-specific models of acquiring knowledge were to be preferred, and the basic forms of representation by which knowledge was acquired seemed to be similar throughout development, even though qualitative changes took place in development in such domains as the understanding of number.

Driver (1978) looked critically at the application of Piagetian theory to science education, stressing that Piaget was concerned with epistemology and the neurophysiological status of cognitive structures and, further, that formal thinking to Piaget was not a vague notion of thinking in abstract terms but was characterized by the existence of integrated structures which could be modeled mathematically. Because studies have shown the theory to be unsatisfactory at this point, Driver thought it better to abandon the concept of structured wholes and look for separate, identifiable skills which develop in adolescence. Evidence about children's thinking needed to be separated from theories based on it, without rejecting the search for underlying patterns of cognitive development, so that problems in specific content areas could be diagnosed. Piaget's idea of learning as equilibration was a reminder that every learner had to tread again well-trodden paths, which need not be boring but become an interesting journey. Returning to the topic, Driver (1982) regarded it as important for science education, since it had implications different from those of traditional learning theories; although the theory could be questioned the results appeared to be replicable. In the group of Australian studies compiled by Keats, Collis, and Halford (1978), Halford, in an introductory chapter, suggested that one factor which worked against a structural approach was the current practice of performing small experiments reported in single papers; such modularization made the study of large-scale systems difficult. Several of the following essays describe new approaches to the study of stages which are broadly supportive of the theory, including that of Jurd (1978), who described findings of tests with historical materials which confirmed a Piagetian developmental sequence similar to those found in science and mathematics by his colleagues.

Johnson and Hooper (1982) in a general survey argued that Piagetian structuralism compared favorably with other learning theories in providing a conceptual basis for educational application, although in the same journal issue Zimmerman (1982) took a more cautious view.

Nagy and Griffiths (1982), in a substantial review of recent fundamental research about Piagetian theory, regarded group tests as easier to administer but less reliable in their results, providing a questionable relationship between the observed products of mental effort and the underlying mental strategies. The validity of a group test of developmental levels needed to be established by comparison with already accepted tests results of the same construct, for example, those that had come from individual interview. They concluded that there was a lack of unity in formal operations, so that a judgment of developmental level might depend to a large extent on the tasks chosen for the assessment. It seemed to them that global measurement of developmental level was not tapping a unique variable, and from the point of view of education it was better to investigate, in specific terms, how developmental levels affected the learning of particular content concepts. It is interesting to notice how closely this suggestion comes to the plea of Kalam (1981) and provides support for him from a quite different perspective.

Hall (1980) reviewed Piaget's theories about the intellectual development of children from an egocentric exclusive self-awareness to the full formal operational thinking which enables them to combine different properties and ideas and formulate results using various perspectives of a situation harmoniously. He cited evidence supporting the development of scientific understanding, with its periods of radical modification, as corresponding epistemologically to Piagetian concepts of assimilation and accommodation. On this theoretical base he asserted that "the discipline of psychology may be the appropriate middle ground on which subjective approaches, such as theology and the humanities, come into dialogue with the natural sciences," and "the Christian faith could exist as an integrative system within psychology." Science and theology were seen by Hall as facets of a continuum of epistemological systems.

The transition from egocentric thinking to objective thinking and its relationship with religious education was discussed by Minney (1985) who considered that it started about the age of six or seven and continued over a long period. He suggested that reading was an accomplishment achieved by somewhat younger children who first regarded it as a hobby and a source of pride but later found it gave them the opportunity to use the power of the written word to stand back and look at events more objectively, so that they slowly relinquished the idea that inanimate objects or machines had a will or purpose of their own. Because religion was shot through with values, a detached objectivity in religion was resisted; this crisis of literacy became embarrassing in the early years of secondary education, and while adolescence brought this crisis, it did not resolve it.

It would seem that as yet there are not sufficient grounds for rejecting the idea of stages as a basis for the study of religious development, providing it is regarded as a performance rather than a competence theory and used with some caution. By whatever means the religious thinking of children is studied, a large measure of agreement between the results remains. Beyond all doubt there are fundamentally different ways of thinking that are characteristic of different periods of mental development, no matter what terminology is used to describe them. Even children's humor (mentioned in Appendix H) is dependent on this development, for a sense of incongruity depends on a logical ability to compare congruent and incongruent situations. The development of logical thinking, which is most clearly seen in the range of experiments with apparatus that bear upon conservation and number, affects the ability to reason in any area, and must of necessity affect the cognitive aspect of religious thinking, just as it does in many other areas of learning.

Knowledge, development, and learning in Piaget's theory

Some reference needs to be made to Piaget's approach to learning, which, apart from general interest, bears upon children's spontaneous religion and their learning of adult religious ideas. Piaget was primarily a biologist and saw his life's work as the study of genetic epistemology. His earlier essays on learning (1959 a, b) are not available in an English translation but are generally known through the account given by Elkind (1981). Two extracts from the first essay are given in his own translation by Furth (1969), and similar ground is covered by Piaget in three other papers (1964a, 1970, and 1977). It is interesting to note that in his own summary of his theory (Piaget, 1970) much more attention is given to the topic than would be expected from its relatively small mention in his major writings.

Piaget's understanding of knowing becomes clear in his discussion of the development of mental imagery (1964b). The traditional understanding of perception is that it provides the individual with a literal copy of reality, and with sufficient repetition a mental image is formed which is stored in memory. Piaget showed that with young children the image recalled in an experiment was affected by what they had come to expect and concluded that there was a double relationship between an individual and an object; not only did the object act on the individual, but the individual acted on the object. To know an object was to act on it, to modify or transform it. This activity, which he called an operation, was of the essence of knowledge, as, for example, in counting, measuring, or classifying. An operation was reversible—the action could be mentally envisaged to return to the starting point—and never isolated from other operations, and these operations were the basis of knowledge. This is quite different from Gestalt theory, for example, in which perception is primary and intelligence derived only from perceptual functioning. Piaget thus distinguished two different kinds of thinking. Figurative thinking concerned the activities which attempted only to represent reality as it appears without seeking to transform it—perception and imitation in a broad sense including graphic imitation of drawing and pictorial representations in mental imagery. By contrast, operational thinking was concerned with the activity that attempts to transform reality, both in physical actions and operations or interiorized actions which focus on the transformation of objects, thus extracting form from content so that it became part of the mental schemata of the subject.

Furth (1977) observed that a person who constructed a chair certainly knew what a chair was, whereas a child might know that the postman delivered letters without any knowledge of the postal system, having a figurative knowledge but a quite inadequate operative knowledge. These were not two different types of knowledge but different aspects or perspectives of the same whole. Figurative knowledge arose from perception, but Piaget recognized that it was not simply a copy of reality, but the individual constructed his own reality, and in this the influence of operative structures was of first importance. The subject and the object could not be dissociated, but knowledge arose from the interaction. The action of things on the individual he called physical (P) experience, whereas the action of the individual on the object he called logico-mathematical (LM) experience. Piaget attached much importance to this distinction, which is to the forefront of his understanding of learning. It has been largely overlooked in discussions about religious thinking, despite Roy (1979) drawing attention to it.

Development was the process which concerned the totality of the structure of knowledge, the development of the body, the nervous system, and the mental functions; it was both biological and psychological. Learning was stimulated by situations usually due to a teacher; it was provoked and was not spontaneous, and was limited to a single problem or structure. Thus, there was an interaction between the biological development of mental structures and the influence of the environment. Development, due to maturation, to experience of the physical environment and the action of the social environment, explained learning. The Piagetian model made clear that children are always "unlearning and relearning as well as acquiring entirely new knowledge" (Elkind, 1981). They arrive at school with a range of ideas about space, causality, and quantity acquired through their spontaneous reaction with the external world. They are thus already motivated to construct a worldview, limited only by their ability and experience, and yet because their ideas are alien to those of adults, they need to modify their existing knowledge as well as gain new information.

In this context Piaget saw learning as a process of mental activity. In the classroom young children may play with water, sand, and clay and use all kinds of objects—this is physical experience, the discovery of qualities and properties—shape, form, color, which are without logical necessity. Logico-mathematical experience is reflection upon what has been done and concerns the relations and properties which do not belong to the things themselves but have a logical necessity. He related a story of a child who counted ten pebbles in a row, then counted them in the other direction, and having repeated the process several times, was fascinated to discover that there were always ten. He then put them in a circle and counted them, in both directions, and finally in many different arrangements, discovering that there were always ten. That was LM experience. P and LM experiences are never isolated, but the two types have always to be distinguished. P experience gives rise to learning in a narrow sense—children learn the names of places and the date of their birthday; such learning is specific to its context. LM experiences give rise to learning in Piaget's broad sense—if children learn to put a set of blocks in order of size they can reverse the process without further learning. Furth (1969) asked, "We learn that Bern is the capital of Switzerland, but do we *learn* that tomorrow what is called today will be yesterday? We learn the vocabulary, but the comprehension of temporal succession is never taught or learned in the same manner as the name of a capital city."

Physical learning, learning in the traditional sense, has been the subject of much research, but Piaget gave little attention to it. Furth (1969) thought it significant that traditional psychology had no term for logico-mathematical learning and observed that while no specialized experience was needed to acquire the conservation judgment of quantity, no special experience sufficed to teach it before the appropriate time. Special teaching was needed to learn the name of Switzerland's capital and was just as necessary for a twelve-year-old as for a three-year-old. With an adult that knowledge was enriched by the knowledge of general concepts such as of country and capital, which implied an operative understanding of which the three-year-old was not capable.

P learning gains in efficiency through the learning process itself—this is normal learning theory. LM learning changes its mode with age and development, and many studies have shown that the development is due to the number of different factors children can deal with simultaneously. At first objects are compared in an undifferentiated way. From about two until seven single dimensions are singled out but are dealt with one at a time without integration. (These issues are very much the concern of more recent studies of information processing theories.) In Elkind's (1961) study of children's conception of religious denomination at this age children said they were either Jewish or American—they could not be both. In middle and later childhood two factors can be coordinated at the same time but not until adolescence can this number be dealt with simultaneously. In physical learning the changes that age brings are really more of the same; in logico-mathematical learning qualitatively distinct processes operate at the different stages. In physical learning, the content is hardly altered by subsequent mental growth;

the date of one's birthday, once learned, does not change. But logico-mathematical learning does change. Young children learn which is their left hand and which is their right, but the concept of left and right evolves over a long period. Not all intelligent adults can easily read a map if tracing a journey from north to south on a north-oriented map. With physical knowledge a child either knows or does not know; logico-mathematical content brings a different conception at successive age-levels. Physical knowledge tends to be analytic, whereas logico-mathematical knowledge is synthetic, enabling events to be organized into larger wholes. Physical learning changes what we see; logico-mathematical learning changes how we see. To study a body of knowledge requires physical learning but to understand it requires logico-mathematical learning. Both are required, but the limitations of ability are clarified by this distinction. The extent of physical learning that is possible depends upon children's experience of such learning and the older the children the greater the content that can be dealt with. With adequate motivation the extent can be dramatically increased. But comprehension is limited by the level of logico-mathematical thinking. In religious education, the difference between P learning and LM learning is the difference between successfully memorizing religious material and what Elkind called spontaneous religion, the freely expressed religious insight children may have. Reflection brings religious understanding of their knowledge of religious material. Much traditional religious education is P learning; some of the newer approaches require LM learning. At every level, religious education needs learners to acquire a sufficient body of knowledge for them to become informed about the topic they are studying, but it also requires this to be organized and related to their wider experience by reflection or by whatever means is appropriate to them as well as to the topic.

Piaget, moral development, and religious development

Quite early in his life Piaget (1932) made his single study of children's moral development. According to Rest (1983) it was not to provide a detailed study of moral judgment but to provide an alternative to Durkheim's point of view. The lively ongoing debate regarding this work has some relevance for religious development. *The Moral Judgement of the Child* relied on children's answers to questions, without the use of materials, except when first establishing the rules of marbles. Their recorded replies, apart from undifferentiated remarks from the youngest children, were classified into two or three types of judgments, characteristic of younger and older children. These were used to describe the heteronomous morality of younger children, based on the constraint of adult rules, and the autonomous morality of older children based on cooperation with their peers; the former was seen as moral realism, the latter as a morality of intention. In this study Piaget distinguished between the two loosely described groups of younger and older children and was aware that there were often overlaps and the development was not clear-cut, nor were there precise stages in it. He wrote, "There are therefore no inclusive stages which define the whole of a subject's mental life at a given point of his evolution; the stages should be thought of as the successive phases of regular processes recurring like a rhythm on the superposed planes of behavior and of consciousness . . . We cannot therefore speak of global or inclusive stages characterized as such by autonomy or heteronomy but only of phases of heteronomy or autonomy which define a process that is repeated for each new set of rules or for each new plane of thought or reflection" (Piaget, 1932).

That in this field Piaget did not speak of stages, but phases, is significant but is often overlooked, even by some of the most careful commentators. Emler (1983) noted the complexity of this development; individual elements taken separately changed with age and relate to mental growth, but taken collectively they did not exhibit true stage characteristics, that is, they were not parts of functionally and structurally unified systems of thought. He noted that Kohlberg did not follow Piaget, yet attempted to base his more complex moral stage development theory on Piaget's concepts of logico-mathematical thinking and development. It appeared to Emler that children acquired specific moral concepts separately and not as elements in the development of integrated structural wholes; each phase showed its own distinctive emphasis, so that there was a family of similarities and differences rather than a single, unequivocal dimension of development. Such a description fits well the results of Piagetian studies of religious development and suggests that some religious concepts, if not all, develop in the same manner as moral insights.

Tamminen, Vianello, Jaspard, and Ratcliff (1988) reviewed Italian research involving more than 2,000 children in which Piaget's studies on immanent justice were replicated with children from four to twelve. Very different results were obtained, conflicting with the conclusion that as they grew older children decreasingly believed that bad actions would be followed by punishment. Far fewer Italian six-year-olds thought like this, but between six and twelve there was an increase in this belief. The authors concluded that by six children's strong causal reasoning led them to deny the link in Piaget's story and that the increased belief in immanent justice after this age was due to teaching that justice was guaranteed by God.

A further point to notice is that Piaget regarded moral development as a product of social learning. He assumed the constraining influence of adults and the different influence of peers, although he made no effort to study or test them. This social influence is different from the linguistic and educational social environment which he saw as one factor operating in the total development process. The actual relationships he described between children and their parents and peers is not of present importance; the dimension of social pressure in achieving moral judgments was clearly identified, so that it is possible to regard them as the discovery by children of the principles by which social relationships are organized, a point which is clarified and elaborated by Wright (1982). Yet this discovery is held within the level of operational thinking at which particular children function. Once more, the importance for a model for religious thinking and its development is evident, as is the finding of Jantz (1973) that those of higher intellectual development were not necessarily those who showed the greater moral development.

Finally, Elkind (1981), in his chapter on "How the mind grows," spoke of two Piagetian paths of mental development, describing areas in which substitution, and not integration, was the pattern. Most Piagetian studies concerned integration, but in areas that are not logical growth tended to be by substitution. This point is reinforced by Pinard and Laurendeau (1969), who noted that cases of substitution were recognized by the fact that the external intervention of cultural, social, or educational forces could change the order of appearance of successive behaviors, even if not altering their basic quality. In the same volume Flavell and Wohlwill (1969) observed that young children's moral concepts do not form part of, or lead to, the qualitatively different concepts that will subsequently be formed; the relation seemed to be simply that of replacement or substitution, and it was possible that the earlier form could coexist with the later one in a state of suppression and could reassert itself from time to time under certain conditions. In moral growth, according to Elkind, concepts of intention are substituted for earlier concepts of culpability; proof that this is not integration comes from the way that adults can revert to judging a child's action on a quantitative basis rather than on intentions, so that a child who accidentally breaks mother's best lamp is in reality likely to be more severely punished than if he breaks an old cup on purpose, even though adult distress does not justify such an action. Similar growth by substitution is seen in the studies of children's understanding of the natural world; the animistic idea of young children that regards inanimate objects as having consciousness is first altered so that only objects that move—the clouds or the sun—are conscious, until about eight or nine, only those things that move of their own accord are endued with consciousness. The argument is not affected by the suggestion that children's animistic thinking is not spontaneous but is acquired from the "baby-talk" of adults. Magical ideas are similarly displaced by ideas of causality, and Elkind cited his own studies of children's ideas of their religious denomination as another substitution process.

In more general terms, moral development is a topic that has attracted so much attention that it is not possible to review it here, although some aspects of it have bearing on religious development. Kohlberg's six stages of moral reasoning are closely related to Piagetian stages of logical development and recently revised methods of scoring responses to the moral dilemmas have provided good evidence to support the stage theory. A detailed discussion of this and much else that is relevant is available in Rest (1983).

A Piagetian model

It thus appears that there is good reason for the continued use of a Piagetian model for the study of religious thinking but with qualifications, as Miles (1983) also concluded. The phenomena of stage theory are not in dispute, although the stages are not as sharply defined as used to be thought. The debate about regarding stage theory as a competence or a performance theory is not relevant to its practical use as a guide to religious thinking. A range of Piagetian studies notably in mathematics, science, history, and geography all show a similar development, and it would be remarkable if religious studies did not share it too. The statistics reproduced earlier based on Elkind's and Goldman's research show that, while particular items show strong stage characteristics, the aggregate learning process for all of them appears to be much more uniform. In assessing religious learning, care needs to be taken to distinguish between physical and logico-mathematical learning; not a few tests of religious thinking deal with an external body of knowledge, material that has been memorized, rather than seeking the logic of comprehension and children's religious explanation of their experience. It is also important to recognize that religious development may share with moral development the substitution of higher level concepts for earlier notions. This could explain the occasional adult reversion to childish religious ideas under stress, but the comment of Rosenberg (1989a, b) must not be forgotten, that substitution characterized the religious ideas of children lacking strong religious socialization. There is sufficient evidence for religious development to be regarded, at least sometimes, as involving substitution and not integration, especially in the earlier years. The importance of social learning emphasized in moral learning is certainly important in religious learning, as also is its lack of insistence on a rigid application of stage theory. The identical nature of responses between Jewish, Catholic, and Protestant children which Elkind found suggests that similar religious ideas develop in similar ways in faiths other than Christian. Unfortunately very little research has as yet been carried out in this area, although Oser (1985) stated that his tests of religious judgment were not culturally specific.

The late development of formal operational thinking about religion must be noticed; it can perhaps be explained as due to unfamiliarity of content for many respondents drawn from a materialistic society. When subjects with a religious background have been identified they frequently show a much better response in religious tests. Studies in Ireland and Northern Ireland have been mainly of attitude to religion, but the higher scores recorded suggest the possibility of an earlier development of formal religious thinking. Meanwhile, the objectivity of much of the argument against a developmental approach to religious thinking remains in question, when so little of it rests on psychological theory and so much of it appears to be due to theological presupposition.

One issue of great importance which requires further investigation concerns younger children in the first years at school. If Goldman has been criticized for questioning young children about material which they were bound to interpret at their own inadequate level, and for the form of questions used, it still remains to be seen what a sensitive study would reveal in this area. Much energy has been spent on debating the issue of the content of religious education for this age-group, but sufficient insight to give full guidance is still lacking. Goldman did not explore the ideas of preschool children, although indications of the use they make of imperfectly understood religious vocabulary are found in chapter 5. Little is known of the origins and nature of their first religious insights, and adult recollections of incidents in these first years of life are incomplete and unreliable. Despite the difficulties involved and the time required, it is from two to seven more than at any other time that a serious longitudinal study is needed. Until then, the overall description of religious thinking set out by Goldman remains the best guide so far available.

Alternative approaches to cognitive development

The application of Piagetian theory has given a significant understanding of cognitive development in religion. But while this remains influential for religious education, it has to be noted that little attempt has been made to instigate research based on more recent studies of cognitive development.

There has been a research explosion about cognitive development and communication, accompanied by a tendency to shift away from Piagetian theory to information processing theory. Modern technology has resulted in cognitive development being regarded as a particular instance of information processing, while simultaneously computer-based studies of artificial intelligence have suggested new approaches to the mental mechanisms of cognition. A full treatment of information processing models is to be found in Newell and Simon (1972). While these studies are general psychological investigations, many of the problems they explore are those met in the development of religious thinking, and for this reason some of them are cited since their methods and conclusions seem appropriate to religious research.

One example of the information processing approach is that of Schroder, Driver, and Streufert (1967) who studied the reactions and responses of adolescent groups in contrived war games situations with varying degrees of complexity and available information. Although the two groups appeared to be very similar they differed significantly in their conceptual levels. One person might only perceive two elements in a particular situation, another three. Yet two elements used with flexibility could offer better insight into a situation than three elements only used independently. Adolescents functioning in this way could view a social situation in terms of two points of view, seeing one in relationship to the other and perceiving the effects of one on the other. They could observe the effects of their own behavior from several points of view which were not compartmentalized. The authors distinguished between adolescents of apparently similar abilities who yet differed in how they used new information to create new ideas or to use it in novel ways. Does this offer a model for teaching strategies in religious education?

Klahr and Wallace (1976) explored the logical processes in cognitive development by artificial intelligence programs. They were related to well-established psychological studies, many of them Piagetian. A considerable number of the tasks required a very detailed analysis, so that children often had to detect the structures of syntax and relate them to semantic structures when the two could be independent. Abstraction was an example of a sudden jump from continuous to discontinuous processing. They advanced a theory of cognitive development that placed the detection of sequential regularities at the core. What mechanisms trigger the spiritual advance associated with releasing religious thinking from concrete categories?

The work of Schank and Abelson (1977) bears on the area where the interests of psychology, linguistics, and artificial intelligence overlap. In common speech implicit meanings are often conveyed without strict grammatical structure. "I like apples" is about eating, although eating is not mentioned. Speech often implies causal chains, and these they investigated by a study of scripts. Their scripts were a growing elaboration of a few simple and often humorous anecdotal sentences, many of them concerned with familiarity about restaurants. They produced a computer program about restaurants that could recognize the implied differences between two similar short statements—"John went to a restaurant. He asked the waitress for *coq au vin*. He paid the bill and left." and "John went into a restaurant. He ordered a Big Mac. He paid for it and found a nice park to eat it." One was explicable only by knowledge of "fancy" restaurants, the other by Fast Food outlets. A script was seen as a structure that described appropriate sequences of events in a particular context, of stylized everyday situations. It took a particular point of view—a customer saw a restaurant one way, a chef another. To understand the actions found in a situation the subject must have been in that situation before, and other peoples' actions made sense only as they were part of a stored program of actions that had been previously experienced. Scripts were acquired only by experience; children learned about restaurants by experiencing them enough times, and the knowledge was acquired gradually. A three-year-old might focus on eating but know nothing about paying. Knowledge of plans and goals facilitated adaptation to new situations, so most understanding was script-based, and new information was understood in terms of old information. Plans describe the set of choices a person has when setting out to accomplish a goal; the authors indicate different categories of goals, some of them immediate, such as the satisfaction of hunger; others long-term, such as achieving a lifelong ambition. These goals were generated by the beliefs individuals held and their life-themes, such as honesty, lifestyle, or political attitude. The study appears to bear very much on religious learning through involvement in the religious activities of church, mosque, synagogue, or temple and indicates the substantial difference between such practical learning of religious scripts and classroom learning of religious material.

Klausmeier and his associates (1979) made an extremely thorough study of concept development in the school years both from a Piagetian stance and from their own theory of conceptual learning development. The care taken over all aspects of testing and the comparison of different types of statistical analysis applied to the results makes the work an outstanding example of the proper use of such procedures.

Concept attainment was seen as a result of acquiring and organizing information, which was an active and constructive process, and then storing and retrieving it. They recognized the importance of neurological maturation but considered that this must interact with learning to provide increasingly powerful mental processes whereby learning became more efficient, so that long after maturation has ceased the cognitive structures continued to develop. Four successive levels of attaining a concept were envisaged: designated concrete, identity, classificatory, and formal. These theoretical levels were described in some detail, and their approach to concepts was further extended and clarified and tested alongside Piagetian theory, in an extended longitudinal study. Their conceptual learning and development theory demonstrated invariant progression through the levels they described. Contrary to Piaget, concurrent development of the levels was fundamental to their theory. Attainment of the four successive levels of the same concept continued for many years and any three successive levels developed concurrently for one or more years. Attaining the higher level of concepts was accompanied by increasing understanding of principles and by more advanced problem-solving skills; individuals of the same age varied greatly in their levels of concept attainment, and this variability became increasingly differentiated according to the content during the junior school years. They cited both Piaget and Bruner to support their stress on the importance of formal education, and an experiment demonstrated that a few carefully planned lessons to teach specific concepts introduced at the proper time to supplement classroom instruction produced large gains by the pupils in a short time. The development shown was relatively unrelated to that described by Piaget, and the development of the cognitive dimensions proceeded quite independently and not as Piagetian theory would expect. The results did not support Piaget's concrete operational stage as descriptive of children's actual cognitive development during ages seven to eleven, nor the stage of concrete operational thought as an empirically verifiable theoretical construct. To the contrary, it was found that by the end of the primary school years the ability to classify was functioning at a mature level. If this was shown to be the case with religious concepts, how important it would be.

Appendix H

Metaphor Comprehension in Childhood

To understand parables and much biblical material requires an ability to understand metaphors. This topic has attracted a good deal of attention recently, and there is a growing interest in the whole area of metaphor; major issues of philosophy, linguistics, and psychology are involved. A brief account of recent studies about children's understanding of metaphors allows the more specific research about biblical material to be set in context and evaluated against objective psychological norms.

Ortony (1979) focused attention on some of the issues. Should metaphors be seen as a deviation from the normal use of language, or do they play an important, even essential, role in language and thought? If truth cannot be narrowly and objectively expressed, is there something of metaphor in any statement of it? Metaphor is an essential element in normal communication, and even in scientific understanding it is important.

Metaphor is the principle whereby one concept is understood in terms of another. Metaphors are not easy to define, although they are simple to illustrate. A metaphor assigns to X a property Y which it could not literally possess in that context. Its tenor is its purpose or general drift of thought; its topic, X, is the subject of the metaphor, and its vehicle, Y, is the image which relates to the tenor. The ground of a metaphor is what its tenor and its vehicle have in common. Many classifications of metaphors have been suggested. Similarity metaphors rely on a shared attribute, as when a submissive person is called a sheep. In a proportional metaphor, at least four elements of a sentence are related proportionally—"put a tiger in your tank" relates the implied fuel to a car as power relates to a tiger. The literary concepts of similarity and relation and their novel integration are also the basis for the psychological processes in metaphor comprehension (Paivio, 1979).

Understanding the metaphoric use of language is a complex activity. It requires the ability to distinguish between analogy and metaphor, to recognize that a literal interpretation is inappropriate, to treat a statement that has the surface structure of a predictive statement as a statement of comparison, and to represent objects with sufficient detail so that their prominent features can be distinguished (Ortony 1986). Miller (1979) argued that in novel metaphors, it was not the meaning of the words which changed but our feelings and beliefs about the things to which the words referred. The claim that metaphor played an important part in learning was disputed by Green (1979), who felt that their use was seldom indispensable, except by religious teachers.

Tourangeau and Sternberg (1982) argued that metaphors correlated two systems of concepts from different domains, and good metaphors involved distant domains. Because the tenor and the vehicle were in different domains they did not share the features involved, and interpreting metaphors required several stages in which the terms of the metaphor were encoded, the domains involved were inferred, the structures to be seen as parallel were found, the correspondences between the structures were mapped, the terms involved were compared, and then the metaphor was reinterpreted, the last particularly if it was ironic or hyperbolic in type. Studies aimed at revealing the psychological processes involved in metaphor comprehension can bear on educational interests; context affected comprehension and plausibility (Waldbrand, 1983), and greater semantic difference between topic and vehicle produced slower comprehension (Christian, 1982). Literal and metaphoric statements were similarly processed and guided by the expectation of meaning so that the properties of a metaphor did not make a significant difference in comprehension, but true-false and absurd statements behaved quite differently (McKoy, 1980). The level of development of operational thinking was significantly related to metaphor comprehension with students (Petrun, 1980). Children aged ten could recall metaphoric passages with greater ease than literal paraphrases of the same material, and those aged seven had no difficulty in relating metaphoric and literal descriptions in familiar passages (Pearson et al., 1979).

Piagetian theory was the basis of some earlier studies. Children from seven to nine could use figurative language at the stage of concrete operational thinking, but it required formal operational thinking in order to explain the relationships (Pollio and Pollio, 1974). When they investigated if children could understood figurative language even when they could not explain it, the developmental sequence showed that cliches were always a little better understood and that the production of figurative language required not only metaphoric understanding but also confidence in their own expressive style (Pollio and Pollio, 1979). Only with the attainment of logical operational thinking were children up to twelve able to paraphrase and explain metaphors and proverbs in common use in a way acceptable to adults; the less common items proved to be the most difficult to understand. Berlese (1983) found that high-school students from sixteen to eighteen with formal operational thinking achieved a significantly better understanding of psychological metaphors.

Because some Piagetian studies regarded metaphoric understanding as only attainable in the final stages of language development while others described the spontaneous use of metaphor and figurative speech by preschool children, Winner, Rosenstiel and Gardner (1976) asked children to explain metaphoric sentences or select a paraphrase. Magic responses showed a peak at eight, after which genuine metaphoric responses were almost all at six or seven; metonymic responses, using words in a transferred sense, rapidly fell off after eight; primitive metaphoric responses increased greatly. Children of ten demonstrated a basic understanding of metaphors but often were unable to explain them, exhibiting metaphoric thinking before they could use words with precision, and were more competent with sensory rather than psychological figures.

Galda (1981) read stories with anomalous endings to children, providing pictures to help find the meaning of each story ending, for a literal or metaphorical or unconnected meaning. Understanding and the ability to explain improved with age, and she found six stages comparable to Piaget's, ranging from difficulty with literal comprehension to immediate understanding and verbal explanation of the metaphoric relationship. Schecter (1980) explored the relationship between animism and the development of metaphoric thinking. Concepts of life and consciousness were tested against the understanding of body metaphors, e.g., describing people as hard-headed or soft-headed. Children of six to eight used anthropomorphic data for attributing or denying life to various objects, whereas older children developed more scientific criteria and an ability to appreciate metaphoric senses of life. The younger children could only understand body metaphors in a literal sense. Longitudinal studies confirmed the observations. The development was compatible with the general properties of cognitive development, and these body metaphors could only be understood when the children had left animistic thinking behind.

A seminal study was by Billow (1975), using similarity metaphors with only two elements and proportionality metaphors with four or more elements. Metaphor comprehension was strongly related to maturing cognitive operations as well as to age, and the significant increase in comprehension of proportional metaphors between seven and thirteen was significantly related to advances in formal operational development. Boys of five scored 29 percent for understanding similarity metaphors, but by seven this had become 66 percent, so that a figurative sense appeared to be developing quite early in life. In a further study (Billow, 1981), he observed groups of children aged two to six, recording their possible metaphoric creations and subsequently asking them about their awareness and understanding of these usages. By this means he was able to demonstrate that metaphoric processes exist quite early in children's development.

Ortony (1979) demonstrated that in metaphor comprehension, which required the comprehension of the nonliteral use of language in general and of metaphor in particular, there were two basic variables—the nature and the extent of contextual support. Measures of metaphor comprehension often confounded general linguistic performance with metaphoric ability (Reynolds and Ortony, 1980). There was an important difference between metaphors and similes; the apparent violation of conversational postulates which was immediately obvious in the case of the metaphor was much less obvious for the simile; children of four could distinguish meaningful expressions from anomalous ones and were aware that terms from the metaphorical expressions were from a different category from the literal ones, so that they showed some rudimentary metaphoric aptitude (Vosniadou and Ortony, 1983a). When some children aged six were asked to paraphrase stories that ended metaphorically while others were asked to play them out, the latter group produced more correct interpretations than the others and showed a much better comprehension. It appeared that paraphrasing underestimated young children's understanding of metaphor (Vosniadou and Ortony, 1983b; Vosniadou, 1984). The experiment was repeated with a control group using literal endings to the stories to ensure that they were fully comprehensible (Vosniadou, Ortony, Reynolds, and Wilson, 1984). The predictability of the story endings and the complexity of the metaphors affected comprehension, but even preschool children showed some evidence of metaphor comprehension. Metaphor comprehension was a progressive development that started quite early in life but did not have a clearly identifiable sequence of stages. In this respect the results were inconsistent with Piagetian theory. Hanson (1982) undertook six experiments to test Ortony's model of the semantic processing underlying metaphor comprehension, and his results gave general support to it.

Research showed that children's ability to produce and understand metaphorical language emerged out of their notions of similarity and developed to encompass many conceptual domains. It was a continuous and not a stage-like process which was restricted by the limitations in their knowledge and their information-processing ability. It required the transfer of knowledge from one conceptual domain to another, and this depended on their conceptual knowledge which was advanced by it (Vosniadou, 1987).

It is studies concerned with metaphor comprehension which bear most directly on religious understanding. Culture affects the comprehension of metaphors; a comparison of American and Colombian children showed that the children performed better when interpreting metaphors that were native to their respective cultures, as Ortony's theory of contextual metaphor comprehension would suggest (Henao, 1983). Children's ability to understand and use metaphors increased with maturity, and increased maturity differentiated between adolescents and adults. Adolescents tended to be more literal and analytic in their thinking, adults exhibited a more synthesizing, integrative, or poetic style of thought. Metaphors were an integral component of ordinary language (Boswell, 1977). Children aged six failed to grasp that metaphors were intended nonliterally, and only at about ten did they begin to give appropriate explanations of them. The ability to articulate the underlying meaning of a word was not a necessary condition for correct paraphrasing, but rather understanding of metaphor arose from knowledge of the real world and a capacity to think analogically (Winner, 1977). In a teaching situation over a few months children aged nine were able to produce and appreciate figurative language to the extent that it quickly became routine. Although individuals varied greatly in their rates of progress, the stages they passed through in this development were remarkably similar (Winner, 1976). When the metaphor comprehension of children of four to six was studied, pictures were found to facilitate the comprehension of perceptual matches and words the comprehension of linguistic matches; the tasks were performed better by six-year-olds. Unexpectedly, appropriate symbolic play did not facilitate comprehension by any of the children (Seitz, 1987). Comprehension of metaphors by children from five to nine involving different conceptual domains emerged at about the same time for terms within the same field and often at very different times for metaphors from different fields. Comprehension developed on a domain by domain basis and depended on the extent of knowledge in the two domains juxtaposed in the metaphor (Keil, 1986).

Several studies have looked at the relative difficulty of understanding different types of metaphors, and their authors have sometimes invented their own phraseology to describe them, which are in themselves not of immediate concern. Their order of difficulty did not change between six and nine. Predictive metaphors and similes were the most difficult to understand, topic-less metaphors were of intermediate difficulty, and analogies and riddles the easiest. The childrens' cognitive skills were insufficient to perceive the resemblance between normal and metaphoric use when a metaphor was based on a physical resemblance, so that some additional pragmatic skill was needed (Winner, 1978). With children aged four the word arrangement of metaphors was important; the directed form, X is like Y, was better understood than the nondirected form, X and Y are alike. The children found similarities by finding properties for one term and then applying them to the other (Cerbin, 1984). Proportional metaphors were more difficult than predictive to understand, but perceptual metaphors and psychological metaphors were of similar difficulty. Older children had better understanding, although the younger children were familiar with the features of the metaphors and recognized literally the topics and vehicles they used. Even children aged seven could deal with proportional metaphors when they had a good grasp of their concepts and vocabulary (Nippold, 1982; Nippold, Leonard, and Kail, 1984). Between the ages of five and seven there was a wide-ranging ability and a steady improvement in children's analogical reasoning and proportional metaphor comprehension, which was related to their vocabulary development (Nippold and Sullivan, 1987). Young children preferred metaphors involving color and shape; in the middle years, movement and sound, and older children preferred metaphors that were not perceptual. Preference for a literal rather than a metaphoric completion to a sentence declined with age (Silberstein, Gardener, Phelps, and Winner, 1982).

While metaphor comprehension appeared to be a cognitive, analytic problem-solving process, metaphor preferences rested on aesthetic judgments and individual differences which were differently processed (Green, 1985). This may partly account for a finding about the developmental trend which did not support the hypothesis that concepts began at a primitive, concrete level and gradually developed to the comprehension of abstract metaphors (Broderick, 1984, 1985). In this developmental trend, dual-function words (e.g., "a cold way") were less well understood than metaphors before age eleven, and proverbs were least well comprehended at every age. Most children aged eight could translate metaphors and dual-function words, but proverbs were not understood until formal operational thinking was achieved. Many of the observed responses showed Piaget's verbal syncretism, by which children erroneously imagine they have understood; e.g., "birds of a feather" meant "feathers are soft" or "the birds are chirping" (Douglas and Peel, 1979).

Understanding idiomatic expressions showed a significant increase with age, and although some idioms were comprehended at six or seven, for most children comprehension increased rapidly after nine, irrespective of their sex (Prinz, 1983). While normal and slow-learning children showed improvement with age in their comprehension, slow-learning children lagged far behind those of normal ability, the older of them achieving less than the younger of the normal group. (Boxerman-Kraemer, 1984). A study was undertaken in which children and adolescents had to describe people or human characteristics either by personification, using inanimate, physical qualities, or by objectification, using psychological qualities. The children aged four were equally likely to objectify as to personify, but at fourteen they tended to personify rahter than objectify (Rosenberg, 1987).

Even children aged five could construct figurative interpretations of metaphors when they were familiar with the context, but older children and adults were progressively less dependent on it. The interpretation of metaphors was not a single ability to distinguish between the literal and the figurative but included both continuous and discontinuous changes in different aspects of interpretive activity at different points in development (Hadley, 1982). There was no apparent difference in difficulty at age ten between interpreting metaphors or similes, but context had an important effect. Metaphors and similes in an irrelevant context proved to be more difficult to understand (Rickelman, 1983). When there was contextual priming about metaphoric meaning there was immediate and automatic metaphor comprehension (Gildea and Glucksberg, 1983). For students the quality of a metaphor was determined by its context and not by its conceptual similarity. Memory for metaphor was related to its structure; tenors and vehicles were recalled to the same extent, and nearly always as a pair, but when recall was by a cue, tenors were consistently recalled more often. It followed that the vehicle is a consistently better prompt for the tenor of a metaphor than the reverse, showing that the vehicle carries more weight in a metaphor (McCabe, 1980). Ortony, Schallert, Reynolds, and Antes (1978) showed that figurative language seemed to be processed in much the same way as literal language, and in comprehending metaphors the degree of contextual support was the chief determinant of difficulty.

In the cognitive processes underlying metaphor comprehension the level of metaphor processing rested both on mental capacity and on the learning that accrues with age (Johnson, 1980). Metaphor comprehension improved with age, without any sex difference. By age eight the metaphors children used were understood regardless of their ground, and at all ages, even adult, abstract metaphors were the least preferred. In the older years more able children performed significantly better than the others (Green, 1985). When familiar concrete nouns were used metaphorically kindergarten children could distinguish genuine metaphors from nonsense; by age seven the metaphors most accepted changed from being perceptually grounded to functionally grounded. By adolescence metaphoric relationships were rejected that were acceptable to younger children and to adults. Overall, many differences were found between individuals in their flexibility in evaluating metaphors (Shantiris, 1983, 1984).

There was a significant age difference between eight and eleven in understanding metaphors; it was associated with reading vocabulary, reading comprehension, and total reading achievement. There was no sex difference (Muller, 1976). Good readers were better at metaphor comprehension and metaphor-related language tasks than poor readers (Seidenberg and Bernstein 1988). At twelve, specific word knowledge arising from vocabulary-based teaching, rather than the traditional ways of teaching about metaphors, proved to be a key factor in interpreting them (Readence, Baldwin, Rickelman, and Miller, 1986). When good and poor readers were asked to predict the content of stories from literal and metaphorical titles and then after reading the stories, to confirm or deny their predictions, many poor readers predicted a literal interpretation based on a metaphoric title, and subsequently confirmed this despite the story content. Most children, given a metaphoric title, chose a response more appropriate for a literal title, rather than one which contained a simile related to the metaphor of the title (Kraus, 1980). Metaphors occurring naturally in a story were processed less successfully than the text as a whole, and different kinds of metaphors were processed in different ways. Average readers aged twelve dealt with the metaphors better than more proficient younger readers or less proficient older readers. Less successful processing of metaphors demonstrated that when there were inherent difficulties in the metaphoric language they affected the reading process (Altwerger, 1982). Good readers were better at metaphor comprehension and metaphor-related language tasks than poor readers (Seidenberg and Bernstein, 1988).

Another group of studies have been concerned with the way that children use metaphors in normal situations, producing them in writing or in conversation. In conversation metaphor was found to be more meaningful than literal utterances in producing a change of perspective about a discussion (Crider, 1984). Children between five and nine could produce and understand metaphors related to their own world and vocabulary, and the types of metaphor produced changed with their mental development. It was apparent that competence with metaphors depended on a complex interaction between semantic, cognitive, and motivational factors (Warnick, 1983). In essay writing, some children aged nine produced metaphors which required formal operational thinking; their metaphor production increased with age; there was no sex difference at this age as there was with graduate students (Fox, 1984). Observation of poetry writing lessons showed that children were influenced by the teacher's use of language, and metaphor affected the way the children interacted; it could be used to structure an environment and to analyze relationships, and to enhance learning (Mayfield, 1986). Metaphor production in children's work was stimulated by filmed scenes which enabled such pairings as a literal (a ballerina spinning and leaping), a metaphorical (a ballerina and a top spinning), and a nonsensical (a ballerina leaping and a top spinning). Literal pairings were frequent and constant for all ages; metaphorical pairings increased with age, and metaphoric language, which also increased with age, was used only when talking about metaphoric pairings. Perceived metaphoric similarity was sufficient to elicit metaphoric language, and this facility increased with age (Dent, 1980). Young children showed symbolic manipulation in their spontaneous metaphors which noted similarity between different objects. These emerged first and were followed by simile, and after this more deliberate proportional metaphor emerged (Harris, 1982).

At times metaphoric understanding is an aid to memory. Among high-school students paraphrases best aided retention of concrete scientific information, but metaphors were more effective in remembering abstract material (Angelo, 1979).

The comprehension of proverbs is a related topic. It was noted earlier that proverbs were less well comprehended at every age (Douglas and Peel, 1979). Another study found that there was no clear association between logical operations and proverb interpretation (Cometa, 1976; Cometa and Eson 1978). Parental education affected the ability of adolescents aged fifteen to understand and apply common proverbs, but the family income level did not. There was a significant difference between black and white groups, so that racial linguistic characteristics constituted a factor in understanding (Fisher, 1981). Working-class black children and middle-class white children from six to nine could reason abstractly and analogically and comprehend and generate metaphors by interpreting proverbs and using them. Ideas generated by other children stimulated abstraction when assisted by the teacher (Pasamanick, 1982). But children aged six to nine were capable of abstracting the basic meaning of proverbs and did so in a variety of credible ways. This was in contrast to Piagetian theory which required a later age for it to happen. It was due to regarding the developmental process as involving an interaction between adults and children (Pasamanick, 1983). Failure to distinguish proverbs as both analogies and metaphors had led to confusing results. There was a developmental basis in comprehending proverbs, but evidence was lacking to indicate the development of any underlying component skills, so that it was inappropriate to derive an essentially linguistic phenomenon from a logic of hierarchical structures imported from the realm of Piagetian operations. Tests indicated that proverbs were perceived as an affectation of speech, and children preferred abstract statements (Resnick, 1977, 1982). Understanding of common proverbs was very significantly related to verbal reasoning; there was a highly significant improvement between the ages of twelve and thirteen, and then little further development until seventeen or eighteen (Jarman, 1985).

It has been suggested that studies of the development of a sense of humor in children might also shed light on their ability to understand some types of religious material. Allport (1937) considered that a sense of humor indicated insight and was similar to religion in providing a different frame of reference for contemplating life's worries and mischances. But he saw this as a mature quality and quite distinct from the cruder sense of humor of children. Even so, there would seem to be common elements in the two even at this level—it is incongruity which provides children with the sense of the absurd or comic, just as there was incongruity in such religious disclosure as Ramsey (1957) described when "the penny dropped." Incongruity also has something in common with metaphor. A definitive study of children's humor was made by Athey (1970), who not only made a competent critical survey of the literature, comparing Freud's work, often regarded as fundamental, with a range of other studies, but compared the responses of children to humorous items at various levels of complexity. Results were significantly related to vocabulary scores. There was no significant difference between boys and girls; laughter and comprehension were strongly associated, and there were marked age differences, which related closely to Piaget's basic stages. The children's recognition of the incongruities in the stories was a central issue, and there were a number of levels at which they were perceived. This perception of incongruity depended on an intellectual ability to shift rapidly within the available congruences, combining the different aspects or concepts in the item.

These studies not only show that metaphoric understanding is a developmental process, but it does not have a clearly identified sequence of stages, so that its relationship to Piagetian stages is not precise. It is affected by them indirectly by the development of vocabulary, especially as indicated by reading ability and by the normal process of maturation with increasing age, which operates in part through the extension of experience which age brings. Metaphoric understanding is affected by the type of metaphor used, and its context is of considerable importance. Ease of comprehension is related to the context, which is another way of describing the related experience and cultural background. These factors probably account for the greater difficulty found at every age in understanding proverbs—these nearly always relate to a comparison outside everyday experience in the present. Some facility with words which appears to involve metaphor has been observed in several studies with preschool children, but before too much stress is placed on this it is well to note the warning of Marti (1986), who argued that since children below the age of four cannot differentiate the relationships involved in identity, resemblance, or difference, any claim that their speech used metaphors had failed to consider their cognitive competence. All of this suggests that great caution is needed when using biblical material involving any sort of metaphoric intention with children below the age of seven or eight. One implication of the contextual theory is that metaphoric religious narratives are more likely to be understood by those children with some experience of religious activities and utterances. It remains for the psychological insights into the nature of metaphors to be related to literary studies of parables and other biblical material, and then for this to be made the basis for further research into biblical understanding.

Appendix I

Attitude to Religion—Theoretical Considerations

Attitude measurement effectively began with Thurstone and the method by which he developed a scale for measuring "Attitude to the Church" (Thurstone and Chave, 1929). Respondents had to tick the items they agreed with from a longer list in which various opinions were expressed. Shortly afterwards Likert (1932) produced an alternative type of scale using items with responses of the type agree strongly, agree, not certain, disagree, disagree strongly. This work produced a rapidly growing literature about attitude measurement and an immediate interest in attitude change. Problems of scale construction soon emerged. The judgment of independent assessors about possible items can be unreliable—the subjects in six widely differing groups assimilated the religious statements toward the position of their own group. A Christian Union student group assimilated statements favorable to its own position at the favorable end of the scale and others to the unfavorable end, whereas a Socialist group assimilated the most unfavorable statements toward its own unfavorable position. (Roiser, 1981).

The problem of adequately defining an attitude in psychological terms and of reconciling expressed attitudes with observed behavior became major issues. Greenwald (1968) made the acute observation that there were three approaches to defining attitudes—to present a new definition, to select the one most favored after reviewing other definitions, or after the review, to despair of finding any consensus. Surveying the contributions he and his colleagues had gathered in their book, he pointed out that there were a limited number of themes expressed in the many definitions—the conditioned, the discriminative, and the reinforcing stimulus functions attributed to attitude objects, and it followed that attitude theory, although complex, had to do with the organization of habits, cognitions, and emotions. Disregard of one or other aspects of this structure could lead to many false paths. Lemon (1973) complained that attitude had become a pot pourri term, with no generally accepted definition but tailored to suit any purpose in hand.

Salomonsen (1972) had defined an attitude simply as an emotional state of readiness that comprised cognitive elements. (His interest had been the analysis of long unstructured interviews about religious education and preparation for confirmation. He extracted key items about the issues and categorized responses to them into positive, negative, or neutral which proved to be scalable). Argyle and Beit-Hallahmi (1975) defined it as the extent to which a person is favorable or unfavorable to the organization or set of practices and judged by his verbal expression. Francis and Kay (1984) regarded attitude to religion as restricted to an affective element but recognized that it was then specific to a particular belief. Francis (1976) defined it as "a relatively permanent and enduring evaluative predisposition to a positive or negative response of an affective nature which is based upon or reflects to some extent evaluative concepts or beliefs learned about the characteristics of a referent or group of referents which come within a definition of the religious." This assumes that attitudes are relatively stable; mean attitude scores of groups tend to show changes over a period of time, but there is evidence that individual children do not have stable attitudes to issues in which they are not personally involved. It is now recognized that attitudes are learned, persist over time, and consist of predispositions to respond to a given object or class of objects, rather than fixed responses (Thomas, 1978). They comprise knowledge regarding the object of the attitude, feelings, likes, or dislikes about the object and behavioral tendency toward the object. The literature regarding the nature of attitudes is considerable.

An early problem was that behavior could not be accurately predicted from an attitude alone but could be contrary to it. The classical illustration was provided by LaPiere (1934) who, while traveling extensively in America with a Chinese student couple, recorded their experiences with hotels and restaurants, only once being refused accommodation. Yet six months later in replying to a written question about accepting Chinese people as guests, only one hotel said that it would offer them accommodation. Much research has subsequently been undertaken about this problem. It was alleged that individuals' attitudes toward an object could be seen as a function of their beliefs about that object, although they could have many beliefs about it which might or might not reinforce each other (Fishbein, 1967).

A definitive theoretical study was that of Ajzen and Fishbein (1970) who concluded that behavior could be predicted with accuracy from expressed intentions, which mediated the effect of the other variables influencing behavior. Intention to perform an act is a joint function of attitude toward performing it and of beliefs about what behavior is expected in that situation; these beliefs are in turn affected by the motivation to comply with what is expected. A persuasive message was insufficient to account for attitude change, which was dependent on changing behavioral intention. Liska (1975) reviewed the changes over several decades whereby the original understanding of attitude was modified by practical considerations of attitude measurement; it had become an affective response in a very select sample to quite particular symbolic objects. Even with this limitation, it was difficult to predict the relevant behavior from the expressed attitude with any degree of consistency. That behavior is the product of many influences, of which attitude is only one, was argued at length by Fishbein and Ajzen (1975)—attitudes vary not only in the degree to which they are favorable or unfavorable, but also in their complexity and strength; they seldom exist in isolation but tend to cluster with other attitudes held by individuals and their groups.

Subsequent studies have added to the complexity of the matter. Thomas and Tuck's (1975) examination of Fishbein's attitude theory cited studies showing that attitudes were equally well predicted by beliefs spontaneously elicited by individuals. Their own experiment, replicating Fishbein's design, showed that a large proportion of the beliefs most frequently expressed by their students were not salient for them, and some sets of beliefs known to be inappropriate for the purpose were still good predictors when using Fishbein's formula. Liska (1984) reviewed the relationship between attitude and behavior and, in particular, the Fishbein-Ajzen model, which he regarded as viewing attitude formation and change as a product of human information processing. This was an inefficient operation which took time, even months and years. The model ignored the effect of behavior on intention and attitude. Intention was not a necessary and sufficient cause of behavior—people frequently did not do what they intended to do. While the conceptual distinction among intention, cognition and attitude was useful, intention did not completely mediate the effect of attitude on behavior, and neither did attitude mediate completely the effect of beliefs on intention—beliefs were frequently too complex for the cognitive ability of people to allow them to proceed completely into attitudes. Contrary to the Fishbein-Ajzen model behavior affected both intentions and attitudes and was not merely the product of them, and an even more complex model was required. Behavior was the result of attitudes, behavioral intention, and subjective norms, each of which was affected by contingent variables, and attitude itself was affected by behavior. Attitudes and subjective norms both arose from beliefs about the specific consequences and social expectations of behavior. These beliefs interacted with each other and were themselves the product of the social situation, which not only affected these beliefs but gave rise directly to the behavior intention.

Subsequently, he used a sophisticated technique to make further studies of the effect of attitudes on behavior and behavior on attitudes; Liska et al. (1984) confirmed that both effects depended on the presence of conditions that accentuated these effects. Davis (1985) tested Liska's model and found that while his results did not entirely support it, neither did they support the Fishbein-Ajzen one. In predicting behavior the centrality of the individual's intention was not lost but neither was the effect on it of social structure. Cooper and Croyle (1984) in another review noted in some areas the cognitive response perspective was dominant, so that in two particular areas of ongoing research the interplay among cognitive, psycho-physiological, and social psychology was reaffirmed.

Behavior can be inconsistent with an expressed attitude; this was once thought to undermine the concept of attitude. But without the recognition that this inherent inconsistency between attitudes and behavior is something to be expected there can still arise somewhat artificial discussions regarding the direction of causation, whether behavior is due to attitude, or attitude is the consequence of behavior. Does a positive attitude to the church motivate an individual to church attendance or is it church attendance that gives rise to the attitude? There cannot be one with-out the other, and both are manifestations of integrated mental structures which do not develop in a fragmentary manner but in which all attitudes and all behav-ioral patterns are related. Influences which give rise to specific behaviors also give rise to the related specific attitudes; the significant association of the two does not imply that one is the cause of the other. However, in a study of students' atti-tudes Kahle and Berman (1979) were able to show that attitudes had causal pre-dominance over behavior for all four issues tested, which implied that if attitudes changed, behavior would also subsequently change.

Another difficulty lay in the interpretation of numerical scores; the significance of a neutral point on a multiple-choice Likert-type scale (ranging from "strongly agree" to "strongly disagree") is not clear. There is no way of saying with certainty that above a certain point all scores indicate a favorable attitude, while below it all scores show an unfavorable one. Westermann (1983) made a critical exam-ination of scoring methods used with different types of attitude scales and showed that there was serious doubt whether attitude scale scores were interval-set mea-surements. Earlier, Edwards (1957) had provided a technique to deal with the dif-fering operational characteristics of items in an attitude scale.

Other problems relevant to religious issues have also been indicated. Olson (1978) compared students' religious behavior with previously expressed attitudes and found much inconsistency except among those professing low religiousness. Brown and Ferguson (1968) asked students first to answer the question "Who am I?" and subsequently to complete an attitude to religion scale. Scale results indicated a higher degree of religiousness than answers to the question. Of the highest scoring students, less than a half gave any place to religion in their answers, and of the lowest scoring students only a quarter gave a religious reply.

The assumption that the public has stable attitudes was tested by Bishop, Hamilton, and McConahay (1980) on political issues. In general they found it unfounded. On matters relatively remote to them the less well educated had nonat-titudes rather than attitudes, but the college-educated had a more coherent belief system, with the interrelatedness of their attitudes remaining consistent, whereas the attitudes of the other group, while relatively stable, were organized in idiosyn-cratic ways. Does it follow that individuals with little or no religious involvement may have less stable attitudes to religion, or even display "nonattitudes" and show inconsistency about related issues?

Ungar (1980) demonstrated that religious behavior is affected by social norms. Under anonymous conditions students' attitudes were not affected by mild reli-gious manipulation whereas under public conditions it had a measurable effect. This was explicable by presuming that the students made attitude statements that were influenced by their wanting to give the most socially desirable response; self-perception seemed only to influence inconsequential issues of little importance. Bryan and Walbek (1970) asked junior age children to play a game which allowed them to make small winnings and also exposed them to one of four people who practiced and preached either charity or greed, or who preached one but practiced the other. They found that while the preaching influenced what the children preached to each other, it did not influence their practice; their practice, but not their preaching, was influenced by the practice of the model. Brinberg (1979) used church attendance to study two different models by which attitude was compared with professed intention and actual behavior and found that one model was better for predicting intention, the other for actual behavior.

The sophistication of measurement can lead to research becoming flawed by misunderstanding the nature of the data unless the relatively crude conceptualizations on which it is based are kept in mind. Lemon (1973) questioned the logic of measuring attitude by a simple scale and then attributing attitude changes to an external influence when some other indicator could have given the same result; it was better to use behavioral criteria. Equally, two individuals might differ markedly in the characteristics they ascribed to an attitude object, yet be identical to each other in the degree of feeling they manifested to it. It was possible for people to hold a neutral position to an issue, being uncertain of their opinion about it, and yet still to regard it as very important. The intensity and extremity of attitudes could be regarded as independent dimensions. It follows that similar responses to an item such as "I find it hard to believe in God" can represent different psychological orientations to different concepts of God. Belief in a benign, loving God is quite different from belief in a harsh, unmerciful God, even if the strength of the attitude is identical in each case. Sadly, no studies on attitude to religion appear to have been undertaken which involve the fundamental distinction between different religious orientations. Long before this Rokeach (1956) argued for a practical link between emotional states and cognitive beliefs, so that, for example, fear of being alone and of isolation could be represented as a cognitive belief that "Man on his own is a helpless and miserable creature," and when stated in this way the distinction between what was cognitive and what was emotional was all but erased. Later (Rokeach 1974), he suggested that there were far too many attitudes and beliefs to give a satisfactory explanation of human behavior whereas the links between values and behavior were strong, long-lasting, and more decisive for behavior. He regarded values as arising from cognitive preferences, and they appeared to give a stronger cognitive basis for behavior than an affective one. Rokeach's stance was recognized by Kitwood and Smithers (1975), although they were critical of the tests he had used.

There is no reason to regard the balance between cognitive understanding of scale items and the affective response to them as constant; it is more likely to vary from item to item, and certainly from scale to scale, but both are always present to some degree. Attitude scores are never a measure of a purely affective response—such a response cannot exist. Because an attitude score can be measured with precision and the reliability of a scale be expressed at a high level, it does not necessarily follow that it measures what it was designed to do. By way of illustration Greer (1982b) used the two attitude to religion scales of Francis

(1976) and of Turner (1970), both of proven statistical reliability. Francis scale was essentially affective and designed for use with children, and with little explicit reference to Christian doctrine; that of Turner included doctrinal statements and opinions about doctrine, intended to emphasize cognitive aspects of Christianity. When Greer used them in Northern Ireland mean scores on both scales were similar, yet there were significantly different types of response between Catholic and Protestant pupils, the Catholics tending to score higher on Francis' affective instrument, while the Protestants tended to score higher on Turner's cognitive instrument. Greer regarded this as indicating that the two scales did not measure the same thing.

A single test instrument is capable of analysis from more than one perspective. When Muthén, Olsson, Pettersson, and Stahlberg (1977) developed and used an attitude to religion scale, the first analysis of their data showed factors of religiousness, such as general, evaluative, Christian, or traditional factors. The second analysis, directed to the subjects tested, showed differences between those who classified themselves as Christian, Christian with reservations, and non-Christian. The third analysis of the concepts underlying the test showed three factors, one related to aspects of the Deity, the second a non-religious-religious continuum, and the third human religious behavior versus divine activity. Such complex structures may well be disguised by simple comparisons of overall test scores secured from two groups not necessarily similar according to the functioning of the test used.

Observed differences between the attitude scores of two groups may not necessarily be due to the variable under investigation. Clift, Hutchings, and Povey (1984) studied boys and girls in four urban primary schools and found that those in spacious class-rooms differed in some respects from those in space-restricted conditions. Those in a better environment showed more positive attitudes toward their own class and its image and claimed to be more conforming and to relate better to their teachers than those in the restricted environment. Would this influence have affected in any way their measured attitude to religion?

Not all agree about the value of attitude studies. Nuttin (1975) regarded the concept of social attitude change as misleading and useless for predicting or understanding behavior. The concept, he argued, could serve only as a parsimonious label for descriptive studies of the way groups said they thought, felt, or were invited to behave with regard to some value, but social and educational studies ought seriously to question any understanding or practice based on these social attitude assumptions.

Attitude scales measure with great precision a somewhat uncertain quantity. Intelligence tests offer a parallel. No other tests have yielded results of greater reliability and precision than those for Intelligent Quotient, but now it is recognized that, apart from disagreement about what it was that they measured, they could not reliably predict children's academic performance a few years later, which is what they were used for in England. Attitude to religion measures an affective response to a general religiousness but indicates little about the beliefs of its respondents or of their religious behavior.

Glossary

ACCOMMODATION
As used by Piaget, the process whereby cognitive mental structures become more complex as they are modified by new experiences.

AFFECTIVE
The mental activity of feelings, motivation, and reactions to others and to oneself, as distinct from the cognitive which is concerned with thought.

ASSIMILATION
As used by Piaget, the cognitive process by which experiences are understood and interpreted.

ASSOCIATION
A less technical term for the statistical measure of correlation.

COGNITIVE
The mental activity of thought, as distinct from the affective, which is concerned with feelings.

CORRELATION
A statistical procedure which determines the strength of the relationship between two distinct measures, as between age and mental development. A correlation coefficient of +1.0 would indicate a perfect positive relationship; 0.0 would indicate no relationship at all. An inverse relationship is indicated by a negative coefficient. Correlation does not imply a causal relationship, but it can be used to predict one measure from the other, and the stronger the correlation, the more accurate the prediction.

Factor analysis

A highly sophisticated statistical technique, greatly facilitated by computer programs, which calculates from the manner in which a number of items in a test are correlated the smaller number of underlying influences which account for them; each of these is called a factor, and the degree to which particular items contribute to each factor is known as their factor loading.

Locus of control

A description of how individuals see themselves in relation to the external world. Those with an external locus of control regard happenings as caused by chance, fate, or other powerful people; those with internal control consider that they have control over their decisions and what happens to them.

Modeling

Learning that arises from observations of the performance of other people.

Path analysis

When all the correlations of a group of variables are known, the direction of causation is assumed where it seems probable, and by a series of repetitions, the strength of causation of all the variables can be determined.

Rank order

The order of a set of scores placed in order from the lowest to the highest.

Reliability

The reliability of a measurement indicates the probable accuracy with which it coincides with the measurement for the whole population. The reliability of a test estimates its consistency in gauging the particular ability of the subjects tested by its freedom from chance errors of measurement. Internal consistency is the extent to which each item in a test measures exactly the same variable being tested.

Scalogram analysis

An analysis of the degree to which a series of test items can be placed in an increasing order of difficulty evident to all respondents. Ideally, for each item there should be a group of respondents who have correctly endorsed it and every preceding item and no following item. The extent to which a set of items fulfills this condition is expressed by a coefficient of reproducibility ranging from 0 to 1.

Schools in England and Wales

Except for independent schools, schools are mainly financed and controlled by a local education authority, which is a committee of the local authority administering the area, either a county, county borough, or a county town.

Grammar schools, some of which have a long history, are secondary schools whose pupils have been selected at age eleven for their above-average mental ability. They tend to be traditional in their ethos and have a strong academic emphasis in their curriculum. Most have now been absorbed into comprehensive schools, but in some local education authority areas a few still remain.

Modern schools were established by the 1944 education act which required secondary education for all children. They offered a curriculum designed for children of average or below-average ability. In practice, they were often regarded as schools for children who had failed to secure a grammar school place, and they have now all been absorbed into comprehensive schools.

Technical schools were established in a few large cities to provide a technical emphasis in education for pupils likely to proceed to some form of industrial employment.

Comprehensive schools are secondary schools for all children regardless of their ability and are now the most frequently found type of secondary school.

Sixth forms comprise pupils above age sixteen who have chosen to remain at school for further study after the school-leaving age. Alternative provisions for education after sixteen are available in colleges of further education.

Primary schools educate children from the age of five up to secondary age; separate infant and junior schools are sometimes found, but infant and junior departments in a primary school are more frequent.

In a few places, schools are organized into first, middle, and high schools; the age of transition between them varies, as does the organization of middle schools.

Church schools are of two types, both primary and secondary. Voluntary aided schools (a few have special agreements with their local education authority) are financed by the local authority, but staff appointments, pupil admissions, religious education, buildings and their use are controlled by the governors who represent the church and provide 15 percent of all capital costs. When a new voluntary aided school is built, or an existing one extended, the governors have to provide 15 percent of the cost. In voluntary controlled schools, the governors have no financial responsibility for capital costs, and only a fifth of them represent the church; they lack any special power, except for being consulted in the appointment of a teacher responsible for church teaching. With a single exception, Catholic schools are always voluntary aided.

SEMANTIC DIFFERENTIAL

A method of testing attitudes devised by Osgood, Succi, and Tannenbaum (1957). Subjects are presented with contrasting pairs of words, such as good/bad, and have to indicate the position between them on a numerical scale (often 1-9) of their own feeling about the object in question.

SIGNIFICANCE

In statistics, significance measures the extent to which a result is due to chance. When the odds against its chance occurrence are 20 to 1 (the 5 percent level, sometimes shown as P(robability) = 0.05) it is regarded as statistically significant. With odds of 100 to 1 (the 1 percent level, P=0.01) it is regarded as highly significant.

REFERENCES

NUMBERS FOLLOWING THE CITATIONS IN PARENTHESES, BOLDFACE,
REFER TO THE LOCATION OF THE CITATIONS IN THE TEXT.

Abraham, K. G.
(1986)   Ego-identity differences among Anglo-American and Mexican-American adolescents,
          Journal of Adolescence, 9,151-166. **(217)**
Abraham, K. L.
(1979)   *The influence of cognitive conflict on religious thinking in fifth and sixth grade children,*
          PhD thesis, Oregon State University. **(32)**
(1981)   Cognitive conflict as a methodology in the design of religious education curriculum,
          Character Potential, 9,207-212. **(32)**
Acklin, M. W.
(1984)   *An ego developmental study of religious cognition*, PhD thesis, Georgia State University. **(358)**
Acock, A. C. and Bengtson, V. L.
(1978)   On the relative influence of mothers and fathers: a covariance analysis of political and
          religious socialization, *Journal of Marriage and the Family*, 40,519-530. **(234)**
(1980)   Socialization and attribution processes; actual versus perceived similarity among parents
          and youths, *Journal of Marriage and the Family*, 42,501-515. **(228)**
Adorno, T. W., Frenkel-Brunswik, E., Levison, D. J., and Sanford, R. N.
(1950)   *The Authoritarian Personality*, New York: Norton. **(350)**
Adulf, E. M. and Smart, R. G.
(1985)   Drug use and religious affiliation, feelings, and behavior, *British Journal of Addiction*,
          80, 163-171. **(289)**
Ahmad, N. H.
(1973)   Religiosity as a function of rigidity and anxiety, *Indian Journal of Experimental Psy-
          chology*, 7,49-50. **(206)**
Ahrendt, C. J.
(1975)   *Relationship between the self-concept of children and their concepts of God*, PhD thesis,
          University of Texas at Austin. **(196)**
Aiken, L. A.
(1979)   *Relationship of extroversion and religion to hierarchical drug use in adolescents*, PhD
          thesis, Loyola University of Chicago. **(195)**
Ainsworth, D.
(1961)   *A study of some aspects of the growth of religious understanding of children aged
          between 5 and 11 years*, DipEd dissertation, University of Manchester. **(17)**, **(38)**, **(117)**
Ajzen, I. and Fishbein, M.
(1970)   The prediction of behavior from attitudinal and normative variables, *Journal of Exper-
          imental Psychology*, 66,466-487. **(392)**

Alatas, S. H.
  (1977)   Problems of defining religion, *International Social Science Journal*, 29,213-234. (**336**)
Alatopoulous, C. S.
  (1968)   *A study of relationships between knowledge and certain social and moral attitudes among school leavers*, MPhil thesis, University of London. (**151**), (**340**)
Albrecht, S. L., Chadwick, B. A., and Alcorn, D. S.
  (1977)   Religiosity and deviance: application of an attitude-behavior contingent consistency model, *Journal for the Scientific Study of Religion*, 16,263-274. (**286**)
Albrecht, S. L. and Cornwall, M.
  (1989)   Life events and religious change, *Review of Religious Research*, 31, 23-38. (**203**)
Alexander, K. L. and Pallas, A. M.
  (1985)   School sector and cognitive performance: when is a little a little? *Sociology of Education*, 58, 115-128. (**301**)
Allen, E. F. and Hites, R. W.
  (1961)   Factors in religious attitudes of older adolescents, *Journal of Social Psychology*, 55,265-273. (**148**)
Allen, R. O. and Spilka, B.
  (1967)   Committed and consensual religion: a specification of religion-prejudice relationships, *Journal for the Scientific Study of Religion*, 6,191-206. (**351**)
Allery, C. H.
  (1985)   *Religion and worship in the Victorian school*, BPhil dissertation, University of Birmingham. (**99**)
Allison, J.
  (1968)   Adaptive regression and intense religious experience, *Journal of Nervous and Mental Disease*, 145,452-463. (**190**)
  (1969)   Religious conversion: regression and progression in an adolescent experience, *Journal for the Scientific Study of Religion*, 8,23-38. (**190**)
Allport, G. W.
  (1937)   *Personality: a Psychological Interpretation*, London: Constable. (**390**)
  (1950)   *The individual and his religion; a psychological interpretation*, New York: Macmillan. (**10**), (**351**)
  (1966)   The religious context of prejudice, *Journal for the Scientific Study of Religion*, 5,447-457. (**351**)
Allport, G. W. and Ross, J. M.
  (1967)   Personal religious orientation and prejudice, *Journal of Personality and Social Psychology*, 5,432-443, reprinted in Malony, H.N. (Ed.) (1977), *op.cit.* (**351**)
Almond, G.
  (1954)   *The Appeals of Communism*, Princeton: Princeton Univeristy Press. (**223**)
Alston, J. P.
  (1975)   Review of the polls, *Journal for the Scientific Study of Religion*, 14, 165-168. (**341**)
  (1977)   Problems of defining religion, *Social Science Journal*, 29, 213-234. (**336**)
Alston, J. P. and Hollinger, R. C.
  (1972)   Review of the polls, *Journal for the Scientific Study of Religion*, 11,401-403. (**244**)
Alston, J. P. and McIntosh, W. A.
  (1979)   An assessment of the determinants of religious participation, *Sociological Quarterly*, 20,49-62. (**243**)
Altwerger, B. I.
  (1982)   *A psycholinguistic analysis of sixth, eighth, and tenth grade readers' processing of naturally occurring text metaphors*, EdD thesis, University of Arizona. (**389**)
Alves, C.
  (1968)   *Religion and the Secondary School*, London: SCM Press. (**140**), (**150**), (**242**), (**256**), (**306**)
Alwin, D. F.
  (1986)   Religious and parental child-rearing orientations: evolution of a Catholic-Protestant convergence, *American Journal of Sociology*, 92,412-440. (**296**)
Ambert, A-M. and Saucier, J-F.
  (1986)   Adolescents' overt religiosity and parents' marital status, *International Journal of Comparative Sociology*, 27,87-95. (**235**)

Amon, J. and Yela, M.
   (1968)   Dimensions de la religiosidad, *Revista de Psicologia General y Aplicada*, 23,989-993. (**351**)
Anderson, D. R.
   (1967)   *The effects of instruction on the development of propositional thinking in young ado-lescents*, DCP dissertation, University of Birmingham. (**143**)
Anderson, D. S.
   (1971)   Do Catholic schools cause people to go to church? *Australian and New Zealand Journal of Sociology*, 7,65-67. (**324**)
   (1988)   Values, religion, social class and the choice of private school in Australia, *International Journal of Educational Research*, 12,351-373. (**332**)
Anderson, D. S. and Western, J. S.
   (1972)   Denominational schooling and religious behavior, *Australian and New Zealand Journal of Sociology*, 8,19-31. (**324**), (**326**)
Andrews, M. M.
   (1981)   *The use of models and metaphors in religious discourse, with special reference to impli-cations for syllabuses in religious education*, MPhil thesis, University of Aston. (**124**)
Ang, A. L.
   (1989)   *The relationship between moral reasoning and religious orientation of Bible college stu-dents in Singapore*, EdD thesis, Biola Univeristy, Talbot School of Theology. (**284**)
Angelo, R. V.
   (1979)   *Effects of metaphors and paraphrases as encodings of verbal information*, PhD thesis, Florida State University. (**389**)
Annis, L. V.
   (1976)   Emergency helping and religious behavior, *Psychological Reports*, 39,151-158. (**358**)
Arbour, L.
   (1977)   *The effectiveness of a high-school theology course on the doctrine of original sin, sal-vation, and grace*, MRE project, University of St. Michael's College. (**28**)
Archer, S. L.
   (1982)   The lower age boundaries of identity development, *Child Development*, 53,1551-1556. (**215**)
Argyle, M.
   (1958)   *Religious Behavior*, London: Routledge and Kegan Paul. (**199**), (**222**), (**249**), (**350**)
   (1964)   Seven psychological roots of religion, *Theology*, 67, 331-339. (**10**), (**217**)
Argyle, M. and Beit-Hallahmi, B.
   (1975)   *The Social Psychology of Religion*, London: Routledge and Kegan Paul. (**248**), (**251**), (**392**)
Ash R. T.
   (1969)   Jewish adolescent attitudes toward religion and ethnicity, *Adolescence*, 4,245-282. (**19**), (**303**)
Ashby, M. LaV.
   (1968)   *The effect of self concept on children's learning in religious education*, PhD thesis, George Peabody College for Teachers. (**211**)
Astey, J.
   (1984)   The role of worship in Christian learning, *Religious Education*, 79,243-251. (**165**)
Athanasou, J. A.
   (1984)   Religious practices and knowledge among Greek Orthodox junior high-school students, *Journal of Christian Education*, Papers 79,17-25. (**242**), (**332**)
Athey, C.
   (1970)   *A theoretical and experimental study of humour in children related to Piaget's theory of intellectual development*, MEd dissertation, University of Leicester. (**390**)
Atkins, J. B.
   (1972)   *The attitude of the young adolescent to religion and religious eduction*, DipRE disser-tation, University of Nottingham. (**153**)
Attfield, D.
   (1974)   A fresh look at Goldman: the research needed today, *Learning for Life*, 14,44-49. (**38**)
   (1976a) Conceptual research in religious education, *Learning for Life*, 16,68-75. (**38**)
   (1976b) Moral thinking in religion — a note on Goldman, *Educational Studies*, 2,29-32. (**38**)
Ausubel, D. P., Montemajor, R., and Svajian, P.
   (1977)   *Theory and Problems of Adolescent Development*, New York: Grune and Stratton. (**286**)
Ausubel, D. P., Sullivan, E. V., and Ives, S. W.

(1980)   *Theory and Problems of Child Development,* (3rd Ed.) New York: Grune & Stratton. **(99), (282)**

Aylwin, T.
(1981)   Using myths and legends in school, *Children's Literature in Education,* 12,82-89. **(125)**

Babin, P.
(1963)   *Crisis of Faith,* New York: Herder & Herder (trans. *Les jeunes et la foi,* Lyons, 1960). **(78)**
(1964)   The idea of God: its evolution between the ages of 11 and 19, in Godin, A. (Ed.) (1964), *op. cit.* **(78)**
(1967)   *Faith and the Adolescent,* London: Burns, Oates (trans. *Dieu et l'adolescent,* Lyons, 1963) **(78)**

Baggot, A. L.
(1978)   *Religious attitudes, authoritarianism, selected personal values and probabilistic upward social-class mobility in working-class adolescents,* PhD thesis, New York University. **(208)**

Bagshaw, D. R.
(1966)   *An inquiry into the quality of adolescent thinking about biblical passages,* DCP dissertation, University of Birmingham. **(29), (135)**

Bahr, H. M. and Martin, T. K.
(1983)   "And thy neighbor as thyself": self-esteem and faith in people as correlates of religiosity and family solidarity among Middletown high-school students, *Journal for the Scientific Study of Religion,* 22,132-144. **(209)**

Baither, R. C. and Saltzberg, L.
(1978)   Relationship between religious attitude and rational thinking, *Psychological Reports,* 43,853-854. **(353)**

Baker, M. and Gorsuch, R.
(1982)   Trait anxiety and intrinsic-extrinsic religiousness, *Journal for the Scientific Study of Religion,* 21,119-122. **(207)**

Balch, R. W.
(1980)   Looking behind the scenes in a cult: implications for the study of conversion, *Sociological Analysis,* 41,137-143. **(189)**

Ballard, S. N. and Fleck, J. R.
(1975)   The teaching of religious concepts: a three stage model, *Journal of Psychology and Theology,* 3,164-171. **(46)**

Bambach, J. D.
(1973)   Relevance in religious and moral education: a study of students' questions and opinions in some English and Canadian schools, *Journal of Christian Education,* Papers 16,108-120. **(327)**

Ban, J. D.
(1986)   Adolescents in Canadian culture: religious development, *Religious Education,* 81,225-238. **(279)**

Barber, L. W.
(1978)   *Celebrating the Second Year of Life,* Birmingham, Alabama: The Religious Education Press. **(99), (102)**
(1981)   *The Religious Education of Preschool Children,* Birmingham, Alabama: The Religious Education Press. **(99), (102)**

Barker, I. R. and Currie, R. F.
(1985)   Do converts always make the most committed Christians? *Journal for the Scientific Study of Religion,* 24,305-313. **(191)**

Barnes, D. and Shemilt, D.
(1974)   Transmission and interpretation, *Educational Review,* 26,213-228. **(142)**

Barnes, E.
(1892)   Theological life of a Californian child, *Pedagogical Seminary,* 2,442-448. **(66)**

Barnes, J. H.
(1984)   *The longitudinal impact of a small, religiously orientated, liberal arts college on the dogmatism and selected value related attitudes and behaviors of its graduates,* EdD thesis, Loyola University of Chicago. **(272)**

Barnes, M.
(1989)   In defense of developmental theories of religion, *Journal for the Scientific Study of Religion,* 28,230-232. **(58)**

Barnes, M. and Doyles, D.
  (1989)   The formulation of a Fowler scale: an empirical assessment among Catholics, *Review of Religious Research*, 30,412-440. **(58)**
Barnes, V. C.
  (1983)   *The influence of religion on the attitudes of West Indian adolescents in Birmingham*, BPhil (Ed.) dissertation, University of Birmingham. **(241)**
Barnsley, G. and Wilkinson, A.
  (1981)   The development of moral judgment in children's writing, *Educational Review*, 33,3-16. **(140)**
Barton, K., Modgil, S., and Cattell, R. B.
  (1973)   Personality variables as predictors of attitude toward science and religion, *Psychological Reports*, 32,223-228. **(195)**
Barton, K. and Vaughan, G. M.
  (1976)   Church membership and personality: a longitudinal study, *Social Behavior and Personality*, 4,11-16. **(196)**
Batres, A. L.
  (1984)   *Parental methods of control/influence as antecedents to belief systems*, PhD thesis, University of Colorado at Boulder. **(233)**
Batson, C. D.
  (1971)   *Creativity and religious development: toward a structural-functional psychology of religion*, ThD thesis, Princeton Theological Seminary. **(17)**
  (1974)   Creative religious growth and pre-formal religious education, *Religious Education*, 69,302-315. **(100)**
  (1975)   Rational processing or rationalization? The effects of disconfirming information on stated religious beliefs, *Journal of Personality and Social Psychology*, 32,178-184. **(162)**
  (1976)   Religion as prosocial: agent or double agent? *Journal for the Scientific Study of Religion*, 15,29-45. **(358)**
Batson, C. D. and Gray, R. A.
  (1981)   Religious orientation and helping behavior: responding to one's own or the victim's needs? *Journal of Personality and Social Psychology*, 40,511-520. **(354), (359)**
Batson, C. D., Naifeh, S. J., and Pate, S.
  (1978)   Social desirability, religious orientation, and racial prejudice, *Journal for the Scientific Study of Religion*, 17,31-41. **(356)**
Batson, C. D. and Raynor-Prince, L.
  (1983)   Religious orientation and complexity about existential concerns, *Journal for the Scientific Study of Religion*, 22,38-50. **(356)**
Batson, C. D. and Ventis, W. L.
  (1982)   *The Religious Experience; A Social-Psychological Perspective*, New York and Oxford: Oxford University Press. **(202), (356)**
  (1985)   Misconception of Quest: a reply to Hood and Morris, *Review of Religious Research*, 26,398-407. **(357)**
Baxter, J.
  (1977)   Models of religious understanding and adolescent reality, *Learning for Living*, 17,25-33. **(360)**
Bayer, G. C.
  (1982)   *The relationship between religious orientation and sex-role identity*, PhD thesis, Rosemead Graduate School of Professional Psychology. **(200)**
Bayley, C.
  (1970)   Relation of religion and racial prejudice in Europe, *Journal for the Scientific Study of Religion*, 9,219-225. **(351)**
Bealer, R. C. and Willits, F. K.
  (1967)   The religious interests of American high-school youth, *Religious Education*, 62,435-444. **(265)**
Beard, R.
  (1969)   *An Outline of Piaget's Developmental Psychology*, London: Routledge and Kegan Paul. **(120)**
Beardsworth, T.
  (1977)   *A Sense of Presence*, Oxford: The Religious Experience Research Unit. **(177), (186)**
Becker, L. B.
  (1977)   Predictors of change in religious belief and behavior during college, *Sociological Analysis*, 38,65-74. **(275)**

Becker, R. J.
 (1971) Religion and psychological health, in Strommen, M. P. (Ed.), *op.cit.* **(201)**
Beechick, R. A.
 (1974) *Children's Understanding of Parables: a Developmental Study*, EdD thesis, Arizona State University. **(38), (120)**
Beiswanger, G. W.
 (1930) The character value of Old Testament stories, *University of Iowa Studies in Character*, 3,1-63. **(17), (99)**
Beit-Hallahmi, B.
 (1973) (Ed.) *Research in Religious Behavior: Selected Readings*, Monterey, California: Brooks/Cole Publishing Co.
 (1974) Self-reported religious concerns of university underclassmen, *Adolescence*, 9,333-338. **(274)**
 (1979) Personal and social components of the Protestant ethic, *Journal of Social Psychology*, 109,263-267. **(237)**
 (1986) Religion as art and identity, *Religion*, 16,1-7. **(168)**
Beit-Hallahmi, B. and Argyle, M.
 (1975) God as a father projection, *British Journal of Medical Psychology*, 48,71-75. **(95), (186)**
Bender, I. E.
 (1958) Changes in religious interest: a retest after 15 years, *Journal of Abnormal and Social Psychology*, 57,41-46. **(271)**
Benoit, A.
 (1969) Valeurs sociales transmises par l'enseignement secondaire des eglises et de l'etat en Colombie, *Social Compass*, 16,29-44. **(298)**
Benson, P. L., Donahue, M. J., and Guerra, M. J.
 (1989) The good news gets better, *Momentum*, Nov. 40-44. **(300)**
Benson, P. and Spilka, B.
 (1973) God image as a function of self esteem and locus of control, *Journal for the Scientific Study of Religion*, 12,297-310. **(210), (212)**
Berger, M. H.
 (1978) *The relationship of religious attitudes and values with personality adjustment*, PhD thesis, University of North Carolina at Chapel Hill. **(203)**
Berger, P. L.
 (1969) *A Rumor of Angels*, London: Allen Lane, The Penguin Press. **(223)**
 (1974) Some second thoughts on substantive versus functional definitions of religion, *Journal for the Scientific Study of Religion*, 13,125-133. **(337)**
Berger, W. and Van Der Lans, J.
 (1979) Stages of human and religious growth, *Concilium*, 122,34-43. **(39)**
Bergin, A. E.
 (1983) Religiosity and mental health: a critical reevaluation and meta-analysis, *Professional Psychology: Research and Practice*, 14,170-184. **(202), (204)**
Bergin, A. E., Stinchfield, R. D. et al.
 (1988) Religious lifestyles and mental health: an exploratory study, *Journal of Counselling Psychology*, 35,91-98. **(202)**
Bergin, A. E., Masters, K. S. and Richards, P. S.
 (1987) Religiousness and mental health reconsidered: a study of an intrinsically religious sample, *Journal of Counselling Psychology*, 34,197-204. **(207)**
Bergline, K.
 (1974) *The Development of Hypothetico-Deductive Thinking in Children*, New York: Halstead Press. **(42)**
Berlese, E. E.
 (1983) *Misunderstanding understanding: an analysis of differences between concrete and formal operational adolescents in their understanding of metaphor in psychotherapy*, PhD thesis, California School of Professional Psychology, Berkeley. **(384)**
Bernt, F. M.
 (1989) Being religious and being altruistic: a study of college service volunteers, *Personality and Individual Differences*, 10, 663-669. **(359)**
Berridge, D. M.

(1969)   *Growing to Maturity*, London: Burns & Oates. **(98)**, **(257)**
Berryman, J. W.
(1979)   Being in parables with children, *Religious Education*, 74,271-285. **(68)**, **(101)**, **(123)**
(1980)   Montessori and religious education, *Religious Education*, 75,294-307. **(123)**
(1985)   Children's spirituality and religious education, *British Journal of Religious Education*,
         7,120-127. **(123)**
Berzonski, M. D.
(1978)   Formal reasoning in adolescence, *Adolescence*, 13,279-290. **(372)**
Best, O. G.
(1967)   *The development of explanatory thought in the adolescent in out of school social sit-
         uations*, DPC dissertation, University of Birmingham. **(137)**
Bibby, R. W.
(1983)   Searching for invisible thread: meaning systems in contemporary Canada, *Journal for
         the Scientific Study of Religion*, 22,101-119. **(348)**
Bible Society
(1978)   *National survey on religious attitudes of young people*, London: Bible Society. **(250)**,
         (248), **(258)**, **(282)**
(1980)   *Prospects for the eighties*, London: Bible Society.
Biggs, J. B. and Collis, K. F.
(1982)   *Evaluating the Quality of Learning*, New York: Academic Press. **(138)**
Biggs, J. B. and Telfer, R.
(1987)   *The Process of Learning*, Sydney: Prentice-Hall. **(138)**
Billow, R. M.
(1975)   A cognitive developmental study of metaphor comprehension, *Developmental Psychol-
         ogy*, 11,415-423. **(385)**
(1981)   Observing spontaneous metaphor in children, *Journal of Experimental Child Psychology*,
         31,430-445. **(385)**
Binkley, L. K.
(1963)   What characterizes religious language? *Journal for the Scientific Study of Religion*, 2,18-
         22. **(361)**
Bishop, G. D., Hamilton, D. L. and McConahay, J. P.
(1980)   Attitudes and nonattitudes in the belief system of mass publics, *Journal of Social Psy-
         chology*, 110,53-64. **(394)**
Black, A. M.
(1968)   *Experiments in developing young children's ideas of God*, DipEd dissertation, University
         of Liverpool. **(141)**
Black, A. W.
(1970)   An investigation into pupils' attitudes to religious instruction in New South Wales sec-
         ondary schools, *Australian Journal of Education*, 14,19-29. **(326)**
Black, M. S. and London P.
(1966)   The dimensions of guilt, religion, and personal ethics, *Journal of Social Psychology*,
         69,39-45. **(232)**
Blair, J. R., McKee, J. S. and Jernigan, L. F.
(1986)   Children's belief in Santa Claus, Easter Bunny, and Tooth Fairy, *Psychological Reports*,
         46,691-694. **(138)**
Blizard, R. A.
(1980)   *The relationships between three dimensions of religious belief and moral development*,
         PhD thesis, California School of Professional Psychology. **(285)**
Blum, P.
(1976)   *A comparative analysis of the impact of family and social role orientation on the devel-
         opment of religious values among adolescents*, PhD thesis, University of Notre Dame. **(154)**
Bock, E. W., Beeghley, L., and Mixon, A. J.
(1983)   Religion, socio-economic status and sexual morality: an application of reference group
         theory, *Sociological Quarterly*, 24,545-559.**(291)**
Bock, G. E.
(1976)   *The Jewish schooling of American Jews: a study of noncognitive educational effects*,
         EdD thesis, Harvard University. **(304)**

Boehm, L.
(1962)   The development of conscience: a comparison of students in Catholic parochial schools
           and in public schools, *Child Development*, 33, 591-602. **(282)**, **(296)**
(1963)   The development of conscience: a comparison of upper-middle class gifted children
           attending Catholic and Jewish parochial schools, *Journal of Social Psychology*, 59,101-
           110. **(282)**, **(296)**
Boivin, M. J., Darling, H. W., and Darling, T. W.
(1987)   Racial prejudice among Christian and non-Christian college students, *Journal of Psy-
           chology and Theology*, 15,47-57. **(354)**
Bolt, M
(1975)   Purpose in life and religious orientation, *Journal of Psychology and Theology*, 3,116-118. **(205)**
Bonney, M. E.
(1949)   A study of friendship choices in college in relation to church affiliation. . ., *Journal of
           Social Psychology*, 29,153-166. **(71)**, **(274)**
Booth, F.
(1965)   *A sample study of the religious ideas of fourth year juniors*, DipChDvt dissertation, Uni-
           versity of London. **(106)**
Borenstein, M. T.
(1982)   *Religious orientation and moral development*, PhD thesis, New York University. **(282)**
Borklund, P. A.
(1980)   *Spiritual transformation/individuation: a descriptive study of the spiritual journeys of
           selected Christians*, PhD thesis, California School of Professional Psychology. **(58)**
Borowitz, E. B.
(1980)   Beyond immanence, *Religious Education*, 75,387-408. **(168)**
Bose, R. G.
(1929)   Religious concepts of children, *Religious Education*, 24,831-837. **(66)**, **(103)**
Boswell, D. A.
(1977)   *Metaphoric processing in maturity*, PhD thesis, Pennsylvania State University. **(386)**
Bouhmama, D.
(1990)   A study of the relationship between moral judgment and religious attitude of Algerian
           university students, *British Journal of Religious Education*, 12, 81-85. **(284)**
Bourque, L. B.
(1969)   Social correlates of transcendental experience, *Sociological Analysis*, 30,151-163. **(168)**
Bowden, J. S.
(1958)   *An enquiry in religious education in the West Midland Counties*, PhD thesis, University
           of Birmingham. **(77)**
Boxerman-Kraemer, S.
(1984)   *The comprehension of idiomatic expressions by normal and borderline children: a devel-
           opmental case study*, PhD thesis, Adelphi University, The Institute of Advanced Psy-
           chological Studies. **(388)**
Boyle, D.
(1982)   Piaget and education: a negative evaluation, in Mogdil, S. and Mogdil, C. (Eds.) (1982),
           op. cit. **(371)**
Boyle, J. J.
(1984)   *Catholic children's attitudes towards Christianity*, MSc thesis, University of Bradford. **(318)**
Boyle, J. J. and Francis, L. J.
(1986)   The influence of differing church aided school systems on pupil attitude toward religion,
           Research in Education, 35,7-12. **(318)**
Bradbury, J. B.
(1947)   *The religious development of the adolescent*, MEd thesis, University of Manchester. **(76)**, **(146)**
Bradford, R. E.
(1978)   *An investigation of religious orientation and mental abnormality*, EdD thesis, East Texas
           State University **(355)**
Bradley, L. R.
(1983)   *An exploration of the relationship between Fowler's theory of faith development and
           Myers-Briggs personality type*, PhD thesis, Ohio State University. **(55)**
Bradshaw, J.

(1949)   *A psychological study of the development of religious beliefs among children and young people*, MSc thesis, University of London. **(76)**

Brandenburg, G. C.
(1915)   The language of a three-year old child, *Pedagogical Seminary*, 22,89-120. **(99)**

Brandling, R.
(1980)   *Christmas in the Primary School*, London: Ward Lock Educational. **(103)**

Brantley, L. S.
(1986)   *Adolescent moral development and religious exposure in a black Seventh-Day Adventist parochial school*, EdD Thesis, George Peabody College for Teachers of Vanderbilt University. **(285)**

Breed, G. and Fagan, J.
(1972)   Religious dogmatism and peak experiences: a test of Maslow's hypothesis, *Psychological Reports*, 31,866. **(171)**

Brimer, J.
(1972)   School worship with juniors, *Learning for Life*, 11,5,6-12. **(307)**

Brinberg, D.
(1979)   An examination of the determinants of intention and behavior: a comparison of two models, *Journal of Applied Social Psychology*, 9,560-575. **(395)**

Brink, T. L.
(1978)   Inconsistency of belief among Roman Catholic girls concerning religion, astrology, and reincarnation, *Review of Religious Research*, 20,82-85. **(267)**

Briscoe, H.
(1969)   *A study of some aspects of the special contribution of Church of England aided primary schools to children's development*, MEd thesis, University of Liverpool. **(313)**

British Council of Churches
(1981)   *Young People and the Church*, London: British Council of Churches. **(251)**

Britton, E. C. and Winanc, J. M.
(1958)   *Growing from Infancy to Adulthood*, New York: Appleton-Century-Crofts. **(99)**

Broderick, V. K.
(1984)   *The development of metaphor comprehension*, paper presented to the annual meeting of the Eastern Psychological Association. **(387)**
(1985)   *The development of metaphor comprehension in preschool children*, PhD thesis, Pennsylvania State University. **(387)**

Broen, W. F.
(1957)   A factor-analytic study of religious attitudes, *Journal of Abnormal and Social Psychology*, 54,176-179. **(345), (346)**

Bron, B.
(1975)   Intoxication and ecstasy: the phenomenon of toxic ecstasy in young people, *Confinia Psychiatrica*, 18,61-72. **(290)**

Bronfenbrenner, U.
(1974)   The origins of alienation, *Scientific American*, 231,2,53-61. **(262)**

Brothers, J. B.
(1964)   Religious attitudes of educated young Catholics in the same school year, in Godin, A. (Ed.) (1964), *op. cit.* **(316), (333)**

Broughton, W.
(1975)   Theistic conceptions in American Protestantism, *Journal for the Scientific Study of Religion*, 14,331-344. **(87), (345), (346)**

Broun, S. N.
(1984)   *An analysis of ego development and religious development*, PhD thesis, University of Texas Health Science Center at Dallas. **(57)**

Brown, C. M. and Furguson, L. W.
(1968)   Self concepts and religious beliefs, *Psychological Reports*, 22,266. **(394)**

Brown, D. M. and Annis, L.
(1978)   Moral development and religious behavior, *Psychological Reports*, 43, 1230. **(283)**

Brown, G.
(1983)   Piaget's theory and educational psychology, in Mogdil, S., Mogdil, C. and Brown, G. (Eds.) (1983) *Jean Piaget: an interdisciplinary critique*, London: Routledge & Kegan Paul. **(371)**

Brown, G. and Desorges, C.
(1979)   *Piaget's Theory: A Psychological Critique*, London: Routledge and Kegan Paul. **(371)**
Brown, K. B.
(1974)   *Relationship between personal religious orientation and positive mental health*, PhD thesis, United States International University. **(202), (209)**
Brown, L. B.
(1962)   A study of religious belief, *British Journal of Psychology*, 53,259-272. **(103), (348)**
(1965a)   Classifications of religious orientation, *Journal for the Scientific Study of Religion*, 4,91-99. **(347), (348)**
(1965b)   Aggression and denominational membership, *British Journal of Social and Clinical Psychology*, 4,175-178. **(221)**
(1966a)   Egocentric thought in petitionary prayer: a cross-cultural study, *Journal of Social Psychology*, 68,197-210. **(112)**
(1966b)   The structure of religious belief, *Journal for the Scientific Study of Religion*, 5,259-272. **(11), (18), (222), (344), (348)**
(1968)   Some attitudes underlying petitionary prayer, in Godin A. (Ed.) (1968a), *op. cit.* **(112), (113)**
(1981a)   Another test of Yinger's measure of nondoctrinal religion, *Journal of Psychology*, 107,3-5. **(347)**
(1981b)   The religionism factor after 25 years, *The Journal of Psychology*, 107,7-10. **(222)**
Brown, L. B. and Forges, J. P.
(1980)   The structure of religion: a multidimensional scaling of informal elements, *Journal for the Scientific Study of Religion*, 19,423-431. **(344), (347)**
Bruce, S.
(1983)   The persistence of religion: conservative Protestantism in the United Kingdom, *Sociological Review*, 31,453-470. **(246)**
Brusselmans, C. and Wakin, E.
(1977)   *A parent's guide: religion for little children*, Huntington, Indiana: Our Sunday Visitor. **(98)**
Bryan, J. and Walbek, N.
(1970)   Preaching and practicing self-sacrifice: children's actions and reactions, *Child Development*, 41,329-353. **(395)**
Bryk, A. S. and Holland, P. B.
(1982)   The implication of Greeley's latest research, *Momentum*, 13,8-11. **(301)**
Bucher, A. A. and Reich, K. H. (Eds.)
(1989)   *Entwicklung von Religiosität*, Freiburg: Universitätsverlag Freiburg Schweiz. **(59)**
Buckalew, L. W.
(1978)   A descriptive study of denominational correlates in psychotic diagnosis, *Social Behavior and Personality*, 6,239-242. **(205)**
Bulkeley, S. G.
(1981)   *The image of God and parental images: a dialogue between theology and psychology*, PhD thesis, University of Glasgow. **(94)**
Bull, N. J.
(1969)   *Moral Education*, London: Routledge & Kegan Paul. **(55), (140)**
Bullen, A.
(1969)   *Exploring God's World*, London: Geoffrey Chapman. **(103)**
Bullivant, B. M.
(1976)   *Competing values and traditions in an Orthodox Jewish Day School: a study of encultural dissonance*, PhD thesis, Monash University, Australia. **(242)**
Burger, G. K. and Allen, J.
(1973)   Perceived dimensions of religious experience, *Sociological Analysis*, 34,255-264. **(346)**
Burgess, W. A.
(1975)   *Church attendance, social orientation, and perception of adult caring among adolescents: a longitudinal study*, PhD thesis, University of Notre Dame. **(327)**
Burkett, S. R.
(1977)   Religion, parental influence, and adolescent alcohol and marijuana use, *Journal of Drug Issues*, 7,263-273. **(289)**
(1980)   Religious belief, normative standards and adolescent drinking, *Journal of Studies on Alcohol*, 41,662-671. **(290)**

Byrnes, D. A. and Kiger, G.
(1988)   Racial attitudes and discrimination: university teacher education students compared to
          the general student population, *College Student Journal*, 22,176-184. **(274)**
Caird, D.
(1987)   Religiosity and personalty: are mystics introverted, neurotic or psychotic? *British Jour-
          nal of Social Psychology*, 26,345-346. **(204)**
(1988)   The structure of Hood's mysticism scale: a factor-analytic study, *Journal for the Sci-
          entific Study of Religion*, 27,122-127. **(173)**
Caird, D. and Law, H. G.
(1982)   Nonconventional beliefs: their structure and measurement, *Journal for the Scientific
          Study of Religion*, 21,152-163. **(344)**, **(347)**
Campbell, O. M.
(1983)   *An investigation into the distinguishing personality correlates of mysticism*, PhD thesis,
          University of Texas at Austin. **(198)**
Caplow, T.
(1985)   Contrasting trends in European and American religion, *Sociological Analysis*, 46, 101-
          108. **(248)**
Capps, D. E.
(1974)   Contemporary psychology of religion; the task of theoretical reconstruction, *Social
          Research*, 41,362-383, reprinted in Malony, H.N. (Ed.) (1977), *op. cit.* **(343)**
Captain, P. A.
(1975)   The effect of positive reinforcement on comprehension, attitudes and rate of Bible read-
          ing in adolescence, *Journal of Psychology and Theology*, 3,49-55. **(233)**
Caputi, N.
(1984)   *Guide to the Unconscious*, Birmingham, Alabama: Religious Education Press. **(9)**
Cardwell, J. D.
(1972)   *On the development and reassessment of the multidimensional theory of religious com-
          mitment: a factor-analytic approach*, PhD thesis, University of Utah. **(344)**, **(345)**, **(346)**
Carter, M.
(1979)   *The development of aspects of the self in adolescence with particular reference to the con-
          tribution of religious and moral education*, MPhil thesis, University of Nottingham. **(210)**
Cater, D. A.
(1976)   *Personality and demographic correlates associated with conceptual religious thinking
          and religious orthodoxy in children and adolescents*, PhD thesis, Fuller Theological Sem-
          inary. **(26)**
Cavallett, S.
(1983)   *The Religious Potential of the Child*, New York: Paulist Press. **(66)**
Cerbin, W. J.
(1984)   *A study of young children's comprehension of metaphorical language*, PhD thesis, Uni-
          versity of Chicago. **(387)**
Cerney, M. S.
(1965)   *The development of the concept of God in Catholic school children*, PhD thesis, The
          Catholic University of America. **(81)**
Chalfant, H. P. and Peek, C. W.
(1983)   Religious affiliation, religiosity, and racial prejudice: a new look at old relationships,
          Review of Religious Research, 25,155-161. **(356)**
Chao, P.
(1980)   *Yinger's substructure of religion; a Chinese replication*, PhD thesis, Loyola University
          of Chicago. **(347)**
Charney, L. A.
(1986)   *Religious conversion: a longitudinal study*, PhD thesis, University of Utah. **(190)**
Chesto, K. O'C.
(1987)   *F.I.R.E. (Family-centered Intergenerational Religious Education): an alternative model
          of religious education*, DMin thesis, Hartford Seminary. **(234)**
Childerston, J. K.
(1985)   *Understanding religious "fundamentalists": a study of typology and moral judgment*,
          PhD thesis, Fuller Theological Seminary. **(198)**, **(283)**

Childs, B. H.
  (1983)   The possible connection between "private speech" and prayer, *Pastoral Psychology*, 32,24-33. (**112**)
Chirban, J.
  (1981)   *Human Growth and Faith: Intrinsic and Extrinsic Motivation in Human Development*, Washington, D.C.: University Press of America. (**52**)
Chlewinski, Z.
  (1981)   Personality and attitude toward religion in Poland, *Personality and Individual Differences*, 2,243-245. (**195**)
Choudhary, S.
  (1989)   A study of the relationship between neuroticism and religiosity, *Journal of Personality and Clinical Studies*, 5, 47-50. (**204**)
Christian, J. T.
  (1982)   *Topic, vehicle, and similarity attributes of metaphor: a model of the comprehension process*, PhD thesis, Vanderbilt University. (**384**)
Christiano, G.
  (1986)   *An analytical assessment of the faith development theory of J. W. Fowler: an approach to moral eduction*, EdD thesis, Rutgers, The State University of New Jersey-New Brunswick. (**57**)
Church of England Central Board of Finance
  (1960, etc)*Church Statistics*, London: Church of England Board of Information. (**249**)
Clark, A. V.
  (1983)   *Meanings and concepts*, in Mussen, P. H. (Ed.), *op. cit.* (**99**)
Clark, C. A., Worthington, E. L. and Danser, D. B.
  (1988)   The transmission of religious beliefs and practices to firstborn early adolescent sons, *Journal of Marriage and the Family*, 50,463-472. (**235**)
Clark, W. H.
  (1958)   *The Psychology of Religion*, New York: Macmillan. (**74**), (**290**), (**343**)
  (1964)   Mysticism as a basic concept, in Godin, A. (1964), *op, cit.* (**165**)
  (1968)   The psychology of religious experience, *Psychology Today*, reprinted in Malony, H. N. (Ed.) (1977), *op. cit.* (**166**), (**342**)
  (1969)   *Chemical Ecstacy*, New York: Sheed and Ward. (**290**)
  (1973)   *Response to Tippett, etc.*, in *Religious Experience; its Nature and Function in the Human Psyche*, The First John G. Finch Symposium on the Psychology of Religion: Springfield, Illinois: Charles Thomas. (**290**)
Clarke, W. D.
  (1974)   *A study of the development of adolescent judgment*, PhD thesis, University of Birmingham. (**137**)
Clarke, W. N.
  (1981)   The natural roots of religious experience, *Religious Studies*, 17,511-523. (**165**)
Clauser, J. A.
  (1966)   Family structure, socialization and personality, in Hoffman, L. W. (Ed.) *Review of Child Development Research*, Vol. II, New York: Russel-Sage Foundation. (**225**)
Clayton, R. R.
  (1968)   Religiosity in 5-D; a Southern test, *Social Forces* 47,80-83. (**345**)
  (1970)   *A scale of scales: is religiosity unidimensional?* paper presented to the 33rd annual meeting of the Southern Sociological Society. (**349**)
Clayton, R. R. and Gladden, J. W.
  (1973)   The five dimensions of religiosity: toward demythologizing a sacred artifact, *Journal for the Scientific Study of Religion*, 13,135-143. (**349**)
Cliff, P. and Cliff, F.
  (1966)   *A Diary for Teachers of Infants*, London: Rupert Hart Davis. (**103**)
Clift, S., Hutchings, R. and Povey, R.
  (1984)   School-related attitudes of 11-year-old pupils in spacious and space-restricted classrooms, *Educational Research*, 26,208-212. (**396**)
Cline, V. B. and Richards, J. M.
  (1965)   A factor-analytic study of religious belief and behavior, *Journal of Personality and*

Social Psychology, 1,569-587. **(156)**, **(198)**, **(344)**, **(346)**

Clippinger, J. A.
  (1973)   Toward a human psychology of personality, *Journal of Religion and Health*, 12,3,241-258, reprinted in Malony, H. N. (Ed.) (1977), *op. cit.* **(167)**

Cochran, J. K.
  (1987)   *The variable effects of religiosity on deviant behavior*, PhD thesis, University of Florida. **(288)**

Cohen, D.
  (1983)   *Piaget: Critique and Reassessment*, London: Croom Helm. **(370)**

Cohen, J.
  (1968)   Multiple regression as a general data-analytic system, *Psychological Bulletin*, 70,426-443. **(339)**

Cole, D. T.
  (1986)   A response to Foster and Moran's "Piaget and parables": the convergence of secular and scriptural views of learning, *Journal of Psychology and Theology*, 14,49-53. **(46)**

Coleman, C. J., Toomey, W. C., and Woodland, R. L.
  (1975)   Cognition, belief and behavior: a study of commitment in a religious institution, *Religious Education*, 70,676-688. **(300)**

Coleman, J. S., Hoffer, T., and Kilgore, S.
  (1981a)   *Public and private schools*, Washington: National Center for Educational Statistics. **(301)**, **(332)**
  (1981b)   Questions and answers: our response, *Harvard Educational Review*, 51,526-545. **(301)**, **(332)**
  (1982)   *High School Achievement: Public, Catholic, and Private Schools Compared*, New York: Basic Books. **(331)**

Colwell, J. C.
  (1986)   *A correlation study of self-concept and spirituality in seminarians*, PhD thesis, Western Conservative Baptist Seminary. **(211)**

Cometa, M. S.
  (1976)   *Logical operations in semantic development: a Piagetian model of metaphor and proverb comprehension*, PhD thesis, State University of New York at Albany. **(389)**

Cometa, M. S. and Eson, M. E.
  (1978)   Logical operations and metaphor interpretation: a Piagetian model, *Child Development*, 49,649-659. **(389)**

Commons, M. L., Richards, F. A., and Kuhn, D.
  (1982)   Systematic and meta-systematic reasoning: a case for levels of reasoning beyond Piaget's stage of formal operations, *Child Development*, 53,1058-1069. **(372)**

Conger, J. J. and Petersen, A. C.
  (1984)   *Adolescence and Youth; Psychological Development in a Changing World* (3rd Ed.) New York: Harper & Row. **(286)**, **(288)**, **(290)**

Conn, W. E.
  (1981)   Affectivity, in Kohlberg and Fowler, *Religious Education*, 76,33-48. **(53)**

Convey, J. J.
  (1984)   Encouraging findings about students' religious values, *Momentum*, 15,47-49. **(300)**

Conway, M. T.
  (1979)   *Adolescent religious development: a study of the beliefs, attitudes and values of students in a suburban post-primary school*, MEd thesis, St. Patrick's College, Maynooth. **(252)**, **(262)**

Cooper, J. and Croyle, R. T.
  (1984)   Attitudes and attitude change, *Annual Review of Psychology*, 35,395-426. **(393)**

Cooper, W. D.
  (1970)   *The concept of God in young children aged 5-9*, MEd thesis, University of Aberdeen. **(84)**

Cornwall, M.
  (1987)   The social bases of religion: a study of factors influencing religious belief and commitment, *Review of Religious Research*, 29,44-56. **(239)**

Cornwall, M., Albrecht, S. L., Cunningham, P. H., and Pitcher, B. L.
  (1986)   The dimensions of religiosity: a conceptual model with an empirical test, *Review of Religious Research*, 27,226-244. **(344)**, **(347)**

Coster, H.
  (1981)   Some developmental characteristics of the parental figures and the representation of God,

in Vergote and Tamayo (1981), *op. cit.* (**92**)

Coursey, R. D.
  (1971)   Liberal and conservative Roman Catholics, *Proceedings of the Annual Conference of the American Psychological Association*, 6,133-134. (**265**)

Cousin, P.
  (1985)   The religious acculturation of Lycee pupils in France, *Lumen Vitae*, 40,270-285. (**334**)

Cove, M. K.
  (1975)   *Developmental trends in religious beliefs, attitudes, and values among adolescents: a longitudinal study*, PhD thesis, University of Notre Dame. (**154**)

Cox, E.
  (1967)   *Sixth Form Religion*, London: SCM Press. (**151**), (**153**), (**199**), (**227**), (**259**), (**260**), (**268**), (**320**), (**340**)
  (1983)   Understanding religion and religious understanding, *British Journal of Religious Education*, 6,3-7 (**362**).

Cox, J.
  (1982)   *The English Church in a Secular Society: Lambeth, 1870-1930*, New York: Oxford University Press. (**244**)

Crandall, V. C. and Gozali. J.
  (1969)   The social desirability responses of children of four religious cultural groups, *Child Development*, 40,751-762. (**231**) (**302**)

Crandell, J. E. and Rasmussen, R. D.
  (1975)   Purpose in life as related to specific values, *Journal of Clinical Psychology*, 31,483-485. (**205**)

Cranford, K. T.
  (1984)   *A multitrait-multisource examination of the relationship between moral judgment and religiousness of eighth-grade students*, PhD thesis, Lousiana State University and Agricultural and Mechanical College. (**284**)

Crawford, M. E., Handel, P. J., and Wiener, P. L.
  (1989)   The relationship between religion and mental health/distress, *Review of Religious Research*, 31, 16-32. (**203**)

Crider, C. M.
  (1984)   *The perspective creating function of metaphors in conversation*, PhD thesis, Clark University. (**389**)

Crockett, J. D.
  (1972)   *A factor-analytic study of the religious beliefs inventory*, PhD thesis, University of Minnesota. (**344**), (**345**), (**346**)

Cronbach, L. J.
  (1984)   *Essentials of Psychological Testing* (4th Ed.), New York: Harper & Row. (**195**)

Crossan, D.
  (1979)   Thought on "A kind of believing," *Bulletin of the Association for Religious Education*, 12,31,7-10. (**258**)

Crotty, R. B.
  (1986)   The teaching of religions in a secular school: the South Australian experience, *Religious Education*, 81,310-321. (**322**)

Csanyi, D. A.
  (1982)   Faith development and the age of readiness for the Bible, *Religious Education*, 77,518-524. (**49**)

Culnane, W. R.
  (1978)   *Erikson, religious education and mid-adolescent attitudes: an interdisciplinary approach*, PhD thesis, Boston College. (**142**), (**143**)

Curcione, N. R.
  (1973)   Family influence on commitment to the priesthood: a study of altar boys, *Sociological Analysis*, 34,265-280. (**227**)

Currie, R., Klug, L. F., and McCombs, C. R.
  (1980)   Intimacy and saliency: dimensions for ordering religious experience, *Review of Religious Research*, 24,19-31. (**176**)

Curtis, C. A.
  (1987)   *A study of private education in a black community: the Concord Baptist Church Ele-*

mentary School in Bedford-Stuyvesant, EdD thesis, Rutgers, The State University of New Jersey-New Brunswick. **(301)**

Cuttance, P. F.
(1981)   School effects research: a synoptic review of past effort and some suggestions for the future, *Australian and New Zealand Journal of Sociology*, 17,65-69. **(329)**

Cygnar, T. E., Jacobson, C. K., and Noel, D. L.
(1977)   Religiosity and prejudice: an interdimensional analysis, *Journal for the Scientific Study of Religion*, 16,183-191. **(347)**

Dache, M.
(1971)   The Lord's apparitions and the resurrection, *Lumen Vitae*, 26,461-468. **(104)**

Dahlin, B.
(1988)   Conceptions of religion among Swedish teenagers: a phenomenological study, *Religious Education*, 83,611-621. **(264)**
(1990)   Conceptions of religion among Swedish teenagers: a phenomenological study, *British Journal of religious Education*, 12, 74-80. **(105)**

Daines, J. W.
(1949)   *A psychological study of the attitude of adolescents to religion and religious instruction*, PhD thesis, University of London. **(146), (168)**
(1962)   *An enquiry into the methods and effects of religious education in sixth forms*, Nottingham: University of Nottingham Institute of Education. **(306)**
(1966)   *Meaning or Muddle*, Nottingham: University of Nottingham Institute of Education. **(106)**

Dale, A. T.
(1966)   *New World*, London: Oxford University Press. **(121)**

Dale, R. R. and Jones, J. A.
(1964)   An investigation into the comparative response of boys and girls to scripture as a school subject in certain coeducational grammar schools in industrial South Wales, *British Journal of Educational Psychology*, 37,132-142. **(148)**

Daly, M. J.
(1982)   *An exploratory investigation of the relationships among self-esteem, irrational beliefs, and dogmatism*, PhD thesis, University of Missouri-Columbia. **(211)**

Daniel, E. F.
(1980)   *Intrinsic-extrinsic religious motivation and patterns of the self-concept: an analysis of selected young adults of the North Caribbean Conference of Seventh-Day Adventists*, EdD thesis, Andrews University. **(353)**

Darcy, F. and Beniskos, J-M.
(1971)   Some people say. . . the themes of resurrection and hell as perceived by 6-8 year old children receiving religious instruction, *Lumen Vitae*, 26,449-460. **(100)**

Darcy-Berube, F.
(1974)   Reflections on the religious and moral awakening of the child, *Religious Education*, 69,381-383. **(171)**

Darley, J. M. and Batson, C. D.
(1973)   From Jerusalem to Jericho: a study of situational and dispositional variables in helping behavior, *Journal of Personality and Social Psychology*, 27,100-108. **(358)**

Daugherty, L. R. and Burger, J. M.
(1984)   The influence of parents, church, and peers on the sexual attitude and behavior of university students, *Archives of Sexual Behavior*, 13,351-359. **(292)**

Davids, L.
(1982)   Ethnic identity, religiosity, and youthful deviation: the Toronto computer dating project - 1979, *Adolescence*, 17,673-684. **(289), (292)**

Davidson, J. D.
(1975)   Glock's model of religious commitment: assessing some different approaches and results, *Review of Religious Research*, 16,83-93. **(346)**

Davies, D.
(1985)   Symbolic thought and religious knowledge, *British Journal of Religious Education*, 7,76-80,54. **(130)**

Davies, G.
(1965)   *Concrete and formal thinking among a group of adolescent children of average ability*,

MEd thesis, University of Birmingham. **(28)**

Davies, J.
(1971)   Shaken with the wind: the effects of group pressure on the expression of moral belief, *Journal of Moral Education*, 1,49-52. **(237)**

Davies, J. W.
(1978)   *A criterion of cognitive meaning for language in religious use*, PhD thesis, University of Waterloo, Canada. **(116), (227)**

Davis, R. A.
(1985)   Social structure, belief, attitude, intention, and behavior: a partial test of Liska's revisions, *Social Psychology Quarterly*, 48,89-93. **(393)**

Davis, R. F.
(1978)   *Levels of religious thinking in young children and religious practices of their families*, PhD thesis, University of North Carolina at Greensboro. **(227)**

Dawes, R. S.
(1954)   *The concepts of God among secondary school children*, MA thesis, University of London. **(76)**

Day, D. N.
(1980)   *Religious orientation, God concept, religious experience, social interest, and self-concept as a function of psychological needs*, PhD thesis, Rosemead Graduate School of Professional Psychology. **(64)**

Day, L. G.
(1980)   *The relationship of self-disclosure and self-actualisation to cognitive and affective God concepts*, PhD thesis, Rosemead Graduate School of Professional Psychology. **(210)**

De Blauwe-Plomteux, M.
(1972)   L'Attitude des adolescents et des jean adultes envers le Christ, *Social Compass*, 19,415-430. **(263)**

De Bord, L. W.
(1969)   Adolescent religious participation: an examination of sibstructure and church attendance, *Adolescence*, 4,557-570. **(254)**

De Jong, E. F., Faulkener, J. E., and Warland, R. H.
(1976)   Dimensions of religiosity reconsidered: evidence from a cross-cultural study, *Social Forces*, 54,866-889. **(344), (345), (346), (349)**

De Neuter, P.
(1972)   Amour, sexualité et religion, *Social Compass*, 19,365-387. **(174), (186)**

De Silva, W. A.
(1969)   *Concept formation in adolscence through contextual clues, with special reference to history material*, PhD thesis, University of Birmingham. **(136), (137)**

De Valensart, G.
(1968)   Modern religious pictures, in Godin, A, (Ed.) (1968a), *op. cit.* **(74)**

De Vaus, D. A.
(1980)   Education and religious change among senior adolescents, I, questioning some common research assumptions, *Journal of Christian Education*, Papers 69,13-24. **(328)**
(1981a)   Education and religious change among senior adolescents, II, findings of an enquiry, *Journal of Christian Education*, Papers, 70,33-45. **(328)**
(1981b)   The impact of Catholic schools on the religious orientation of boys and girls, *Journal of Christian Education*, Papers, 71,44-51. **(328)**
(1982a)   Does tertiary education produce religious change? *Australian Journal of Education*, 26,101-104. **(273)**
(1982b)   The impact of children on sex-related differences in church attendance, *Sociological Analysis*, 43,145-154. **(199)**
(1983)   The relative importance of parents and peers for adolescent religious orientation, *Adolescence*, 18,147-158. **(229)**
(1984)   Workforce participation and sex differences in church attendance, *Review of Religious Research*, 25,247-256. **(199)**
(1985)   The impact of tertiary education on religious education, *Journal of Christian Education*, Papers 84,9-26. **(273)**

De Vaus, D. and McAllister, I.

(1987)   Gender differences in religion: a test of the structural location theory, *American Sociological Review*, 52,472-481. (**199**)

De Witt, C. A

(1987)   *Ego identity status, religious orientation and moral development of students from Christian colleges*, PsyD, Rosemead School of Psychology. (**216**)

Debot-Sevrin, M.-R.

(1968)   An attempt at experimental teaching, in Godin, A. (Ed.) (1968a), *op. cit.* (**119**)

Dechambre, G.

(1983)   Bible stories in the nursery school, *Lumen Vitae*, 38,177-184. (**102**)

Deconchy, J-P.

(1964)   The idea of God: its emergence between 7 and 16 years, Lumen Vitae, 19,285-296. (**77**)

(1967)   *Structure genetique de l'idee de Dieu chez des catholique francois*, Brussels: Lumen Vitae. (**77**)

(1968)   God and the parental images, in Godin, A, (Ed.) (1968a) *op. cit.* (**84**)

(1978)   Le Theorie du "Locus of Control" et l'etude des attitude et des comportements religieux: Bibliographie, *Archives de Sciences Sociales des Religions*, 23,153-160. (**212**)

(1984)   From the onset of "dogmatism" to the construct of "orthodoxy": the articulation of the subject and the group within the ideological field, *High School Journal*, 68,327-334. (**242**)

Degelman, D., Mullen, P., and Mullen, N.

(1984)   Development of abstract thinking: a comparison of Roman Catholic and Nazarene youth, *Journal of Psychology and Theology*, 3,44-49. (**32**)

Demaria, T. P.

(1986)   *Predicting guilt from religion, religiosity and irrational beliefs*, PhD thesis, Hofstra University. (**205**)

Dempsey, K. C.

(1966)   The religious attitude of first year university students, *Australian Journal of Higher Education*, 2,243-251. (**271**), (**323**)

Dempsey, K. C. and Pandey, J.

(1967)   School and religion, *Australian Journal of Education*, 11,268-275. (**323**), (**324**)

Dempsey, K. and Poole, M.

(1970)   Changes in religious attitude and belief among students of the University of New England, *Australian Journal of Social Issues*, 5,201-297. (**271**)

Dendinger, V. K.

(1983)   *Religious mystical experience: a comparison of frequency of occurrence among intuitive feelers and nonintuitive feelers*, PhD thesis, United States International University. (**198**)

Dennison, F.

(1962)   *An examination of the junior child's understanding of religious terms*, DipEd dissertation, University of Birmingham. (**106**)

Dent, C, H.

(1980)   *Perceiving and describing metaphoric and literal similarity*, PhD thesis, University of California, Los Angeles. (**389**)

Department of Education and Science

(1988)   *Statistics of Schools, January 1987*, London:HMSO (**305**)

Deshen, S.

(1972)   The variety of abandonment of religious symbols, *Journal for the Scientific Study of Religion*, 11,33-41. (**244**)

Desjardins, L. and Tamayo, A.

(1981)   Parental and divine figures of Christians and Hindus according to belief systems, in Vergote and Tamayo (1981) *op. cit.* (**92**)

Devolder, J.

(1979)   Religious values and practices of college freshmen, *Counseling and Values*, 23, 159-164. (**275**)

Di Giuseppe, R. A.

(1971)   Dogmatism correlation with strength of religious conservatism, *Psychological Reports*, 28,14. (**208**)

Dicker, H. I.

(1975)   *Extrinsic-intrinsic religious orientation and ethnocentrism in charitable volunteering*,

PhD thesis, St John's University. **(352)**, **(353)**

Dickinson, G. E.
(1976) Religious practices of adolescents in a Southern college: 1964-1974, *Journal for the Scientific Study of Religion*, 15,361-363. **(266)**
(1982) Changing religious behavior of adolescents 1964-1979, *Youth and Society*, 13,283-288. **(266)**

Dillistone, F. W.
(1989) Narrative theology, *Modern Churchman*, 31,40-42. **(44)**

Diorio, J. A.
(1978) Sailing to Byzantium: issues in religious education, *British Journal of Educational Studies*, 26,247-262. **(362)**

Dirks, D. H.
(1988) Moral development in Christian higher education, *Journal of Psychology and Theology*, 16,342-338. **(283)**

Dittes, J.
(1965) An editorial comment, *Journal for the Scientific Study of Religion*, 4,47. **(21)**, **(167)**
(1969) Psychology of religion, in Lindzey, G. and Aronson, E. (Eds.) *The Handbook of Social Psychology*, Vol. Five, Reading Mass.: Addison-Wesley. **(194)**, **(343)**, **(344)**, **(352)**
(1971) Two issues in measuring religion, in Strommen, M. (Ed.) (1971), *op. cit.* **(48)**, **(196)**, **(212)**, **(344)**

Dobbins, R. D.
(1975) Too much, too soon, *Christianity Today*, 20,41-42. **(79)**

Dockrell, J., Campbell, R., and Neilson, I.
(1980) Conservation accidents revisited, *International Journal of Behavioral Development*, 3,423-429. **(370)**

Dodrill, C. B.
(1976) Personality differences between Christian and secular college students, *Journal of Pastoral Theology*, 4,152-154. **(196)**

Doerrer, P.
(1970) *Lutheran elementary school students' concepts of God as father*, PhD thesis, St. Paul University. **(85)**

Donahue, M. J.
(1985a) Intrinsic and extrinsic religiousness: the empirical research, *Journal for the Scientific Study of Religion*, 24,418-423. **(352)**, **(356)**, **(357)**, **(358)**, **(359)**
(1985b) Intrinsic and extrinsic religiousness: review and meta-analysis, *Journal of Personality and Social Psychology*, 48,400-419. **(353)**

Donaldson, M.
(1978) *Children's Minds*, London: Fontana. **(40)**, **(370)**

Donnelly, K.
(1979) *Residual religion in an urban community*, MA thesis, University of Leicester. **(246)**

Doran, F. D.
(1978) *Myth, Bible and religious education*, PhD thesis, University of Exeter. **(126)**

Douglas, J. D. and Peel, B.
(1979) The development of metaphor and proverb translation in children grades 1 through 7, *The Journal of Educational Research*, 73,116-119. **(387)**, **(389)**

Douglas-Smith, B.
(1971) An empirical study of religious mysticism, *British Journal of Psychiatry*, 118, 549-554. **(169)**

Dowd, D. C.
(1985) *A conceptual analysis and exploratory investigation of Christian development*, PhD thesis, University of North Dakota. **(57)**

Downton, A.
(1980) An evolving theory of spiritual conversion and commitment: the case of the Divine Light Mission, *Journal for the Scientific Study of Religion*, 19,381-396. **(188)**

Dreger, R. M.
(1952) Some personality correlates of religious attitudes as determined by projective techniques, *Psychological Monographs*, 66, No 335. **(209)**

Driver, R.

(1978)   When is a stage not a stage? *Educational Research*, 21,54-61. (**373**)
(1982)   Piaget and science education: a state of decision, in Mogdil, S. and Mogdil, C. (Eds.), *op. cit.* (**373**)

Dry, L. W.
(1989)   *A study of the relationship between perceived nurturance of fathers and the intrinsic religious orientation of their fifth and sixth grade children*, EdD thesis, Southwestern Baptist Theological Seminary. (**234**)

Dudley, R. L.
(1978)   Alienation from religion in adolescents from fundamentalist religious homes, *Journal for the Scientific Study of Religion*, 17,389-398. (**233**)

Dudley, R. L. and Dudley, M. G.
(1986)   Transmission of religious values from parents to adolescents, *Review of Religious Research*, 28,3-15. (**234**)

Dudley, R. L. and Laurent, C. R.
(1984)   Alienation from religion in church-related adolescents, *Sociological Analysis*, 49,408-420. (**254**)

Dudley, R. L., Mutch, P. B., and Cruise, R. J.
(1987)   Religion, faith, and drug use among Seventh-Day Adventist youth in North America, *Journal for the Scientific Study of Religion*, 26, 218-233. (**289**)

Dufton, B. D. and Perlman, D.
(1986)   The association between religiosity and the Purpose-in-Life test: does it reflect purpose or satisfaction? *Journal of Psychology and Theology*, 14,42-48. (**205**)

Dumoulin, A. and Jaspard, J-M
(1973)   *Les mediation religieuses dans l'universe de l'enfant (Priest and Eucharist in the Perception of the Divine)*, Brussels-Louvain: Lumnen Vitae-Louvain University Press. (**105**)

Dundas-Grant, V.
(1975)   Moments of revelation? Reflections on "Inglorious Wordsworths" by Michael Paffard, *Learning for Living*, 15,67-70. (**178**)

Dunn, R. A.
(1984)   *Moral judgment among high-school freshmen and seniors in selected Seventh-Day Adventist schools*, PhD thesis, University of Southern Mississippi. (**284**)

Dunning, J. B.
(1973)   *Human creativity: a symbol of transcendence in contemporary psychology and the theology of Karl Rahner: implications for religious education*, PhD thesis, The Catholic University of America. (**17**)

Dykstra, C.
(1981)   Understanding the place of "understanding," *Religious Education*, 76, 187-194. (**362**)

Dykstra, C. and Parks, S. (Eds.)
(1988)   *Faith Development and Fowler*, Birmingham, Alabama: Religious Education Press. (**62**)

Eckstein, S. L.
(1978)   Adolescent drug use: a commentary, *Ontario Psychologist*, 10,11-14. (**289**)

Edwards, A. L.
(1957)   *Techniques of Attitude Scale Construction*, New York: Appleton-Century-Crofts. (**394**)

Edwards, J. B.
(1959)   *A study of certain moral attitudes among boys in a secondary modern school*, MA thesis, University of Birmingham. (**147**)

Edwards, S. E.
(1984)   *Factors of reading attitude, religious background, class standing and type of school related to the Bible-reading habits of college students*, PhD thesis, Indiana University. (**274**)

Egan, J. and Francis, L. J.
(1986)   School ethos in Wales: the impact of non-practicing Catholic and non-Catholic pupils on Catholic secondary schools, *Lumen Vitae*, 41,159-174. (**318**)

Eisenberg-Berg, N. and Roth, K.
(1980)   Development of young children's prosocial moral judgment: a longitudinal follow up, *Developmental Psychology*, 16,375-376. (**99**)

Elias, J. L.
(1979)   Evaluation and the future of religious education, *Religious Education*, 74,656-667. (**334**)

Elkind, D.
  (1961)   The child's conception of his religious denomination: I, The Jewish child, *Journal of Genetic Psychology*, 99,209-225. **(18), (44)**
  (1962)   The child's conception of his religious denomination: II, The Catholic child. *Journal of Genetic Psychology*, 101, 185-193. **(18)**
  (1963)   The child's conception of his religious denomination: III, The Protestant child, *Journal of Genetic Psychology*, 103,291-304. **(18)**
  (1964a)   Piaget's semi-clinical interview and the study of spontaneous religion, *Journal for the Scientific Study of Religion*, 4,40-47. **(18), (25)**
  (1964b)   Age change and religious identity, *Review of Religious Research*, 6,36-40. **(18), (25)**
  (1970)   The origins of religion in the child, *Review of Religious Research* 12, 1, 35-42. **(220)**
  (1978)   *The Child's Reality: Three Developmental Themes*, Hillsdale, New Jersey: Lawrence Erlbaum. **(18)**
  (1980)   The role of play in religious education, *Religious Education*, 75,282-293. **(101)**
  (1981)   *Children and Adolescents: Interpretive Essays in honor of Jean Piaget*, New York: O.U.P. **(40), (370), (374), (375), (376), (378)**
Elkind, D. and Elkind, S.
  (1963)   Varieties of religious experience in young adolescents, *Journal for the Scientific Study of Religion*, 2,102-112. **(171), (176), (186)**
Elkind, D. and Flavell, J. H. (Eds.)
  (1969)   *Studies in Cognitive Development*, New York: O.U.P.
Elkind, D., Spilka, B., and Long, D.
  (1968)   The child's concept of prayer, in Godin, A. (Ed.) (1968a), *op. cit.* **(21)**
Ellis, J. I.
  (1970)   *Response to literature: a study of the responses of thirteen- and fifteen-year-olds to five passages on a theme of violence*, MEd dissertation, University of Birmingham. **(137)**
Ellis, L. and Thompson, R.
  (1989)   Relating religion, crime, arousal, and boredom, *Socioliogy and Social Research*, 73,132-139. **(288)**
Emler, N.
  (1983)   Approaches to moral development: Piagetian influences, in Mogdil, S. and Mogdil, C. (Eds.) (1982), *op. cit.* **(378)**
Ennis, P. H.
  (1967)   Ecstasy and everyday life, *Journal for the Scientific Study of Religion*, 6,40-48. **(167)**
  (1978)   Conceptualization of children's logical competence: Piaget's propositional logic and an alternative proposal, in Siegal, L. S. and Brainerd, C. J. (Eds.) *Alternatives to Piaget: Critical Essays on the Theory*, New York: Academic Press. **(370)**
Entner, P. D.
  (1976)   *Religious orientation and mental health*, PhD thesis, Rosemead Graduate School of Psychology. **(353)**
Erickson, D. A.
  (1964)   Religious consequences of public and sectarian schooling, *School Review*, 72,21-33. **(301)**
Ernest, J. R.
  (1982)   *Personal religious orientation and God-concepts as a function of remembered family authoritarianism*, PhD thesis, Rosemead Graduate School of Professional Psychology. **(231)**
Ernsberger, D. J. and Manaster, G. J.
  (1981)   Moral development, intrinsic/extrinsic religious orientation and denominational teachings, *Genetic Psychology Monographs*, 104,23-41. **(282), (353)**
Esawi, A. R.
  (1968)   *Ethico-religious attitudes and emotional adjustment in children aged 11-18 years*, PhD thesis, University of Nottingham. **(152), (196)**
Evans, C. K.
  (1985)   *Religion and cognitive style: an exploration of Jung's typology among A. R. E. study group members*, PhD thesis, University of Michigan. **(197)**
Evans, D. B.
  (1968)   *Religious concepts and their development in students at colleges of education during their training course*, MEd thesis, University of Nottingham. **(81), (110)**

Eve, R. A. and Harrold, F. B.
  (1986)   Creationism, cult archaeology, and other pseudo-scientific beliefs: a study of college
            students, *Youth and Society*, 17,396-421. **(196)**, **(276)**
Ezer, M.
  (1962)   The effect of religion upon children's responses to questions involving physical causality,
            in Rosenblith, J. F. and Allinsmith, W. (Eds.) *The Causes of Behavior*, reprinted in Beit-
            Hallahmi, M. (Ed.) (1973), *op. cit.* **(17)**
Fagerlind, I.
  (1974)   Research on religious education in the Swedish school system, *Character Potential*, 7,38-
            47. **(118)**, **(264)**
Fahs, S. L.
  (1930)   The beginnings of religion in baby behavior, *Religious Education*, 25,896-903. **(80)**
  (1950)   The beginnings of mysticism in children's growth, *Religious Education*, 45,139-147. **(166)**
Fahy, P. S.
  (1976)   School and home perceptions of Australian adolescent males attending Catholic schools,
            Our Apostolate, 24,167-188. **(330)**
  (1978)   Religious beliefs of 15,900 youths attending Australian Catholic schools, *Word in Life*,
            26,66-72. **(330)**
  (1980a)   *The effectiveness on Christian criteria of 17 Australian Catholic high schools*, PhD the-
            sis, Boston College. **(330)**
  (1980b)   The religious effectiveness of some Australian Catholic high schools, *Word in Life*,
            28,86-99. **(330)**
  (1982)   Predictors of religious vocational interest among 3431 Australian Catholic adolescents,
            Word In Life, 30,149-160. **(331)**
Falbo, T. and Shepperd, J. A.
  (1986)   Self-righteousness: cognitive power and religious characteristics, *Journal of Research
            in Personality*, 20,145-157. **(198)**
Farmer, L. J.
  (1988)   *Religious experience in childhood: a study of adult perspectives on early spiritual aware-
            ness*, EdD thesis, University of Massachusetts. **(171)**
Faulkner, J. E. and De Jong, G. F.
  (1966)   Religiosity in 5-D: an empirical analysis, *Social Forces*, 45,246-254. **(347)**, **(349)**
Fawcett, T.
  (1970)   *The Symbolic Language of Religion*, London: SCM Press. **(130)**
Fay, B. W.
  (1977)   *Religious experience as related to psycho-pathology and maladjustment*, PhD thesis,
            Adelphi University. **(202)**
Fay, L. F.
  (1974)   Catholics, parochial schools, and social stratification, *Social Science Quarterly*, 55,520-
            527. **(296)**
Fay, M. A.
  (1983)   *An object relations exercise at the conscious symbolic and memory content levels of the
            maternal and paternal components of the representation of God in five Christian women*,
            PhD thesis, Boston University Graduate School. **(93)**
Fee, J. L., Greeley, A. M., McCready, W. C., and Sullivan, T. A.
  (1981)   *Young Catholics in the United States and Canada*, Los Angeles: Sadlier. **(300)**
Fehr, L. A. and Heintzelman, M. E.
  (1977)   Personality and attitude correlates of religiosity: a source of controversy, *Journal of Psy-
            chology*, 95,63-66. **(208)**, **(209)**, **(345)**
Feldman, K. A.
  (1969)   Change and stability of religious orientations during college, *Review of Religious
            Research*, 12,40-60, reprinted in Malony, H.N. (Ed.) (1977), *op.cit.* **(270)**, **(274)**
Ferguson, T.
  (1952)   *The Young Delinquent in his Social Setting*, Oxford: Oxford University Press. **(286)**
Festinger, L., Riecken, H. W., and Schachter, S.
  (1956)   *When Prophecy Fails*, Minneapolis: University of Minnesota Press. **(162)**, **(220)**, **(222)**
Fichter, J. H.

(1969)   Sociological measurement of religiosity, *Review of Religious Research*, 12,169-177. **(344)**
Filsinger, E. E., Faulker, J. E., and Warland, R. H.
(1979)   Empirical taxonomy of religious individuals: an investigation among college students, *Sociological Analysis*, 40,136-146. **(345), (348)**
Finker, R. and Stark, R.
(1986)   Turning pews into people: estimating 19th century church membership, *Journal for the Scientific Study of Religion*, 25,180-192. **(253)**
Finney, J. M.
(1978)   A theory of religious commitment, *Sociological Analysis*, 39,19-35. **(223), (344)**
Finney, J. R. and Malony, H. N.
(1985)   Means, end and quest: a research note, *Review of Religious Research*, 26,408-412. **(358)**
Fishbein, M.
(1967)   Attitudes and the prediction of behavior, in Fishbein, M. (Ed.) *Readings in Attitude Theory and Measurement Part III*, New York: Wiley. **(392)**
Fishbein, M. and Ajzen, I.
(1975)   *Belief, Attitude, Intention and Behavior,* Reading, Massachusetts: Addison-Wesley. **(393)**
Fishburn, J. E.
(1983)   The family as a means of grace in American theology, *Religious Education*, 78,90-102. **(236)**
Fisher, J. T.
(1981)   *Adolescent proverb comprehension: racial similarities and differences,* PhD thesis, Florida State University. **(390)**
Flakoll, D. A.
(1974)   *Self-esteem, psychological adjustment, and images of God.* Paper presented to the Convention for the Scientific Study of Religion, Washington, D.C. **(209)**
Flavell, J. H.
(1963)   *The Developmental Psychology of Jean Piaget,* New York: Van Nostrand. **(370), (371)**
(1970)   Concept development, in Mussen, P.H. (Ed.) *Carmichael's Manual of Child Psychology* (3rd ed.), Vol I, New York: Wiley. **(37)**
(1977)   *Cognitive Development,* Englewood Cliffs, New Jersey: Prentice-Hall. **(371)**
Flavell, J. H. and Wohlwill, J. F.
(1969)   Formal and functional aspects of cognitive development, in Elkind, D and Flavell, J. H. (1969) (Eds.), *op. cit.* **(379)**
Fleck, J. R., Ballard, S. N., and Reilly, J. W.
(1975)   The development of religious concepts and maturity: a three-stage model, *Journal of Psychology and Theology*, 3,156-163. **(46)**
Flemming, C. M.
(1966)   Research evidence and Christian education, *Learning for Living*, 6,1,10-13. **(36)**
Florian, V. and Har-Even, D.
(1983)   Fear of personal death: the effects of sex and religious beliefs, *Omega: Journal of Death and Dying*, 14,83-91. **(199)**
Flyn, M. and MacNamara, M.
(1975)   *The idea of God in Catholic children: a comparison between those who have used the Canadian Catechism and those who have not,* Toronto: MRE project, St Michael's College. **(72)**
Flynn, P. F.
(1974)   *Some Catholic schools in action: a survey of sixth form students at 21 Catholic boys' high schools in New South Wales and the A.C.T.,* MA thesis, Macquarie University, Sydney, Australia. **(330)**
(1985)   *The Effectiveness of Catholic Schools,* Sydney: A Saint Paul Publication. **(330)**
Ford-Grabowsky, M.
(1986)   What developmental phenomena is Fowler's study? *Journal of Psychology and Christianity*, 5,5-13. **(55)**
(1987)   Flaws in faith-development theory, *Religious Education*, 82,80-93. **(55)**
(1988)   The journey of a pilgrim: an alternative to Fowler, *Living Light*, 24,242-254. **(55)**
Forliti, J. E. and Benson, P. L.
(1986)   Young adolescents: a national study, *Religious Education*, 81,199-224. **(233)**

Forrester, J. F.
   (1946)   A study of the attitude of some secondary modern school pupils toward religious instruc-
             tion, PhD thesis, University of London. **(146)**
Foster, J. D. and Moran, G. T.
   (1985)   Piaget and the parables: the convergence of secular and scriptural views of learning,
             Journal of Psychology and Theology, 13,97-103. **(46)**
   (1986)   Piaget and parables assimilated: a response to Cole, Journal of Psychology and Theology,
             14,54-58. **(46)**
Fowler, J. W.
   (1980)   Faith and the structuring of meaning, in The First International Conference on Moral
             and Religious Development, op. cit. **(50)**
   (1981)   Stages of Faith: The Psychology of Human Development and the Quest for Meaning,
             San Francisco: Harper & Row. **(44), (51), (100), (263)**
   (1984a)   A gradual introduction into the faith, Concilium, 174,47-53. **(59)**
   (1984b)   Being Adult, Being Christian, San Francisco: Harper & Row. **(214)**
Fowler, J. and Keen, S.
   (1978)   Life Maps: Conversations on the Journey of Faith, Waco, Texas: Word books. **(50)**
Fowlkes, M. A.
   (1988)   Religion and socialization, in Ratcliff, D. (Ed.), op cit. **(225), (239)**
Fox, R.
   (1984)   A study of metaphor in the writing of nine- and thirteen-year-olds, college freshmen,
             and graduate students in the humanities and in the sciences, PhD thesis, University of
             California, San Diego. **(389)**
Fox, W. S. and Jackson, E. F.
   (1973)   Protestant-Catholic differences in educational achievement and persistence in school,
             Journal for the Scientific Study of Religion, 12,65-84. **(299)**
Francis, L. J.
   (1976)   An Enquiry into the Concept "Readiness for Religion," PhD thesis, University of Cam-
             bridge. **(99), (157), (392), (395)**
   (1977a)   Readiness for research in religion, Learning for Living, 16,109-114. **(157)**
   (1977b)   School influence and pupil attitude in religious education, MSc thesis, University of Lon-
             don. **(157)**
   (1978a)   Attitude and longitude: a study in measurement, Character Potential, 8,119-130. **(159), (321)**
   (1978b)   Measurement reapplied: research into the child's attitude toward religion, British Journal
             of Religious Education, 1,45-51. **(159)**
   (1978c)   Teenage values today, New Society, 45,687-688. **(282), (290)**
   (1979a)   The child's attitude toward religion and religious education: a review of research, Edu-
             cational Research, 21,103-108. **(162)**
   (1979b)   The priest as test administrator in attitude research, Journal for the Scientific Study of
             Religion, 18,78-81. **(158)**
   (1979c)   School influence and pupil attitude toward religion, British Journal of Educational Psy-
             chology, 49,107-123. **(143), (159), (161), (308), (321)**
   (1979d)   Theology and education: a research perspective, Scottish Journal of Theology, 32,61-
             70. **(311)**
   (1979e)   Research and the development of religious thinking, Educational Studies, (Oxford)
             5,109-115. **(362)**
   (1980a)   Paths of holiness: attitudes toward religion among 9-11 year old children, Character
             Potential, 9,129-138.**(157), (308)**
   (1980b)   The young person's religion: a crisis of attitude, Scottish Journal of Theology, 33,159-
             169. **(157)**
   (1980c)   Christianity and the child today, Occasional Papers: Farmington Institute for Christian
             Studies, No. 6. **(157)**
   (1981)   Anonymity and attitude scores among ten and eleven year old children, Journal of
             Experimental Education, 49,74-76. **(158)**
   (1982)   Youth in Transit: a profile of 16-25 year olds, Aldershot: Gower. **(252), (273), (277)**
   (1983a)   School influence and pupil attitude: a decade's progress, Abingdon: Culham College
             Institute. **(308), (309)**

(1983b) *Church of England Schools and Teacher Attitudes,* Abingdon: Culham College Institute. **(314)**

(1983c) Anglican voluntary primary schools and children's church attendance. *Research in Education,* 30,1-9. **(314)**

(1984a) *Monitoring the Christian development of the child,* Abington: Cullham College Institute, reprinted in *Family, School and Church in Religious Education,* Department of Christian Ethics and Practical Theology, University of Edinburgh. **(157), (159), (160), (251)**

(1984b) Roman Catholic schools and pupil attitudes in England, *Lumen Vitae,* 39,99-108. **(159), (308)**

(1984c) Dimensions of Christian belief, *Educational Studies,* 10,103-111. **(159)**

(1984d) Christianity and beliefs about religious education: a research note, *Journal of Christian Education,* Papers, 81,21-26. **(160)**

(1986a) Denominational schools and pupil attitude toward Christianity, *British Educational Research Journal,* 12,145-152. **(309)**

(1986b) *Partnership in Rural Education,* London: Collins Liturgical Publications. **(314)**

(1986c) Roman Catholic secondary schools: falling rolls and pupil attitudes, *Educational Studies,* (Oxford), 12,119-127. **(318)**

(1986d) Are Catholic schools good for non-Catholics? *The Tablet,* 240,170-172. **(319)**

(1987a) Measuring attitude toward Christianity among 12-18-year-old pupils in Catholic schools, *Educational Research,* 29,230-233. **(318)**

(1987b) The decline in attitudes toward religion among 8-15 year olds, *Educational Studies,* (Oxford) 13,125-134. **(160)**

(1987c) *Religion in the Primary School: a partnership between church and state?* London: Collins Liturgical Publications. **(310)**

(1989a) Drift from the churches: secondary school pupils' attitudes toward Christianity, *British Journal of Religious Education,* 11,76-86. **(310)**

(1989b) Monitoring changing attitudes toward Christianity among secondary school pupils between 1974 and 1986, *British Journal of Educational Psychology,* 59,86-91. **(159), (250), (310)**

Francis, L. J. and Carter, M.

(1980) Church aided secondary schools: religious education as an examination subject and pupil attitudes toward religion, *British Journal of Educational Psychology,* 50,297-300. **(159), (211)**

Francis, L. J. and Egan, J.

(1987) Catholic schools and the communication of faith—an empirical inquiry, *Catholic School Studies,* 60,27-34. **(319), (332)**

Francis, L. J. and Kay, W. K.

(1984) Attitude toward religion: definition, measurement, and evaluation, *British Journal of Educational Studies,* 32,45-50. **(392)**

Francis, L. J., Lankshear, D. W., and Pearson, P. R.

(1989) The relationship between religiosity and the short form of the JEPQ (JEPQ-S) indices of E, H, L, and P among eleven year olds, *Journal of Personality and Individual Differences,* 10,763-769. **(204)**

Francis, L. J. and Pearson, P. R.

(1985) Extroversion and religiosity, *Journal of Social Psychology,* 125,269-270. **(195)**

(1987) Empathetic development during adolescence: religiosity the missing link, *Personality and Individual Differences,* 8,145-148. **(197)**

(1988) Religiosity and the short-scale EPQ-R indices of E, N & L compared with the JEPI, JEPQ and EPQ, *Personality and Individual Differences,* 9,653-657. **(204)**

Francis, L. J., Pearson, P. R., Carter, M., and Kay, W. K.

(1981a) The relationship between neuroticism and religiosity among English 15- and 16-year-olds, *Journal of Social Psychology,* 114,99-102. **(195)**

(1981b) Are introverts more religious? *British Journal of Social Psychology,* 20,101-104. **(195)**

Francis, L. J., Pearson, P. R., and Kay, W. K.

(1982) Eysenck's's personality quadrants and religiosity, *British Journal of Social Psychology,* 21,262-264. **(195)**

(1983a) Are religious children bigger liars? *Psychological Reports,* 52,551-554. **(158)**

(1983b) Neuroticism and religiosity among English school children, *Journal of Social Psychology,* 121,149-150. **(204)**

(1983c) Are introverts still more religious? *Personality and Individual Differences,* 4,221-222. **(195)**

(1988) Religiosity and lie scores: a question of interpretation, *Social Behavior and Personality,*

16,91-95. **(197)**

Francis, L. J., Pearson, P. R., and Stubbs, M. T.
(1985)   Personality and religion among low ability children in residential special schools, *British Journal of Mental Subnormality*, 31,41-45. **(205)**

Francis, L. J. and Stubbs, M. I.
(1987)   Measuring attitude toward Christianity: from childhood into adulthood, *Personality and Individual Differences*, 8,741-743. **(160)**

Francis, L. J., Wesley, C. B., and Rust, J. N.
(1978)   Research in progress: an account of the religious attitude research project at the London Institute of Education, *Bulletin of the Association for Religious Education*, 11,10-15. **(157)**

Francis, S.
(1987)   The application of Fowler's faith development theory to teaching religion in a voluntary context, *Journal of Christian Education*, Papers 90,45-50. **(59)**

Franklin, S. P.
(1928)   Measurement of the comprehension difficulty of the precepts and parables of Jesus, *The University of Iowa Studies in Character*, Vol. 2, No. 1. **(117)**

Franks Davis, C. E.
(1986)   *The evidential force of religious experience*, DPhil thesis, University of Oxford. **(169)**

Fraser, R. S. and Stacey, B. G.
(1973)   A psychological investigation of the influence of attitude on the judgement of social stimuli, *British Journal of Social and Clinical Psychology*, 12,337-352. **(149)**

Freeman, H. A.
(1931)   First graders' religious ideas, *School and Society*, 34,733-735. **(66)**

Friedman, M.
(1985)   Abraham, Socrates, and Heinz: where are the women? in Harding, C. G. (Ed.), *op. cit.* **(54)**

Friedman, S. I.
(1983)   *The effect of Jewish religious education on the moral reasoning and social interest of Yeshiva high school students*, PhD thesis, Fordham University. **(284)**

Friedman, W. J., Robinson, A. B., and Friedman, B. L.
(1986)   Sex differences in moral judgment? A test of Gilligan's theory, *Psychology of Women Quarterly*, 11,37-46. **(55)**

Fuchs, J. L.
(1978)   *Relationship of Jewish day school education to student self-concepts and Jewish identity*, EdD thesis, University of California. **(304)**

Fukuyama, Y.
(1961)   The major dimensions of church membership, *Review of Religious Research*, 2,154-161. **(348)**

Fullerton, J. T. and Hunsberger, B.
(1982)   A unidimensional measure of Christian orthodoxy, *Journal for the Scientific Study of Religion*, 21,317-326. **(346)**

Fulljames, P. and Francis, L. J.
(1988)   The influence of creationism and scientism on attitudes toward Christianity among Kenyan secondary school students, *Educational Studies*, (Oxford), 14,77-96. **(160)**

Funk, R. B. and Willits, F. K.
(1987)   College attendance and attitude change: a panel study 1970-81, *Sociology of Education*, 60,224-231. **(273)**

Furnham, A. F
(1985)   Why do people save? Attitudes to, and habits of, saving money in Britain, *Journal of Applied Social Psychology*, 15,354-373. **(344)**

Furth, H. G.
(1969)   *Piaget and Knowledge: Theoretical Foundations*, Englewood Cliffs, New Jersey: Prentice-Hall. **(374)**, **(376)**
(1977)   The operative and figurative aspects of knowledge in Piaget's theory, in Geber, B.A. (Ed.) (1977), *op. cit.* **(40)**, **(375)**

Furushima, R. Y.
(1983)   *Faith development theory: a cross-cultural research project in Hawaii*, EdD thesis, Columbia University Teachers College. **(57)**
(1985)   Faith development in a cross-cultural perspective, *Religious Education*, 80,414-420. **(57)**

Gabbard, C. E.
(1986)   Assessing locus of control with religious populations, *Journal of Research in Personality,* 20,292-308. **(212)**

Galanter, M., Rabkin, R., Rabkin, J., and Deutsch, A.
(1979)   The "Moonies": a psychological study of conversion and membership in a contemporary religious sect, *The American Journal of Psychiatry,* 136,165-170. **(203)**

Galda, S. L.
(1981)   *The development of the comprehension of metaphor.* Paper presented to the annual meeting of the American Educational Research Association: Resources in Education. **(385)**

Galloway, E. R.
(1981)   *Religious beliefs and practices of Maroon children of Jamaica,* EdD thesis, New York University. **(110)**

Gallup, G. and Jones, S.
(1989)   *Religion in America,* Princeton, New Jersey: The Princeton Religion Research Center. **(175), (190), (254)**

Gannnon, T. M.
(1972)   In the eye of the hurricane: religious implications of contemporary trends, *Social Compass,* 19,213-228. **(338)**

Garrity, F. D.
(1960)   *A study of the attitude of some secondary modern school pupils toward religious education,* MEd thesis, University of Manchester. **(148), (153)**

Gartrell, C. D. and Shannon, Z. K.
(1985)   Contacts, cognitions, and conversion: a rational choice approach, *Review of Religious Research,* 27,32-48. **(188)**

Gaskins, L. E.
(1978)   *Locus of control: its relationship to religious denominations and leader-follower perceptions of behavior,* PhD thesis, University of Florida. **(212)**

Gates, B. E.
(1976)   *Religion in the Developing World of Children,* PhD thesis, University of Lancaster. **(31), (177)**
(1977)   Religion in the child's own core curriculum, *Learning for Living,* 17,1,9-15. **(31)**

Geber, B. A. (Ed.)
(1977)   *Piaget and Knowledge: Studies in Genetic Epistemology,* London: R.K.P.

Geist, C. R. and Bangham, W. R.
(1980)   Locus of control and religious affiliation, *Psychological Reports,* 47,1281-1282. **(212)**

Gellard, J.
(1978)   Major trends in recent French religious research, *Journal for the Scientific Study of Religion,* 17,449-455. **(243)**

Gelman, R. and Baillargeon, R.
(1983)   A review of some Piagetian concepts, in Mussen, P.H. (Ed.), *op. cit.,* 167-230. **(372)**

General Synod Board of Education
(1989)   *Children in the Way: New Directions for the Church's Children,* London: National Church House Publishing. **(249)**

George, S.
(1977)   *Stage theory: a model for curriculum development in religious education,* MA dissertation, University of London. **(46)**

Gerber, F.
(1988)   Des structures et des hommes: le courent néo-Piagétien en psychologie religieuse, *Revue de Thelogie et de Philisophie,* 120,195-216. **(62)**

Gerkin, C. V. and Cox, D. G.
(1955)   The religious story test as a tool for evaluating religious growth, *Journal of Pastoral Care,* 9,21-26. **(104)**

Gerkin, C. V. and Weber, G. H.
(1953)   A religious story test: some findings with delinquent boys, *Journal of Pastoral Care,* 2,77-90. **(104)**

Gessell, A., Ilg, F. L., and Ames, L. B.
(1977)   *The Child from Five to Ten,* New York: Harper & Row. **(158)**

Getz, I. R.

(1984)   Moral judgment and religion: a review of the literature, *Counseling and Values*, 28,84-116. **(214)**, **(285)**

Gibbons, D. and De Jarnette, J.
(1972)   Hypnotic susceptibility and religious experience, *Journal for the Scientific Study of Reii-gion*, 11,152-156. **(191)**

Gibbs, D. R., Mueller, S. A., and Wood, J. R.
(1973)   Doctrinal orthodoxy, salience, and the consequential dimension, *Journal for the Scientific Study of Religion*, 12,33-52. **(347)**

Gibson, H. M. and Francis, L. J.
(1989)   Measuring the attitude toward Christianity among 11-16 year old pupils in Catholic schools in Scotland, *Educational Research*, 31,65-69. **(320)**

Gildea, P. and Glucksberg, S.
(1983)   On understanding metaphor: the role of context, *Journal of Verbal Learning and Verbal Behavior*, 22,577-590. **(388)**

Gilkey, R. W.
(1977)   *Peak experiences and adaptive regression: one man's ceiling is another man's door*, PhD thesis, University of Michigan. **(172)**

Gillespie, V. B.
(1973)   *Religious conversion and identity: a study in relationship*, PhD thesis, Claremont Graduate School. **(191)**

(1979)   *Religious conversion and personal identity: how and why people change*, Birmingham, Alabama: Religious Education Press. **(191)**

Gilligan, C.
(1977)   In a different voice: women's conceptions of self and morality, *Harvard Educational Review*, 47,481-517. **(54)**

(1980)   Justice and responsibility: thinking about real dilemmas of moral conflict and choice, in The First International Cinference on Moral and Religious Development, *op. cit.* **(54)**

Gilliland, A. R.
(1940)   The attitude of college students toward God and the church, *Journal of Social Psychology*, 11,11-18. **(274)**

Ginsburg, H. and Opper, S.
(1979)   *Piaget's Theory of Intellectual Development*, Englewood Cliffs, New Jersey: Prentice-Hall. **(370)**

Gladding, S. T. and Clayton, G. A.
(1986)   The Gladding, Lewis, and Adkins scale of religiosity: differences among a sample of Protestants, Catholics, Jews, and nonaffiliates, *Psychological Reports*, 59,995-998. **(194)**

Gladding, S. T., Lewis, E. L., and Adkins, L.
(1981)   Religious beliefs and positive mental health: the GLA scale and counseling, *Counseling and Values*, 25,206-215. **(354)**

Glass, K. D.
(1971)   Denominational differences in religious belief, practice, anxiety, and dogmatism, *Religious Education*, 66,204-206. **(206)**, **(207)**

Glassey, W.
(1945)   The attitude of grammar school pupils and their parents to education, religion, and sport, *British Journal of Educational Psychology*, 15,101-104. **(145)**

Glen, N. D.
(1987)   The trend in "no religion" respondents to U. S. national surveys, late 1950s to early 1980s, *Public Opinion Quarterly*, 51,293-314. **(253)**

Glock, C. Y. and Stark, R.
(1965)   *Religion and Society in Tension*, Chicago: Rand and McNally. **(10)**, **(265)**, **(328)**, **(343)**, **(344)**, **(345)**, **(349)**, **(354)**

Glock, C. Y., and Wuthnow, R.
(1979)   Departures from conventional religion: the nominally religious, the nonreligious, and the alternatively religious, in Wuthnow, R. (Ed.) (1979), *op. cit.* **(175)**, **(186)**

Glueck, S. S. and Glueck, E. T.
(1968)   *Delinquents and Nondelinquents in Perspective*, Cambridge, Mass: Harvard University Press. **(286)**

Godin, A.
(1962)   Importance and difficulty of scientific research in religious education: the problem of the "criterion," *Religious Education*, 57,161-171. **(342)**
(1964)   (Ed.) *From Religious Experience to Religious Attitude*, Brussels: Lumen Vitae, and (1965) Chicago: Loyola University Press.
(1968a)   (Ed.) *From Cry to Word*, Brussels: Lumen Vitae.
(1968b)   Genetic development of the symbolic function: meaning and limits of the work of R. Goldman, *Religious Education*, 63,439-445. **(32), (36)**
(1971)   Some developmental tasks in Christian education, in Strommen, M. (Ed.) (1971), *op. cit.* **(45)**
(1975)   Words of man—Word of God, *Lumen Vitae*, 30,55-60. **(93)**
(1985)   *The Psychological Dynamics of Religious Experience*, Birmingham, Alabama: Religious Education Press. **(84), (119), (170), (186), (348)**
Godin, A. and Coopez, A.
(1957)   Religious projection pictures, *Lumen Vitae*, 12,260-274. **(342)**
Godin, A. and Hallez, M.
(1964)   Parental images and divine paternity, in Godin, A. (1964), *op. cit.* **(85), (86), (88)**
Godin, A. and Marthe, S.
(1960)   Magic mentality and sacramental life in children of 8-14 years, *Lumen Vitae*, 15,277-296. **(105)**
Goldman, R. G.
(1962)   *Some aspects of the development of religious thinking in childhood and adolescence*, PhD thesis, University of Birmingham. **(23), (135), (364)**
(1963a)   The development of religious thinking, *Learning for Living*, 2,5,6-9. **(23)**
(1963b)   What is religious knowledge? *National Froebel Foundation Bulletin*, No. 117. **(23), (44), (102)**
(1964)   *Religious Thinking from Childhood to Adolescence*, London: Routledge and Kegan Paul. **(23), (24), (27), (47), (62), (112)**
(1965a)   *Readiness for Religion*, London: Routledge and Kegan Paul. **(23), (41)**
(1965b)   The implications of developmental education, *Learning for Living*, 4,5,6-9. **(23)**
(1965c)   Dr. Goldman replies, *Learning for Living*, 5,1,24-26. **(23), (36), (48)**
(1966)   The reformation of religious and moral education, *Learning for Living*, 5,5,21-25. **(23)**
(1967)   Two kinds of fundamentalists, *Learning for Living*, 6,3,14-16. **(36)**
(1969)   Dr. Beeching, I presume? *Religious Education*, 64,47-52. **(37)**
Gonzalez-Anleo, J.
(1987)   Los jovenes y las religion "light," *Cuadernos de Realidades Sociales*, 29-30,5-34. **(263)**
Goodenough, E. R. and Goodenough, E. W.
(1962)   Myths and symbols of children, *Religious Education*, 57,172-177. **(133)**
Goodman, F. D., Henney, J. H., and Pressel, E.
(1974)   *Trance, Healing and Hallucination: Three Field Studies in Religious Experience*, New York: John Wiley. **(172)**
Goodman, I. M.
(1978)   *Jewish education and religious attitudes: a correlation study of college-age Jewish students*, EdD thesis, Yeshiva University. **(304)**
Goodnow, J.
(1977)   *Children's Drawings*, London: Open Books. **(75)**
Goring, P.
(1980)   A personality comparison of evangelical seminarians, Catholic nuns and university graduates in a Colombian setting, *Journal of Pastoral Psychology*, 8,323-327. **(202)**
Gorman, M.
(1977)   Moral and faith development in seventeen year old students, *Religious Education*, 72,491-504. **(55)**
(1978)   *Moral and Faith Development in Seventeen Year Old Students*, Washington, D. C.: Spons Agency-Joseph P. Kennedy Foundation. **(55)**
Gorsuch, R. L.
(1967)   Dimensions of the conceptualization of God, *International Yearbook for the Sociology of Religion*, 3,187-199. **(65)**
(1968)   The conceptualization of God as seen in adjective ratings, *Journal for the Scientific Study*

of Religion, 7,56-64. **(65)**, **(88)**

(1984)   Measurement: the boon and bane of investigating religion, *American Psychologist*, 39,228-236. **(339)**, **(360)**

(1988)   Psychology of religion, *Annual Review of Psychology*, 39,201-221. **(96)**, **(197)**, **(202)**, **(288)**, **(359)**

Gorsuch, R. L. and Aleshire, D.
(1974)   Christian faith and ethnic prejudice: a review and interpretation of research, *Journal for the Scientific Study of Religion*, 13,281-307. **(353)**

Gorsuch, R. L. and McFarland, S. G.
(1972)   Single vs. multiple-item scales for measuring religious variables, *Journal for the Scientific Study of Religion*, 11,53-64. **(352)**

Gorsuch, R. L. and McPherson, S. E.
(1989)   Intrinsic/Extrinsic measurement: I/E-Revised and single item scale, *Journal for the Scientific Study of Religion*, 28,348-354. **(356)**

Gorsuch, R. L. and Smith, C. S.
(1983)   Attributions of responsibility to God: an interaction of religious beliefs and outcomes, *Journal for the Scientific Study of Religion*, 22,340-352. **(219)**

Gorsuch, R. L. and Venable, G. D.
(1983)   Development of an "Age-Universal" I-E scale, *Journal for the Scientific Study of Religion*, 22,181-187. **(352)**

Graebner, O. E.
(1964)   Child concepts of God, *Religious Education*, 59,234-241. **(67)**, **(75)**

Graham, T. W.
(1978)   Frequency of church attendance and blood pressure elevation, *Journal of Behavioral Medicine*, 1,37-43. **(344)**

Grannell, A. P.
(1977)   *Toward a theory of religious faith development*, PhD thesis, Boston University Graduate School. **(55)**

Gray, M.
(1963)   *Religious beliefs and attitudes in training college students*, MEd thesis, University of Nottingham. **(276)**

Greeley, A. M.
(1964)   A note on the origins of religious differences, *Journal for the Scientific Study of Religion*, 3,21-31. **(275)**

(1969)   Continuities in research on the "religious factor", *American Journal of Sociology*, 75,355-359. **(298)**

(1974)   *Ecstasy: A Way of Knowing*, Englewood Cliffs, New Jersey: Prentice-Hall. **(175)**

(1975)   *The Sociology of the Paranormal: A Reconnaissance*, Beverly Hills and London: Sage. **(182)**

(1979)   Ethnic variations in religious commitment, in Wuthnow, R. (Ed.) (1979), *op. cit.* **(300)**

(1981)   *The Religious Imagination*, New York: Sadlier. **(95)**, **(224)**

(1982a)   *Catholic High Schools and Minority Students*, New Brunswick: Transaction Books. **(300)**

(1982b)   *Religion: a Secular Theory*, New York: The Free Press. **(223)**

Greeley, A. M. and Gockel, G. L.
(1971)   The religious effects of parochial education, in Strommen, M. P. (Ed.), *op. cit.* **(298)**

Greeley, A. M., McCready. W. C., and McCourt, K.
(1976)   *Catholic Schools in a Declining Church*, Kansas City: Sheed and Ward. **(298)**, **(331)**

Greeley, A. M. and Rossi, P. H.
(1966)   *The Education of Catholic Americans*, Chicago: Aldine. **(297)**, **(300)**, **(316)**, **(328)**

Green, C. W. and Hoffman, C. L.
(1989)   Stages of faith and perception of similar and dissimilar others, *Review of Religious Research*, 30,246-259. **(58)**

Green, M.
(1985)   *The development of metaphoric comprehension and preference*, EdD thesis, Boston University. **(387)**, **(388)**

Green, T. F.
(1979)   Learning without metaphor, in Ortony, A. (Ed.), *op. cit.* **(384)**

Greenacre, I.

(1971)   *The response of young people to religious allegory,* DipEd dissertation, University of Birmingham. **(120)**

Greenwald, A. G.
(1968)   On defining attitude and attitude theory, in Greenwald, A. G., Brock, T. C., and Ostrom, T. M. (Eds.), *Psychological Foundations of Attitudes,* New York: Academic Press. **(391)**

Greenwood, D. M.
(1984)   *The relation of religious experience to teaching religion in school,* PhD thesis, University of Birmingham. **(183)**

Greer, J. E.
(1970a)   *Sixth form religion in Northern Ireland: a study of the religious beliefs, practices, and attitudes and of the moral judgment of sixth form pupils attending county and Protestant voluntary schools in Northern Ireland,* MPhil thesis, Queens University, Belfast. **(259)**
(1970b)   The attitudes of parents and pupils to religion in school, *Irish Journal of Education,* 4,39-46. **(259)**
(1971)   Religious belief and church attendance of sixth form pupils and their parents, *Irish Journal of Education,* 5,98-106. **(260)**
(1972a)   Sixth form religion in Northern Ireland, *Social Studies: Irish Journal of Sociology,* 1,325-340. **(199), (260), (320)**
(1972b)   The child's understanding of creation, *Educational Review,* 24,99-110. **(128)**
(1980a)   The persistence of religion: a study of adolescents in Northern Ireland, *Character Potential,* 9,139-149. **(42), (261)**
(1980b)   Stages in the development of religious thinking, *British Journal of Religious Education,* 3,1,24-28. **(39)**
(1981a)   Religious attitudes and thinking in Belfast pupils, *Educational Research,* 23,177-189. **(183)**
(1981b)   Religious experience and religious education, *Search,* 4,23-34. **(183)**
(1982a)   The religious experience of Northern Irish pupils, *The Irish Catechist,* 6,49-58. **(184), (186)**
(1982b)   A comparison of two attitudes to religion scales, *Education Research,* 24,226-227. **(395)**
(1983a)   Attitude to religion reconsidered, *British Journal of Educational Studies,* 31,18-28. **(145), (161)**
(1983b)   A critical study of "Thinking about the Bible," *British Journal of Religious Education,* 5,113-125. **(41)**
(1984a)   Moral cultures in Northern Ireland, *Journal of Social Psychology,* 123,63-70. **(261)**
(1984b)   Fifty years of the psychology of religion in religious education; I, *British Journal of Religious Education,* 6,93-97. **(47)**
(1985)   Viewing "the other side" in Northern Ireland: openness and attitudes to religion among Catholic and Protestant adolescents, *Journal for the Scientific Study of Religion,* 24,275-292. **(321)**
(1988)   *Hardest to Accept,* Coleraine, N. Ireland: University of Ulster Faculty of Education Resource Centre. **(261)**

Greer, J. E. and Brown, C. A.
(1973)   The effects of new approaches to religious education in the primary school, *Journal of Curriculum Studies,* 5,73-78. **(309)**

Gregory, H. M.
(1966)   *Parables in the secondary school,* DipRE dissertation, University of Nottingham. **(117)**

Greil, A. L. and Ruddy, D. R.
(1984)   What have we learned from process models of conversion? An examination of case studies, *Sociological Forces,* 17,305-323. **(188)**

Griffin, G. A., Gorsuch, R. L., and Davis, A. L.
(1987)   A cross-cultural investigation of religious orientation, social norms, and prejudice, *Journal for the Scientific Study of Religion,* 26,358-365. **(354)**

Griffiths, K. M.
(1977)   *An investigation into the development of concepts of animism in selected primary school children,* PhD thesis, University of Birmingham. **(139)**

Grocock, T. A.
(1940)   *Religious instruction in secondary schools, an enquiry and some suggestions,* MA thesis, University of Birmingham. **(145)**

Gronblom, G.
(1984)   *Dimensions of religiosity: the operationalization and measurement of religiosity with*

special regard to the problem of dimensionality, Abo Akademi, Finland. **(344)**, **(345)**, **(346)**, **(347)**

Grossman, H.
(1975)   On Peter Berger's definition of religion, *Journal for the Scientific Study of Religion,* 14,289-292. **(337)**

Gruber, A.
(1957)   Differences in religious evolution of adolescents, *Lumen Vitae,* 12,301-302. **(198)**

Gruis, T. E.
(1979)   *An inquiry into some relationships between church attendance and school participation beyond regular classroom activity,* EdD thesis, Aquinas Institute of Theology. **(267)**

Habib, R. R.
(1988)   *Religiosity and its relationship to self-concept, locus of control, and dogmatism,* PhD thesis, University of Southern California. **(210)**

Hacker, R. G.
(1984)   A hierarchy of intellectual development in science, *British Journal of Educational Psychology,* 54,137-151. **(139)**, **(370)**

Hadaway, C. K.
(1989)   Identifying American apostates: a cluster analysis, *Journal for the Scientific Study of Religion,* 28,201-205. **(255)**

Hadaway, C. K., Elifson, K, W., and Peterson, D. H.
(1984)   Religious involvement and drug use among urban adolescents, *Journal for the Scientific Study of Religion,* 23,109-128. **(288)**

Hadley, M. J.
(1982)   *The realization of metaphor in context: a developmental study of interpretation,* PhD thesis, City University of New York. **(388)**

Hall, E.
(1988)   Fantasy in religious education: a psychological perspective, *British Journal of Religious Education,* 10,41-48. **(101)**

Hall, G. C.
(1980)   An integration of science and theology in a Piagetian epistemology, *Journal of Pastoral Theology,* 8,243-302. **(373)**

Hallam, R. N.
(1966)   *An investigation into some aspects of the historical thinking of children and adolescents,* MEd thesis, University of Leeds. **(135)**
(1967)   Logical thinking in history, *Educational Review,* 19,183-202. **(135)**
(1968)   Piaget and moral judgments in history, *Educational Research,* 11,200-206. **(136)**
(1969)   Piaget and the teaching of history, *Educational Research,* 12,3-12. **(135)**
(1972)   Thinking and learning in history, *Teaching History,* 337-346. **(135)**
(1975)   *A study of the effect of teaching method on the growth of logical thought,* PhD thesis, University of Leeds. **(135)**
(1978)   An approach to teaching history in primary schools, *Teaching History,* June, 9-14. **(136)**, **(143)**
(1979a)   Attempting to improve logical thinking in school history, *Research in Education,* 21,1-24. **(136)**
(1979b)   Children's responses on historical passages and two Piagetian tasks, *The Durham and Newcastle Research Review,* 8,42,9-14. **(136)**

Hamby, J.
(1973)   *Some personality correlates of four religious orientations,* PhD thesis, University of Tennessee. **(352)**, **(353)**, **(355)**

Hamlyn, D. W.
(1978)   *Experience and the Growth of Understanding,* London: Routledge & Kegan Paul. **(370)**

Hammersla, J. F., Andrews-Quells, L. S., and Frease, L.
(1986)   God concept and religious commitment among Christian university students, *Journal for the Scientific Study of Religion,* 25,424-435. **(65)**

Hanford, J. T.
(1975)   A synoptic approach: resolving problems in empirical and phenomenological approaches to the psychology of religion, *Journal for the Scientific Study of Religion,* 14,219-227. **(341)**

Hanlon, K.

(1989) A survey of religious education in Roman Catholic secondary schools in England and Wales, *British Journal of Religious Education*, 11,154-162. **(318)**

Hansen, I. V.
(1968) *The independent school ethos: a first sample of the independent boys' schools of Australia, comprising six "Public Schools" in the State of Victoria*, PhD thesis, University of Melbourne, Australia. **(324)**
(1971) *Nor Free, nor Secular*, Melbourne: Oxford University Press. **(324)**

Hanson, B. A.
(1987) *Attitude-treatment interactions with religiously orientated subjects*, PhD thesis, Rosemead School of Psychology. **(212)**

Hanson, R. H.
(1982) *An investigation of the similarity and contrast models of metaphorical and categorical semantic processing*, PhD thesis, Purdue University. **(386)**

Hardin, J. F.
(1978) *A study of the relationship of moral development to school setting, comparing students in a church related school with students in a public school*, EdD thesis, Oklahoma State University. **(283)**

Hardin, K. N. and Gold, S. R.
(1988) Relationship of sex, sex guilt, and experience to written sexual fantasies, *Imagination, Cognition, and Personality*, 8,155-163. **(201)**

Harding, C. G. (Ed.)
(1985) *Moral Dilemmas*, Chicago: Precedent Publishing.

Hardy, A.
(1970) A request for accounts of a certain type of religious experience to be sent to help research, *Learning for Living*, 9,4,27-28. **(177)**
(1975) *Biology of God*, London: Jonathan Cape. **(177)**

Harms, E.
(1944) The development of religious experience in children, *American Journal of Sociology*, 50,112-122. **(46), (74), (99)**

Harriman, J. F.
(1978) *Patterns of thinking on five religious questions among two samples of university students*, PhD thesis, University of Washington. **(275)**

Harris, A. T.
(1981) *A study of the relationship between stages of moral development and the religious factors of knowledge, belief, and practice in Catholic high-school adolescents*, PhD thesis, University of Oregon. **(284)**

Harris, D. B.
(1963) *Children's Drawings and Measures of Intellectual Maturity*, New York: Harcourt, Brace and World. **(75)**

Harris, P. G.
(1982) *The development of the use and comprehension of metaphor by "preschool" children*, PhD thesis, Texas A & M University. **(389)**

Harrison, M. I.
(1974) Sources of recruitment to Catholic pentecostalism, *Journal for the Scientific Study of Religion*, 13,49-64. **(170)**

Hart, J. G.
(1985) LAWSEQ: its relation to other measures of self-esteem and academic ability, *British Journal of Educational Psychology*, 55,167-169. **(206)**

Hartley, K. J.
(1984) *R.E. in English Catholic Secondary Schools: Catechesis or Education?*, MEd dissertation, University of Birmingham. **(319)**

Hartman, S. G.
(1971) *Eleverna och skolans religionsundervisning* (School pupils and religious education), Stockholm: Utbildningsforlaget, cited in Fagerlind (1974), *op. cit.* **(264)**

Hartman, S. G., Pettersson, S., and Westling, G.
(1973) *Vad funderar barn pa?* (What do children think about?), Stockholm: Utbildningsforlaget. **(264)**

Harvey, O. J. and Felknor, C.
  (1970)   Parent-child relations as an antecedent to conceptual functioning, in Hoppe, R.A., Milton,
           G.A., and Simmel, E.C. (Eds.) *Early Experiences and the Process of Socialization,* New
           York: Academic Press. **(226)**
Hassan, M. K. and Khalique, A.
  (1981)   Religiosity and its coordinates in college students, *Journal of Psychological Research,*
           25,129-136. **(206), (207)**
  (1987)   Impact of parents on children's religious prejudice, *Indian Journal of Current Psycho-
           logical Reports,* 2,47-55. **(231)**
Hastings, P. K. and Hoge, D. R.
  (1976)   Changes in religion among college students, 1948 to 1974, *Journal for the Scientific
           Study of Religion,* 15,237-249. **(271), (274)**
  (1981)   Religious trends among college students, 1948-79, *Social Forces,* 60,517-531. **(271)**
  (1986)   Religious and moral attitude trends among college students, 1948-84, *Social Forces,*
           65,370-377. **(271)**
Hauser, J.
  (1981)   Adolescents and religion, *Adolescence,* 16,309-320. **(206), (267), (284)**
Hausner, R. J.
  (1973)   *The value of Abraham H. Maslow's personality theory for understanding the approach
           to Christian prayer in selected writings of Thomas Merton,* PhD thesis, Catholic Uni-
           versity of America. **(165)**
Havens, J.
  (1963)   Memo on the religious implications of the consciousness-changing drugs, *Journal for
           the Scientific Study of Religion,* 2,216-226. **(172)**
  (1964)   A study of religious conflict in college students, *Journal of Social Psychology,* 64,77-
           82. **(274)**
Havers, N.
  (1972)   *Der Religionsunterricht - Analyse eines unbeliebter Fachs,* Munich: Kosel. **(334)**
Hawes, G. K.
  (1965)   (Mis)leading questions, *Learning for Living,* 4,4,28-30. **(41)**
Hawkins, J. P. and Pratt, D. L.
  (1988)   And robins I have never seen. . .*Educational Studies* (Oxford), 14,97-103. **(132)**
Hay, D.
  (1977)   Religious experience and education, *Learning for Life,* 16,4,156-160. **(181)**
  (1979a) The spiritual experience of the British, *New Society,* 48,862,Ap12,72-74. **(181)**
  (1979b) Religious experience among a group of postgraduate students—a qualitative survey,
           Journal for the Scientific Study of Religion, 18,164-182. **(181)**
  (1982)   *Exploring Inner Space,* Harmondsworth: Penguin. **(181), (186), (202)**
  (1983)   Numinous experiences: frequent or rare? *Journal of Analytic Psychology,* 28,17-32. **(182)**
  (1986a) Asking questions about religious experience, *Religion,* 18,217-229. **(165)**
  (1986b) Religious experience as liberation, *Faith and Freedom: a Journal of Progressive Reli-
           gion,* 39,137-150. **(165)**
  (1988)   *The bearing of empirical studies of religious experience on education,* PhD thesis, Uni-
           versity of Nottingham. **(181)**
Hay, D. and Morisy, A.
  (1978)   Reports of ecstatic, paranormal, or religious experience in Great Britain and the United
           States—a comparison of trends, *Journal for the Scientific Study of Religion,* 17,255-
           268. **(182)**
  (1985)   Secular society, religious meanings: a contemporary paradox, *Review of Religious
           Research,* 26,213-227. **(181)**
Hayden, B.
  (1987)   Alliances and ritual ecstasy: human responses to resource stress, *Journal for the Sci-
           entific Study of Religion,* 26,81-91. **(168)**
Hayes, E. L.
  (1969)   Centrality of the Bible in Christian education, *Bibliotheca Sacra,* 126,224-231. **(129)**
Hayes, R. L.
  (1982)   A re-review of adolescent identity formation: implications for education, *Adolescence,*

17,153-165. **(214)**

Hebron, M. E.
  (1957)   The research into the teaching of religious knowledge, *Studies in Education*, 2,420-446. **(119)**
  (1959)   Religious instruction for the less able pupil in a secondary modern school, *Religion in Education*, 26,101-105. **(119)**

Heimbrock, H-G.
  (1986)   The development of symbols as a key to the developmental psychology of religion, *British Journal of Religious Education*, 8,150-154. **(131)**

Heirich, M.
  (1977)   Change of heart: a test of some widely held theories about religious conversion, *American Journal of Sociology*, 83,653-686. **(191)**

Heller, D. I.
  (1986)   *The Children's God*, Chicago: University of Chicago Press. **(72)**

Henao, A. O.
  (1983)   *A cross-cultural study of the effects of culture-specific schemata of children's comprehension of metaphoric language*, PhD thesis, University of Wisconsin-Madison. **(386)**

Hendrick, S. S. and Hendrick, C.
  (1987)   Love and sex attitudes and religious belief, *Journal of Social and Clinical Psychology*, 5,391-398. **(291)**

Hendricks, L. E. and Fullilove, R. E.
  (1983)   Locus of control and the use of contraception among unmarried black adolescent fathers and their controls, *Journal of Youth and Adolescence*, 12,225-233. **(291)**

Henry, R. M.
  (1987)   Moral belief structure and context, self-identity and parental favoriteness as determinants of moral judgment stage, *Journal of Moral Education*, 16,3-17. **(231)**

Hepburn, L. R.
  (1971)   Religion in the social studies: the question of religious attitudes, *Religious Education*, 66,172-179. **(152)**

Herek, G. M.
  (1987)   Religious orientation and prejudice: a comparison of racial and sexual attitudes, *Personality and Social Psychology Bulletin*, 13,34-44. **(354)**

Hertel, B.
  (1973)   Some dimensions of Sanskritization: belief, practice, and egalitarianism among Hindus of the Gangetic Plain, *Journal for the Scientific Study of Religion*, 12,17-32. **(344), (349)**

Hertel, B. R. and Nelsen, H. M.
  (1974)   Are we entering a post-Christian era? Religious belief and attendance in America, 1957-1968, *Journal for the Scientific Study of Religion*, 13,409-419. **(266)**

Heskested, S.
  (1984)   Religiosity and mental health: an empirical study, *Nordisk Psykiatrisk Tidsskrift*, 38,353-361. **(205)**

Hess, R. D. and Terney, J. V.
  (1962)   Religion, age, and sex in children's perceptions of family, *Child Development*, 33,781-789. **(234)**

Heywood, B.
  (1973)   The teaching of skills, *Learning for Life*, 13,2,62-63. **(142)**

Heywood, D.
  (1985)   Piaget and faith development: a true marriage of minds? *British Journal of Religious Education*, 8,72-78. **(54)**

Hick, J. H.
  (1963)   Comment, *Journal for the Scientific Study of Religion*, 2,22-24. **(361)**

Hickey, A. V.
  (1977)   *A study of the relationships between faculty perceptions of the dimensions of organizational climate and their perceptions of the dimensions of religiosity in selected Catholic high schools*, EdD thesis, St John's University. **(329)**

Hickman, D. C.
  (1971)   The effectiveness of religious and moral education, in *Moral education and the formation of attitudes* , in Nurser, J. S. (Ed.), Canberra: Australian National University Centre

for Continuing Education. **(328)**

Hill, C. I.
(1986)   A developmental perspective on adolescent "rebellion" in the church, *Journal of Psychology and Theology,* 14,306-318. **(213), (214), (216)**

Hill, M.
(1968)   *RI and Surveys: Opinion Polls on Religious Education in State Schools,* London: National Secular Society. **(236)**

Hill, S.
(1985)   Religion and region in America, *The Annals of the American Academy of Political and Social Sciences,* 480,132-141. **(243)**

Hilliard, F. H.
(1959)   The influence of religious education upon the development of children's moral ideas, *British Journal of Educational Psychology,* 29,50-59. **(146), (257), (282)**
(1965)   Children's religious thinking, *Learning for Living,* 5,2,13-15. **(36)**

Hilty, D. M.
(1988)   Religious belief, participation, and consequences: an exploratory and confirming analysis, *Journal for the Scientific Study of Religion,* 27,243-259. **(348)**

Hilty, D. M. and Morgan, R. L.
(1985)   Construct validation for the religious involvement inventory: replication, *Journal for the Scientific Study of Religion,* 24,75-86. **(344)**

Hilty, D. M., Morgan, R. L., and Burns, J. E.
(1984)   King and Hunt revisited: dimensions of religious involvement, *Journal for the Scientific Study of Religion,* 23,252-266. **(344), (345), (346)**

Hilty, D. M., Morgan, R., and Hartman, W.
(1985)   A structural equation modeling analysis of the means, end, and quest orientations, *Journal for the Scientific Study of Religion,* 24,424-436. **(357)**

Hilty, D. M. and Stockman, S. J.
(1986)   A covariance structure analysis of the DeJong, Faulkener, and Warland religious involvement model, *Journal for the Scientific Study of Religion,* 25,483-493. **(344), (349)**

Himmelfarb, H. S.
(1974)   *The impact of religious schooling: the effects of Jewish education upon adult religious involvement,* PhD thesis, University of Chicago. **(304)**
(1975a)   *The long-range effectiveness of different types of Jewish education.* Paper presented to the 70th Annual Meeting of the American Sociological Association. **(304), (344), (345), (346), (350)**
(1975b)   Measuring religious involvement, *Social Forces,* 53,606-618. **(304), (345), (346)**
(1977)   The interaction effect of parents, spouse, and schooling: comparing the impact of Jewish and Catholic schools, *Sociological Quarterly,* 18,464-477. **(304)**

Hinchliffe, D. W.
(1973)   *Attitudes to religion, morality, and worship of a sample of fifth form boys and girls,* DipEd dissertation, University of Birmingham. **(153)**

Hindley, A. H.
(1965)   *The religious concepts of secondary modern children tested by their art work,* AdCertEd dissertation, University of Sheffield. **(75)**
(1970)   *The effect of a study of adolescence, by adolescents, on their attitude to the Christian faith,* MEd thesis, University of Manchester. **(152)**

Hinkle, D. E. and Oliver, J. D.
(1983)   How large should the sample be? A question with no simple answer? or. . *Educational and Psychological Measurement,* 43,1051-1060. **(340)**

Hirschberg, G. and Gilliard, A. R.
(1942)   Parent-child relationships in attitudes, *Journal of Abnormal and Social Psychology,* 37,125-130. **(228), (295)**

Hirschberg, J. C.
(1955)   Some comments on religion and childhood, *Bulletin of the Menninger Clinic,* 19,227-228. **(231)**

Hoagland, D. D.
(1984)   *Moral judgment and religious belief: an investigation of the "moral majority,"* PhD the-

sis, Fuller Theological Seminary, School of Psychology. (285)

Hoelter, J. W.
(1980)   *Self-integration and religiosity: an empirical investigation.* Paper presented at the annual
          meeting of the North Central Sociological Association. (211)

Hoffman, M. L.
(1971)   Development of internal moral standards in children, in Strommen, M. P. (Ed.), *op. cit.* (227)

Hoge, D. R.
(1972)   A validated intrinsic religious motivation scale, *Journal for the Scientific Study of Reli-
          gion,* 11,369-376. (352)
(1976)   The outlines of an "invisible religion": the multiple commitments of Protestants, *Char-
          acter Potential,* 8,3-11. (353)

Hoge, D. R. et al.
(1981)   Desired outcomes of religious education and youth ministry in six denominations, *Living
          Light,* 18,18-25. (254)
(1982)   Desired outcomes of religious education, in Wyckoff, D. C. and Richter, D. (Eds.), *op.
          cit.* (254)

Hoge, D. R. and De Zulveta, E.
(1985)   Salience as a condition for various social consequences of religious commitment, *Jour-
          nal for the Scientific Study of Religion,* 24,21-28. (290)

Hoge, D. R. and Keeter, L. G.
(1976)   Teachers' religious beliefs and participation, *Journal for the Scientific Study of Religion,*
          15,221-235. (230)

Hoge, D. R. and Petrillo, G. H.
(1978a)   Development of religious thinking in adolescence: a test of Goldman's theories, *Journal
          for the Scientific Study of Religion,* 17,139-154. (43)
(1978b)   Determinants of church participation and attitudes among high-school youth, *Journal
          for the Scientific Study of Religion,* 17,359-379. (227), (231), (233)
(1979)   Youth and the church, *Religious Education,* 74,305-313. (233), (237), (254)
(1982)   Transmission of religious and social values from parents to teenage children, *Journal
          of Marriage and the Family,* 44,569-580. (228)

Hoge, D. R. and Smith, E. I.
(1982)   Normative and nonnormative religious experience among high-school youth, *Sociolog-
          ical Analysis,* 43,69-82. (176), (254)

Holland, E. G.
(1968)   *Adolescent attitudes, values, and conflicts in a West Midland town,* DPC dissertation,
          University of Birmingham. (279)

Holland, V. M. and Rohrman, N. L.
(1979)   Distribution of the feature (+Antimate) in the lexicon of the child, *Journal of Psycholin-
          guistic Research,* 8,367-388. (370)

Holley, R.
(1971)   Learning religion, *Learning for Living,* 10,4,14-19. (361)
(1978)   *Religious Education and Religious Understanding,* London: Routledge and Kegan Paul. (361)

Holm, J. L.
(1973)   What shall we tell the children? *Theology,* 76,141-148. (34)
(1975)   *Teaching Religion in School: A Practical Approach,* London: Oxford University Press. (34)

Holm, N. G.
(1982)   Mysticism and intense experiences, *Journal for the Scientific Study of Religion,* 21,268-
          276. (170)

Holm, N. G. (Ed.)
(1982)   *Religious Ecstasy,* Stockholm: Almquist and Wikell. (170)

Holt, J. G.
(1986)   *Religious experience: a psychological interpretation of first-hand accounts from the per-
          spective of object relations and narcissism theories,* PhD thesis, Boston University. (185)

Homan, R. and Youngman, J.
(1982)   School and church as agencies of religious socialization, *British Journal of Religious
          Education,* 5,22-27. (250)

Hood, R. W.

(1970)   Religious orientation and the report of religious experience, *Journal for the Scientific Study of Religion*, 9,285-291. **(172)**, **(202)**

(1971)   A comparison of the Allport and Feagin scoring procedure for intrinsic/extrinsic religious orientation, *Journal for the Scientific Study of Religion*, 10,370-374. **(172)**, **(351)**

(1972)   Normative and motivational determinants of reported religious experience in two Baptist samples, *Review of Religious Research*, 13,192-196. **(172)**, **(186)**

(1973a)   Religious orientation and the experience of transcendence, *Journal for the Scientific Study of Religion*, 12,441-448. **(172)**

(1973b)   Forms of religious commitment and intense religious experience, *Review of Religious Research*, 15,29-36. **(173)**

(1973c)   Hypnotic susceptibility and reported religious experience, *Psychological Reports*, 33,549-550. **(173)**

(1974)   Psychological strength and the report of intense religious experience, *Journal for the Scientific Study of Religion*, 13,65-71. **(173)**

(1975)   The construction and validation of a measure of reported mystical experience, *Journal for the Scientific Study of Religion*, 14,29-41. **(173)**, **(175)**

(1976)   Mystical experience as related to present and anticipated church participation, *Psychological Reports*, 39,1127-1136. **(173)**

(1977a)   Differential triggering of mystical experience as a function of self actualization, *Review of Religious Research*, 18,264-270. **(173)**

(1977b)   Eliciting mystical states of consciousness with semistructured nature experience, *Journal for the Scientific Study of Religion*, 16,155-163. **(173)**

(1978a)   The usefulness of the indiscriminate pro and anti categories of religious orientation, *Journal for the Scientific Study of Religion*, 17,419-431. **(355)**

(1978b)   Anticipatory set and setting: stress incongruities as elicitors of mystical experience in solitary nature situations, *Journal for the Scientific Study of Religion*, 17,279-287. **(174)**, **(353)**

(1980)   Social legitimacy, dogmatism, and the evaluation of intense experiences, *Review of Religious Research*, 21,184-194. **(174)**

(1985)   The conceptualization of religious purity in Allport's typology, *Journal for the Scientific Study of Religion*, 24,413-417. **(357)**

Hood, R. W. and Hall, J. R.
(1980)   Gender differences in the description of erotic and mystical experiences, *Review of Religious Research*, 21,195-203. **(174)**, **(186)**

Hood, R. W., Hall, J. R., Watson, P. J., and Biderman, M.
(1977)   Comparison of reported religious experience in Caucasian, American Indian and two Mexican-American samples, *Psychological Reports*, 41,657-658. **(174)**

(1979)   Personality correlates of the report of mystical experience, *Psychological Reports*, 44,804-806. **(175)**

Hood, R. W. and Morris, R. J.
(1981a)   Knowledge and experience criteria in the report of mystical experiences, *Review of Religious Research*, 23,76-84. **(175)**

(1981b)   Sensory isolation and the differential elicitation of religious imagery in intrinsic and extrinsic religious persons, *Journal for the Scientific Study of Religion*, 20,261-273. **(175)**

(1983)   Toward a theory of death transcendence, *Journal for the Scientific Study of Religion*, 22,353-365. **(353)**

(1985)   Conceptualization of Quest: a critical rejoinder to Batson, *Review of Religious Research*, 26,391-397. **(357)**

Hood, R. W., Morris, R. J., and Watson, P. J.
(1987)   Religious orientation and prayer experience, *Psychological Reports*, 60,1201-1202. **(173)**

(1989)   Prayer experience and religious orientation, *Review of Religious Research*, 31,39-45. **(112)**

Hopkins, J. R.
(1977)   Sexual behavior in adolescence, *Journal of Social Issues*, 33,67-85. **(290)**

Hopson, D. S.
(1982)   *The relationship of religious commitment, life stress, and psychological adjustment*, PhD thesis, Southern University at Carbondale. **(204)**

Hornsby-Smith, M. P.
(1978)   *Catholic Education: The Unobtrusive Partner*, London: Sheed & Ward. **(298)**, **(315)**

Hornsby-Smith, M. P., Lee, R. M., and Reilly, P. A.
    (1985)   Common religion and customary religion: a critique and a proposal, *Review of Religious Research*, 26,244-252. **(277)**, **(337)**

Hornsby-Smith, M. and Petit, M.
    (1975)   Social, moral, and religious attitudes of secondary school children, *Journal of Moral Education*, 4,261-272. **(314)**, **(333)**

Hoult, T. F. and Peckham, C. W.
    (1957)   Religion as a cultural factor in one aspect of the personality of selected college students, *Journal of Education Sociology*, 31,75-81. **(276)**

Howe, L. T.
    (1978)   Religious understanding from a Piagetian perspective, *Religious Education*, 73,569-581. **(364)**

Howells, J. C.
    (1978)   Religious education in Victoria today, *Learning for Living*, 17,3,118-122. **(322)**

Howkins, K. G.
    (1966)   *Religious Thinking and Religious Education*, London: Tyndale Press. **(25)**, **(41)**
    (1972)   *The Challenge of Religious Studies*, London: Tyndale Press. **(41)**

Huber, M. A.
    (1988)   Learning through fantasy games, *British Journal of Religious Education*, 10,72-78. **(101)**

Hughes, G. H.
    (1953)   *An enquiry into the effect of religious education on the moral attitudes of children*, DipEd dissertation, University of Birmingham. **(146)**

Hummel, R. and Roselli, L.
    (1983)   Identity status and academic achievement in female adolescents, *Adolescence*, 18,17-27. **(215)**

Hundelby, J. D., Carpenter, R. A., Ross, R. A., and Mercer, G. W.
    (1982)   Adolescent drug use and other behaviors, *Journal of Child Psychology and Psychiatry and Allied Disciplines*, 23,61-68. **(289)**

Hunsberger, B.
    (1987)   More on the development of Christian orthodoxy, *Journal for the Scientific Study of Religion*, 26,256-259. **(347)**

Hunsberger, B. and Brown, L. B.
    (1984)   Religious socialization, apostasy, and the impact of family background, *Journal for the Scientific Study of Religion*, 23,239-251. **(231)**, **(234)**

Hunsberger, B. and Ennis, J.
    (1982)   Experimenter effects in studies of religious attitude, *Journal for the Scientific Study of Religion*, 21,131-137. **(158)**

Hunsberger, B. and Platonow, E.
    (1986)   Religiousness and helping charitable causes, *Journal of Psychology*, 120,517-528. **(359)**

Hunsberger, B. E.
    (1973)   *Religious denomination, education, and university students' reported agreement with parents' religious beliefs*, PhD thesis, University of Manitoba. **(229)**
    (1976)   Background religious denomination, parental emphasis, and the religious orientation of university students, *Journal for the Scientific Study of Religion*, 15,251-255. **(229)**
    (1978)   The religiosity of college students: stability and change over years at university, *Journal for the Scientific Study of Religion*, 17,159-164. **(272)**
    (1980)   A reexamination of the antecedents of apostasy, *Review of Religious Research*, 21,158-170. **(231)**
    (1985)   Parent-university student agreement on religious and nonreligious issues, *Journal for the Scientific Study of Religion*, 24,314-320. **(226)**

Hunt, L. L. and Hunt, J. G.
    (1975)   A religion factor in secular achievement among blacks: the case of Catholics, *Social Forces*, 53,595-605. **(301)**

Hunt, R. A.
    (1972)   Mythological-symbolic religious commitment: the LAM scales, *Journal for the Scientific Study of Religion*, 11,42-52.**(204)**, **(344)**, **(346)**

Hunt, R. A. and King, M.

(1971)   The intrinsic-extrinsic concept; a review and evaluation, *Journal for the Scientific Study of Religion*, 10,339-356. **(351)**, **(352)**
Hunter, E. F
(1956)   *The Questioning Child and Religion*, Boston: Beacon Press. **(98)**
Hunter, J. P.
(1982)   Operationalizing evangelism: a review, critique, and proposal, *Sociological Analysis*, 42,363-372. **(79)**
Hurlock, E. B.
(1969)   *Developmental Psychology*, New York: McGraw-Hill. **(99)**
Hutsebaut, D.
(1972)   The representation of God: two complementary approaches, *Social Compass*, 19,389-406. **(87)**, **(88)**, **(89)**
Hyde, D.
(1977)   Relating God to the world of secondary students, *Journal of Christian Education*, Papers, 58,48-54. **(326)**
Hyde, K. E.
(1959)   *The communication of religious ideas and attitudes among secondary school children*, PhD thesis, University of Birmingham. **(27)**, **(80)**, **(106)**, **(147)**, **(158)**, **(339)**
(1963)   Religious concepts and religious attitudes, *Educational Review*, 15,132-141, 217-227. **(80)**, **(147)**
(1965)   *Religious Learning in Adolescence*, Edinburgh: Oliver and Boyd for the University of Birmingham Institute of Education. **(29)**, **(80)**, **(147)**, **(198)**
(1968)   A critique of Goldman's research, *Religious Education*, 63,429-435. **(37)**
(1969)   *Religion and Slow Learners: A Research Study*, London: SCM Press. **(119)**
(1984)   Twenty years after Goldman's research, *British Journal of Religious Education*, 7,5-7. **(34)**
Iisager, H.
(1949)   Factors influencing the formation and change of political and religious attitudes, *Journal of Social Psychology*, 29,253-265. **(228)**
Inhelder, B. and Piaget, J.
(1958)   *The Growth of Logical Thinking from Childhood to Adolescence*, London: Routledge and Kegan Paul. **(42)**
Inhelder, B. and Sinclair, H.
(1969)   Learning cognitive structures, in Mussen, P. et al. (Eds.) *Trends and Issues in Developmental Psychology*, New York: Holt, Rinehart. **(364)**
Inskeep, K. W.
(1986)   *Religious organizational socialization in the Evangelical Free Church of America*, PhD thesis, Loyola University of Chicago. **(229)**
Isert, L.
(1969)   Religious education in the light of recent psychological concepts of development, *Catholic Educational Review*, 66,656-663. **(23)**
Jackson, L. E. and Coursey, R. D.
(1988)   The relationship of God centered and internal locus of control to intrinsic religious orientations, coping, and purpose in life, *Journal for the Scientific Study of Religion*, 27,399-410. **(212)**
Jacques, J. M. and Chason, K. J.
(1978)   Cohabitation: a test of reference group theory among black and white college students, *Journal of Comparative Family Studies*, 9,147-165. **(292)**
Jahoda, G.
(1951)   Development of unfavorable attitudes toward religion, *Quarterly Bulletin of the British Psychological Society*, 2,35-36. **(239)**
Jalali-Tehrani, S. M-M.
(1985)   *Religious commitment as a factor in personality integration—a factor in mental health*, PhD thesis, Saybrook Institute. **(204)**
James, J.
(1974)   *Some differences in religious attitudes and concepts in boys and girls of secondary school age*, DCP dissertation, University of Birmingham. **(147)**
Jan, I.

(1973)   *On Children's Literature,* London: Penguin. **(132)**

Jantz, R. K.
(1973)   An investigation of the relation between moral development and intellectual development in male elementary school students, *Theory and Research in Social Studies,* 1,75-81. **(378)**

Jarman, R. L.
(1985)   *The development of proverb comprehension: a preliminary investigation,* MSc thesis, University of London. **(390)**

Jarvis, P.
(1972)   *Religious socialization in the junior school: an enquiry among class teachers.* MSocSc thesis, University of Birmingham. **(307), (311)**
(1974)   Religious socialization in the junior school, *Educational Research,* 16,100-106. **(307)**

Jarvis, W. L.
(1967)   *A limited study of the continued participation of recent confirmands of the American Lutheran Church,* STM thesis, Wartburg Theological Seminary. **(227)**

Jaspard, J-M.
(1971)   The 6 to 12 year-old children's appreciation of the Eucharistic Presence, *Luman Vitae,* 26,237-262. **(105)**
(1972)   Loi rituelle et structuration de l'attitude religieuse chez l'enfant, *Social Compass,* 19,459-471. **(87)**
(1980)   The relation to God and the moral development of the young child, in The First International Conference on Moral and Religious Development, *op. cit.* **(80)**

Jebb, P. (Ed.)
(1968)   *Religious Education: Drift or Decision?* London: Darton, Longman & Todd.

Jencks, C.
(1985)   How much do high-school students learn? *Sociology of Education,* 58,128-135. **(301)**

Jensen, G. F. and Maynard, L. E.
(1979)   The religious factor and delinquency: another look at the Hell Fire hypotheses, in Wuthnow, R. (Ed.) (1979), *op. cit.* **(287)**

Jersild, A. T., Brook, J. S., and Brook, D. W.
(1978)   *The Psychology of Adolescence,* New York: Macmillan. **(266)**

Johnsen, M. W.
(1986)   *Personality change resulting from a religious conversion experience,* PhD thesis, Texas Technical University. **(207)**

Johnson, A. C., Brekke, M. L., Strommen, M. P., and Underwager, R. C.
(1974)   Age differences and dimensions of religious behavior, *Journal of Social Issues,* 30,43-67. **(254)**

Johnson, J. E. and Hooper, F. H.
(1982)   Piagetian structuralism and learning: reflections on two decades of educational application, *Contemporary Educational Psychology,* 7,217-237. **(373)**

Johnson, J. F.
(1955)   *An enquiry into some of the religious ideas of six-year-old children,* DipEd dissertation, University of Birmingham. **(67)**

Johnson, J. M.
(1980)   *The development of metaphor comprehension: its mental-demand measurement and its process-analytic models,* PhD thesis, York University, (Canada). **(388)**

Johnson, M. A.
(1973)   Family life and religious commitment, *Review of Religious Research,* 14,144-150. **(109), (353), (354)**
(1974)   *The relationship between religious knowledge and selected cognitive and personality variables,* DEd thesis, Temple University. **(109), (354)**

Johnson, M. R.
(1985)   "Race," religion and ethnicity: religious observance in the West Midlands, *Ethic and Racial Studies,* 8,426-437. **(243)**

Johnson, S.
(1984)   *Religious experience as creative, revelatory, and transforming event: the implications of intense Christian experience for the Christian educational process,* PhD thesis, Princetown Theological Seminary. **(167)**

Johnson, W. P.
  (1966)   *The religious attitude of secondary modern county school pupils,* MEd thesis, University of Manchester. **(149)**
Johnstone, R. L.
  (1966)   *The effectiveness of Lutheran elementary and secondary schools as agencies of Christian education,* St. Louis: Condoria Seminary. **(302)**
Jones, J. A.
  (1962)   *An investigation into the responses of boys and girls respectively to Scripture as a school subject in certain coeducational grammar schools in industrial South Wales,* MEd thesis, University of Wales, Swansea. **(148)**
  (1974)   *A study of the changes in the attitudes of students in a college of education to the Bible and to the teaching of it, in relation to certain personality factors,* PhD thesis, University College Cardiff. **(154)**
Jones, M. C.
  (1960)   A comparison of the attitudes and interests of ninth-grade students over two decades, *Journal of Educational Psychology,* 51,175-186. **(266)**
Jordan, D.
  (1941)   The attitude of central school pupils to certain school subjects and the correlation between attitude and attainment, *British Journal of Educational Psychology,* 11,28-44. **(152), (155)**
Josephina, F. A.
  (1961)   A study of some religious terms for six-year old children, *Religious Education,* 56,24-25. **(99), (100)**
Joubert, C. E.
  (1978)   Sex, church attendance, and endorsement of Ellis's irrational beliefs, *Psychological Reports,* 42,1318. **(198)**
Jurd, M. F.
  (1978)   An empirical study of operational thinking in history-type material, in Keats, J. A., Collis, K. F., and Halford, G. S. (Eds.) (1978), *op. cit.* **(373)**
Justice, W. G. and Lambert, W.
  (1986)   A comparative study of the language people use to describe the personalities of God and their earthly parents, *Journal of Pastoral Care,* 40,166-172. **(93)**
Kahle, L. R. and Berman, J. J.
  (1979)   Attitudes cause behavior: a cross-lagged panel analysis, *Journal of Personality and Social Psychology,* 37,315-321. **(394)**
Kahoe, R. D.
  (1974)   Personality and achievement correlates of intrinsic and extrinsic religious orientation, *Journal of Personality and Social Psychology,* 29,812-818. **(209), (352), (353)**
  (1977)   Intrinsic religion and authoritarianism: a differentiated relationship, *Journal for the Scientific Study of Religion,* 16,179-183. **(209)**
  (1985)   The development of the intrinsic and extrinsic religious orientation, *Journal for the Scientific Study of Religion,* 24,408-422. **(354)**
  (1989)   A concluding unscientific postscript on religious development, *Journal for the Scientific Study of Religion,* 28,230-232. **(59)**
Kaiser, R. G.
  (1978)   *A study of selected religious practices, beliefs, and knowledge of eighth-grade students in the Lutheran schools of Michigan,* EdD thesis, Wayne State University. **(302)**
Kalam, T. P.
  (1981)   *The myth of stages and sequences in moral and religious development,* PhD thesis, University of Lancaster. **(56), (373)**
Kane, A. L.
  (1988)   *Religious orientation, moral development and ego identity status,* PhD thesis, Yeshiva University. **(284)**
Kanger, K. E.
  (1972)   *Change in religious attitudes of freshmen Catholic women after one year on a small religiously orientated campus, a large religiously oriented campus and a secular campus,* PhD thesis, University of N. Colorado. **(275)**

Kassim, P. A.
    (1980)   *The interrelationship of language, maturity of judgment and the level of abstract thought in young adolescents,* MEd thesis, University of Birmingham. **(137)**

Kay, W. K.
    (1981a)   *Religious thinking, attitudes, and personality among secondary school pupils in England and Ireland,* PhD thesis, University of Reading. **(42), (43), (160), (195)**
    (1981b)   Marital happiness and children's attitude to religion, *British Journal of Religious Education,* 3,102-105. **(160)**
    (1981c)   Psychoticism and attitude to religion, *Personality and Individual Differences,* 2,249-252. **(204), (235)**

Kay, W. K. and Francis, L. J.
    (1983)   Progress in the psychology of religious development, *Lumen Vitae,* 38,342-346. **(157)**

Keats, J. A., Collis, K. F., and Halford, G. S.
    (1978)   *Cognitive Development: Research Based on a Neo-Piagetian Approach,* Chichester: Wiley. **(373)**

Kedem, P. and Cohen, D. W.
    (1987)   The effects of religious education on moral judgment, *Journal of Psychology and Judaism,* 11,4-14. **(283)**

Keil, F. C.
    (1986)   Conceptual domain and the acquisition of metaphor, *Cognitive Development,* 1,73-96. **(387)**

Kelly, H. H. and Michela, J. L.
    (1980)   Attribution theory and research, *Annual Review of Psychology,* 31,457-501. **(219)**

Kent, R. R.
    (1987)   *The religiosity and parent/child socialization connection with adolescent substance abuse,* PhD thesis, Brigham Young University. **(289)**

Keown, D.
    (1986)   What Utah children believe, *The Humanist,* 46,21-26. **(267)**

Kerry, T.
    (1980)   Demands made by religious education on pupils' thinking, *British Journal of Religious Education,* 3,46-52. **(142)**

Kesteven, S. W.
    (1967)   *An enquiry into attitudes to religion of youth club members in Stafford and district,* MEd thesis, University of Birmingham. **(150)**

Keys, W. P. and Ormerod, M. B.
    (1976)   Some factors affecting pupils' subject preference, *Durham Research Review,* 36,1109-1115. **(161)**

Kharari, K. and Harmon, T. N.
    (1982)   The relationship between the degree of professed religious belief and use of drugs, *International Journal of the Addictions,* 17,847-857. **(288)**

Kibble, D.
    (1980)   Is religious knowledge possible in RE? *Bulletin of the Association for Religious Education,* 13,34,4-16. **(362)**

Kibble, D., Parker, S., and Price, C.
    (1982)   The age of uncertainty: religious belief among adolescents, *British Journal of Religious Education,* 4,31-35. **(259)**

Kieren, D. K. and Munro, B.
    (1987)   Following the leader: parents influence and adolescent religious activity, *Review of Religious Research,* 26,249-255. **(234)**

Kildahl, J. P.
    (1965)   The personality of sudden religious converts, *Pastoral Psychology,* 16,37-44, reprinted in Malony, H. N. (Ed.) (1977), *op. cit.* **(190)**

Kilpatrick, D. G., Sutker, L. W., and Sutker, P. B.
    (1970)   Dogmatism, religion and religiosity, a review and reevaluation, *Psychological Reports,* 26,15-22. **(243)**

King, K., Abernathy, T. J., Robison, I. E., and Balswick, J. O.
    (1976)   Religiosity and sexual attitudes among college students, *Adolescence,* 11,535-539. **(291)**

King, M. B.
    (1967)   Measuring the religious variable: nine proposed dimensions, *Journal for the Scientific Study of Religion,* 6,173-190. **(344)**
    (1969)   Measuring the religious variable: ammended findings, *Journal for the Scientific Study of Religion,* 8,321-323. **(344)**
King, M. and Hunt, R.
    (1973)   *Measuring Religious Dimensions,* Dallas: Southern Methodist Studies in Social Science No. 1. **(344)**
    (1975)   Measuring the religious variable: national replication, *Journal for the Scientific Study of Religion,* 14,13-22. **(344), (360)**
Kingan, B. A.
    (1969)   *A study of some factors hindering the religious education of a group of primary school children,* MEd thesis, University of Liverpool. **(25)**
Kirkpatric, C. and Stone, S.
    (1935)   Attitude measurement and the comparison of generations, *Journal of Applied Psychology,* 19,564-582. **(81), (229)**
Kirkpatric, L. A.
    (1986a)   *Empirical research on images of God: a methodological and conceptual critique,* paper presented at the Annual Meeting of the Society for the Scientific Study of Religion, Savannah, Georgia. **(96)**
    (1986b)   *Multidimensionality of extrinsic religiousness,* paper presented at the Annual Meeting of the American Psychological Association, Washington, D. C. **(356)**
Kish, L.
    (1978)   Some statistical problems in research design, in Brynner, J. and Stribley, K. M. (Eds) *Social Research: Principles and Procedures,* London: Longman/Open University Press. **(339)**
Kitwood, T.
    (1978)   The morality of interpersonal values; an aspect of values in adolescent life, *Journal of Moral Education,* 7,189-198. **(279)**
    (1980)   *Disclosure to a Stranger,* London: Routledge & Kegan Paul. **(279)**
Kitwood, T. and Smithers, A. G.
    (1975)   Measurement of human values: an appraisal of the work of Milton Rokeach, *Educational Research,* 17,175-179. **(395)**
Klahr, D. and Wallace, J. G.
    (1976)   *Cognitive Development: An Information-Processing View,* Hillsdale, New Jersey: Lawrence Erlbaum. **(381)**
Klausmeier, H. J. and Associates
    (1979)   *Cognitive Learning and Development: Information-Processing and Piagetian Perspectives,* Cambridge, Massachusetts: Ballinger. **(382)**
Klinberg, G.
    (1959)   A study of religious experience in children from 9 to 13 years of age, *Religious Education,* 54,211-216. **(185)**
Knight, G. D. and Sedlacek, W. E.
    (1981a)   *The religious orientation of college students,* Maryland University Counseling Center. **(352)**
    (1981b)   *Religious orientation and the concepts of God held by university students,* Maryland University Counseling Center. **(353), (355)**
Knowles, P. A.
    (1975)   *An analysis of mystic experience,* PhD thesis, Claremond Graduate School. **(168)**
Kojetin, B. A., McIntosh, D. M., Bridges, R. A., and Spilka, B.
    (1987)   Quest: constructive search or religious conflict? *Journal for the Scientific Study of Religion,* 26,111-115. **(357)**
Kolls, M.
    (1980)   *Childrens' drawings: readiness measure and resource for learning.* Paper presented at the annual meeting of the Claremont Reading Conference. **(75)**
Koplin, M. D.
    (1987)   *Family, religiousness, and peer influence on adolescent drug-use,* PhD thesis, Brigham Young University. **(289)**
Koppe, W.

(1973) *How Persons Grow in Christian Community,* Yearbook in Christian Education, IV, Philadelphia: Fortress Press. **(107)**

Kousoulas, E. P.
(1973) *The relation between the development of Piagetian concepts of God and rain and age, religion and sex among suburban children,* PhD thesis, New York University. **(30)**

Kraft, W. A., Litwin, W. J., and Barber, S. E.
(1986) Relationship of intrinsic-extrinsic religiousness and assertiveness, *Psychological Reports,* 59,1115-1118. **(352)**

Kraus, C. A.
(1980) *An investigation of the effects of literal and metaphoric titles on good and poor readers' comprehension of text,* PhD thesis, University of Maryland. **(389)**

Krausz, E.
(1977) The religious factor in Jewish identification, *International Social Science Journal,* 29,250-260. **(244)**

Kristo, J.
(1982) The interpretation of religious experience: what do mystics intend when they talk about their experiences? *The Journal of Religion,* 62,21-38. **(166)**

Kròl, J.
(1982) [Young people's image of father and its influence on their image of God], *Roczniki Filozoficzne: Psychologia,* 30,73-103. **(95)**

Krull, K. H.
(1984) *Religious orientation and interpersonal God concept as a function of cognitive style,* PsyD thesis, Rosemead School of Psychology. **(64)**

Krych, M. A.
(1985) *Communicating "justification" to elementary-age children: a study in Tillich's correlational method and transformational narrative for Christian education,* PhD thesis, Princeton Theological Seminary. **(45)**

Kuhlen, R. G. and Arnold, M.
(1944) Age differences in religious beliefs and problems during adolescence, *Journal of Genetic Psychology,* 65,291-300. **(106)**

Kuhre, B. E.
(1971) The religious involvement of the college student from a multidimensional perspective, *Sociological Analysis,* 32,61-69. **(348)**

Kuiper, H. P.
(1976) *Teacher self-disclosure and advocacy, compared to neutrality, their effect on learning, with special reference to religious studies,* Fort Lauderdale: Nova University. **(140)**

Kukuyama, Y.
(1963) Wonder letters: an experimental study of the religious sensibility of children, *Religious Education,* 58,377-383. **(132)**

Kuriakose, W. M.
(1960) *The development of the idea of God among secondary school children,* DCP dissertation, University of Birmingham. **(80)**

Kurtines, W. and Pimm, J. B.
(1983) The Moral Development Scale: a Piagetian measure of moral judgement, *Educational and Psychological Measurement,* 43,89-105. **(367)**

Kwilecki, S.
(1988a) A scientific approach to religious development: proposals and a case illustration, *Journal for the Scientific Study of Religion,* 27,307-325. **(58)**
(1988b) Personal religion and belief development: the "articulate authoritarian" type, *Religion,* 18,231-253. **(58)**
(1989) Reply to Barnes and Kahoe, *Journal for the Scientific Study of Religion,* 28,233-236. **(59)**

Lafuente Benaches, M. J. and Valcarcel Gonzalez, M. P.
(1984) Actitudes frente a la sexualidad de una maestra de universitarios valencuanos, *Piscológica,* 5,81-99. **(291)**

Langdon, A. A.
(1969) A critical examination of Dr. Goldman's research study on religious thinking from child-

hood to adolescence, *Journal of Christian Education,* Papers 12,37-63. **(37)**
LaPiere, R. T.
   (1934)   Attitudes vs. actions, *Social Forces,* 15,232-237. **(392)**
Larivière, J-J,
   (1964)   Religious knowledge among pupils of secular and religious catechists: a comparative study, in Godin, A. (Ed.) (1964), *op. cit.* **(296)**
Larson, L. and Knapp, R. H.
   (1964)   Sex differences in symbolic conceptions of the deity, *Journal of Projective Techniques and Personality Assessment,* 28,303-306. **(84)**
Laurent, C. R.
   (1986)   *Selected variables related to alienation from religion among church-related high-school students,* PhD thesis, Andrews University. **(228)**
Lawrence, J. A.
   (1979)   *The component procedures of moral judgment making,* PhD thesis, University of Min nesota. **(283)**
Lawrence, P. J.
   (1965)   Children's thinking about religion: a study of concrete operational thinking, *Religious Education,* 60,111-116. **(23)**
Leavey, M. C.
   (1972a)   *Religious education, school climate, and achievement: a study of nine Catholic sixth form girls' schools,* PhD thesis, Australian National University, Canberra, Australia. **(328)**
   (1972b)   The transmission of religious and moral values in nine Catholic girls' schools, *Twentieth Century,* 27,3,167-184. **(328)**, **(330)**
Lee, J. M.
   (1973)   *The Flow of Religious Instruction,* Birmingham, Alabama: Religion Education Press. **(141)**, **(224)**
   (1988)   How to teach: foundations, processes, procedures, in Ratcliff, D. (Ed.), *op. cit.* **(45)**
Lee, S. W.
   (1985)   *The orthodoxy of Christian beliefs and Jungian personality type,* EdD thesis, University of South Dakota. **(195)**, **(198)**
Leean, C.
   (1988)   Faith development, adult life cycle, and "Habits of the Heart," *Religious Education,* 83,571-585. **(53)**
Lemert, C. C.
   (1975)   Defining nonchurch religion, *Review of Religious Research,* 16,186-197. **(337)**
Lemieux, R.
   (1970)   *L'enseignement catechetique a l'elementaire dans le diocese de Quebec,* Quebec: Laval University Centre of Religious Sociology. **(299)**
Lemon, N.
   (1973)   *Attitudes and their Measurement,* London: Batsford. **(242)**, **(392)**, **(395)**
Lenski, G.
   (1961)   *The Religious Factor,* Garden City, New York: Doubleday. **(232)**, **(295)**, **(359)**
Léonard, A.
   (1957)   Religious psychology today, *Lumen Vitae,* 12,233-243. **(99)**
Levin, J. S. and Schiller, P. L.
   (1987)   Is there a religious factor in health? *Journal of Religion and Health,* 26,9-36. **(201)**
Levine, S. V.
   (1978)   Youth and religious cults: a societal and clinical dilemma, *Adolescent Psychiatry,* 6,75-89. **(203)**
Lewis, E.
   (1956)   The development of the religious attitude in children, in Mairet, P. (Ed.), *op. cit.* **(85)**
Lewis, E. C. and Gladding, S. T.
   (1983)   Test-retest reliability of the Gladding, Lewis, Adkins scale of religiosity: a longitudinal study, *Psychological Reports,* 52,34. **(345)**
Lewis, G.
   (1982)   *A case study which examines the purposes of writing in five main subject areas. . .in the first year of secondary education,* MEd dissertation, University of Birmingham. **(142)**

Lewis, J. F.
(1974)   *Ecstatic experience: a classification*, PhD thesis, University of Arizona. **(174)**
Liebman, C. H.
(1983)   Extremism as a religious norm, *Journal for the Scientific Study of Religion*, 22,275-86. **(244)**
Liege, P-A.
(1968)   Religion which is not faith, in Godin, A. (Ed.) (1968a), *op. cit.* **(167)**
Likert, R.
(1932)   Techniques for measuring attitudes, *Archives of Psychology*, 140. **(391)**
Lin, N.
(1976)   *Foundations of Social Research*, New York: McGraw-Hill. **(340)**
Lindquist, B. E.
(1980)   *Relationships among personal religion, dimensions of moral character, and parent-child interactions*, PhD thesis, California School of Professional Psychology. **(232)**
Lindsey, D. B., Sirotnik, B. W., and Heeren, J.
(1986)   Measuring Christian orthodoxy: reassessing the idea of undimensionality, *Journal for the Scientific Study of Religion*, 25,328-338. **(344), (346)**
Linnemann, E.
(1966)   *Parables of Jesus: Introduction and Exposition*, London: S.P.C.K. **(122)**
Linner, S.
(1979)   Literary symbols and religious belief, in Biezais, H. (Ed.) *Religious Symbols and their Function*, Stockholm: Almquist and Wiksell. **(124)**
Liska, A. E.
(1975)   (Ed.) *The Consistency Controversy: Readings on the Impact of Attitude on Behavior*, Cambridge, Massachusetts: Schenkman.
(1984)   A critical examination of the causal structures of the Fishbein/Ajzen attitude behavior model, *Social Psychology Quarterly*, 47,61-74. **(393)**
Liska, A. E., Felson, R. B., Chamlin, M., and Baccaglini, W.
(1984)   Estimating attitude-behavior reciprocal effects within a theoretical specification, *Social Psychology Quarterly*, 47,15-23. **(393)**
Litherland, N. R.
(1969)   Comments on a survey of teachers' attitudes to religious education, *Educational Research*, 11,235-237. **(140)**
Lloyd, I.
(1981)   Teaching religious understanding, *Religious Studies*, 17,253-259. **(140)**
Loder, J. E.
(1980)   Negation and transformation: a study in theology and human development, in The First International Conference on Moral and Religious Education, *op. cit.* **(53)**
(1981)   *The Transforming Moment: Understanding Convictional Experiences*, San Francisco: Harper & Row. **(168)**
Lodwick, A. B.
(1957)   *An investigation of the question whether the inferences that children draw in learning history correspond to the stages of mental development that Piaget postulates*, DipEd dissertation, University of Birmingham. **(135)**
Loewenthal, K.
(1985)   Attributes of religious commitment: difference between the religious and nonreligious, *Journal of Social Psychology*, 125,519-520. **(242)**
(1986)   Factors affecting religious commitment, *Journal of Social Psychology*, 126,121-123. **(242)**
Lofland, J.
(1966)   *Doomsday Cult*, Englewood Cliffs, New Jersey: Prentice Hall. **(188)**
Lofland, J. and Skonovd, H.
(1981)   Conversion motifs, *Journal for the Scientific Study of Religion*, 20,373-385. **(188)**
Long, D., Elkind, D. and Spilka, B.
(1967)   The child's conception of prayer, *Journal for the Scientific Study of Religion*, 6,101-109. **(21), (25), (112)**
Loomba, R. M.
(1942)   The religious development of children, *Indian Journal of Psychology*, 17,161-167. **(101)**
Lorch, B. R. and Hughes, R. H.

(1985)   Religion and youth substance use, *Journal of Religion and Health*, 24,197-208. **(289)**
Loukes, H.
(1961)   *Teenage Religion,* London: SCM Press. **(255)**
(1965)   *New Ground in Christian Education,* London: SCM Press. **(256)**
Luber, M.
(1986)   *Peak experiences: an exploratory study of positive experiences recounted by children and adolescents,* PhD thesis, Bryn Mawr College. **(171)**
Ludwig, D. J. and Blank, T.
(1969)   Measurement of religion as a perceptual set, *Journal for the Scientific Study of Religion,* 8,319-321. **(349)**
Ludwig, D. J., Weber, T., and Iben, D.
(1974)   Letters to God: a study of children's religious concepts, *Journal of Psychology and Theology,* 2,31-35. **(70), (99)**
Luft, G. and Sorell, G. T.
(1987)   Parenting style and parent-adolescent religious value consensus, *Journal of Adolescent Research,* 2,53-68. **(232)**
Lukoff, D. and Lu, F. G.
(1988)   Transpersonal psychology research review topic: mystical experience, *Journal of Transpersonal Psychology,* 20,161-184. **(171)**
Lupton, H. E.
(1974)   *The psychometric assessment of religious awareness among adolescents,* MEd thesis, University of Manchester. **(38), (106)**
Luther, D. E.
(1979)   *A comparative study of self-concepts and God concepts among selected groups of graduate students,* PhD thesis, Michigan State University. **(283)**
Maas, R. M.
(1985a)   *New foundations for biblical education with children: a challenge to Goldman,* PhD thesis, The Catholic University of America. **(41), (43)**
(1985b)   Biblical catechesis and religious development: the Goldman project twenty years later, *Living Light,* 22,124-144. **(41), (43)**
McAllister, E. W.
(1981)   Religious attitudes among women college students, *Adolescence,* 16,587-612. **(272)**
(1985)   Religious attitudes of women college students: a follow-up study, *Adolescence,* 20,797-804. **(272)**
McAllister, I.
(1988)   Religious change and secularization: the transmission of religious values in Australia, *Sociological Analysis,* 3,249-263. **(244)**
McBride, A.
(1976)   A reaction to Fowler; fears about procedure, in Hennessy, T. C. (Ed.) *Values and Moral Development,* New York: Paulist Press. **(57)**
McCabe, A. L.
(1980)   *A rhetoric of metaphor; similarity, goodness, memory, and interpretation,* PhD thesis, University of Virginia. **(388)**
McCall, C. V.
(1981)   *An investigation of the differences in religious conflict and anxiety among religiously fundamentalist students enrolled in Hiwassee College, Johnson Bible College and the University of Tennessee, Knoxville,* EdD thesis, University of Tennessee. **(207)**
McClain, E. W.
(1978)   Personality differences between intrinsically religious and nonreligious students: a factor analytic study, *Journal of Personality Assessment,* 42,159-166. **(197)**
McClure, R. F. and Lodea, M.
(1982)   Religious activity, denominational membership, and life satisfaction, *Psychology: A Quarterly of Human Behavior,* 9,12-17. **(203)**
McConahay, J. B. and Hough, J. C.
(1973)   Love and guilt-orientated dimensions of Christian belief, *Journal for the Scientific Study of Religion,* 12,53-64. **(352)**
McCormick, H., Izzo, A., and Folcik, J.

(1985)   Adolescent's values, sexuality, and contraception in a rural New York county, *Adolescence,* 20,385-395. **(291)**

McCready, W.
(1979)   The family and socialization, in Greeley, A. (Ed.) *The Family in Crisis or in Transition,* New York: Seabury Press. **(228)**

McCready, W. C. and Greeley, A. M.
(1976)   *The Ultimate Values of the American Population,* Beverly Hills: Sage Publications. **(172), (202), (215), (229), (337), (338)**

MacCuish, D.
(1970)   *An enquiry into some aspects of the religious thinking of a group of children in Aberdeen,* MEd dissertation, University of Aberdeen. **(25)**

McDill, E. L., Meyers, E. D., and Rigsby, L. C.
(1967)   Institutional effects on the academic behavior of high-school students, *Sociology of Education,* 40,181-199. **(328)**

MacDonald, C. B. and Luckett, J. B.
(1983)   Religious affiliation and psychiatric diagnosis, *Journal for the Scientific Study of Religion,* 22,15-37. **(205)**

McDonald, G. W.
(1980)   *Adolescent characteristics affecting parental power perception in the family,* paper presented to the Southern Sociological Society. **(235)**

MacDonald, L.
(1969)   *Social Class and Delinquency,* London: Faber and Faber. **(225), (286)**

McDowell, J. B.
(1952)   The development of the idea of God in the Catholic child, *Educational Research Monthly,* Washington: The Catholic University of America. **(79)**

McFarland, G.
(1984)   Psychology of religion; a call for a broader paradigm, *American Psychologist,* 39,321-329. **(342)**

McFarland, S.
(1989)   Religious orientations and the targets of discrimination, *Journal for the Scientific Study of Religion,* 28,324-336. **(354)**

McGarrigle, J. and Donaldson, M.
(1974)   Conservation accidents, *Cognition,* 3,341-350. **(40), (370)**

McGrady, A.
(1983)   Teaching the Bible, research from a Piagetian perspective, *British Journal of Religious Education,* 5,126-133. **(40), (41)**
(1987)   A metaphor and model paradigm of religious thinking, *British Journal of Religious Education,* 9,84-94. **(117)**

McGrath, M.
(1974)   *Replication of the child's concept of prayer: a developmental study,* MRE project, University of St Michael's College, Ontario. **(23)**

McIntosh, W. A., Fitch, S. D., Wilson, J. B., and Myberg, K. L.
(1981)   The effect of mainstream religious controls on adolescent drug use in rural areas, *Review of Religious Research,* 23,54-75. **(288)**

McKenzie, D. W.
(1987)   *The symbolic parent versus actual parent approaches in the examination of similarities between parent and God concept,* PhD thesis, United States International University. **(94)**

McKoy, J. B.
(1980)   *Metaphor and metaphoric processing,* PhD thesis, New York University. **(384)**

MacLean, A. M.
(1930)   *The Idea of God in Protestant Religious Education,* Contributions to Education, 410, New York: Teachers College, Columbia University. **(80)**

McLeish, J.
(1984)   Children's superstitions: British and Canadian, *Canadian Journal of Education,* 19,425-436. **(139)**

McLeod, H.
(1973)   Class, community, and religion: the religious geography of nineteenth-century England,

in Hill, M. (Ed.) *A Sociological Yearbook of Religion in Britain,* 6, London: SCM Press. **(243), (244)**

(1974)   *Class and Religion in the Late Victorian City,* London: Croom Helm. **(248)**

MacMahon, B.

(1981)   *A study of dimensions of religion among Roman Catholic adolescents living in Dublin,* PhD thesis, University of Manchester. **(252), (262)**

MacMain, J. S.

(1980)   *An empirical study of the reasons for young adult participation or nonparticipation within local churches,* DMin thesis, Easter Baptist Theological Seminary. **(216)**

MacRae, D. R.

(1977)   *The relationship of psychological needs to God concept and religious perceptions,* PhD thesis, Rosemead Graduate School of Psychology. **(64)**

McSweeney, R. V.

(1971a)   *Adolescent values: their nature and correlance,* PhD thesis, University of Queensland, Brisbane, Australia. **(326)**

(1971b)   Values of Queensland students from different types of schools, *Journal of Christian Education,* Papers, 14,3,132-139. **(326)**

Machalek, R. and Martin, M.

(1976)   "Invisible religions": some preliminary evidence, *Journal for the Scientific Study of Religion,* 15,311-32. **(347)**

Maddock, R. C. and Kenny, C. Y.

(1972)   Philosophies of human nature and personal religious orientation, *Journal for the Scientific Study of Religion,* 11,277-281. **(353)**

Madge, V.

(1964)   Prayer remembered, *Learning for Life,* 4,1,15-18. **(111)**

(1965)   *Children in Search of Meaning,* London: SCM Press. **(98)**

Madsen, G. E. and Vernon, G. M.

(1983)   Maintaining the faith during college: a study of campus religious group participation, *Review of Religious Research,* 25,127-141. **(272)**

Magee, D. M.

(1985)   *Story in religious education,* MA(Ed) thesis, Queen's University, Belfast. **(132)**

Maier, H. W.

(1978)   *Three Theories of Child Development,* New York: Harper & Row. **(50), (51)**

Mailhiot, B.

(1962)   And God became a child; the reactions of children and child-groups under school age, *Lumen Vitae,* 16,277-288. **(66)**

Main Mein, J. R.

(1982)   *A pilot study investigating aspects of transcendental experiences,* MA thesis, University of Hull. **(182), (186)**

Mairet, P. (Ed.)

(1956)   *Christians Essays in Psychiatry,* London: SCM Press.

Malony, H. N. (Ed.)

(1977)   *Current Perspectives in the Psychology of Religion,* Grand Rapids, Michigan: Eerdmans.

Malony, H. N.

(1985)   Assessing religious maturity, *Psychological Patient,* 1,25-33. **(344)**

Mandler, J. M.

(1983)   Representation, in Mussen, P.H. (Ed.), *op. cit.* 420-494. **(372)**

Maneso, J. E. and Sedlacek, W. E.

(1985)   Changes in religious behavior and attitudes of college students from 1973 to 1983, *Counseling and Values,* 30,74-77. **(272)**

Marchant, H. C.

(1970)   *An investigation into the attitudes of young people to religious and moral education with special reference to five schools and colleges of further education in mid-Wales,* MA thesis, University of Wales, Aberystwyth. **(307)**

Marcia, J. E.

(1966)   Development and validation of ego-identity status, *Journal of Personality and Social Psychology,* 3,551-558. **(213), (216)**

Maret, S. M. and Maret, L. D.
(1982) Attitudes of fundamentalists toward nonmarital sex, *Psychological Reports*, 51,921-922. **(291)**
Margaro, P. A. et al.
(1984) Personality style in posttraditional religious organizations, *Psychology: A Quarterly Journal of Human Behavior*, 21,10-14. **(203)**
Margolis, R. D. and Elfinson, K. W.
(1979) A typology of religion experience, *Journal for the Scientific Study of Religion*, 18,61-67. **(166), (186)**
Mark, T.
(1979) *A study of cognitive and affective elements in the religious development of adolescents*, PhD thesis, University of Leeds. **(155)**
(1982a) Compassionate attitudes in two comprehensive schools, *Journal of Moral Education*, 11,128-132. **(155)**
(1983b) A study of religious attitudes, religious behavior and religious cognition, *Educational Studies*, 8,209-216. **(155)**
Marron, D. J.
(1984) *The relationship between religious-mindedness and ego-strength in Roman Catholic sisters*, PhD thesis, United States International University. **(210), (358)**
Marsh, H.
(1981) *An empirical exploration of the occurrence of superstitious habits in a sample of the British population*, PhD thesis, University of Birmingham. **(207)**
Marsh, R. P.
(1986) *The effect of training on the helping behavior of religiously orientated persons*, PhD thesis, Western Conservative Baptist Seminary. **(359)**
Martell, B.
(1972) Religion in the schools: how useful are the surveys? *Religious Education*, 67,268-272. **(341)**
Marthai, R.
(1980) *Construction and validation of a measure of phenomenal process religious maturity*, PhD thesis, University of Southern Mississippi. **(211)**
Marti, E.
(1986) First metaphors in children: a new hypothesis, *Communication and Cognition*, 19,337-346. **(391)**
Martin, B. and Pluck, R.
(1977) *Young People's Beliefs*, London: General Synod Board of Education. **(132), (246), (257), (279)**
Martin, C. and Nichols, R.
(1962) Personality and religious belief, *Journal of Social Psychology*, 56,3-8. **(195)**
Martin, D.
(1967) *Sociology of English Religion*, London: Heinemann. **(328)**
(1980) Age and sex variations of church attenders, in Bible Society, (1980), *op. cit.* **(248)**
Martin, F. D.
(1972) *Art and the Religious Experience: the "Language" of the Sacred*, Lewisberg: Backnell University Press. **(168)**
Martin, J.
(1985) *A longitudinal study of self-concept and school-related attitude during the adolescent years*, MEd dissertation, University of Birmingham. **(214)**
Martinsson, S.
(1968) *Religionsundervisning och mognad*, (Religious education and readiness. . .) Stockholm School of Education (cited by Bergline, K (1974), *op. cit.*) **(25)**
Marto, R. P.
(1984) *A father's locus of control, spiritual well-being, and self-esteem and their relationship to his child's self-esteem in a Catholic parochial high-school population*, PhD thesis, Western Conservative Baptist Seminary. **(234)**
Martyn, D.
(1967) *The idea of God among Roman Catholic children age 7 and 8*, MEd thesis, University of Manchester. **(68)**
Marvell, J.

(1973)   *Religious beliefs and moral values of immigrant children,* MEd thesis, University of
          Leicester. **(312)**
(1974a)   Religious beliefs and moral values: the influence of the school, *Educational Research,*
          16,94-99. **(312)**
(1974b)   Moral socialization in a multiracial community, *Journal of Moral Education,* 3,244-257. **(312)**
(1975)   The formation of religious belief in a multiracial community, *Learning for Living,* 15,17-
          23. **(312)**
(1976)   Phenomenology and the future of religious education, *Learning for Life,* 16,4-8. **(348)**
Mason, J. S.
(1974)   Adolescent judgment as evidenced in response to poetry, *Educational Review,* 26,124-
          139. **(137)**
Mathes, E. W.
(1982)   Mystical experiences, romantic love, and hypnotic suggestibility, *Psychological Reports,*
          50,701-702. **(172)**
Mathes, E. W., Zevon, M. A., Michael, A., Roter, P. M., and Joerger, S. M.
(1982)   Peak experience tendencies: scale development and theory testing, *Journal of Human-
          istic Psychology,* 22,92-108. **(172)**
Mathias, W. D.
(1943)   *Ideas of God and conduct,* New York: Teachers College Contributions to Education,
          Columbia University. **(70)**
Mauss, A. L.
(1969)   Dimensions of religious defection, *Review of Religious Research,* 10,128-135. **(254)**
Mavor, I. G.
(1987)   A "study of religion" course in Queensland secondary schools, *Journal of Christian Edu-
          cation,* Papers 88,34-38. **(322)**
May, P. R.
(1968)   Attitudes of County Durham teachers to religious and moral education, *Durham
          Research Review,* 5,288-294, 351-357. **(140)**
(1977)   Religious judgments in children and adolescents: a research report, *Learning for Living,*
          16,3,115-122. **(250)**
(1979)   Religious thinking in children and adolescents, *Durham and Newcastle Research Review,*
          8,42,15-28. **(250)**
May, P. R. and Johnston, O. R.
(1967)   Parental attitude to religious education in state schools, *Durham Research Review,*
          18,127-138. **(236)**
Mayfield, N. L.
(1986)   *The bridge to the other side: the language of metaphor,* Phd thesis, Stanford University. **(389)**
Meadow, M. J.
(1976)   *The structure of religious attitudes: a factor-analytic study,* PhD thesis, University of
          Minnesota. **(344), (345)**
Meissner, W. W.
(1984)   Developmental aspects of religious experience, in Meissner, W. W., (Ed.) *Psychoanalysis
          and Religious Experience,* New Haven and London: Yale University Press. **(169), (213)**
Melchert, N.
(1977)   Mystical experience and ontological claims, *Philosophy and Phenomenological
          Research,* 37,445-463. **(168)**
(1981)   "Understanding" as a purpose of religious education, *Religious Education,* 76,178-186. **(362)**
Meltz, H. E.
(1980)   *A study of the academic achievement and religious effectiveness of Seventh-Day Adven-
          tist education,* EdD thesis, Oklahoma State University. **(303)**
Menegusso, E. N.
(1980)   *An investigation of the relationship between religiosity, amount of exposure to Seventh-
          Day Adventist parochial education, and other selected variables among Seventh-Day
          Adventist secondary students in Sao Paulo, Brazil,* EdD thesis, Andrews University. **(303)**
Meyer, P. G.
(1975)   *Intellectual development of college students as measured by analysis of religious content,*
          PhD thesis, University of Minnesota. **(275)**

Meyer, R. A.
    (1974)   *Multivariate analysis of social and religious attitudes,* PhD thesis, The Louisiana State University. **(352)**, **(353)**
    (1976)   *Development of a committed-nominal religious attitude scale,* paper presented at the annual meeting of the Southeastern Psychological Association, New Orleans. **(355)**
Middleton, R. and Putney, S.
    (1962)   Religion, normative standards, and behavior, *Sociometry,* 25,141-152. **(225)**, **(280)**, **(286)**
Miles, G. B.
    (1971)   *A study of logical thinking and moral judgment in G.C.E. Bible knowledge candidates,* MEd thesis, University of Leeds. **(27)**, **(36)**, **(138)**
    (1983)   *A critical and experimental study of adolescent's attitudes and understanding of transcendental experience,* PhD thesis, University of Leeds. **(42)**, **(53)**, **(184)**, **(186)**, **(372)**, **(379)**
Miller, D. E
    (1981)   Lifestyle and religious commitment, *Religious Education,* 76,49-63. **(279)**
Miller, G.
    (1977)   Attitudes of schoolchildren to the church, *Lumen Vitae,* 32,71-93. **(155)**
Miller, G. A.
    (1979)   Images and models, similes and metaphors, in Ortony, A. (Ed.), *op. cit.* **(384)**
Miller, K. L.
    (1976)   *The relationship of stages of development in children's moral and religious thinking,* EdD thesis, Arizona State University. **(31)**
Miller, W. K.
    (1974)   *The construction of an agreement-disagreement item scale: a contemporary survey of the religious sentiments of college students,* EdD thesis, University of Northern Colorado. **(344)**, **(345)**, **(350)**
Minder, W. E.
    (1985)   *A study of the relationship between church sponsored K-12 education and church membership in the Seventh-Day Adventist Church,* EdD thesis, Western Michigan University. **(303)**
Minney, R.
    (1979)   Do young people believe? *Bulletin of the Association for Religious Education,* 12,31,4-6. **(258)**
    (1985)   Religious education and the crisis of literacy, *Religious Education,* 80,29-36. **(374)**
Minney, R. and Potter, M.
    (1984)   *Awe and Wonder in the Classroom,* Durham: University of Durham School of Education. **(170)**
Mischey, E. J.
    (1976)   *Faith development and its relationship to moral reasoning and identity status in young adults,* PhD thesis, University of Toronto. **(215)**
    (1981)   Faith, identity, and morality in late adolescence, *Character Potential,* 9,175-185. **(215)**
Mitchell, A. A.
    (1977)   *Attitudes toward certain school subjects of secondary school boys classified by year group and type of school,* MEd thesis, University of Manchester. **(155)**
Mobbs, F.
    (1981)   What, exactly, is a Catholic school? *Word in Life,* 29,68-71. **(322)**
Moberg, D. O. and Hoge, D. R.
    (1986)   Catholic college students' religious and moral attitudes 1961-1982; effects of the sixties and seventies, *Review of Religious Research,* 28,104-117. **(273)**
Moberg, D. O. and McEnery, J. H.
    (1976)   Changes in church-related behavior and attitude of Catholic students, *Sociological Analysis,* 37,53-62. **(271)**
Moberg, D. O., Zylak, J., and Robzien, J.
    (1972)   *Religious attitudes and practices of Catholic students,1961 and 1971,* paper presented to the 67th annual meeting of the American Sociological Association. **(271)**
Mocciaro, R.
    (1983)   Sriluppo del pensiero e immagine di Dio nel fanciullo e nel preadolescente, *Sociologia,* 17,297-303. **(30)**
Moehle, D. L.

(1983)   Cognitive dimensions of religious experience, *Journal of Social Psychology,* 19,122-145. **(176), (186)**

Mogdil, S. and Mogdil, C.
(1982)   *Jean Piaget: Consensus and Controversy,* London: Holt, Rinehart and Winston. **(372)**

Mol, H. (J. J.)
(1972)   Australia, in Mol, H. (Ed.) *Western Religion: A Country by Country Inquiry,* The Hague: Moulton. **(323)**
(1983)   *Meaning and Place: An Introduction to the Social Scientific Study of Religion,* New York: The Pilgrim Press. **(224)**

Mol, J. J. (H.)
(1968)   The effects of denominational schools in Australia, *Australian and New Zealand Journal of Sociology,* 4,18-35. **(323)**
(1971a)   *Religion in Australia,* Melbourne: Nelson. **(323), (326)**
(1971b)   A rejoinder, *Australian and New Zealand Journal of Sociology,* 7,68-69. **(324)**

Monaghan, R. R.
(1967)   Three faces of the true believer, *Journal for the Scientific Study of Religion,* 6,237-245. **(350)**

Montgomery, S. M. and Montgomery, R.
(1975)   Religious practices and orthdoxy among Catholic students as a function of parental beliefs and religious behavior, *Psychological Reports,* 37,706. **(227)**

Moore, J.
(1976)   Is the Old Testament for children? *I, Living Light,* 13,374-378. **(141)**

Moore, K. and Stoner, S.
(1977)   Adolescent self-respect and religiosity, *Psychological Reports,* 4,55-56. **(210)**

Moore, M. E.
(1979)   *The differential effect of a church-related college environment and a state college or university environment on the moral development of self-described religious students,* EdD thesis, University of Virginia. **(284)**

Moreton, F. E.
(1944)   Attitudes to religion among adolescents and adults, *British Journal of Educational Psychology,* 14,69-77. **(145), (149), (306)**

Morgan, S. P.
(1981)   *The intergenerational transmission of religious behavior: the effect of parents on their children's frequency of prayer.* Paper presented at the annual meeting of the American Sociological Association, Toronto: **(228)**

Moriarty, J. B.
(1972)   *Religious understanding, religious attitudes and self-esteem of parochial school and Confraternity of Christian Doctrine students,* EdD thesis, Northern Illinois University. **(298)**

Morley, H. C.
(1975)   Religious concepts of slow learners: an application of the findings of Ronald Goldman, *Learning for Living,* 14,107-110. **(26)**

Morris, R. J. and Hood, R. W.
(1980)   Religious and unity criteria of Baptists and Nones in reports of mystical experience, *Psychological Reports,* 46,728-730. **(175)**
(1981)   The generalizability and specificity of intrinsic/extrinsic orientation, *Review of Religious Research,* 22,245-254. **(354)**

Morris, R. J., Hood, P. W., and Watson, P. J.
(1989)   A second look at religious orientation, social desirability, and prejudice, *Bulletin of the Psychonomic Society,* 27,81-84. **(355)**

Morrison, G.
(1985)   Parental reasons for choosing Anglican schools, *Journal of Christian Education* Papers, 83,21-32. **(322)**

Moseley, R. M. and Brockenbrough, K.
(1988)   Faith development in the preschool years, in Ratcliff, D. (Ed.), *op. cit.* **(53), (225)**

Moser, C. A. and Kalton, G.
(1971)   *Survey Methods in Social Investigation,* London: Heinemann Educational. **(48)**

Mostul, B. L.
(1980)   *The relationship of ambiguity tolerance to trait anxiety, self-esteem, purpose in life, and*

religious orientation, PhD thesis, California School of Professional Psychology, Fresno. (**206**)

Moulton, R. W., Burstein, E., Liberty, P. G. Jr, and Altacher, H.
(1971)   Patterning of parental affection and disciplinary dominance as a determinant of guilt and sex typing, in Dager, E. Z. (Ed.) *Socialization, Process, Product, and Change*, Chicago: Markham. (**231**)

Mudge, E. L.
(1923)   *The God Experience*, Cincinnati: The Caxton Press. (**66**), (**67**)

Mueller, C. W.
(1980)   Evidence on the relationship between religion and educational attainment, *Sociology of Education*, 53,140-152. (**301**)

Mueller, D. J.
(1967)   Effects and effectiveness of parochial elementary schools: an empirical study, *Review of Religious Research*, 9,48-51. (**302**)

Mueller, G. H.
(1980)   The dimensions of religiosity, *Sociological Analysis*, 41,1-24. (**348**)

Mukhopadhyay, L.
(1986)   *Development of religious identity and prejudice in children*, paper presented to the 11th World Congress of the International Sociological Association. (**241**)

Muller, D. H.
(1976)   *An investigation of the precision of metaphorical language interpretation of students in grade four through six*, PhD thesis, Florida State University. (**388**)

Mumford, C.
(1982)   *Young Children and Religion*, London: Arnold. (**103**), (**111**)

Munkachy, L. D.
(1974)   *Peak experiences and self-actualization in traditional and alternative styles of education: an exploratory survey*, PhD thesis, University of Michigan. (**167**), (**171**), (**186**)

Murphy, R.
(1977a)   Does children's understanding of parables develop in stages? *Learning for Living*, 16,4,168-172. (**38**), (**120**), (**371**)

(1977b)   The development of religious thinking in children in three easy stages? *Learning for Living*, 17,1,16-19. (**38**), (**41**), (**120**)

(1978)   A new approach to the study of the development of religious thinking in children, *Educational Studies*, 4,1,19-22. (**108**), (**134**)

(1979)   *An investigation into some aspects of the development of religious thinking in children aged between six and eleven years*, PhD thesis, University of St. Andrews. (**39**), (**138**)

Murray, A. V.
(1953)   *Education into Religion*, London: Nisbet. (**343**)

Murray, C.
(1978)   The moral and religious beliefs of Catholic adolescents: scale development and structure, *Journal for the Scientific Study of Religion*, 17,439-447. (**317**)

Musgrave, P. W.
(1971)   The relationship between the family and education in England: a sociological account, *British Journal of Educational Studies*, 19,17-31. (**236**)

(1973)   *Knowledge, Curriculum and Change*, London: Angus & Robertson. (**109**)

Mussen, P. H. (Ed.)
(1983)   *Handbook of Child Psychology*, Vol III Cognitive Development, New York: Wiley.

Muthén, B., Olsson, U., Pettersson, T., and Stahlberg, G.
(1977)   Measuring religious attitudes using the semantic differential technique: an application of three-mode factor analysis, *Journal for the Scientific Study of Religion*, 16,275-288. (**347**), (**396**)

Muyskens, L. A.
(1982)   *The relationship between religious beliefs and aesthetic preferences of community college humanities students*, PhD thesis, East Texas State University. (**168**)

Myers, I. B.
(1962)   *The Myers-Briggs Type Indicator Manual*, Princeton, New Jersey: Educational Testing Services. (**198**)

Nagy, P. and Griffiths, A. K.
(1982)   Limitations of recent research relating Piaget's theory to adolescent thought, *Review*

of Educational Research, 52,513-556. **(373)**

Neff, T.
(1977)   Image of God and psychic structure, *Lumen Vitae,* 32,399-422. **(65)**, **(95)**

Nelsen, H. M.
(1972)   Sectarianism, worldview and anomie, *Social Forces,* 51,226-233. **(78)**
(1980)   Religious transmission versus religious formation: preadolescent-parent interaction, *Sociological Quarterly,* 21,207-218. **(228)**, **(234)**
(1981)   Gender differences in the effects of parental discord on pre-adolescent religiousness, *Journal for the Scientific Study of Religion,* 20,351-360. **(235)**
(1982)   The influence of social and theological factors upon the goals of religious education, *Review of Religious Research,* 23,255-263. **(228)**

Nelsen, H. M., Cheek, N. H. and Au, P.
(1985)   Gender differences in images of God, *Journal for the Scientific Study of Religion,* 24,396-402. **(95)**

Nelsen, H. M., Everett, R. F., Mader, P. D., and Hamby, W. C.
(1976)   A test of Yinger's measure of nondoctrinal religion: implications for invisible ratings as a belief system, *Journal for the Scientific Study of Religion,* 15,263-267. **(156)**

Nelsen, H. M. and Kroliczak, A.
(1984)   Parental use of the threat "God will punish": replication and extension, *Journal for the Scientific Study of Religion,* 23,267-277. **(232)**

Nelsen, H. M. and Potvin, R. H.
(1977)   The rural church and rural religion: analysis of data from children and youth, *The Annals of the American Academy of Political and Social Science,* 429,103-114. **(241)**
(1980)   Toward disestablishment: new patterns of social class, denomination and religiosity among youth? *Review of Religious Research,* 22,137-154. **(255)**
(1981)   Gender and regional differences in the religiosity of Protestant adolescents, *Review of Religious Research,* 22,268-285. **(199)**

Nelsen, H. M., Potvin, R. H., and Shields, J.
(1977)   *The Religion of Children,* Washington, D. C.: United States Catholic Conference. **(71)**, **(299)**

Nelsen, H. M. and Rizva, A.
(1984)   Gender and religious socialization: comparison of Pakistan and the United States, *Journal of Comparative Family Studies,* 15,281-290. **(226)**

Nelsen, H. M., Waldron, T. W., and Stewart, K.
(1973)   Image of God and religious ideology and involvement: a partial test of Hill's Southern culture-religion thesis, *Review of Religious Research,* 15,37-44. **(78)**

Nelsen, H. M., Yokley, R. L., and Madron, T. W.
(1971)   Rural-urban differences in religiosity, *Rural Sociology,* 36,389-396. **(243)**

Nelson, L. D. and Dynes, R. R.
(1976)   The impact of devotionalism and attendance on caring and helping behavior, *Journal for the Scientific Study of Religion,* 15,47-59. **(359)**

Nelson, M. O.
(1971)   The concept of God and feelings toward parents, *Journal of Individual Psychology,* 27,46-49. **(86)**, **(88)**

Nelson, M. O. and Jones, E. M.
(1957)   An application of the Q-technique to the study of religious concepts, *Psychological Reports,* 3,293-297. **(85)**, **(86)**

Ness, L.
(1980)   *Jewish attitudes of the 1979 graduates of Suffolk conservative afternoon schools,* EdD thesis, Yeshiva University. **(305)**

Neufeld, K.
(1979)   Child-rearing, religion, and abusive parents, *Religious Education,* 74,234-244. **(236)**

Neuwien, R. A. (Ed.)
(1966)   *Catholic Schools in Action: The Notre Dame Study of Catholic Elementary and Secondary Schools in the United States,* Notre Dame, Indiana: University of Notre Dame Press. **(296)**

Neville, G. K.
(1982)   Culture, youth, and socialization in American Protestantism, in Wyckoff, D. C. and Richter, D. (Eds.), *op. cit.* **(239)**

Newcome, T. and Sevehla, G.
    (1973)   Intra-family relationships in attitude, *Sociometry*, 1,180-205. (**228**)

Newell, A. and Simon, H. A.
    (1972)   *Human Problem Solving*, Englewood Cliffs, New Jersey: Prentice-Hall. (**381**)

Nias, D. K.
    (1972)   The structuring of social attitudes in children, *Child Development*, 43,211-219. (**240**)

Nieratka, D. M.
    (1984)   *Religious development and cognitive/affective maturity in adolescents and adults*, PhD thesis, Wayne State University. (**216**)

Ninnes, A. H.
    (1978)   Two steps forward, one step back: religious education in South Australia, *Learning for Living*, 17,145-148. (**322**)

Nipkow, K. E.
    (1986)   *Erwachsenwerden ohne Gott? Gotteserfahrung im Lebenslauf*, Munich: Kaiser. (**47**)

Nipkow, K. E., Schweitzer, F., and Fowler, J. W. (Eds)
    (1988)   *Glaubensentwicklung und Erziehung*, Gütersloh: Gütersloher Verlagshaus Gerd Mohn. (**59**), (**62**)

Nippold, M. A.
    (1982)   *Perceptual and psychological concepts in children's understanding of predictive versus proportional metaphors: a developmental investigation*, PhD thesis, Purdue University. (**387**)

Nippold, M. A., Leonard, L. B., and Kail, R.
    (1984)   Syncretic and conceptual factors in children's understanding of metaphors, *Journal of Speech and Hearing Research*, 27,197-205. (**387**)

Nippold, M. A. and Sullivan, M. P.
    (1987)   Verbal and perceptual analogical reasoning and proportional metaphor comprehension in young children, *Journal of Speech and Hearing Research*, 30,367-376. (**387**)

Nordberg, R. B.
    (1971)   Developing the idea of God in children, *Religious Education*, 66,204-206. (**100**)

Notzer, N., Levran, D., Mashiach, S., and Soffer, S.
    (1984)   Effect of religiosity on sex attitudes, experience and contraception among university students, *Journal of Sex and Marital Therapy*, 10,57-62. (**292**)

Nowotny, E.
    (1978)   *Young people's ideas about God, religion, and the meaning of life*, Melbourne: Dove Communications. (**327**)

Nowparast, N.
    (1980)   *A comparative personality study of Moslem, Jewish, and Christian college students in Iran*, PhD thesis, Florida Institute of Technology. (**208**)

Nucci, L. P.
    (1985)   Children's conceptions of morality, societal convention, and religious prescription, in Harding, C.G. (Ed.), *op. cit.* (**281**)

Nudelman, A. E.
    (1971)   Dimensions of religiosity: a factor-analytic view of Protestants, Catholics and Christian Scientists, *Review of Religious Research*, 13,42-56. (**346**)

Nunn, C. Z.
    (1964)   Child control through a "coalition with God," *Child Development*, 35,417-432. (**232**)

Nuttin, J. M.
    (1975)   *The Illusion of Attitude Change: toward a response contagion theory of persuasion*, London and New York: Academic Press. (**396**)

Nye, F. I.
    (1958)   *Family Relationships and Delinquent Behavior*, New York: Wiley. (**286**)

Nye, W. C. and Carlson, J. S.
    (1984)   The development of the concept of God in children, *Journal of Genetic Psychology*, 145,137-142. (**33**)

Nye, W. C., Keys, K. S., and Carlson, J. S.
    (1981)   *The development of the concept of God in children*, paper presented to the 11th Annual Interdisciplinary USC-UAP International Conference on Piagetian Theory and the Helping Professions, Los Angeles. (**33**)

O'Connell, B. J.
  (1975)   Dimensions of religiosity among Catholics, *Review of Religious Research*, 16,198-207. **(344), (345), (346), (347)**
O'Gorman, T. P.
  (1979)   *An investigation of moral judgment and religious knowledge scores of Catholic high school boys from Catholic and public schools*, PhD thesis, Boston College. **(284)**
Oh, C. S.
  (1984)   *The impact of religiosity on academic achievement among high school students*, EdD thesis, Columbia University Teachers College. **(267)**
O'Keefe, B.
  (1986)   *Faith, Culture, and the Dual System*, London: The Falmer Press. **(312)**
Oliker, D. M.
  (1979)   *Personality dimensions of the father and their effect on his son: adolescent son's level of moral reasoning as a function of his father's locus of control and self-esteem*, PhD thesis, California School of Professional Psychology, Los Angeles. **(234)**
Olson, D. V.
  (1989)   Church friendships: boon or barrier to church growth? *Journal for the Scientific Study of Religion*, 28,432-447. **(239)**
Olson, J. M.
  (1978)   *Attitude-behavior consistency: an individual difference perspective*, Resources in Education, ERIC ED 172 052. **(394)**
Orlowski, C. D.
  (1979)   Linguistic dimensions of religious measurement, *Journal for the Scientific Study of Religion*, 18,306-311. **(346)**
Ortony, A.
  (1979)   *Some psycholinguistic aspects of metaphor*, Technical Report no. 112, Cambridge, Mass: Bolt, Beranek and Newman. **(383), (385)**
  (1986)   Some problems for models of metaphor comprehension and their developmental implications, *Communication and Cognition*, 19,347-366. **(384)**
Ortony, A. (Ed.)
  (1979)   *Metaphor and Thought*, Cambridge: Cambridge University Press. **(116)**
Ortony, A., Schallert, D. L., Reynolds, R. E., and Antes, S. J.
  (1978)   Interpreting metaphors and idioms: some effects of context on comprehension, *Journal of Verbal Learning and Verbal Behavior*, 17,465-477. **(388)**
Oser, F.
  (1980)   Stages of religious judgment, in The First International Conference on Moral and Religious Development, *op. cit.* **(59), (60), (61)**
  (1985)   Religious dilemmas: the development of religious judgement, in Harding, C. G. (Ed.), *op. cit.* **(59), (60), (380)**
  (1988)   Genese und Logik der Entwickling des religiösen Bewußeins: Eine Entgegnung auf Kritiken, in Nipkow, D. E., Schweitzer, F., and Fowler, J. W. (Eds), *op. cit.* **(59), (61)**
Oser, F. and Gmünder, P.
  (1988)   *Der Mensch - Stufen seiner religiösen Entwicklung: Ein strukturgenitischer Ansatz*, Gütersloh: Gütersloher Verlagshaus Gerd Mohn. **(59), (61), (285)**
Oser, F. and Reich, K. H.
  (1987)   The challenge of competing explanations: the development of thinking in terms of complementarity, *Human Development*, 30,178-186. **(47)**
  (1990)   Moral judgment, religious judgment, worldview, and logical thought: a review of their relationship, *British Journal of Religious Education*, 12,94-101. **(285)**
Osgood, C. E., Succi, G. J., and Tannenbaum, P. H.
  (1957)   *The Measurement of Meaning*, Urbana: University of Illinois Press. **(94), (399)**
Ostron, R. M., Larzelere, R. E., and Reed, S. K.
  (1982)   The views of selected evangelical Christians on sex education, *Journal of Psychology and Christianity*, 1,17-22. **(292)**
Oswald, R.
  (1970)   *The relationship between certain personality variables and theological belief*, Texas: North Texas State University. **(209)**

Otto, R.
(1950)   *The Idea of the Holy,* London: Oxford University Press. **(128)**
Otwell, A. G.
(1988)   *The possible predictor effects of religious belief, locus of control, and certain demographic variables on academic achievement,* EdD thesis, East Texas State University. **(196)**
Ouellett, F.
(1983)   Religious understanding: an obsolete concept in the public school context? *British Journal of Religious Education,* 6,8-13. **(363)**
Overall, C.
(1982)   The nature of mystical experiences, *Religious Studies,* 18,47-54. **(166)**
Ozorak, E. W.
(1987)   *The development of religious beliefs and commitment in adolescence,* PhD thesis, Harvard University. **(267)**
(1989)   Social and cognitive influences on the development of religious beliefs in adolescence, *Journal for the Scientific Study of Religion,* 28,448-463. **(229)**
Paffard, M.
(1970)   Creative activities and "peak" experiences, *British Journal of Educational Psychology,* 40,283-290. **(177), (178)**
(1973)   *Inglorious Wordsworths: a study of some transcendental experiences in childhood and adolescence,* London: Hodder and Staughton. **(178), (186)**
Paivio, A.
(1979)   Psychological processes in the comprehension of metaphor, in Ortony, A. (Ed.), *op. cit.* **(383)**
Palmer, G.
(1978)   *An investigation of the function of myth in religious education, with particular reference to the changing role of Christian myth,* MPhil thesis, University of London. **(125)**
Palmer, V. J.
(1965)   *Religious education in Church of England and non-church primary schools,* DipEd dissertation, University of Birmingham. **(313)**
Paloutzian, R. F.
(1981)   Purpose in life and value changes following conversion, *Journal of Personality and Social Psychology,* 41,1153-1160. **(191)**
Paloutzian, R. F., Jackson, S. L., and Crandall, J. E.
(1978)   Conversion experience, belief systems, and personal and social attitudes, *Journal of Psychology and Theology,* 6,266-275. **(191)**
Pargament, K. I. and De Rosa, D. V.
(1985)   What was that sermon about? Predicting memory for religious meaning from cognitive psychology theory, *Journal for the Scientific Study of Religion,* 85,180-193. **(118)**
Pargament, K. I. and Hahn, J.
(1986)   God and the just world: causal and coping attribution to God in health situations, *Journal for the Scientific Study of Religion,* 25,193-207. **(220)**
Pargament, K. I. et al.
(1987)   Indiscriminate proreligiousness: conceptualization and measurement, *Journal for the Scientific Study of Religion,* 26,182-200. **(355)**
Parker, C. A.
(1971)   Changes in religious beliefs of college students, in Strommen, M. P. (Ed.), *op. cit.* **(271), (274)**
Parker, M. and Gaier, E. L.
(1980)   Religion, religious beliefs, and religious practices among conservative Jewish adolescents, *Adolescence,* 15,361-374. **(305)**
Parker, M. S.
(1977)   *Dimensions of religious conversion during adolescence,* PhD thesis, State University of New York at Buffalo. **(190)**
Pasamanick, J. R.
(1982)   *The proverb moves the mind: abstraction and metaphor in children six-nine,* PhD thesis, Yeshiva University. **(390)**
(1983)   Talk *does* cook rice: proverb abstraction through social interaction, *International Journal of the Sociology of Language,* 44,5-25. **(390)**
Passman, W.

(1980) *Sensitization and religious education in the junior school,* MEd thesis, University of Birmingham. **(129)**

Patino, L.
(1961) A religious attitude scale for children of 10-13 years, *Lumen Vitae,* 16-257-276. **(148)**

Pazhayapurakal, E. J.
(1989) *The influence of parents, peers, and schools on the religious attitudes and practices of Catholic school students,* PhD thesis, Fordham University. **(237)**

Pearce, R. T.
(1979) Religious education and emotion, *British Journal of Religious Education,* 1,136-140. **(170)**

Pearson, P. D. et al.
(1979) *The function of metaphor in children's recall of expository passages,* Cambridge, Mass,: Bolt, Beranack and Newman. **(384)**

Peatling, J. H.
(1973) *The incidence of concrete and abstract religious thinking in the interpretation of three Bible stories,* PhD thesis, New York University. **(30), (41), (42)**
(1974) Cognitive development in pupils grades four through twelve: the incidence of concrete and abstract religious thinking, *Character Potential,* 7,52-61. **(30), (41), (42)**
(1975) The slow learner and religious education: a research note, *Learning for Living,* 14,102-106. **(30)**
(1976) Finn and American: reflections on a comparison, *Character Potential,* 7,220-225. **(31)**
(1977) Cognitive development: religious thinking in children, youth and adults, *Character Potential,* 8,100-115. **(31)**
(1979) The particularity of potential; religious thinking as an example of a developmental problem, *Character Potential,* 9,45-55. **(31)**

Peatling, J. and Laabs, C.
(1975) Cognitive development in pupils in grades four through twelve: a comparative study of Lutheran and Episcopalian children and youth, *Character Potential,* 7,107-115. **(31)**

Peatling, J., Laabs, C., and Newton, T.
(1975) Cognitive development: a three-sample comparison of means on the Peatling scale of religious thinking, *Character Potential,* 7,159-162. **(31)**

Peek, C. W. et al.
(1985) Religiosity and delinquency over time: deviance deterrence and deviance amplification, *Social Science Quarterly,* 66,120-131. **(287)**

Peel, E. A.
(1959) Experimental examination of some of Piaget's schemata concerning children's perception and thinking, and a discussion of their educational significance, *British Journal of Educational Psychology,* 29,89-103. **(24), (48), (135)**
(1971) *The Nature of Adolescent Judgment,* London: Staples. **(29), (121), (134), (143)**

Perkins, H. W.
(1985) A research note on religiosity as opiate or prophetic stimulant among students in England and the United States, *Review of Religious Research,* 26,269-280. **(208)**
(1987) Parental religion and alcohol use problems as intergenerational predictors of problem drinking among college youth, *Journal for the Scientific Study of Religion,* 26,340-347. **(290)**

Perry, F. A.
(1979) *An experimental study of the value of family worship in the lives of children as judged by their parents,* DMin thesis, Eastern Baptist Theological Seminary. **(228)**

Petersen, L. R. and Takayama, K. P.
(1984) Community and commitment among Catholics: a test of local-cosmopolitan theory, *Sociological Quarterly,* 25,97-112. **(243)**

Peterson, S.
(1960) *Retarded Children: God's Children,* Philadelphia, Pennsylvania: Westminster Press. **(119)**

Petrovich, O.
(1988) Re-review: Ronald Goldman's "Religious Thinking from Childhood to Adolescence," *Modern Churchman,* 30,44-49. **(62)**

Petrun, C. J.
(1980) *Metaphor Comprehension and Cognitive Development in College Students,* Paper pre-

sented at the Annual Meeting of the Midwestern Psychological Association. **(384)**

Pettersson, S.
(1970) *Mognad och abstrakt stoff,* (Readiness and abstract learning), Stockholm, School of Education (cited by Bergline, K. (1974), *op. cit.*) **(25)**
(1975) *The Retention of Religious Experience,* Stockholm: Almqvist and Wiksell. **(180)**

Philben, K. M.
(1988) *The transmission of religiosity from parents to their young adult children,* PhD thesis, Illinois Institute of Technology. **(234)**

Philibert, P. J.
(1985) Symbolic and diabolic images of God, *Studies in Formative Spontaneity,* 6,87-101. **(100)**
(1988) Kohlberg and Fowler revisited: an interim report on moral structuralism, *Living Light,* 24,162-171. **(54)**

Phillips-Bell, M.
(1983) Justification and multifaith religious education, *British Journal of Religious Education,* 5,87-95. **(363)**

Phoon, C. Y.
(1987) *A correlational study of Jungian psychological types and nineteen spiritual gifts,* PhD thesis, Andrews University. **(198)**

Piaget, J.
(1930) *Immanentisme et Foi religieuse,* Geneva: Groupe romand des Anciens Membres de l'Association Chretiénne d'Etudiants. **(15), (369)**
(1932) *The Moral Judgment of the Child,* London: Routledge. **(15), (54), (281), (377), (378)**
(1959a) Apprentissage et connaissance (première partie), in Greco, P. and Piaget, J. (Eds.) *Études d'épistémologies génétique,* Vol. 7, *Apprentissage et Connaissance,* Paris: Presses Universitaries de France. **(374)**
(1959b) Apprentissage et connaissance (seconde partie), in Greco, P. and Piaget, J. (Eds.) *Études d'épistémologies génétique,* Vol. 10, *La logique des apprentissages,* Paris: Presses Universitaries de France. **(374)**
(1964a) Development and learning, in Ripple, R. E. and Rockcastle, K. V. (Eds.) (1964), *op. cit.* **(374)**
(1964b) The development of mental imagery, in Ripple, R. E. and Rockcastle, K. V. (Eds.) (1964), *op, cit.* **(375)**
(1965) *The Child's Conception of the World,* London: Routledge. **(97)**
(1969) *The Psychology of the Child,* New York: Basic Books. **(42)**
(1970) Piaget's theory, in Mussen, P. H. (Ed.) *Carmichael's Manual of Child Psychology,* New York: Wiley. **(374)**
(1974) *The Child and Reality,* New York: Viking Press. **(371)**
(1977) The role of action in the development of thinking, in Overton W. F. and Gallagher, J. M. (Eds.) *Knowledge and Development, I, Advances in Research and Theory,* New York: Plenum Press. **(374)**
(1981) *Intelligence and Affectivity: Their Relationship During Child Development,* Palo Alto, California: Annual Reviews Inc. **(46)**

Piazza, T. and Glock, C. Y.
(1979) Images of God and their social meanings, in Wuthnow, R. (Ed.), *op. cit.* **(248)**

Pilkington, G. W., Poppleton, P. K., Gould, J. B., and McCourt, M. M.
(1976) Changes in religious belief, practices and attitudes among university students over an eleven year period. . .,*British Journal of Social and Clinical Psychology,* 15,1-9. **(149)**

Pinard, A. and Laurendeau, M.
(1969) "Stage" in Piaget's cognitive-developmental theory: exegesis of the concept, in Elkind, D. and Flavell, J. H. (Eds.) (1969), *op. cit.* **(378)**

Pinkenson, R. S.
(1987) *The impact of the Jewish day care experience on parental Jewish identity,* EdD thesis, Temple University. **(230)**

Pitts, V. P.
(1976) Drawing the invisible: children's conceptualization of God, *Character Potential,* 8,12-24. **(74)**
(1977) *The God Concept in the Child: a bibliography,* New York: Character Research Press. **(10)**

Ploch, D. R.

(1987) Method for the time being, *Sociological Analysis,* 47,43-51. **(338)**
Pollio, M. R. and Pollio, H. R.
  (1974) The development of figurative language in children, *Journal of Psycholinguistic Research,* 3,185-201. **(384)**
  (1979) A test of metaphoric comprehension and some preliminary developmental data, *Journal of Child Language,* 6,111-120. **(384)**
Poloma, M. M. and Pendleton, B. F.
  (1989) Exploring types of prayer and quality of life: a research note, *Review of Religious Research,* 31,46-53 **(112)**
Ponton, M. O. and Gorsuch, R. L.
  (1988) Prejudice and religion revisited: a cross-cultural investigation with a Venezuelan sample, *Journal for the Scientific Study of Religion,* 27,260-271. **(352), (353), (354), (357)**
Poole, J. W.
  (1986) *An investigation into the effect of the method of teaching a Bible story on the cognitive domain of fourth year pupils in secondary schools,* MEd thesis, University of Birmingham. **(142)**
Poole, M. E.
  (1983) *Youth: expectations and transition,* Melbourne: Routledge and Kegan Paul. **(326)**
Poppleton, P. K. and Pilkington, G. W.
  (1963) The measurement of religious attitudes in a university population, *British Journal of Social and Clinical Psychology,* 2,20-36. **(149), (152), (218)**
Potvin, R. H.
  (1977) Adolescent God images, *Review of Religious Research,* 19,43-53. **(210), (241)**
Potvin, R. H. and Lee, C-F.
  (1981) Religious development among adolescents, *Social Thought,* 7,47-61. **(226)**
  (1982) Adolescent religion: a developmental approach, *Sociological Analysis,* 43,131-144. **(224), (238)**
Potvin, R. H. and Sloane, D. M.
  (1985) Parental control, age, and religious practice, *Review of Religious Research,* 27,3-14. **(233)**
Povall, C. H.
  (1971) *Some factors affecting pupils' attitudes to religious education,* MEd thesis, University of Manchester. **(153)**
Powell, G. and Stewart, R. A.
  (1978) The relationship of age, sex, and personality to social attitudes in children aged 5-15 years, *British Journal of Social and Clinical Psychology,* 17,307-317. **(240), (321)**
Power, F. C. and Kohlberg, L.
  (1980) Religion, morality, and ego development, in The First International Conference on Moral and Religious Development, *op. cit.* **(53)**
Poythress, N. G.
  (1975) Literal, antiliteral, and mythological religious orientations, *Journal for the Scientific Study of Religion,* 14,271-284. **(349)**
Prais, S. J.
  (1974) A sample survey on Jewish education in London, *Jewish Journal of Sociology,* 16,133-154. **(319)**
Prentice, N. M.
  (1978) Imaginary figures of early childhood: Santa Clause, Easter Bunny, and the Tooth Fairy, *American Journal of Orthopsychiatry,* 48,618-628. **(138)**
Preston, C.
  (1987) Meaning and organization in religious experience: an exploratory study, *Review of Religious Research,* 28,252-267. **(219)**
Preston, J. D.
  (1969) Religiosity and adolescent drinking behavior, *Sociological Analysis,* 10,372-383. **(232)**
Prezyna, W.
  (1969) [Religious attitudes and personality traits analyzed on the basis of the data supplied by R. B. Cattel's 16 factor questionnaire]. *Roszniki Filozoficzne: Annales de Philisophie,* 17,99-124. **(196)**
Price, J. H.

(1970) *A study of the God concepts of emotionally disturbed children at a child care center and the God concepts of children in three Methodist church schools*,EdD thesis, Syracuse University. **(78)**

Priestley, J. G.
(1981) Religious story and the literary imagination, *British Journal of Religious Education*, 4,17-24. **(132)**
(1983) Concepts with blurred edges: story and the religious imagination, *Religious Education*, 78,377-389. **(44), (132)**

Primaveia, L. H., Tantillo, J., and DeLisio, T.
(1980) Religious orientation, religious behavior and dogmatism as correlates of irrational beliefs, *Rational Living*, 15,35-37. **(209)**

Prince, J. R.
(1972) Religious and social attitudes in church and state schools in Western Australia, *Journal of Christian Education*, Papers 15,1,34-55. **(325)**

Prinz, P. M.
(1983) The development of idiomatic meaning in children, *Language and Speech*, 26,263-272. **(387)**

Proudfoot, W. and Shaver, P.
(1975) Attribution theory and the psychology of religion, *Journal for the Scientific Study of Religion*, 14,317-330. **(219)**

Pruyser, P. W.
(1977) The seamy side of current religious beliefs, *Bulletin of the Menninger Clinic*, 41,329-348. **(204)**

Purkey, S. C. and Smith, M. S.
(1982) *Effective schools - a review*, Washington, D. C.: Spons Agency—National Academy of Education. **(295)**

Putney, S. and Middleton, R.
(1961a) Dimensions and correlates of religious ideologies, *Social Forces*, 39,285-290. **(280), (346)**
(1961b) Rebellion, conformity, and parental religious ideologies, *Sociometry*, 24,125-135. **(232)**

Quin, P. V.
(1965) Critical thinking and openmindedness in pupils from public and Catholic secondary schoos, *Journal of Social Psychology*, 66,23-30. **(295)**

Radke, M. and Sutherland, J.
(1949) Children's concepts and attitudes about minority and majority American groups, *Journal for Educational Psychology*, 40,449-468. **(240)**

Radke, M., Trager, H. B., and Bavis, H.
(1949) Social perception and attitudes of children, *Genetic Psychology Monographs*, 40,327-447. **(239)**

Raduka, G. G
(1980) *An investigation of hypothesized correspondence between Fowlerian stages of faith development and Jungian stages of personality development*, PhD thesis, University of Maryland. **(55)**

Rambo, L. P.
(1982) Charisma and conversion, *Pastoral Psychology*, 31,96-108. **(189)**

Ramsey, I. T.
(1957) *Religious Language*, London: SCM Press. **(390)**

Randall, T. M. and Desrosiers, M.
(1980) Measurement of supernatural belief: sex differences and locus of control, *Journal of Personality Assessment*, 44,493-498. **(199)**

Randour, M. L. and Bondanza, J.
(1987) The concept of God in the psychological formation of females, *Psychoanalytic Psychology*, 4,301-303. **(94)**

Ranwez, P.
(1964) Discernment of children's religious experience, in Godin, A. (Ed.) (1964), *op. cit.* **(171), (178)**

Raschke, V.
(1973) Dogmatism and committed and consensual religiosity, *Journal for the Scientific Study of Religion*, 12,339-344. **(209)**

Ratcliff, D.

(1985a) The use of play in Christian education, *Christian Education Journal*, 6,26-33. **(101)**
(1985b) The development of children's religious concepts: research review, *Journal of Psychology and Christianity*, 1,35-43. **(10)**
(1987) Teaching the Bible developmentally, *Christian Education Journal*, 7,21-32. **(122), (133)**
(1988) (Ed.) *Handbook of Preschool Religious Education*, Birmingham, Alabama: Religious Education Press. **(98), (103)**

Raudenbush, S. W. and Bryk, A. S.
(1989) Methodological advances in analyzing the effects of schools and classrooms on students' learning, in Rothkopf, E. Z. (Ed.) *Review of Research in Education*, Washington, D.C.: American Educational Research Association. **(339)**

Ray, J. J. and Doratis, D.
(1971) Religiocentrism and ethnocentrism: Catholic and Protestant in Australian schools, *Sociological Analysis*, 32,170-179. **(323)**

Readence, J. E., Baldwin, R. S., Rickelman, R. J., and Miller, G. M.
(1986) The effect of vocabulary instruction on interpreting metaphor, *National Reading Conference Yearbook*, 35,87-96. **(388)**

Rees, D. G.
(1967) *A psychological investigation into denominational concepts of God*, MA thesis, University of Liverpool. **(269)**

Rees, R. J.
(1967) *Background and Belief*, London: SCM Press. **(77), (204)**

Reese, J. R.
(1988) *Routes of conversion: a sociopsychological study of the varieties of individual religious change*, PhD thesis, University of Iowa. **(191)**

Reich, K. H.
(1987) Religiöse and naturwissenschaftlich Weltbilder: Entwicklung einer komplementären Betrachtungsweise in der Adoleszenz, *Unterrichtswissenschaft*, 3,332-343. **(47)**
(1989) Between religion and science: complementarity in the religious thinking of young people, *British Journal of Religious Education*, 11,62-69. **(47)**

Reid, I.
(1977) Sunday school attendance and moral attitudes, knowledge and practice, *Learning for Living*, 17,3-8. **(250)**
(1980) *Sunday Schools: A Suitable Case for Treatment*, London: Chester House Publications. **(250)**

Reid, L. A.
(1961) *Ways of Knowledge and Experience*, London: Allen and Unwin. **(165)**

Resnick, D. A.
(1977) *The development of children's comprehension of proverbs*, PhD thesis, Columbia University. **(390)**
(1982) A developmental study of proverb comprehension, *Journal of Psycholinguistic Research*, 11,521-538. **(390)**

Rest, J. R.
(1979a) *Development in Judging Moral Issues*, Minneapolis: Minnesota University Press. **(281), (283)**
(1979b) *Revised Manual for the Defining Issues Test*, Minneapolis: Minnesota Moral Research Project. **(281), (283), (285)**
(1983) Morality, in Mussen, P. H. (Ed.) *Handbook of Child Psychology Vol.III*, New York: Wiley, 556-629. **(377), (379)**

Reynolds, R. E. and Ortony, A.
(1980) Some issues in the measurement of children's comprehension of metaphorical language, *Child Development*, 51,1110-1119. **(385)**

Rhoades, H. G.
(1979) *Religious involvement, symptom of pathology or signal of health - a social psychological study*, PhD thesis, Ball State University. **(205)**

Rhymer, J.
(1984) Religious attitudes of Roman Catholic pupils in Scotland, in *Family, School, and Church in Religious Education*, Department of Christian Ethics and Practical Theology, University of Edinburgh. **(319)**

Rhymer, J. and Francis, L. F.
    (1985)   Roman Catholic secondary schools in Scotland and pupil attitude toward religion, *Lumen Vitae*, 40,103-110. **(319)**
Rhys, W. T.
    (1966)   *The development of logical thought in the adolescent with reference to the teaching of geography in the secondary school,* MEd thesis, University of Birmingham. **(137)**
Riccards, M. L.
    (1979)   The structure of religious development, *Lumen Vitae*, 34,97-120. **(50)**
Richardson, J. G. and Weatherby, G. A.
    (1983)   Belief in an afterlife as symbolic action, *Review of Religious Research*, 25,162-169. **(268)**
Richardson, R. and Chapman, J.
    (1973)   *Images of Life: Problems of religious belief and human relationships in schools,* London: SCM Press. **(197)**, **(270)**
Richardson, S.
    (1965)   *Manual, study of values,* Slough, Bucks: National Foundation for Educational Research. **(154)**
Richek, H. G.
    (1971)   *A note on anxiety, depression, and religiousness in American college sudents,* Resources in Education, ERIC ED 146 530. **(206)**
Richmond, R. C.
    (1972)   Maturity of religious judgment and differences of religious attitude between the ages of 13 and 16 years, *Educational Review*, 24,3,225-236. **(29)**, **(135)**
    (1974)   *Some factors associated with the maturity of religious judgment among 15 year old adolescents,* MEd thesis, University of Birmingham. **(29)**
Rickelman, R. J.
    (1983)   *The effects of context on sixth graders' ability to interpret metaphors and similes,* PhD thesis, University of Georgia. **(388)**
Ridder, N. F.
    (1985)   *The religious beliefs and practices of Catholic graduates of Catholic and public high schools in the state of Nebraska from 1972-1981,* DEd thesis, University of Nebraska-Lincoln. **(299)**
Rigby, K. and Densley, T. R.
    (1985)   Religiosity and attitude toward institutional authority among adolescents, *Journal of Social Psychology*, 125,723-728. **(230)**
Ripple, R. E. and Rockcastle, K. V. (Eds.)
    (1964)   *Piaget Rediscovered: A Report of the Conference on Cognitive Studies and Curriculum Development,* Cornell University.
Ritzema, R. J.
    (1979)   Attribution to supernatural causation: an important component of religious commitment? *Journal of Psychology and Theology*, 7,286-293. **(346)**
Rixon, L. D.
    (1959)   *An experimental and critical study of the teaching of Scripture in secondary schools,* PhD thesis, University of London. **(146)**
Rizzuto, A-M.
    (1974)   Object relations and the formation of the image of God, *British Journal of Medical Psychology*, 47,83-99. **(65)**, **(86)**
    (1979)   *The Birth of the Living God: A Psychoanalytic Study,* Chicago: University of Chicago Press. **(65)**, **(84)**
    (1980)   The psychological foundations of belief in God, in The First International Conference on Moral and Religious Development, *op. cit.* **(86)**
Roazen, P.
    (1976)   *Erik H. Erikson: The Power and Limits of a Vision,* New York: The Free Press. **(50)**
Roberts, F. J.
    (1965)   Some psychological factors in religious conversion, *British Journal of Social and Clinical Psychology*, 4,185-187. **(190)**
Roberts, M. K. and Davidson, J. D.
    (1984)   The nature and sources of religious involvement, *Review of Religious Research*, 25,334-

350. **(224)**, **(241)**

Robertson, J. D.
(1989)   *An investigation of religiosity and mental health measures in Bible college students*, PhD thesis, University of Tennessee. **(203)**

Robertson, R.
(1975)   On the analysis of mysticism: pre-Weberian, Weberian, and post-Weberian perspectives, *Sociological Analysis*, 36,241-266. **(167)**

Robinson, E. A.
(1971)   Religious education: a shocking business, *Learning for Life*, 11,5-8. **(179)**
(1975)   The necessity for dreams: religious education and the imagination, *Learning for Living*, 14,194-197. **(179)**
(1977a)   *The Original Vision*, Oxford: Religious Experience Research Unit, Manchester College. **(44)**, **(46)**, **(178)**, **(186)**
(1977b)   Education and unreality, *Learning for Living*, 16,162-167. **(179)**
(1978)   *Living the Questions: studies in the childhood of religious experience*, Oxford: Religious Experience Research Unit. **(179)**
(1982)   Professionalism and the religious imagination, *Religious Education*, 77,628-641. **(179)**
(1984)   Religious experience, in Sutcliffe, J. M. (Ed.) (1984), *op. cit.* **(166)**

Robinson, E. A. and Jackson, M.
(1987)   *Religion and Values at Sixteen Plus*, Oxford: Alister Hardy Research Centre, and London: Christian Education Movement. **(180)**

Robinson, M. D.
(1983)   *Stage development theories and the learning process with special reference to religious and moral development in the comprehensive school: an analysis and proposed model*, MEd thesis, University of Hull. **(46)**

Robinson, R.
(1964)   Prayer in childhood, *Learning for Life*, 4,1,7-11. **(111)**

Robinson, W. L. and Calhoun, K. S.
(1983)   Sexual factors, attitudes, and behavior as a function of race, gender, and religiosity, *Imagination, Cognition, and Personality*, 2,281-290. **(291)**

Robinson, W. P.
(1979)   *The effects of cognitive complexity, locus of control, and openness on the communication process in adult conversion to Christianity*, PhD thesis, University of Pittsburgh. **(188)**

Rogers, W. R.
(1980)   Interdisciplinary approaches to moral and religious development: a critical overview, in The First International Conference on Moral and Religious Development, *op. cit.* **(105)**

Rohrbaugh, J. and Jessor, R.
(1975)   Religiosity in youth: a personal control against deviant behavior, *Journal of Personality*, 18,136-155. **(212)**, **(287)**, **(288)**

Roiser, M.
(1981)   A psychological approach to the explanation of displacement effects in the judgment of attitude statements, *British Journal of Social Psychology*, 20,37-40. **(391)**

Roke, P. A.
(1985)   *An enquiry into pupil perceptions as to the relative value of curriculum subjects in general and of geography in particular*, MA thesis, University of London. **(161)**

Rokeach, M.
(1956)   Political and religious dogmatism: an alternative to the authoritarian personality, *Psychological Monographs*, 425,70,18. **(207)**, **(395)**
(1969)   Religion, values, and compassion, *Review of Religious Research*, 11,24-39. **(156)**
(1970)   Faith, hope, and bigotry, *Psychology Today*, 3,33-37,58. **(351)**
(1974)   *The Nature of Human Values*, New York: The Free Press. **(395)**

Rommertveit, R.
(1953)   *Social Norms and Roles*, Oslo: Universitetsforlaget, cited by V. Aubert (1968) *Elements of Sociology*, London: Heinman Educational. **(238)**

Roof, W. C.
(1978)   Alientation and apostacy, *Society*, 15,41-45. **(266)**
(1979)   Concepts and indicators of religious commitment: a critical review, in Wuthnow, R.

(Ed.), *op. cit.* (**339**), (**359**), (**360**)
(1984)   American religion in transition: a review and interpretation of recent trends, *Social Compass,* 31,273-289. (**273**)
Roof, W. C., Hadaway, C. K., Hewitt, M. L., McGaw, D., and Morse, R.
(1977)   Yinger's measure of nondoctrinal religion; a Northeastern test, *Journal for the Scientific Study of Religion,* 16,403-408. (**347**)
Roof, W. C. and Roof, J. L.
(1984)   Review of the polls: images of God among the Americans, *Journal for the Scientific Study of Religion,* 23,201-205. (**93**)
Rosander, A. C.
(1939)   Age and sex patterns of social attitudes, *Journal of Educational Psychology,* 30,481-496. (**239**)
Rosenberg, L. M.
(1987)   *A developmental study of psycho-physical metaphor,* PhD thesis, University of North Carolina at Chapel Hill. (**388**)
Rosenberg, R.
(1977)   *Die Entwicklung des Gebotsbigriffs bei judischen Kindern in Israel,* Jerusalem. (**113**)
(1989a) Die Entwicklung von Gebetskonzepten, in Bucher, A. A. and Reich, K. H., *op. cit.* (**49**), (**113**), (**380**)
(1989b) The development of the concept of prayer in Jewish Israeli children and adolescents, in Tanerbaum, A. (Ed.) *Studies in Jewish Education,* Vol. V, Jerusalem: Magnus Press, Hebrew University. (**49**), (**113**), (**380**)
Rosenblatt, R.
(1984)   Children of war, *American Educator: The Professional Journal of the American Federation of Teachers,* 8,37-41. (**238**)
Rosengrant, J.
(1976)   The impact of set and setting on religious experience in nature, *Journal for the Scientific Study of Religion,* 15,301-310. (**174**)
Rosolato, G.
(1980)   Presente mystique, *Nouvelle Revue de Psychoanalyse,* 22,5-36. (**168**)
Ross, T. A. and McTaggart, E. A.
(1983)   Organizational climate in Catholic schools, *Australian Journal of Education,* 27,78-93. (**333**)
Rossi, P. H. and Rossi, A. S.
(1957)   Some effects of parochial school education in America, *Harvard Educational Review,* 27,168-199. (**295**)
(1961)   Some effects of parochial school education in America, *Daedalus, Journal of the American Academy of Arts, and Sciences,* 90,300-328. (**295**)
Rossiter, G. M.
(1981)   *Religious Education in Australian Schools,* Canberra. (**323**)
(1983)   *An interpretation of normative theory for religious education in Australian Schools,* PhD thesis, Macquarie University, Australia. (**322**), (**328**), (**331**), (**334**)
(1985)   Studying religion in Australian schools: the interface with tertiary religious studies, *Journal of Christian Education,* Papers 82,47-57; Papers 83,33-44. (**323**)
Rothenberg, D. J.
(1986)   *Psychological dimensions of rapid religious change,* PhD thesis, Yeshiva University. (**191**)
Roulston, J. F.
(1971)   *Attitudes to religious instruction in state high schools in Ipswich, Queensland,* LitB thesis, The University of New England, Armnidale, Australia. (**326**)
(1975)   Attitudes of a sample of senior students to religious instruction in Queensland State High Schools, *Journal of Christian Education* Papers, 53,39-46. (**326**)
Rowe, A. J.
(1981)   Children's thinking and the Bible, *Journal of Christian Education,* Papers, 70,18-32. (**40**)
Rowins, C. H.
(1987)   *Measuring the effectiveness of preaching in parables,* DMin thesis, Princeton Theological Seminary. (**122**)
Roy, P. R.
(1979)   *Application of Piaget's theory of cognitive development to religious thinking, with special*

reference to the work of Dr. R. G. Goldman, MEd thesis, University of Liverpool. **(39), (375)**

Ruffy, M.
(1981)   Influence of social factors in the development of the young child's moral judgments, *European Journal of Social Psychology,* 11,61-75. **(99), (240)**

Russell, A.
(1978)   *The attitude of primary school children to religious education,* MPhil thesis, University of Nottingham. **(157), (311)**

Rytting, M. and Christensen, H. T.
(1980)   The effect of religious orthodoxy: a statistical analogy, *Journal of Pastoral Theology,* 8,4,314-322. **(208)**

Sabell, M. H.
(1983)   *A comparative study of relationship between religious understanding and certain social and moral attitudes among hearing-impaired school-leavers,* MSc dissertation, University of Surrey. **(111)**

Saigh, P. A.
(1986)   Religious symbols and the WISC-R performance of Roman Catholic junior-high-school students, *Journal of Genetic Psychology,* 147,417-418. **(158)**

Saigh, P. A., O'Keefe, T., and Antoun, F.
(1984)   Religious symbols and the WISC-R performance of Roman Catholic junior-high-school students, *Journal of Genetic Psychology,* 145,159-166. **(158)**

St. Clair, S. and Day, H. D.
(1979)   Ego identity status and values among high school females, *Journal of Youth and Adolescence,* 8,317-326. **(215)**

St. George, A. and McNamara, P. H.
(1984)   Religion, race, and psychological well-being, *Journal for the Scientific Study of Religion,* 23,351-363. **(202)**

Salman, H. D.
(1965)   Summary and critique of Goldman's research, *Revue des Sciences Philosophiques et Theologiques,* 49,699-700. **(36)**

Salomonsen, P.
(1972)   Attitude measurement: some methodological problems, *Social Compass,* 19,507-518. **(48), (392)**

Satler, C. A. and Routledge, L. M.
(1974)   Intelligence and belief in the supernatural, *Psychological Reports,* 34,299-302. **(196)**

Sanderson, S. K.
(1973)   *Religion, politics, and morality: an approach to religious and political belief systems and their relation through Kohlberg's cognitive-developmental theory of moral judgment,* PhD thesis, University of Nebraska, Lincoln. **(283)**

Santilli, N. R. and Meacham. J. A.
(1982)   Structuralist perspectives on social development in youth, *Human Development,* 25,34-37. **(221)**

Sapp, G. L. and Gladding, S. T.
(1989)   Correlates of religious orientation; religiosity and moral judgment, *Counseling and Values,* 33,140-145. **(357)**

Sapp, G. L. and Jones, L.
(1986)   Religious orientation and moral judgment, *Journal for the Scientific Study of Religion,* 25,208-214. **(282), (357)**

Saussy, C.
(1988)   Faith and self-esteem, *Journal of Pastoral Care,* 42,125-137. **(209)**

Savin-Williams, R. C.
(1977)   Age and sex differences in the adolescent image of Jesus, *Adolescence,* 12,353-366. **(110)**

Schank, R. and Abelson, R.
(1977)   *Scripts, Plans, Goals, and Understanding,* Hillsdale, New Jersey: Lawrence Erlbaum **(381)**

Schecter, B. A.
(1980)   *Animism and the development of metaphoric thinking in children,* PhD thesis, Columbia University. **(385)**

Schimpf, A. L.

(1972)   *An analysis of the functions of narrative forms in biblical literature and their relationship to religious education*, PhD thesis, University of Pittsburgh. **(121)**

Schmidt, C. E.

(1981)   *The relationship of parents' belief systems to their parenting practices and to the belief systems of their children*, PhD thesis, University of Colorado at Boulder. **(234)**

Schoenfeld, E.

(1984)   Religiosity and salience of religious values: an exploratory study, *Humbadt Journal of Social Relations*, 12,49-67. **(274)**

(1987)   Images of God and man: an exploratory study, *Review of Religious Research*, 28,224-235. **(64)**

Schönbach, P., Gollwitzer, P., Stiepel, G., and Wagner, U.

(1981)   *Education and Intergroup Attitudes*, London: Academic Press. **(230)**

Schools Council

(1971)   Working Paper No. 36, *Religious Education in Secondary Schools*, London: Evan/Methuen Educational. **(343)**

(1977)   Religious Education in Primary Schools Project, *Discovering an Approach*, London: Macmillan Educational. **(103)**

Schroder, R. H., Driver, M. J., and Streufert, S.

(1967)   *Human Information Processing*, New York: Holt, Rinehart and Winston. **(381)**

Schroeder, W. W. and Obenhaus, V

(1964)   *Religion in American Culture*, New York: Crowell-Collier, The Free Press of Glencoe. **(117), (196)**

Schubert, F. D.

(1987)   *From theology to religion: a study in American Roman Catholic secularization as reflected in selected American Roman Catholic college religious curricula*, PhD thesis, Boston University. **(246)**

Schurter, D. D.

(1987)   Fowlers's faith stages as a guide for ministry to the mentally retarded, *Journal of Pastoral Care*, 41,234-240. **(59)**

Scobie, G. E.

(1973)   Types of Christian conversion, *Journal of Behavioral Science*, 1,265-271. **(189)**

(1975)   *Psychology of Religion*, London: Batsford. **(189), (208), (276)**

(1978)   Teaching in social attitude areas, *A.E.P. Journal* 4,8,13-20. **(240)**

Scott, E. and Orr, K.

(1967a)   Values in the secondary school—A Queensland inquiry, II, Development of an instrument for the measurement of some adolescent values, *Journal of Christian Education*, Papers 10,1,7-18. **(324)**

(1967b)   Values in the secondary school—a Queensland inquiry, III, research findings, *Journal of Christian Education*, Papers10,3,130-150. **(324)**

Seck, A. R., Keller, J. F., and Hinkle, D. E.

(1984)   Premarital sexual intercourse: a test of the effects of peer group, religiosity, and sexual guilt, *Journal of Sex Research*, 20,168-185. **(292)**

Seidenberg, P. L. and Bernstein, D. K.

(1988)   Metaphor comprehension and performance on metaphor-related language tasks: a comparison of good and poor readers, *RASE: Remedial and Special Education*, 9,39-45. **(388), (389)**

Seitz, J. A.

(1987)   *Precursors of creativity: metaphor, symbolic play, and categorization in early childhood*, PhD thesis, City University of New York. **(386)**

Selig, S. and Teller, G.

(1975)   The moral development of children in three different school settings, *Religious Education*, 70,406-415. **(305)**

Seppo, S.

(1971)   [*The attitude of students toward religious education in secondary schools*] Juväskylä Studies in Education, Psychology and Social Research, 25, Finland: University of Juväskylä. **(311)**

Sevigny, R.

(1971)   *L'expérience religieuse chez les jeunes,* Montreal, University Press. **(210)**

Seyfarth, L. H., Larsen, K. S. et al.
(1984)   Attitude toward evangelism: scale development and validation, *Journal of Social Psychology,* 123,55-61. **(191)**

Shackle, E.
(1974)   *Personality function, cognitive style, and orientation to religions and religious education of trainee teachers of religion,* MPhil thesis, University of London. **(197)**

Shantiris, K.
(1983)   *Developmental changes in metaphor evaluation; the tropic rose,* PhD thesis, University of California, Los Angeles. **(388)**
(1984)   *Developmental changes in metaphor comprehension: it's not all uphill.* Paper presented at the Biennial Meeting of the Society for Research in Child Development, Detroit. **(388)**

Shapiro, H. M. and Dashefsky, A.
(1974)   Religious education and ethnic identification: implications for ethnic pluralism. *Review of Religious Research,* 15,93-102. **(303)**

Sharkey, P. W. and Malony, H. N.
(1986)   Religiosity and emotional disturbance: a test of Ellis' theories in his own counseling center, *Psychotherapy* 23,640-641. **(205)**

Shaver, D. G.
(1987)   Moral development of students attending a Christian liberal arts college and a Bible college, *Journal of College Student Personnel,* 28,211-218. **(284)**

Shaw, B. W.
(1970)   Religion and conceptual models of behavior, *British Journal of Social and Clinical Psychology,* 9,320-327. **(18)**

Sheffield University Institute of Education
(1961)   *Religious Education in Secondary Schools,* London: Nelson. **(255)**

Sheppard, E. M.
(1986)   *A correlational study of the relationship between adolescent religiosity and adolescent perception of parental behavior in Antigua and Barbuda,* EdD thesis, Andrews University. **(233)**

Shields, J. J.
(1984)   *Religion and delinquent behavior: a study of adolescents,* PhD thesis, The Catholic University of America. **(287)**

Shippey, F. A.
(1970)   Clique structure in religious youth groups, *Sociology and Social Review,* 54,371-377. **(237)**

Shortridge, J. R.
(1977)   A new regionalism of American religion, *Journal for the Scientific Study of Religion,* 16,143-153. **(243)**

Shrauger, J. S. and Silverman, R. E.
(1971)   The relationship of religious background and participation to locus of control, *Journal for the Scientific Study of Religion,* 10,11-16. **(212)**

Shulik, R. N.
(1979)   *Faith development, moral development, and old age: an assessment of Fowler's Faith Development paradigm,* PhD thesis, University of Chicago. **(52)**

Shuttleworth, A.
(1959)   *Children's concepts of God,* DCP dissertation, University of Birmingham. **(79)**

Siegal, L. S.
(1982)   Development of quantity concepts: perceptual and linguistic factors, in Brainerd, C. J. (Ed.) *Childrens' Logical and Mathematical Cognition,* New York: Springer-Verlag. **(372)**

Siegal, L. and Hodkin, B.
(1982)   The garden path to the understanding of cognitive development: has Piaget led us into the poison ivy? in Mogdil, S. and Mogdil, C. (Eds.) (1982), *op. cit.* **(372)**

Siglag, M. W.
(1986)   *Schizophrenic and mystical experiences: similarities and differences,*PhD thesis, University of Detroit. **(205)**

Silberstein, L., Gardener, H., Phelps, E., and Winner, E.
(1982)   Autumn leaves and old photographs: the development of metaphor preferences, *Journal*

of Experimental Child Psychology, 34,135-150. **(387)**

Silverman, I. J.
 (1977)   A survey of cohabitation on two college campuses, *Archives of Sexual Behavior,* 6,11-20. **(291)**

Silverstein, S. M.
 (1988)   A study of religious conversion in North America, *Genetic, Social, and General Psychology Monographs,* 114,261-305. **(186), (192), (235)**

Simmonds, R. B.
 (1977)   *The people of the Jesus movement: a personality assessment of members of a fundamentalist religious community,* PhD thesis, University of Nevada. **(203)**

Simmonds, R. J.
 (1986)   *Content and structure in faith development: a case examination of James Fowler's theory,* PhD thesis, The Southern Baptist Theological Seminary. **(56)**

Simmons, C. and Wade, W.
 (1982)   "What is the good?": a comparison of young people's responses to two unfinished sentences about values, *Educational Studies,* 8,113-121. **(279)**

Simmons, H. C.
 (1983)   The religious becoming of the child, *Living Light,* 20,71-79. **(225)**

Simon, A. L. and Ward, L. D.
 (1975)   Age, sex, intelligence, and religious beliefs in 11- to 15-year old pupils, *Irish Journal of Education,* 9,108-114. **(106)**

Singer, R. E.
 (1959)   *A study of the God concepts of children in three suburban religious schools.* PhD Thesis, Northwestern University. **(71)**

Singh, B. K.
 (1980)   Trends in attitudes toward premarital sexual relationships, *Journal of Marriage and the Family,* 42,387-393. **(291)**

Sipps, G. J. and Alexander, R. A.
 (1987)   The multifactorial nature of extraversion-introversion in the Myers-Briggs Type Indicator and Eysenck Personality Inventory, *Educational and Psychological Measurement,* 47,543-552. **(195)**

Skinner, P. J.
 (1983)   *The interaction between formal operational thought and ego identity development in late adolescence and early adulthood,* PhD thesis, Texas Technical University. **(213)**

Slattery, P. J.
 (1974)   The religion teacher in the classroom, *Religious Education,* 69,665-679. **(330)**
 (1979)   Religious education and classroom climate, *Word in Life,* 27,1,19-24. **(330)**

Slee, N.
 (1983)   Parable teaching: exploring new worlds, *British Journal of Religious Education,* 5,3,134-138. **(121), (122)**
 (1986)   Goldman yet again—assessing his significance, *British Journal of Religious Education,* 8,84-93. **(47), (48)**
 (1987)   The development of religious thinking: some linguistic considerations, *British Journal of Religious Education,* 9,120-123. **(48)**
 (1988)   Religious development and education: report on the first symposium on religious development and education, *Journal of Beliefs and Values,* 9,1-16. **(62)**

Sloane, D. M. and Potvin, R. H.
 (1983)   Age differences in adolescent religiousness, *Review of Religious Research,* 25,142-154. **(255)**
 (1986)   Religion and delinquency: cutting through the maze, *Social Forces,* 65,87-105. **(288)**

Slocumb, F. G.
 (1981)   *An attributional analysis of religious explanations,* PhD thesis, Virginia Commonwealth University. **(219)**

Smart, N.
 (1969)   *The Religious Experience of Mankind,* New York: Charles Scribner's Sons. **(10), (343)**
 (1973)   *The Science of Religion and the Sociology of Knowledge: Some methodological questions,* Princeton, New Jersey: Princeton University Press. **(343)**

Smidt, C.

(1980)   Civil religious orientations among elementary school children, *Sociological Analysis*, 41,25-40. **(240)**, **(267)**
Smith, C. B., Weigert, A. J., and Thomas, D. L.
(1979)   Self-esteem and religiosity: an analysis of Catholic adolescents from five cultures, *Journal for the Scientific Study of Religion*, 18,51-56. **(210)**
Smith, Catherine S.
(1982)   *God-concept, sex role perceptions, and religious experience*, PhD thesis, Fuller Theological Seminary, School of Psychology. **(200)**
Smith, Craig S.
(1983)   *Sanctioning and causal attributions to God: a function of theological position and actors' characteristics*, PhD thesis, Fuller Theological Seminary, School of Psychology. **(220)**
Smith, D. T.
(1976)   *The relationship between the moderately retarded's God concept and their parental concepts*, MA thesis, Ohio State University. **(76)**
Smith, J. J.
(1941)   Religious development of children, in Skinner, C. E. and Harriman, P. L. (Eds.) *Child Psychology*, New York: Macmillan. **(103)**
Smith, M.
(1985)   Answers to some questions about faith development, *British Journal of Religious Education*, 8,79-83. **(54)**
Smith, N. A.
(1985)   *The background object as fundamental to psychoanalytic theory and faith*, PhD thesis, Rosemead School of Psychology. **(166)**
Smith, W. M.
(1977)   *The effects of two kinds of religious experience in relation to religious orientation and sex role identification*, PhD thesis, University of Washington. **(174)**
Snow, D. A. and Machalek, R.
(1983)   The convert as a social type, in Collins, R. (Ed.) *Sociological Theory*, San Francisco: Jossey-Bass. **(189)**
Snow, D. A. and Philips, C. L.
(1980)   The Lofland-Stark conversion model: a critical reassessment, *Social Problems*, 27,430-447. **(188)**
Soderstrom, D.
(1977)   *Religious orientation and meaning in life*, PhD thesis, United States University. **(353)**
Soderstrom, D. and Wright, E. W.
(1977)   Religious orientation and meaning in life, *Journal of Clinical Psychology*, 33,65-68. **(353)**
Sohn, L. E.
(1985)   *God concepts in children: beliefs about the attributes of God and implications for Lutheran curriculum and instruction*, PhD thesis, Marquette University. **(75)**
Sonada, T. and Norbeck, E.
(1975)   Prophecy continues to fail: a Japanese sect, *Journal of Cross-Cultural Psychology*, 6,331-345. **(220)**
Soskis, J. M.
(1987)   *Metaphor and Religious Language*, Oxford: Claredon Press. **(116)**
Sowell, J. J.
(1977)   *Factors influencing learning in Christian education: a study of seventeen seventh-grade Sunday school classes*, PhD thesis, Northwestern University. **(141)**
Spatti, R. J.
(1978)   *Religiosity among worshiping Catholic university students*, PhD thesis, University of Pittsburgh. **(275)**
Spellman, C. M., Baskett, G. D., and Byrne, D.
(1971)   Manifest anxiety as a contributing factor in religious conversion, *Journal of Consulting and Clinical Psychology*, 36,245-247, reprinted in Malony, H. N. (Ed.) (1977), *op. cit.* **(206)**
Spencer, A. E
(1968)   An evaluation of Roman Catholic educational policy in England and Wales 1900-1960, in Jebb, P. (Ed.), *op. cit.* **(316)**
(1971)   *The Future of Catholic Education in England and Wales*, London: Catholic Renewal

Movement. **(316)**

Sperber, D.
(1975) *Rethinking Symbolism,* Cambridge: Cambridge University Press. **(130)**

Spilka, B.
(1976) The complete person—some theoretical views and research findings for a theological-psychology of religion, *Journal of Psychology and Theology,* 4,15-24. **(353)**
(1977) Utilitarianism and personal faith, *Journal of Psychology and Theology,* 5,226-233. **(353)**

Spilka, B., Addison, J., and Rosensohn, M.
(1975) Parents, self, and God: a test of competing theories of individual-religion relationships, *Review of Religious Research,* 16,154-165. **(86), (218)**

Spilka, B., Armatas, P., and Nussbaum, J.
(1964) The concept of God: a factor analytic approach, *Review of Religious Research,* 6,28-36. **(86), (88)**

Spilka, B., Hood, R. W., and Gorsuch, R. L.
(1985) *The Psychology of Religion: An Empirical Approach,* Englewood Cliffs, New Jersey: Prentice-Hall. **(46), (52), (97), (219)**

Spilka, B., Kojetin, B., and McIntosh, D.
(1985) Forms and measures of personal faith: questions, correlates, and distinctions, *Journal for the Scientific Study of Religion,* 24,437-442. **(357)**

Spilka, B., Minton, B., Sizemore, D., and Stout, L.
(1977) Death and personal faith: a psychometric investigation, *Journal for the Scientific Study of Religion,* 16,169-178. **(353)**

Spilka, B. and Mullin, M.
(1977) Personal religion and psychological schemata: a research approach to a theological psychology of religion, *Character Potential,* 8,57-66. **(353)**

Spilka, B. and Reynold, J. F.
(1965) Religion and prejudice: a factor-analytic study, *Review of Religious Research,* 6,163-168. **(207)**

Spilka, B. and Schmidt, G.
(1983) General attribution theory for the psychology of religion: the influence of event-character on attributions to God, *Journal for the Scientific Study of Religion,* 22,326-339. **(220)**

Spilka, B., Shaver, P., and Kirkpatrick, L. A.
(1985) A general attribution theory for the psychology of religion, *Journal for the Scientific Study of Religion,* 24,1-20. **(219)**

Spiro, M. E. and D'Andrade, R. G.
(1958) A cross-cultural study of some supernatural beliefs, *American Anthropologist,* 60,456-466. **(96)**

Stace, W. T.
(1960) *Mysticism and Philosophy,* Philadelphia and New York: Macmillan. **(166), (172), (175)**

Stack, S.
(1983) The effect of the decline in institutionalized religion on suicide, *Journal for the Scientific Study of Religion,* 22,239-252. **(348)**

Stanger, R. L.
(1978) *Religious change in college students in three differential church-related college environments,* PhD thesis, University of Michigan. **(275)**

Stanley, G.
(1965) Personality and attitude correlates of religious conversion, *Journal for the Scientific Study of Religion,* 4,60-63. **(190)**

Staples, C. L. and Mauss, A. L.
(1987) Conversion or commitment? a reassessment of the Snow and Machalek approach to the study of conversion, *Journal for the Scientific Study of Religion,* 26,133-147. **(189)**

Stark, R.
(1963) On the incompatibility of religion and science: a survey of American graduate students, *Journal for the Scientific Study of Religion,* 3,3-20. **(212)**
(1965) A taxonomy of religious experience, *Journal for the Scientific Study of Religion,* 5,97-116. **(166), (170), (176), (186)**

Stark, R. and Glock, C. Y.

(1968)   *American Piety: The Nature of Religious Commitment,* Berkeley: University of California Press. **(176), (349)**
Stark, R., Kent, L., and Doyle, D. P.
(1982)   Religion and delinquency: the ecology of a "lost" relationship, *Journal of Research in Crime and Delinquency,* 19,4-24. **(287)**
Stark, R. and Lofland, J.
(1965)   Becoming a world saver: a theory of conversion to a deviant perspective, *American Sociological Review,* 30,862-875. **(188)**
Stephens, B. and Simpkins, K.
(1974)   *The reasoning, moral judgment, and moral conduct of the congenitally blind; final report,* Philadelphia: Temple University. **(111)**
Sternberg, C. F.
(1979)   *Belief systems and the conceptualization of God,* PhD thesis, University of Colorado at Boulder. **(64)**
Stevens, A.
(1986)   Thoughts on the psychology of religion and the neurobiology of archetypal experience, *Zygon: Journal of Religion in Science,* 21,9-29. **(177)**
Stevens, R.
(1983)   *Erik Erikson: An Introduction,* Milton Keynes: The Open University Press. **(50)**
Stevens, V.
(1975)   *An application of attitude testing to the identification of religious sentiment in adolescents,* MPhil thesis, University of Nottingham. **(81)**
Stockholm School of Education
(1977)   *Children and ideology: an introduction to a research and developmental project and some preliminary findings,* Stockholm. **(105)**
Stone, C. A. and Day, M. C.
(1980)   Competence and performance models and the characteristics of formal operational skills, *Human Development,* 23,323-353. **(372)**
Stones, S. K.
(1965)   *An analysis of the growth of adolescent thinking in relation to the comprehension of school history material,* DPC dissertation, University of Birmingham. **(135)**
Stoop, D. A.
(1979)   *The relation between religious education and the process of maturity through the developmental stages of moral judgments,* PhD thesis, University of Southern California. **(284)**
Strader, M. and Thornton, A.
(1987)   Adolescent religiosity and contraceptive usage, *Journal of Marriage and the Family,* 49,117-128. **(291)**
Stratton, J. H.
(1981)   *The moral and religious beliefs of Catholic adolescents residing in the diocese of Shrewsbury,* MEd thesis, University of Manchester. **(317)**
Straus, R. A.
(1981)   The social-psychology of religious experience: a naturalistic approach, *Sociological Analysis,* 42,57-67. **(169)**
Streeter, H. C.
(1981)   *The place of religious education in the curriculum of young children,* MA thesis, Roehampton Institute of Higher Education. **(121)**
Strickland, B. R. and Shaffer, S.
(1971)   I-E, I-E & F. *Journal for the Scientific Study of Religion,* 10,366-369. **(209), (353)**
Strommen, M.
(1971)   (Ed.) *Research on Religious Development,* New York: Hawthorn. **(10)**
(1974)   *Five Cries of Youth,* New York: Harper & Row. **(266)**
Stroup, G. W.
(1981)   *The Promise of Narrative Theology,* Atlanta: John Knox Press. **(44)**
Strunk, O.
(1958)   Relationship between self-respect and adolescent religiosity, *Psychological Reports,* 4,683-686. **(209)**
(1959)   Perceived relationships between parental and deity concepts, *Psychological Newsletter,*

10,222-226. **(85)**, **(88)**

Stubblefield, H. W. and Richard, W. C.
(1965)   The concept of God in the mentally retarded, *Religious Education*, 60,184-188. **(81)**

Stuhlmueller, C.
(1976)   Is the Old Testament for children - II, *Living Light*, 13,379-385. **(141)**

Stump, R. S.
(1984)   Regional migration and religious commitment in the United States, *Journal for the Scientific Study of Religion*, 23,292-303. **(243)**
(1986)   Regional variations in the determinants of religious participation, *Review of Religious Research*, 27,208-225. **(243)**

Sturgeon, R. S. and Hamley, R. W.
(1979)   Religiosity and anxiety, *Journal of Social Psychology*, 108,137-138. **(206)**

Sutcliffe, J. M. (Ed.)
(1984)   *A Dictionary of Religious Education*, London: SCM Press.

Sutherland, P.
(1988)   A longitudinal study of religious and moral values in late adolescence, *British Educational Research Journal*, 14,73-78 **(273)**

Sutherland, P. A.
(1986)   *An investigation into the attainment of physical and biological science concepts across the school-age range*, PhD thesis, University of Birmingham. **(28)**

Suziedelis, A. and Potvin, R. H.
(1981)   Sex difference in factors affecting religiousness among Catholic adolescents, *Journal for the Scientific Study of Religion*, 20,38-51. **(211)**, **(228)**

Swainson, B. M.
(1939)   Elementary school children and ideas of God, *Religion in Education*, 6,94-99. **(70)**

Sweigart, N. L.
(1986)   *The relationship between client religiousness and the clinical perceptions of psychotherapists*, PhD thesis, the Florida State University. **(205)**

Sweitzer, E. K.
(1984)   *The symbolic use of religious language among evangelical Protestant Christians from the perspective of James Fowler's faith development theory*, PhD thesis, Boston University. **(58)**

Swickard, D. L.
(1963)   *A factor-analytic study of the patterns of religious belief, degree of prejudice and perceived parent-child rearing practices*, PhD thesis, University of Denver. **(206)**, **(231)**

Swindell, D. H. and L'Abate, L.
(1970)   Religiosity, dogmatism, and repression-sensitization, *Journal for the Scientific Study of Religion*, 9,249-251. **(207)**

Tabachnik, S.
(1986)   *Jewish identity development in young adulthood*, PhD thesis, The Wright Institute (Berkeley). **(211)**

Tamayo, A.
(1981)   Cultural differences in the structure and significance of the paternal figures, in Vergote and Tamayo (1981), *op. cit.* **(91)**

Tamayo, A. and Cooke, S.
(1981)   The influence of age on the parental figures and the representation of God, in Vergote and Tamayo (1981), *op. cit.* **(93)**

Tamayo, A. and Desjardins, L.
(1976)   Belief systems and conceptual images of parents and God, *The Journal of Psychology*, 92,131-140. **(90)**, **(93)**

Tamayo, A. and Dugas, A.
(1977)   Conceptual representation of mother, father, and God according to sex and field of study, *The Journal of Psychology*, 97,79-84. **(91)**

Tamayo, A. and St. Arnaud, P.
(1981)   The parental figures and the representation of God of schizophrenics and delinquents, in Vergote and Tamayo (1981), *op. cit.* **(91)**

Tamminen, K.

(1976)   Research concerning the development of religious thinking in Finnish students, *Character Potential*, 7,206-219. **(31)**, **(42)**

(1977)   What question of life do Finnish school children reflect on? *Learning for Life*, 16,148-155. **(264)**

(1979)   Pupils' questions and interests: material for problem-centered education, *Character Potential*, 9,5-16. **(264)**

(1981)   *Religious Experience among Children and Youth: Project on the Religious Development of Children and Youth, Report II*, University of Helsinki, Department of Practical Theology. **(185)**

(1991?)   *Religious Development in Childhood and Youth: An Empirical Study*, unpublished manuscript. **(25)**

Tamminen, K., Vianello, R., Jaspard, J-M, and Ratcliff, D.

(1988)   The religious concepts of preschoolers, in Ratcliff, D. (Ed.), *op. cit.* **(68)**, **(111)**, **(185)**, **(378)**

Tanner, A. E.

(1906)   Children's religious ideas, *Pedagogical Seminary*, 13,511-513. **(66)**

Tanuwidjaja, F. H.

(1974)   Religious thinking of Indonesian children from childhood to adolescence, *South East Asia Journal of Theology*, 15,117-118. **(30)**

Taylor, G. R.

(1953)   *Sex in History*, London: Thames and Hudson. **(200)**

Taylor, H. P.

(1970)   *A comparative study of the religious attitudes, beliefs, and practices of sixth formers in Anglican, state, and Roman Catholic grammar schools*, MPhil thesis, University of London. **(269)**, **(306)**

Taylor, P. J.

(1988)   Structural determinants of religious participation among black Americans, *Review of Religious Research*, 30,114-125. **(253)**

Tebbi, C. K., Mallon, J. C., Richards, M. E., and Bigler, L. R.

(1987)   Religiosity and locus of control of adolescent cancer patients, *Psychological Reports*, 61,683-696. **(213)**

Telford, C. W.

(1950)   A study of religious attitudes, *Journal of Social Psychology*, 31,217-230. **(145)**, **(241)**

Terrance, F.

(1987)   *Religiousness, ego development, and adjustment*, PhD thesis, Miami University. **(216)**

Terry, J. P.

(1983)   *Construction and validation of the Peck-Terry-Layton scale of religious values*, PhD thesis, Iowa State University. **(348)**

TeSelle, S. M.

(1975)   *Speaking in Parables: A Study in Metaphor and Theology*, Philadelphia: Fortress Press. **(124)**

The Academy of Religion and Mental Health.

(1969)   *Todays Youth and Moral Values; report of the tenth annual meeting*, New York. **(265)**

The First International Conference on Moral and Religious Development,

(1980)   *Toward Moral and Religious Maturity*, Morristown, New Jersey: Silver Burdett.

Thilagaraj, R.

(1983)   Parent-child relationship and juvenile delinquency, *Social Defense*, 19,20-6. **(233)**

Thomas, K. and Tuck, M.

(1975)   An explanatory study of determinant and indicant beliefs in attitude measurement, *European Journal of Social Psychology*, 5,167-168. **(393)**

Thomas, K. C.

(1978)   *Attitude Assessment: Rediguide 7, Guides in Educational Research:* University of Nottingham School of Education. **(392)**

Thomas, L. E. and Cooper, P. E.

(1978)   Measurement and incidence of mystical experiences: an exploratory study, *Journal for the Scientific Study of Religion*, 17,433-437. **(175)**

(1980)   Incidence and psychological correlates on intense spiritual experiences, *Journal of Transpersonal Psychology*, 12,75-85. **(175)**

Thomas, L. E., Cooper, P. E., and Suscovich, D. J.

(1982) Incidence of near-death and intense spiritual exercises in an intergenerational sample, *Omega, Journal of Death and Dying*, 13,35-41. (**176**)

Thompson, A. D.
(1974) Open-mindedness and indiscrimiate antireligious orientation, *Journal for the Scientific Study of Religion*, 13,471-477. (**353**), (**355**)

Thompson, D. D.
(1973) *A study of the relationship of Rokeach's dogmatism with the religious orientation and religious orthodoxy of Catholic high school students and their parents*, PhD thesis, The Catholic University of America. (**232**)

Thompson, R. C., Michel, J. B., and Alexander, T. J.
(1970) Christian orthodoxy, authoritarianism, and prejudice, *Rocky Mountains Social Science Journal*, 7,117-123. (**208**)

Thouless, R. H.
(1935) The tendency to certainty in religious belief, *British Journal of Psychology*, 26,16-31. (**103**)

Thurstone, L. L.
(1929) Theory of attitude measurement, *Psychological Review*, 36,222-241. (**145**)

Thurstone, L. L. and Chave, E. J.
(1929) *The Measurement of Attitudes*, Chicago: University of Chicago Press. (**145**), (**391**)

Tickner, M. F.
(1981) *A pilot study investigating aspects of children's experiences which might be termed religious*, MA thesis, University of Hull. (**180**)

Tipton, R. M., Harrison, B. M., and Mahoney, J.
(1980) Faith and locus of control, *Psychological Reports*,46,1151-1154. (**212**)

Tisdale, J. R.
(1966) Selected correlates of extrinsic religious orientations, *Review of Religious Research*, 7,78-84. (**232**)
(1967) Students with extrinsic religious values: a study in contrasting groups, *Review of Religious Research*, 9,11-15. (**352**), (**353**)

Tittle, C. R. and Welch, M. R.
(1983) Religiosity and deviance: toward a contemporary theory of constraining effects, *Social Forces*, 61,653-682. (**286**)

Tjart, D. and Boersma, F. J.
(1978) A comparative study of religious values of Christian and public school eighth graders, *Journal of Psychology and Theology*, 6,132-140. (**303**)

Tobacyk, J.
(1983) Parental identification and religious beliefs, *Psychological Reports*, 52,402. (**234**)

Tobacyk, J., Miller, M. J., and Jones, G.
(1984) Paranormal beliefs of high-school students, *Psychological Reports*, 55,255-261. (**267**)

Toch, H.
(1966) *The Social Psychology of Social Movements*, London: Methuen. (**222**), (**224**), (**244**)

Toch, H. and Anderson, R.
(1960) Religious belief and denominational affiliation, *Religious Education*, 55,193-200. (**265**)

Torrance, E. P., Goldman, R. G., and Torrance, J. P.
(1974) The meaning and relevance of learning readiness for curriculum construction in Christian education: a study paper, *Character Potential*, 7,118-142. (**37**)

Tourangeau, R. and Sternberg, R. J.
(1982) Understanding and appreciating metaphors, *Cognition*, 11,203-244. (**384**)

Towler, R. and Chamberlain, A.
(1973) Common Religion, in Hill, M. (Ed.) *A Sociological Yearbook of Religion in Britain 6*, London: SCM Press. (**337**)

Treston, K.
(1973) *An investigation of the relationship between youth role orientation and religiosity*, PhD thesis, University of Notre Dame. (**327**)

Treston, K., Whiteman, R. G., and Florent, J. G.
(1975) Catholic school religious training versus adolescent background and orientation: two comparative studies, *Notre Dame Journal of Education*, 6,1,59-64. (**327**)

Trevelyan, J. A.

(1978)   *The religious dimension of life during adolescence: a study of the relationship between psychological perspectives in the works of Erikson, Jung, Kohlberg, and Tillich, and clinical perspectives in two research settings*, EdD thesis, Harvard University. **(56)**

Tulloch, E. F

(1985)   *A study of faith stage transition in adults*, PhD thesis, East Texas State University. **(59)**

Turner, E. B.

(1970)   Religious understanding and religious attitudes in male urban adolescents, PhD thesis, Queen's University of Belfast. **(108), (321), (395)**

(1978)   Toward a standardized test of religious language comprehension, *British Journal of Religious Education*, 1,1,14-21. **(108)**

(1980a)   General cognitive ability and religious attitude in two school systems, *British Journal of Religious Education*, 2,136-141. **(108), (321)**

(1980b)   Intellectual ability and the comprehension of religious language, *Irish Journal of Psychology*, 4,182-109. **(108)**

Turner, E. B., Turner, I. F., and Reid, A.

(1980)   Religious attitudes in two types of secondary school: a decade of change? *Irish Journal of Psychology*, 4,43-52. **(321)**

Turner, I. F. and Davies, J.

(1982)   Religious attitudes in an integrated primary school: a Northern Ireland case-study, *British Journal of Religious Education*, 5,28-32. **(321)**

Turner, L. N.

(1963)   *The certainty of belief as a variable of personality*, PhD thesis, University of California. **(208)**

Ungar, S.

(1980)   Attitude inferences from behavior performed under public and private conditions, *Social Psychology Quarterly*, 43,81-89. **(394)**

Union College Character Research Project

(1959)   *Children's Religious Concepts*, Schenectady, New York: Union College Character Research Project. **(104)**

Vaatainen, R. L.

(1974)   7 ja 8 vuotiaiden uskonnolliset kasitykset, *Uskonnonpedasgogiikan julkaisuja A 10/1974*, University of Helsinki, Department of Practical Theology. **(68)**

Vaillancourt, P. M.

(1973)   Stability of children's survey responses, *Public Opinion Quarterly*, 37,373-387. **(158)**

Van Aerde, M.

(1972)   The attitude of adults toward God, *Social Compass*, 19,407-413. **(88)**

Van Bunnen, C.

(1964)   The burning bush, in Godin, A. (Ed.) (1964), *op. cit.* **(128)**

Vanden, H. A.

(1985)   *Faith development and family interaction*, PhD thesis, Union for Experimenting Colleges. **(56)**

VanderPlate, C.

(1973)   Religious orientations in psychiatric patients and normals, *Christian Association for Psychological Studies: Proceedings of the Twentieth Annual Conference*. **(205)**

Vanecko, J. J.

(1966)   Religious behavior and prejudice: some dimensions and specification of the relationship, *Review of Religious Research*, 8,27-36. **(351)**

Vannesse, A.

(1977)   Religious language and relation to the mother, *Lumen Vitae*, 32,423-433. **(92)**

Vannesse, A., and Neff, T.

(1981)   Parental images and the representation of God in seminarians and women religious, in Vergote and Tamayo (1981), *op. cit.* **(92)**

Vannesse, A. and De Neuter, P.

(1981)   The Semantic Differential Parental Scale, in Vergote and Tamayo (1981), *op. cit.* **(88)**

Varma, C. K.

(1959)   *A study of the attitudes of school children towards six school subjects*, DCP dissertation, University of Birmingham. **(146)**

Vegelius, J. and Bäckström, A.

(1981)   An enquiry about religion, analyzed by a nominal scale truncated component analysis, *Educational and Psychological Measurement*, 41,717-724. **(339)**

Venable, G. D.
(1984)   *Intrinsic and extrinsic religiosity in developmental perspectives,* PhD thesis, Fuller Theological Seminary, School of Psychology. **(383)**

Vercruysse, G.
(1972)   The meaning of God: a factor-analytic study, *Social Compass*, 19,347-364. **(87), (88)**

Vercruysse, G. and De Neuter, P.
(1981)   Maternal and paternal dimensions in the parental and divine figures, in Vergote and Tamayo (1981), *op. cit.* **(88)**

Vergote, A.
(1964)   Religious experience, in Godin, A. (1964), *op. cit.* **(167)**
(1980)   The dynamics of the family and its social significance for moral and religious education, in The First International Conference on Moral and Religious Development, *op. cit.* **(80), (227)**
(1981)   Overview and theoretical perspectives, in Vergote and Tamayo, *op. cit.* **(90), (91)**

Vergote, A. and Aubert, C.
(1972)   Parental images and representation of God, *Social Compass*, 19,431-444. **(87), (90)**

Vergote, A. and Tamayo, A.
(1981)   *The Parental Figures and the Representation of God,* The Hague: Mouton. **(80), (94)**

Vergote, A., Tamayo, A., Pasquali, L., Bonami, M., Pattyn, M-R., and Casters, A.
(1969)   Concept of God and parental images, *Journal for the Scientific Study of Religion,* 8,79-87. **(87), (91), (96)**

Verma, O. P. and Upadhyay, S. H.
(1984)   Religiosity and social-distance, *Indian Psychological Review,* 26,29-34. **(241)**

Vernon, G. M.
(1962)   Measuring religion; two methods compared, *Review of Religious Research,* 3,159-165. **(341)**
(1968)   The religious "nones": a neglected category, *Journal for the Scientific Study of Religion,* 7,219-229. **(337), (341)**

Vetter, G. B. and Green, M.
(1932)   Personality and group factors in the making of atheists, *Journal of Abnormal and Social Psychology,* 27,179-194. **(232)**

Veverka, F. B.
(1984)   *"For God and Country" : Catholic schooling in the 1920s,* EdD thesis, Columbia University Teachers College. **(295)**

Vianello, R.
(1980)   *Riserche psicologiche sulla religiosita infantile,* Firenze: Giunti. **(69)**

Vianello, R. and Marin-Zanovello, M. L.
(1980)   Ricerca di sondaggio sull'atteggiamento magic infantile, *Eta Evolutiva,* 7,24-39. **(69)**

Vick, T. E.
(1975)   *A study of the relationship between the principal's management style and school climate,* PhD thesis, University of California, Riverside. **(328)**

Villeneuve, C. M.
(1984)   *Religious value transmission among Seventh-Day Adventist white American families: a cognitive approach to parental values and relationship as perceived by youth,* EdD thesis, Andrews University. **(233)**

Vosniadou, S.
(1984)   *Testing the metaphoric competence of the young child: paraphrase versus enactment,* paper presented to the Biennial Meeting of the Society for Research in Child Development. **(386)**
(1987)   Children and metaphors, *Child Development,* 58,870-885. **(386)**

Vosniadou, S. and Ortony, A.
(1983a)   The emergence of the literal-metaphorical-anamalous distinction in young children, *Child Development,* 54,154-161. **(385)**
(1983b)   *Testing the Metaphoric Competence of the Young Child; Paraphrase versus Enactment,* Cambridge, Mass.: Bolt, Beranek, and Newman. **(386)**

Vosniadou, S., Ortony, A., Reynolds, R. E., and Wilson, P.
(1984)   Sources of difficulty in the young child's understanding of metaphoric language, *Child*

*Development, 55,*1588-1606. **(386)**

Voye, L. and Remy, J.
(1986)   De religiositeit bij de jeugd, *Tijdschrift voor Sociologie,* 7,315-338. **(263)**

Wadsworth, M. F. and Freeman, S. R.
(1983)   Generation differences in beliefs: a cohort study of stability and change in religious beliefs, *British Journal of Sociology,* 34,416-437. **(277)**

Wahrman, I. S.
(1981)   The relationship of dogmatism, religious affiliation and moral judgment development, *Journal of Psychology,* 108,151-154. **(208)**

Waldbrand, W.
(1983)   *Understanding metaphor,* PhD thesis, University of New York. **(384)**

Walker, D. J.
(1950)   *A study of children's conceptions of God,* EdB thesis, University of Glasgow. **(77)**

Walker, H. E.
(1985)   *Study of the attitudes concerning church standards expressed by Seventh-Day Adventists in relation to selected personality traits,* PhD thesis, Andrews University. **(197)**

Walker, L. T.
(1966)   *A study of the attitudes of training college students toward religious education and religion,* PhD thesis, University of London. **(149)**

Wall, M.
(1983)   *Religious education and its assumptions in the comprehensive school,* MEd dissertation, University of Birmingham. **(142)**

Walley, P. B.
(1984)   *The effect of religious orientation on attitudes toward seeking professional psychological help,* PhD thesis, University of Georgia. **(358)**

Wallin, G. J.
(1978)   *Learning disabilities, religious training and moral judgment of Jewish high-school boys,* PhD thesis, Fordham University. **(305)**

Warnick, A. P.
(1983)   *A developmental study of metaphor production and comprehension,* PhD thesis, Ohio State University. **(389)**

Warren, J. F.
(1980)   *An investigation of children's beliefs in transcendent figures,* PhD thesis, Duke University. **(138)**

Warren, N. C.
(1970)   *Empirical studies in the psychology of religion; an assessment of the period 1960-1970,* paper from the Symposium on Methods in the Psychology of Religion, reprinted in Malony, H. N. (Ed.) (1977), *op. cit.* **(340)**

Warren, T.
(1988)   *An exploration of Holland's personality types and associated religious orientations,* PhD thesis, Texas Technological University. **(357)**

Washburn, D. A.
(1982)   Dimensions of spiritual attachment, *Journal of Psychology and Christianity,* 1,2-11. **(206)**

Wason, P. C.
(1977)   The theory of formal operations—a critique, in Geber, B. A. (Ed.) *Piaget and Knowing: Studies in Genetic Epistemology,* London: Routledge and Kegan Paul. **(371)**

Waters, K.
(1974)   Religious education in South Australia, *Learning for Living,* 13,200-202. **(322)**

Watkins, A. J.
(1977)   *Evaluation of religious arguments in relation to religious attitude and logical thinking,* EdD thesis, Lehigh University. **(275)**

Watkins, D.
(1979)   Changes in the religious practices and beliefs of students at an Australian university: 1965-1977, *Australian Journal of Social Issues,* 14,211-217. **(274)**

Watson, P. J., Hood, R. W., Foster, S. G., and Morris, R. J.
(1988)   Sin, depression and narcissism, *Review of Religious Research,* 29,295-305. **(204)**

Watson, P. J., Hood, R. W., and Hall. J. R.

(1987)   The relation between religiosity and narcissism, *Counseling and Values*, 31,179-184. **(353)**

Watson, P. J., Hood, R. W., and Morris, R. J.
(1984)   Religious orientation, humanistic values, and narcissism, *Review of Religious Research*, 25,257-264. **(353), (355)**
(1985)   Dimensions of religiosity and empathy, *Journal of Psychology and Christianity*, 4,73-85. **(357)**

Watson, P. J., Hood, R. W., Morris, R. J., and Hall, J. R.
(1984)   Empathy, religious orientation, and social desirability, *Journal of Psychology*, 117,211-216. **(359)**

Watson, P. J., Howard, R., Hood, R. W., and Morris, R. J.
(1988)   Age and religious orientation, *Review of Religious Research*, 29,271-280. **(358)**

Watson, P. J., Morris, R. J., and Hood, R. W.
(1987)   Antireligious humanistic values, guilt, and self-esteem, *Journal for the Scientific Study of Religion*, 26,353-546. **(211), (353)**
(1989)   Interactional factor correlates with Means and End religion, *Journal for the Scientific Study of Religion*, 28,337-347. **(358)**

Wearing, A. J. and Brown, L. B.
(1972)   The dimensionality of religion, *British Journal of Social and Clinical Psychology*, 11,143-148. **(349)**

Webb, S. C.
(1965)   An exploratory investigation of some needs met through religious experience, *Journal for the Scientific Study of Religion*, 5,51-58. **(344)**

Webster, C. M.
(1975)   *Toward a cognitive developmental approach in religious education*, PhD thesis, University of Toronto. **(31)**

Webster, D. H.
(1984)   James Fowler's theory of faith development, *British Journal of Religious Education*, 7,14-18. **(53)**

Weddell, S. C.
(1972)   Religious orientation, racial prejudice, and dogmatism: a study of Baptists and Unitarians, *Journal for the Scientific Study of Religion*, 11,395-399. **(352)**

Weigert, A. J. and Thomas, D. L.
(1969)   Religiosity in 5-D: a critical note, *Social Forces*, 48,260-263. **(344), (349)**
(1970a)   Secularization: a cross-cultural study of Catholic male adolescents, *Social Forces*, 49,28-35. **(245)**
(1970b)   Secularization and religiosity: a cross-cultural analysis of Catholic adolescents, *Sociometry*, 33,305-326. **(245)**
(1972)   Parental support, control, and adolescent religiosity: an extension of previous research, *Journal for the Scientific Study of Religion*, 11,389-393. **(232)**
(1974)   Secularization and religiosity: a cross-national study of Catholic adolescents in five societies, *Sociological Analysis*, 35.1-23. **(245)**
(1979)   Family socialization and adolescent conformity and religiosity: an extension to Germany and Spain, *Journal of Comparative Family Studies*, 10,371-383. **(245)**

Weis, A. G.
(1987)   Psychological distress and well-being in Hare Krishnas, *Psychological Reports*, 61,23-35. **(203)**

Welch, M. L.
(1988)   *An analysis of desired student outcomes of Catholic elementary schools as perceived by principals, teachers, parents, and board members*, EdD thesis, Loyola University of Chicago. **(334)**

Weller, L., Levinbok, S. Maimon, R., and Shaham, A.
(1975)   Religiosity and authoritarianism, *Journal of Social Psychology*, 95,11-18. **(208)**

Westbury, J. I.
(1975)   *Religious beliefs and attitudes of pupils in an East London comprehensive school*, MEd thesis, University of Leicester. **(258)**

Westermann, R.
(1983)   Interval-scale measurement of attitude: some theoretical considerations and empirical

testing methods, *British Journal of Mathematical and Statistical Psychology,* 36,228-239. (**394**)

Westling, G., Pettersson, S., and Fagerlind, I.
   (1973)   *Mognad och undervisning i religionskunskap* [Readiness and the teaching of religion], Stockholm: Utbildningforlaget (cited in Fagerlind (1974), *op, cit.*). (**118**)

Wheeler, L. R. and Wheeler, V. D
   (1945)   Differences in religious ideas and attitudes of children who go to church and those who never attend, *Religious Education* 40,149-161. (**104**)

White, F. P.
   (1970)   *The God of childhood,* PhD thesis, Duquesne University. (**71**)

White, R. E.
   (1985)   *Christian schooling and spiritual growth and development,* EdD thesis, Northern Arizona University. (**56**), (**303**)

White, V. M.
   (1985)   *Faith stages, affiliation, and gender: a study of the faith development of Catholic college undergraduates,* EdD thesis, Boston University. (**225**)

Whitehouse, J.
   (1970)   *Children's reactions to the Zacchaeus story,* DipEd dissertation, University of Birmingham. (**26**)
   (1972)   Children's reactions to the Zaccheaus story, *Learning for Living,* 11,4,19-24. (**26**)

Whiteman, R. G.
   (1973)   *An analysis of the relationship between selected interpersonal and institutional variables and the value systems of youth,* PhD thesis, University of Notre Dame. (**327**)

Whiteman, T. H. and Kosier, K. P.
   (1964)   Development of children's moralistic judgements: age, sex, I. Q. and certain personal-experiential variables, *Child Development,* 35,843-850. (**282**)

Wiebe, B. and Vraa, C. W.
   (1976)   Religious values of students in religious and in public high schools, *Psychological Reports,* 38,709-710. (**303**)

Wiebe, K. F. and Fleck, J. R.
   (1980)   Personality correlates of intrinsic, extrinsic and non-religious orientations, *Journal of Psychology,* 105-181-187. (**352**), (**353**), (**355**)

Wieting, S. G.
   (1975)   An examination of intergenerational patterns of religious belief and practice, *Sociological Analysis,* 30,137-149. (**226**)

Wilhoit, J.
   (1982)   Memory: an area of difference between Piaget and Goldman, *Journal of Christian Education (U.S.),* 2,11-14. (**40**)

Wilkinson, F.
   (1965a)   Religion and young children, *Learning for Living,* 4,3,6-8. (**44**)
   (1965b)   The parables in an infant classroom, *Learning for Living,* 4,4,21-23. (**102**), (**119**)

Wilkinson, M. L. and Tanner, W. C.
   (1980)   The influence of family size, interaction, and religiosity on family affection in a Mormon sample, *Journal of Marriage and the Family,* 42,297-304. (**230**)

Williams, D. L.
   (1989)   Religion in adolescence: dying, dormant, or developing? *Source* 54,41-3. (**253**)

Williams, J. L.
   (1972)   *An analysis of the similarities and disparities of religiosity between college students and their parents as related to family solidarity,* PhD thesis, Louisiana State University. (**234**)

Williams, M. L.
   (1974)   *Children's concepts of God and self: developmental sequences,* PhD thesis, University of Texas. (**75**)

Williams, R.
   (1971)   A theory of God-concept readiness: from the Piagetian theories of child artificialism and the origin of religious feeling in childhood, *Religious Education,* 66,62-66. (**23**)

Willits, F. K. and Crider, D. M.
   (1989)   Church attendance and trraditional beliefs in adolescence and young adulthood: a panel

study, *Review of Religious Research*, 31,68-81. (**238**)

Wills, E.
(1971) Religious education in the primary schools: the infant school, *Learning for Living*, 10,3,10-12. (**102**)

Wilson, B.
(1977) How religious are we? *New Society*, 42,176-178. (**245**)
(1978) When prophecy failed, *New Society*, 42,183-184. (**220**)

Wilson, D. F.
(1928) *Child Psychology and Religious Education*, London: SCM Press. (**98**)

Wilson, P. J., Morris, R. J., Foster, F. E., and Hood, R. W.
(1986) Religiosity and social desirability, *Journal for the Scientific Study of Religion*, 25,215-232. (**359**)

Wilson, R. W.
(1976) *A social-psychological study of religious experience with special emphasis on conversion*, PhD thesis, University of Florida. (**192**)
(1984) Christianity-biased and unbiased dogmatism, relationship to different Christian commitment, including conversion, *High School Journal*, 68,374-388. (**208**)

Wilson, S. D.
(1988) *A comparison of evangelical Christian adult children of alcoholics and non-alcoholics on selected personality and religious variables*, PhD thesis, The Union for Experimenting Colleges and Universities. (**290**)

Wilson, W. and Miller, H. W.
(1968) Fear, anxiety and religionism, *Journal for the Scientific Study of Religion*, 7,111. (**206**)

Wilson, W. C.
(1960) Extrinsic religious values and prejudice, *Journal of Abnormal and Social Psychology*, 60,286-288. (**351**)

Wiltshire, K. W.
(1973) Social and religious attitudes of Nonconformist Protestant youth, *Journal of Christian Education*, Papers 16,3,179-197. (**327**)

Wimberley, R. C.
(1978) Dimensions of commitment: generalizing from religion to politics, *Journal for the Scientific Study of Religion*, 17,225-240. (**345**)

Winand, P.
(1972) Le Symbole du feu dans la vie des adolescents et dans leur univers religieux, *Social Compass*, 19,445-458. (**129**)

Wingert, M. L.
(1973) *Effects of preschool education on early personality adjustment*, PhD thesis, George Peabody College for Teachers. (**196**)

Wingrove, E. R. and Alston, J. P.
(1974) Cohort analysis of church attendance 1939-1969, *Social Studies*, 53,324-331. (**252**)

Winkelman, M.
(1986) Trance states: a theoretical model and cross-cultural analysis, *Ethos*, 14,174-243. (**167**)

Winner, E.
(1976) *Can adolescents produce metamorphic figures? A training study*, Resources in Education, ED 112 407. (**386**)
(1977) *What does it take to understand a metaphor?* Paper presented at a Symposium on Metaphor and Analogy, The Society for Research in Child Development, New Orleans, Louisiana. (**386**)
(1978) *Misunderstanding metaphor: cognitive problem or pragmatic problem?* Washington, D.C.: Spons Agency, National Institute of Education. (**387**)

Winner, E., Rosenstiel, A. K., and Gardner, H.
(1976) The development of metaphoric understanding, *Developmental Psychology*, 12,289-297. (**384**)

Witt, D. D. and Smith, R. R.
(1978) *The influence of education of religiosity*, paper presented to the 53rd meeting of the Southwestern Sociological Association. (**196**)

Wolf, R. J.

(1979)   A study of the relationship between religious education, religious experience, maturity, and moral development, PhD thesis, New York University. (283)

Woodroof, J. T.
(1984)   Premarital sexual behavior and religion in adolescence, Journal for the Scientific Study of Religion, 24,343-366. (291)
(1986)   Reference groups, religiosity and premarital sexual behavior, Journal for the Scientific Study of Religion, 25,436-460. (229)

Worten, S. A. and Dollinger, S. J.
(1986)   Mothers' intrinsic motivation, disciplining preferences, and different conceptions of prayer, Psychological Reports, 58,218. (23)

Wright, D.
(1962)   A study of religious belief in sixth form boys, Researches and Studies, University of Leeds, 24,19-27. (178), (234), (268)
(1965)   The moral judgments of sixth form boys and girls, Learning for Living, 4,4,14-16. (280)
(1972)   The Psychology of Religion: a review of empirical studies, Sutton Coldfield, Warwickshire: The Association for Religious Education. (10), (200), (354)
(1982)   Piaget's theory of practical morality, British Journal of Psychology, 73,279-283. (378)

Wright, D. and Cox, E.
(1967a)   Religious belief and coeducation in a sample of sixth form boys and girls, British Journal of Social and Clinical Psychology, 6,23-31. (153), (320)
(1967b)   A study of the relationship between moral judgement and religious belief in a sample of English adolescents, Journal of Social Psychology, 27,135-144. (280)
(1971)   Changes in attitudes towards religious education and the bible among sixth-form boys and girls, British Journal of Educational Psychology, 41,328-331. (261), (269), (281), (321)

Wright, H. D. and Koppe, W. A.
(1964)   Children's potential religious concepts, Character Potential, 2,83-90. (64), (82)

Wuthnow, R. (Ed)
(1979)   The Religious Dimension, New York: Academic Press. (341)

Wyckoff, D. C. and Richter, D. (Eds.)
(1982)   Religious Education Ministry with Youth, Birmingham, Alabama: Religious Education Press.

Yeatts, J. R.
(1988)   Variables related to the recall of the English Bible, Journal for the Scientific Study of Religion, 27,593-608. (123)

Yeatts, J. R. and Asher, W.
(1982)   Factor analysis of religious variables: some methodological considerations, Review of Religious Research, 24,49-54. (339)

Yeatts, J. R. and Linden, K. W.
(1984)   Text comprehension of various versions of the Bible, Journal for the Scientific Study of Religion, 23,1-18. (123)

Yeaxlee, B.A.
(1939)   Religion and the Growing Mind, London: Nisbet. (98)

Yinger, J. M.
(1969)   A structural examination of religion, Journal for the Scientific Study of Religion, 8,88-99. (337)
(1970)   The Scientific Study of Religion, New York: Macmillan. (170), (199), (222), (299), (337), (347)

Young, M.
(1982)   Religiosity, sexual behavior, and contraceptive use of college females, Journal of American College Health, 30,216-220. (291)

Young, R. C,
(1981)   Values differentiation as stage transition; an extension of Kohlberg's moral stages, Journal of Psychology and Theology, 9,164-174. (214)

Youniss, J.
(1978)   Dialectical theory and Piaget on social knowledge, Human Development, 21,234-247. (221)

Youniss, J. and Smoller, J.

(1985)   *Adolescent Relations with Mother, Father, and Friends,* Chicago: University of Chicago Press. (**235**)

Zaenglein, M. M., Vener, A. M., and Stewart, C. S.
(1975)   The adolescent and his religion: beliefs in transition, *Review of Religious Research,* 17,51-60. (**266**)

Zern, D. S.
(1987a)   The relationship of religious involvement to a variety of indicators of cognitive ability and achievement in college students, *Adolescence,* 22,883-895. (**196**)
(1987b)   Positive links among obedience pressure, religiosity, and measures of cognitive accomplishment: evidence for the secular value of being religious, *Journal of Psychology and Theology,* 15,31-39. (**231**)

Zimmerman, B. J.
(1982)   Piaget's theory and instruction; how compatible are they? *Contemporary Educational Psychology,* 7,204-216. (**373**)

Zimmerman, S. C.
(1977)   *The religious motivation of church-affiliated believers, nonaffiliated believers, and non-believers,* PhD thesis, Saint Louis University. (**344**)

Zinsser, C. F.
(1985)   *Teaching children in a fundamentalist church: an ethnographic study,* PhD thesis, University of Pennsylvania. (**225**)

Index of Associate Authors

THE ASTERISKS INDICATE THAT THERE IS OTHER WORK BY THE AUTHOR LISTED IN THE REFERENCES UNDER HIS LEADING NAME.

485

INDEX OF SUBJECTS